W9-CPC-938

# Equity
# Portfolio
# Management

**Frank J. Fabozzi, Ph.D., CFA**

**James L. Grant, Ph.D.**

**with contributions from Bruce M. Collins, Ph.D.**

**Published by Frank J. Fabozzi Associates**

**FJF**
*To my wife Donna,*
*and our children, Francesco, Patricia, and Karly*


**JLG**
*To my wife Barbara and our family,*
*Erica, Meredith, Hannah, Joel, and Kathryn*

© 1999 By Frank J. Fabozzi Associates
New Hope, Pennsylvania

Editorial consultant: Megan Orem
Cover designer: Scott C. Riether

This publication is designed to provide accurate and authoritative information in regard to the subject matter covered. It is sold with the understanding that the publisher is not engaged in rendering legal, accounting, or other professional services.

ISBN: 1-883249-40-6

Printed in the United States of America

# Preface

*Equity Portfolio Management* is designed to (1) provide a rigorous foundation in modern portfolio theory and capital market theory principles for those seeking to enter the dynamic world of equity portfolio management and (2) provide security analysts and portfolio managers with practical and quantitative insights on the latest equity management tools and strategies.

We provide an integrated approach to equity portfolio management by emphasizing that a properly designed investment management process consists of five fundamental elements. These elements include setting investment objectives, establishing investment policy, selecting the equity portfolio management strategy (active versus passive management, or a combination of the two approaches), selecting stocks, and measuring and evaluating overall investment performance. Furthermore, as emphasized by a major vendor of analytical portfolio systems, BARRA, an integrated approach to equity portfolio management requires a systematic focus on four key elements that determine superior investment performance — namely, forming reasonable return expectations, managing portfolio risk, achieving trading cost efficiency, and monitoring the overall investment process. In this context, the bulk of this book (Chapters 1 to 10) focuses on the first two elements — returns expectations and portfolio risk control — while the last four chapters (Chapters 11 to 14) of this book emphasize the importance of achieving trading cost efficiencies — using, for example, equity derivative strategies to enhance return and effectively manage risk, as well as measuring and evaluating investment performance.

The foundations and insights offered in *Equity Portfolio Management* include rigorous discussions of the following investment topics: tenets of modern portfolio theory and capital market theory, statistical concepts used in equity management, the latest developments on equity style management, traditional and value-based metric approaches to equity fundamental analysis, discounted cash flow equity valuation models (such as dividend discount, free cash flow, economic profit, and sales franchise models), prominent fundamental and macroeconomic factor models, and equity-based derivatives strategies used in today's rapidly changing world of portfolio management.

We also cover the latest developments in models designed to measure equity trading costs. A unique feature of *Equity Portfolio Management* is our profile of the portfolio management strategies of five money management firms and their equity managers — Jacobs Levy Equity Management, State Street Global Advisors, Boston Partners Asset Management, Credit Suisse Asset Management, and Columbia Management Company.

We are grateful to the following individuals for various forms of assistance: Wayne Archambo of Boston Partners Asset Management, Lawrence Viehl of Columbia Management Company, James Abate of Credit Suisse Asset Management, Bruce Jacobs and Kenneth Levy of Jacobs Levy Equity Management, Dan diBartolomeo of Northfield Information Services, Eric Sorensen of Salomon

Smith Barney, Frank Jones of The Guardian Life, Ronald Kahn of Barclays Global Investors, Robert Jones of Goldman Sachs Asset Management, Peter Stonberg of State Street Global Advisors, and Dan Anderson of Wilshire Associates Inc.

We thank Meredith Grant — a Ph.D. candidate in physics at Carnegie Mellon University — for her quantitative research assistance.

A section in Chapter 8 on dividend discount models is adapted from pages 108 to 115 of William J. Hurley and Frank J. Fabozzi, "Dividend Discount Models," in Frank J. Fabozzi (ed.), *Selected Topics in Equity Portfolio Management* (Frank J. Fabozzi Associates, 1998). We are grateful to Professor Hurley for his permission to use this coauthored work.

Last, but certainly not least, we are grateful to Dr. Bruce M. Collins for his contributions to this book. Prior to joining the faculty of Western Connecticut State University, he was vice president and head of equity derivatives products research at Lehman Brothers and First Boston Corporation. His contributions to this book include Chapters 12 and 13, adapted from Bruce M. Collins and Frank J. Fabozzi, *Derivatives and Equity Portfolio Management* (Frank J. Fabozzi Associates, 1998), and parts of the discussion in Chapter 11, adapted from Bruce M. Collins and Frank J. Fabozzi, "A Methodology for Measuring Transaction Costs," published in the *Financial Analysts Journal* (March/April 1991). These contributions warrant his identification on the cover and title page of this book.

*Frank J. Fabozzi*
*James L. Grant*

# Table of Contents

Preface iii

About the Authors vi

1. Introduction 1

2. Modern Portfolio Theory, Capital Market Theory, and Asset Pricing Models 11

3. Statistical Measures and Their Applications 43

4. Blueprint for Passive-Active Investing 65

5. Equity Management Styles 97

6. Traditional Fundamental Analysis 125

7. Security Analysis Using Value-Based Metrics 153

8. Discounted Cash Flow Equity Valuation Models 199

9. Factor-Based Portfolio Models 229

10. Profiles in Equity Management 261

11. Equity Trading 299

12. Derivative Instruments and Their Characteristics 329

13. Applications of Derivatives to Equity Portfolio Management 365

14. Performance Evaluation 393

Index

# About the Authors

*Frank J. Fabozzi* is editor of the *Journal of Portfolio Management* and an Adjunct Professor of Finance at Yale University's School of Management. He is a Chartered Financial Analyst and Certified Public Accountant. Dr. Fabozzi is on the board of directors of the Guardian Life family of funds and the BlackRock complex of funds. He earned a doctorate in economics from the City University of New York in 1972 and in 1994 received an honorary doctorate of Humane Letters from Nova Southeastern University. Dr. Fabozzi is a Fellow of the International Center for Finance at Yale University.

*James L. Grant* is president of JLG Research — a company specializing in economic profit research and customized seminars in investment management. Dr. Grant holds a Ph.D. in Business from the University of Chicago's Graduate School of Business, and has been a featured speaker at industry conferences on value-based metrics. Dr. Grant is a research consultant to Credit Suisse Asset Management — providing quantitative advice on several of the investment management strategies described in this book. He has published several articles in investment journals, including the *Journal of Portfolio Management* and the *Journal of Investing*. Dr. Grant is the author of *Foundations of Economic Value Added* (published in 1997 by Frank J. Fabozzi Associates), which has been translated into Japanese, and the coeditor with Frank Fabozzi of *Value-Based Metrics: Foundations and Practice* (to be published in 2000 by Frank J. Fabozzi Associates).

# Chapter 1

# Introduction

The purpose of this book is to describe the state-of-the-art strategies for the management of equity portfolios. While the principles that we describe apply equally to the management of portfolios for all investors, our main focus is on the management of portfolios of institutional investors. The entities include pension funds, investment companies (i.e., mutual funds), insurance companies, and pooled fund accounts.

In this chapter we provide an overview of the investment management process and then discuss an integrated approach to equity portfolio management. With this background we can place the chapters that follow in their proper context. A summary of the chapters in this book is provided at the end of the chapter.

## OVERVIEW OF THE INVESTMENT MANAGEMENT PROCESS

The investment management process involves the following five steps:

1. setting investment objectives
2. establishing investment policy
3. selecting an equity portfolio strategy
4. selecting the stocks
5. measuring and evaluating performance

The investment process is a continuous process whereby performance evaluation may result in changes to the objectives, policies, strategies, and composition of a portfolio.

### Setting Investment Objectives

The first step in the investment management process, setting investment objectives, depends on the institution. For example, a pension fund that is obligated to pay specified amounts to beneficiaries in the future would have the objective of generating sufficient funds from its investment portfolio so as to satisfy its pension obligations. As another example, life insurance companies sell a variety of products, most of which guarantee a dollar payment at some time in the future or a stream of dollar payments over time. Therefore, the investment objective of the life insurance company would be to satisfy the obligations stipulated in the policy and to generate a profit. For an investment company (i.e., mutual fund), the investment objective is set forth in the fund's prospectus.

It is common in practice to find that the investment objective of the institution is different from that of the manager hired to manage the funds. A good

1

example is a defined benefit pension fund. For this type of pension fund, the liabilities are the obligations of the sponsor of the pension fund (i.e., plan sponsor). The objective of the plan sponsor is to invest those funds so as to satisfy the projected liabilities to the plan beneficiaries. Often, a plan sponsor will hire one or more investment management firms to manage the funds. However, the firms engaged to manage the funds are given an investment objective that is often far different from the plan sponsor's investment objective. Typically, the investment objective is to outperform (i.e., earn a higher rate of return than one of the stock market indexes described in Chapter 5. The implicit assumption of the plan sponsor is that the stock market index selected as the benchmark for the manager will at least generate a rate of return that will be sufficient to satisfy the projected liabilities that have to be paid to beneficiaries.

In this book, we do not focus on the investment objectives of institutional investors. Rather, we assume that a manager is given an investment objective by the client that is cast in terms of some stock market index. The investment objective may be to simply match the performance of the stock market index or to outperform that index. In the case of outperforming an index, the equity manager is seeking to "add value." The amount of outperformance is referred to in the jargon of the investment management business as the manager's alpha.

## Establishing Investment Policy

The second step in the investment management process is establishing investment policy to satisfy the investment objectives. Setting policy begins with the asset allocation decision. That is, the appropriate individual or board of the institution must decide how the institution's funds should be distributed among the major classes of assets in which it may invest. The major asset classes typically include stocks, bonds, real estate, and foreign securities. Client and regulatory constraints must be considered in establishing an investment policy. Since our focus in this book is on equity portfolio management, we take the asset allocation decision among the major asset classes as given.

In setting policy guidelines, the client will specify its risk tolerance. At one time, risk tolerance was defined in a "soft" way. For example, an investment policy that a client might give to a manager it retained could state that the client wants the manager to follow a "low risk investment policy" or an "aggressive policy." Such mandates are difficult to implement because the terms can be interpreted differently by each manager. Today, clients attempt to define risk tolerance in a quantitative fashion. Modern portfolio theory, as we describe in Chapter 2, provides the tools that can be used to quantify risk.

In setting policy guidelines, the client must also specify whether or not the manager is permitted to use derivative instruments and the circumstances under which they may be used. Derivative instruments such as options, futures, and swaps are explained in Chapter 12, while their application in equity portfolio management is described in Chapter 13.

# Selecting a Portfolio Strategy

Selecting an equity portfolio strategy that is consistent with the investment policy guidelines of the client or institution is the third step in the investment management process. Portfolio strategies can be classified as either active or passive.

An active portfolio strategy uses available information and forecasting techniques to seek a better performance than a portfolio that is simply diversified broadly. In Chapter 9 we will describe the factors that appear to be responsible for generating the returns on common stock. Essential to all active equity portfolio strategies are expectations about the factors that could influence the performance of stocks. For example, with active equity portfolio strategies this may include forecasts of future earnings, cash flows, dividends, or price-earnings and price-book value ratios.

A passive portfolio strategy involves minimal expectational input, and instead relies on diversification to match the performance of some stock market index. Because a passive portfolio strategy involves matching some stock market index, this strategy is commonly referred to as indexing. In effect, an indexing strategy assumes that the marketplace will reflect all available information in the price paid for securities.

Between these extremes of active and passive/indexing strategies, new strategies have sprung up that have elements of both. For example, the core of a portfolio may be passively managed with the balance actively managed. An enhanced indexing strategy is one in which the portfolio is actively managed but the degree to which the portfolio differs from the characteristics of the specified stock market index is small. In Chapter 4 we will discuss the factors in deciding whether a client may elect to have its manager(s) actively or passively manage its funds. In Chapter 4, we also describe an active-passive strategy that attempts to mine the best of both the passive and active approaches to equity portfolio management.[1]

# Selecting Stocks

Once an equity portfolio strategy is selected, the next step is stock selection or stock picking. It is in this step that the manager attempts to construct an efficient portfolio. As we explain in Chapter 2, in modern portfolio theory an efficient portfolio is one that provides the greatest expected return for a given level of risk, or equivalently, the lowest risk for a given expected return. The specific meaning of return and risk cannot be provided at this time. As we develop our understanding of modern portfolio theory in Chapter 2 and equity factor models in Chapter 9, we will be able to quantify what we mean by these terms.

---

[1] It is interesting to note that the College Retirement Equities Fund (CREF) now employs a combination of active and quantitative (or passive oriented) techniques. In a recent newsletter to TIAA-CREF participants it was stated that "the two approaches complement each other, with funds in each account shifting between active and quantitative segments in response to investment opportunities." For a brief description of portfolio management products at CREF, see *Investment Forum*, TIAA-CREF, Volume 3, Number 1, Winter 1999.

## Exhibit 1: The Investing Process

| Information Value | *less* | Implementation Cost | *equals* | Captured Value |
|---|---|---|---|---|

Source: See Wayne H. Wagner and Mark Edwards, "Implementing Investment Strategies: The Art and Science of Investing," Chapter 11 in Frank J. Fabozzi (ed.), *Active Equity Portfolio Management* (New Hope, PA: Frank J. Fabozzi Associates, 1998).

## Measuring and Evaluating Performance

The measurement and evaluation of investment performance is the last step in the investment management process. Actually, it is misleading to say that it is the last step since the investment process is an ongoing process. This step involves measuring the performance of the portfolio and then evaluating that performance relative to some benchmark. A benchmark is simply the performance of a predetermined set of securities, obtained for comparison purposes. The benchmark may be a popular stock market index such as the Standard & Poor's 500. Institutional investors have worked with consultants to develop customized benchmarks that better reflect their investment objectives.

Although a portfolio manager may have performed better than a benchmark portfolio, this does not necessarily mean that the portfolio satisfied the client's investment objectives. For example, suppose that the sponsor of a pension fund established as its objective the maximization of portfolio return and allocated 75% of the fund to stocks and the balance to bonds. Suppose further that the manager retained to manage the stock portfolio earned a return over a 1-year horizon that was 300 basis points greater than the established benchmark. Assuming that the risk of the portfolio was similar to that of the benchmark, it would appear that the manager outperformed the benchmark. However, suppose that in spite of this performance, the pension fund cannot meet its liabilities. Then the failure was in establishing the investment objectives and setting policy, not the manager's performance.

## INTEGRATED APPROACH TO PORTFOLIO MANAGEMENT

We have set forth the investment management process as a series of five distinct steps. However, equity portfolio management requires an integrated approach. There must be recognition that superior investment performance results when valuable ideas are implemented in a cost efficient manner. Wayne Wagner and Mark Edwards [2] emphasize that the process of investing — as opposed to the process of investment — includes innovative stock selection and portfolio strategies as well as efficient

---

[2] See Wayne H. Wagner and Mark Edwards, "Implementing Investment Strategies: The Art and Science of Investing," Chapter 11 in Frank J. Fabozzi (ed.), *Active Equity Portfolio Management* (New Hope, PA: Frank J. Fabozzi Associates, 1998).

cost structures for the implementation of any portfolio strategy. Exhibit 1 highlights the importance of an integrated approach to managing equity portfolios with the recognition that the value added is the result of information value less the implementation cost of trading. Wagner and Edwards refer to this value as "captured value."

This view that an investing process requires an integrated approach to portfolio management is reinforced by BARRA, a vendor of analytical systems used by portfolio managers. BARRA emphasizes that superior investment performance is the product of careful attention paid by equity managers to the following four elements:[3]

- forming reasonable return expectations
- controlling portfolio risk to demonstrate investment prudence
- controlling trading costs
- monitoring total investment performance

Accordingly, the investing process that includes these four elements are all equally important in what BARRA refers to as the "apex" of superior investment performance. We discussed the role of the last element—namely, monitoring investment performance — earlier. Below we'll briefly describe the role of the first three of these investing elements for managing equity portfolios.

## Formation of Expected Returns

Forecasting expected security and portfolio returns — whether directly or indirectly — is the essence of what most equity managers do. Central to the formation of those return expectations is the manager's perception of the degree of pricing efficiency in the capital market.[4] The concept of "pricing efficiency" and its implications in managing equity portfolios are explained in Chapter 2. If a manager believes that the capital market (or any sub-component thereof) is largely price inefficient, then he or she has an incentive to employ active management strategies that seek to generate abnormal returns — where abnormal or "excess returns" are measured relative to a benchmark index such as the S&P 500, or a customized benchmark that is consistent with the equity manager's "style" of investing. Along this line, many active strategies employ fundamental and/or quantitative tools of the type explained in this book to identify mispriced securities in the marketplace.

Conversely, if the equity manager believes that the capital market is mostly price efficient, then he or she has an incentive to form return expectations that are consistent with the holdings of well diversified or "efficient portfolios" — which as we noted earlier in the jargon of modern portfolio theory is a portfolio that provides the maximum expected return for a given level of risk. In effect, if

---

[3] These portfolio management elements are the foundation for BARRA's Market Impact Model™. A brief description of their equity trading model is covered in a three-part newsletter series — see Nicolo Torre, "The Market Impact Model™," Equity Trading: Research, BARRA Newsletters 165-167, (BARRA, 1998).

[4] A capital market that is "price efficient" is one where current security prices "fully reflect" all available information that is relevant to the pricing of securities.

stock prices reflect full information, then it makes little sense for the equity manager to spend time (and money) in a research activity that is on the average doomed to produce inferior performance. In this instance, according to modern portfolio theory, the equity manager has an incentive to form a portfolio that consists of efficient combinations of a "risk-free" asset and a portfolio consisting of all risky securities. The portfolio of all risky securities is called the market portfolio. The combination of all possible combinations of the risk-free asset and the market portfolio— as generally displayed in a graph showing expected return versus risk — is called the capital market line. It represents that alternative set of (two asset) efficient portfolio choices for a passive equity manager.

## Portfolio Risk Management

Controlling risk is a primary responsibility of portfolio managers. Risk in equity management has several connotations and is often viewed in the context of:

- Probability of loss in portfolio value (downside risk)
- Volatility of portfolio returns (without indication of price direction)
- Fundamental risk to security value when companies "miss" consensus estimates (earnings, cash flow, dividends, etc.)
- Risk of failure to produce a given level of active reward (performance over-and-above a representative passive benchmark)

At this introductory juncture, it is perhaps most beneficial to focus on the risk of failing to produce a given level of active portfolio return. In this context, Bruce Jacobs and Kenneth Levy suggest that traditional equity managers face a portfolio management dilemma involving a tradeoff between the depth, or "goodness," of their equity management insights and the breadth or scope of their equity management ideas.[5] According to Jacobs and Levy, the breadth of active research conducted by equity managers is constrained in practical terms by the number of investment ideas (or securities) that can be implemented (researched) in a timely and cost efficient manner. This tradeoff is shown in Exhibit 2.

The exhibit displays the relationship between the depth of equity manager insights (vertical axis) and the breadth of those insights (horizontal axis). The depth of equity manager insights is measured in formal terms by the information coefficient (IC, on the vertical axis of Exhibit 2), while the breadth (BR) of manager insights can be measured by the potential number of investment ideas or the number of securities in the capital market.[6] When the breadth of equity man-

---

[5] See Bruce I. Jacobs and Kenneth N. Levy, "Investment Management: An Architecture for the Equity Market," Chapter 1 in Frank J. Fabozzi (ed.), *Active Equity Portfolio Management* (New Hope, PA: Frank J. Fabozzi Associates, 1998).
[6] The information coefficient, IC, measures the association (or correlation) between forecasted and actual portfolio returns. We cover the information coefficient, and its close performance measurement associate, the information ratio (investment return/risk ratio) in Chapter 14.

ager insights is low — as in the case of traditional equity management, according to Jacobs and Levy—then the depth, or "goodness" of each insight needs to be high in order to produce a constant level of investment reward-to-investment risk. Exhibit 2 shows that this low breadth/high depth combination produces the same level of active reward that would be associated with a pair-wise high number of investable ideas (or securities) and a relatively low level of equity manager insights.

In a risk management context, one can say that the probability of failure to achieve a given level of active reward is quite high when the breadth of investment ideas or securities to be analyzed is very low. That scenario is likely in the traditional "bottom up" approach to active equity management that we discuss in Chapter 4. On the other hand, the risk of not achieving a given level of active reward is low when the breadth of implementable manager ideas is high. That can happen in a world where active managers employ what Jacobs and Levy refer to as the "engineered" approach to active portfolio management.[7] However, if the capital market is largely price efficient, then the probability of failing to produce any level of active reward is high (near unity). With market efficiency, investable ideas are transparent, and their active implications are already fully impounded in security prices.

---

## Exhibit 2: Combination of Breadth (Number) of Insights and Depth, or "Goodness," of Insights Needed to Produce a Given Investment Return/Risk Ratio

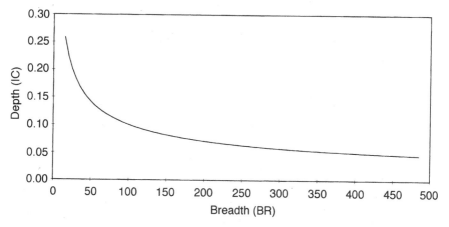

Source: See Bruce I. Jacobs and Kenneth N. Levy, "Investment Management: An Architecture for the Equity Market," Chapter 1 in Frank J. Fabozzi (ed.), *Active Equity Portfolio Management* (New Hope, PA: Frank J. Fabozzi Associates, 1998).

---

[7] See Jacobs and Levy, "Investment Management: An Architecture for the Equity Market."

## Equity Trading Considerations

Over the 10-year period 1987 to 1996 one mutual fund (the Vanguard Index 500) that follows a particular passive approach to investing called indexing outperformed some 80% of actively managed portfolios.[8] If equity managers have good stock selection skills, then why are they losing to more passive-oriented strategies? According to Wagner and Edwards, the cost of implementing valuable investment ideas has been both misunderstood and underestimated — such that equity managers have incurred sub-par performance despite the presence of better than average investment ideas.[9]

Equity trading costs consist of more than just the explicit fee charged by brokers to handle and clear trades. As explained in Chapter 11, there are direct and indirect trading costs that can be measured in the context of:

- Commissions and other direct charges (custody fees, taxes, etc.)
- Price impact that reflects the cost of finding liquidity by the broker/dealer
- Trader timing costs that arise from liquidity probing by the firm's trader(s)
- Opportunity cost arising from incomplete or failed trades

Wagner and Edwards estimate that these trading cost are equal to about 2.76% of potential active performance. Because of the magnitude of these costs, one can see why today's equity managers may have seemingly "winning" ideas, yet losing investment results — especially when performance is compared to a passive indexing strategy having substantially lower turnover rates for the underlying securities in a buy and hold portfolio. Indeed, this highlights the importance of what Wagner and Edwards call an investing process (recall Exhibit 1), where "captured value" consists of the information value from creative ideas (a reflection of the investment process) less the cost of getting those ideas into equity portfolios.

## OVERVIEW OF BOOK

Having described the process for managing equity portfolios and why the process should viewed as an integrated one, our goal in this book is to explain the methodologies and issues surrounding (1) the active and passive approaches to equity portfolio management and (2) the cost-efficient ways of implementing valuable investment ideas. We begin by explaining the theories, models, and equity strategies that lay the foundation for what equity managers do in practice when selecting stocks and constructing portfolios. That is an essential component of the investment management process, and it constitutes a large portion of the material covered in this book. The rest of our coverage of equity management is devoted to

---

[8] Lipper Analytical Services. Ten-year comparisons as of December 31, 1996. Investment results include only managers with 10-year histories.
[9] See Wagner and Edwards, "Implementing Investment Strategies: The Art and Science of Investing."

equity trading issues and strategies — including the role of derivative securities — that seek to enhance or protect the economic value of investable ideas.

Chapters 2 and 3 focus on the theoretical and statistical tenets of three important theories: modern portfolio theory, capital market theory, and asset pricing theory. Taken together, the investment concepts introduced in developing these theories and the implications and models that are the products of these theories provide a framework for evaluating the design of both passive and active approaches to managing equity portfolios.

The central issue as to whether to passively or actively manage an equity portfolio is the degree to which the capital market is price efficient. In Chapter 4 we explain what is meant by a price efficient market and then provide evidence that suggests that the capital market is neither 100% price efficient, nor 100% price inefficient. Based on that evidence, we develop in Chapter 4 a "blueprint" for a passive-active approach to investment management. In a nutshell, the passive- active model recognizes — in a systematic manner — that some sectors of the global equity market may be highly price efficient while other sectors may be price inefficient. Indeed, organizing for passive-active investing allows the passive and active frameworks to exist simultaneously in the overall investment program.

We then devote several chapters to explaining traditional and modern approaches to active equity management. In Chapter 6 we focus on traditional fundamental analysis. In Chapter 7 we explore the emerging role of "value-based metrics" (including EVA® and CFROI®) in securities analysis and equity portfolio management, an approach that has had an increased following by practitioners in recent years. In Chapter 8 we look at the theory and application of discounted cash flow models. In this context, we cover the traditional dividend discount model and free cash flow approaches to equity valuation, along with the modern "economic profit" and "sales franchise" approaches to corporate (enterprise) valuation and stock price estimation.

The role of multiple factor models in assessing portfolio returns and controlling equity risk is our focus in Chapter 9. These models can be categorized as macroeconomic factor models and fundamental factor models. The macroeconomic factor models that we review are the Burmeister, Ibbotson, Roll, and Ross model, the Salomon Risk Attribute Model, and the Northfield Information Services Macroeconomic Factor model. The prominent fundamental factor models we review include the BARRA, Wilshire, and Goldman Sachs Asset Management models.

In Chapter 10, we profile the active management strategies of five equity management firms: Jacobs Levy Equity Management, State Street Global Advisors, Credit Suisse Asset Management, Boston Partners Asset Management, and Columbia Management Company. The real time investment approaches of these five companies are not only interesting in their own right, but they also serve to show that many of the investment concepts and models explained in this book are used in the practice of managing equity portfolios.

In Chapter 11 we cover the process of equity trading and its strategic role in the implementation of valuable investment ideas. In the same chapter we present alternative equity trading strategies. In Chapters 12 and 13 we explain the role of derivative instruments in implementing a strategy in a cost efficient way and for controlling portfolio risk.

Our focus in Chapter 14 is on the measurement of investment performance. We present some traditional measures of performance — Sharpe, Treynor, and Jensen measures — and their limitations in assessing the performance of a money manager. We then explain how equity factor models are used to develop return attribution models that can be used to assess a manager's performance.

Finally, the combination of returns management, portfolio risk control, trading cost efficiency, and total process control are the essence of an integrated approach to managing equity portfolios. An understanding of these elements presented in this book should go a long way in the effort to build equity portfolios to meet client dictated investment objectives.

# Chapter 2

# Modern Portfolio Theory, Capital Market Theory, and Asset Pricing Models

In this chapter, we set forth theories that are the underpinnings for the management of portfolios: modern portfolio theory and capital market theory. *Modern portfolio theory* deals with the selection of portfolios that maximize expected returns consistent with individually acceptable levels of risk. Using quantitative models and historical data, modern portfolio theory defines "expected portfolio returns" and "acceptable levels of portfolio risk," and shows how to construct an "optimal portfolio."

*Capital market theory* deals with the effects of investor decisions on security prices. More specifically, it shows the relationship that should exist between security returns and risk if investors constructed portfolios as indicated by modern portfolio theory. Together, modern portfolio theory and capital market theory provide a framework to specify and measure investment risk and to develop relationships between expected security return and risk (and hence between risk and required return on an investment). These relationships are called *asset pricing models*.

Modern portfolio theory and capital market theory have revolutionized the world of investment management by allowing managers to quantify the investment risk and expected return of a portfolio. Moreover, these theories tell us that the focus of portfolio management should be the risk of the entire portfolio, not the risk of the individual assets. That is, it is possible to combine risky assets and produce a portfolio whose expected return reflects its components, but with considerably lower risk.

Our purpose in this chapter is to present the basic principles and implications. We do not attempt to provide a rigorous derivation of the relationships presented. In Chapter 4, we discuss the implications of these theories for selecting an equity management strategy.

## MODERN PORTFOLIO THEORY

Prior to modern portfolio theory, practitioners would often speak of risk and return, but the failure to quantify these important measures made the goal of constructing an optimal portfolio highly subjective and provided no insight about the return investors should expect. Moreover, portfolio managers would focus on the risks of individual assets without understanding how combining them into a portfolio can affect the portfolio's risk.

11

# Some Basic Concepts

The theories presented in this chapter draw on concepts from two fields: financial economic theory and probability and statistical theory. Chapter 3, provides a review of some of the basic concepts of probability and statistics that we use in this chapter. In this section we will describe several concepts from financial economic theory that will be used. Many of the concepts have a more technical or rigorous definition. Our goal here is to keep the explanation simple enough to appreciate the importance and applicability of these concepts to the development of modern portfolio theory and capital market theory.

## Efficient Portfolios and an Optimal Portfolio

In constructing a portfolio, investors seek to maximize the expected return from their investment given some level of risk they are willing to accept.[1] Portfolios that satisfy this requirement are called *efficient portfolios*. The concepts of expected return and risk will be defined more specifically as we proceed in the development of modern portfolio theory.

To construct an efficient portfolio, it is necessary to make some assumption about how investors behave in making investment decisions. A reasonable assumption is that investors are risk averse. A *risk-averse investor* is one who when faced with two investments with the same expected return but two different risks will prefer the one with the lower risk. Given a choice of efficient portfolios from which an investor can select, an *optimal portfolio* is the one that is most preferred.

## Utility Function and Indifference Curves

In economic theory, there are many situations where individuals and firms face choices. The "theory of choice" describes the decision-making process with the help of a concept called the *utility function*. A utility function is a mathematical expression that assigns a value to all possible choices. The higher the value, the greater the utility. Simply put, in portfolio theory the utility function expresses the preferences of economic entities with respect to perceived risk and expected return.

A utility function can be expressed in graphical form by an indifference curve. Exhibit 1 shows indifference curves labeled $u_1$, $u_2$, and $u_3$. The horizontal axis measures risk, and the vertical axis measures expected return. Each curve represents a set of portfolios with different combinations of risk and return. All the points on a given indifference curve indicate combinations of risk and expected return that will give the same level of utility to a given investor. For example, on utility curve $u_1$, there are two points $u$ and $u'$, with $u$ having a higher expected return than $u'$, but also having a higher risk. An investor has an equal preference for (or is indifferent to) any point on the curve, because the curve reflects the investor's level of risk aversion. The slope of an indifference curve reflects the fact that investors require a higher expected return in order to accept higher risk.

---

[1] Alternatively stated, investors seek to minimize the risk that they are exposed to given some target expected return.

## Exhibit 1: Indifference Curves

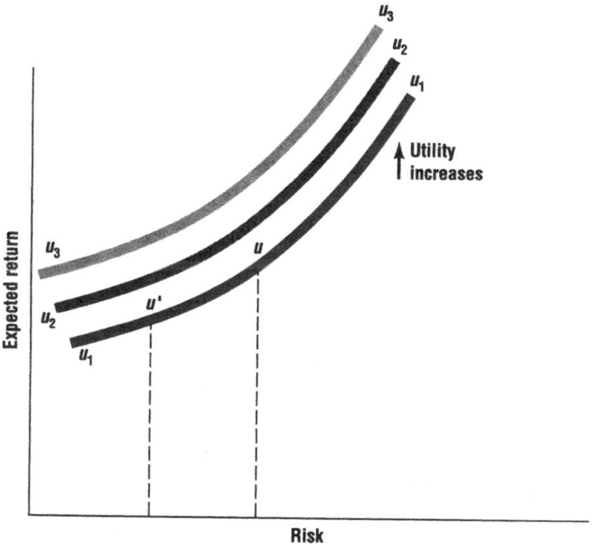

For the three indifference curves shown in Exhibit 1, the utility the investor receives is greater the further the indifference curve is from the horizontal axis, because that curve represents a higher level of return at every level of risk. Thus, for the three indifference curves shown in the figure, $u_3$ has the highest utility and $u_1$ the lowest.

### Risky Assets versus Risk-Free Assets

A risky asset is one for which the return that will be realized in the future is uncertain. For example, suppose an investor purchases the stock of Merck today and plans to hold the stock for one year. At the time the investor purchases the stock, he or she does not know what return will be realized. The return will depend on the price of Merck stock one year from now and the dividends that the company pays during the year. Thus, the pharmaceutical stock, and indeed the stock of all companies, is a risky asset.

There are assets, however, for which the return that will be realized in the future is known with certainty today. Such assets are referred to as *risk-free* or *riskless assets*. The risk-free asset is commonly defined as short-term obligations of the U.S. government. For example, if an investor buys a U.S. government security that matures in one year and plans to hold that security for one year, then there is no uncertainty about the return that will be realized. The investor knows that in one year, the maturity date of the security, the government will pay a specific amount to retire the debt.

# Measuring a Portfolio's Expected Return

Investors are most often faced with choices among risky assets. Here we will look at how to measure the expected return of a risky asset and the expected return of a portfolio of risky assets.

## Measuring Single-Period Portfolio Return

The *actual* return on a portfolio of assets over some specific time period is straightforward to calculate, as shown below:

$$R_p = w_1 R_1 + w_2 R_2 + ... + w_G R_G \qquad (1)$$

where

$R_p$ = rate of return on the portfolio over the period
$R_g$ = rate of return on asset g over the period
$w_g$ = weight of asset g in the portfolio (i.e., asset g as a proportion of the market value of the total portfolio)
$G$ = number of assets in the portfolio

Equation (1) states that the return on a portfolio of $G$ assets ($R_p$) is equal to the sum of the individual asset weights in the portfolio times its return, for each asset g. The portfolio return $R_p$ is sometimes called the *holding period return*, or the *ex post return*. For example, consider the following portfolio consisting of three assets:

| Asset | Market value | Rate of return |
|-------|-------------|----------------|
| 1 | $6 million | 12% |
| 2 | $8 million | 10% |
| 3 | $11 million | 5% |

The portfolio's total market value is $25 million. Therefore,

$R_1 = 12\%$  and  $w_1 = \$6$ million/$25 million = 0.24 or 24%
$R_2 = 10\%$  and  $w_2 = \$8$ million/$25 million = 0.32 or 32%
$R_3 = 5\%$  and  $w_3 = \$11$ million/$25 million = 0.44 or 44%

and the portfolio's return is then

$$R_p = 0.24 \,(12\%) + 0.32 \,(10\%) + 0.44 \,(5\%) = 8.28\%$$

## The Expected Return of a Portfolio of Risky Assets

Equation (1) shows how to calculate the actual return of a portfolio over some specific time period. In portfolio management, the investor also wants to know the expected (or anticipated) return from a portfolio of risky assets. The expected portfolio return is the weighted average of the expected return of each asset in the portfolio. The weight assigned to the expected return of each asset is the percentage of the market value of the asset to the total market value of the portfolio. That is,

$$E(R_p) = w_1 \, E(R_1) + w_2 \, E(R_2) + ... + w_G \, E(R_G) \qquad (2)$$

The $E(\ )$ signifies expectations, and $E(R_P)$ is sometimes called *ex ante return,* or the expected portfolio return over some specific time period.

The expected return on a risky asset is calculated as follows. First, a probability distribution for the possible rates of return that can be realized must be specified. A probability distribution is a function that associates the probability of occurrence to a possible outcome for a random variable. Given the probability distribution, the expected value of a random variable is simply the weighted average of the possible outcomes, where the weight is the probability associated with the possible outcome. Rather than use the term "expected value of the return of an asset," we simply use the term *expected return.* Mathematically, the expected return of asset $i$ is expressed as

$$E(R_i) = p_1\, r_1 + p_2\, r_2 + \ldots + p_N\, r_N \qquad (3)$$

where

$r_n$ = the $n$-*th* possible rate of return for asset $i$
$p_n$ = probability of attaining rate of return $n$ for asset $i$
$N$ = number of possible outcomes for the rate of return

In practice, the probability distribution is based on historical returns.

Assume that an individual is considering an investment, stock XYZ, which has a probability distribution for the rate of return for some time period as given below:

| $n$ | Rate of return (%) | Probability of occurrence |
|---|---|---|
| 1 | 15 | 0.50 |
| 2 | 10 | 0.30 |
| 3 | 5 | 0.13 |
| 4 | 0 | 0.05 |
| 5 | −5 | 0.02 |

Substituting into equation (3), we get

$$E(R_{XYZ}) = 0.50\,(15\%) + 0.30(10\%) + 0.13\,(5\%) + 0.05\,(0\%) + 0.02\,(-5\%)$$
$$= 11\%$$

Thus, 11% is the expected value or mean of the probability distribution for the rate of return on stock XYZ.

## Measuring Portfolio Risk

Investors have used a variety of definitions of risk. Professor Harry Markowitz changed how the investment community thought about risk by quantifying the concept of risk.[2] He defined risk in terms of a well-known statistical measure

---

[2] Harry M. Markowitz, "Portfolio Selection," *Journal of Finance* (March 1952), pp. 77-91, and *Portfolio Selection*, Cowles Foundation Monograph 16 (New York: John Wiley & Sons, 1959).

known as the *variance*. Specifically, Markowitz quantified risk as the variance about an asset's expected return.

### Variance as a Measure of Risk

The variance of a random variable is a measure of the dispersion of the possible outcomes around the expected value. In the case of an asset's return, the variance is a measure of the dispersion of the possible outcomes for the rate of return around the expected return.

The equation for the variance of the return for asset $i$, denoted var$(R_i)$, is

$$\text{var}(R_i) = p_1[r_1 - E(R_i)]^2 + p_2[r_2 - E(R_i)]^2 + ... + p_N[r_N - E(R_i)]^2 \qquad (4)$$

Using the probability distribution of the return for stock XYZ we can illustrate the calculation of the variance:

$$\text{var}(R_{XYZ}) = 0.50[15\% - 11\%]^2 + 0.30[10\% - 11\%]^2 + 0.13[5\% - 11\%]^2$$
$$+ 0.05[0\% - 11\%]^2 + 0.02[-5\% - 11\%]^2 = 24\%$$

The variance associated with a distribution of returns measures the tightness with which the distribution is clustered around the mean or expected return. Markowitz argued that this tightness or variance is equivalent to the uncertainty or riskiness of the investment. If an asset is riskless, it has a dispersion of zero around the expected return.

Since the variance is squared units, it is common to see the variance converted to the standard deviation or square root of the variance:

$$SD(R_i) = \sqrt{\text{var}(R_i)}$$

For stock XYZ, then, the standard deviation is:

$$SD(R_{XYZ}) = \sqrt{24\%} = 4.9\%$$

The two are conceptually equivalent; that is, the larger the variance or standard deviation, the greater the investment risk.

There are two criticisms of the use of the variance as a measure of risk. The first criticism is that since the variance measures the dispersion of an asset's return around its expected return, it considers the possibility of returns above the expected return and below the expected return. Investors, however, do not view possible returns above the expected return as an unfavorable outcome. In fact, such outcomes are quite favorable. Because of this, some have argued that measures of risk should not consider the possible returns above the expected return.

Markowitz recognized this limitation and, in fact, suggested a measure of downside risk — the risk of realizing an outcome below the expected return — called the *semi-variance*. The semi-variance is similar to the variance except that in the calculation no consideration is given to returns above the expected return. However, because of the computational problems with using the semi-variance and the limited resources available to him at the time, he compromised and used the variance in developing portfolio theory.

Today, various measures of downside risk are currently being used by practitioners. However, regardless of the measure used, the basic principles of portfolio theory developed by Markowitz are applicable. That is, the choice of the measure of risk may affect the calculation but doesn't invalidate the theory.

The second criticism is that the variance is only one measure of how the returns vary around the expected return. When a probability distribution is not symmetrical around its expected return, then a statistical measure of the skewness of a distribution should be used in addition to the variance. The variance can be justified based on empirical evidence which suggests that the historical distribution of the returns on stocks is approximately symmetrical.[3] Because expected return and variance are the only two parameters that investors are assumed to consider in making investment decisions, the Markowitz formulation of portfolio theory is often referred to as a *two-parameter model*.

### Measuring the Portfolio Risk of a Two-Asset Portfolio

Equation (4) gives the variance for an individual asset's return. The variance of a portfolio consisting of two assets is a little more difficult to calculate. It depends not only on the variance of the two assets, but also upon how closely one asset tracks the other asset. The formula is

$$\text{var}(R_p) = w_i^2 \ \text{var}(R_i) + w_j^2 \ \text{var}(R_j) + 2 \ w_i \ w_j \ \text{cov}(R_i,R_j) \tag{5}$$

where

$$\text{cov}(R_i,R_j) = \text{covariance between the return for assets } i \text{ and } j$$

In words, equation (5) states that the variance of the portfolio return is the sum of the weighted variances of the two assets plus the weighted covariance between the two assets.

The covariance is a new term in this discussion and has a precise mathematical translation. However, its practical meaning is the degree to which the returns on two assets vary or change together. The covariance is not expressed in a particular unit, such as dollars or percent. A positive covariance means the returns on two assets tend to move or change in the same direction, while a negative covariance means the returns move in opposite directions.

The covariance is analogous to the correlation between the returns for two assets. Specifically, the correlation between the returns for assets $i$ and $j$ is defined as the covariance of the two assets divided by the product of their standard deviations:

$$\text{cor}(R_i, R_j) = \frac{\text{cov}(R_i, R_j)}{\text{SD}(R_i)\text{SD}(R_j)}$$

---

[3] See Chapters 1 and 2 in Eugene Fama, *Foundations of Finance* (New York: Basic Books, 1976).

The correlation and the covariance are conceptually equivalent terms. Dividing the covariance by the product of the standard deviations simply (but importantly) makes the correlation a number that is comparable across different assets. The correlation coefficient can have values ranging from +1.0, denoting perfect comovement in the same direction, to −1.0, denoting perfect comovement in opposite directions.

In our illustration of how to calculate the expected return, variance, and standard deviation, we used the probability distributions for the stock. As such, they are truly "expected values," since they were derived probabilistically. In practice, the estimation of these statistical measures is typically obtained from *historical* observations on the rate of returns. We show how this is done in the next chapter.

Now let's look at the implications of the variance of the portfolio as given by equation (5). The equation tells us that since the variance of a portfolio depends on the covariances of its constituent securities, a portfolio's risk can be low despite the fact that the risk of individual assets making up the portfolio can be quite high. This principle has important implications for managing portfolios, as we shall see below.

### Measuring the Risk of a Portfolio with More Than Two Assets

Thus far we have given the portfolio risk for a portfolio consisting of two assets. The extension to three assets — $i$, $j$, and $k$ — is as follows:

$$\text{var}(R_p) = w_i^2 \ \text{var}(R_i) + w_j^2 \ \text{var}(R_j) + w_k^2 \ \text{var}(R_k) + 2 \, w_i \, w_j \, \text{cov}(R_i, R_j)$$
$$+ \ 2 \, w_i \, w_k \, \text{cov}(R_i, R_k) + 2 \, w_j \, w_k \, \text{cov}(R_j, R_k) \tag{6}$$

In words, equation (6) states that the variance of the portfolio return is the sum of the weighted variances of the individual assets plus the sum of the weighted covariances of the assets. Hence, the variance of the portfolio return is the weighted sum of the individual variances of the assets in the portfolio plus the weighted sum of the degree to which the assets vary together.

In general, for a portfolio with $G$ assets, the portfolio variance is

$$\text{var}(R_p) = \sum_{g=1}^{G} w_g^2 \text{var}(R_g) + \sum_{g=1}^{G} \sum_{h=1}^{G} w_g w_h \, \text{cov}(R_g, R_h) \tag{7}$$
$$\text{for } h \neq g$$

## Portfolio Diversification

Often, one hears investors talking about "diversifying" their portfolio. By this an investor means constructing a portfolio in such a way as to reduce portfolio risk without sacrificing return. This is certainly a goal that investors should seek. However, the question is how does one do this in practice.

Some investors would say that a portfolio can be diversified by including assets across all asset classes. For example, one investor might argue that a portfolio should be diversified by investing in stocks, bonds, and real estate. While that might be reasonable, two questions must be addressed in order to construct a diversified portfolio. First, how much should be invested in each asset class? Should 40% of the portfolio be in stocks, 50% in bonds, and 10% in real estate, or is some other allocation more appropriate? Second, given the allocation, which specific stocks, bonds, and real estate should the investor select?

Some investors who focus only on one asset class such as common stock argue that such portfolios should also be diversified. By this they mean that an investor should not place all funds in the stock of one corporation, but rather should include stocks of many corporations. Here, too, several questions must be answered in order to construct a diversified portfolio. First, which corporations should be represented in the portfolio? Second, how much of the portfolio should be allocated to the stocks of each corporation?

Prior to the development of portfolio theory, while investors often talked about diversification in these general terms, they never provided the analytical tools by which to answer the questions posed above. A major contribution of portfolio theory is that using the concepts discussed above, a quantitative measure of the diversification of a portfolio is possible, and it is this measure that can be used to achieve the maximum diversification benefits.

## Markowitz Diversification

The Markowitz diversification strategy is primarily concerned with the degree of covariance between asset returns in a portfolio. Indeed a key contribution of Markowitz diversification is the formulation of an asset's risk in terms of a portfolio of assets, rather than in isolation. *Markowitz diversification* seeks to combine assets in a portfolio with returns that are less than perfectly positively correlated, in an effort to lower portfolio risk (variance) without sacrificing return. It is the concern for maintaining return, while lowering risk through an analysis of the covariance between asset returns, that separates Markowitz diversification from the naive approaches mentioned above and makes it more effective.

Markowitz diversification and the importance of asset correlations can be illustrated with a simple two-asset portfolio example. To do this, we will first show the general relationship between the risk of a two-asset portfolio and the correlation of returns of the component assets. Then we will look at the effects on portfolio risk of combining assets with different correlations.

**Portfolio Risk and Correlation**  In our two-asset portfolio, assume that common stock C and common stock D are available with expected returns and standard deviations as shown:

|          | $E(R)$ | $SD(R)$ |
|----------|--------|---------|
| Stock C  | 10%    | 30%     |
| Stock D  | 25%    | 60%     |

If an equal weighting (50%) is assigned to both stocks $C$ and $D$, the expected portfolio return can be calculated as:

$$E(R_p) = 0.50(10\%) + 0.50(25\%) = 17.5\%$$

The variance of the return on the two-stock portfolio is

$$\mathrm{var}(R_p) = w_C^2\ \mathrm{var}(R_C) + w_D^2\ \mathrm{var}(R_D) + 2\ w_C\ w_D\ \mathrm{cov}(R_C,R_D)$$
$$= (0.5)^2\ (30\%)^2 + (0.5)^2\ (60\%)^2 + 2(0.5)(0.5)\mathrm{cov}(R_C,R_D)$$

From the relationship between correlation and covariance we have

$$\mathrm{cor}(R_C, R_D) = \frac{\mathrm{cov}(R_C, R_D)}{\mathrm{SD}(R_C)\mathrm{SD}(R_D)}$$

so

$$\mathrm{cov}(R_C,R_D) = \mathrm{SD}(R_C)\ \mathrm{SD}(R_D)\ \mathrm{cor}(R_C,R_D)$$

Since $\mathrm{SD}(R_C) = 30\%$ and $\mathrm{SD}(R_D) = 60\%$, then

$$\mathrm{cov}(R_C,R_D) = (30\%)(60\%)\ \mathrm{cor}(R_C,R_D)$$

Substituting into the expression for $\mathrm{var}(R_p)$, we get

$$\mathrm{var}(R_p) = (0.5)^2(30\%)^2 + (0.5)^2(60\%)^2 + 2(0.5)(0.5)(30\%)(60\%)\ \mathrm{cor}(R_C,R_D)$$

Taking the square root of the variance:

$$\mathrm{SD}(R_p) = \sqrt{(0.5)^2(30\%)^2 + (0.5)^2(60\%)^2 + 2(0.5)0.5(30\%)(60\%)\mathrm{cor}(R_C, R_D)}$$
$$= \sqrt{0.1125 + (0.09)\mathrm{cor}(R_C, R_D)}$$

***The Effect of the Correlation of Asset Returns on Portfolio Risk*** How would the risk change for our two-asset portfolio with different correlations between the returns of the component stocks? Let's consider the following three cases for $\mathrm{cor}(R_C,R_D)$: $-1.0$, $0$, and $+1.0$. Substituting into the equation for the standard deviation of the portfolio as given above for these three cases of $\mathrm{cor}(R_C,R_D)$, we get

| $\mathrm{cor}(R_C,R_D)$ | $E(R_p)$ | $\mathrm{SD}(R_p)$ |
|---|---|---|
| +1.0 | 17.5% | 45.0% |
| 0 | 17.5% | 33.5% |
| -1.0 | 17.5% | 15.0% |

As the correlation between the returns on stocks C and D decreases from +1.0 to 0.0 to −1.0, the standard deviation of the portfolio return also decreases from 45% to 15%. However, the expected portfolio return remains 17.5% for each case.

This example clearly illustrates the effect of Markowitz diversification which states that as the correlation (covariance) between the returns for assets that are combined in a portfolio decreases, so does the variance (hence the standard deviation) of the return for that portfolio. This is due to the degree of correlation between the asset returns. The good news is that investors can maintain expected portfolio return and lower portfolio risk by combining assets with lower (and preferably negative) correlations. However, the bad news is that very few assets have small to negative correlations with other assets! The problem, then, becomes one of searching among large numbers of assets in an effort to discover the portfolio with the minimum risk at a given level of expected return or, equivalently, the highest expected return at a given level of risk. The stage is now set for a discussion of Markowitz efficient portfolios and their construction.

## Choosing a Portfolio of Risky Assets

Diversification in the manner suggested by Professor Markowitz leads to the construction of portfolios that have the highest expected return at a given level of risk. Such portfolios are called *Markowitz efficient portfolios* or, simply, *efficient portfolios*. In order to construct Markowitz efficient portfolios, the theory makes some basic assumptions about asset selection behavior.

First, it assumes that the only two parameters that affect an investor's decision are the expected return and the variance. That is, investors make decisions using the two-parameter model formulated by Markowitz. Second, it assumes that investors are risk averse (i.e., when faced with two investments with the same expected return but different risk levels, investors will prefer the one with the lower risk). Third, it assumes that all investors seek to achieve the highest expected return at a given level of risk. Fourth, it assumes that all investors have the same expectations regarding expected return, variance, and covariances for all risky assets. This assumption is referred to as the *homogeneous expectations assumption*. Finally, it assumes that all investors have a common one-period investment horizon.

### *Constructing Markowitz Efficient Portfolios*

The technique of constructing Markowitz efficient portfolios from large groups of stocks requires a massive number of calculations. In a portfolio of $G$ securities, there are $(G^2 - G)/2$ unique covariances to calculate. Hence, for a portfolio of just 50 securities, there are 1,225 covariances that must be calculated. For 100 securities, there are 4,950. Furthermore, in order to solve for the portfolio that minimizes risk for each level of return, a mathematical technique called *quadratic programming* (and a computer) must be used.[4] A discussion of this technique is

---

[4] Alternative methods that require less computer time can be used by investors who want a useful approximation to the Markowitz efficient frontier. The basic idea behind these alternative methods is that an estimated relationship between the return on a stock and some common stock market index or indexes can be used in lieu of the variance and covariance of returns. One of the approaches suggested by Sharpe uses one common stock index, and the approach is referred to as the *single-index market model*. (See William F. Sharpe, "A Simplified Model for Portfolio Analysis," *Management Science* (January 1963), pp. 277-293.) Multiple indexes have been suggested in Kalman J. Cohen and Jerry A. Pogue, "An Empirical Evaluation of Some Alternative Portfolio Selection Models," *Journal of Business* (April 1967), pp. 166-193.

beyond the scope of this chapter. However, it is possible to illustrate the general idea of the construction of Markowitz efficient portfolios by referring again to the simple two-asset portfolio consisting of stocks C and D.

Recall that for two assets, common stocks C and D, $E(R_C) = 10\%$, $SD(R_C) = 30\%$, $E(R_D) = 25\%$, and $SD(R_D) = 60\%$. We now further assume that $cor(R_C,R_D) = -0.5$. The expected portfolio return and standard deviation are calculated for five different proportions of C and D in the portfolio in Exhibit 2. Given these available combinations of stocks C and D, it is now possible to introduce the notion of a feasible portfolio and a Markowitz efficient portfolio.

## Feasible and Efficient Portfolios

A *feasible portfolio* is a portfolio that an investor can construct given the assets available. The collection of all feasible portfolios is called the *feasible set of portfolios*. With only two assets, the feasible set of portfolios is graphed as a curve that represents those combinations of risk and expected return that are attainable by constructing portfolios from the available combinations of the two assets. In Exhibit 3, the feasible set of portfolios is defined by the combinations of stocks C and D producing the $E(R_p)$ and $SD(R_p)$ given in Exhibit 2, and is represented by the curve 1–5. If combinations of more than two assets were being considered, the feasible set is no longer the curved line. It would be approximated by the shaded area in Exhibit 4.

In contrast to a feasible portfolio, a Markowitz efficient portfolio is one that gives the highest expected return of all feasible portfolios with the same risk. A Markowitz efficient portfolio is also said to be a *mean-variance efficient portfolio*. Thus, for each level of risk there is a Markowitz efficient portfolio. The collection of all efficient portfolios is called the *Markowitz efficient set of portfolios*.

## Exhibit 2: Portfolio Expected Returns and Standard Deviations for Varying Proportions of Stocks C and D

Data for stock C: $E(R_C) = 10\%$   $SD(R_C) = 30\%$
Data for stock D: $E(R_D) = 25\%$   $SD(R_C) = 60\%$
Correlation between stock C and stock D = –0.5

| Portfolio | Proportion of stock C ($w_C$) | Proportion of stock D ($w_D$) | $E(R_p)$ | $SD(R_p)$ |
|---|---|---|---|---|
| 1 | 100% | 0% | 10.0% | 30.0% |
| 2 | 75 | 25 | 13.8 | 19.8 |
| 3 | 50 | 50 | 17.5 | 26.0 |
| 4 | 25 | 75 | 21.3 | 41.8 |
| 5 | 0 | 100 | 25.0 | 60.0 |

## Exhibit 3: Feasible and Efficient Sets of Portfolios for Stocks C and D

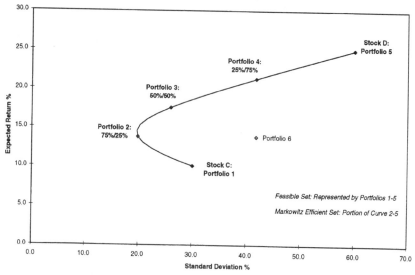

## Exhibit 4: Feasible and Efficient Sets of Portfolios When There Are More Than Two Assets

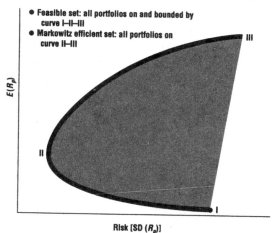

This can be seen graphically in Exhibit 3. Efficient combinations of stocks C and D lie on the curve section 2–5 in the exhibit. These Markowitz efficient combinations of stocks C and D offer the highest expected return at a given level of risk. Notice that portfolio 1 [with $E(Rp) = 10\%$ and $SD(Rp) = 30\%$] is not included in the Markowitz efficient set, since there are two portfolios, for example, in the

Markowitz efficient set (portfolios 2 and 3) that have higher expected returns and lower risk levels. Portfolios to the left of section 2-3-4-5 are not attainable from combinations of stocks C and D and are, therefore, not candidates for the Markowitz efficient set. Portfolios to the right of section 2-3-4-5 are not included in the Markowitz efficient set, since there exists some other portfolio that would provide a higher expected return at the same level of risk or, alternatively, a lower level of risk at the same expected return. To see this, consider portfolio 6 in Exhibit 3. Portfolios 4 and 6 have the same level of risk, but portfolio 4 has a higher expected return. Likewise, portfolios 2 and 6 have the same expected returns, but portfolio 2 has a lower level of risk. Thus, portfolios 4 and 2 are said to dominate portfolio 6.

Exhibit 4 also shows the Markowitz efficient set. All the portfolios on the Markowitz efficient set dominate the portfolios in the shaded area.

The Markowitz efficient set of portfolios is sometimes called the *Markowitz efficient frontier*, because graphically all the Markowitz efficient portfolios lie on the boundary of the set of feasible portfolios that have the maximum return for a given level of risk. Any portfolios above the Markowitz efficient frontier cannot be achieved. Any portfolios below the Markowitz efficient frontier are dominated by portfolios on the Markowitz efficient frontier.

### Choosing a Portfolio in the Markowitz Efficient Set

Now that we have constructed the Markowitz efficient set of portfolios, the next step is to determine the optimal portfolio.

An investor will want to hold one of the portfolios on the Markowitz efficient frontier. Notice that the portfolios on the Markowitz efficient frontier represent trade-offs in terms of risk and return. Moving from left to right on the Markowitz efficient frontier, the expected risk increases, but so does the expected return. The question is, which is the best portfolio to hold? The best portfolio to hold of all those on the Markowitz efficient frontier is the optimal portfolio.

Intuitively, the optimal portfolio should depend on the investor's preference or utility as to the trade-off between risk and return. As explained at the beginning of this chapter, this preference can be expressed in terms of a utility function.

In Exhibit 5, three indifference curves and the efficient frontier are drawn on the same diagram. In our application, the indifference curve indicates the combinations of risk and expected return that give the same level of utility. Moreover, the farther from the horizontal axis the indifference curve, the higher the utility.

From Exhibit 5, it is possible to determine the optimal portfolio for the investor with the indifference curves shown. Remember that the investor wants to get to the highest indifference curve achievable given the Markowitz efficient frontier. Given that requirement, the optimal portfolio is represented by the point where an indifference curve is tangent to the Markowitz efficient frontier. In Exhibit 5, that is the portfolio $P_{MEF}^*$. For example, suppose that $P_{MEF}^*$ corresponds to portfolio 3 in Exhibit 3. From Exhibit 2 we see that this portfolio is a combination of 50% of stock C and 50% of stock D, with $E(R_p) = 17.5\%$ and $SD(R_p) = 26\%$.

## Exhibit 5: Selection of the Optimal Portfolio

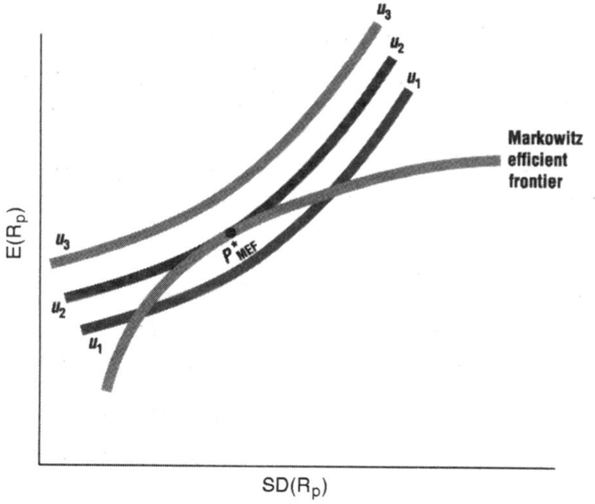

$u_1$, $u_2$, $u_3$ = indifference curves with $u_1 < u_2 < u_3$

$P^*_{MEF}$ = optimal portfolio on Markowitz efficient frontier

Consequently, for the investor's preferences for risk and return as determined by the shape of the indifference curves, and his or her expectations for returns and covariance of stocks C and D, portfolio 3 maximizes utility. If this investor had a different preference for expected risk and return, there would have been a different optimal portfolio.

At this point in our discussion, a natural question is how to estimate an investor's utility function so that the indifference curves can be determined. Unfortunately, there is little guidance about how to construct one. In general, economists have not been successful in measuring utility functions.

The inability to measure utility functions does not mean that the theory is flawed. What it does mean is that once an investor constructs the Markowitz efficient frontier, the investor will subjectively determine which Markowitz efficient portfolio is appropriate given his or her tolerance to risk.

## CAPITAL MARKET THEORY AND ASSET PRICING MODELS

Having introduced the principles of modern portfolio theory, we will now describe capital market theory and the implications of both that theory and modern portfolio theory for the pricing of financial assets. We first focus on one well-known asset pricing model called the *capital asset pricing model* (CAPM) and then another popular asset pricing model. The asset pricing models we describe in this chapter are equilibrium models. That is, given assumptions about the behavior and expectations of investors, and assumptions about capital markets, these models predict the theoretical equilibrium price of an asset.

## Assumptions

Just like the model for the selection of Markowitz efficient portfolios, capital market theory and asset pricing models are abstractions of the real world and, as such, are based upon some simplifying assumptions. Some of these assumptions may even seem unrealistic. However, these assumptions make the theory more tractable from a mathematical standpoint. The assumptions to derive the CAPM are that (1) investors rely on two factors in making their decisions: expected return and variance; (2) investors are rational and risk averse and subscribe to Markowitz methods of portfolio diversification; (3) investors all invest for the same period of time; (4) investors share all expectations about assets (the "homogeneous expectations assumption"); (5) there is a risk-free investment and investors can borrow and lend any amount at the risk-free rate; and (6) capital markets are completely competitive and frictionless.

The theory assumes all investors make investment decisions over some single-period investment horizon. How long that period is (i.e., six months, one year, two years, etc.) is not specified. In reality, the investment decision process is more complex than that, with many investors having more than one investment horizon — such as short-term and long-term planning horizons. Nonetheless, the assumption of a one-period investment horizon is necessary to simplify the mathematics of the theory.

The first four assumptions deal with the behavior of investors in making investment decisions. It is also necessary to make assumptions about the characteristics of the capital market in which investors transact. These are covered by the last two assumptions.

## Capital Market Theory

Earlier in this chapter we distinguished between a risky asset and a risk-free asset. We described how to create Markowitz efficient portfolios from risky assets. We did not consider the possibility of constructing Markowitz efficient portfolios in the presence of a risk-free asset, that is, an asset where the return is known with certainty.

In the absence of a risk-free rate, portfolio theory tells us that Markowitz efficient portfolios can be constructed based on expected return and variance and that the optimal portfolio is the one that is tangent to the investor's indifference curve. Once a risk-free asset is introduced and assuming that investors can borrow and lend at the risk-free rate (assumption 5, above), the conclusion of Markowitz portfolio theory can be qualified as illustrated in Exhibit 6. Every combination of the risk-free asset and the Markowitz efficient portfolio $M$ is shown on the *capital market line* (CML). The line is drawn from the vertical axis at the risk-free rate tangent to the Markowitz efficient frontier. The point of tangency is denoted by $M$. All the portfolios on the capital market line are feasible for the investor to construct. Portfolios to the left of *M* represent combinations of risky assets and the risk-free asset. Portfolios to the right of *M* include purchases of risky assets made with funds borrowed at the risk-free rate. Such a portfolio is called a *levered portfolio* since it involves the use of borrowed funds.

Now compare a portfolio on the capital market line to the portfolio on the Markowitz efficient frontier with the same risk. For example, compare portfolio $P_A$, which is on the Markowitz efficient frontier, with portfolio $P_B$, which is on the capital market line and therefore some combination of the risk-free asset and the Markowitz efficient portfolio *M*. Notice that for the same risk the expected return is greater for $P_B$ than for $P_A$. A risk-averse investor will prefer $P_B$ to $P_A$. That is, $P_B$ will dominate $P_A$. In fact, this is true for all but one portfolio on the line: portfolio *M*, which is on the Markowitz efficient frontier.

Recognizing this, we must modify the conclusion from portfolio theory that an investor will select a portfolio on the Markowitz efficient frontier, the particular portfolio depending on the investor's risk preference. With the introduction of the risk-free asset, we can now say that an investor will select a portfolio on the line representing a combination of borrowing or lending at the risk-free rate and purchasing the Markowitz efficient portfolio *M*.

The particular efficient portfolio that the investor will select on the line will depend on the investor's risk preference. The investor will select the portfolio on the line that is tangent to the highest indifference curve. In the absence of a risk-free asset, it would not be possible to construct such a portfolio.

## Exhibit 6: The Capital Market Line

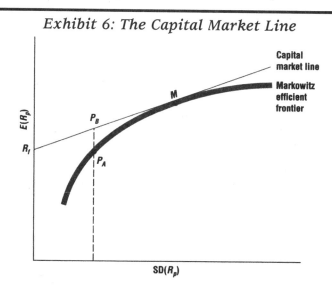

Portfolios to the left of *M* are combinations of
risk-free asset and market portfolio.

Portfolios to the right of *M* are leveraged portfolios
(borrowing at a risk-free rate to buy a market portfolio)

Several researchers demonstrated that the opportunity to borrow or lend at the risk-free rate implies a capital market where risk-averse investors will prefer to hold portfolios consisting of combinations of the risk-free asset and some portfolio *M* on the Markowitz efficient frontier.[5] William Sharpe, one of the developers of the theory, called the line from the risk-free rate to portfolio *M* on the efficient frontier the *capital market line,* and this is the name that has been adopted in the industry.

One more key question remains: How does an investor construct portfolio *M*? Eugene Fama answered this question by demonstrating that *M* must consist of all assets available to investors, and each asset must be held in proportion to its market value relative to the total market value of all assets.[6] So, for example, if the total market value of some asset is $200 million and the total market value of all assets is $X, then the percentage of the portfolio that should be allocated to that asset is $200 million divided by $X. Because portfolio *M* consists of all assets, it is referred to as the market portfolio.

Now we can restate how a risk-averse investor who makes investment decisions as suggested by Markowitz and who can borrow and lend at the risk-free rate should construct efficient portfolios. This should be done by combining an investment in the risk-free asset and the market portfolio. While all investors will select a portfolio on the capital market line, the optimal portfolio for a specific investor is the one that will maximize that investor's utility function.

The capital market line can be derived algebraically. We will dispense with the proof here and simply indicate the formula for the capital market line below:

$$E(R_p) = R_F + \frac{E(R_M) - R_F}{SD(R_M)} SD(R_p) \tag{8}$$

where

$E(R_M)$ = expected return for the market
$R_F$ = risk-free return
$SD(R_M)$ = standard deviation of the market return
$SD(R_P)$ = standard deviation of the portfolio

Under the assumptions stated earlier, equation (8) is a straight line representing the efficient set for all risk-averse investors.

As we mentioned, both capital market theory and the derivation of the Markowitz efficient frontier assume that all investors have the same expectations for the inputs into the model. With homogeneous expectations, $SD(R_M)$ and

[5] William F. Sharpe, "Capital Asset Prices," *Journal of Finance* (September 1964), pp. 425-442; John Lintner, "The Valuation of Risk Assets and the Selection of Risky Investments in Stock Portfolio and Capital Budgets," *Review of Economics and Statistics* (February 1965), pp. 13-37; Jack L. Treynor, "Toward a Theory of Market Value of Risky Asset," Unpublished Paper, Arthur D. Little, 1961; and, Jan Mossin, "Equilibrium in a Capital Asset Market," *Econometrica* (October 1966), pp. 768-783.
[6] Eugene F. Fama, "Efficient Capital Markets: A Review of Theory and Empirical Work," *Journal of Finance* (May 1970), pp. 383-417.

$SD(R_p)$ are the market's consensus for the return distributions for the market portfolio and portfolio $p$. The slope of the CML is

$$\frac{E(R_M) - R_F}{SD(R_M)}$$

Let's examine the economic meaning of the slope. The numerator is the expected return of the market in excess of the risk-free return. It is a measure of the *risk premium*, or the reward for holding the risky market portfolio rather than the risk-free asset. The denominator is the risk of the market portfolio. Thus, the slope measures the reward per unit of market risk. Since the CML represents the return offered to compensate for a perceived level of risk, each point on the line is a balanced market condition, or equilibrium. The slope of the line determines the additional return needed to compensate for a unit change in risk. That is why the slope of the CML is also referred to as the *equilibrium market price of risk*.

The CML says that the expected return on a portfolio is equal to the risk-free rate plus a risk premium equal to the price of risk (as measured by the difference between the expected return on the market and the risk-free rate divided by the standard deviation of the market return) times the quantity of market risk for the portfolio (as measured by the standard deviation of the portfolio). That is,

$$E(R_p) = R_F + \text{Market price of risk} \times \text{Quantity of market risk}$$

## Capital Asset Pricing Model

Up to this point, we know how a risk-averse investor who makes decisions based on two parameters (expected return and variance) should construct an efficient portfolio: using a combination of the market portfolio and the risk-free rate. Based on this result, a model can be derived that shows how a risky asset should be priced. In the process of doing so, we can fine-tune our thinking about the risk associated with an asset. Specifically, we can show that the appropriate risk that investors should be compensated for accepting is not the variance of an asset's return but some other quantity. In order to do this, let's take a closer look at the risk.

### Systematic and Unsystematic Risk

In the development of portfolio theory, Professor Markowitz defined the variance of the portfolio rate of return as the appropriate measure of risk. This risk measure can be divided into two general types of risk: systematic risk and unsystematic risk.

Professor William Sharpe defined *systematic risk* as the portion of an asset's variability that can be attributed to a common factor.[7] It is also sometimes called *undiversifiable risk* or *market risk*. Systematic risk is the minimum level of risk that can be obtained for a portfolio by means of diversification across a large number of randomly chosen assets. As such, systematic risk is that which results from general market and economic conditions that cannot be diversified away.

---

[7] William F. Sharpe, "A Simplified Model for Portfolio Analysis," *Management Science* (January 1963), pp. 277-293.

## *Exhibit 7: Systematic and Unsystematic Portfolio Risk*

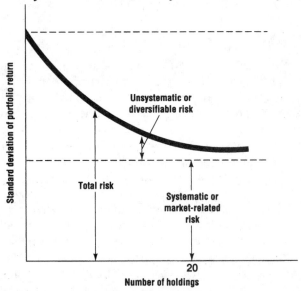

Sharpe defined the portion of an asset's variability that can be diversified away as *unsystematic risk*. It is also sometimes called *diversifiable risk, unique risk, residual risk,* or *company-specific risk.* This is the risk that is unique to a company, such as a strike, the outcome of unfavorable litigation, or a natural catastrophe. As examples of this type of risk, one need only recall the case of product tampering involving Tylenol capsules (manufactured by Johnson & Johnson, Inc.) in October 1982 or the chemical accident at the Union Carbide plant in Bhopal, India, in December 1984. Both of these unforecastable and hence unexpected tragedies had negative impacts on the stock prices of the two companies involved.

How diversification reduces unsystematic risk for portfolios can be illustrated with a graph. Exhibit 7 shows that at a portfolio size of about 20 randomly selected stocks, the level of unsystematic risk is almost completely diversified away.[8] Essentially, all that is left is systematic, or market, risk.

Therefore the total risk of an asset can be measured by its variance. However, the total risk can be divided into its systematic and unsystematic risk components. Next we will show how this can be done so as to be able to quantify both components.

### *Market Model*

The market model or single-index market model developed by Sharpe can be used to isolate the systematic and unsystematic components of an asset's return.[9] The linear relationship can be expressed as follows:

---

[8] Empirical evidence for Exhibit 7 is provided in Wayne H. Wagner and Sheila Lau, "The Effect of Diversification on Risks," *Financial Analysts Journal* (November-December 1971), p. 50.

[9] Sharpe, "A Simplified Model for Portfolio Analysis."

$$R_{it} = \alpha_i + \beta_i R_{Mt} + e_{it} \tag{9}$$

where

$R_{it}$   =   return on asset $i$ over the period $t$

$R_{Mt}$   =   return on the market portfolio over the period $t$

$\alpha_i$   =   a term that represents the nonmarket component of the return on asset $i$

$\beta_i$   =   a term that relates the change in asset $i$'s return to the change in the market portfolio

$e_{it}$   =   random error term that reflects the unique risks associated with investing in an asset over period $t$

The market model given by equation (9) says that the return on an asset depends on the return on the market portfolio and the extent of the asset's responsiveness as measured by beta ($\beta_i$). In addition, the return will also depend on conditions that are unique to the firm as measured by $e_{it}$.

The term $\beta$, or beta, is the slope of the market model for the asset, and measures the degree to which the historical returns on the asset change systematically with changes in the market portfolio's return. Hence, beta is referred to as an index of that systematic risk due to general market conditions that cannot be diversified away. For example, if a stock has a beta of 1.5, it means that, on average, on the basis of historical data, the stock had a return equal to 1.5 times that of the market portfolio's return. The beta for the market portfolio is 1.0.

The term in the market model, popularly referred to as *alpha* is equal to the average value over time of the unsystematic returns for the stock. For most stocks, alpha tends to be small and unstable.

Recall from our earlier discussion, the total risk of an asset can be decomposed into market or systematic risk and unique or unsystematic risk. We can use the market model to quantify these two risks. To see how, let's look at the total risk of the return of stock $i$ as measured by the variance of its return. This is done by determining the variance of equation (9). We show without proof that the variance would be

$$\text{var}(R_i) = \beta_i^2 \ \text{var}(R_M) + \text{var}(e_i) \tag{10}$$

Equation (10) says that the total risk as measured by $\text{var}(R_i)$ is equal to the sum of (1) the market or systematic risk as measured by $\beta_i^2 \ \text{var}(R_M)$, and (2) the unique risk as measured by $\text{var}(e_i)$

In Chapter 3 we explain how the market model is estimated by applying statistical techniques to historical data on returns. Another product of the statistical technique used to estimate beta is the percentage of systematic risk to total risk. In statistical terms, it is measured by the *coefficient of determination* ($R^2$) from the regression, which indicates the percentage of the variation in the return of the asset explained by the market portfolio return. The value of the coefficient ranges from 0 to 1. For example, a coefficient of determination of 0.3 for an asset means that 30% of the variation in the return of that asset is explained by the return of the market portfolio. Unsystematic or unique risk is then the amount not explained by the market portfolio's return. That is, it is 1 minus the coefficient of determination $(1 - R^2)$.

Studies have shown that for the average New York Stock Exchange (NYSE) common stock, systematic risk is about 30% of return variance, while unsystematic risk is about 70%. In contrast, the coefficient of determination for a well-diversified portfolio of stocks will typically exceed 90%, indicating that unsystematic risk is less than 10% of total portfolio return variance. This supports the point made in Exhibit 7 that with a well-diversified portfolio, most of the port-folio risk is systematic risk.

### The Security Market Line

The capital market line represents an equilibrium condition in which the expected return on a portfolio of assets is a linear function of the expected return on the market portfolio. A directly analogous relationship holds for individual security expected returns:

$$E(R_i) = R_F + \frac{[E(R_M) - R_F]}{SD(R_M)} SD(R_i) \tag{11}$$

Equation (11) simply uses risk and return variables for an individual security in place of the portfolio values in the formula for the CML in equation (8). This ver-sion of the risk- return relationship for individual securities is called the *security market line* (SML). As in the case of the CML, the expected return for an asset is equal to the risk-free rate plus the product of the market price of risk and the quantity of risk associated with the security.

Another more common version of the SML relationship uses the beta of a security. To see how this relationship is developed, look back at equation (10). In a well-diversified portfolio (i.e., Markowitz diversified), the unique risk is elimi-nated. Consequently, equation (10) can be rewritten as $var(R_i) = \beta_i^2 \, var(R_M)$ and the standard deviation as $SD(R_i) = \beta_i \, SD(R_M)$.

If $\beta_i \, SD(R_M)$ is substituted into equation (11) for $SD(R_i)$, we have the beta version of the SML or the capital asset pricing model as shown in equation (12):

$$E(R_i) = R_F + \beta_i [E(R_M) - R_F] \tag{12}$$

Equation (12) states that, given the assumptions of the CAPM, the expected (or required) return on an individual asset is a positive linear function of its index of systematic risk as measured by beta. The higher the beta, the higher the expected return. Notice that it is only an asset's beta that determines its (differential) expected return.

## Exhibit 8: The Security Market Line

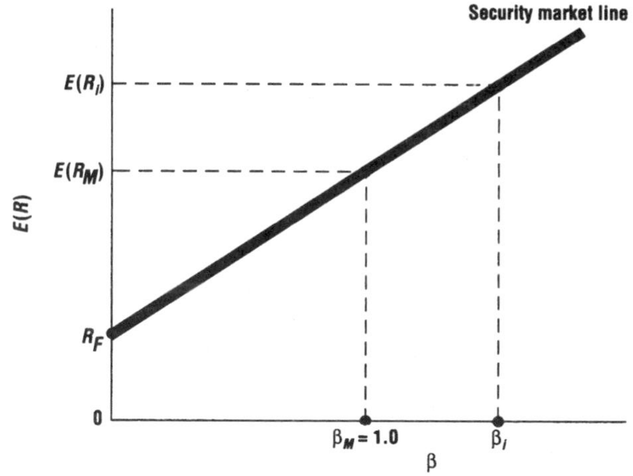

Let's look at the prediction of the CAPM for several values of beta. The beta of a risk-free asset is zero, because the variability of the return for a risk-free asset is zero and therefore it does not covary with the market portfolio. So if we want to know the expected return for a risk-free asset, we would substitute zero for $\beta_i$ in equation (12). Thus, the return on a risk-free asset is simply the risk-free return. Of course, this is what we expect. The beta of the market portfolio is 1. If asset $i$ has the same beta as the market portfolio, then substituting 1 for $\beta_i$ in equation (12) gives a value equal to $E(R_M)$. In this case, the expected return for the asset is the same as the expected return for the market portfolio. If an asset has a beta greater than the market portfolio (i.e., greater than 1), then the expected return will be higher than for the market portfolio. The reverse is true if an asset has a beta less than the market portfolio. A graph of the SML is presented in Exhibit 8.

In equilibrium, the expected return of individual securities will lie on the SML and *not* on the CML. This is true because of the high degree of unsystematic risk that remains in individual securities that can be diversified out of portfolios of securities.

It follows that the only risk that investors will pay a premium to avoid is market risk. Hence, two assets with the same amount of systematic risk will have the same expected return. In equilibrium, only efficient portfolios will lie on both the CML and the SML. This underscores the fact that the systematic risk measure, beta, is most correctly considered as an *index* of the contribution of an individual security to the systematic risk of a well-diversified portfolio of securities.

There is one more version of the SML that is worthwhile to discuss. It can be demonstrated that SML can be expressed as:

$$E(R_i) = R_F + \frac{\text{Cov}(R_i, R_M)}{\text{var}(R_M)}[E(R_M) - R_F] \tag{13}$$

This version of the SML emphasizes that it is not the variance or standard deviation of an asset that affects its return. It is the covariance of the asset's return with the market's return that affects its return. An asset that has a positive covariance will have a higher expected return than the risk-free asset; an asset with a negative covariance will have a lower expected return than the risk-free asset. The reason has to do with the benefits of diversification we discussed earlier in this chapter. If the covariance is positive, this increases the risk of an asset in a portfolio and therefore investors will only purchase that asset if they expect to earn a return higher than the risk-free asset. If an asset has a negative covariance, recall from our discussion earlier in this chapter that this will reduce the portfolio risk and investors would be willing to accept a return less than the risk-free asset.

Finally, it is important to point out the difference between the market model and the CML and SML. The CML and the SML represent an *ex ante*, or predictive, model for expected returns. The market model is an *ex post*, or descriptive, model used to describe historical data. Hence, the market model makes no prediction of what expected returns should be.

### Tests of the CAPM

The number of articles found under the general heading "tests of the CAPM" is impressive. One bibliographic compilation lists almost 1,000 papers on the topic.

The major implication that is tested is that beta should be the only factor that is priced by the market. That is, other factors such as the variance or standard deviation of the returns, and variables that we will discuss in later chapters such as the price-earnings ratio, dividend yield, and firm size, should not be significant in explaining the return on stocks. However, the empirical evidence finds that beta is not the only factor priced by the market. Several studies have discovered other factors that explain stock returns. These include the other factors that we just cited.

One of the most controversial papers written on the CAPM is Richard Roll's "A Critique of the Asset Pricing Theory's Tests."[10] The CAPM is a general equilibrium model based upon the existence of a market portfolio that is defined as the value-weighted portfolio of all investment assets. Furthermore, the market portfolio is defined to be *ex ante* mean-variance efficient. Roll argues that this means that the market portfolio lies on the *ex ante* Markowitz efficient frontier for all investors and demonstrates that the only true test of the CAPM is whether the market portfolio is in fact *ex ante* mean-variance efficient. However, the true market portfolio is, in fact, *ex ante* mean-variance efficient since it includes all investment assets (e.g., stocks, bonds, real estate, art objects, and human capital). The consequences of this "non-observability" of the true market portfolio are that the CAPM is not testable until the exact composition of the true market portfolio is known, and the only valid test of the CAPM is to observe whether the *ex ante* true market portfolio is mean-variance efficient. As a result of his findings, Roll states

---

[10] Richard Roll, "A Critique of the Asset Pricing Theory's Tests," *Journal of Financial Economics* (March 1977), pp. 129-176

that he does not believe there ever will be an unambiguous test of the CAPM. He does not say that the CAPM is invalid. Rather, Roll says that there is likely to be no unambiguous way to test the CAPM and its implications due to the non-observability of the true market portfolio and its characteristics.

Does this mean that the CAPM is useless to the financial practitioner? The answer is no, it does not. What it means is that the implications of the CAPM should be viewed with caution.

### Zero-Beta Version of the CAPM

As explained earlier, in a world without a risk-free asset, an investor will select some portfolio on the Markowitz efficient frontier. When a risk-free asset is assumed, the CML can be generated and dominates the Markowitz efficient frontier. From the CML, the CAPM is derived.

Not only is the existence of a risk-free asset important in developing the CAPM, but there are two related assumptions. First, it is assumed that investors can borrow or lend at the risk-free rate. The risk-free asset is one in which there is no uncertainty about the return that will be realized over some investment horizon. To realize that return, it is assumed the borrower will not default on its obligation. In the United States the short-term obligations of the federal government are viewed as default-free and therefore risk-free assets. There is not just one interest rate in an economy but a structure of interest rates. The U.S. government pays the lowest interest rate, and individual borrowers pay a higher rate. The greater the perceived risk that the borrower will default, the higher the interest rate. Thus, while the U.S. government may be able to borrow at the risk-free rate, an individual investor must pay a higher rate. Consequently, this assumption does not reflect the situation facing investors in the real world.

The second related assumption is that investors can borrow and lend at the same risk-free rate. In real-world markets, investors typically lend and borrow money at different rates, the former being less than the latter. Again, the assumption does not reflect the economic situation facing investors in real-world capital markets.

Fischer Black examined the implications for the original CAPM, when there is no risk-free asset in which the investor can borrow and lend.[11] He demonstrated that neither the existence of a risk-free asset nor the requirement that investors can borrow and lend at the risk-free rate is necessary for the theory to hold. However, without the risk-free asset a different form of the CAPM will result.

Black's argument is as follows. The beta of a risk-free asset is zero. That is, since there is no variability of the return on a risk-free asset, it cannot covary with the market. Suppose that a portfolio can be created such that it is uncorrelated with the market. This portfolio would have a beta of zero. We shall refer to any portfolio with a beta of zero as a *zero-beta portfolio*. Black demonstrated how a zero-beta portfolio can be constructed and that the CAPM would be modified as follows:

---

[11] Fischer Black, "Capital Market Equilibrium with Restricted Borrowing," *Journal of Business* (July 1972), pp. 444-455.

$$E(R_p) = E(R_Z) + \beta_p [E(R_M) - E(R_Z)] \tag{14}$$

where $E(R_Z)$ is the expected return on the zero-beta portfolio and $[E(R_M) - E(R_Z)]$ is the market risk premium.

The version of the CAPM as given by equation (14) is the same as equation (12) except that the expected return for the zero-beta portfolio is substituted for the risk-free rate. Black's zero-beta version of the CAPM is called the *two-factor model*. Empirical tests of the two-factor model suggest that it does a better job in explaining historical returns than the pure CAPM.[12]

The basic principle in developing the zero-beta portfolio is that by means of short selling, a zero-beta portfolio can be created from a combination of securities. The reason why short selling is a necessary assumption is that since assets such as stocks are positively correlated, the only way to get a portfolio that is uncorrelated with the market portfolio is to create a portfolio in which stocks are owned and stocks are shorted. Thus, when the price of stocks increases, there will be a gain on the stocks owned in the portfolio, giving a positive return; however, there will be a loss on the stocks that have been shorted and therefore a negative return. The zero-beta portfolio is created such that this combination of stocks owned and stocks shorted will have a beta of zero.

Unfortunately, not all investors are permitted to sell short. Many institutional investors are prohibited or constrained from selling short. Thus, the two-factor version of the CAPM avoids relying on the myth of "borrowing and lending at a risk-free rate." It still cannot reflect the real world for all investors, however, because it does require unrestricted short selling, which is not available to everyone.

## Arbitrage Pricing Theory Model

Professor Stephen Ross developed an alternative asset pricing model based purely on arbitrage arguments, and hence called the *arbitrage pricing theory* (APT) *model*.[13] While we do not spend as much time in developing the underlying theory for this asset pricing model, in Chapter 9 we discuss in more detail how factor models are used in practice.

The arbitrage pricing theory model postulates that a security's expected return is influenced by a variety of factors, as opposed to just the single market index of the CAPM. Specifically, look back at equation (9), which states that the return on a security is dependent on its market sensitivity index and an unsystematic return. The APT in contrast states that the return on a security is linearly related to $H$ "factors." The APT does not specify what these factors are, but it is assumed that the relationship between security returns and the factors is linear.

---

[12] Fischer Black, Michael C. Jensen, and Myron Scholes, "The Capital Asset Pricing Model," in Michael C. Jensen (ed.), *Studies in the Theory of Capital Markets* (New York: Praeger 1972).

[13] Stephen A. Ross, "The Arbitrage Theory of Capital Asset Pricing," *Journal of Economic Theory* (December 1976), pp. 343-362,

The following notation will be used:

$\tilde{R}_i$ = the random rate of return on security $i$

$E(R_i)$ = the expected return on security $i$

$\tilde{F}_h$ = the $h$-th factor that is common to the returns of all assets ($h$ = 1, ..., $H$)

$\beta_{i,h}$ = the sensitivity of the $i$-th security to the $h$-th factor

$H$ = number of factors

$\tilde{e}_i$ = the unsystematic return for security $i$

The APT model asserts that the random rate of return on security $i$ is given by the following relationship:

$$\tilde{R}_i = R_F + \beta_{i,1}\tilde{F}_1 + \beta_{i,2}\tilde{F}_2 + ... + \beta_{i,H}\tilde{F}_H + \tilde{e}_i \tag{15}$$

For equilibrium to exist, the following condition to insure no arbitrage profits must be satisfied: using no additional funds (wealth) and without increasing risk, it should not be possible, on average, to create a portfolio to increase return. In essence, this condition states that there is no "money machine" available in the market.

Ross has shown that the following risk and return relationship will result for each security $i$ in a no-arbitrage world:

$$E(R_i) = R_F + \beta_{i,F1}[E(R_{F1}) - R_F] + \beta_{i,F2}[E(R_{F2}) - R_F]$$
$$+ ... + \beta_{i,FH}[E(R_{FH}) - R_F] \tag{16}$$

where

$\beta_{i,Fh}$ = the sensitivity of security $i$ to the $h$-th factor, and

$E(R_{Fh}) - R_F$ = the expected excess return of the $h$-th systematic factor over the risk-free rate, and can be thought of as the price (or risk premium) for the $h$-th systematic risk.

Equation (16) is the APT model. It states that investors want to be compensated for all the factors that *systematically* affect the return of a security. The compensation is the sum of the products of each factor's systematic risk ($\beta_{i,Fh}$), and the risk premium assigned to it by the financial market [$E(R_{Fh} - R_F)$]. As in the case of the CAPM, an investor is not compensated for accepting unsystematic risk.

Examining the equations, we can see that the CAPM as given by equation (12) is actually a special case of the APT model as given by equation (16). If the only factor in equation (16) is market risk, the APT model reduces to equation (12).

Supporters of the APT model argue that it has several major advantages over the CAPM. First, it makes less restrictive assumptions about investor preferences toward risk and return. CAPM theory assumes investors trade off between risk and return solely on the basis of the expected returns and standard deviations of prospective investments. The APT, in contrast, simply requires that some rather unobtrusive bounds be placed on potential investor utility functions. Second, no assumptions are made about the distribution of security returns. Finally, since the APT does not rely on the identification of the true market portfolio, the theory is potentially testable.

The disadvantage is the identification of the factors. The factors must be determined statistically. We'll discuss this further when we look at the APT model in Chapter 9 where we explain how factor models are used by practitioners.

## SOME PRINCIPLES TO TAKE AWAY

In this chapter, we have covered the heart of what is popularly called modern portfolio theory and capital market theory. We have emphasized the assumptions and their critical role in the development of these theories. While you may understand the topics covered, you may still be uncomfortable as to where we have progressed in investment management given the lack of theoretical and empirical support for the CAPM or the difficulty of identifying the factors in the APT model. You're not alone. There are a good number of practitioners and academics who feel uncomfortable with these models, particularly the CAPM.

Nevertheless, what is comforting is that there are several general principles of investing that are derived from these theories that very few would question. All of these principles are used in later chapters.

1. Investing has two dimensions, risk and return. Therefore, focusing only on the actual return that a manager has achieved without looking at the risk that had to be accepted to achieve that return is inappropriate.
2. It is inappropriate to look at the risk of an individual asset when deciding whether it should be included in a portfolio. What is important is how the inclusion of an asset into a portfolio will affect the risk of the portfolio.
3. Whether investors consider one risk or 1,000 risks, risk can be divided into two general categories: systematic risks that cannot be eliminated by diversification, and unsystematic risk which can be diversified.
4. Investors should only be compensated for accepting systematic risks. Thus, it is critical in formulating an investment strategy to identify the systematic risks.

# QUESTIONS

1. "A portfolio's expected return and variance of return are simply the weighted average of the individual asset's expected returns and variances." Explain why you agree or disagreement with this statement?

2. Professor Harry Markowitz, co-recipient of the 1990 Nobel Prize in Economic Science, wrote the following: "A portfolio with sixty different railway securities, for example, would not be as well diversified as the same size portfolio with some railroad, some public utility, mining, various sort of manufacturing, etc." Why is this true?

3  a. What is meant by a Markowitz efficient frontier?
   b. Explain why all feasible portfolios are not on the Markowitz efficient frontier.

4. Two portfolio managers are discussing modern portfolio theory. Manager A states that the objective of Markowitz portfolio analysis is to construct a portfolio that maximizes expected return for a given level of risk. Manager B disagrees. He believes that the objective is to construct a portfolio that minimizes risk for a given expected return. Which portfolio manager is correct?

5. Explain the critical role of the correlation between assets in determining the potential benefits from diversification.

6. Suppose that you are evaluating the global diversification opportunities of a portfolio consisting of the following four asset classes: U.S. large cap stocks, U.S. small cap stocks, stocks of developed foreign countries, and stocks of emerging market countries.

   a. Write out the rate of return variance for this 4-asset global portfolio.
   b. How many unique covariances are there in this portfolio having four asset classes? Verify your answer by using the following formula:

   $$\text{Unique covariances} = (G^2 - G)/2$$
   $$(G = \text{Number of asset classes})$$

   c. Should a risk averse investor prefer a high or low return correlation among U.S. equities and, say, the stocks of emerging market countries? Explain your answer using an efficient frontier.

7. A well-known mutual fund company offers an investment product called "The 30 Percent Solution — A Global Guide For Investors Seeking Better Performance with Reduced Portfolio Risk." The investment product recommends investing 70% in U.S. equities and 30% in international equities.

Use the following average return and risk information for U.S. and international equities over a recent 20-year period to verify the risk management accuracy (or inaccuracy) of the proposed "30 Percent Solution."

| | U.S. Equities | International Equities | "70/30 Solution" |
|---|---|---|---|
| Average Return | 15% | 17% | ? |
| Standard Deviation | 14% | 22% | ? |

The figures are based on S&P 500 and Morgan Stanley EAFE (Europe, Australia, and Far East) total return indexes during 20-year period, 1977-1996.

Assume a correlation of 0.3 between domestic U.S. and international equity returns in answering this question. Explain your findings.

8. The following excerpt is from Warren Bailey and Rene M. Stulz, "Benefits of International Diversification: The Case of Pacific Basin Stock Markets," *Journal of Portfolio Management* (Summer 1990):

> Recent international diversification literature uses monthly data from foreign stock markets to make the point that American investors should hold foreign stock to reduce the variance of a portfolio of domestic stocks without reducing its expected return. (p. 57)

a. Why would you expect that the justification of diversifying into foreign stock markets would depend on empirical evidence regarding the ability to "reduce the variance of a portfolio of domestic stocks without reducing its expected return"?

b. Typically in research papers that seek to demonstrate the benefits of international diversification by investing in a foreign stock market, two efficient frontiers are compared. One is an efficient frontier constructed using only domestic stocks; the other is an efficient frontier constructed using both domestic and foreign stocks. If there are benefits to diversifying into foreign stocks, should the efficient frontier constructed using both domestic and foreign stocks lie above or below the efficient frontier constructed using only domestic stocks? Explain your answer.

9. The following excerpt is from John E. Hunter and T. Daniel Coggin, "An Analysis of the Diversification from International Equity Investment," *Journal of Portfolio Management* (Fall 1990):

> The extent to which investment risk can be diversified depends upon the degree to which national markets were completely dominated by a single world market factor (i.e., if all cross-national correlations were 1.00, then international diversification would have no benefit). If all national markets were completely independent (that

is, if all cross-national correlations were zero), then international diversification over an infinite number of countries would completely eliminate the effect of variation in national markets. (p. 33)

a. Why are the "cross-national correlations" critical in justifying the benefits from international diversification?

b. Why do Hunter and Coggin state that there would be no benefit from international diversification if these correlations are all 1.00?

10 a. In the "real world" the investor's borrowing rate of interest is higher than the lending rate. Show how this capital market imperfection impacts the set of efficient portfolios that are available to risk averse investors. (Hint: the "Capital Market Line" now consists of two linear segments.)

b. In a world where investors can borrow and lend at the same (risk-free) rate of interest, we learned that there is one tangency portfolio consisting of all risky assets called the market portfolio, $M$. Illustrate where the market portfolio, $M$, would be positioned in the portfolio opportunity set when there exists a divergence between borrowing and lending rates of interest in the economy. Explain your answer.

11. What is the single factor that is used to explain the expected return for a security or portfolio in the traditional CAPM?

12 a. How does the Black "zero-beta" model differ from the traditional CAPM? Be sure to discuss the underlying logic of the Black portfolio model.

b. Show where Black's "zero beta" portfolio lies on the boundary of feasible investment portfolios. (Hint: Portfolio "Z," for zero-beta portfolio, plots directly across from a line drawn tangent to the market portfolio $M$ and intersecting the expected return axis (vertical axis) in expected return and portfolio risk space.)

13 a. What is a multi-factor asset-pricing model?

b. Why were multi-factor models developed, and what are their potential benefits and limitations?

14. One of the major challenges for corporate pension plan (defined benefit) sponsors is to be sure that there are sufficient assets in a portfolio to cover projected payment of future benefits to retired (and retiring) employees. From a "surplus risk management" perspective, should plan sponsors prefer positive or negative return correlation in a portfolio having both assets and liabilities?

Explain your answer in the context of the rate of return variance for a "2-asset" portfolio—namely, a portfolio consisting of a conventional asset class like common stocks and a liability (or negative asset) having the payoff characteristics of a "fixed income" security.

# Chapter 3

# Statistical Measures and Their Applications

After having read Chapter 2, it should be apparent that investment managers rely on statistical tools in their analysis of the risk characteristics of stocks and stock portfolios. In this chapter, we will expand and apply some of the statistical measures introduced in Chapter 2. In later chapters we will require an understanding of other statistical measures. We introduce those measures in this chapter.

## DESCRIPTIVE STATISTICS

Suppose that you — as an equity analyst or manager — are interested in knowing about the financial merits of large capitalization stocks along the popular value and growth styles of investing. After some preliminary research, you decide that the S&P/BARRA indexes would be a meaningful source of return/risk data for large cap stocks of varying equity styles. Further, suppose that your research produces a *sample* of annual total returns on the S&P/BARRA growth and value indexes, and the S&P 500 Index over the 18 years covering 1980 to 1997. The sample total returns (i.e., dividends plus change in market value) are shown in Exhibit 1.[1]

A quick look at Exhibit 1 shows that equity investing — whether value, blend, or growth style — can be quite volatile on a yearly basis. For example, during 1980 large cap growth stocks earned 39.4% while their value-oriented counterpart earned 23.59%. Likewise, the 1980 return to the S&P 500 — a capitalization weighted *blend* of both value and growth stocks — was also positive and high, at 32.27%. In contrast, during 1981 all three stock market indexes were down substantially from the attractive return performance observed in the previous year. For 1981, large cap growth stocks had negative total returns, −9.81%, while the return to value investing in that year was about zero. Also, the blended large cap return — as measured by the S&P 500 index — was down at −5.01%.

In more recent times, Exhibit 1 shows similar return volatility in the growth and value styles of equity investing. During 1994 — a year of heightened interest rate uncertainty — the performance of value stocks was down at -0.64%, while large cap growth stocks had a low positive return, at 3.13%. Not surprisingly, the overall return to large cap equity investing as measured by the S&P 500 return was also low, at only 1.32%. In contrast, during 1995 — a year of falling interest

---

[1] The annual total returns shown in Exhibit 1 were listed in the *S&P 500 Directory* (New York: Standard & Poor's, 1998).

rates and robust corporate profits — the return to growth and value stock investing was up quite substantially. Large cap growth stocks earned 38.13%, while value stocks earned 37% during that year of economic growth and declining interest rates. Although market volatility is evident in recent years, it is also apparent that U.S. stock market performance was quite exceptional during the last few years of the period analyzed. Indeed, the S&P 500 had a cumulative total return (unadjusted for reinvested earnings) of some 94% during the 1995 to 1997 period.[2]

## Arithmetic Average Return

The arithmetic average rate of return on a portfolio can be viewed as both a measure of central tendency and investment performance (with certain limitations),[3] while the standard deviation can be viewed as a measure of portfolio risk. These return/risk measures are frequently used from a performance measurement perspective because (1) the mean and standard deviation are the two key parameters that can be used to identify the location of any outcome in the normal distribution, and (2) the empirical evidence on common stock returns supports the notion — although not totally so due to "fat tails" in daily return distributions — that the distribution of common stock returns is largely normal.

## Exhibit 1: Annual Total Returns on Large Cap Value, Blend, and Growth Stocks (1980 to 1997)

|  | Growth (%) | Value (%) | S&P500 (%) |
|---|---|---|---|
| 1980 | 39.4 | 23.59 | 32.27 |
| 1981 | −9.81 | 0.02 | −5.01 |
| 1982 | 22.03 | 21.04 | 21.44 |
| 1983 | 16.24 | 28.89 | 22.38 |
| 1984 | 2.33 | 10.52 | 6.1 |
| 1985 | 33.31 | 29.68 | 31.57 |
| 1986 | 14.5 | 21.67 | 18.56 |
| 1987 | 6.5 | 3.68 | 5.1 |
| 1988 | 11.95 | 21.67 | 16.61 |
| 1989 | 36.4 | 26.13 | 31.69 |
| 1990 | 0.2 | −6.85 | −3.1 |
| 1991 | 38.37 | 22.56 | 30.47 |
| 1992 | 5.06 | 10.52 | 7.62 |
| 1993 | 1.67 | 18.6 | 10.08 |
| 1994 | 3.13 | −0.64 | 1.32 |
| 1995 | 38.13 | 37 | 37.58 |
| 1996 | 23.97 | 21.99 | 22.96 |
| 1997 | 36.53 | 29.99 | 33.36 |
| Average | 17.77 | 17.78 | 17.83 |
| Std. Dev. | 16.13 | 12.21 | 13.59 |

[2] With compounding (discussed shortly), U.S. large cap stocks were up 126% in the three years since 1994.
[3] We cover the benefits and limitations of alternative investment performance measures in Chapter 14.

In our case, the arithmetic average or mean return is calculated by adding up the 18 yearly returns on the relevant value, blend, and growth indexes and then dividing by the number of observations, 18 in our sample. Mathematically, this is expressed as:

$$\text{Avg}(R) = \frac{\sum R_t}{n}$$

where

| | | |
|---|---|---|
| Avg $(R)$ | = | arithmetic average return |
| $R_t$ | = | observed total return for year $t$ |
| $n$ | = | number of years in the sample |
| $\Sigma$ | = | summation from year 1 to year $n$ |

The idea of dividing each return observation by the sample size is not to say that each yearly return outcome is equally likely, but rather to recognize that relative frequencies ($1/n$) in classical statistics approximate population probabilities.

Applying this to the yearly returns on large cap value stocks, the arithmetic average yearly return is

$$\text{Avg}(R) = \frac{23.59 + 0.02 + \dots + 29.99}{18} = 17.78\%$$

Applying this formula to large cap growth stocks and the S&P 500 provides average yearly return estimates of 17.77% and 17.83%, respectively.

If we use the subscripts $v$, $g$, and $m$ to denote value, growth and blend indexes, then we can write:

$$\text{Avg}(R_v) = 17.78\%, \text{Avg}(R_g) = 17.77\%, \text{Avg}(R_m) = 17.83\%$$

These average yearly return estimates reveal that large cap value stocks had similar average return performance when compared to growth stocks over the 18-year period. The six years of large cap growth returns in excess of 30% — three that occurred during the 1990s (1991, 1995, and 1997) — made a significant positive contribution to the 17.77% average return earned on the S&P/BARRA large cap growth index. Although a close inspection of return outcomes during the 1980 to 1997 period reveals that there was only one year when large cap value stocks had a realized return that exceeded 30% (specifically, 1995), the 10 years of favorable returns to value investing in the 21% to 30% range made a meaningful contribution to the average yearly return on this large cap value index.

## Sample Variance and Standard Deviation

Let's now look at the risk or volatility associated with the popular growth and value styles of investing. For the most part, the standard deviation of portfolio return is used as a quantitative measure of risk. The standard deviation is calculated by first estimating the variance, and then taking the square root of this statistical figure. As mentioned before, using the return variance to measure investment uncertainty makes sense when the probability distribution of security returns is reasonably normal.

The variance of returns, denoted var(R), is computed as follows

$$var(R) = \frac{\sum [R_t - \text{Avg}(R)]^2}{n-1}$$

The variance of the return to value investing over the 1980 to 1997 years is:

$$var(R) = \frac{(23.59 - 17.78)^2 + (0.02 - 17.78)^2 + \ldots + (29.99 - 17.78)^2}{18 - 1} = 149.08$$

Since variance is measured in squared units, it is helpful to convert this figure to the standard deviation by taking its square root. The square root of the variance is in turn the return standard deviation, denoted SD(R). That is,

$$SD(R) = [var(R)]^{0.5}$$

For large cap value investing, we have

$$SD(R) = [149.08]^{0.5} = 0.1221 \text{ or } 12.21\%$$

Likewise — using the variance and standard deviation formulas — the annual risk of large cap growth investing over the 18-year period was 16.13%, while the risk of large cap investing more generally—as measured by blended return fluctuations on the S&P 500 — was 13.59%. Again, using the subscripts $v$, $g$, and $m$ to denote the particular style index, we have

$$SD(R_v) = 12.21\%, SD(R_g) = 16.13\%, SD(R_m) = 13.59\%$$

Taken together, the average return and portfolio risk estimates over the years 1980 to 1997 indicate that the value style of investing is especially attractive because it offers both high returns with comparatively low risk — that is, favorable returns combined with low volatility means more sleep at night for the equity portfolio manager!

## Sample Coefficient of Variation

Another helpful measure for the equity manager's tool-kit is the *coefficient of variation* (CV). This performance measure looks at the risk *per* unit of expected return and is computed as follows:

$$CV = \text{Risk/Reward}$$
$$= SD(R)/\text{Avg}(R)$$

Since the standard deviation is in the numerator of this formula, the risk-averse investor would prefer portfolios that offer low volatility per return unit (that is, low *CV*), since these portfolios also have high expected return per unit of risk (or high, 1/*CV*).

The coefficient of variation for the S&P/BARRA large cap value index over the 1980 to 1997 period is:

$$CV = 12.21/17.78 = 0.69$$

During this period, the coefficient of variation for the S&P/BARRA large cap growth index and the S&P 500 were 0.91 and 0.76, respectively. Consistent with the findings reported in Chapter 5, these risk to reward figures point to the risk-adjusted return superiority of the value style of investing over reasonably long periods of time.

## The Combined Results

Exhibit 2 shows the combined performance/risk results for the S&P 500 and the S&P/BARRA growth and value indexes for the 18 years covering 1980 to 1997. Additionally, the exhibit reports the average return and risk estimates on long-term U.S. Treasury bonds, while we note in discussion the performance of large cap stocks over the 1960 to 1997 period.

With average returns in excess of 17% for all three S&P-based return series during the 1980 to 1997 years, the return to U.S. equity investing has been especially attractive in recent years. From a historical perspective, this finding is interesting in light of the fact that for the past 38 years, the yearly average return on U.S. large cap stocks was 12.7%. Another look at Exhibit 2 reveals that the high average returns in recent years were earned with mostly lower return volatility (risk) — except for the S&P/BARRA large cap growth index.

*Exhibit 2: Performance and Risk Estimates for Large Cap Value, Blend and Growth Stocks (1980-1997)*

| Equity Index | Average Return % | Return Standard Deviation % | Coefficient of Variation |
|---|---|---|---|
| | 1980 to 1997 Period | | |
| S&P/BARRA Value | 17.78 | 12.21 | 0.69 |
| S&P/BARRA Growth | 17.77 | 16.13 | 0.91 |
| S&P 500 | 17.83 | 13.59 | 0.76 |
| L.T. Treasury Bonds | 12.36 | 13.66 | 1.11 |

* Equity indexes were obtained from Standard and Poor's. The average return and risk estimates for U.S. treasury bonds are based on the Lehman Brothers Long Term Treasury Bond Index.

While not shown in the exhibit, the annualized return standard deviation on the value and blend S&P indexes were less than the 15.8% risk figure observed on the S&P 500 index over the years 1960 to 1997. Based on recent results, U.S. large cap equities across the value, blend, and growth spectrum had relatively high risk-adjusted reward (low $CV$, or high $1/CV$) during the 18-year observation period. Also, the risk-adjusted return to equity investing in recent years — whether growth, value, or blend (large cap U.S. indexing) — was noticeably better than the risk-adjusted performance for long-term Treasury bonds. In this context, the coefficient of variation on long-term Treasury bonds, 1.11, was higher than the risk-to-expected reward ratio for large cap equities in recent years — ranging from 0.70 to about 0.90 during the 1980 to 1997 period.

When the equity manager looks at the relative performance of U.S. large cap growth and value stocks in recent years, it is also important to emphasize a key investment finding. Exhibit 2 shows that large cap value stocks — as measured by the S&P/BARRA large cap value index — outperformed the growth-oriented counterpart from a risk-adjusted return perspective during the 1980 to 1997 period. At 17.78% and 17.77%, respectively, the average return to large cap value investing was similar to the average return observed on large cap growth stocks, while Exhibit 2 shows that the volatility of large cap value investing, 12.21%, was noticeably lower than the risk to large cap growth investing, 16.13%.

These risk-adjusted performance findings support the often mentioned performance assertion by some equity portfolio managers that "*value wins.*" Statistically speaking, the S&P/BARRA value index has the lowest coefficient of variation, at 0.69, among the coefficient of variation (risk to average reward) estimates reported in Exhibit 2.

## RELATED DESCRIPTIVE MEASURES

When providing information about the risk of equity investing, the manager may find it instructive to form a "confidence interval" (or probability range) about the estimated average return on a portfolio. In this context, information can be provided to investors about the downside risk of equity investing, as well as the statistically based upside potential due to the inherent volatility of the underlying investment. Assuming a normal distribution for stock returns and that the distribution is unchanged in the future, approximately 68% of the return outcomes for any given year should fall within 1 standard deviation of the average return, while 95% of the possible return outcomes should lie within two standard deviations of the average annual total return.

Exhibit 3 shows the estimated confidence interval for the annual total return outcomes for value, blend, and growth styles of equity investing. These performance ranges are based on the average annual return and standard deviation figures that were calculated over the 1980 to 1997 period reported in Exhibit 1. As can be seen, the confidence intervals provide information about the large return uncertainty that is present when investing in common stocks more generally.

## Exhibit 3: Confidence Intervals for Annual Total Returns for Large Cap Value, Blend, and Growth Stocks (1980-1997)

| Equity Index | 68% Confidence Interval Avg($R$) ±1 × SD($R$) | 95% Confidence Interval Avg($R$) ±2 × SD($R$) |
|---|---|---|
| S&P/BARRA Value | 5.57% to 29.99% | −6.64% to 42.20% |
| S&P/BARRA Growth | 1.64% to 33.90% | −14.49% to 50.03% |
| S&P 500 | 4.24% to 31.42% | −9.35% to 45.01% |

Exhibit 3 reveals that with 95% confidence, the return to value investing for any given year ranges from a low of −6.64% on up to 42.2% (based on sample statistics covering 1980 to 1997). Large cap growth stocks had an even wider range with performance outcomes running from −14.49% on up to 50.03%. The confidence interval for large cap domestic indexing (namely, the S&P 500) is also quite wide, running from −9.35% on the downside, up to 45.01% upside stock market potential. These 95% confidence intervals also serve as a reminder to the equity manager that stocks are especially volatile, and that predicting return outcomes (and therefore, stock prices) for any given year can be a challenging if not fruitless task. Moreover, wide ranges in the return outcomes for common stocks are even quite evident when a 68% confidence interval is computed.

## Sample Correlation Analysis

Another interesting statistical measure for the equity manager's research kit is return correlation. Correlation measures the strength of the *linear* statistical association between two variables. In our case, it might be interesting to examine the correlation between large cap value and growth stocks as well as the overall impact of the domestic market index on these popular equity styles. The statistical formula for the correlation between large cap value returns and the market proxy can be expressed as:

$$\text{cor}(R_v, R_m) = \frac{\text{cov}(R_v, R_m)}{\text{SD}(R_v)\text{SD}(R_m)}$$

where $SD(R_v)$ and $SD(R_m)$ are standard deviation estimates for the respective large cap value and U.S. market indexes, and $\text{cov}(R_v, R_m)$, denoting covariance, is a statistical measure of the comovement between the respective return series.

To apply the correlation concept, Exhibit 4 shows a *3×3* correlation matrix (actually, half of it) for the S&P/BARRA large cap value and growth indexes and the S&P 500. Each observation in this exhibit represents a correlation estimate between two paired return series. The equity manager should notice the "1's" that lie along the "diagonal" of the correlation matrix. Simply put, this means that the correlation of a security or portfolio with itself is, by definition, unity. For example, the correlation between the return on the S&P 500 and the S&P 500, cor($R_m$,$R_m$), is by definition 1.[4]

---

[4] On the other hand, the covariance between the return on a market index and itself, $\text{cov}(R_m, R_m)$ is the market variance, $\text{var}(R_m)$.

## Exhibit 4: Correlation Matrix for Large Cap Return Indexes

| Index | Value* | Growth* | S&P 500 |
|---|---|---|---|
| Value | 1.00 | | |
| Growth | 0.81 | 1.00 | |
| S&P 500 | 0.93 | 0.97 | 1.00 |

\* S&P/BARRA Large Cap Return Index (estimated over 1980-1997 period)

The equity manager should also note that only one set of "off-diagonal" elements is shown in the correlation matrix. This occurs because the correlation of the return to the S&P/BARRA value index with the S&P 500, for example, is the same as the statistical comovement between the S&P 500 and the S&P/BARRA value series, namely, $cor(R_v, R_m) = cor(R_m, R_v)$. By statistical design, the correlation between any two variables ranges from $-1$ for perfect negative correlation to $+1$ for perfect positive comovement. Zero correlation indicates that no (*linear*) association is present in the variables.

Exhibit 4 shows that there is a high positive return correlation between the S&P/BARRA large cap style indexes and the S&P 500 index. At 0.97, the correlation between the S&P/BARRA growth index is slightly higher than the (high) positive association between the return to large cap value stocks and the representative market index, at 0.93. These high correlation figures should not be surprising to the equity manager since the S&P 500 itself is comprised of the large cap value and growth stocks that make up these popular style indexes.

On the other hand, Exhibit 4 shows that the correlation between the large cap value and growth indexes is noticeably lower, at 0.81. The relatively lower — but still high positive — return association between the S&P/BARRA value and growth indexes is capturing the somewhat dampened cross-effect of the (domestic) market index on these equity styles indexes.

## Wealth Accumulation

One of the most common ways of conveying performance results is to show how an investment of say $10,000 has grown over time. In this context, the initial investment is assumed to grow at the annual total rates of return, with "compound interest" so to speak being earned on reinvested earnings. In mathematical terms, the growth of an initial investment can be represented by:

$$FV = PV \times (1 + R_1) \times (1 + R_2) \dots \times (1 + R_n)$$

where *FV* denotes future value and is the wealth accumulation from the initial (present value) investment, and the $R_t$'s represent the observed total returns on the investment series in question.

Applying this formula to the S&P/BARRA large cap growth series over the 18-year period 1980 to 1997, we obtain:

$$FV_g = \$10,000 \times (1.3940) \times (0.9019) \dots \times (1.3653)$$
$$= \$161,756$$

Likewise, the wealth accumulation in the S&P/BARRA value and the S&P 500 over this 18-year period were $172,837 and $170,761, respectively.

Hence, over the 1980 to 1997 period the growth of $10,000 invested in relatively low volatility (as far as equities are concerned) value stocks was $11,081 more than the wealth accumulation in large cap growth stocks, and some $2,076 higher than the dollar accumulation in the S&P 500. The yearly wealth accumulation in these large cap indexes is shown in Exhibit 5.

## Time-Weighted Average Return

A corollary measure that is often cited along with a growth of $10,000 chart is the *time-weighted average return*. This number measures that one compound yearly return figure — also known as the *internal rate of return* (IRR) — that allows the initial investment to grow to its future terminal value. The time-weighted average return is computed as follows:

$$IRR = [FV/PV]^{1/n}$$

where *FV* is the terminal value.

Applying this formula to compute the time-weighted average return on the S&P/BARRA large cap growth index over the 1980 to 1997 period we get 16.87% as shown below:

$$
\begin{aligned}
IRR_g &= [FV_g/PV]^{1/n} - 1.0 \\
&= [161{,}756/10{,}000]^{1/18} - 1.0 = 0.1687 \text{ or } 16.87\%
\end{aligned}
$$

## Exhibit 5: Growth of $10,000: Large Cap Value, Blend, and Growth Portfolios: 1980-1997

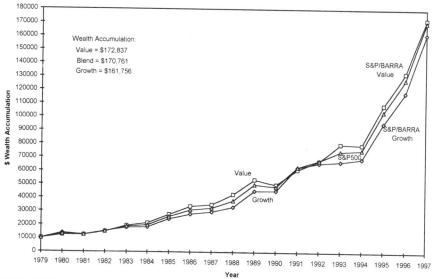

Upon inserting the respective present and future value figures into the IRR formula for large cap value stocks, one finds that the time-weighted average return to value investing was 17.30%, while the annualized return on the S&P 500 index was 17.22% for the 18-year reporting period.

# REGRESSION ANALYSIS

Another statistical tool that is frequently used in equity management is *regression analysis*. This form of statistical analysis is commonly used to quantify the sensitivity of a particular security or portfolio to movements in a market index — or other systematic pervasive factor. For instance, suppose that you were interested in knowing the return sensitivity of growth or value stocks to fluctuations in the broad market, as well as the percentage of movement in these portfolios that can be attributed to this market factor. In this context, one could examine the "market model" relationship between, say, large cap growth stocks — as measured by the S&P/BARRA large cap growth return — and the return to the S&P 500.

The single factor regression equation for the return to growth stocks and the representative market portfolio can be expressed as:

$$R_g = \alpha + \beta\, R_m + e$$

where $R_g$ is the return (annual in our illustration) on growth stocks, $\alpha$ is the constant or intercept term, $\beta$ is the beta sensitivity of the portfolio to movement in the market, and $e$ is the residual (or unexplained) component of $R_g$ that accounts for presumably *random* factors. Otherwise, there would be missing *factors* that statistically impact the portfolio's return outcome for any given year.

Exhibit 6 shows a scatter plot of the return to large cap growth stocks (vertical axis) and the return to large cap blend stocks (horizontal axis) — as measured by returns earned on the S&P/BARRA growth index and the S&P 500 over the 1980 to 1997 period. An initial look at the exhibit suggests that a strong *positive* (linear) relationship exists between these portfolio return series. Low returns on growth stocks (below 10%) are associated with low performance in the marketplace, while at the high performing end of the return spectrum, large cap growth stocks have high annual return outcomes when the stock market is also high.

Exhibit 7 presents the "fitted versus actual" display of the market model relationship between the return to large cap growth stocks and the S&P 500. The exhibit also shows regression statistics — including the intercept ($\alpha$), slope ($\beta$), and percentage of variation explained ($R^2$) by the estimated linear regression model. Specifically, $R^2$ (called the *coefficient of determination*) measures the percentage of variation in the dependent variable that is explained by the independent variable (in this instance, the market factor).

## Exhibit 6: S&P/BARRA Growth versus S&P 500 Index: 1980-1997

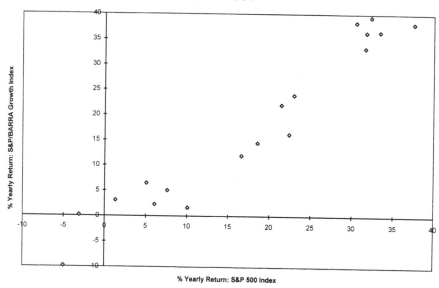

## Exhibit 7: Fitted Line Plot: S&P/BARRA Growth versus S&P 500: 1980-1997

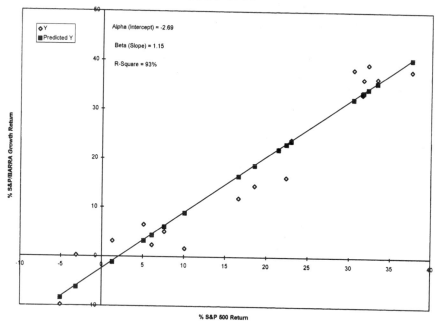

At 1.15, the estimated return sensitivity, or beta, of the S&P/BARRA large cap growth index is higher than the average beta in the marketplace, which is 1. This suggests that — other things the same — if the U.S. stock market were to rise by 10%, then large cap growth stocks would rise by 11.5%. Since beta also implies a symmetric return response on the downside, growth stocks should fall by this same percentage if large cap stocks (namely, the S&P 500) were to decline by 10%.

The intercept term in Exhibit 7 for the estimated market model relationship between large cap growth stocks and the S&P 500 is −2.69%. This finding is not too encouraging for large cap U.S. investors because it suggests that if the stock market were "flat" for any year, then this growth style of investing would fall short of the market performance by some 269 basis points. Given that growth stocks are more volatile than the overall stock market, this negative intercept term seems doubly problematic from an expected return-risk perspective.

On balance, the $R^2$ (which is the correlation, $cor(R_g, R_m)$, squared) between these portfolio return series is quite high. In this context, the linear regression results suggest that 93% of the movement in return on the S&P/BARRA growth index is statistically explained by large cap return fluctuations more broadly. Alternatively, the linear regression results indicate that only 7% of the yearly fluctuation in large cap growth returns is explained by non-market factors (possibly sector or industry related return effects).

In a similar manner, the market model can be used to assess the importance of the S&P 500 on large cap value stocks. A visual inspection of Exhibit 8 suggests that a positive association exists between the return to large cap value stocks and the observed return to the market factor. That is, high positive return in the stock market is associated with high return to value investing, while a low positive return outcome is apparent for value stocks when the market return is relatively low. The findings during the 1980 to 1997 years also point to the possibility that the return to large cap value stocks has a *non*-linear relationship with the market index — as the paired return pattern in Exhibit 8 displays some "curvature." Although important, the statistical (and financial) question of non-linear association between the underlying stock market variables is beyond the scope of this chapter.

Exhibit 9 shows the regression results for the estimated *linear* relationship in return to large cap value stocks and the S&P 500 over the 1980 to 1997 period. In this fitted relationship, the intercept term is positive at 2.82% per year, while the market model beta is less than 1. At 0.84, the estimated beta suggests that if the market were to rise by, say, 10%, then the price of value stocks would follow by 8.4%. Conversely, if the stock market were to fall by 10%, then large cap value stocks — as measured by the S&P/BARRA value index — would fall by 8.4%. This defensive aspect of value stocks as manifested in their relatively low beta (compared with that of large cap growth stocks) is one of the more attractive features of this style of equity investing.

*Exhibit 8: S&P/BARRA Value versus S&P 500 Index: 1980-1997*

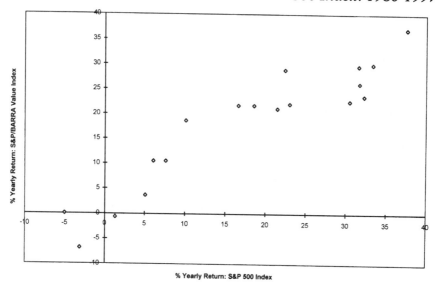

*Exhibit 9: Fitted Line Plot: S&P/BARRA Value versus*
*S&P 500: 1980-1997*

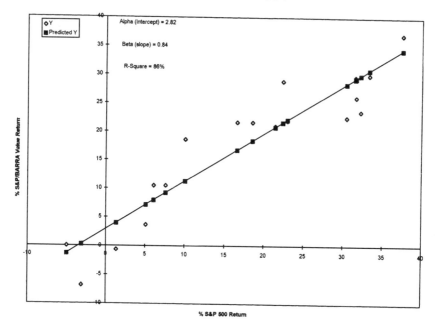

In light of the observation concerning a possible non-linear association between the return to value stocks and market factor, it is not surprising to see that the coefficient of determination ($R^2$ value) at 0.86, is somewhat lower than the 0.93 figure observed for large cap growth stocks. This means that approximately 86% of the movement in the S&P/BARRA large cap value index is explained by movements in the general level of the stock market, while some 93% of the return fluctuation for growth stocks is explained by the inherent volatility in the (large cap) market factor. One can also see in Exhibit 9 that the estimated slope in the fitted relationship is lower for value stocks in comparison with the estimated beta for growth stocks.

## Hypothesis Testing

Another interesting feature of the reported regression results is the "$t$-statistic." This measure is calculated by forming a ratio of the estimated alpha (or beta) to the "standard error," $SE(\alpha)$, of the intercept term (or $SE(\beta)$) that was estimated in the regression relationship. In effect, the $t$-statistic can be used to assess whether or not the estimated alpha and beta values are significantly different from zero. The regression "$t$-statistics" for the estimated alpha and beta are given by:

$$t(\alpha) = \alpha/SE(\alpha)$$
$$t(\beta) = \beta/SE(\beta)$$

where the estimated regression parameter — either alpha or beta — is statistically different from zero when the absolute value of the computed $t$-value exceeds 2. In these conventional $t$-tests, the implied hypothesis for alpha or beta is zero. (The critical $t$-value is actually higher than "2" for our sample since there are less than 30 observations.)

Suppose that the equity manager is interested in knowing whether the estimated alpha/beta values in the market model regression for large cap value stocks are statistically distinguishable from zero. Based on the ($\alpha$) and ($\beta$) estimates reported in Exhibit 9, the $t$-values are:

$$t(\alpha_v) = 2.82/1.79 = 1.58$$
$$t(\beta_v) = 0.84/0.08 = 10.50$$

Due to high standard error on the estimated $\alpha_v$, $SE(\alpha_v)$ at 1.79, the $t$-value on alpha for value stocks, $t(\alpha_v)$ at 1.58 is statistically indistinguishable from zero — even though the estimated $\alpha$ is positive at 2.82% per year. In contrast, the estimated $\beta_v$ for value stocks, 0.84, is highly significant when the "null hypothesis" is that there is no (linear) statistical relationship between the return to value stocks and the market factor — as the estimated $t$ value, $t(\beta_v)$ at 10.50, far exceeds the critical value for statistical significance of 2. This is not surprising since a high positive return relationship would be expected as the S&P/BARRA value index is constructed from stocks that comprise the S&P 500.

Given that there should be a high positive relationship between these indexes, a perhaps more meaningful question is whether or not the estimated β for value stocks is statistically different from the (large cap) market beta of 1. This question can be addressed by setting the hypothesized value of β at 1. The following $t$-value shows how this works:

$$t(\beta_v) = (0.84 - 1.0)/0.08$$
$$= -2.00$$

Although the estimated beta for large cap value stocks is less than 1 — as one might reasonably expect for value stocks — the $t$-value just barely confirms this result with "95% confidence." Given the high return volatility of stocks more generally, one often finds a conflict between the concept of practical significance and statistical significance. These conflicts are especially problematic in the equity management area when incentives and bonuses are based on the statistical significance of a particular performance measure applied to a portfolio of common stocks.

## Regression Analysis for Individual Stocks

The above discussion focuses on the market model relationship between well diversified portfolios of value and growth stocks using total returns on the S&P/BARRA large cap growth/value indexes. Let's now look at how the results might differ when one examines the statistical association between an individual value (or growth) stock and the return on the market factor.

Exhibit 10 shows how "BLOOMBERG" reports the estimated regression results in its "Historical Beta" module. In this exhibit, the market model relationship for Eastman Kodak is revealed for the weekly period covering November 3, 1995 to October 31, 1997. The BLOOMBERG regression analysis shows both the estimated intercept (alpha) and slope (beta) parameters, along with a scatter plot of *weekly* returns on the company stock versus "fitted" S&P 500 values. BLOOMBERG's representation of the fitted relationship for Eastman Kodak (Y-variable) and the weekly return to the market factor (X-variable) is given by:

$$Y = 0.83\, X - 0.37$$

where the intercept term is −0.37 (for −0.37% per week) and the "raw beta" is 0.83. At 0.89, the BLOOMBERG "adjusted beta" is somewhat higher than the estimated raw beta in the sample regression.

In turn, the "adjusted beta" is a weighted average of the estimated beta from the regression, 0.83, and the average beta of stocks in the reference S&P 500 index, 1. The beta weights are 67% on the raw beta and 33% on the market beta. The adjusted beta attempts to account for a well-known regression tendency of beta moving towards the grand average of 1.[5]

---

[5] See Marshall E. Blume, "On the Assessment of Risk," *Journal of Finance* (March 1971), pp. 1-10.

### Exhibit 10: BLOOMBERG Regression Analysis for Eastman Kodak (K)
#### Historical Data

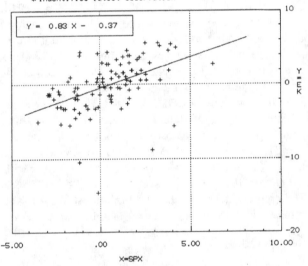

```
              EK          US

     Relative Index   SPX

     Period
     Range  11/ 3/95  To  10/31/97
     Market  Trade


     ADJ  BETA           .89
     RAW  BETA           .83
     Alpha (Intercept)  -.37
     R2 (Correlation)    .19
     Std Dev of Error   3.23
     Std Error of Beta   .17
     Number of Points   104


     Adj beta = (0.67) * Raw Beta
              + (0.33) * 1.0

   * Indentifies latest observation
```

Y = 0.83 X - 0.37

Source: COPYRIGHT BLOOMBERG L.P. ALL RIGHTS RESERVED.

Since Eastman Kodak's beta is less than 1, the stock — by this risk metric — can be considered a *value* stock. This is due to the comparably low sensitivity of the company's return with the market factor. At –0.37, the estimated alpha is negative, although the standard error of alpha is not shown for hypothesis testing. It is also instructive to note that the coefficient of determination ($R^2$ value) between the weekly return to the market factor and Kodak's rate of return is noticeably low, at 0.19. This 19% variation explained in the weekly return to Eastman Kodak stock and the market is not that unusual since "company specific" and "industry effects" loom large when explaining the return performance of any given stock — especially, over a short time interval.

On the other hand, the equity manager should expect that the correlation between a portfolio of value (or growth) stocks and the market index is considerably higher as company and industry specific events tend to get diversified away. This happens because the portfolio takes on more characteristics of the market when the number of stocks increases. One needs only to recall (see Exhibit 4) the high positive correlation, at 0.93, between the total return on the S&P/BARRA large cap value index and the S&P 500 during the sample period.

## Regression Analysis for a Growth Stock

Exhibit 11 shows the regression results reported by BLOOMBERG for a large cap growth stock — Cisco Systems, Inc. Among the statistical findings, it is interesting to see that the adjusted beta, 1.43, is now lower than the estimated raw beta, at 1.65. This happens because the BLOOMBERG adjusted relative risk formula accounts for the known tendency of high beta stocks to regress toward the market beta of 1. It is also interesting to see that the coefficient of determination ($R^2$) between the return to Cisco stock and the S&P 500 over the 104 weeks is 0.34 — somewhat higher than that observed for Eastman Kodak.

Although the estimated beta on Cisco Systems' stock is greater than 1 — a relative risk characteristic for a growth stock — the low correlation between Cisco's stock and the market point to strong company and/or industry specific happenings ("residual effects") that largely influence the return behavior of the firm's securities. The BLOOMBERG market model relationship for Cisco Systems, Inc. ($Y$-variable) and the S&P ($X$-variable) was found to be:

$$Y = 1.65\,X + 0.05$$

This regression equation suggests that if the weekly market return were, say, 1% (100 basis points) then the weekly return to Cisco stock would be 1.7% (about 88% per year — which is not uncommon for that high tech growth stock!). However, since the correlation between Cisco Systems' stock return and the market return — as measured by the S&P 500 return — is low, the confidence in achieving this estimated weekly statistical association for any *given* week is somewhat low. For the most part, the source of divergent predictive implications between beta and correlation can usually be traced to high "own return volatility" (or high standard deviation) in a firm's stock.

## SUMMARY

Statistical concepts can be helpful to equity analysts and managers alike in gauging the return/risk characteristics of investment securities and portfolios. At the very least, this requires a familiarity with descriptive statistics that characterize the probability distribution of return outcomes — including the mean and standard deviation of portfolio return — as well as various correlative estimates between security returns.

Armed with a statistical background, the equity manager can also focus on the regression characteristics of individual securities and portfolios relative to a market index by emphasizing the concepts of (1) alpha, (2) beta, and (3) $R^2$, or coefficient of determination. These regression metrics — among others, including the Sharpe ratio covered in Chapter 14 — are reported regularly for individual securities and mutual funds by such familiar names as Bloomberg, Morningstar, O'Neill & Company, and Value Line. Moreover, a detailed understanding of how a simple regression model works is a prerequisite to understanding the basic elements of a multiple factor model covered in Chapter 9.

### Exhibit 11: BLOOMBERG Regression Analysis for Cisco Systems, Inc. (CSCO)
#### Historical Beta

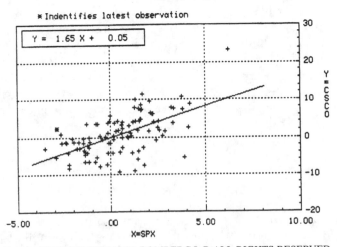

| | | |
|---|---|---|
| ADJ BETA | 1.43 |
| RAW BETA | 1.65 |
| Alpha (Intercept) | .05 |
| R2 (Correlation) | .34 |
| Std Dev of Error | 4.36 |
| Std Error of Beta | .23 |
| Number of Points | 104 |

Source: COPYRIGHT 1998 BLOOMBERG L.P. ALL RIGHTS RESERVED.

# QUESTIONS

1. What statistical measures are used in calculating the risk of an asset and a portfolio?

2. What is a "wealth accumulation" statistic used for?

3. What is the coefficient of determination ($R^2$) and what information does it provide an investor interested in estimating the relationship between a factor thought to affect the return on stocks?

4. a. Why is a "t-statistic" an important statistical measure in attempting to demonstrate whether or not each of three factors is an important independent variable in explaining stock returns in the following relationship?

$$r_j = a + b_1 \text{ Factor } 1 + b_2 \text{ Factor } 2 + b_3 \text{ Factor } 3 + \text{error term}$$

where $r_j$ is the return on stock $j$ and $b_1$, $b_2$, and $b_3$ are the parameters of the regression model to be estimated.

b. Suppose that the t-statistics are estimated to be as follows:

$$b_1 \text{ t-statistic} = 3.7 \quad b_2 \text{ t-statistic} = 1.0 \quad b_3 \text{ t-statistic} = 2.8$$

Which factors are statistically significant in explaining stock returns.

5. Below is the Bloomberg screen for Merck & Co., Inc.

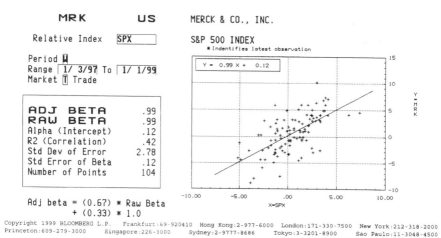

    a. What is meant by an "adjusted beta"?

    b. Why is an adjusted beta calculated for a stock?

    c. In the box on the screen there is a value for "R2" (used to denote $R^2$). The value shown is 0.42. How do you interpret this value?

    d. In the box you will see "R2 (Correlation)." Is the $R^2$ the same thing as the "Correlation"?

6. Suppose that you are interested in gaining some statistical insight on the return to large cap value and growth stocks in the aftermath of the October Crash of 1987. Specifically, you hypothesize that due to excess market volatility during Black Monday, October 19, 1987, that investors—to the extent that they were willing to stay in stocks—would naturally gravitate to a relatively low risk equity strategy that is captured by the large cap "value" style of investing.

    Further suppose that you will base your research on portfolio performance in excess of that which can be explained by the Capital Asset Pricing Model. In this context, your research analysis will focus on large cap value and growth stock returns in excess of the "risk-free" interest rate according to:

$$(R_p - R_F) = a + b\,(R_M - R_F) + e_p$$

where $(R_p - R_F)$ is the annual portfolio premium and $(R_M - R_F)$ is the market risk premium. According to CAPM, $a$ (alpha) should be equal to zero, and $b$ is the sensitivity of the excess portfolio return to fluctuation in the excess market return.

    You have gathered the following data for U.S. Treasury bill returns for the years 1988 to 1997:

| Year | Return % |
| --- | --- |
| 1988 | 6.3 |
| 1989 | 8.4 |
| 1990 | 7.8 |
| 1991 | 5.6 |
| 1992 | 3.5 |
| 1993 | 2.9 |
| 1994 | 3.9 |
| 1995 | 5.6 |
| 1996 | 5.3 |
| 1997 | 5.3 |

    Use the 10 years of Treasury bill returns along with the corresponding large cap value, growth, and market returns — see Exhibit 1 of this chapter — for the 10 years covering 1988 to 1997 to answer questions (a through h) below.

    To answer the questions, a linear regression package such as that available in EXCEL is necessary to answer these questions in a manner that corresponds with the statistical formulas and discussion in Chapter 3.

a. What is the average excess return to large cap value and growth stocks in the 10 years after the Crash of 1987?

b. What is the standard deviation of the excess return to large cap value and growth stocks during the 1988 to 1997 period?

c. What is the coefficient of variation for value and growth stocks in the aftermath of the Crash of 1987? Explain your findings.

d. Calculate a 95% confidence interval for the (excess) return to large cap value and growth stocks?

e. What are the estimated "alpha" values for the large cap growth and value styles of equity management in the 10 years following the Crash of 1987? Are these alpha values statistically significant?

f. What are the estimated "beta" values for the large cap growth and value stocks during the 10 years since the Crash of 1987?

g. What percentage of the movement in the excess return to large cap value and growth stocks in the 10-year period can be explained by movements in the excess market returns (over the risk-free rate)?

h. Are the statistical findings for large cap value and growth stocks consistent with your initial hypothesis about investor behavior in the aftermath of Black Monday (October 1987)? Be sure to support your overall research assessment with a focus on the "risk-adjusted" return to large cap value (and growth) investing.

# Chapter 4

# Blueprint for Passive-Active Investing

Today's world of equity management is often classified along *two* broad investment themes: namely, active investing and passive investing. Yet with few exceptions there seems to be little discussion among investment practitioners about what constitutes a *jointly* passive-active approach to equity portfolio management.[1] To fill this architectural void, this chapter develops a set of "blueprints" for the passive and active approaches to equity management. By understanding the differences between the two seemingly polar investment approaches, it is hoped that investors will see why a jointly passive-active approach to equity management makes sense in today's real-time capital markets.

We begin with a discussion of the role of capital market efficiency in the passive-versus-active management debate. Following this, the chapter is organized as follows. First, we provide an organized framework for the passive approach to equity portfolio management. In this context, a "blueprint" for passive equity management is developed having both theoretical and empirical foundations. Second, we provide a blueprint for the active approach to investing along with the primary classifications — "bottom-up" and "top-down" investing — that traditionally define this popular approach to equity management. Finally, we provide an integrated "architecture" for the passive-active approach that depends on the *degree* of capital market efficiency.[2]

## CAPITAL MARKET EFFICIENCY

At the heart of today's passive-versus-active debate is the degree of pricing efficiency in the capital market. *Pricing efficiency* refers to a market where current security prices "fully reflect" all available information that is relevant to the valuation of securities. When a market is price-efficient, strategies pursued to outper-

---

[1] For two exceptions, that do point to the benefits of passive-active investing, see: Bruce I. Jacobs and Kenneth N. Levy, "Investment Management: An Architecture for the Equity Market," *Active Equity Portfolio Management* (Frank J. Fabozzi Associates: New Hope PA, 1998) pp. 1-20; and Robert Jones, "The Active versus Passive Debate: Perspectives of an Active Quant," *Active Equity Portfolio Management.* pp. 37-56.

[2] In practice, one can distinguish between two "kinds" of capital market efficiency: (1) an operationally-efficient market, and (2) a pricing-efficient capital market. In an operationally-efficient (internally-efficient) market transactions services can be obtained at their *true* intrinsic value. In a pricing-efficient (externally-efficient) market, prices "fully reflect" all available information that is relevant to security pricing. A complete discussion of the two types of market efficiency can be found in Richard R. West, "Two Kinds of Market Efficiency," *Financial Analysts Journal* (November/December 1975), pp. 30-34.

form a broad-based stock market index will not consistently produce superior returns after adjusting for (1) risk or volatility, and (2) transaction costs. In his seminal article on capital market efficiency, Eugene Fama points out that in order to test whether or not the stock market is price-efficient, two definitions are necessary: First, it is necessary to define what it means for prices to "fully reflect" all available information, and second, the "relevant" set of information that is assumed to be absorbed in security prices must be appropriately defined.[3]

In defining the "relevant" information set that current security prices should fully reflect, Fama classified the pricing efficiency of the stock market into three general forms: (1) weak form, (2) semistrong form, and (3) strong form. The distinction between these forms of capital market efficiency lies in the particular information set that is hypothesized to be impounded in equilibrium security prices. *Weak-form efficiency* means that the price of the stock reflects the past price and volume history. *Semi-strong form* market efficiency suggests that current security prices "fully reflect" all publicly available information (which includes historical price and trading patterns, as well as publicly available information about companies, industries, and even the macro-economy). Finally, *strong-form efficiency* exists in a capital market where the price of a security reflects all information, whether or not it is publicly available.

The active versus passive implications of the efficient market hypothesis emerge when one looks at varying *degrees* of capital market efficiency. If the capital market is largely efficient, then an investor's "optimal portfolio" should consist of passive security holdings as defined by some appropriate model of capital market equilibrium. In principle, this means holding a capitalization-weighted portfolio of *all* risky securities in the marketplace. Such a passive-based market portfolio is not restricted to U.S. equities alone, but includes international stocks, bonds, and real estate as well. On the other hand, if sizable pockets of pricing inefficiencies are present in real-time capital markets, then the investor's optimal portfolio should be largely active. A *jointly* passive-active approach to equity management emerges when the capital market is somewhat price inefficient, but not to the degree where the investor faces a 100% passive *or* all-active approach to equity management. We believe that this "middle of the road" position on pricing efficiency is a defining characteristic of real world capital markets.

## Formulating Empirical Tests

Tests of the efficient market hypothesis investigate whether it is possible to generate abnormal returns on securities or portfolios. An *abnormal return* (or *excess return*) is defined as the difference between the actual return and the expected return from a predetermined model of capital market equilibrium. As such, the expected return used in empirical tests is one predicted from an *equilibrium* pricing model — such as the Capital Asset Pricing Model or the Arbitrage Pricing

---

[3] See Eugene F. Fama, "Efficient Capital Markets: A Review of Theory and Empirical Work," *Journal of Finance* (May 1970), pp. 383-417.

Theory explained in Chapter 2. Consequently, expected return models consider the risk associated with a particular equity investment. In principle, the equilibrium expected return model should consider systematic or non-diversifiable risk factors that are inherent to *all* securities in the marketplace.

As Fama points out, tests of the efficient market hypothesis are really "joint tests" of (1) the degree of pricing efficiency in the capital market when measured *relative* to some assumed model of capital market equilibrium, and (2) a test of the specific model of capital market equilibrium *given* that the capital market is informationally efficient. In tests of the efficient market hypothesis, calculation of the "excess" return on a security or portfolio should take transaction costs from commissions and fees into account. In general, the abnormal return in such tests is calculated by subtracting the *equilibrium* expected return from the actual return according to:

$$AER = AR - ER$$

where *AER* is the abnormal excess return on a security or portfolio, *AR* is the actual return *net* of transaction costs, and *ER* is the expected return from some *equilibrium* return-generating model.

In practice, the expected-return generating model used in empirical tests of market efficiency may be misspecified for many reasons. First, the model may fail to consider all appropriate risk measures. This can happen, for example, if the Capital Asset Pricing Model is used in the empirical analysis when the Arbitrage Pricing Model is the more descriptive model of capital market equilibrium. Second, the appropriate market risk parameter (such as *beta*) may not be estimated properly — that is, the incorrect market index (domestic rather than global index, for example) may be used in the risk estimation process. Also, spurious regularities may arise if the return-generating process is best described by a *nonlinear* model, as opposed to a *linear* model that is frequently used in many tests of the efficient market hypothesis. In these instances, abnormal return regularities pointing to pricing inefficiencies (with seemingly large active return benefits over passive investing) would be questionable.

## BLUEPRINT FOR PASSIVE INVESTING

If the capital market is largely "efficient" in the sense that current security prices reflect full information, then investors have an obvious incentive to go *passive* with their equity allocations. Having said that, one is left wondering about the particular form of the passive investor's portfolio holdings. In view of theoretical and recent empirical considerations, the investor may (1) hold a globally-diversified portfolio of U.S. and international securities, (2) hold a well-diversified portfolio of U.S. securities alone, or possibly (3) follow a "buy and hold" strategy using one of the three equity management styles described by Bruce Jacobs and Kenneth Levy.[4] For passive (as opposed to active)-minded investors, this means holding indexed-value, indexed-growth, or perhaps indexed-small capitalization portfolios.

Exhibit 1 presents a "blueprint" for the passive approach to equity portfolio management. This blueprint reveals that there are three generic approaches to passive investing: namely, global-indexing, local-indexing, and style-passive investing. The nucleus of the passive "architecture" consists of global-passive investing. This strict form of passive investing is based on two key assumptions: (1) the capital market is price-efficient worldwide, and (2) equilibrium security prices are set in accordance with an established global-based model of capital market equilibrium — such as the portfolio model of Markowitz and the CAPM as described in Chapter 2. In turn, deviations from *global* market efficiency help to define other forms of passive (as well as active) investing, including local and style-passive approaches to equity portfolio management.

Before delving into the foundation behind the three general types of passive equity management, it is helpful to note that there are several reasons why today's investors might depart from the global nucleus of the passive-equity management blueprint. First, global indexing is a relatively new phenomena and sufficient indexing opportunities may not be present in the international capital markets — especially in the emerging financial markets. Second, recent empirical anomalies point to the performance superiority of the U.S. equity market over the developed and emerging markets of the world. Third, and possibly worse yet, passive-minded investors may not realize that real passive investing means holding a well-diversified portfolio of securities on a global basis.

---

## Exhibit 1: Passive Investing

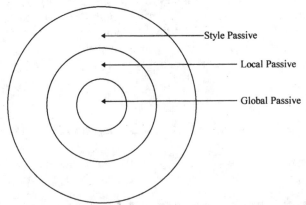

Source: Adapted from Exhibit 4 in Bruce I. Jacobs and Kenneth N. Levy, "Investment Management: An Architecture for the Equity Market," Chapter 1 in Frank J. Fabozzi (ed.), *Active Equity Portfolio Management* (New Hope, PA: Frank J. Fabozzi Associates, 1998), p. 5.

---

[4] See Jacobs and Levy, "Investment Management: An Architecture for the Equity Market," p. 2.

Finally, empirical anomalies also suggest that uncertainty exists among today's investors (and today's academics) about the *correct* model of capital market equilibrium. For example, in Chapter 5 we will discuss two equity style strategies — value and growth. Studies by Eugene Fama and Kenneth French, as well as Rex Sinquefield, suggest that "value wins" from both a U.S. domestic and international perspective.[5] Style-passive investing therefore emerges (see Exhibit 1) as an alternative to local or global indexing due to suspected empirical regularities (or inefficiencies) that point to a misspecification of the true model of capital market equilibrium. Also, the "just right" model of capital market equilibrium may involve non-linearities that are not captured in the linear-based conventional models.

# Global-Passive Investing

If a high degree of capital market efficiency is present in real-time financial markets, then it is reasonable to ask what constitutes the globally-efficient portfolio holdings of passive investors. Considerable insight on this passive equity management question can be obtained by understanding the investment implications of established models of capital market equilibrium. Along this line, several models of capital market equilibrium that we have described in Chapter 2 have evolved over the years to address such portfolio management issues — the Capital Asset Pricing Model (CAPM), the "zero-beta" CAPM model, and the Arbitrage Pricing Theory (APT) model. These well-known asset pricing models grew largely out of Harry Markowitz's pioneering work on portfolio selection.

## Insights from the Markowitz and Sharpe Models

We'll begin the passive investing journey by taking another look at the portfolio models of Harry Markowitz and William Sharpe. Before proceeding, it is important to realize that *two* concepts of "efficiency" are required for their combined model to become operational: (1) the capital market is indeed "efficient" in the sense of Fama's pricing-efficiency hypothesis, and (2) that risk-averse investors strive to hold "efficient portfolios" that maximize expected return while minimizing risk. In the absence of the price efficiency assumption, active investors could of course design portfolios that outperform similar risk-indexed passive strategies. With these efficiency considerations in mind, Exhibit 2 illustrates the passive implications of the combined portfolio models of Markowitz and Sharpe.

Exhibit 2 shows that in a well-functioning capital market, the "market portfolio," M, is the *one* risky component of every rational investors' mean-variance efficient portfolio. In the combined Markowitz-Sharpe framework, investors hold varying proportions of the "risk-free" asset in conjunction with tangency portfolio, M. In this *jointly* efficient setting, "M" is the capitalization-weighted portfolio of all risky securities in the global marketplace. As revealed by the line

---

[5] Eugene F. Fama and Kenneth R. French, "The Cross Section of Expected Stock Returns," *Journal of Finance* (June 1992), pp. 427-465, and Rex A. Sinquefield, "Where Are the Gains from International Diversification?" *Financial Analysts Journal* (January/February 1996).

labeled "*CML*," for *capital market line*, this risky market index held in linear combination with the "riskless asset" provides (passive) investors with the highest expected return for any given (unlevered or levered) level of global portfolio risk.

Since tangency portfolio *M* is the *only* risky component of every investor's efficient portfolio, it must therefore be the value-weighted index of all risky securities — including stocks, bonds, real estate, and any other tradable capital asset. If this were not the case, then a logical inconsistency would exist in the sense there would be some assets trading with positive prices that were not being held by investors in the financial markets. In principle, any risky subset of the world portfolio (*M*) — such as a domestic-only passive index like the S&P 500 — must therefore offer *lower* risk-adjusted performance in comparison with efficient combinations of the risk-free asset and *risky* tangency portfolio, *M*.[6]

Along this line, Exhibit 2 reveals that domestic portfolio *m* — which might reflect the capitalization-weighted holdings of a local index fund like Vanguard's Index 500, or even Vanguard's broader Extended Market index — is, in principle, an *inefficient* portfolio in the combined works of Markowitz and Sharpe. This occurs because a linear combination of the riskless asset and domestic-index portfolio necessarily provides investors with lower risk-adjusted expected returns. In more formal terms, the slope of the *CML* connecting the risk-free asset with domestic index, *m*, is *flatter* than the risk-adjusted performance that would be available on a globally diversified portfolio holding of risky tangency portfolio, *M*, and the riskless asset.[7] At this point, it becomes an empirical issue as to whether the globally-diversified portfolio makes sense for real world investors.

## Local-Passive Investing

For passive investors, the "just right" type of portfolio indexing in recent years seems quite obvious — especially when viewed in terms of U.S. cumulative returns for large capitalization stocks that exceeded 90% in the 3-year period, 1995 to 1997. From an empirical perspective, the correct approach to passive investing seems abundantly clear: simply go passive using an index fund that tracks U.S. large capitalization stocks rather than holding a globally-diversified portfolio position. Although the domestic-indexing solution for investors may look quite appealing, the "just right" approach to passive investing (aside from active investing discussed later) is often more complicated than the recent empirical evidence might suggest. In this latter context, we'll look at the empirical cases for and against the local-passive form of equity management.

---

[6] The share of U.S. equity capitalization in developed world markets at year-end 1997 was 49.8%. This is consistent with a 50/50 (see *M*) mix of U.S. and international equities for global-mided (equity) investors. This equity share figure is reported in *MSCI Perspectives* (New York: Morgan Stanley Capital International, January 1998). As we will shortly see though, the risk-adjusted return benefits from global equity investing are sensitive to the estimation period.

[7] This can also be restated in terms of the Sharpe ratio defined in Chapter 14.

## Exhibit 2: Global Efficient Frontier

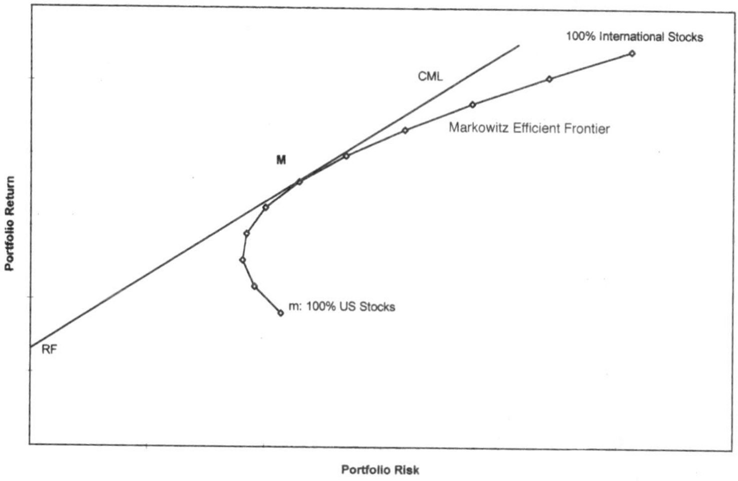

## Empirical Case for U.S. Large-Cap Indexing

Building an empirical case for U.S. large-cap indexing over the past few years is a rather straightforward task. Exhibits 3a and 3b show the return performance of five asset classes during 1997 and 1996, respectively. Three equity and two bond return series are shown in the exhibit, along with the U.S. inflation rate. Equity assets include U.S. large capitalization stocks, small-cap stocks, and the return performance on the Morgan Stanley-EAFE (Europe, Australia, and the Far East) index. EAFE returns are reported here to shed empirical light on international equity opportunities in the developed foreign markets. The bond return series cover long-term government bonds and U.S. Treasury bills.

Exhibit 3a shows that U.S. large-cap stocks had a 33.4% total return in 1997. This performance is considerably higher than the 20.3% earned on U.S. small capitalization stocks, as well as the paltry 1.2% return on international stocks comprising EAFE. Likewise, Exhibit 3b shows that U.S. large caps went to the head of the investment class in 1996 as they achieved a total return performance of 23%. With a return of 16.5% for that year, U.S. small capitalization stocks did well too. However, the small cap return performance in 1996 fell short of that earned on U.S. large capitalization stocks. Moreover, at 6.4% for 1996, the weighted-average return performance for the developed countries comprising the MSCI-EAFE index was again *lower* than that available on the S&P 500.

Exhibits 3a and 3b also point to substantial fluctuation in U.S. long-term government bond returns. During 1997, bond prices rose due to low inflation and falling interest rates. Consequently, the total return on Treasury bonds for that year was quite attractive, at 13.2%. In contrast, interest rates largely went up during 1996, with Treasury bonds providing a marginal return of only −0.9%. During these years, the return on long-term government bonds was volatile and lower than that available on U.S. equities. Taken together, the empirical evidence shown in Exhibits 3a and 3b, respectively, reinforce the popular notion that U.S. large capitalization indexing is a viable (passive) portfolio strategy for the future.

### Exhibit 3a: Return Performance in U.S. and Developed Foreign Markets: 1997

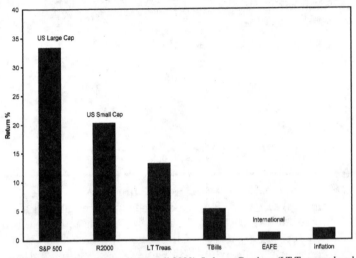

Source: Standard & Poor's, Frank Russell (Russell 2000), Lehman Brothers (LT Treasury bonds), Federal Reserve estimates, and *MSCI Perspectives*

### Exhibit 3b: Return Performance in U.S. and Developed Foreign Markets: 1996

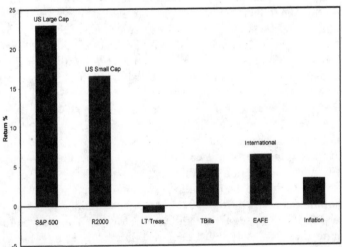

Source: Standard & Poor's, Frank Russell (Russell 2000), Lehman Brothers (LT Treasury bonds), Federal Reserve estimates, and *MSCI Perspectives*

## Exhibit 4: Growth of $10,000 in U.S. and Developed Foreign Markets: 1988 to 1997

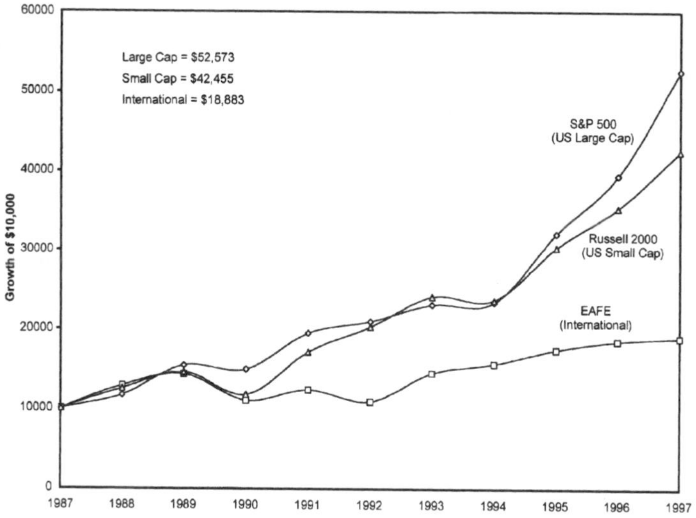

Large Cap = $52,573
Small Cap = $42,455
International = $18,883

S&P 500
(US Large Cap)

Russell 2000
(US Small Cap)

EAFE
(International)

Source: Standard & Poor's, Frank Russell (Russell 2000), and *MSCI Perspectives*

### Ten Years of Equity Investing

The case for large-cap indexing is also evident when the performance window is expanded to cover ten years of equity investing. Exhibit 4 shows the growth of $10,000 invested in U.S. large capitalization stocks, small cap stocks, and the Morgan Stanley EAFE index from year-end 1987 through December 1997.

Exhibit 4 shows that the initial $10,000 invested in U.S. large cap stocks grew to $52,573, thereby providing investors with an 18.1% compound yearly return. This 10-year large-cap growth is considerably better than the $42,455 reported on U.S. small capitalization stocks and the dismal-looking (from a longer-term growth perspective) $18,883 provided to investors from the developed foreign countries comprising EAFE. At 15.6% and 6.6% respectively, the 10-year annualized return performance on these equity classes — U.S. small cap and international stocks — were substantially lower than the compound yearly return, 18.1%, available on U.S. large capitalization stocks.

### Anomalies in the 10-Year Global Frontier

U.S. large-cap indexing from (year-end) 1987-1997 was also attractive because of anomalous behavior in the average return/risk relationship observed in the developed foreign markets. In this context, Exhibit 5 shows the global portfolio frontier that results from a "two-asset" holding of S&P 500 stocks in combination with the international equities comprising EAFE. With a correlation of 0.319 between these equity return series during the 1988 to 1997 period, the exhibit shows that international equity investing was both risk reducing *and* performance decreasing.

Portfolios that lie on the Markowitz efficient frontier to the left of the 100% domestic U.S. point (Exhibit 5) — such as the 90/10 combination down to the 70/30 mix — have comparatively lower return standard deviations with lower average returns. For obvious reasons, portfolio combinations that lie on the negatively-sloping portion of the empirically based global frontier would not be chosen by passive investors seeking to maximize expected return per unit of risk.

The 10-year empirical finding contrasts sharply with the celebrated benefits of global investing — namely, performance enhancement with lower risk through international diversification. In the oft-recommended "70/30 solution"[8] — consisting of 70% U.S. equities and 30% EAFE stocks — one *normally* expects to see rising average returns and reduced return volatility as the investor (initially) moves *leftward* from the 100% domestic equity position. This after all is the major risk-adjusted performance prediction of the combined models of Markowitz and Sharpe.

However, global performance superiority during the 10-year estimation period is clearly not revealed in Exhibit 5. The diversified 70/30 mix of U.S. and international equities (shown as G70/30 in the exhibit) has lower average return in comparison with the return/risk position for U.S. equities alone. In this context, the average return-risk estimates for the "70/30 solution" were 15.51% and 12.62%, while the average return/volatility estimates for S&P 500 stocks during the ten years were 18.86% and 14.43%, respectively.

## Exhibit 5: Global Portfolio Frontier: S&P 500 and EAFE: 1988 to 1997

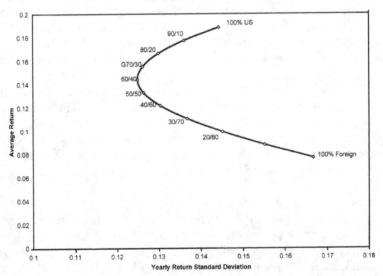

---

[8] It is interesting to note that the "30 Percent Solution" for real-time global investing is an investment product of a well-known mutual fund company. Also, the investor now sees why the U.S. equity cap weight in developed world markets, near 50% at year-end 1997, is empirically problematic.

## Exhibit 6: Benefit of Global Investing: 1970-1997 Period

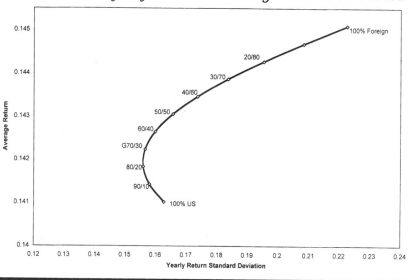

Based on numerous risk-reducing alternatives that were present in the domestic U.S. market over the 10 years 1988 to 1997 — via relatively low-volatility Treasury and high-quality corporate debt securities — it's difficult to imagine that investors would hold international securities or international portfolios like EAFE for diversification reasons *alone*. Hence, given the empirical results (Exhibits 4 and 5 together) for the January 1988 to December 1997 period, one is left wondering why *passive*-minded (or active for that matter) investors would bother with an equity management strategy that deviates in any meaningful way from the U.S. equity market.

### Empirical Case Against U.S. Large-Cap Indexing

As the performance evaluation period lengthens, the case for U.S. large-cap indexing begins to weaken — as anticipated long-term return/risk relationships in domestic and international capital markets strengthen. Exhibit 6 shows the global portfolio frontier — based on average return/risk combinations of S&P 500 and EAFE stocks — for the 28-year period January 1970 to December 1997.[9] As the investor moves to the left of the 100% U.S. equity position, average portfolio return rises while return volatility declines. For instance, the 80/20 mix of U.S./ EAFE equities has an average return of 14.18% with a return standard deviation of 15.60%. In contrast, the 100% U.S. equity point has a 28-year average return of

---

[9] We admit that an element of "data mining" occurred in the production of Exhibit 6. Because of high positive returns earned on U.S. large cap stocks during the 1995 to 1997 period, the long-term global efficient frontier — based on the 20-year period 1978 to 1997 — results in a "backward bending" frontier like that shown in Exhibit 5 for the 1988 to 1997 years. Forward bending global efficient frontiers result when (1) using average return and risk data during the 20-year period 1977 to 1996 and (2) using return/volatility data during the 28-year period (1970-1997) shown in Exhibit 6.

14.10% with an *own*-return volatility of 16.27% — hence, (slightly) lower average return to domestic indexing with higher risk.

Exhibit 6 also shows that the "70/30 solution" of U.S. and international equities (shown as G70/30) is consistent with long-term performance expectations — as this portfolio mix not only enhances performance while reducing risk, but it also lies on the *positively-sloping* portion of the global frontier. The long-term average return and risk combination for this portfolio mix was 14.22% and 15.66%, respectively. Indeed, the 28-year evidence revealed in Exhibit 6 suggests that no rational investor would hold just S&P 500 stocks when the diversified 60/40 mix of U.S. large cap and international equities has higher average return (historically, at 14.26%) for about the same amount of equity portfolio risk.

### Small-Cap Impact on the Efficient Frontier
Rather than diversifying globally, one might ponder whether long-term performance benefits were available by simply diversifying within the U.S. equity market. Exhibit 7 shows the efficient frontier for a two-asset class combination of U.S. large cap and U.S. small cap stocks over the 1979 to 1997 period — again, using the Russell 2000 index to represent small cap stock performance (recall Exhibit 3a). Unlike the international diversification opportunity shown in Exhibit 6, the domestic frontier shows that when small caps are added to the portfolio opportunity set that performance goes down and risk goes up. At 17.66% and 13.78%, for example, the 70/30 domestic pairing of U.S. large and small caps has a lower average return and higher volatility when compared to a 100% allocation to U.S. large cap stocks, at 17.85% and 13.21%.

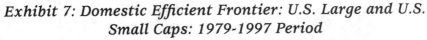

## Exhibit 7: Domestic Efficient Frontier: U.S. Large and U.S. Small Caps: 1979-1997 Period

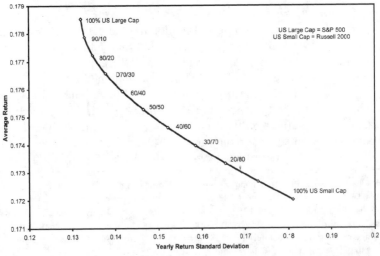

This global risk view that EAFE stocks have greater diversification (or risk reducing) potential than U.S. small cap stocks is supported by the 19-year correlation between the S&P 500 and EAFE indices, at 0.32, in comparison with the higher U.S. large cap/small cap correlation of 0.746 estimated over the 1979 to 1997 period. As we learned in Chapter 2, low correlation is preferred to high correlation when combining volatile assets — like U.S. small caps and EAFE stocks — into investment portfolios. Before moving on, it is important to emphasize that the "backward bending" frontier shown in Exhibit 7 is not a pervasive long-term finding for U.S. small and large cap stocks. Performance data going back to 1970 reveal that U.S. small caps outperformed U.S. large caps — which is the pre-condition for a "forward bending" efficient frontier. However, due to high correlation between U.S. large and small cap stocks, global diversification still prevails.

## Style-Passive Investing

Given that tests of the efficient market hypothesis are only meaningful in the context of some assumed model of capital market equilibrium, it is important to note that numerous studies have questioned the empirical validity of the single-factor CAPM. In one of the well-known studies, Eugene Fama and Kenneth French find that two easily measured variables — including size and book yield — adequately describe the cross section of U.S. security returns in the 1963 to 1990 period.[10] This recognition that fundamental factors beyond the single-factor beta model can influence security and portfolio returns in a systematic non-market fashion is also observed in a rigorous study by Richard Roll.[11]

Since the empirical findings suggest that stocks having high yields — book, earnings, and even dividend yield — tend to outperform stocks having comparatively lower yields when compared to CAPM, this implies that a *style*-passive strategy — in this case, a "value" strategy — may be superior to (1) a global-indexed strategy, (2) a local or domestic-indexed strategy, and (3) a "growth stock" strategy. Although a *value* strategy can — and in most practical instances does — have active components (discussed later), it can be classified as passive if once the position is formed it remains that way following the "buy and hold" acquisition of stocks of companies having relatively low price relatives and high yields. Moreover, that passive investors hold style-indexed portfolios need not be a sign of a profit-making inefficiency unless of course it can be shown that they earn abnormal returns relative to the true (obviously not CAPM) model of capital market equilibrium.

### Range of Equity Style Opportunities

Exhibit 8 introduces a 5×3 matrix that can be used to classify well-known and emerging equity management styles.[12] This matrix can be viewed from both a passive and

---

[10] Fama and French, "The Cross Section of Expected Stock Returns," and Sinquefield, "Where Are the Gains from International Diversification?"

[11] See Richard Roll, "Style Return Differentials: Illusions, Risk Premiums, or Investment Opportunities," Chapter 5 in T. Daniel Coggin, Frank J. Fabozzi, and Robert Arnott (eds.), *The Handbook of Equity Style Management* (New Hope, PA: Frank J. Fabozzi Associates, 1997), pp. 93-120.

[12] We cover the investment fundamentals and return-risk aspects of various equity styles in Chapter 5.

active investing perspective. At this point, we'll look at the range of equity style possibilities from a passive approach to investing. Specifically, investors already familiar with mutual fund reports produced by Morningstar[13] will notice the 3×3 equity-style submatrix shown in Exhibit 8. This portion of the equity style matrix consists of large cap opportunities — ranging from domestic (and/or international) large-cap value, blend, and growth portfolios — on down to similar style-indexed classifications for mid cap and small capitalization stocks. Additionally, the enhanced (5×3) matrix allows for a variety of equity management strategies including passive (and active) opportunities in the micro- and maxi-cap universe of securities.

In terms of equity style definitions, conventional wisdom holds that large cap stocks have an average market capitalization of more than $5 billion. Mid-cap stocks often range from $1 to $5 billion on the size scale, while the small caps have an equity capitalization of less than $1 billion. As shown in Chapter 5, indexed (or passive)-value portfolios typically have low price-to-earnings and low price-to-book value ratios, along with relatively high dividend yields. On the other hand, indexed-growth portfolios have high price relatives, low dividend payout ratios, and, consequently, high corporate plowback and earnings-growth rates. Additionally, growth stocks like technology stocks often have low debt-to-capital ratios while so-called value stocks have comparably higher (due to the debt) corporate leverage ratios.

Exhibit 8 expands the range of passive (and active) opportunities for equity investors. In this context, *maxi*-capitalization value- and growth-stock opportunities have been added to the equity style matrix to account for the growing realization that another equity size classification is needed — namely "giant cap" stocks — as U.S. large capitalization firms — like Cisco Systems, Coca-Cola, General Electric, and Microsoft — continue to soar in value. At September 30 1996, Ibbotson Associates reports that General Electric had an equity capitalization of some $150 billion.[14] That figure is 30 times the popular Morningstar base for large cap stocks, and some five times the recent average (equity) capitalization for S&P 500 firms. Also, at the lowest end of the equity size spectrum, *micro*-cap stocks have an equity capitalization of about $200 million, or less. In this context, Ibbotson Associates reports micro-cap size values of $197 million and $94 million, respectively, for selected 9*th* and 10*th* decile firms listed on the New York Stock Exchange.

## Exhibit 8: Range of Equity Management Styles

|            | Value | Blend | Growth |
|------------|-------|-------|--------|
| Maxi-Cap   | Max V | Max B | Max G  |
| Large-Cap  | Lge V | Lge B | Lge G  |
| Mid-Cap    | Mid V | Mid B | Mid G  |
| Small-Cap  | Sm V  | Sm B  | Sm G   |
| Micro-Cap  | Mic V | Mic B | Mic G  |

[13] Morningstar provides performance analysis for several thousand mutual funds.
[14] Ibbotson Associates, *Stocks, Bonds, Bills and Inflation — 1997 Yearbook* (Chicago: Ibbotson Associates, 1997).

### Style-Passive Investing: A Closer Look

From a strict passive perspective — namely, complete price efficiency — Exhibit 8 suggests that equity securities from *all* 15 components of the generalized equity style matrix should be held in proportion to their outstanding capitalization in the world market portfolio, *M* (recall Exhibit 2). However, unless a suitable indexed-passive global fund exists, then investors would have to "round out" their *undiversified* equity positions with a series of passive-domestic index funds. Otherwise, the portfolio holdings of passive-minded investors would be lacking in assessed (world) return per unit of expected portfolio risk.

Real world passive investors may look at Exhibit 8 to discover local indexing or style indexing opportunities. From a domestic-indexing perspective, Gus Sauter of the Vanguard Group has pioneered several domestic-indexed products (characterized as "blend" opportunities in the generalized equity style matrix) including Vanguard's popular S&P 500 Index Trust, Extended Market Index that tracks the Wilshire 5000 index, to Vanguard's recent indexing efforts in the medium and small capitalization universes.[15] With an asset base of some $45 billion in the investable S&P 500 at year-end 1997, Vanguard's indexing initiatives over the 10-year period 1988-1997 have been very successful. They also represent a formidable challenge for actively-managed equity mutual funds such as the giant Magellan Fund of Fidelity Investments.

Given that *value* stocks seem to earn abnormal returns when measured relative to the single-factor CAPM, passive-minded investors may buy and hold the stocks of small, mid, and large capitalization firms to obtain a diversified return to value investing. From a style-passive perspective, investors would hold indexed portfolios of stocks on the *leftmost* rim of the 5×3 equity style matrix. Sufficient indexed-value opportunities would need to exist in real-time capital markets for the style-passive investor to generate a diversified return to value investing. The passive performance goal might be to earn a return that is consistent with the S&P/BARRA Large-Cap Value Index,[16] or possibly a return to value investing that matches the performance of the Russell 2000 Value Index. In style-indexed situations like this, passive investors have an expected return and risk incentive to deviate from the *strict* global-passive solution to equity portfolio management.

## BLUEPRINT FOR ACTIVE INVESTING

Active investing makes sense when a moderate to low degree of capital market efficiency is present in the financial markets (or specific areas thereof). This hap-

---

[15] For an insightful discussion of mid-cap and small-cap indexing, see George U. Sauter, "Medium and Small Capitalization Indexing," Chapter 7 in Frank J. Fabozzi (ed.), *Professional Perspectives on Indexing* (New Hope PA: Frank J. Fabozzi Associates, 1998), pp. 80-97.

[16] Recall that in Chapter 3 we noted that the S&P/BARRA Large-Cap Value Index had greater risk-adjusted return performance than the S&P/BARRA Large-Cap Growth Index over the 1980 to 1997 period.

pens when the active investor has (1) better information than most other investors (namely, the "consensus" investors), and/or (2) the investor has a more productive way of looking at a given information set to generate active rewards. Observed "anomalies" or regularities in the global marketplace need *not* be a sign of real market inefficiencies since many investors can incorporate the known return/risk effects into the investment decision-making process used to estimate abnormal returns. As Russell Fogler points out, true abnormal returns are "idiosyncratic" and therefore cannot be known or predicted by the consensus investor.[17]

Exhibit 9 presents a "blueprint" for the active approach to equity management. The specific active method chosen by the investment manager is dependent on the *degree* of pricing inefficiencies within the capital market(s). As mentioned before, passive investors hold indexed portfolios of varying types (global passive, local passive, and style passive) depending on their understanding of the true model of capital market equilibrium and systematic *non*-market regularities that may be present in the capital market. On the other hand, active investors become "active" with their equity allocations precisely because of perceived market inefficiencies that have not been recognized by consensus investors.

## Exhibit 9: Active Investing

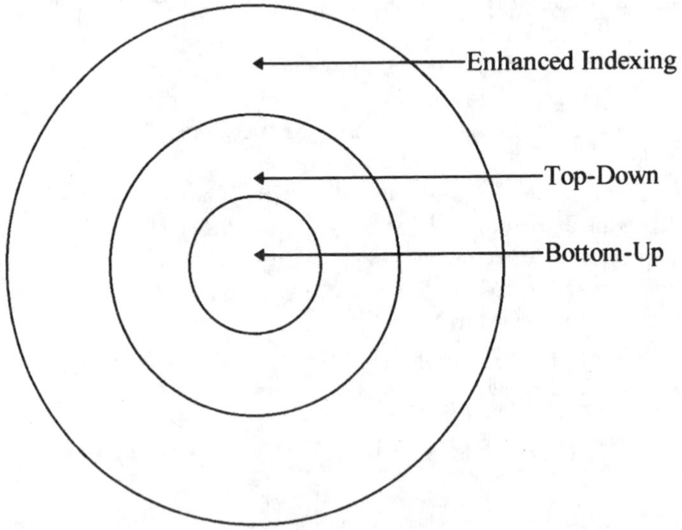

Source: Adapted from Exhibit 4 in Bruce I. Jacobs and Kenneth N. Levy, "Investment Management: An Architecture for the Equity Market," Chapter 1 in Frank J. Fabozzi (ed.), *Active Equity Portfolio Management* (New Hope, PA: Frank J. Fabozzi Associates, 1998), p. 5.

---

[17] See H. Russell Fogler, "Common Stock Management During the 1990s," *Journal of Portfolio Management* (Winter 1990), p. 26.

The outer rim of the active blueprint shown in Exhibit 9 consists of the "enhanced indexing" approach to equity management. As emphasized by John Loftus of PIMCO, the goal of an enhanced indexing strategy is to outperform a passive benchmark within some predetermined percentage, say 2% over the targeted index on a risk-adjusted basis.[18] This approach recognizes the difficulty of achieving high abnormal return (alpha) in the presence of a moderate to high degree of capital market efficiency. Looking inward — with greater pricing inefficiencies — we see the "top-down" approach to active equity management. As introduced below, top-down investing uses macroeconomic factors and quantitative analysis in the quest (or possibly, zest) for positive alpha. Finally, the *good-ole-fashioned* "stock picking" approach — namely, "bottom-up" stock selection — comprises the *nucleus* of the active equity blueprint.[19] It is associated with the *highest* degree of capital market inefficiency and, consequently, the highest amount of equity portfolio risk.

## Top-Down Approach to Active Investing

With the *top-down approach* to active investing, an equity manager begins by assessing the macroeconomic environment and forecasting its near-term outlook.[20] Based on this assessment and forecast, an equity manager decides on how much of the portfolio's funds to allocate among the different sectors of the equity market and how much to cash equivalents (i.e., money market instruments). For a manager who is permitted to purchase fixed-income securities, the manager must first decide on how much of the portfolio's funds to allocate among equities, bonds, and cash equivalents.

Given the amount of the portfolio's funds to be allocated to the equity market, the manager must then decide how much to allocate among the sectors and industries of the equity market. These sectors can be classified as follows: basic materials, communications, consumer staples, financials, technology, utilities, capital goods, consumer cyclicals, energy, health care, and transportation.[21] Industry classifications give a finer breakdown and include, for examples, aluminum, paper, international oil, beverages, electric utilities, telephone and telegraph, etc.

---

[18] For an insightful discussion of this limited-risk active strategy, see John S. Loftus, "Enhanced Equity Indexing," Chapter 4 in *Professional Perspectives on Indexing*, pp. 34-53.

[19] It is interesting to note that James Abate of Credit Suisse Asset Management uses the term *nucleus* to describe the "bottom-up" portion of his active equity strategy, and the term *peripherals* to describe the "top-down" segment of the overall strategy. For a discussion of CSAM's innovative approach to active equity management, see James A. Abate, "Select Economic Value Portfolios," *U.S. Equity Product Overview* (New York: Credit Suisse Asset Management, January 1998).

[20] In Chapter 10, we cover an interesting top-down thematic approach to equity management by Lawrence Viehl of Columbia Management Company. Viehl's top-down model incorporates both macro-economic and political considerations in the security selection and portfolio construction process. For a complete discussion, see Lawrence S. Viehl, "Top Down/Thematic Equity Management," in T. Daniel Coggin and Frank J. Fabozzi (eds.), *Applied Equity Valuation* (New Hope, PA: Frank J. Fabozzi Associates, 1999), pp. 37-48.

[21] These are the categories used by Standard & Poor's. There is another sector labeled "miscellaneous" that includes stocks that do not fall into any of the other sectors.

In making the active asset allocation decision, a manager who follows a top-down approach often relies on an analysis of the equity market to identify those sectors and industries that will benefit the most on a relative basis from the anticipated economic forecast. Once the amount to be allocated to each sector and industry is made, the manager then looks for the individual stocks to include in the portfolio. The top-down approach looks at changes in several macroeconomic factors to assess the expected excess return (anticipated performance over risk-free return) on securities and portfolios. Prominent economic variables include changes in commodity prices, interest rates, inflation, and economic productivity.

Additionally, the top-down approach can be both quantitative and quali-tative in nature. From the former perspective, equity managers employ "factor models" in their top-down attempt at generating abnormal returns (that is, posi-tive alpha). Two of the more sophisticated and proprietary *macro*-factor models are the Burmeister, Ibbotson, Roll and Ross (BIRR) model, and the Salomon Smith Barney RAM (Risk Attribute Model) model. Although these models, dis-cussed in Chapter 9, differ in terms of input and output, they effectively capture the risk of a portfolio by estimating the sensitivity of its return to a statistically-determined set of macroeconomic risk measures.

The power of top-down factor models is that given the macroeconomic risk measures and factor sensitivities, a portfolio's risk exposure profile can be quantified and controlled. In this way, it is possible to see why a portfolio is likely to generate abnormally high or low returns in the marketplace. One of the practi-cal limitations of these quantitatively based approaches to equity management is that their can be disagreement about the "just right" number of macro-risk pricing factors. Without standardization across models, this makes return performance comparisons among equity portfolios somewhat problematic.

## Bottom-Up Approach to Active Investing

At the *nucleus* of the active blueprint (Exhibit 9) is the *bottom up approach* to equity management. This form of active investing makes sense when substantial pricing inefficiencies exist in the capital markets (or components thereof). An investor who follows a bottom-up approach to investing focuses on the analysis of individual companies, and therefore gives relatively less weight to the signifi-cance of economic and market cycles. The primary research tool used in this form of investing is called *security analysis*. Three types of security analysis can now be distinguished in practice: (1) traditional fundamental analysis, (2) quantitative fundamental analysis, and (3) security analysis using "value-based" metrics.

### Traditional Fundamental Analysis

*Traditional fundamental analysis* often begins with the financial statements of a company in order to investigate its revenue, earnings, and cash flow prospects, as well as its overall corporate debt burden. Growth in revenue, cash flow, and earn-ings on the income statement side (current and pro-forma) as well as corporate leverage ratios (debt-to-capital ratio, etc.) from current and anticipated future balance sheets are frequently used by fundamental equity analysts in forming an opinion of the investment merits of a particular company's stock.

In this form of security analysis, the investor also looks at the firm's product lines, the economic outlook for the products (including existing and potential opportunities), and the industries in which the company operates. Based on the growth prospects of earnings, the fundamental analyst attempts to determine the fair market value of the stock, using, for example, a price-to-earnings or price-to-book value multiplier. The estimated "fair value" of the firm is then compared to the actual market price to see if the stock is correctly priced. "Cheap stocks" or potential buy opportunities have a market price below the estimated *intrinsic value*, while "expensive" or overvalued stocks have a trade price that exceeds the estimated fair value of the stock. Notable investors who have successfully employed the traditional approach to security analysis include Warren Buffet (Berkshire Hathaway, Inc.) and Peter Lynch (formerly of Fidelity Management & Research Co). The traditional approach to security analysis was developed by Benjamin Graham and David Dodd.[22]

### Quantitative Fundamental Analysis

One of the more sophisticated approaches to security analysis is the *fundamental factor model approach* employed by BARRA. The present-day version of this quantitative approach to active equity investing (and performance evaluation) evolved out of pioneering research during the 1970s by Barr Rosenberg and Vinay Marathe.[23] Without getting into the details here,[24] the BARRA model is both jointly quantitative and fundamental in nature because it has 13 systematic non-market factors as well as 52 industry designators that can be used to identify active rewards on individual securities and portfolios.

Residual factors such as size and earnings and book yields are prominent factors that may be used by active investors to generate excess return. In fact, one of the key benefits of the BARRA model is that it provides a quantitative, fundamental explanation as to why the observed alpha — a measure of abnormal return performance based on the single-factor CAPM — on a portfolio is nonzero. As such, these "common factors" or "extra-market covariance" effects should be built into the equity-security selection process.

### Value-Based Metrics Approach to Security Analysis

A rapidly emerging form of security analysis is based on an "economic profit" measure called *EVA* (for Economic Value Added).[25] The EVA metric was devel-

---

[22] See Benjamin Graham and David Dodd, *Security Analysis* (New York: McGraw-Hill: 1934 original edition).

[23] Barr Rosenberg and Vinay Marathe, "The Prediction of Investment Risk: Systematic and Residual Risk," *Proceedings of the Seminar on the Analysis of Security Prices*, University of Chicago, November 1975.

[24] We cover the BARRA fundamental equity risk model in Chapter 9.

[25] EVA® is a registered trademark of Stern Stewart & Co.

oped commercially by Stern Stewart & Co. during the early 1980s as a modern tool for measuring corporate financial success. EVA (and its close associate, *Cash Flow Return on Investment*, or CFROI) analysis falls into the realm of equity security analysis because this economic profit approach is related to the firm's underlying net present value (NPV).[26] In this context, EVA is an innovative approach to looking at the firm's real profitability as corporate earnings are calculated *net* of the overall dollar cost of debt and equity capital. Companies having positive discounted-average EVA — or equivalently, positive NPV — are viewed as "wealth creators," while firms with negative EVA are looked upon as "wealth wasters" due to their negative NPV outcomes.

From a security selection perspective, companies with positive EVA momentum are considered buy opportunities, while the stocks (and risky bonds) of negative-average EVA firms are possible sell candidates. To date, major corporate players like Coca-Cola and AT&T have embraced this economic profit measure, while investment banking firms such as CS First Boston, Goldman Sachs, and Merrill Lynch are either using it or taking a serious look at the potential benefits of this rapidly emerging form of security analysis. In more recent developments, the Goldman Sachs U.S. Research Group estimates EVA with the forward-looking betas produced by the BARRA fundamental factor model and Credit Suisse Asset Management uses economic profit concepts in their security selection decisions.[27] Moreover, one of the authors has advanced the EVA model in a company and industry analysis context using quantitative techniques that include the Markowitz portfolio model.[28]

## Style-Active Investing

The enhanced equity style matrix shown in Exhibit 8 has many active management implications. For example, if abnormal return opportunities exist in the maxi-cap universe — due perhaps to further corporate restructurings and acquisitions — then investors could tilt their portfolios in the relevant "giant-cap" value or growth direction. If untapped opportunities also exist down in "micro-cap land," then active equity allocations might result in a "perimeter" portfolio of sorts, whereby pro-active investors allocate their funds according to the value or growth styles that lie along the *outer* rim of the 5×3 equity style matrix.

From a style-active perspective, it is interesting to note that many studies document the return superiority of value investing over growth investing. Recent studies by Fama and French,[29] Roll,[30] and Sinquefield[31] point to the risk-adjusted

---

[26] CFROI® is the investment and financial advisory product of HOLT Value Associates, LP.

[27] See Steven G. Einhorn, Gabrielle Napolitano, and Abby Joseph Cohen, "EVA: A Primer," *U.S. Research* (Goldman Sachs, September 10, 1997), and Abate, "Select Economic Value Portfolios."

[28] See James L. Grant, *Foundations of Economic Value Added* (New Hope, PA: Frank J. Fabozzi Associates, 1997).

[29] Fama and French, "The Cross Section of Expected Stock Returns."

[30] Roll, "Style Return Differentials: Illusions, Risk Premiums, or Investment Opportunities."

[31] Sinquefield, "Where Are the Gains from International Diversification?"

return benefits (measured using the CAPM) of this apparently *low* volatility style of equity investing.[32]

Among the most widely cited studies, Fama and French show that stocks of small companies having low price-to-book value ratios were the *best* performing U.S. equities over the 1963 to 1990 period. They also observe that over the past half-century the traditionally-celebrated CAPM relationship between average investment return and beta risk is "weak and perhaps non-existent." In addition, Roll employs a series of factor model tests over the 10-year period covering March 1984 to March 1994 to assess the possible performance difference between the value and growth styles of investing. His empirical results clearly demonstrate the performance superiority of the value style of investing after controlling for suspected risk factors. Using efficient frontier analysis, Grant observes that during the 1980 to 1992 years the low-volatility, high dividend yield (another well-known value indicator) stock portfolios consisting of both small and large U.S. firms were attractive investments on a risk-adjusted basis.[33]

### Caveats on the Value Style of Investing

Although the empirical evidence is quite compelling about the return superiority of the value style of investing, the findings are problematic in some respects. First, the empirical findings contradict the long-established view in finance that investors should be compensated for bearing market or systematic risk. From a performance perspective, the findings also imply that value managers may be penalized over growth managers for their low risk investment successes because their equity style benchmarks — due to unexplained empirical regularities — have comparatively high expected returns.

Alternatively, if passive style benchmarks are employed in practice then active growth managers may be unduly rewarded for their relatively low performance. This happens because it is easier to outperform the high volatility, and low expected return, indexed-growth benchmark in comparison with a performance standard that evolves from an established equilibrium framework — such as the *levered* portion of the capital market line, CML, that requires high expected returns for portfolios having relatively high return volatility.

Exhibit 10 shows how active managers might be unduly rewarded when they are benchmarked according to equity style as opposed to an equilibrium model that posits a positive expected return and portfolio-risk relationship (although not necessarily linear). For convenience, the equilibrium return/risk relationship is assumed to be described by the capital market line, labeled *CML*. Based on the empirical evidence on the performance merits of value over growth investing, the benchmarked-value and growth combinations are shown as points

---

[32] Other studies documenting the performance superiority of value investing over growth investing are reported in Coggin, Fabozzi, and Arnott (eds.), *The Handbook of Equity Style Management*.

[33] See James L. Grant, "A Yield Effect in Common Stock Returns," *Journal of Portfolio Management* (Winter 1995), pp. 35-41.

B-V and B-G in the exhibit. In a similar manner, the return performances of two hypothetical active managers are shown as points A-V and A-G, respectively.[34]

Exhibit 10 shows that the return performance for the actively managed value portfolio, A-V, is higher than the corresponding average return/low-risk combination on the capital market line. In this situation, the manager has outperformed the market on a risk-adjusted basis — therefore the manager deserves a bonus for having such security selection (alpha) and portfolio management insights. On the other hand, the active growth manager has underperformed the traditional return/risk model of capital market equilibrium — hence, the manager deserves to be dismissed from a *strict* security selection and active portfolio management interpretation.

However, Exhibit 10 reveals that the value manager's skill actually falls short of the benchmarked-value performance due to the *empirically based* findings that value stocks outperform their more growth-oriented counterparts. Thus, the security selection measures (alpha values) for the active value strategy give conflicting signals about the manager's true ability to generate abnormal return. Likewise, for the active growth manager, the security selection measure would be negative when measured against the *levered* market index, while positive alpha would be observed when active return performance is compared to the presumed high volatility and low performing growth-style index — represented by point B-G in Exhibit 10.

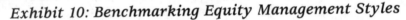

## Exhibit 10: Benchmarking Equity Management Styles

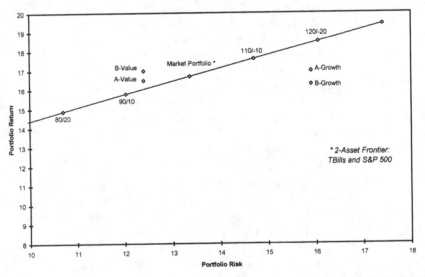

---

[34] The benchmarked value and growth points, B-V and B-G, shown in Exhibit 10 are based on average return and risk estimates for the Russell Large Cap Value and Growth indexes over the 1979 to 1995 period. The CML is actually a "two asset" efficient frontier based on average return and standard deviation estimates for the S&P 500 index and U.S. Treasury bills estimated over the comparable time period.

This empirically driven view that it may be easier for growth managers to outperform their equity-style benchmarks, while value managers have an added measure of return responsibility is supported in a study by Coggin and Trzcinka.[35] They find that institutional equity managers not only outperformed the stock market in general, but that their active selectivity figures (alpha) for benchmarked-growth portfolios were higher than the corresponding security selection measures for value-focused managers.

## Nonlinear and Behavioral Considerations

As explained before, if the capital market is price efficient then passive investors have a clear incentive to hold the risky market portfolio in combination with risk-free Treasury securities. When this happens, individual securities will be priced in a *linear* fashion according to their beta-risk in the market portfolio, *M*. This after all is the essence of CAPM. Likewise, if the equilibrium relationship between equity return and risk is more adequately described by the APT model, then individual securities in the market will again be priced in a linear manner according to their estimated sensitivity to relevant risk factors.

### Nonlinear Dynamic Models

Some market observers — like Edgar Peters of PanAgora Asset Management[36] — believe that the pattern of stock price behavior is so complex that *linear* (simple, or otherwise) mathematical models are insufficient for detecting historical price patterns and developing models for forecasting future return volatility. While stock prices may appear to change randomly, there could be an undiscovered *nonlinear* pattern that is missed when using simple mathematical tools. Scientists have developed complex mathematical models for detecting patterns from observations of some phenomenon that appear to be random. Generically, these models are called *nonlinear dynamic models* because the mathematics used to detect any structure or pattern is based on a system of nonlinear equations.

Nonlinear dynamic models have been suggested for analyzing stock price patterns. In recent years, there have been several studies that suggest that stock prices exhibit the characteristics of a nonlinear dynamic model.[37] The particular form of nonlinear dynamic models that has been suggested is *chaos theory*. At this stage, the major insight provided by chaos theory is that stock price movements that appear to be random may in fact have a structure that can be used to generate abnormal returns. At the time of this writing, however, the actual application seems to have fallen short of the mark. Interviews with market players by Sergio

---

[35] See T. Daniel Coggin and Charles Trzcinka, "Analyzing the Performance of Equity Managers: A Note on Value versus Growth," Chapter 9 in *The Handbook of Equity Style Management.*

[36] See Edgar E. Peters, *Chaos and Order in the Capital Markets: A New View of Cycles, Prices, and Market Volatility* (New York: John Wiley & Sons, 1991).

[37] See José Scheinkman and Blake LeBaron, "Nonlinear Dynamics and Stock Returns," *Journal of Business* (1989), pp. 311-337, and Peters, *Chaos and Order in the Capital Markets.*

Focardi and Caroline Jonas in 1996 found that "chaos theory is conceptually too complex to find much application in finance today."[38]

### Nonlinearities and Market Overreaction

To benefit from favorable news or to reduce the adverse effect of unfavorable news, investors must react quickly to new information. Cognitive psychologists have shed some light on how people react to extreme events.[39] In general, people tend to overreact to such events. People tend to react more strongly to recent information, and they tend to heavily discount older information. The real question for active investors then is: do these overreacting investors follow the same pattern? That is, do "uninformed" investors systematically overreact to extreme financial events?

The *overreaction hypothesis* suggests that when investors react to unanticipated news that will benefit a company's stock, the price rise will be greater than it should be given that information, resulting in a subsequent and sharp decline in the price of the stock. In contrast, the overreaction to unanticipated news that is expected to adversely affect the economic well-being of a company will force the price down too much, followed by a subsequent correction that will increase the price. These overreaction scenarios are illustrated in Exhibit 11.

## Exhibit 11: Overreaction Pattern of Stock Price Behavior

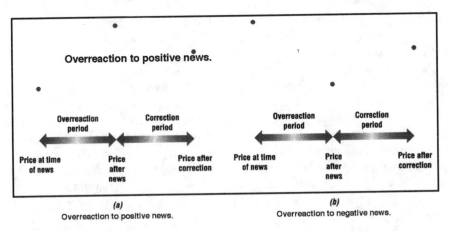

(a) Overreaction to positive news.

(b) Overreaction to negative news.

---

[38] See Sergio Focardi and Caroline Jonas, *Modeling the Market: New Theories and Techniques* (New Hope, PA: Frank J. Fabozzi Associates, 1997), p. 14.

[39] For an extensive treatment of the "behavioral" approach to looking at the world of finance and investments, see Robert A. Haugen, *The New Finance: The Case Against Efficient Market* (Englewood Cliffs, NJ: Prentice Hall, 1995).

If, in fact, the market does overreact then informed investors may be able to exploit this to realize positive abnormal returns if they can (1) identify an extreme event and (2) determine when the effect of the overreaction has been impounded in the market price and is then ready to reverse course. Investors who are capable of doing this will pursue the following strategies. When positive news is identified, they will buy the security and subsequently sell it before the correction to the overreaction. In the case of negative news, investors will short the stock and then buy it back to cover the short position before the correction to the overreaction.

As originally formulated by Werner DeBondt and Richard Thaler, the overreaction hypothesis can be described by two propositions.[40] First, the extreme movement of a stock price will be followed by a movement in the stock price in the opposite direction. This is called the "directional effect." Second, the more extreme the initial price change (i.e., the greater the overreaction), the more extreme the offsetting reaction (i.e., the greater the price correction). This is called the "magnitude effect." However, the directional effect and the magnitude effect may simply mean that investors overweight short-term sources of information.[41] To rectify this, Keith Brown and W. V. Harlow added a third proposition, called the "intensity effect," which states that the shorter the duration of the initial price change, the more extreme the subsequent response will be.[42]

Several empirical studies support the directional effect and the magnitude effect.[43] Brown and Harlow tested for all three effects (directional, magnitude, and intensity) and found that for intermediate and long-term responses to *positive* events, there is only mild evidence that market pricing is inefficient; however, evidence on short-term trading responses to *negative* events is strongly consistent with all three effects. Thus, they conclude that "the tendency for the stock market to correct is best regarded as an asymmetric, short-run phenomenon." It is asymmetric because investors appear to overreact to negative rather than positive extreme events.

## BLUEPRINT FOR PASSIVE-ACTIVE INVESTING

Having introduced separate blueprints for passive and active approaches to equity portfolio management, it is now time to look at a suggested architecture for passive-active investing. This integrated approach to equity management recognizes that at any given moment in time, varying degrees of price efficiency exist in real-

---

[40] See Werner DeBondt and Richard Thaler, "Does the Market Overreact?" *Journal of Finance* (July 1985), pp. 793-805.

[41] See Peter L. Bernstein, "Does the Market Overreact?: Discussion," *Journal of Finance* (July 1985), pp. 806-808.

[42] See Keith C. Brown and W.V. Harlow, "Market Overreaction: Magnitude and Intensity," *Journal of Portfolio Management* (Winter 1988), p. 7.

[43] See DeBondt and Thaler, "Does the Market Overreact?"; Werner DeBondt and Richard Thaler, "Further Evidence on Investor Overreaction and Stock Market Seasonality," *Journal of Finance* (July 1987), pp. 557-581; John Howe, "Evidence of Stock Market Overreaction," *Financial Analysts Journal* (July-August 1986), pp. 74-77; and, Brown and Harlow, "Market Overreaction: Magnitude and Intensity," pp. 6-13.

time financial markets. The expanded investment possibilities provided by the *jointly* passive-active approach to equity management are illustrated in Exhibit 12.

The proposed blueprint for passive-active investing consists of two dynamic wheels that are connected by a pricing efficiency axle. At the center of the axle is an information sensor that distributes the passive-active equity weights according to the *degree* of capital market efficiency (noted as DCME in Exhibit 12). To see how this works, consider a hypothetical investor who believes — after extensive information processing — that a 30% degree of pricing efficiency exists in real-time financial markets. From a passive-active perspective, this means that 70% of the portfolio funds will be managed in an active context, while 30% of the equity moneys will be distributed to a form of passive strategy — such as style passive or local indexing. In turn, the *integrated* passive-active portfolio return can be expressed as:

$$E(R_I) = w_p E(R_p) + w_a E(R_a)$$
$$= w_p E(R_p) + (1-w_p)E(R_a)$$

where, $E(R_I)$ is the integrated portfolio return, $w_p$ and $w_a$ reflect the passive and active equity weights, while $E(R_p)$ and $E(R_a)$ reflect the anticipated return to passive and active components of the equity portfolio strategy.

As shown, the passive weight, $w_p$, is central to the jointly passive-active strategy and is a reflection of the degree of market efficiency that is present in the global capital markets. In a similar manner, it is possible to assess the riskiness of the passive-active portfolio in the context of (1) "own volatility" considerations associated with the passive return component, (2) "own volatility" aspects of the active strategy, and (3) "covariance effects" in the returns associated with passive-active investing.

Specifically, the "riskiness" or return variance of the integrated portfolio, var $(R_I)$, can be expressed in formal terms as:

$$\text{var}(R_I) = w_p^2 \text{var}(R_p) + (1 - w_p)^2 \text{var}(R_a) + 2w_p(1 - w_p)\text{cov}(R_p, R_a)$$
$$= w_p^2 \text{SD}(R_p)^2 + (1 - w_p)^2 \text{SD}(R_a)^2$$
$$+ 2w_p(1 - w_p)\text{SD}(R_p)\text{SD}(R_a)\text{cor}(R_p, R_a)$$

## Exhibit 12: Passive — Active Investing

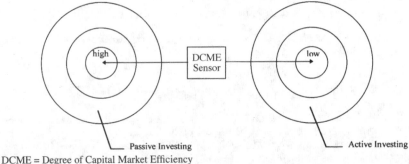

DCME = Degree of Capital Market Efficiency

where, in the first expression, the "var" terms on the right hand side of the integrated risk equation represent "own" return variances, and $cov(R_p, R_a)$ is the covariance between passive and active return components. In turn, the "SD" terms in the second expression represent return standard deviations, while $cor(R_p, R_a)$ is the correlation between the passive and active return elements in the integrated portfolio strategy.

Once the *passive* weight ($w_p$) is set, the investor selects the components of the passive-active portfolio. In this context, the investor selects specific types of passive and active approaches to equity management — like those we introduced in this chapter. Within the passive component, local indexing and/or style-passive investing may make sense for, say, the U.S. equity market. Within the active equity component, the investor may choose active international investing — namely, a top-down or bottom-up international equity theme — to round-out the integrated passive-active strategy. The benefit of this synthesized approach to equity management is that it recognizes that *neither* polar extremes — all passive or all active — make sense for today's real world investor.

## Practical Considerations

In practice, it would seem that revealed investor portfolios would have both passive and active elements. This real-time active-passive expectation is based on a variety of considerations. First, even if today's investors felt that the stock market were 100% efficient, they may not realize the full ramifications of the classic Markowitz and Sharpe portfolio models — in the sense that the global portfolio, $M$, is the one optimal portfolio of all risky securities. In addition, given their equity risk fears, they may be unwilling to "stay the course" with the global market portfolio if it means placing a seemingly abnormal weighting on unusually volatile regions of the world.

On this score, one needs only to consider the popularity of equity "ex indexes" — like the MSCI-EASEA and KOKUSAI indexes — to account for the low return per unit of risk in Japan during the post 1989 years. Due to "own volatility" considerations, as opposed to real diversification reasons, investors may also shy away from the appropriate mix of emerging market securities. Hence, *organizing* for passive-active investing is a formal way of recognizing that most real-time investment portfolios have both passive and active components. In this way, the synthesized equity strategy offers a pragmatic solution to the seemingly impossible dilemma posed by the question of active versus passive investing.

## The "Catch 22" of Market Efficiency

Finally, the concept of passive-active investing is not — as some equity managers might think — just a theoretical or academic construct. Robert Jones of Goldman Sachs Asset Management points out that active versus passive investing — namely, the efficient markets controversy — is really a matter of *degrees* rather than a 100% passive or all-active equity decision.[44] He argues that in order for the

---

[44] See Robert C. Jones, "The Active Versus Passive Debate: Perspectives of an Active Quant," Chapter 3 in *Active Equity Portfolio Management.*

capital market to be price efficient, there needs to be a sufficient number of investors who in fact think that it is inefficient. Consequently, their active information gathering and active investment decisions help ensure that the capital market is indeed price efficient. Jones, like others, calls this the "Catch 22" of market efficiency in the sense that without some degree of active investing, the capital market inefficiency door would remain wide open.

Also, because of documented market regularities and behavioral considerations, Jones notes that an investor's optimal portfolio should have both passive and active elements. In this context, the passive-active investor can earn a normal return in areas of the capital market that are deemed price efficient, while still taking advantage of possible abnormal return opportunities due possibly to investor overreaction (or underreaction) to unanticipated events and known empirical regularities in U.S. and international capital markets.

As an application of how this might work for institutional investors that are authorized to use futures contracts and short sell securities, Jones suggests that they could go long a particular small cap fund and an S&P 500 futures contract, while simultaneously going short the Russell 2000 small cap index futures contact.[45] In this way, the passive-active investor earns the S&P 500 return on the highly efficient large cap component of the U.S. stock market while earning a positive expected alpha on the small cap fund measured relative to the Russell 2000 index. Moreover, such abnormal return-generating strategies (commonly referred to as "portable alpha strategies") can be transported to other areas of the global marketplace — such as EAFE and/or emerging market countries — that show evidence of capital market inefficiencies.

# SUMMARY

A "crisis in equity management" seems to exist in today's high-tech world of finance. This observation is based on the fact that sophisticated empirical tests have not yet produced the *one* model of capital market equilibrium that adequately describes the real-world trade-off between investment return and portfolio risk. If anything, there remains more questions for today's investors about the question of passive versus active investing in comparison with those raised when the efficient market hypothesis was first introduced by Eugene Fama in the early 1970s. In days gone by, passive investing was more of an academic construct as opposed to a serious real-time investment consideration in today's world of information technology.

However, as Robert Jones points out, the real world of investing would be all too boring if capital markets were in fact 100% efficient. In such a world there would be little, if any, incentive for investors to seek out active investment opportu-

---

[45] We cover "derivatives" (futures and options) and their applications in equity management in Chapters 12 and 13.

nities as the resulting return performances would fall short of that earned on similar risk indexed-passive strategies. On the other hand, it is important to recognize that if capital markets were largely inefficient, then the world of investing might be plagued by the "hubris" of active money managers, with all too many looking for the latest "get rich" scheme to outperform the stock market on a risk-adjusted basis.

For better or worse, the equity market probably lies somewhere between these market efficiency extremes, with the real world implication that investor portfolios should have *jointly* passive-active components. This view of the world of equity investing is one of the guiding themes of this book. With this in mind, let's continue building our equity management foundation with a closer look at equity management styles.

# QUESTIONS

1. a. What is meant by a capital market that is "price efficient"?
   b. What are the implications of the degree of price efficiency for the active versus passive forms of investing?

2. What is meant by an "abnormal return"?

3. In a recent newsletter to participants, the College Retirement Equities Fund (CREF) provided an update on its innovative approach to equity portfolio management. CREF's general approach to equity portfolio management is captured by the following statement:

   > "... the two (investment) approaches complement each other, with funds in each account shifting between active and quantitative (passive) in response to investment opportunities." [Source: *Investment Forum*, TIAA-CREF, Volume 3, Number 1, Winter 1999.]

   a. Is the CREF approach to investment management best described by (i) the passive approach, (ii) the active approach, or (iii) the passive-active approach to equity portfolio management? Explain why.
   b. Which exhibit in Chapter 4 captures the essence of the above-mentioned CREF approach to equity management — Exhibit 1, Exhibit 9, or Exhibit 12? Explain why.

4. Many real world depictions of the efficient frontier are based on a 2-asset class combination of U.S. large cap equities (the S&P 500) and the equities of developed foreign countries — namely, EAFE (see Exhibit 2, for example). Discuss the benefits and limitations of the 2-asset class representation of the passive approach to equity portfolio management. Be sure to mention the role of the market portfolio, $M$, in explaining your answer.

5. In 1996 and 1997, U.S. small cap stocks underperformed U.S. large cap stocks (see Exhibits 3a and 3b).

   a. Is this small cap underperformance consistent with the historical experience in U.S. capital markets?
   b. What are the active management implications of the 1996 and 1997 underperformance of U.S. small cap stocks for investors with near to long-term investment horizons?

6. Compare and contrast the following active approaches to equity portfolio management:

a. Traditional fundamental analysis
b. Quantitative fundamental analysis
c. Value based metrics approach to equity management
d. Behavioral approach to equity management

7. Look again at the "backward bending" efficient frontier shown in Exhibit 5. What happens to the global opportunity set when a risk-free asset such as U.S. Treasury bills is introduced into the analysis?

8. Exhibit 10 suggests that it is easier for large cap growth stock managers to out-perform their performance benchmarks in comparison with large cap value managers.

a. What is the reasoning behind this performance attribution statement?
b. Is this growth stock performance advantage (relative to growth stock bench-mark) permanently cast in stone? Explain your reasoning.

9. Use the average return and equity risk data provided below to answer the fol-lowing questions:

|  | S&P 500 | EAFE | Active Fund X |
|---|---|---|---|
| Average Return | 15% | 17% | 16% |
| Standard Deviation | 14% | 22% | 13% |

S&P 500 and EAFE figures are based on the Morgan Stanley EAFE (Europe, Aus-tralia, and the Far East) total return indexes during the 20-year period, 1977-1996. Active Fund X is a hypothetical actively managed fund.

a. Construct a "2-asset" global efficient frontier consisting of the domestic passive opportunity (S&P 500) and the international passive opportunity as repre-sented by EAFE. Assume that the return correlation among these indexes, at 0.3, over a 20-year period (1977-1997) is representative of international equity index comovement for the future.
b. Construct a "passive-active" efficient frontier consisting of the domestic passive opportunity (S&P 500) and the actively managed portfolio, Active Fund X. For convenience, assume a return correlation of 0.3 among the domestic passive and active opportunities. Combine the efficient frontiers constructed in parts a and b into one graph showing the comparative investment approaches.
c. What are the portfolio management implications of the comparative portfolio efficient frontiers — namely, the global passive frontier versus the passive-active efficient frontier? What are the critical assumptions underlying these investment results?

# Chapter 5

# Equity Management Styles

Today's world of equity management is often characterized by distinct "styles" of investing. Three general themes that have emerged over the past quarter-century are the value, growth, and equity-size approaches to investment management. These equity management styles have evolved since the 1970s from research showing that portfolio managers often invest in certain types of stocks having similar investment fundamentals — for examples, small capitalization stocks along the size dimension, low price-relative stocks in the case of value investing, and stocks with high earnings growth rates for growth stock investors. Today's interest in equity styles is also due to empirical anomalies which suggest that equity performance benchmarks are not well described by known return/risk models of capital market equilibrium.

Consider the price-to-earnings ratio as a simple way to distinguish between the popular growth and value styles of equity investing. In the value style of investing, the research focus is generally on the "P" rather than the "E." The investment presumption here is that the firm's stock price has been driven down to a level that is inconsistent with its true earnings capabilities. By investing in these presumably undervalued stocks, the informed investor anticipates receiving a windfall capital gain when consensus investors realize that the firm's real earnings potential is much greater than had been previously anticipated. Also, if the firm's stock price is too low before the price revision, then these stocks will have correlated "value clusters" based on low price-to-earnings and book-value ratios, and perhaps high dividend yields. Given their precarious financial situation, value-oriented firms may have (historically) low earnings-growth rates and return on equity, and relatively high debt to capital ratios.

In the growth style of investing, the research focus is primarily on the "E" for earning per share. The investment insight here is that earnings growth is a key financial driver that reflects the success of management in producing products or services that are in high demand by consumers. Consequently, if growth firms — in industries such as health care and technology — have an uncanny ability to grow their revenue and earnings at abnormal rates, then it's not that much of a "leap of faith" to expect that their stock prices will grow rapidly as well. This price prediction is largely independent of current growth-stock valuations which might look high when viewed in a price-relative context. Unlike their value counterparts, growth stocks are often characterized by high price/earnings and price/book ratios, high earnings growth rates, and low dividend yields. Dividend yield is low, and corporate plowback ratio is high, because these firms reinvest most of their earnings into (hopefully) wealth-creating projects. Growth firms also have relatively low corporate leverage ratios as long-term debt often plays a minor role in the financing of their real growth opportunities.

## EVOLUTION OF EQUITY STYLES

In the early 1970s, several studies found that there were categories of stocks that had similar characteristics and performance patterns. Moreover, the returns of these stock categories performed differently than other categories of stocks. That is, the returns of stocks within a category were highly correlated and the returns between categories of stocks were relatively uncorrelated. The first such study was by James Farrell who called these categories of stocks "clusters."[1] He found that for stocks there were at least four such categories or clusters — growth, cyclical, stable, and energy. In the later half of the 1970s, there were studies that suggested even a simpler categorization by size (as measured by total capitalization) produced different performance patterns.

Practitioners began to view these categories or clusters of stocks with similar performance as a "style" of investing. Some managers, for example, held themselves out as "growth stock managers" and others as "cyclical stock managers." Using size as a basis for categorizing style, some managers became "large cap" investors while others were "small cap" investors. Moreover, there was a commonly held belief that a manager could shift "styles" to enhance performance return.

Today, the notion of an equity investment style is widely accepted in the investment community. The acceptance of equity style investing can also be seen from the proliferation of style indices published by several vendors and the introduction of futures and options contracts based on some of these style indices.

In this chapter, we will look at the practical aspects of style investing. First, we look at the popular style types and the difficulties of classifying stocks according to style. Second, we look at the empirical evidence on style management. Third, we discuss active style management and how it can be implemented.

## TYPES OF EQUITY STYLES

Stocks can be classified by style in many ways. The most common is in terms of one or more measures of "growth" and "value." Within a growth and value style there is a sub-style based on some measure of size. The most plain vanilla classification of styles is as follows: (1) large value, (2) large growth, (3) small value, and (4) small growth.

---

[1] James L. Farrell Jr., "Homogenous Stock Groupings: Implications for Portfolio Management," *Financial Analysts Journal* (May-June 1975), pp. 50-62.

The motivation for the value/growth style categories can be explained in terms of the most common measure for classifying stocks as growth or value — the price-to-book value per share (P/B) ratio.[2] Earnings growth will increase the book value per share. Assuming no change in the P/B ratio, a stock's price will increase if earnings grow. A manager who is growth oriented is concerned with earnings growth and seeks those stocks from a universe of stocks that have higher relative earnings growth. The growth manager's risks are that growth in earnings will not materialize and/or that the P/B ratio will decline.

For a value manager, concern is with the price component rather than with the future earnings growth. Stocks would be classified as value stocks within a universe of stocks if viewed as cheap in terms of their P/B ratio. By cheap it is meant that the P/B ratio is low relative to the universe of stocks. The expectation of the manager who follows a value style is that the P/B ratio will return to some normal level and thus even with book value per share constant, the price will rise. The risk is that the P/B ratio will not increase.

Each quarter the Mobius Group surveys institutional money managers and asks their style. In June 1996, there were 1,526 domestic equity money managers in the survey who responded that they follow an active strategy. Of these survey participants, 503 indicated that growth was an "accurate" or a "very accurate" description of their style. Moreover, these managers indicated that it was wrong to classify them as value managers. There were 460 managers of the 1,526 surveyed that responded that value was an "accurate" or a "very accurate" description of their style and that it would be wrong to classify them as growth managers.

Within the value and growth categories there are sub-styles. As mentioned above, one sub-style is based on size. The sub-styles discussed below are based on other classifications of the stocks selected.

## Sub-Styles of Value Category

In the value category, there are three sub-styles: low price-to-earnings (P/E) ratio, contrarian, and yield.[3] The *low-P/E manager* concentrates on companies trading at low prices relative to their P/E ratio.[4] The P/E ratio can be defined as the current P/E, a normalized P/E, or a discounted future earnings. The *contrarian manager* looks at the book value of a company and focuses on those companies that are selling at low valuation relative to book value. The companies that fall into this category are typically depressed cyclical stocks or companies that have little or no current earnings or dividend yields. The expectation is that the stock is on a cyclical rebound or

---

[2] Support for the use of this measure is provided in the following study: Eugene F. Fama and Kenneth R. French, "Common Risk Factors on Stocks and Bonds," *Journal of Financial Economics* (February 1993), pp. 3-56.

[3] Jon A. Christopherson and C. Nola Williams, "Equity Style: What it is and Why it Matters," Chapter 1 in T. Daniel Coggin, Frank J. Fabozzi, and Robert D. Arnott (eds.), *The Handbook of Equity Style Management: Second Edition* (New Hope, PA: Frank J. Fabozzi Associates, 1997).

[4] For a discussion of an approach based on low price-earnings, see Gary G. Schlarbaum, "Value-Based Equity Strategies," Chapter 7 in *The Handbook of Equity Style Management*.

that the company's earnings will turn around. Both these occurrences are expected to lead to substantial price appreciation. The most conservative value managers are those that look at companies with above average dividend yields that are expected to be capable of increasing, or at least maintaining, those yields. This style is followed by a manager who is referred to as a *yield manager.*

## Sub-Styles of Growth Category

Growth managers seek companies with above average growth prospects. In the growth manager style category, there tends to be two major sub-styles.[5] The first is a growth manager who focuses on high-quality companies with consistent growth. A manager who follows this sub-style is referred to as a *consistent growth manager.* The second growth sub-style is followed by an *earnings momentum growth manager.* In contrast to a growth manager, an earnings momentum growth manager prefers companies with more volatile, above-average growth. Such a manager seeks to buy companies in expectation of an acceleration of earnings.

## Hybrid Styles: Value-Growth Managers

There are some managers who follow both a growth and value investing style but have a bias (or tilt) in favor of one of the styles. The bias is not sufficiently identifiable to categorize the manager as growth or value managers. Most managers who fall into this hybrid style are described as *growth at a price managers* or *growth at a reasonable price managers.* These managers look for companies that are forecasted to have above-average growth potential selling at a reasonable value.

As noted above, the Mobius Group surveys institutional money managers quarterly and asks them to classify their style. In the June 1996 survey, 503 indicated they were growth managers and 460 value managers. There were 252 managers who indicated that both value and growth styles were an "accurate" or "very accurate" description of their styles. Most of these managers probably fell into the category of growth at a price managers.

## STYLE CLASSIFICATION SYSTEMS

Now that we have a general idea of the two main style categories, growth and value, and the further refinement by size, let's see how a manager goes about classifying stocks that fall into the categories. We call the methodology for classifying stocks into style categories as a *style classification system.* Vendors of style indices have provided direction for developing a style classification system. However, managers will develop their own system.

Developing such a system is not a simple task. To see why, let's take a simple style classification system where we just categorize stocks into value and

---

[5] Christopherson and Williams, "Equity Style."

growth using one measure, the price-to-book value ratio. The lower the P/B ratio the more the stock looks like a value stock. The style classification system would then be as follows:

> *Step 1:* Select a universe of stocks.
> *Step 2:* Calculate the total market capitalization of all the stocks in the universe.
> *Step 3:* Calculate the P/B ratio for each stock in the universe.
> *Step 4:* Sort the stocks from the lowest P/B ratio to the highest P/B ratio.
> *Step 5:* Calculate the accumulated market capitalization starting from the lowest P/B ratio stock to the highest P/B ratio stock.
> *Step 6:* Select the lowest P/B stocks up to the point where one-half the total market capitalization computed in Step 2 is found.
> *Step 7:* Classify the stocks found in Step 6 as value stocks.
> *Step 8:* Classify the remaining stocks from the universe as growth stocks.

While this style classification system is simple, it has both theoretical and practical problems. First, from a theoretical point of view, in terms of the P/B ratio there is very little distinguishing the last stock on the list that is classified as value and the first stock on the list classified as growth. From a practical point of view, the transaction costs are higher for implementing a style using this classification system. The reason is that the classification is at a given point in time based on the prevailing P/B ratio and market capitalizations. At a future date, P/B ratios and market capitalizations will change, resulting in a different classification of some of the stocks. This is often the case for those stocks on the border between value and growth that could jump over to the other category. This is sometimes called "style jitter." As a result, the manager will have to rebalance the portfolio to sell off stocks that are not within the style classification sought.

## Refinements to the Basic Style Classification System

There are two refinements that have been made to style classification systems in an attempt to overcome these two problems. First, more than one categorization variable has been used in a style classification system. Two types of categorization variables have been used: deterministic and expectational. Deterministic variables are those derived from historical data. These variables include dividend/price ratio (i.e., dividend yield), cash flow/price ratio (i.e., cash flow yield), return on equity, and earnings variability. Expectational variables are those based on expectations or forecasts. Examples are earnings growth estimates or variables which rely on some stock valuation model (such as a dividend discount model or a factor model).

As examples of this refinement, consider the style classification system developed by one vendor of style indices, Frank Russell, and one developed by a broker/dealer, Salomon Brothers Inc. For the Frank Russell style indices, the universe of stocks (either 1,000 for the Russell 1000 index or 2,000 for the Russell 2000 index) were classified as part of their value index or growth index using two categorization variables. The two variables are the B/P ratio (a deterministic variable) and a long-term growth forecast (an expectational variable).[6] The latter variable is obtained from the Institutional Brokerage Estimates Survey (IBES). Salomon Brothers uses more than two variables. The variables included are P/B ratio, earnings growth, P/E ratio, dividend yields, and historical returns.[7]

When using several variables in the style classification system, a score is developed for each stock. The classification is then done as follows:

*Step 1:* Select a universe of stocks.

*Step 2:* Calculate the total market capitalization of all the stocks in the universe.

*Step 3:* Using the variables for classification, develop a score for each stock, with the highest score being value.

*Step 4:* Sort the stocks from the highest score to the lowest score.

*Step 5:* Calculate the capitalization-weighted median of the scores.

*Step 6:* Select the stocks with a score above the capitalization-weighted median found in Step 5 and classify them as value stocks.

*Step 7:* Classify the remaining stocks in the universe as growth stocks.

With this system, half of the market capitalization is in each group.

The second refinement has been to develop better procedures for making the cut between growth and value. This involves not classifying every stock into one category or the other. Instead, stocks may be classified into three groups: "pure value," "pure growth," and "middle-of-the-road" stocks. The three groups would be such that they each had one third of the total market capitalization. The two extreme groups, pure value and pure growth, are not likely to face any significant style jitter. The middle-of-the road stocks are assigned a probability of being value or growth. This style classification system is used by Frank Russell and Salomon Brothers Inc.

We will illustrate this approach using the Salomon Brothers model, called the *Growth/Value* (GV) *Model* for distinguishing between growth and value stocks.[8] The model uses a statistical technique called discriminant analysis to "discriminate" between growth and value stocks. Discriminant analysis gives a score, called the "discriminant score," and it is this score that is used to make the cut-off between growth and value. The bottom line output of the model is a ranking of a universe of stocks based on the probability that any particular stock will be a growth stock. This probability is called the "growth stock probability" and its

---

[6] "Russell Equity Indices: Index Construction and Methodology," Frank Russell Company, July 8, 1994 and September 6, 1995.

[7] Sergio Bienstock and Eric H. Sorensen, "Segregating Growth from Value: It's Not Always Either/Or," Salomon Brothers Inc., Quantitative Equities Strategy, July 1992.

[8] Bienstock and Sorensen, "Segregating Growth from Value: It's Not Always Either/Or."

complement, 1 minus the growth stock probability, is the "value stock probabil-ity." When the growth stock probability of a particular stock approaches 1, then it is concluded that that particular stock is a growth stock. Similarly, when the value stock probability of a particular stock approaches 1, then it is concluded that that particular stock is a value stock. Stocks that do not clearly fall into the growth or value categories are identified by the model based on these probabilities.

The product of the model is illustrated in Exhibit 1. The results of the GV model shown in the figure are the result of an application to the largest 3,000 cap-italization stocks in 1991. The horizontal axis shows the discriminant score. The vertical axis shows the growth-stock probability. As the discriminant score increases, the growth-stock probability increases. The dots in Exhibit 1 are spe-cific stocks from the 3,000 analyzed with the GV model. Because most of the stocks analyzed fall near the middle, it looks like a solid curve in that area. There are five vertical lines in the figure. These lines indicate the percentage of the 3,000 stocks that fall below the line. Specifically, moving from left to right, the first line represents 10%, the second 25%, the third 50%, the fourth 75%, and the last 90%. This means that 10% of the 3,000 stocks fell below the first line and 10% were above the last line. Salomon Brothers views stocks that fall below the 10% line as being unambiguously value stocks (because they have a low growth stock probability) and those that are above the 90% line as being unambiguously growth stocks (because they have a high growth stock probability). The stocks that fall in between are unassigned.

## Exhibit 1: Product of Salomon Brothers Growth-Value Model for Probability Ranking of 3,000 Largest Capitalization Stocks in 1991

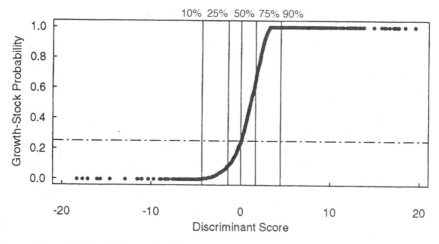

Source: Figure 2 in Sergio Bienstock and Eric H. Sorensen, "Segregating Growth from Value: It's Not Always Either/Or," Salomon Brothers Inc., Quantitative Equities Strategy, July 1992, p. 5.

Thus far our focus has been on style classification in terms of value and growth. As we noted earlier, sub-style classifications are possible in terms of size. Within a value and growth classification, there can be a model determining large value and small value stocks, and large growth and small growth stocks. The variable most used for classification of size is a company's market capitalization. To determine large and small, the total market capitalization of all the stocks in the universe considered is first calculated. The cutoff between large and small is the stock that will give an equal market capitalization.

This simple classification based on size with value and growth has been refined by creators of style indices. For example, Wilshire Associates creates broad-based style indices. The broadest based index is the Wilshire 5000. Wilshire's approach to size was to limit the stocks to the largest 2,500 because it was felt that they better represent stocks held by institutional investors. This index is called the Wilshire Top 2500. Studies of the performance profile of the stocks in this index by Wilshire's Institutional Services/Equity Division found that there was different performance between the 700th and 800th stocks. Wilshire selected the 750th largest stock as the cut-off for the large category. This is the Wilshire Top 750 stocks. Stocks 751 to 2,500 are included in the Wilshire Next 1750.

## RELATIVE PERFORMANCE OF VALUE AND GROWTH

Now that we understand the various style classification systems, we next look at the most important question associated with style management: is style management worth the effort and cost? To answer this question, we can look at the evidence on the relative performance of value and growth stocks. We look first at the U.S. experience, followed by the empirical evidence for value and growth stocks in several developed countries including Canada, Germany, Japan, and the United Kingdom.

### Value and Growth: The U.S. Experience

The performance of U.S. value and growth stocks is presented in terms of the empirical findings by Melissa Brown and Claudia Mott.[9] In their comprehensive study, they show the investment fundamentals (price/earnings and price/book ratios, earnings growth rates and ROE, etc.) and total returns earned on prominent U.S. growth and value indexes over the 17 years covering 1979 to 1995. Equity style indexes used in the Brown and Mott study include the Prudential Securities Growth and Value Indexes, the S&P/BARRA Growth and Value Indexes, the Growth/Value Indexes of Frank Russell Company, and the Growth and Value Indexes constructed by Wilshire Associates, Brown and Mott show the historical return to value and growth by equity size sub-classifications — including U.S. large-cap, mid-cap, and small capitalization portfolios.

---

[9] See Melissa R. Brown and Claudia E. Mott, "Understanding the Differences and Similarities of Equity Style Indexes," Chapter 2 in *The Handbook of Equity Style Management*.

## Exhibit 2: Selected Fundamentals for U.S. Large Cap Growth and Value Indexes

| | PSI-G | PSI-V | Wil-G | Wil-V | S/B-G | S/B-V | Rus-G | Rus-V |
|---|---|---|---|---|---|---|---|---|
| 5-Yr EPS Growth | 20.1 | 7.6 | 17.4 | 5.1 | 11.4 | 7.4 | 14.5 | 6.4 |
| ROE | 23.4 | 19.7 | 25 | 16.7 | 25.2 | 15.2 | 23.7 | 16.4 |
| Yield | 0.6 | 2.9 | 1.2 | 3.9 | 1.7 | 2.7 | 1.3 | 2.9 |
| Debt/Cap | 29.1 | 51.9 | 34.9 | 56.9 | 41.7 | 47.1 | 38 | 52.1 |
| P/E | 26.9 | 14.5 | 23.9 | 12.7 | 25.3 | 15.7 | 27.2 | 15.4 |
| P/BV | 4.4 | 3.1 | 4.7 | 2.2 | 5.2 | 2.3 | 5 | 2.6 |

Source: Prudential Securities, Inc.; calculations as of June 28, 1996

## Fundamentals for U.S. Large Cap Value and Growth

Exhibit 2 reports selected fundamentals for U.S. large cap growth and value stocks as of June 1996. As reported, the differences in investment fundamentals for value and growth stocks are quite noticeable. For example, the 5-year earnings growth for Prudential Securities Large Cap Growth is 20.1%, while the corresponding earnings growth for their value index is only 7.6%. Likewise, at 17.4%, the 5-year earnings growth for Wilshire Large Cap Growth is substantially higher than the earnings growth figure for their large cap value index, at 5.1%.

The return on equity for Wilshire Large Cap Growth, 25%, is higher than the ROE figure of 16.7% for their large cap value index. Along this corporate performance line, the ROE figures for S&P/BARRA Growth and Russell Growth indexes, 25.2% and 23.7%, are considerably higher than the reported ROE figures for their value indexes, at 15.2% and 16.4%, respectively. With high earnings growth and ROE figures — and presumably high corporate plowback ratios — it's not surprising to see that the dividend *yield* observed on large cap growth stocks is substantially lower than the yield figures observed on the respective value indexes. As of June, 1996, the dividend yield on Wilshire's Large Cap Growth index was only 1.2%, while their large cap value index had an average yield of 3.9%.

Exhibit 2 also shows that growth stocks have noticeably high price relatives — including the price-to-earnings and price/book value ratios. For instance, the Prudential Securities Large Cap Growth index has a price-to-earnings ratio of 26.9, while the PSI Large Cap Value index has a price/earnings average of 14.5. Similarly, at 25.3, the price-to-earnings ratio for S&P/BARRA Large Cap Growth index is higher than the price/earnings ratio for their large cap value portfolio, at 15.7. Exhibit 2 also shows that the price-to-book value ratios are substantially higher for growth stocks than value stocks. In this context, the S&P/BARRA and Frank Russell Associates large cap growth indexes have high price/book ratios, around 5 times, while their large cap value indexes have price-to-book ratios at 2.3 and 2.6, respectively. Considerable price/book differences also apply for the Prudential Securities and Wilshire large cap growth and value indexes.

## Exhibit 3: Growth of $10,000 in U.S. Large Cap Growth and Value Indexes: 1979-1995

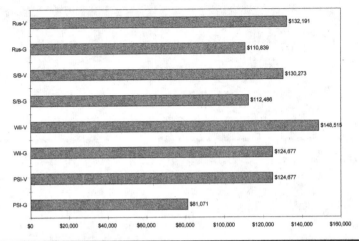

Finally, Exhibit 2 reveals that the average firm in a large cap growth index has a *low* debt-to-capital ratio in comparison with the typical firm that shows up in a portfolio of value-oriented companies. For instance, the average firm in the Wilshire Large Cap Value index finances growth (to the extent that it has any) with 56.9% debt, while the typical company in Wilshire Large Cap Growth finances its corporate investment activities with 34.9% debt.

## Wealth Accumulation in U.S. Large Cap Value and Growth

Given that "growth stocks" have relatively high earnings growth, one might reasonably expect that their return performance would outshine the performance of value stocks — where the observed earnings growth rates and ROE figures are much lower. However, the empirical evidence on growth versus value investing is inconsistent with this performance expectation — since the long-term dollar-accumulation in large cap value portfolios is often higher than the wealth accumulation observed for growth stocks.[10]

Exhibit 3 reveals that $10,000 invested at year-end 1978 in the Wilshire Large Cap Value index grew to $148,515 by year-end 1995, while this initial investment in Wilshire's growth index grew to $124,677. Similarly, during the 17-year reporting period, $10,000 invested in the S&P/BARRA Value index grew to $130,273, while this deposit grew to $112,486 in the large cap growth portfolio.

---

[10] However, the empirical findings of Jacobs and Levy suggest that the performance advantage of value over growth is biased by the investor's interpretation of the "long term." According to Jacobs and Levy, value, growth, and size approaches to equity investing may come *and* go in cycles. For their insightful research, see Bruce I. Jacobs and Kenneth N. Levy, "Investment Management: An Architecture for the Equity Market," Frank J. Fabozzi (ed.), *Active Equity Portfolio Management* (Frank J. Fabozzi Associates: New Hope PA, 1998), pp. 1-20.

Although the exhibit shows that value investing outperforms growth, it is also interesting to see that performance differences exist *within* the universe of firms that are classified by the well-known suppliers of growth and value indexes.

At $148,515, the wealth accumulation in Wilshire Large Cap Value is considerably higher than the dollar figure observed for Prudential Securities Value, at $124,677. As mentioned before, these commercial vendors have — albeit similar in some respects — different fundamental screening criteria on both earnings and relative valuations in the assignment of securities to value and growth stock portfolios. Within the large cap value universe, it is interesting to see that Wilshire Large Cap Value — which is tilted toward *high* yield stocks — resulted in the highest wealth accumulation over the 17-year reporting period. This view that high-yielding stocks offer an attractive return potential for investors is also consistent with the risk-adjusted performance findings observed by one of the authors.[11]

Exhibit 4 reports the compound yearly returns that were used to construct the growth of $10,000 chart for large cap growth and value stocks. Looking at performance this way, one sees that the annualized return on large cap growth stocks falls consistently short of that found on value stocks. The compound yearly return on value stocks ranges from 16% for the Prudential Securities Large Cap Value up to 17.2% for Wilshire Large Cap Value. In contrast, the performance of growth stocks during the 1979 to 1995 period ranges from a low of 13.1%, observed on the Prudential Securities Large Cap Growth, up to 16% for the Wilshire Large Cap Growth portfolio. The S&P/BARRA and Russell large cap growth performances were 15.3% and 15.2%, respectively.

### Exhibit 4: Compound Yearly Returns on U.S. Large-Cap Growth and Value Indexes:1979-1995

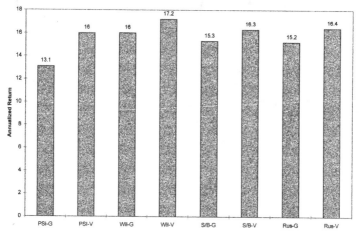

---

[11] See, James L. Grant, "A Yield Effect in Common Stock Return," *Journal of Portfolio Management* (Winter 1995).

## Exhibit 5: Efficient Frontiers for U.S. Large Cap Value and Growth: 1979-1995

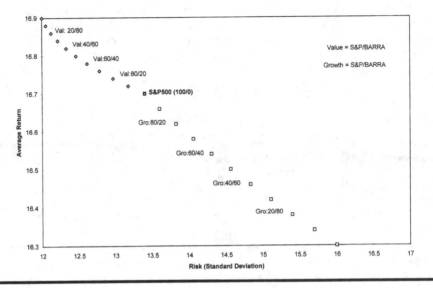

## Efficient Frontiers for U.S. Large Cap Value and Growth

There are two competing reasons that can help explain why growth stocks have underperformed value stocks over reasonably long periods of time. First, if the capital market were price *inefficient*, then it is possible that investors were overly optimistic about the future earnings potential of growth stocks, and therefore overly pessimistic about the future earnings prospects of firms whose securities are classified as value stocks.[12] After all, there must be some justification for abnormally high price-to-earnings and price/book ratios observed on growth stocks in view of the correspondingly low price relatives (and high yields) on the so-called value stocks.

On the other hand, if a large degree of pricing efficiency exists in the financial markets, then the superiority of large cap value over growth investing could possibly be due to some missing risk factor in the equilibrium expected return-risk relationship described in the combined portfolio models of Markowitz-Sharpe. Unfortunately, two well-known measures of equity risk, including beta and return standard deviation, do *not* seem to account for the unusual returns observed on value stocks. This view that U.S. large cap value stocks have attractive risk-adjusted return performance is visually evident in the portfolio "efficient frontiers" shown in Exhibit 5.

---

[12] As explained later, Bauman and Miller argue that earnings biases result from analysts placing too much reliance on recent past earnings trends in forecasting future earnings. See W. Scott Bauman and Robert E. Miller, "Investment Styles, Stock Market Cycles, Investor Expectations, and Portfolio Performance," Chapter 8 in *The Handbook of Equity Style Management*.

Specifically, Exhibit 5 shows average return and risk estimates resulting from "two asset" portfolio combinations of (1) U.S. large cap value stocks — measured by S&P/BARRA Large Cap Value — and the S&P 500, and (2) U.S. large cap growth stocks — measured by S&P/BARRA Large Cap Growth — in combination with S&P 500 stocks, estimated over the 17-year time period covering 1979 to 1995. The domestic-passive, or S&P 500, performance is represented in Exhibit 5 by the point representing a (simple) average return of 16.7% and a equity risk (return standard deviation) estimate of 13.4%. For our purpose, this local-passive position also represents an *implied* "asset mix" consisting of 100% U.S. large cap equities — a "blend" of large cap value and growth stocks — with a zero investment allocation to either U.S. large cap value and growth per se.

Exhibit 5 shows what happens to average portfolio return and risk when an investor deviates from the domestic-passive index. Movements to the left of the S&P 500 point show the return-risk impact of *increasing* equity allocations to U.S. large cap value stocks, while movements to right of the U.S. passive point represent the risk-adjusted return impact of *increasing* equity allocations to U.S. growth stocks. Indeed, the efficient frontiers reveal that two-asset combinations of U.S. value stocks (style-passive) and the S&P 500 (local passive) were both performance enhancing and risk reducing. In sharp contrast, two-asset combinations of U.S. large cap growth and S&P 500 stocks over the reporting period were performance decreasing and risk increasing.

That "value wins" during the 1979-1995 years is clearly evident in the return/risk combination represented by the 60/40 value portfolio (see, Val:60/40 in Exhibit 5) compared with the 60/40 portfolio performance of U.S. large cap growth (see, Gro:60/40). In this context, the average return/risk combination for Val:60/40 was 16.78% and 12.62%, while the return/risk combination for Gro:60/40 was noticeably lower, at 16.54% and 14.31%, respectively. Moreover, the slightly greater "convexity" in the portfolio efficient frontier for large cap value stocks versus the efficient frontier for growth stock is due to a slightly lower return correlation. At, 0.927, the return correlation between large cap value stocks and the S&P 500 during the sample years was slightly lower than the return correlation between U.S. large cap growth stocks and the domestic-passive index, at 0.963.

## U.S. Small Cap Value and Growth

We'll now look at the empirical findings for U.S. small cap value and growth stocks to see if the risk-adjusted return benefit of value stocks transcend the large (and mid) cap size dimension.[13] In this context, Exhibit 6 shows the growth of $10,000 invested in U.S. small cap growth and value stocks over the 1979 to 1995 period. The empirical findings for small cap value and growth portfolios are interesting for

---

[13] Performance findings for U.S. mid cap stocks are mentioned in the text discussion, but not shown in separate chapter exhibits. For a detailed examination of the investment fundamentals and return performance of U.S. mid cap stocks, see Brown and Mott, "Understanding the Differences and Similarities of Equity Style Indexes."

several reasons. Specifically, there appears to exist an *inverse* relationship between firm size and return to the value style of investing. This observation is reinforced by noting that the wealth accumulation in U.S. small cap value stocks — $241,493 for Wilshire and $198,014 for PSI small cap value indexes — during the sample period is the highest among the overall universe of value-oriented securities.

This comparative wealth finding is noteworthy because small cap value stocks had earnings and ROE measures that were approximately the same as the historical earnings figures observed for U.S. mid and large cap value stocks. Yet, the small cap value performance outdistances the wealth accumulation in both U.S. mid cap and large cap value stocks by a fairly wide margin. At $241,493, the dollar accumulation in Wilshire Small Cap Value during the 1979 to 1995 period is some $37,750 higher than the wealth accumulation in their mid cap value index (not shown in the exhibits).

Wilshire's Small Cap Value grew to $241,493 during the 17-year accumulation years, while the initial $10,000 invested in the PSI Small Cap Value portfolio grew to $198,014 — still quite attractive, yet $43,479 lower than the dollar-return performance observed on Wilshire's small cap value product. The small cap performance difference revealed in Exhibit 6 between these value indexes is interesting in light of the fact that (1) earnings growth rates and ROE metrics for Wilshire Small Cap Value portfolio are near-to-lower than the underlying corporate performance figures observed on the PSI Small Cap Value, and (2) the dividend yield, 3.8%, for Wilshire Small Cap Value is historically higher than the yield factor, at 1.4%, observed on the PSI Small Cap Value index.

## Exhibit 6: Growth of $10,000 in U.S. Small Cap Growth and Value Indexes: 1979-1995

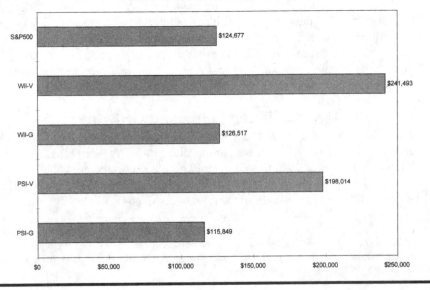

## Exhibit 7: Compound Yearly Returns on U.S. Small-Cap and Value Indexes: 1979-1995

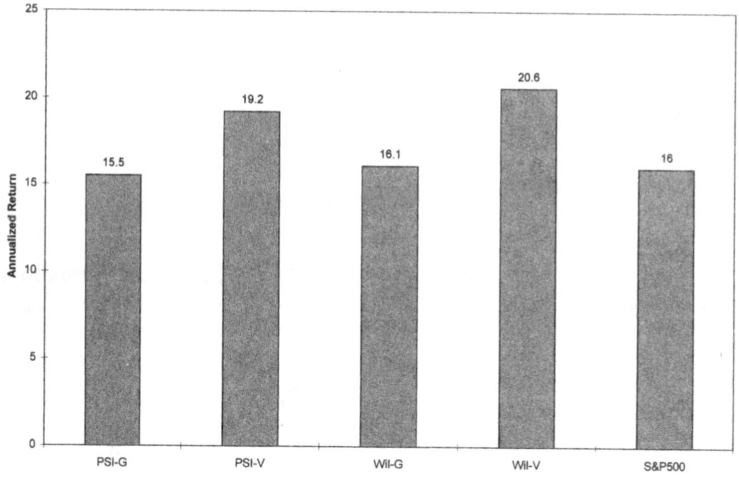

Also, one might reasonably expect that U.S. small cap growth stocks would have comparatively strong investment performance. There are at least two reasons for this. First, small cap growth companies are more entrepreneurial in nature and are not shackled by organizational inefficiencies that might impair the ability of mid to large size firms (especially) to pursue wealth-enhancing activities. Second (as we will soon see), small company growth (and value) portfolios have volatile equity returns. From an equilibrium expected return-risk perspective, they should therefore offer investors comparatively high average returns to compensate for the added risk.

However, Exhibit 6 shows that this relative performance anticipation for small cap growth stocks did not happen over the 17-year reporting period. During this period, the investment performance of U.S. small cap growth stocks was dramatically *lower* than that observed on small cap value stocks. At $126,517 and $115,849, the Wilshire and PSI small cap growth accumulations were substantially lower than the wealth accumulation during the 1979 to 1995 period in their small cap value indexes, at $241,493 and $198,014, respectively. Also, Exhibit 6 reveals that the performance of U.S. small cap growth stocks was either near — or short of — the wealth accumulation of an initial $10,000 invested in the S&P500, at $124,677.

Exhibit 7 shows the compound annual returns that were used to construct the growth of $10,000 chart for the U.S. small cap portfolios. At 19.2% and 20.6%, the annualized returns on PSI and Wilshire small cap value indexes were substantially higher than the compound yearly returns observed on the corresponding small cap growth indexes, at 15.5% and 16.1%, respectively. Moreover, at 16%, the annualized return to large cap stocks — as measured by the S&P 500 — was competitive with the return performance of volatile small cap growth stocks.

## Exhibit 8: Return-Risk Analysis for U.S. Small Cap Stocks

|  | PSI-G | PSI-V | Wil-G | Wil-V | S&P500 |
|---|---|---|---|---|---|
| St.Dev | 20.9 | 18.3 | 21.4 | 17.1 | 13.4 |
| Average | 17.3 | 20.7 | 18 | 21.9 | 16.7 |
| Coef. Var. | 1.21 | 0.88 | 1.19 | 0.78 | 0.80 |

## Return-Risk Considerations for U.S. Small Cap Value and Growth

Exhibit 8 shows the average return and risk estimates for the PSI and Wilshire small cap growth and value portfolios. Looking at U.S. small cap performance by investment style, it's interesting to see that small cap value stocks have attractive risk-adjusted returns, especially when compared with small cap growth stocks. At 21.9%, Exhibit 8 reveals that the (simple) average return on the Wilshire Small Cap Value index is 390 basis points *higher* than the average return performance on their small cap growth index. Yet the Wilshire Small Cap Value portfolio has a return standard deviation estimate, 17.1%, that is *lower* than the volatility figure, 21.4%, observed on the corresponding small cap growth portfolio. Likewise, the PSI small cap value portfolio has an attractive average return, at 20.7%, in the presence of a risk estimate, 18.3%, that is noticeably lower than volatility figure for the PSI small cap growth portfolio.

As with U.S. mid cap and large cap stocks, this small cap value finding is interesting because these firms have comparatively low historical earnings growth rates along with low price-to-earnings and price/book ratios. The relative performance benefit of the value style of investing (over growth) is especially reinforced by the coefficient of variation on the PSI and Wilshire small cap value indexes, 0.88 and 0.78, in the presence of the high risk/reward ratios observed on their small cap growth products, at 1.21 and 1.19, respectively. On the other hand, investors should realize that small cap (and mid cap value) stocks are quite volatile, as their return standard deviations are considerably higher than the 13.4% annualized risk estimate for the S&P 500. It is also worth mentioning that the coefficient of variation for the PSI and Wilshire small cap value portfolios, 0.88 and 0.78, are near the risk/reward estimate, at 0.8, observed on this popular U.S. large capitalization index.

## Combining the Results for U.S. Value and Growth

Let's now look at the combined returns to U.S. value and growth by equity size sub-classifications. For the value group, Exhibit 9 shows that compound yearly returns over the 1979 to 1995 years were inversely related to firm size. This means that when equity size goes down — as one moves from PSI and Wilshire large- to mid- to small-cap value portfolios — the return to value investing goes up. Also, since U.S. small cap value stocks have the highest return standard deviation — followed by mid cap and large cap value stocks — the apparent inverse association between firm size and return to value investing is consistent with a positive average return-risk relationship *within* the overall universe of value-oriented companies.

## Exhibit 9: The Return to Value Investing: 1979-1995
## (Ranked by Large, Mid, and Small Cap Size Sub-Classifications)

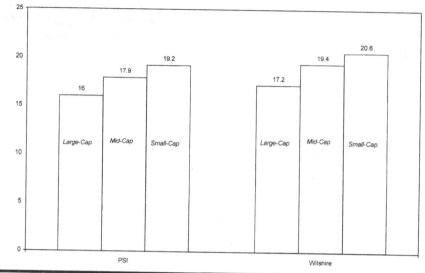

This segmented, or style-based, view of the real-time expected return-risk relationship is interesting because a more general equilibrium framework would suggest otherwise. In this context, the relatively low-volatility U.S. value stocks should on the average underperform the high risk (as measured by beta or return standard deviation) growth stocks. However, Exhibit 10 shows that (1) from a historical perspective, U.S. growth stocks underperformed value stocks, and (2) U.S. small cap stocks were especially problematic because their average return performance even within the growth group was low, while the return volatility in small caps was quite high. Taken together, one is left in a quandary about the equilibrium expected return-risk relationship between value and growth stocks, as well as the risk-adjusted performance within the universe of U.S. growth stocks more generally.

## VALUE AND GROWTH:
## THE INTERNATIONAL EXPERIENCE

From an international perspective, Robert Arnott, David Leinweber, and Christopher Luck present evidence on the performance of value and growth for the United States, Japan, United Kingdom, and Germany.[14] Using the simple measure

---

[14] See, David J. Leinweber, Robert D. Arnott, and Christopher G. Luck, "The Many Sides of Equity Style: Quantitative Management of Core, Value, and Growth Portfolios," Chapter 11 in *The Handbook of Equity Style Management*.

of value and growth based on the P/B ratio, they calculated the growth of $1 invested in growth stocks and value stocks from January 1975 to June 1995. The results are reported in Exhibit 11. For the U.S. analysis, the universe of stocks included are those in the S&P 500. As can be seen from Exhibit 11 in every country, value outperformed growth based on the simple definition of growth and value. Exhibit 12 presents this superior performance over the entire time period in terms of the difference in the cumulative return between value stocks and growth stocks for the markets of the same five countries.

## Exhibit 10: The Return to Growth Investing: 1979-1995 (Ranked by Large, Mid, and Small Cap Size Sub-Classifications)

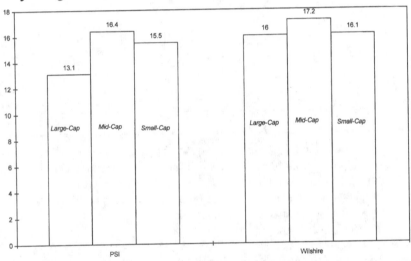

## Exhibit 11: Growth of $1 Invested in Growth Stocks and Value Stocks Using Simple Price/Book Classification: January 1975 to June 1995

| Country | Growth of $1 invested in | | | Portion of monthly returns where Growth exceeded Value |
|---|---|---|---|---|
| | Value Stocks | Growth Stocks | Best of Value-or-Growth | |
| U.S. | $23 | $14 | $42 | 45% |
| U.K. | 42 | 24 | 82 | 44 |
| Japan | 37 | 10 | 89 | 39 |
| Canada | 12 | 5 | 31 | 39 |
| Germany | 14 | 9 | 30 | 45 |

Source: Exhibit 10 in David J. Leinweber, Robert D. Arnott, and Christopher G. Luck, "The Many Sides of Equity Style: Quantitative Management of Core, Value, and Growth Portfolios," Chapter 11 in T. Daniel Coggin, Frank J. Fabozzi, and Robert D. Arnott (eds.), *The Handbook of Equity Style Management: Second Edition* (New Hope, PA: Frank J. Fabozzi Associates, 1997), p. 188.

*Exhibit 12: Cumulative Returns of Value Minus Growth Stocks for Five Countries: January 1975 to June 1995*

A: U.S. S&P500 Value – Growth

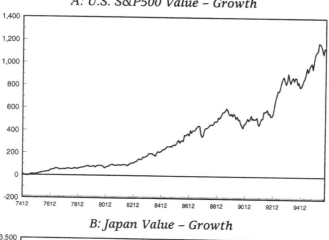

B: Japan Value – Growth

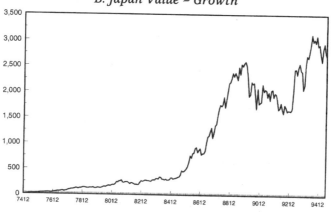

C: U.K. Value – Growth

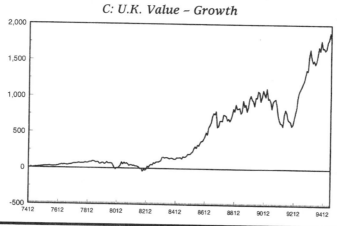

### Exhibit 12 (Continued)
#### D: Canada Value – Growth

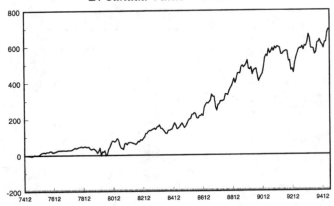

#### E: Germany Value – Growth

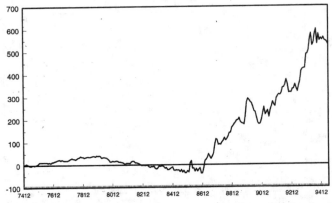

Source: Exhibit 5, 6, 7, 8, and 9 in David J. Leinweber, Robert D. Arnott, and Christopher G. Luck, "The Many Sides of Equity Style: Quantitative Management of Core, Value, and Growth Portfolios," Chapter 11 in T. Daniel Coggin, Frank J. Fabozzi, and Robert D. Arnott (eds.), *The Handbook of Equity Style Management: Second Edition* (New Hope, PA: Frank J. Fabozzi Associates, 1997), pp. 185- 187.

## THE ROLL STUDY

While the results are informative, they are largely based on raw returns. That is, they make no adjustment for differences in risk that might exist between growth and value stocks. A comprehensive analysis that addresses this issue was performed by Richard Roll.[15] He addressed the following three questions:

---

[15] Richard Roll, "Style Return Differentials: Illusions, Risk Premiums, or Investment Opportunities," Chapter 5 in *The Handbook of Equity Style Management*.

1. Are the observed differences in the performance between equity styles just statistical aberrations and therefore not likely to be repeated?
2. Are the observed differences in performance between equity styles simply a reflection of the compensation for the differences in the risks associated with each equity style?
3. Are the observed differences in performance between equity style truly an investment opportunity that can generate an enhanced return without incurring any additional exposure to loss?

To empirically address these questions, Roll used the following three categorization variables: (1) large or small size; (2) high or low earnings per share/price (E/P) ratio; and, (3) high or low book equity/market equity (B/M) ratio. A low relative P/E ratio is viewed as an indicator of value, therefore a high relative E/P ratio is a measure of value. A low relative P/B ratio is an indicator of value. It has the same meaning when expressed in terms of the B/M ratio (i.e., a low relative B/M ratio is an indicator of growth); therefore a high relative B/M ratio is an indicator of value.

Only U.S. stocks were included in Roll's study. The universe of stocks included all listed NYSE and AMEX stocks available from the CRSP database. The period covered was April 1984 to March 1994. The number of stocks in the universe varied each month.

## Roll's Style Classification Scheme

Each month the stocks in the universe were classified into one of eight portfolios. This was done as follows. The stocks were ranked separately from low to high based on a given style categorization variable. Then a stock was assigned to one of eight style portfolios as follows. Each portfolio was designated by three letters. Each letter represented the stock assignment within a style classification variable as either "low" denoted by "L" or "high" denoted by "H." The first letter for a portfolio indicated size, the second letter E/P ratio, and the third letter B/M ratio. For example, a portfolio designated LHL meant the stocks in this portfolio were the smallest capitalization stocks with the highest E/P ratio, and the lowest B/M ratio. Each month the stocks in the style portfolio changed based on their classification according to the style categorization variable.

For each of the eight style portfolios, a value-weighted monthly total return was calculated. The total return included price change, dividends, and reinvestment of dividends. Exhibit 13 shows the growth of $1 invested in each style portfolio over the period and ranks the performance of the style portfolios. The best performing style portfolio was "LHH." This is a small capitalization portfolio that has a high E/P and a high B/M. This is clearly a value portfolio and the findings are therefore consistent with the results presented in Exhibit 11 of the superior performance of value stocks based on raw returns. The worst performing style portfolio was "LLL." The low E/P and low B/M indicate that this style portfolio is biased in the direction of growth. In terms of return performance, the best performing style portfolio outperformed the worst performing style portfolio by more than 15% annually.

### Exhibit 13: 4-Growth of $1 Invested and Performance of Style Portfolios from March 31, 1985 to March 31, 1994

| Rank | Growth of $1 | Style Size | Earnings/Price | Book/Market |
|------|--------------|-----------|----------------|-------------|
| 1 | $6.85 | Low | High | High |
| 2 | 5.34 | High | High | High |
| 3 | 5.15 | Low | High | Low |
| S&P 500 | 3.96 | — | — | — |
| 4 | 3.49 | High | High | Low |
| 5 | 3.05 | High | Low | Low |
| 6 | 2.76 | High | Low | High |
| 7 | 2.02 | Low | Low | High |
| 8 | 1.64 | Low | Low | Low |

Source: Richard Roll, "Style Return Differentials: Illustrations, Risk Premiums, or Investment Opportunities," Chapter 5 in T. Daniel Coggin, Frank J. Fabozzi, and Robert D. Arnott (eds.), *The Handbook of Equity Style Management: Second Edition* (New Hope, PA: Frank J. Fabozzi Associates, 1997), p. 102.

Roll then statistically tested whether the monthly excess returns on the style portfolios (i.e., the difference between the return on a style portfolio and the risk-free rate) was significantly different. Using an elaborate statistical test, Roll found that they were statistically significant.

However, the empirical results in Exhibit 13 (as well as those in Exhibit 11) are based on raw returns. No adjustment was made in the results reported to account for the risks associated with each portfolio style. Roll takes this into account by analyzing the risk-adjusted returns for the style portfolios. He used two different equity risk models: the capital asset pricing model and a factor model. Roll does not find that accounting for risk can explain the difference in performance of the style portfolios. That is, he found that there were still differences in return performance after adjusting for risk. This suggests that equity style provided extra return without incurring additional risk.

## Why Have Value Stocks Outperformed Growth Stocks?

There is considerable debate as to why it has been empirically observed that value stocks have outperformed growth stocks over extended periods. The results may merely be the result of data mining. There are other explanations that have been proffered.

The first explanation is that there are one or more risks that are not being recognized in the analysis.[16] If there are risks that are not identified, then it is possible that the premium realized by value stocks over growth stocks is a risk premium to compensate for such risks. While one can never be sure of capturing all the risks, the study by Roll described above uses the latest technology in asset pricing modeling and still finds differential performance. The second explanation

---

[16] Eugene F. Fama and Kenneth R. French, "The Cross-Section of Expected Returns," *Journal of Finance* (June 1992), pp. 427-465.

is that there are systematic errors in forecasts that cause the difference in performance.[17]

A partial explanation for the difference in performance of growth and value stocks where the criteria for classification is the price-earnings ratio has been suggested by Scott Bauman and Robert Miller.[18] They looked at the earnings forecast and found that earnings were consistently underestimated for the lowest price-earnings stocks and consistently overestimated for the highest price-earnings stocks. The low price-earnings stocks are value stocks. An underestimate of future earnings means that such stocks will perform better than expected. In the case of growth stocks, which are the high price-earnings stocks, an overestimate of earnings will result in worse performance than expected. Why does this bias exist? Bauman and Miller argue that it is the result of too much reliance by analysts on recent past earnings trends in formulating forecasted earnings.

## ACTIVE STYLE MANAGEMENT

The results of the studies by Brown and Mott, Arnott-Leinweber-Luck, and Richard Roll suggest that a value style outperforms a growth style. The outperformance of value over growth, however, did not occur for every time period studied. For example, in the Arnott-Leinweber-Luck study, even though the cumulative return differential favored value stocks, there were dips in their reported curves shown in Exhibit 12 (A) through (E). A dip means that there were periods where growth stocks outperformed value stocks. The last column in Exhibit 11 shows the percentage of months over the January 1975 to June 1995 period in which growth stocks outperformed value stocks.

The implication of this is that there are opportunities to switch styles based on expectations of what will be the best performing style. This portfolio strategy is called *active style management* or *tactical style management*. (Selecting one style and sticking with it is referred to as *passive style management*.)[19] The potential for enhanced performance by pursuing such a strategy can be seen by looking at what a style switching strategy would have done in terms of the growth of $1 if a manager could *perfectly predict* the better performing of the two styles each month and invested in that style. This is shown in the fourth column of Exhibit 11. For example, in the United States a perfect foresight style switching strategy would have generated a growth of $1 equal to $42 at the end of 20 years compared to $23 for value stocks.

---

[17] This explanation has been suggested in the following studies: Josef Lakonishok, Andrei Shleifer, and Robert Vishny, "Contrarian Investment, Extrapolation, and Risk," *Journal of Finance* (December 1994), pp. 1541-1578; and, Robert A. Haugen, *The New Finance: The Case Against Efficient Markets* (Englewood Cliffs, NJ: Prentice Hall, 1995).

[18] W. Scott Bauman and Robert E. Miller, "Investment Styles, Stock Market Cycles, Investor Expectations, and Portfolio Performance."

[19] See Bruce I. Jacobs and Kenneth N. Levy, Chapter 2 of this book, for more on style and active equity management.

Now we know that with perfect foresight a style switching strategy which ignores transaction costs would have produced a significantly enhanced return compared to a passive style management. The question is how to implement a real-world style switching strategy to enhance returns. To do so, it is necessary to accurately forecast returns to style. Moreover, any realistic style switching strategy must recognize the costs of trading large positions in one style into a large position of another style.

## Implementing a Style Switching Strategy

Typically, the costs of implementation of style switching do not make it economic to pursue a style switching strategy over short time periods. There are more effective ways to implement a style switching strategy.[20] Rather than a style switching strategy from value to growth or growth to value, a policy of tilting a portfolio toward a style can be employed. For example, a style switching strategy means that at a given time either (1) 100% is allocated to a value portfolio and 0% to a growth portfolio or (2) 0% is allocated to a value portfolio and 100% to a growth portfolio. In a style tilting strategy, there is some allocation to each style, the percentage allocation based on the expected relative performance of the two styles. In addition to reducing transaction costs, style tilting reduces the size of the bet made on a style.

There are two additional ways to effectively implement an active style management strategy. First, as noted earlier, a probabilistic style classification system can be used so as to focus only on the strongest value stocks or growth stocks. This increases the probability that the manager is achieving the target style exposure and reduces transaction costs from stocks at the border crossing over. Second, a style switching or style tilting strategy should occur only based on longer-term forecasted better return performance of a style. The reason is that transaction costs associated with the frequent shifting of the portfolio between styles for short periods will more than likely eat up the potential enhanced return.

Transaction costs are critical in a strategy. Futures contracts provide a cost effective means for altering an exposure to an asset. Because of the increased interest in style investing, futures on style indices have been developed and are currently trading. Futures on style indices provide a means for reducing the transaction costs associated with active style management.[21]

## SUMMARY

Many studies have emerged that look at the relative merit of the value versus growth style of equity investing. In this chapter, the average return and risk estimates reported in the Brown-Mott and Roll studies for U.S. equities — as well as

---

[20] Leinweber, Arnott, and Luck, "The Many Sides of Equity Style."
[21] See, Joanne M. Hill and Maria E. Tsu, "Value and Growth Index Derivatives," Chapter 19 in *The Handbook of Equity Style Management.*

the international equity style findings of Arnott, Leinweber, and Luck — were used to demonstrate the return superiority of the well-known *value* style of investing. Although differences exist in the construction of major growth and value indexes — such as the growth/value indexes constructed by Prudential Securities, Inc., Frank Russell Associates, S&P/BARRA, and Wilshire Associates — the empirical results suggest that "value wins" (over growth) whether one looks at equity style sub-classifications by large cap, mid cap, and even small capitalization firms.

Within the U.S. value universe, it is interesting to see that an inverse association seems to exist between firm size and average return performance. Although the return to value is quite exceptional in any case, a ranking within the value group suggests that small cap value stocks outperform the mid cap value group, while the stocks of large capitalization value firms underperform both groups. This inverse association between firm size and performance does not appear to be present in the U.S. growth stock area since mid cap growth stocks outperformed the comparatively low performing and highly volatile small cap growth stocks over the 1979 to 1995 years.

Based on recent empirical evidence, one is left wondering why relatively low-risk value stocks have comparatively high average returns, while the high-risk growth stock portfolios have lower return performance. From an efficient market's perspective, it would seem that investors would bid up the prices of the presumably undervalued stocks in the value group, while selling-off the seemingly overpriced securities in the growth group — especially, the stocks of small cap growth companies! Of course, this financial *disintermediation* argument only makes sense to the degree that the capital market is efficient in the risk-pricing sense (beta and return standard deviation) described by the Markowitz and Sharpe portfolio models.

# QUESTIONS

1. Compare and contrast the value and growth styles of equity management. Be sure to discuss (i) the sub-categories within the value and growth styles, (ii) the investment fundamentals of value and growth, and (iii) the return and risk characteristics that define these two popular styles of equity management.

2. In developing a style classification system, what are the problems of using one variable to classify stock?

3. Discuss in general terms how the following value and growth stock indexes are constructed:

   • the S&P/BARRA value and growth indexes
   • the Frank Russell Associates indexes of value and growth
   • the Prudential Securities approach
   • the Wilshire approach to equity style construction

4. Use the information provided below to identify the equity management styles (value versus growth) of "mystery" funds X and Y. (Mystery funds X and Y are assumed to be style-based index funds having the same investment fundamentals as those supplied by one of the major providers of growth and value indexes.)

| | Mystery Funds | |
|---|---|---|
| | Fund X | Fund Y |
| P/BV | 2.6 | 5 |
| P/E | 15.4 | 27.2 |
| Debt/Cap | 52.1 | 38 |
| Yield | 2.9 | 1.3 |
| ROE | 16.4 | 23.7 |
| EPS Growth | 6.4 | 14.5 |

5. Use the S&P/BARRA approach to develop value and growth indexes for the four stocks shown below. Be sure to answer the questions that follow:

| Stock | Price/Book | ROE | Market Cap% |
|---|---|---|---|
| W | 5.0 | 20% | 30% |
| X | 2.0 | 10% | 15% |
| Y | 4.5 | 15% | 20% |
| Z | 2.5 | 15% | 35% |

   a. What is the capitalization-weighted price/book ratio for a portfolio consisting of all four stocks?
   b. What is the rank order for the four stocks using the S&P/BARRA sorting procedure?
   c. Which of the four stocks would be included in a growth stock index? Why?
   d. Which of the four stocks would be included in a value stock index? Why?

6. Use the following information to construct style-based efficient frontiers like those shown in Exhibit 5. Assume that (i) the core passive opportunity is a representative market index like the S&P 500, (ii) the correlation between the market index and the growth stock opportunity is 0.8, and (iii) the correlation among the value stock portfolio and the market index is 0.6.

|  | Average Return % | Standard Deviation % |
|---|---|---|
| Market Index | 15% | 14% |
| Value Stocks | 17% | 12% |
| Growth Stocks | 13% | 18% |

7. In a classic study titled "Homogeneous Stock Groupings: Implications for Portfolio Management" (*Financial Analysts Journal*, May-June 1975), James Farrell, Jr. found that there were four general clusters of stocks within the U.S. equity market. The four homogeneous groups include growth stocks, cyclical stocks, stable stocks, and energy stocks. The findings had significant active management implications because they suggested that portfolio managers could earn abnormal returns (positive alpha) by "rotating" their portfolios toward those homogeneous stock groups that were currently "in favor" and away from those stock groupings that were "out of favor" with investors.

In today's world of equity management, portfolio managers are often classified by three broad equity management styles — namely, value, growth, and small cap stock managers. As a result, some portfolio managers feel that their active management strategies to produce abnormal returns have been constrained by the emergence of pre-defined equity styles such as value and growth. These equity styles seem to prevent active managers from "thinking out of the box" in an attempt to build portfolios having abnormal returns for the future.

a. What are the benefits and limitations of looking at the world of equity portfolio management from the perspective of James Farrell, Jr.?

b. What are the benefits and limitations of the current style-based classification to equity portfolio management — large cap value, large cap growth, and small cap?

c. Is it possible that another cluster might emerge in today's dynamic world of information technology and global competitiveness?

8. Charles Trczinka has set forth some guidelines for deciding whether style makes sense ["Is Equity Style Management Worth the Effort? Some Critical Issues for Plan Sponsors" Chapter 20 in T. Daniel Coggin, Frank J. Fabozzi, and Robert D. Arnott (eds.), *The Handbook of Equity Style Management: Second Edition* (New Hope, PA: Frank J. Fabozzi Associates, 1997)]. Since the greatest interest in style has been in the pension fund community that hires "style managers" the guidelines are cast in terms of the sponsor. In his discussion, he explains the purposes of style management. Comment on the following purposes:

a. "By identifying the investment style of a money manager the sponsor is obtaining information about the money manager's expertise, organization and possibly the manager's likely success."

b. "The second purpose of style management is to measure the manager's performance. A manager with an objectively identifiable style may earn a higher return than other managers with the same style but the same style may do poorly. If measured against broad market benchmarks the manager will be a poor performer."

c. "The fourth use of style management occurs when a sponsor wishes to share some of the control over the portfolio allocation. Sponsors may believe they have an ability to predict which style will earn the higher return or sponsors may decide that some styles are simply not worthy of attention."

# Chapter 6

# Traditional Fundamental Analysis

Investors need to have a keen understanding of the financial characteristics of the companies that they invest in. This need for accurate and timely financial information transcends the investor's active management style, because in the absence of any measurable information on the firm's real profitability, it is difficult to know objectively which companies are likely to succeed and those that will ultimately fail. With this profitability consideration in mind, this chapter looks at some of the more important traditional measures of corporate financial success, with an eye toward assessing their information content in securities valuation.

## TRADITIONAL MEASURES OF CORPORATE SUCCESS

With numerous financial measures available, the investor is sometimes left wondering which metrics are the most important to focus on from the shareholder's perspective. Broad ratio categories include activity, liquidity, debt, and profitability measures — with many ratio selections within each general category. From the investor's perspective, profitability ratios and growth rates combined with relative valuation measures based on accounting and market data are often used by equity analysts when assessing the attractiveness of a firm's common stock. Some of the traditional growth and profitability measures include:

- revenue growth
- earnings and cash flow growth
- dividend growth
- book value and asset growth
- return on equity (ROE)
- return on assets or capital

Likewise, the key valuation measures that are frequently discussed by equity analysts include:

- price/revenue ratio
- price/earnings ratio
- price/cash flow ratio
- price/book value ratio

- value/replacement cost ratio[1]
- dividend yield

We'll begin the traditional focus by looking at how to calculate revenue and earnings growth rates for selected companies in the financial services and beverages industries. Then the research focus will move to the "Dupont formula" with its emphasis on the packaging of a firm's return on equity. This formula can be used to *jointly* highlight the information content of the firm's return on assets (among others) and corporate leverage (debt-related) ratios.[2] We'll continue the traditional focus by viewing *ex ante* profitability ratios in the context of well known valuation measures such as the price/book value ratio, and we'll see how profitability and valuation measures from published reports — such as Bloomberg and Value Line — can be used to assess the attractiveness of the firm's outstanding securities.

## SELECTED PERFORMANCE MEASURES

Equity analysts often speak in terms of revenue, earnings, and cash flow growth, as well as the firm's return on equity and capital. Although revenue is *not* profit, a company must still produce and market a meaningful product in order to have positive earnings. Likewise, the firm's revenue must grow over time for it to show sustainable profit growth. For excessive expense-cutting and a dearth of corporate investment simply to show higher short-term profits will eventually negatively impact the firm's long-term revenue and earnings-generating capabilities. These profit and investment considerations also apply to the firm's need to generate a solid rate of return on its equity capital. After all, it is the shareholders who are the firm's ultimate owners, and it is their financial capital that is at most risk in the life of any on-going business.

### Revenue and Earnings Growth Rates

To illustrate the importance of growth, we'll use a real-world example of the revenue and earnings growth rates for State Street Corporation. In the 1996 Letter to the Shareholders (see Exhibit 1), CEO Marshall Carter and COO David Spina emphasize the strategic financial goals of the banking and financial services company in terms of (1) sustainable real revenue and earnings growth of 12.5% for the 1990s, and (2) a target return on equity (ROE) of 18% for the decade.[3]

---

[1] Given the availability of accounting data, we'll focus on the price/book value ratio as opposed to the price-to-replacement cost of assets ratio called *Tobin's Q*. For an interesting discussion of the conceptual and practical application (with measurement limitations) of this economic valuation ratio, see Pamela P. Peterson and David R. Peterson, *Company Performance and Measures of Value Added* (Charlottesville, VA: The Research Foundation of the ICFA, AIMR, 1996).

[2] Peterson and Peterson (*Company Performance and Measures of Value Added*) point out that the decomposition of return ratios into profit margin and turnover ratios is attributed to E.I. duPont de Nemours & Company (American Management Association 1960).

[3] Financial information for State Street Corporation was obtained from the bank's 1996 Annual Report.

## Exhibit 1: State Street Corporation
### 1996 Letter to the Shareholders

"Our primary financial goal remains sustainable real earnings per share growth, supported by a goal of realizing 12.5% real revenue growth per year in the decade of the 90s. For the decade-to-date we have achieved 15.5% per year nominal growth, which translates to 12.8% real growth when adjusted for inflation. We believe the benefits of our focus on revenue are clear, and we will continue to emphasize revenue growth. Our second supporting goal is an 18% return on common stockholders' equity."

|                          |                        |
|--------------------------|------------------------|
| Marshall N. Carter       | David A. Spina         |
| Chairman and             | President and          |
| Chief Executive Officer  | Chief Operating Officer |

Source: State Street 1996 Annual Report, page 5.

## Exhibit 2: State Street Corporation Selected Income and
### Balance Sheet Information

| (U.S. $Billions, Except Per Share Figures) | | | | | | |
|------------|--------|--------|--------|--------|--------|--------|
| Year       | 1991   | 1992   | 1993   | 1994   | 1995   | 1996   |
| Revenue    | 0.909  | 1.052  | 1.212  | 1.423  | 1.575  | 1.882  |
| Net Income | 0.151  | 0.170  | 0.189  | 0.220  | 0.247  | 0.293  |
| $ EPS      | 1.87   | 2.07   | 2.30   | 2.66   | 2.98   | 3.59   |
| Equity     | 0.844  | 0.970  | 1.125  | 1.284  | 1.483  | 1.618  |
| Assets     | 12.194 | 16.255 | 18.927 | 22.795 | 26.182 | 29.483 |

Source: 1996 Annual Report, page 7.

To see whether State Street's *actual* performance is consistent with its strategic financial goals, Exhibit 2 reports selected income and balance sheet items obtained from the bank's Annual Report for the 1991 to 1996 period — including revenue, net income, and per share earnings on the income statement and equity and assets on the bank's balance sheet, respectively.

State Street's 1996 revenue, $1.882 billion, can be viewed as the future value (FV) of the initial 1991 sales figure of $0.909 billion. In this context, the bank's 1996 revenue figure results from five years of compounding on the initial present value figure such that:

$$FV = PV \times (1 + g_r)^5$$

Upon inserting the bank's revenue figures into the future value expression, and solving for the 5-year *annualized* growth rate, $g_r$, one obtains:

$$g_r = (FV/PV)^{1/5} - 1.0$$
$$= (1.882/0.909)^{0.2} - 1.0 = 0.157 \text{ or } 15.7\%.$$

Additionally, State Street's 5-year earnings growth rate, $g_e$, can be determined in a similar manner. At 13.9%, this annualized nominal earnings growth is calculated according to:

$$g_e = (3.59/1.87)^{0.2} - 1.0 = 0.139 \text{ or } 13.9\%$$

In order to obtain the *real* growth rates for State Street Corporation, we need to *subtract* the annualized inflation rate from the nominal revenue and earning growth rates. With inflation running at 2.8% for the December 1991 to December 1996 years, the real revenue and earnings growth rates for the bank were 12.9% and 11.1%, respectively.[4] Since these percentages either exceed or are near the 12.5% real growth target set by State Street's Board of Directors (see Exhibit 1), the actual revenue and earnings growth figures are largely consistent with the strategic financial goals of the bank.

Indeed, State Street Corporation's name changes in recent years — from State Street Bank and Trust Company to State Street Boston to its present name — were largely designed to emphasize the global growth orientation of the bank. This is consistent with the bank's growing dominance in the *non*-lending and fee-generating areas of global master trust/custody, securities processing, global securities lending, and global asset management. Moreover, the 1996 Annual Report also reveals that State Street Corporation derives about 70% of its yearly revenue from these high-growth and relatively stable income sources.

## ROE Insights from the Dupont Formula

Let's now look at the information content of ROE as a traditional measure of corporate financial success. From an accounting perspective, return on equity is simply net income divided by stockholder's equity (SE). The Dupont formula expands this basic definition by showing that the firm's return on equity is determined by *multiplying* its return on assets (ROA) by a corporate leverage ratio — as measured by the ratio of total assets to stockholders' equity. The firm's return on assets (ROA) is in turn measured by net income (NI) divided by total assets:

$$\text{ROE} = \text{ROA} \times \text{Leverage} = \frac{\text{NI}}{\text{A}} \times \frac{\text{A}}{\text{SE}}$$

To illustrate this concept, we'll look again at State Street Corporation in the banking and financial services sector. At year-end 1996, CEO Marshall Carter and COO David Spina reported that the firm's 18.1% return on equity was consistent with the strategic financial goals of the bank for the 1990s. To the unsuspecting investor, this corporate announcement might seem surprising, especially since the bank's return on assets figure for that year was only 1%:

$$\text{ROA} = \frac{\text{NI}}{\text{A}} = \frac{\$0.293}{\$29.483} = 0.01 \text{ or } 1\%$$

Fortunately, the Dupont formula can be use to explain the seemingly large discrepancy between State Street's ROE and its underlying ROA. According

---

[4] Inflation rate based on Bureau of Labor Statistics' estimates.

to the Dupont formula, the *implied leverage factor* for the banking and financial services company should be 18.1. This implied leverage factor is calculated according to:

$$\text{Implied leverage factor} = \frac{\text{ROE}}{\text{ROA}} = \frac{0.181}{0.01} = 18.1$$

A quick look at State Street's 1996 Annual Report (selected items in Exhibit 2) reveals that stockholders' equity was $1.618 billion, while total assets equaled $29.483 billion. Rounding differences aside, these figures yield a leverage factor of 18 that is consistent with the implied leverage factor.

The Dupont formula reveals that State Street's seemingly low return on assets, at 1%, has been "geared up" to a figure that is consistent with the 18% strategic financial goal of the bank. With a leverage factor near 18, it should be apparent that anything the bank's managers can do to improve its operating efficiency — either through higher margins or asset turnover (AT) — will have a multiplied ROE effect. This happens because ROE is also related to the net profit margin (NPM) and the asset turnover ratio according to:

$$\text{ROE} = \text{ROA} \times \text{Leverage} = (\text{NPM} \times \text{AT}) \times \left(\frac{\text{A}}{\text{SE}}\right)$$

$$= (\text{NPM} \times \text{AT}) \times \left(\frac{1}{1 - \text{DR}}\right)$$

In this instance, ROA is expressed as the net profit margin (net income over revenue) times the firm's asset turnover — measured by the revenue-to-assets ratio. Moreover, the last expression in the ROE expression shows that the leverage factor, A/SE, can be written as the inverse of one-minus the debt ratio (DR). The corporate debt ratio in the Dupont formula results from dividing total liabilities (including a firm's current liabilities) by total assets.

## FUNDAMENTAL STOCK RETURN

Given that ROE sheds some key insights on how companies make money, the analyst may be wondering how to move from underlying company data to assessing the rate of return on the firm's common stock. Another meaningful company-based calculation for equity analysts arises from an understanding of the relationship between the *fundamental* return on a firm's stock (FSR) and its underlying return on equity.

The fundamental stock return is equal to the sum of the assessed dividend yield (*dy*) plus the expected internal capital generation rate, *icgr*.[5] In more formal terms, the firm's fundamental rate of return on stock can be estimated according to:

$$\text{FSR} = dy + icgr = \frac{d}{p} + (1 - \text{DPR}) \times \text{ROE} = \frac{d}{p} + \text{PBR} \times \text{ROE}$$

In this expression, DPR is the firm's dividend payout ratio, while d/p is the dividend yield on its outstanding common stock. In turn, PBR is the plowback ratio, measured by one minus DPR.

Since PBR is the fraction of earnings that are retained by the firm for investment in real assets, the fundamental stock return equation shows how growth is related to financial happenings at the company level. That is, the firm's internal capital generation rate (*icgr*) derives its value from the product of the fraction of earnings retained for future investment (PBR), which is a reflection of added equity capital resulting from re-investment of the firm's profit — times the estimated return that the firm's managers can generate on those retained earnings. ROE in the traditional realm of financial analysis is that likely return on the stockholders' equity.

## Illustration of the ROE-FSR Linkage

Let's return again to State Street Corporation to see how the investor can assess the fundamental stock return from knowledge of key financial ratios at the company level. Unlike most firms, it is interesting to see that the bank directly reports the internal capital generation rate, icgr, in its financial reports.[6] At 14.3%, this figure can be combined with State Street's annual dividend per share and year-end stock price to arrive at the fundamental return on the stock for 1996:

$$FSR = dy + icgr = \frac{0.76}{64.63} + 0.143 = 0.155 \text{ or } 15.5\%$$

With these developments, one now sees the financial implications of the ROE-FSR linkage. In particular, the internal capital generation rate can be expressed as the product of the plowback ratio, at 79% (alternatively, one minus DPR of 0.21), times the return on stockholders' equity (ROE) of 18.1%:

$$icgr = PBR \times ROE$$
$$= 0.79 \times 0.181 = 0.143 \text{ or } 14.3\%$$

Additionally, since ROE is the product of return on assets times the leverage factor, the bank's internal capital generation rate can be expressed as:

$$icgr = PBR \times \left[ ROA \times \left( \frac{A}{E} \right) \right] = 0.79 \times [0.01 \times 18.1] = 0.143$$

Thus, the 1996 Annual Report of State Street Corporation reports some meaningful figures to the shareholders — including ROE, leverage, the internal

---

[5] If one makes the convenient assumption that a firm's dividends and earnings grow at a *constant* rate each year over time, then the fundamental stock return described here is the same as the "internal rate of return (IRR)" on the company's stock. With variable growth, the IRR formula is, of course, the more appropriate representation of the *implied* return on a firm's stock, as it reflects that rate which sets the present value of anticipated future cash flows (dividends or otherwise) equal to the firm's current stock price. Variable growth models are covered in Chapter 8.

[6] See page 7 of the 1996 Annual Report of State Street Corporation.

capital generation rate, and the dividend payout ratio. There is, however, no formal attempt by the bank to show the linkage between the company accounting data and the fundamental rate of return on the stock.

## Coke's Classic "ROE Formula"

Before proceeding to look at traditional valuation measures, let's (for fun!) contrast State Street's 1996 ROE and fundamental stock return in the banking and financial services industry with that of Coca-Cola in the soft drinks and beverages sector.[7] At 56.7% (underlying data not shown), Coke's return on equity is not only dramatically higher than State Street's — due to higher growth opportunities — but the "packaging" of the ROE figures is noticeably different. In contrast with the bank, Coca-Cola's 1996 financial leverage multiplier (Assets/Stockholders' Equity) and return on assets were 2.625 and 21.6%, respectively. With these figures, Coke's classic "ROE-formula" consists of:

$$ROE = ROA \times Leverage = 0.216 \times 2.625 = 0.567 \text{ or } 56.7\%$$

Hence, the beverage firm's exceptional return on equity largely results from its ROA of 21.6%. This powerful ROA figure is fundamentally-related to Coke's ability to generate abnormal profits on its assets — as evidenced by an attractive net profit margin, 18.8%, in the presence of an asset turnover ratio of 1.15. From a comparative perspective, Coke's "classsic" ROE, 56.7%, is due to its *high* return on assets, while State Street's lower, yet still attractive ROE figure, 18.1%, is due to favorable profits being earned on a relatively *small* amount of bank equity capital — in the presence of their worldwide asset base of $29.483 billion.

## Coke's Fundamental Stock Return

The same FSR-ROE procedure can be used to link Coca-Cola's company data with its fundamental stock return. In 1996, the beverage firm's dividend yield was 1.1%, while the plowback and ROE ratios were 64% and 56.7%, respectively. With these figures, Coke's internal capital generation rate was 36.3%:

$$icgr = PBR \times ROE = 0.64 \times 0.567 = 0.363 \text{ or } 36.3\%$$

Additionally, upon adding the dividend yield, 1.1%, to the firm's estimated internal growth rate, one obtains Coke's 1996 fundamental stock return at 37.4%:

$$FSR = dy + icgr = 0.011 + 0.363 = 0.374 \text{ or } 37.4\%$$

With explosive growth, the beverage company's fundamental stock return is largely determined by its return on assets (or return to capital). For Coca-Cola, this means that ROE, *icgr*, and most importantly, *FSR*, are all primarily deter-

---

[7] Financial data used in the Coca-Cola illustration was obtained from a Value Line Report dated September 5, 1997.

mined by the two key components of ROA — including, the net profit margin and the asset turnover ratio. Company, industry, and economy-wide developments that cause these latter financial ratios to rise or fall for Coca-Cola will in turn influence the beverage firm's internal capital generation rate and return on equity.

## TRADITIONAL VALUATION MEASURES

In order to assess whether a firm's stock is mispriced, equity analysts often look at profit-to-valuation measures such as the price/earnings, price/cash flow, and price/book value ratios. This relative valuation assessment is important because investors should (1) look unfavorably at stocks of companies that are selling at *excessive* multiples of earnings or book value, while (2) they should look favorably at the securities of those firms that have *unjustifiably* had their stock price driven down too low relative to the company's fundamental earning potential. In the traditional view, stocks with abnormally high earnings/price, book/price, and dividend yields may be attractive buy opportunities while stocks of firms having excessively low earnings and book yields may be sell or short-sell opportunities.

To examine the price relative — or alternatively yield — concepts we'll use information listed in the 1996 Annual Report for State Street Corporation. The annual report to shareholders provides summary data that can be used to calculate some of the key valuation measures. The pertinent per share figures for the bank are shown in Exhibit 3. With knowledge of the bank's 1996 closing stock price, $64.63, we can convert the per share figures to some key valuation measures and yields as shown in Exhibit 4.

The obvious question at this point is how to interpret either the price relative or yield information. The investor should ask, for example, whether State Street's stock should be selling at 18 times earnings, as well as a multiple of 85 times its per share dividend. These price relatives may seem out of line since Value Line reports that bank stocks typically sell at 10 times earnings with a dividend yield that averages about 3%. If one views State Street as a typical "bank," then the stock is obviously overvalued due to the excessive price relatives and (therefore) abnormally low yields.

---

## Exhibit 3: State Street Corporation Selected Per Share Information at Year-End 1996

| Revenue per share[*] | $22.87 |
|---|---|
| Earnings per share | $3.59 |
| Dividends per share | $0.76 |
| Book value per share | $21.87 |
| Closing stock price | $64.63 |

* Using the "fully diluted shares" figure shown on page 7 of the 1996 Annual Report gives State Street's revenue per share at $22.87 ($1.882 billion/0.0823 billion shares).

Source: 1996 Annual Report, page 7.

### Exhibit 4: State Street Corporation Price Relatives and Yields at Year-End 1996

| Price/Revenue Ratio | Revenue Yield |
|---|---|
| 2.8× | 35.7% |
| Price/Earnings Ratio | Earnings Yield |
| 18× | 5.6% |
| Price/Dividend Ratio | Dividend Yield |
| 85× | 1.2% |
| Price/Book Ratio | Book Yield |
| 3× | 0.3% |

Data for calculations: Annual Report, page 7.

---

On the other hand, the 1996 Annual Report reveals that about 70% of State Street's revenue is generated from the high-growth "fee revenue" side of the business — namely, master trust/custody, global securities lending, securities processing, and global asset management. From this perspective, the seemingly high price relatives and low yields (dividend and earnings' yields, for examples) are a sign that investors were optimistic — although not necessarily overly so — about the firm's *future* growth opportunities in servicing financial assets world-wide. Also, State Street's 1996 loan-to-asset ratio is only 15%, while Value Line reports an average of about 55% for firms they cover in the banking sector. Hence, the observed price relatives and yield figures for State Street Corporation may be a *fundamental* way of saying that the company is not simply your typical "bank."

## ROLE OF ANALYST REPORTS

A company's annual report — and of course quarterly and other periodic reports — is a helpful source of information to see how a firm has performed during the most recent fiscal year and over time. However, when buying stocks, investors are most concerned with the firm's *future* revenue and earnings outlook in light of its historical experience. In this context, there are many sources of information that equity analysts can turn to when assessing the firm's likely growth prospects — including Bloomberg, First Call, IBES, Value Line, and Zacks. We'll use information from Value Line reports as a *guide* to showing how traditional-based financial metrics can be used to assess the likely performance of a company's stock.

Exhibit 5 shows a Value Line report for State Street Corporation dated September 5, 1997. Although there are numerous items of interest, it is helpful to get a "big picture" assessment of the bank's likely performance. In this context, the investor should consider asking the following performance-based questions when looking over the Value Line (or any other) report:

1. Do *you* like what you see in the historical price chart? Why?
2. How does Value Line score the company in terms of expected price performance and expected risk?

3. What are the firm's annualized growth rates in revenue, cash flow, earnings, dividends, book value, and assets?
4. What is the firm's return on equity and return on assets?
5. What is the company's fundamental stock return based on the underlying accounting data?
6. Is the firm's expected performance attractive in light of its current valuation and that of competitors?
7. What is the "rest of the story" in terms of other *quantitative* and *qualitative* considerations that might support, or shed conflicting light on, the firm's growth opportunities?

We address each of these questions below.

## Historical Price Chart

The historical price chart for State Street Corporation shows consistent movement upward over time. The price volatility about the Value Line trend line seems low, with the exception of three distinct declines in the bank's stock price — two of which were either market or sector based and one which was uniquely related to State Street specific happenings. In particular, Exhibit 5 shows that State Street stock dropped in tandem with the general market during the Crash of October 1987. After gaining positive momentum in the 1987 aftermath, the stock dropped again in late 1990 due to the market decline in the period preceding the Gulf Conflict as well as "problem loans" arising from a real estate crisis that had a significant impact on bank stocks more generally. However, State Street's precipitous decline (at 20%) in 1993 was due to an analyst's report pointing to heightened technology costs leading to an anticipated decline in the firm's projected return on equity (as mentioned before, a key measure used by State Street's management in measuring its corporate financial success).[8]

## Value Line Scoring

Price momentum and earnings momentum are two primary considerations in the Value Line scoring system on expected price performance which Value Line defines as *Timeliness*. Exhibit 5 shows that State Street receives a "1" on this measure which, on a scale of 1 to 5, represents the highest score that a stock can receive for expected price performance over the next 12 months. With respect to expected risk which Value Line calls safety, Value Line gives State Street Corporation an average score of "3." This may be due to the sharp price declines at the previously mentioned periods of time as well as the beta of 1.15. This beta risk measure suggests that if the general market were to decline by 10%, then State Street's stock would fall by about 11.5% (1.15 *times* the 10% market decline). Taken together, the Value Line "Timeliness" and "Safety"scores (as of September 1997) suggest that State Street's stock has *exceptional* near-term price potential in the presence of average price volatility.

---

[8] This latter observation is based on company research beyond the Value Line report shown in the text.

# Exhibit 5: Value Line Report for State Street Corporation

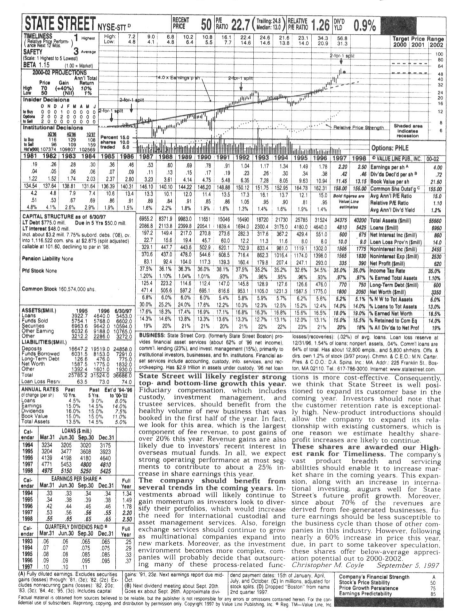

Source: Value Line Investment Survey, New York, NY.

### Exhibit 6: State Street Corporation Expected Internal Capital Generation Rates (%)

| Year | % All Dividends to Net Profit (% DPR) | Plowback Ratio (1-DPR) | % Earned Net Worth (ROE) | icgr %* |
|------|---------|---------|---------|---------|
| 1997 | 20 | 80 | 18 | 14.4 |
| 1998 | 18 | 82 | 19 | 15.6 |
| 2001** | 19 | 81 | 18.5 | 15.0 |

* icgr = (1 − All Dividends to Net Profit) × % Earned Net Worth
** Mid point of year-end values for years 2000-2002.
Estimates based on Value Line Report dated September 5, 1997

## Growth Rates

The upward price trend for State Street's stock shown in Exhibit 5, along with Value Line's optimistic future price assessment *must* in some sense be supported by the firm's underlying growth rates. As we learned from State Street's 1996 Annual Report, revenue over the 1991 to 1996 years was growing at an annualized rate of 15.7%. A look at the *Annual Rates* box in the Value Line report shows that over the past five years the bank's earnings, dividends, book value, and assets were all growing on the order of 14% to 15% per annum. This favorable growth finding is also consistent with the bank's performance over the past 10 years, although the forward-looking Value Line earnings and asset growth estimates show variability out to the millennium (00-'02 growth estimates).

## Return on Equity and Assets

The earnings growth estimate for State Street Corporation, 14%, for year-end 2001 (mid point of 00-'02 years) combined with the book value and asset growth rate estimates — at 11% and 5%, respectively — implies that the bank will be using relatively less "capital" to generate a strong return on equity and assets for the future. For instance, Value Line reports that ROE (*% Earned Net Worth*) should rise from 16.5% at year-end 1996 up to 19% for year-end 1998, while settling at 18.5% out to the year 2001. Likewise, their estimates reveal that State Street's return on assets (*% Earned Total Assets*) should rise from 0.93% (a rate that is below the 1% figure for the banking industry) up to 1.10% by year-end 2001 in the presence of relatively *lower* asset growth of 5%.

## Fundamental Stock Return

With knowledge of the anticipated dividend yield along with the internal capital generation rate, we can assess the fundamental return on State Street stock given the underlying company data reported by Value Line. As shown before, the internal capital generation rate is equal to the corporate plowback ratio times the firm's return on equity. Exhibit 6 shows these forecast calculations using Value Line data for the years 1997, 1998, and 2001.

## Exhibit 7: State Street Corporation Fundamental Stock Returns (FSR %)

| Year | Dividend Yield % (dy%) | Internal Capital Generation Rate (icgr%) | Fundamental Stock Return (FSR%) * |
|------|------------------------|------------------------------------------|-----------------------------------|
| 1997 | 0.9 | 14.4 | 15.3 |
| 1998 | 0.9 | 15.6 | 16.5 |
| 2001** | 1.2 | 15.0 | 16.2 |

* FSR% = dy% + icgr%
** Mid point of year-end values for years 2000-2002.

---

If, for convenience, we assume a dividend yield of 0.9% for both 1997 (see the top of the Value Line report) and 1998, along with the average annual dividend yield of 1.2% shown on the Value Line report to the year 2001, we can obtain estimates of the fundamental stock return (FSR%) for State Street Corporation as revealed in the calculations shown in Exhibit 7.

Not surprisingly, the forward-looking company data obtained from a Value Line report shows that most of State Street's fundamental stock return is based on its *strong* internal capital generation rate of about 15% per annum. This results from the combination of a high plowback of earnings ratio — running at about 80% — along with the bank's strong projected return on equity figures hovering around 18.5% out to the millenium.

## Valuation Considerations

State Street's internal capital generation rate and fundamental stock return projections look attractive for the near future. However, it's also important to look at these performance projections *relative* to the price that one has to pay for the stock — as one of the goals in active investing is to avoid overpaying for the firm's anticipated future growth. From a performance/valuation perspective, Exhibit 8 shows the internal capital generation rates for State Street along with the corresponding growth figures for some of its competors and the relevant price-to-book value ratios. The Value Line figures for Bank of New York are included in the equity analysis for two reasons: (1) like State Street Corporation, Bank of New York has a "formidable" securities processing operation, and (2) it was building a position in State Street stock for possible acquisition in early 1997. Northern Trust is shown here as a representative competitor of State Street because of its "booming" asset management and custody businesses.

Exhibit 8 shows that State Street's price-to-book value ratio is 4.4. If the Value Line estimate of book value is correct, then investors are being asked to pay $4.40 for every $1 of "book equity capital" — measured by total bank assets *net* of both its short-term liabilities (primarily deposits, fed funds purchased, and repurchase agreements) and the small amount of long-term liabilities.[9] On a com-

---

[9] Like other banks, State Street uses repurchase agreements (actually, "reverse repos") as a form of short-term financing.

parative basis, State Street's price/book ratio, 4.4, is higher than the corresponding price relatives for Bank of New York and Northern Trust Company, at 3.2 and 4.1, respectively. Although State Street has the highest price/book ratio among the three banks shown in Exhibit 8, this does not necessarily mean that the stock is overvalued — since the higher price/book ratio may be a sign of the firm's strong expected future growth opportunities.

At 3.5, it's interesting to see that State Street's fundamental stock return *per* unit price/book ratio is (rounding differences aside) the same as the performance-to-relative valuation measure for Northern Trust Company. This is due to the former bank's attractive *FSR* that helps offset its seemingly high price-to-book value ratio. Along this line, the anticipated internal capital generation rate for State Street Corporation is the highest among the three banks shown in Exhibit 8. Moreover, the favorable internal capital generation rate for State Street results from its attractive ROE projection, at 18%, combined with the highest plowback ratio, 80%, among the competing banks under consideration.

However, Exhibit 8 suggests that as of September 1997, Bank of New York (BNY) was the best anticipated "buy" opportunity among the three reported banks. In this context, BNY has the highest return on equity projection, 21%, along with an internal capital generation rate, 14.1%, that bests that of Northern Trust Company. Strong anticipated performance combined with the *lowest* of price/book ratios, 3.2, reveals that BNY has the *highest* fundamental stock return performance *per* unit valuation relative, FSR/(P/BV) ratio at 5.1. On balance, the security selection ranking using this form of traditional analysis places BNY on top of the list followed by State Street Corporation and Northern Trust Company holding equal rank because of their similar performance-to-relative value scores.

## Exhibit 8: Bank Valuation Analysis (1997E) *

| Company: | Bank of New York | Northern Trust Company | State Street Corporation |
|---|---|---|---|
| *Performance %:* | | | |
| Plowback Ratio % | 67.0 | 73.0 | 80.0 |
| Return on Equity % | 21.0 | 18.0 | 18.0 |
| Internal Capital Generation Rate % | 14.1 | 13.1 | 14.4 |
| Dividend Yield % | 2.2 | 1.4 | 0.9 |
| Fundamental Stock Return (FSR) % | 16.3 | 14.5 | 15.3 |
| *Valuation:* | | | |
| Stock Price | 46.0 | 59.0 | 50.0** |
| Book Value Per Share | 14.2 | 14.4 | 11.5 |
| Price/Book Value | 3.2 | 4.1 | 4.4 |
| *Performance/Valuation:* | | | |
| FSR/(P/BV) | 5.1 | 3.5 | 3.5 |

\* Data Source: Value Line reports dated September 5, 1997.
\*\* Reflects 2 for 1 stock split incurred during first quarter of 1997.

## "The Rest of the Story"

In addition to looking at the "numbers," the analyst should make an assessment of any *qualitative* benefits or costs that may impact the firm's stock performance. In this context, the analyst should look at the firm's underlying products as well as management's committment to producing shareholder value. With respect to State Street's product line, the bank goes "to the head of the class" with its state-of-the-art offerings in global custody/master trust, global securities lending, securities processing, and global asset management services, respectively. Commenting on State Street's financial product line, CEO Marshall Carter and COO David Spina have on several occasions stated that the bank is committed to being the "number 1" servicer of financial assets worldwide.

In this context, State Street's committment to shareholders is clearly evidenced in the opening statements of the 1996 Letter to the Stockholders by CEO Carter and COO Spina:[10]

> State Street's consistently strong performance is attributable to the successful execution of our strategies for creating stockholder value...

Management's words of course should be a reflection of their concrete actions and performance realities.[11] On this score, Exhibit 9 shows that State Street Corporation has in fact produced considerable shareholder value over time. Indeed, an initial investment of $10,000 in the bank's stock on October 31, 1987 (just after Black Monday, October 19) grew to $118,345 as of October 31, 1997. At 28.03%, the 10-year compound annual return on State Street stock was higher than the (already attractive) S&P 500 return of 17.22% per annum, as well as the noticeably *lower* annualized return, at only 11.62%, earned on bank stocks covered in the Value Line universe.

## ESTIMATING THE REQUIRED RETURN

As we will shortly see in the "value-based" metrics chapter, one of the problems with the traditional approach to security analysis is that it doesn't make a formal connection between the expected return on a stock and its inherent risk. For example, State Street's 1996 Annual Report provides investors with meaningful information about the banking and financial service firm's ROE *and* internal capital generation rate. Yet, nothing is shown in the report about how this information can be used by analysts to see if the firm's fundamental stock return is greater than some pre-established benchmark, as formally measured by the expected or *required* return on the firm's outstand-

---

[10] State Street Annual Report, p.3

[11] It's interesting to see that State Street Corporation uses traditional financial metrics — like revenue/earnings growth rates and ROE — to emphasize the importance of creating shareholder value added. Although the next chapter focuses on "value-based" measures of corporate financial success, it's important to recognize that managerial actions combined with innovative strategic decisions may be the "real key" to corporate financial success.

ing stock. This omission is important because the fundamental stock return is based on underlying accounting data — such as plowback ratio and ROE — while the required return is based (or should be) on an equilibrium model of return and risk.[12]

One simple, yet formal approach to estimating the expected return is obtained by using the capital asset pricing model (CAPM). In this context, the required return on the stock is estimated according to:

$$ER = R_f + MRP \times Beta$$

where, $R_f$ is the risk-free rate of interest, MRP is the expected market risk premium, and beta measures the systematic or relative risk of the firm's stock. When beta is greater than unity — as in the case of *growth* stocks — the expected return on the stock is higher than that projected for the market portfolio. Conversely, when beta is less than one — most notably for value stocks — the required or expected stock return (ER), falls short of the anticipated return on the representative market portfolio (M).

## Exhibit 9: Growth of $10,000 Investment for State Street Corporation

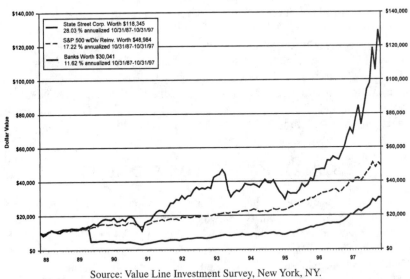

Source: Value Line Investment Survey, New York, NY.

[12] In view of the many benefits of the traditional approach to security analysis, the investor should realize that one of its major limitations is that there is no formal mechanism which describes the *equilibrium* relationship between expected return and risk. Without this, the investor is left in a quandary about the appropriate benchmark that a measure like the fundamental stock return should be compared with to see if a stock provides an appropriate "risk-adjusted" return in the marketplace.

Along this line, Sharpe's Capital Asset Pricing Model (CAPM) is one of the most widely known *equilibrium* approaches to understanding the expected return on a firm's stock. Although CAPM helps resolve the expected return void in traditional financial analysis, the single-factor market model has come under significant empirical challenges in recent years.

## Exhibit 10: Fundamental Stock Return versus CAPM: Selected Company Estimates for 1997

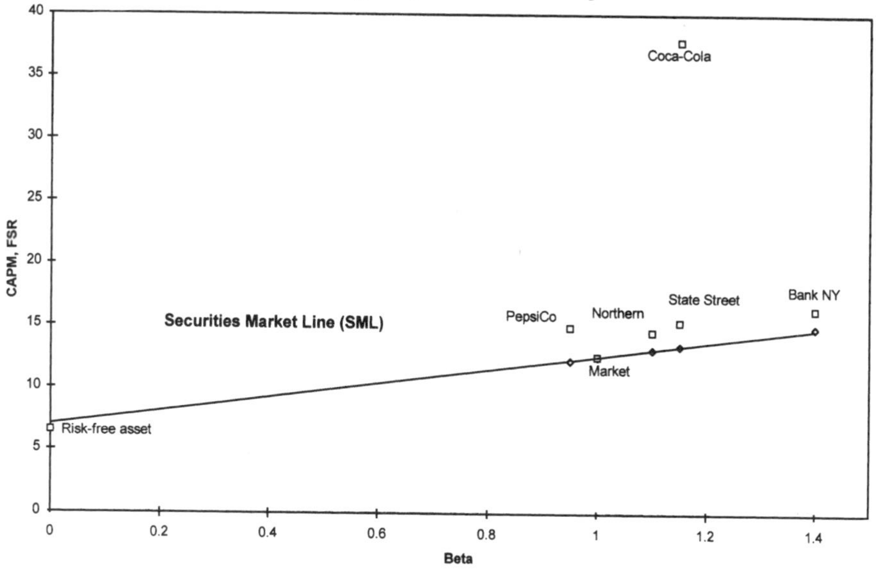

With a risk-free rate of 6.5%, and a market risk premium of 6%, that places the expected return on the market portfolio at 12.5%. In turn, State Street Corporation — with a beta of 1.15 — has a CAPM expected return of 13.4%. Although the bank's required return on its stock exceeds the market's anticipated return, the 13.4% CAPM figure falls *below* the 1997 anticipated stock return, at 15.3%, that is *implied* by the company's underlying fundamentals. In this sense, active investors were not only expecting State Street stock to outperform the general market in 1997 — as measured by the anticipated return performance on an investable market fund like Vanguard's S&P 500 product — but they were also expecting it — due to the relatively attractive company fundamentals — to outperform the required rate of return, at 13.4%, that was associated with this banking company's beta risk class.

## The Combined Result: *FSR*-versus-CAPM

Exhibit 10 provides a display of fundamental stock returns versus CAPM returns for three banks — including Bank of New York, Northern Trust Company, and State Street Corporation — as well as the FSR-CAPM relationship for two powerful beverage firms — namely Coca-Cola and PepsiCo, Inc. In Exhibit 10, the vertical axis reveals the *FSR* and CAPM values for the banking and softdrinks' companies respectively, as well as the projected return to a market index fund such as Vanguard's Index 500. The horizontal axis reports the relative risk, or beta, measures for the selected firms and the market index (at unity). Also, the line labeled SML, for Securities Market Line, represents *unlevered* and *levered* return combinations of the risk-free asset and the market portfolio, measured in expected return and beta-risk space. [13]

In principle, securities with fundamental stock returns that exceed the expected return from the SML are attractive investments because their ROE-induced growth prospects make an abnormally-positive contribution to their implied stock returns. Likewise, any stock whose FSR falls short of the one-factor CAPM benchmark is considered unattractive in this security selection framework. This happens because the sum of its expected dividend yield and internal capital generation rate is not sufficiently high enough for the company's fundamental stock return to lie either above *or* on the Securities Market Line.

In effect, the FSR-CAPM linked model indicates that investors should buy securities of those firms having a fundamental stock return that lies above the CAPM line, as their prices seem low when evaluated in terms of the firm's underlying earnings capabilities. In contrast, they should sell or possibly short-sell the shares of companies with FSR's that falls below the SML, because stock price appears to be high when measured relative to the firm's dividend yield and anticipated growth opportunities. By inference, stocks that lie on the SML are priced "just right," in the sense that their fundamental return could be *synthetically* replicated with a levered or unlevered passive-index fund.

With our previous assumptions about the risk-free rate and market risk premium, Exhibit 10 shows the 12.5% expected return on the market portfolio. Based on projected positive internal growth opportunities, the three bank stocks looked like attractive *buy* opportunities as of September 1997. At 16.3%, the exhibit shows that Bank of New York's fundamental stock return is higher than the CAPM return, 14.9%, for a volatile security having a beta of 1.4. Northern Trust's FSR, at 14.5%, is higher than the albeit lower CAPM return for a stock with a beta estimate of 1.1. Indeed, when risk is factored into the analysis, it's interesting to see that Bank of New York's fundamental stock return *per* unit beta, 11.6, is actually lower than the corresponding risk-adjusted FSR's for State Street Corporation and Northern Trust Company, at 13.3 and 13.2, respectively.[14]

Within the beverage sector, Exhibit 10 shows that Coca-Cola was the clear expected performance winner over PepsiCo. With a fundamental stock return projection for 1997 of 37.9%, Coke easily outperforms the CAPM return of 13.4% for a security having a beta of 1.15. Looking across the beverage and banking sectors at this systematic risk level, it's interesting to see that *both* Coca-Cola and State Street Corporation would be efficiently priced with an expected annual return of 13.4% — even though they operate in two different sectors of the econ-

---

[13] The Treynor index can be used to assess the slope of the SML. We cover this performance ratio in Chapter 14.

[14] We are now getting into performance measurement issues that are beyond the scope of this chapter. We will cover *risk-adjusted* performance measures like the Sharpe index, Treynor index, and the Jensen index in Chapter 14.

omy.[15] Again though, Coke is clearly the more attractive opportunity as its fundamental stock return is considerably higher than that observed for State Street Corporation at the same beta risk level. Moreover, at 37.9%, the powerful beverage firm's fundamental stock return is noticeably higher than the anticipated return that could be achieved by an equivalent-risk *levered* combination of the risk-free asset and the market portfolio.[16]

## TRADITIONAL ROLE OF LEVERAGE

Equity analysts often look at corporate leverage ratios — such as debt-to-equity and debt-to-asset ratios — when evaluating a firm's securities. In the traditional model, leverage can be value-increasing because higher levels of corporate debt lead to both higher ROE and per-share-earnings. However, professional investors are also keenly aware that *excessive* amounts of debt beyond some company *target* level may be wealth-destroying for the shareholders. This negative side of debt is generally due to abnormal earnings volatility associated with a rising probability of corporate bankruptcy and default.[17]

As an example of the positive view of corporate debt policy, an investor need only consider the reference in the financial media to the term "leverage buyouts," with the implication that there exists a doubly beneficial gain to the shareholders resulting from both the buyout itself and the particular form of corporate debt financing — in many instances with high yield bonds of low investment quality. On the notion that firms have an "optimal capital structure," the investor may also recall the popular media's reference to excessive amounts of corporate debt that was issued by U.S. corporations in the 1980s, with the leftover capital structure implication that substantial deleveraging benefits were available to shareholders for the 1990s. [18]

The traditional view that a larger proportion of corporate debt in the firm's capital structure leads to *higher* profitability ratios can be seen in the context of the Dupont formula. In this context, recall that return on equity (ROE) can

---

[15] This of course presumes that investors use the single-factor CAPM in setting equilibrium security prices — and, therefore, equilibrium expected returns.

[16] With a Value-Line beta of 1.4, it's interesting to see that Bank of New York stock has the highest expected (CAPM) return among the companies shown in Exhibit 10. The bank's fundamental stock return is still sufficient enough though to cover the required return on the firm's outstanding common stock.

[17] It is interesting to note that "financial leverage" is one of the residual or "common factors" that drive security and portfolio returns in BARRA's *fundamental* factor model. The pricing implications of this well-known multi-factor model are described in Chapter 9.

[18] The traditional view of corporate debt policy clashes significantly with the Miller-Modigliani (M&M) view. In the equilibrium model described by M&M, corporate leverage *per se* has no effect whatsoever on the market value of the firm and its outstanding shares. For their classic article on the valuation of corporate debt policy, see Franco Modigliani and Merton H. Miller, "The Cost of Capital, Corporation Finance, and the Theory of Investment," *American Economic Review* (June 1958).

be expressed in terms of return on assets (ROA) and the inverse of one minus the corporate debt ratio according to:

$$\text{ROE} = \frac{\text{ROA}}{1 - (\text{D}/\text{A})}$$

where ROA is the return on assets ratio, and D/A is the debt-to-asset measure of corporate leverage.

With a proportionately higher level of fixed financial obligations in the firm's capital structure, the Dupont formula shows that ROE goes up — since the denominator in the return on equity expression falls as D/A rises. Likewise, as debt/asset ratio declines relative to the firm's return on assets, its return on equity (ROE) goes down — as the denominator in the Dupont formula now goes up. In effect, when debt/asset ratio rises relative to ROA, a *smaller* amount of equity capital is now generating the same amount of corporate profitability — thus the shareholder return on equity rises. A declining return on equity (ROE) effect of course happens when a *larger* equity base is earning the same amount of after-tax corporate profit.

## ROE and Leverage: A Numerical Illustration

As a simple example of the ROE and corporate debt linkage, assume that the firm's after-tax profit is $10, and its asset base is $100. Also assume that the firm is initially equity financed such that debt/asset ratio is, for all practical purposes, zero. With 100% equity financing, the *unlevered* firm's return on equity (ROE) is obviously the same as its ROA, at 10%:[19]

$$\text{ROE} = \frac{0.1}{1 - 0} = 0.1 \text{ or } 10\%$$

Let's now assume that the firm's corporate treasurer decides to engage in a financing strategy that effectively swaps the equity shares for more debt, such that D/A rises to say, 40%. With this *pure* capital structure change, the firm's return on equity rises from 10% to 16.7%:[20]

$$\text{ROE} = \frac{0.1}{1 - 0.4} = 0.167 \text{ or } 16.7\%$$

As the firm moves to what it perceives to be its optimal capital structure, we see that the stockholder's ratio of profit-to-equity capital goes up. With this leverage

---

[19] The concept of *unlevered* firms (companies that finance growth primarily with equity — like technology firms) and *levered* firms (companies that finance growth with debt) is a cornerstone of the value-based metrics chapter that follows.

[20] Based on Morningstar figures, the "debt to capital" ratio for companies in the S&P 500 was about 43% as of September 1997. The equity capitalization for the "average firm" in this large cap index was around $32 billion at that time.

Based on the capital structure discussion in the text, one is left wondering whether the 43% debt/capital ratio is the "optimal" capital structure for the U.S. economy — or whether the 43% leverage factor is a statistical artifact (along the M&M lines) with no significant pricing implications.

change, it can also be shown that the firm's per-share earnings would rise as well. Consequently, in the traditional view, investors should be willing to pay more for the firm's now seemingly dearer shares.

## Target Capital Structure: A Graphical Depiction

Exhibit 11 shows the pricing implications of the traditional capital structure position in corporate valuation (vertical axis) and leverage (horizontal axis) space. In the exhibit, $V_u$ is the market value of the *unlevered* firm — a firm having no long-term debt outstanding — while $V_l$ denotes the *levered* firm's corporate value. When the debt-to-asset ratio rises from zero to the target level of, say, 40%, the market value of the levered firm and its outstanding shares go up. In this corporate debt range, stock price rises as the presumably "good news" to the shareholders resulting from the positive ROE and earnings-per-share happenings — with a corresponding *small* change in perceived equity risk — causes investors to pay more for the firm's outstanding shares.[21]

### Exhibit 11: Traditional Capital Structure Model

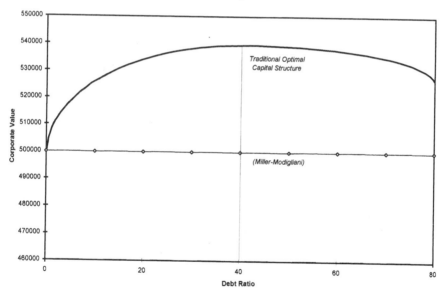

---

[21] In the Modigliani-Miller model, the higher EPS generated by higher corporate leverage is offset by a rise in the investor's required rate of return (in CAPM, for example, beta is linearly related to leverage) on the firm's outstanding stock. Consequently, in a *perfect* capital market, the company's stock price remains *unchanged* in the presence of the debt-induced rise in EPS and ROE. In their economic profit framework, corporate value is only impacted by real growth opportunities as opposed to leverage policies which may give investors the illusion of value creation.

## Exhibit 12: ROE Impact of Corporate Debt Policy in a Changing Economy

| | Corporate Debt Ratio * | | | | | | | |
|---|---|---|---|---|---|---|---|---|
| | 0.0% | 10% | 20% | 30% | 40% | 50% | 60% | 70% |
| | ROE % | | | | | | | |
| Expansion: ROA = 10% | 10 | 11.1 | 12.5 | 14.3 | 16.7 | 20 | 25 | 33.3 |
| Contraction: ROA = -10% | −10 | −11.1 | −12.5 | −14.3 | −16.7 | −20 | −25 | −33.3 |

\* The average "debt/cap" ratio for S&P 500 firms at September 1997 was 43%.

On the other hand, if debt-to-asset ratio exceeds the 40% leverage target (see Exhibit 11), then stock price and firm value *falls* as the heightened financial risk — due to ever-rising fixed obligations that place the firm in financial jeopardy — offsets the leverage-induced ROE and per-share-earnings benefits to the shareholders. With a 60% debt load, for example, the corporate managers have pushed debt *beyond* the optimal level, and should therefore engage in "delevering" activities that effectively swap bonds for more equity shares. Moreover, if the 40% debt level is in fact an optimal one, then stock price declines with any sizable movement to the left *or* right of this target capital structure position.

## Financial Risk Considerations

The Dupont formula can also be used to illustrate the underlying volatility of return on equity at varying debt levels. Exhibit 12 shows the projected return on equity (ROE) ratios with corporate debt levels ranging from zero to 70% in the presence of return on asset ratios varying from 10% to −10%, respectively. As business expands or contracts — that is, ROA goes from 10% down to −10%, respectively — with a 10% debt load, the exhibit shows that ROE fluctuates from 11.1% on the high side down to −11.1% on the downside.

Exhibit 12 also shows that with an economywide debt load of 40%, the ROE numbers range from 16.7% down to −16.7%. As the economy expands or contracts with a 60% debt load, the stockholders' return on equity is even more volatile, with ROE figures ranging from 25% to −25%. On balance, the exhibit reveals that increasing leverage in good times conveys positive benefits to the shareholders, while rising corporate debt loads in bad times is a source of heightened volatility and financial concern. In an attempt to take advance of these leverage swings though, the investor may reap windfall capital gains by buying into the securities of firms with reasonable amounts of debt outstanding in anticipation of an expansionary economy, while trading out of those companies whose securities — namely, the stocks of consumer durable and "industrial cyclical" firms — will be penalized by abnormal levels of corporate debt in a slow growth to recessionary economy.

## Caveats

As a cautionary word on the pricing role of corporate debt policy, it may seem odd that investors should somehow feel better off with higher leverage, even though the firm's return on assets (or capital) remains constant at, say, 10%. This brings up a hopefully obvious point in equity securities valuation. For unless the corporate debt change is associated with a rise in real profitability (due to cash flow benefits from a higher debt-tax subsidy) or a perceived decline in equity risk (when, for example, the firm moves from a position of too much debt back to its target level) then nothing of real significance has changed for the shareholders. Without a meaningful change, investors have little incentive to pay a higher (or lower) price for the firm's shares due to leverage changes *per se*. Moreover, it can be shown from an efficient markets perspective that the stockholder benefits resulting from higher corporate leverage can be offset by a *rise* in the expected (or required) rate of return on the firm's common stock.

## SUMMARY

This chapter looks at performance and valuation measures that are often used in traditional fundamental analysis. Financial measures like growth in revenue, earnings, and book value — as well as return on equity (ROE) and asset ratios — are at the heart of this bottom up approach to security analysis. Along this line, the Dupont formula goes a long way in showing how profitability and leverage changes at the company level impact — either positively or negatively — the shareholders' return on equity capital. Likewise, valuation measures such as price/earnings and price/book value ratios can be used by equity analysts to see if a company's internal growth opportunities are correctly priced in the marketplace. In this context, active investors should avoid overpaying for the firm's perceived future growth opportunities, while they should consider buying those securities where stock price has been incorrectly driven down to a level that is inconsistent with the firm's fundamental earning potential.

We learned that with knowledge of a firm's return on equity and corporate plowback ratio, it is possible to estimate its internal capital generation rate. Upon adding this projected growth figure to the company's estimated dividend yield, the investor obtains the fundamental rate of return on the firm's common stock. From a security selection viewpoint, it was argued that if the fundamental stock return is greater than (CAPM) required return, then the stock price seems low when measured relative to the firm's revenue and earnings growth opportunities. On the other hand if the fundamental stock return falls short of the required return, then the stock appears to be overvalued. Consequently, the investor should consider selling or short-selling, if permitted, these presumably mispriced shares. In this expected return-risk framework, the firm's common stock is priced just right when the projected fundamental stock return equals the required rate of return.

We also examined the traditional valuation role of corporate debt policy. In general, this view holds that pricing gains are available to security holders of those firms that are moving toward their "optimal capital structure," while share price declines are imposed on investors when the firm moves away from the "just right" mix of corporate debt and equity capital. A word of caution was issued to equity analysts when examining the pricing role of corporate debt policy *per se*. In this context, it was noted that equity analysts needs to figure out whether a seemingly favorable change in ROE is due to changes in the firm's real growth opportunities, or possibly due to an *illusionary* shareholder benefit resulting from rising corporate debt — *especially* when the firm's corporate leverage goes beyond the target level.

It seems reasonable to say that a "value-enhancing" return on equity change results from increased profitability on the firm's existing (*and* future) assets in the presence of a relatively stable leverage ratio. The source of beneficial return on assets (ROA) comes from a higher expected net profit margin (NPM) and asset turnover ratio. Depending on where the firm is currently positioned relative to its "optimal capital structure," questionable ROE and per share earnings occurrences may be associated with increases (or decreases) in a variety of corporate debt ratios, including debt/asset, debt/equity, and debt-to-capital ratios, respectively. We also learned that volatility in the underlying economy can impact the valuation of firms and industries having varying degrees of corporate leverage in disproportionate ways.

# QUESTIONS

1. What is traditional fundamental analysis?

2. a. What is the Dupont formula?
   b. Why is the Dupont formula an important research tool when evaluating a company's return on equity (ROE)?

3. a. What is the internal capital generation rate (icgr)?
   b. What is the fundamental stock return (FSR)?
   c. What is the difference between the concept of fundamental stock return (FSR) and expected CAPM return?

4. Suppose that you are evaluating the stocks of two companies having the same return on equity (ROE). Use the Dupont formula to explain (a) why these companies may differ significantly in financial terms even though they have the same ROE, and (b) why in financial terms the two companies may operate in entirely different sectors of the economy — technology and financial service sectors, for example. Be sure to discuss the relationship between a company's return on assets (ROA) and its implied leverage factor in your ROE explanations.

5. Use the following information to calculate the 1998 financial ratios listed below for ABC Energy Corporation.
   Selected financial information for ABC Energy Corporation. All dollar figures are in $000.

|  |  |
|---|---|
| *Balance Sheet:* |  |
| Total Assets | $3600 |
| Stockholder's Equity | $2000 |
| Shares Outstanding (000) | 70 |
|  |  |
| *Income Statement:* |  |
| Revenue | $3200 |
| Net Income | $300 |
| Dividends | $120 |
|  |  |
| *Market Information:* |  |
| Price/Earnings Ratio | 10× |
| Beta | 0.8 |
| Market Risk Premium | 5.0% |
| Risk-free Rate | 5.0% |

a. Calculate:

    i. net profit margin
    ii. Asset turnover

iii. Return on assets (use your results from parts a and b)

iv. Leverage

v. Return on equity (Dupont approach)

vi. Dividend yield*

vii. Plowback ratio (PBR)

viii. Internal capital generation rate (icgr)

ix. Fundamental stock return (FSR)

x. Expected CAPM return

* A simple estimate of ABC Energy Corp's stock price is obtained by multiplying the price/earnings ratio by earnings per share.

b. Based on an overall assessment of the fundamental stock return (FSR) versus the expected CAPM return, does the stock of ABC Energy Corporation appear to be an attractive or unattractive investment? Explain why.

6. The "just right" mix of debt versus equity on a company's balance sheet is a controversial issue in the study of finance. What is the traditional view of corporate debt policy on the valuation of the firm and its outstanding equity shares, and why should a portfolio manager be concerned about the leverage issue in the evaluation of equity securities? (Hint: recall the valuation impact of corporate leverage shown in Exhibit 11.)

7. Since technology firms typically finance their growth with 100% equity — via retained earnings and new stock issues — does it follow that these firms are missing a strategic way of increasing the value of their shares by foregoing debt on their corporate balance sheets?

8. Use the Value Line report on the next page for Intel Corporation (dated April 23, 1999) to answer the following questions regarding the financial success of this well-known producer of computer chips.

a. Do you like what you see in the historical price chart for Intel? Why?

b. How does Value Line score Intel's common stock in terms of expected price performance (*Timeliness*) and expected risk (conversely, *Safety*)? What do these ratings mean?

c. What is Intel's annualized growth rate in sales, cash flow, earnings, and book value? Compare the 10-year and 5-year growth rates reported on the Value Line report in answering this question.

d. What is Intel's estimated ROE ("Return on Shareholders Equity," shown in table) and return on total capital ("Return on Total Capital") for years 1999 and 2000? Why are these company performance ratios similar?

e. How does Intel finance its growth opportunities? Specifically, would you classify this technology firm as an "unlevered" or "levered" firm? Why?

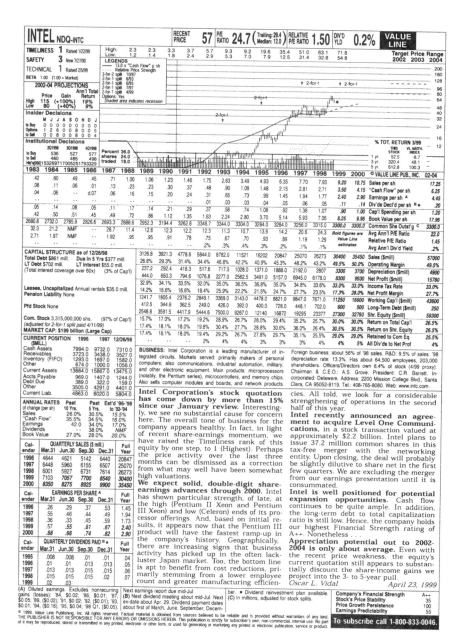

To subscribe call 1-800-833-0046.

f. What is Intel's fundamental stock return (FSR) for year 2000? How does this compare to Intel's required return using CAPM? (Assume a risk-free rate of 5% and a market risk premium of 5%)?

g. Is Intel's expected stock performance attractive in light of its current valuation and that of its competitors? Assume that the price/earnings ratio of related technology firms ranged from 30× to 35× at the Value Line report date.

h. What is the "rest of the story" in terms of other quantitative and qualitative considerations that might support, or shed conflicting light on, your fundamental assessment of Intel's future growth opportunities?

i. Based on your traditional fundamental analysis, how would you score Intel for "Timeliness" and "Safety" as of the Value Line report date?

# Chapter 7

# Security Analysis Using Value-Based Metrics

The world of security analysis is undergoing a revolution of sorts with increased focus on "value-based" metrics that are designed to give shareholders their due. Chief among these measures of corporate financial success is a metric called *economic value added* (EVA). EVA and related value-based measures like *cash flow return on investment* (CFROI) are now making significant inroads into the realm of security analysis and equity portfolio management. These metrics are also paving the way for a "modern" school of equity fundamental analysis that departs from the traditional method, with its prior focus on accounting-based measures like earnings per share (EPS) and return on equity (ROE).[1]

## VALUE-BASED METRICS: MOTIVATION

Although competing measures exist, value-based metrics emphasize the importance of giving *shareholders* their due. The theory behind these measures of corporate financial success is quite simple and compelling: when investors contribute moneys to a firm, they expect to earn a return on those contributed funds which is commensurate with the risk. The firm's managers are thereby charged to invest in real assets (both physical and human) having a return on invested capital that exceeds the overall cost of capital. As recently explained by one of the authors, wealth creating firms have positive residual profitability, while wealth wasters lose market value because their productive returns fall short of the overall cost of debt *and* equity capital. Indeed, wealth destroyers may lose market value even though their after-tax return on invested capital exceeds the cost of corporate debt financing.[2]

---

[1] EVA® is a registered trademark of Stern Stewart & Co. For insightful discussions of their economic profit measure along with many applications in a corporate finance setting, see G. Bennett Stewart III, *The Quest for Value* (New York: Harper Collins, 1991) and Al Ehrbar, *EVA: The Real Key to Creating Wealth* (New York: John Wiley & Sons, Inc., 1998).

CFROI® is a value-based metric (in percentage form, much like an IRR) developed by HOLT Value Associates and promoted by HOLT, Boston Consulting Group (BCG), and Deloitte & Touche. For a rigorous discussion of CFROI with investment applications, see Bartley J. Madden, *CFROI Valuation: A Total Systems Approach to Valuing the Firm* (Reed Educational and Professional Publishing, Ltd., 1998).

[2] James L. Grant, *Foundations of Economic Value Added* (New Hope, PA: Frank J. Fabozzi Associates, 1997).

## Current Interest in Value-Based Metrics

This heightened awareness among corporate managers that "profit" should be measured *net* of the investor's opportunity cost is hardly a new concept to economists. In fact, it dates back to the economic profit notion developed by Alfred Marshall, the famous Cambridge economist, over 100 years ago.[3] Having recognized that, one is left wondering about the source of today's rapidly growing interest in value-based metrics since (1) these concepts have been known to the business and financial communities for many years, and (2) capital markets in the United States and abroad seemed to have performed quite well over the years in the absence of such *formal* measures of corporate financial success.

There are at least *three* developments that have led to the rising utilization of value-based metrics by corporate managers and investors in recent years. As David Young of INSEAD points out, during the 1980s — and still continuing at the time of this writing — there has been a significant deregulation of *commercial* markets, starting in the United States and eventually spreading to the developed and emerging markets of Europe.[4] With deregulation comes competition and innovation as new firms have entry opportunities that were previously blocked by arcane governmental regulations and product market imperfections. Also, old or existing firms must change their inefficient ways since consumers can buy from competing firms that offer either better quality for the same price, or possibly lower prices for the same quality of product.

Second, the growing interest in value-based metrics is due in large part to the deregulation of *financial* markets in the United States and abroad. With open capital markets, investors — just like consumers with added opportunities in product markets — can shop around the world for companies that offer the best "risk-adjusted" expected returns on their outstanding (debt and equity) securities. Indeed with competitive capital markets worldwide, the financial success (or failure) of companies, industries, and even entire nations is impacted by the willingness of corporate (and even governmental) managers to embrace *value-based* principles of wealth maximization that emphasize giving the firm's owners their due.

Also, today's growing interest in value-based metrics is supported by Nobel prize-winning economic research on the academic front — including, for examples, George Stigler's work on industrial re-organization to Merton Miller's and Franco Modigliani's pioneering work on the theory of the firm and the irrelevance of corporate debt policy in competitive or well-functioning capital markets. In the famous "M&M" model — developed originally in 1958 with a significant enhancement by Miller in 1977 — they argue that the wealth-effect of corporate investment-production decisions lies *primarily* in the ability of the firm's manag-

---

[3] Alfred Marshall, *Principles of Economics* (New York: Macmillan, vol 1, 1890).
[4] S. David Young, "Value-Based Management and Economic Value Added: A Global Perspective," in Frankk J. Fabozzi and James L. Grant (eds.), *Value-Based Metrics: Foundations and Practice* (New Hope, PA: Frank J. Fabozzi Associates, 2000).

ers to make *positive* net present value (namely, value-based) decisions for their shareholders.[5]

Indeed, the awarding of the 1990 Nobel Prize in Economic Sciences — to Merton Miller, Harry Markowitz, and William Sharpe — was a watershed event in corporate finance and investment management. The announcement tied a competitive (efficient) market's thread around prominent *equilibrium* financial theories, including Miller's long-held view on the importance of real corporate investment decisions, Sharpe's CAPM to measure expected security returns (the cost of equity capital), and Markowitz's innovative asset-allocation model. Commenting on the financial significance of the October 1990 announcement, the late Fisher Black was quoted as saying, "Finally, finance is no longer a sideshow, but now an integral part of economics proper."[6]

## Implications for Securities Analysts

The academic developments that have emerged over the past 40 years combined with the recent commercial developments *jointly* support the growing use of value-based metrics in security analysis. Indeed, the worldwide movement in recent years toward competitive commercial and financial markets enhances the *real-time* importance of the theory of the firm in the context of creating shareholder value added. From this wealth-creating NPV perspective, one can argue that a modern approach to equity security analysis is one that employs — as a matter of capital market equilibrium — *value-based* metrics in the evaluation of the real earnings prospects (profit net of all capital costs) of individuals firms and sectors.

This capital market equilibrium interpretation should not be taken by security analysts to mean that traditional financial metrics — such as EPS, ROE, and corporate leverage ratios — are now somehow irrelevant. Rather, their economic justification arises in today's competitive market structures when managers and investors alike use them to enhance their financial performance in the context of the NPV benchmarks established in the equilibrium theory of the firm. Moreover, these traditional performance measures can be used along with the modern

---

[5] The importance of NPV analysis *and* the irrelevance of capital structure decisions in a perfect capital market is spelled out by Modigliani and Miller in their classic 1958 and 1961 papers. (See Franco Modigliani and Merton H. Miller, "The Cost of Capital, Corporation Finance, and the Theory of Investment," *American Economic Review* (June 1958); and "Dividend Policy, Growth and the Valuation of Shares," *Journal of Business* (October 1961).

Also, Peter Bernstein eloquently captures the essence of the "M&M" capital structure principles when he states that "the cost of capital depends far more on the quality of corporate earning power than on the structure of paper [debt and equity] claims. For Bernstein's insightful comment on corporate debt policy *and* the implied relevance of NPV analysis, see Peter L. Bernstein, "Pride and Modesty," *Journal of Portfolio Management* (Winter 1991).

[6] Fischer Black's comment on the economic significance of the awarding of the 1990 Nobel Prize in Economic Sciences to three well-known financial economists was cited in Bernstein, "Pride and Modesty."

financial metrics — like EVA and CFROI — in the development of jointly *passive-active* approaches to investment management.

## THE EVA MEASURE OF CORPORATE SUCCESS

Perhaps the best known value-based metric among today's corporate and investment players is a measure called EVA® — for Economic Value Added.[7] Hatched commercially in 1982 by Joel Stern and G. Bennett Stewart, this economic profit measure gained early acceptance among the corporate financial community because of its innovative way of looking at profitability *net* of the dollar weighted cost of debt *and* equity capital. Indeed, many firms — including corporate giants like AT&T and Coca-Cola — have used EVA to design incentive payment schemes that lead managers to make wealth-enhancing investment decisions in the interest of shareholders.

EVA is also gaining popularity in the investment community, as evidenced by the establishment in 1996 of CS First Boston's annual conference on "Economic Value Added." Spearheaded by renowned equity strategists like Abby Joseph Cohen and Steven Einhorn, the U.S. Equity Research Group at Goldman Sachs now uses EVA to evaluate the performance potential of many sectors of the economy, while James Abate at Credit Suisse Asset Management Group uses real economic profit concepts to actively manage investment portfolios from both a bottom-up and top-down perspective.[8]

The financial significance of using a value based metric like EVA from a corporate valuation perspective is crystal clear. As explained (and demonstrated empirically) by one of the authors, wealth-creating firms have positive EVA because their expected net after-tax operating profit exceeds the dollar weighted average cost of debt and equity capital.[9] On the other hand, wealth wasters lose market value *and* incur share price declines because their corporate profitability falls short of their overall capital costs. As mentioned before, this wealth loss can occur even though the firm's profitability is sufficiently high enough to cover its cost of debt financing. Moreover, it is shown how to select individual companies and industries by examining the quantitative relationship between the NPV-to-Capital and EVA-to-Capital ratios in the marketplace.

---

[7] EVA® is the registered trademark of Stern Stewart & Co. Their financial metric is a practitioner's tool for measuring the firm's economic profit or economic value added. Stewart-Stern refers to the present value equivalent of this profit measure as the firm's *market value added* (MVA).

[8] A growing number of investment firms now look at companies, industries and/or the macro-economy in an economic profit context. For examples, see Al Jackson, Michael J. Mauboussin, and Charles R. Wolf, "EVA Primer," *Equity-Research Americas* (CS First Boston: February 20, 1996); Steven G. Einhorn, Gabrielle Napolitano, and Abby Joseph Cohen, "EVA: A Primer," *U.S. Research* (Goldman Sachs, September 10, 1997); and, James A. Abate, "Select Economic Value Portfolios," *U.S. Equity Product Overview* (Credit Suisse Asset Management, January 1998).

[9] Grant, *Foundations of Economic Value Added.*

# THE BASIC EVA FORMULATION

Central to the EVA (and therefore, NPV) calculation is the distinction between levered and unlevered firms.[10] A *levered* firm, like most real-world firms, is one that partly finances its growth with long-term debt. In contrast, equivalent business-risk *unlevered* firms are, in principle, 100% equity financed. This firm-type classification is helpful because EVA is calculated by subtracting the firm's dollar weighted average cost of debt *and* equity financing from its *unlevered* net operating profit after tax, UNOPAT.

$$EVA = UNOPAT - \$COC$$

*unlevered net op. profit after tax*
*− $Cost of capital*

UNOPAT is used in the EVA formulation for two reasons. First, emphasis on this unlevered term serves as a modern-day reminder that the firm largely receives its profitability from the desirability (or lack thereof) of its overall products and services. Second, since most firms have some form of debt outstanding, they receive a yearly interest tax subsidy — measured by the corporate tax rate times the firm's interest expense — that is already reflected in the dollar cost of capital ($COC) calculation.

This latter distinction is important. An incorrect focus by corporate managers on the levered firm's net operating profit after taxes, LNOPAT, rather than its equivalent business risk profit measure, UNOPAT, would lead to an *upward* bias in the firm's reported economic value added. By avoiding the "double counting" of the firm's yearly debt-interest tax subsidy, the research analyst avoids imparting a *positive* bias in not only the firm's real corporate profitability but also its overall corporate valuation and underlying stock price.

In simple terms, the firm's unlevered net operating profit after tax, UNOPAT, can be expressed in terms of its tax-adjusted earnings before interest and taxes, EBIT, according to:[11]

$$UNOPAT = EBIT \times (1 - t)$$
$$= [S - CGS - SGA - D] \times (1 - t)$$

---

[10] The concept of levered and unlevered firms is central to the development of the Modigliani-Miller principles of corporation finance. These firm-type classifications were also used extensively by Eugene F. Fama and Merton H. Miller in their pioneering book, *The Theory of Finance* (New York: Holt, Rinehart, and Winston, 1972).

[11] If gross capital employed is used to measure capital costs (rather than capital net of accumulated depreciation assumed in the text), then the firm's after-tax operating profit can be expressed in a way that emphasizes the depreciation tax subsidy, $tD$, received by the unlevered firm. We can express the firm's unlevered gross operating profit after tax, UGOPAT, according to:

$$UGOPAT = EBIT(1 - t) + D$$
$$= EBITD + tD$$

In Chapter 8, we drop the "U" notation that denotes the unlevered firm, thereby focusing directly on either GOPAT or NOPAT.

A basic discussion of the EVA model is also provided by Thomas P. Jones, "The Economic Value Added Approach to Corporate Investment," in *Corporate Financial Decision Making and Equity Analysis* (Charlottesville, VA: AIMR, The Research Foundation of the ICFA, 1995).

where, in the first expression, EBIT $\times (1 - t)$ is the unlevered firm's net operating profit after tax. This profit term is a reflection of the firm's earnings before interest and taxes, EBIT, less its *unlevered* corporate taxes; namely, EBIT less $t$ times EBIT. Likewise, the terms, $S$, CGS, and SGA in the UNOPAT specification refer to the firm's sales, cost of goods sold, and selling, general and administrative expenses, respectively. In principle, the depreciation term, $D$, should be a charge that reflects the *economic* obsolescence of the firm's assets.

In turn, the firm's *dollar* cost of capital, $COC, can be expressed as:

$$\$COC = [COC\%/100] \times TC$$

where %COC is its weighted-average percentage cost of debt *and* equity capital, while TC is the firm's total operating capital. The weighted capital cost percentage, %COC, is given by:

$$\%COC = \% \text{ After-tax Debt Cost} \times \text{Debt Weight}$$
$$+ \% \text{ Equity Cost} \times \text{Equity Weight}$$

Taken together, these financial developments show that the firm's "economic value added" for any given year can be expressed as:

$$EVA = UNOPAT - \$COC$$
$$= EBIT \times (1 - t) - COC \times TC$$
$$= [S - CGS - SGA - D] \times (1 - t) - COC \times TC$$

This expression shows that the firm's EVA is equal to its *unlevered* net operating profit after tax less the dollar cost of all capital employed in the firm. In the next section of this chapter, a simple income statement and balance sheet are used for a hypothetical firm named "OK-Beverage Company" to show how to measure a firm's "economic value added." The equity analyst who is already familiar with how to estimate a firm's economic profit in a basic setting may prefer to go to the section after that focusing on real-world EVA measurement challenges.

## "OK-BEVERAGE COMPANY"

Let's use the basic financial statements for OK-Beverage Company (OK-B) to see how they can be interpreted in a traditional versus value-based context using EVA. Exhibits 1 and 2 show the income and balance sheets for OK-B at an established point in time.[12]

---

[12] As we will shortly see, OK-Beverage Company looks like a profitable company from a traditional (accounting) perspective. However, the value-based approach to measuring OK-B's corporate profitability shows that the beverage firm has *negative* economic value added. By present value extension, OK-B is a wealth *destroyer* in its status quo position.

## Exhibit 1: Income Statement for OK-B Corporation

|  | Status Quo Position |
|---|---|
| Sales | $130,000 |
| CGS | 90,000 |
| SGA | 23,000 |
| Interest Expense | 3,312 |
| Pretax Profit | 13,688 |
| Taxes (at 40%) | 5,475 |
| Net Income | $8,213 |
| | |
| Shares Outstanding | 6,250 |
| EPS | $1.31 |

## Exhibit 2: Balance Sheet for OK-B Corporation

| | | | | | |
|---|---|---|---|---|---|
| Cash | $7,000 | | Accounts Payable | $8,000 | |
| U.S. Govt. securities | 8,000 | | Wages Payable | 3,000 | |
| Accounts Receivable | 15,000 | | Tax Accruals | 3,000 | |
| Inventory | 52,000 | | Current Liabilities | | $14,000 |
| Current Assets | | $82,000 | (non-interest bearing) | | |
| | | | | | |
| Property | $4,000 | | Long-Term Debt (8% Coupon) | | 41,400 |
| Plant | 16,000 | | | | |
| Equipment | 50,000 | | Common Stock at Par | 625 | |
| Fixed Assets | | $70,000 | (par value $0.10; 6,250 | | |
| | | | shares auth./outstanding) | | |
| | | | Addit. Paid in Capital | 14,000 | |
| | | | Retained Earnings | 81,975 | |
| | | | Stockholders' Equity | | $96,600 |
| | | | | | |
| Total Assets | | $152,000 | Liab. and Stk. Equity | | $152,000 |

Looking at OK-B from a traditional accounting perspective, one sees that the firm appears to be a profitable beverage producer. Based on the income statement shown in Exhibit 1, the firm's management reports *positive* total and per share earnings, at $8,213 and $1.31, respectively. In addition, with stockholders' equity at $96,600 the company's return on equity (ROE) is positive, at 8.5% ($8,213/$96,600). From the traditional viewpoint, this ROE figure also results from multiplying OK-B's return on assets, 5.4%, by its equity-leverage multiplier (assets/equity) of 1.57.

## A Look at OK-B's "Economic Profit"

To see if OK-Beverage Company is in fact a wealth creator having positive EVA, let's first calculate the firm's *unlevered* net operating profit after taxes. Upon substituting the firm's sales, cost of goods sold, selling, general, and administrative and tax rate figures into the UNOPAT formula, one obtains:[13]

$$UNOPAT = [S - CGS - SGA] \times (1 - t)$$
$$= [\$130,000 - \$90,000 - \$23,000] \times (1 - 0.4) = \$10,200$$

Also, in order to calculate OK-B's projected *dollar* cost of capital, one needs to know something about (1) the after-tax cost of debt, (2) the estimated cost of equity capital, and (3) the "target" debt weight, *if any*, in the firm's capital structure, and (4) the amount of operating capital employed in the beverage business. With respect to the first requirement, OK-B's post-tax debt cost can be estimated according to:

$$After\text{-}tax\ Debt\ Cost = Pre\text{-}tax\ Debt\ Cost \times (1 - t)$$
$$= 0.08 \times (1 - 0.4) = 0.048\ or\ 4.8\%$$

where the pre-tax debt percentage, 8%, is taken as the firm's average coupon rate on the balance sheet. Of course, OK-B's pre-tax borrowing cost, at 8%, can also be obtained by dividing the firm's interest expense, $3,312, by the book value of the firm's long-term debt, at $41,400.

In turn, OK-B's cost of *equity* capital can be estimated according to the Capital Asset Pricing Model developed by William Sharpe, et al. With a risk-free interest rate ($R_f$) of 6.5%, a market risk premium (MRP) of 6%, and the firm's stock beta at 1.0, its Sharpe-based cost of equity becomes:[14]

$$CAPM = R_f + MRP \times Beta$$
$$= 0.065 + 0.06 \times 1.0 = 0.125\ or\ 12.5\%$$

Assuming that OK-B's "target debt-to-capital" ratio is, say, 30%, the firm's *percentage* cost of capital can be estimated according to:

$$\%\ COC = \%\ After\text{-}tax\ Debt\ Cost \times Debt\ Weight$$
$$+ \%\ Equity\ Cost \times Equity\ Weight$$
$$= 4.8\% \times (0.3) + 12.5\% \times (0.7) = 10.2\%$$

---

[13] Depreciation is assumed to equal zero in the basic income statement shown in Exhibit 1. For a rigorous examination of the shareholder value impact of properly accounting for economic depreciation (as well as acquisition goodwill) in the EVA calculation, see Stephen F. O'Byrne, "Does Value-Based Management Discourage Investment in Intangibles?" in *Value-Based Metrics: Foundations and Practice*.

[14] The "just right" way of calculating a firm's cost of equity capital has come under numerous empirical challenges in recent years — see, for example, Eugene F. Fama and Kenneth R. French, "The Cross Section of Expected Stock Returns," *Journal of Finance* (June 1992). However, it should be emphasized that the validity of the NPV (and therefore EVA) model does *not* require that security prices are set according to the single-factor CAPM.

Given that significant empirical challenges to CAPM exist, one might consider alternative approaches to estimating the cost of equity capital, including factor models and equity style (value/growth) approaches. Some alternative approaches to estimating the required return on equity capital are suggested at a later point in the text.

### Exhibit 3: OK-B Operating and Financial Capital
#### (Aggregate Results)

| Operating Capital: | | Financing Capital: | |
|---|---|---|---|
| Net Working Capital | | | |
| Current Assets | $82,000 | | |
| Current Liabilities | | | |
| (non-interest bearing) | ($14,000) | | |
| | $68,000 | Long-Term Debt | $41,400 |
| Fixed Assets | $70,000 | Stockholders' Equity | 96,600 |
| Totals: | $138,000 | | $138,000 |

## Repackaging the Balance Sheet

With knowledge of OK-B's operating capital it would be possible to calculate the dollar-cost of capital, $COC, figure and then its underlying EVA. In this context, it is helpful to recognize that the firm's balance sheet can be "repackaged" in a way that shows the *equivalency* between the firm's operating and financial capital. Exhibit 3 illustrates this result.

The exhibit shows that OK-B's operating (and financing) capital is $138,000. The firm's overall dollar-cost of capital can be calculated by applying the percentage capital cost, 10.2%, to either the firm's physical operating capital or its equivalent financing capital. Whichever capital concept is chosen by the research analyst, OK-B's *dollar* cost of capital is $14,076:

$$\$COC = [COC\%/100] \times TC$$
$$= [10.2/100] \times \$138,000 = \$14,076$$

Most importantly, since OK-B's dollar-cost of financing is higher than its unlevered net after-tax operating profit, UNOPAT, the firm has *negative* projected EVA:

$$EVA = UNOPAT - \$COC$$
$$= \$10,200 - \$14,076 = -\$3,876$$

While OK-B *looks* like a profitable company from a traditional accounting perspective, the insight offered by EVA reveals that the firm is a wealth destroyer. This happens because the firm's operating profitability is not sufficient enough to cover the dollar weighted average cost of debt *and* equity capital.

## The Residual Return on Capital (RROC)

It should also be noted that OK-B has negative EVA because its underlying "*residual* (or *surplus*) return on capital" (RROC), is negative. This wealth wasting situation occurs when the firm's after-tax return on productive capital, ROC, falls short of the weighted average capital cost, COC. To illustrate this, simply define RROC as the firm's EVA-to-Capital ratio. At −2.8%, one sees that OK-B's adverse residual return on capital is caused by its negative economic value added:

$$RROC = EVA/Total\ Capital$$
$$= -\$3,876/\$138,000 = -0.028\ or\ -2.8\%$$

Likewise, since EVA can be expressed as the firm's initial capital, TC, times the residual return on capital, RROC, this same result is obtained by focusing on the *spread* between the firm's after-tax return on capital, ROC, and its weighted average cost of debt and equity capital, COC:

$$RROC = EVA/TC = [ROC - COC]$$
$$= [0.074 - 0.102] = -0.028 = -2.8\%$$

where ROC, at 7.4%, in the expression results by dividing UNOPAT, $10,200, by the firm's total capital, $138,000. The COC term (in decimal format) is the familiar capital cost percentage of 10.2%.

## OK-B's Interest Tax Subsidy

When looking at the firm's profitability *net* of its capital costs, it is important to emphasize that its unlevered net operating profit after tax, UNOPAT, must be used in the *first* step of the EVA calculation. This consideration is important because the dollar cost of capital (step *two* in the EVA calculation) already reflects the interest tax subsidy received from the firm's outstanding debt obligations. By *double counting* the firm's interest tax subsidy, the analyst would not only overestimate the firm's real cash flows, but he would also — from a pricing perspective — impart a positive bias in the firm's market value and its outstanding shares.

To show the source of this cash flow bias, it is helpful to note that the *levered* firm's net operating profit after tax, LNOPAT, can be expressed in terms of the equivalent business-risk *unlevered* firm's operating profit *plus* the yearly interest tax subsidy. Looking at OK-B in this levered (with corporate debt) and unlevered (without long-term debt) fashion yields:

$$LNOPAT = UNOPAT + t \times Interest$$
$$= \$10,200 + 0.4 \times \$3,312$$
$$= \$10,200 + \$1,325 = \$11,525$$

where, $t \times$ Interest (at $1,325), is the yearly interest tax subsidy that OK-B receives as a levered firm, as opposed to a debt-free company. However, this *same* interest tax benefit is already reflected in the firm's overall capital cost through the reduced cost of corporate debt financing.

To show this, recall that OK-B's after tax cost of debt was previously expressed as:

$$After\text{-}tax\ Debt\ Cost = Pre\text{-}tax\ Debt\ Cost \times (1 - t)$$
$$= 0.08 \times (1 - 0.4) = 0.048\ or\ 4.8\%$$

In this formulation, the firm's pre-tax cost of debt, 8%, is reduced by 320 basis points due to the tax benefit that OK-B receives from deductibility of its corporate interest expense. Expressing this leverage-induced percentage reduction in the firm's dollar cost of capital yields the *same* yearly interest tax benefit that is already reflected in OK-B's levered cash flows.

$$\$COC \text{ Tax Subsidy} = t \times [\text{Pre-tax Debt Cost}] \times \text{Debt}$$
$$= 0.4 \times [3{,}312/41{,}400] \times 41{,}400 = \$1{,}325$$

Therefore, to avoid the positive earnings bias, OK-B's EVA must be calculated by *first* estimating what its net operating profit after tax, UNOPAT, would be as an equivalent business-risk unlevered firm — namely, a "OK-B like" firm with no long-term debt — and *then* subtracting the overall dollar cost of debt and equity capital from this unlevered cash flow figure.

## OK-B's EVA on a Pre-Tax Basis

If the equity analyst were inclined to calculate OK-B's EVA on a pretax basis, then the firm's unlevered net operating profit before taxes, at $17,000, would be used in conjunction with the *pre*-tax cost of capital.[15] The only real complication here is that the after-tax cost of equity capital needs to be "grossed up" by one *minus* the corporate tax rate to convert it to a pre-tax financing rate. To see this pre-tax EVA development, first note that OK-B's weighted average cost of capital on a *before* tax basis can be expressed as:

$$\text{Pre-tax COC} = \text{Debt Weight} \times \text{Pre-tax Debt Cost}$$
$$+ \text{Equity Weight} \times \text{Pre-tax Equity Cost}$$
$$= 0.3 \times 0.08 + 0.7 \times [0.125/(1 - 0.4)]$$
$$= 0.3 \times 0.08 + 0.7 \times [0.208] = 0.17 \text{ or } 17\%$$

where in this formulation, the firm's *pre-tax* cost of equity capital is 20.8%, and its pre-tax cost of capital is 17%.

With this development, OK-B's *pre-tax* EVA is therefore:

$$\text{Pre-tax EVA} = \text{Pre-tax Unlevered Net Operating Profit} - \text{Pre-tax }\$COC$$
$$= \text{EBIT} - \text{Pretax COC} \times \text{TC}$$
$$= \$17{,}000 - 0.17 \times \$138{,}000$$
$$= \$17{,}000 - \$23{,}460 = -\$6{,}460$$

---

[15] The pre-tax approach to estimating a firm's economic profit is helpful because the equity analyst focuses directly on the unlevered firm's operating profit without getting tangled up on tax issues arising from depreciation and related accounting complexities. However, tax considerations *do* arise when converting the after-tax cost of equity capital (CAPM or otherwise) to a pre-tax required rate of return — as shown in the illustration that follows.

From a real world perspective, it is interesting to note that Polaroid Corporation looks at EVA on a pretax basis when making strategic corporate decisions.

Likewise, the firm's pre-tax EVA is also equal to its after-tax EVA "grossed up" by one *minus* the corporate tax rate:

$$\text{Pretax EVA} = \frac{\text{After Tax EVA}}{1 - t}$$

$$= \frac{-\$3,876}{1 - 0.4} = -\$6,460$$

## Role of OK-B's Growth Opportunities

Given that OK-B has negative EVA, the firm has a clear need for a *positive* growth opportunity. In this context, let's suppose the firm's managers discover (finally!) that they can invest $20,000 in new technology that will increase the firm's sales each year by $40,000. Further suppose that OK-B's cost of goods sold and selling, general, and administrative expenses will rise by $25,000 and $5,000 per annum, respectively. With these assumptions, the firm's forecasted annual UNOPAT will go up by $6,000:

$$\Delta\text{UNOPAT} = \Delta[S - CGS - SGA] \times (1 - t)$$
$$= [\$40,000 - \$25,000 - \$5,000] \times (1 - 0.4) = \$6,000$$

Since the firm's operating capital rises by $20,000 to support the increased sales forecast, OK-B's estimated (annual) capital costs rise by $2,040:

$$\Delta\$COC = COC \times \Delta TC$$
$$= 0.102 \times \$20,000 = \$2,040$$

Taken together, the $\Delta$UNOPAT and $\Delta\$COC$ figures reveal that OK-B's growth opportunity is a *desirable* real investment for the firm's shareholders. With these figures, OK-B's EVA rises by $3,960:

$$\Delta\text{EVA} = \Delta\text{UNOPAT} - \Delta\$COC$$
$$= \$6,000 - \$2,040 = \$3,960$$

As a result of OK-B's real growth opportunity, it is interesting to see that the firm has moved from a wealth-destroyer to a wealth-neutral position. Among other things, this implies that the firm's revised return on capital, 10.3% ($16,200/$158,000) is now close to the overall cost of capital, 10.2%. Likewise, in this wealth neutral situation, the firm's residual capital return, RROC, is nearly zero. With further growth opportunities, its seems that OK-B has the *potential* to become a wealth creator with (discounted) positive-average EVA. In this latter context, the interested reader is referred to the appendix to this chapter for an examination of the basic valuation consequences of OK-B's growth opportunities — including an estimate of its stock price using economic profit concepts.

# EVA MEASUREMENT CHALLENGES

The OK-B illustration discussed above is helpful in showing how a value-based metric like EVA differs from a traditional measure of profit such as accounting net income. However, the basic example belies the complexity of the economic profit calculation in practice. This oversimplification is sometimes missed by real world EVA proponents as well. For instance, in a popular article in *Fortune*, the author states that "EVA is simply after-tax operating profit, a widely used measure, minus the total annual cost of capital." As with the OK-B example, this basic approach to calculating EVA is simple enough yet difficulties can arise when trying to implement the economic profit concept in practice.[16]

Specifically, Goldman Sachs U.S. Equity Research Group and David Young of INSEAD point out that there are some 160 accounting adjustments that can be made to a firm's accounting statements to convert them to a *value-based* format emphasizing cash operating profit and asset replacement cost considerations.[17] Many of the potential adjustments can have a material impact on the analyst's estimate of a company's after-tax return on capital through their *joint* impact on the firm's unlevered net operating profit after tax and the dollar-based capital estimate. Additionally, there are significant empirical anomalies and academic issues involved when estimating the firm's weighted average cost of debt *and* equity capital.

As we learned previously, the firm's after-tax return on capital is calculated by dividing its *unlevered* net operating profit after tax by the *economic* capital employed in the business. In practice, however, there are numerous accounting items that *jointly* impact the numerator and the denominator of the ROC ratio. These potential distortions arise from the accounting-versus-economic treatment of depreciation, intangibles (including research and development expenditures and goodwill arising from corporate acquisitions), deferred taxes, and inventory and other reserves. Such measurement issues are important because they impact the analyst's estimate of cash operating profit in the numerator of the ROC ratio (e.g., profit impact of accounting depreciation versus economic obsolescence) and the economic capital estimate used in the denominator (e.g., impact of net fixed assets on the balance sheet versus economic replacement cost of assets).[18]

# ESTIMATING UNOPAT IN PRACTICE

The major EVA players — including CS First Boston and Goldman Sachs on the investment side, and Stern Stewart & Co. on the corporate advisory side — have

---

[16] See Shawn Tully, "The Real Key to Creating Wealth," *Fortune* (September 20, 1993).

[17] See Einhorn, Napolitano, and Cohen, "EVA: A Primer," and Young, "Economic Value Added."

[18] Goldman Sachs and Stern Stewart do not make any explicit cash adjustments to accounting depreciation on the income statement and (therefore) accumulated depreciation on the balance sheet. This approach to handling accounting depreciation seems at odds with the long established view that managers can manipulate earnings by the judicious use of accounting depreciation policies.

narrowed the list of accounting adjustments to a firm's financial statements. In this context, Exhibit 4 shows Stern Stewart's "bottom up" and "top down" income statement approaches to calculating a firm's unlevered net operating profit after tax while Exhibit 5 shows how capital can be estimated in practice with some key balance sheet adjustments based on the equivalent "asset approach" and "financing sources of assets" approaches to measuring the firm's economic capital.[19]

## Exhibit 4: Calculation of NOPAT from Financial Statement Data

> A. Bottom-up approach
> Begin:
>     Operating profit after depreciation and amortization
> Add:
>     Implied interest expense on operating leases
>     Increase in LIFO reserve
>     Goodwill amortization
>     Increase in bad-debt reserve
>     Increase in net capitalized research and development
> Equals:
>     Adjusted operating profit before taxes
> Subtract:
>     Cash operating taxes
> Equals:
>     NOPAT
> B. Top-down approach
> Begin:
>     Sales
> Add:
>     Increase in LIFO reserve
>     Implied interest expense on operating leases
>     Other income
> Subtract:
>     Cost of goods sold
>     Selling, general, and administrative expenses
>     Depreciation
> Equals:
>     Adjusted operating profit before taxes
> Subtract:
>     Cash operating taxes
> Equals:
>     NOPAT

Note: Exhibit based on information in G. Bennett Stewart III, *The Quest for Value* (New York: Harper Collins, 1991).

---

[19] Numerous EVA-based accounting adjustments can be found in Stewart, *The Quest for Value*. The distinction between *levered* and *unlevered* firms in an economic profit context is emphasized by Grant, *Foundations of Economic Value Added*.

## Exhibit 5: Calculation of Capital Using Accounting Financial Statements

```
A. Asset approach
Begin:
        Net operating assets
Add:
        LIFO reserve
        Net plant and equipment
        Other assets
        Goodwill
        Accumulated goodwill amortization
        Present value of operating leases
        Bad-debt reserve
        Capitalized research and development
        Cumulative write-offs of special items
Equals:
        Capital
B. Source of financing approach
Begin:
        Book value of common equity
Add equity equivalents:
        Preferred stock
        Minority interest
        Deferred income tax reserve
        LIFO reserve
        Accumulated goodwill amortization
Add debt and debt equivalents:
        Interest-bearing short-term debt
        Long-term debt
        Capitalized lease obligations
        Present value of noncapitalized leases
Equals:
        Capital
```

Note: Exhibit based on information in G. Bennett Stewart III, *The Quest for Value* (New York: Harper Collins, 1991).

## The Stern Stewart Approach

In Stern Stewart's "bottom up" approach to estimating UNOPAT, the equity analyst begins with a firm's operating profit after depreciation and amortization. Accounting items that get added back to this figure include the increase in LIFO reserve, goodwill amortization, and the change in *net* capitalized research and development. Two other accounting figures that are shown in Exhibit 4 include the *implied* interest expense on operating leases as well as the increase in bad-debt reserve.

The rise in LIFO reserve is added back to the firm's accounting-based operating profit to give the analyst a better gauge of the actual cost of inventory units used to manufacture the firm's product. In a period of rising prices (inflation), LIFO inventory cost understates corporate profit due to the higher cost of goods sold figure resulting from inventory costing (last in, first out) of newly produced product at near-to-current market prices. Coincidentally, current assets on the firm's balance sheet are understated due to an *incorrect* assumption about the replacement cost of inventory — namely, those units still in inventory having an assumed purchase cost based on the initial inventory units.

Also, the goodwill amortization on the income statement is added back to the operating profit because the companion accumulated figure on the firm's balance sheet — arising from patents, copyrights, internal software, and even corporate acquisitions (price paid for target firm in excess of underlying value of target's *physical* assets) — is viewed as a form of economic capital or asset investment. Since research and development are also viewed as capital investment, the value-based convention is to "capitalize" it on the balance sheet while slowly writing it off over an extended period of time (typically 40 years) on the income statement — rather than "expense" all R&D expenditures in the year incurred. With these adjustments, the analyst arrives at UNOPAT by subtracting "cash taxes" from the firm's estimated pretax cash operating profit. In practice, this means that the accrual-based "income tax expense" item on the income statement needs to be increased by (1) the interest tax subsidy on debt (as well as debt equivalents like leases), and (2) the tax on the firm's *non*-recurring income sources.

Exhibit 4 shows Stern Stewart's "top down" approach to estimating the firm's unlevered net operating profit after tax. As shown here, the analyst begins with sales (revenue), then subtracts the usual operating expenses such as cost of goods sold and selling, general, and administrative expenses. The LIFO reserve is added to the revenue figure, while accounting depreciation (in the Stern Stewart approach) is subtracted on the path to UNOPAT. Since the benefits of corporate debt financing (if any) are already reflected in the dollar cost of capital, $COC, the cash tax figure should be based on the marginal tax rate paid by the unlevered firm. A rigorous application of Stewart's approach to adjusting the firm's accounting operating profit to a cash operating profit figure for the EVA calculation is shown in an Association for Investment Management and Research (AIMR) publication by Pamela Peterson and David Peterson.[20]

## Impact on Invested Capital

As Stewart points out, the amount of capital employed within a firm can be estimated by making adjustments to the left hand or right hand side of the firm's balance sheet. As revealed in Exhibit 5, it is possible to estimate the firm's operating capital using the "asset approach" or the equivalent "sources of financing

---

[20] Using the 1993 Annual Report for Hershey Foods Corporation, Peterson and Peterson provide a step-by-step instruction on how to calculate the firm's cash operating profit, dollar cost of capital, and economic value added (EVA). This practical guide can be found in Pamela P. Peterson and David R. Peterson, *Company Performance and Measures of Value Added* (Charlottesville, VA: The Research Foundation of the Institute of Chartered Financial Analysts, 1996).

approach." The asset approach begins with the "net (short-term) operating assets." This figure represents current assets less *non*-interest bearing current liabilities (accounts/taxes payables, and accrued expenses for examples). To this amount, Stewart adds familiar items like the accumulated LIFO reserve, net plant and equipment, and goodwill-related items. The capitalized value of research and development and cumulative write-offs from special items are also figured into their asset-based view of capital.

In the equivalent "sources of financing" approach, the firm's economic capital estimate is obtained by adding "equity equivalents" to the firm's book value of common equity, along with debt and "debt equivalents." Exhibit 5 shows that in the Stern Stewart model, equity equivalents consist of preferred stock, minority interest, deferred income tax reserve, LIFO reserve, and accumulated goodwill amortization. Likewise, debt and debt equivalents consist of interest bearing short-term liabilities, long-term debt, as well as capitalized lease obligations. With the income statement (Exhibit 4) and balance sheet (Exhibit 5) converted to a cash operating basis, an analyst is able to *jointly* estimate the firm's unlevered net operating profit after tax and the economic capital employed within the firm. As mentioned before, the firm's after-tax return on capital is calculated by dividing UNOPAT by total capital.

## Overview of Goldman Sachs' Approach

Like Stern Stewart and others, Goldman Sachs has narrowed the field from 160 possible accounting adjustments down to a select number of accounting adjustments that can have a meaningful impact on the firm's assessed cash operating profit and its economic capital.[21] The key "equity equivalents" used by Goldman's U.S. Equity Research Group to measure the firm's economic capital (or equivalent financing thereof) are shown in the top portion of Exhibit 6. Based on the "sources of financing approach," they begin with stockholders equity on the firm's balance sheet and then "add back" (if any) the listed equity equivalents. On the income side, the increase in equity equivalents is added back to accounting net income as shown in the lower portion of Exhibit 6.

As shown in Exhibit 6, accounting-based items like deferred tax liabilities (and deferred assets resulting from *non*-recurring restructuring and environmental cleanup costs), minority interests, and LIFO reserves have balance sheet and income statement consequences that can impact the correct estimation of the firm's after-tax return on capital — through their *joint* impact on UNOPAT and economic capital. Also, the taxes used in measuring a company's post-tax capital returns should be a reflection of the cash taxes actually paid by the *unlevered* firm — as the interest tax subsidy (if any) is already reflected in the cost of capital calculation for the levered firm. On the tax issue, Goldman Sachs uses the *statutory* corporate tax rate rather than the firm's effective tax rate.

---

[21] See Einhorn, Napolitano, and Cohen, "EVA: A Primer."

## Exhibit 6: Equity Equivalents Approach Used by Goldman Sachs U.S. Research Group

### Derivation of Total Adjusted Capital Employed

Common Equity
+ Equity Equivalents*
+ Preferred Stock
+ Minority Interest
+ Long-Term Debt
+ Short-Term Debt
+ Current Portion of Long-Term Debt
= Total Capital Employed

### Derivation of NOPAT

Net Income Available to Common
+ Increase in Equity Equivalents
+ Preferred Dividend
+ Minority Interest Provision
+ After-Tax Interest Expense
− ESOP Accrual
= NOPAT

* Includes: Accumulated amortization of intangibles, deferred taxes, cumulative non-recurring charges, LIFO reserves, and ESOP accruals.
Source: Tables 4 and 5 on page 16 of Steven G. Einhorn, Gabrielle Napolitano, and Abby Joseph Cohen of Goldman Sachs, "EVA: A Primer," *U.S. Research* (September 10, 1997).
Copyright 1997 by Goldman Sachs.

---

## Final Comments on UNOPAT Estimation in Practice

Hence, there are many accounting adjustments that an analyst can make when attempting to measure a firm's after-tax return on capital, ROC (measured by the UNOPAT/TC ratio). These ROC challenges are independent of the empirical and academic issues that arise when attempting to calculate the firm's cost of capital, COC (to be discussed shortly). Because the economic profit message can get muted as the number of accounting adjustments grows, it is important for equity analysts to find a practical balance between the number of UNOPAT and capital adjustments while still protecting the integrity of the EVA model. Conformity in the number of accounting adjustments also makes economic profit comparisons across firms and sectors more reliable.

In general, important items like research and development expenditures should be capitalized on the balance sheet and amortized on the income statement over a long period of time — rather than "expensed" in the current year. Also, goodwill which arises from corporate acquisitions (namely, the acquisition "premium" paid by acquirers) should be treated as economic capital. An inspection of Exhibits 4 through 6 reveals that the *major* adjustments to the accounting income statement and balance sheets made by U.S. Equity Research Group at Goldman Sachs as well as Stern Stewart & Co. are similar in scope and interpretation.

# COST OF CAPITAL ESTIMATION CHALLENGES

Aside from any further accounting difficulties that may arise when calculating the firm's economic profit, there remains many challenging "cost of capital" issues that can impact the estimation of the EVA metric. These COC challenges have both theoretical and empirical foundations. In the former context, the standard approach — used by EVA players like CS First Boston, Goldman Sachs, and Stern Stewart — to calculate the cost of capital presumes that corporate debt financing is a "cheaper" source of financing in comparison with equity financing — thereby giving corporate managers an incentive to finance growth with debt versus equity.

Yet Merton Miller argues that even in a world of taxes with deductibility of debt interest expense, levered firms should be priced *as if* they were equivalent business-risk unlevered firms.[22] In his well-known "Debt and Taxes" model, the pre-tax rate of interest on taxable corporate bonds rises in the capital market to a level that offsets any perceived gains from corporate leverage at the firm level. As a result, Miller re-establishes the "capital structure irrelevance" predictions of the original MM (Miller-Modigliani) framework. These powerful principles of corporation finance suggest corporate debt policy has *no* meaningful impact on the value of the firm. In this view, the levered firm's weighted average cost of capital is the same as the capital cost estimate for the equivalent business-risk unlevered firm.

To illustrate the EVA-importance of Miller's arguments in a more direct way, consider the familiar expression of the relationship between the cost of capital for levered and unlevered firms. In this context, the levered firm's after-tax capital cost can be expressed in terms of (1) the after-tax cost of capital for the *equivalent* business-risk unlevered firm (UCOC), and (2) the expected tax benefit available to the company from the perceived debt-interest tax subsidy. In more formal terms, the levered firm's cost of capital (LCOC) can be represented as:

$$LCOC = UCOC \, [1 - t_e \times (D/C)]$$

where UCOC is the unlevered firm's cost of capital, $t_e$ is the *effective* debt tax subsidy rate, and $D/C$ is the firm's "optimal or target" debt-to-capital ratio.

In Miller's "Debt and Taxes" model, he argues that competition in the market for taxable and tax-exempt bonds dictates that the levered firm's cost of capital (LCOC) will be the same as the capital cost for the equivalent business risk unlevered firm, UCOC. This implies that the firm's weighted debt tax subsidy term, $t_e \times (D/C)$, in the cost of capital formulation must be *zero*. In effect, Miller's pioneering work throughout the years reveals that corporate debt policy *per se* has no impact whatsoever on the firm's after-tax cost of capital, and therefore, its overall market capitalization. In this sense, only real corporate investment opportunities (positive NPV projects) can have a material impact on shareholder wealth.

---

[22] See Merton H. Miller, "Debt and Taxes," *Journal of Finance* (May 1977).

Suffice it to say that the effective debt tax subsidy rate, $t_e$, that applies in the real world is considerably lower than the statutory corporate tax rate that managers and investors alike might use in the estimation of the firm's cost of capital. EVA estimates that are calculated in this simple way would of course be biased upward. This measurement error would result from the inherent downward bias in the levered firm's cost of capital due to the presumed debt-interest tax subsidy. Moreover, unless this seemingly favorable subsidy to the levered firm's cost of capital is noticed by investors, then the debt-induced EVA bias could lead to an overly optimistic assessment of the market value of the levered firm and its outstanding shares.[23]

## Using the CAPM

An especially problematic cost of capital issue arises for the equity analyst in the context of estimating the required return on the firm's common stock. In principle, using CAPM to estimate the firm's anticipated cost of equity seems reasonable enough because this *single factor* model is an integral component of established financial theory. However, in recent years CAPM has been challenged by many empirical studies that question the validity of the one-factor expected return-risk predictions of the model.

Specifically, in this asset pricing framework, *beta* is considered to be the systematic (or relative) risk factor that drives the expected rate of return on the firm's outstanding common stock which is an estimate of the cost of equity capital. In this model, stocks of companies with high betas — due, perhaps, to volatile operating and/or leverage conditions — should offer relatively high expected returns, while stocks of firms with low betas should offer comparably lower anticipated returns. Over time, these positive expected return-risk anticipations should be revealed in *real-time* capital markets. However, recent empirical research does not seem to verify the predictions of the single-factor CAPM.[24]

## CAPM Alternatives

Fortunately, there are alternative approaches to using CAPM when estimating a firm's cost of equity capital. In this context, James Abate at Credit Suisse Asset Management (CSAM) has developed a proprietary model that estimates a firm's required return on capital (largely, the expected return on equity capital) based on a model that incorporates (1) the market risk premium, (2) well-known fundamental factors including size and leverage considerations, and (3) the growth and stability in the firm's economic profit over time. Holding the first two equity risk considerations the same, firms that have demonstrated stability in their real eco-

---

[23] The equity analyst should also be aware that even the unlevered firm's cost of capital (UCOC) is impacted by economywide changes in interest rates and the market-based business risk premium. This means that a firm's required return on capital (therefore EVA) can change *independently* of company specific happenings at the micro level. This macro economic concern is also voiced by Peterson and Peterson, *Company Performance and Measures of Value Added.*

[24] See, for example, Fama and French, "The Cross Section of Expected Stock Returns."

nomic profit growth will be assigned a *lower* cost of capital score than firms that otherwise demonstrate substantial specific volatility in their economic profit.[25]

Exhibit 7 shows how the required return on invested capital (cost of capital) is estimated in the CSAM model. As with CAPM, the firm's cost of equity is based on a market driven "base risk premium." To their estimate of the systematic market premium, CSAM adds a "company specific" premium to arrive at the firm's overall cost of capital — based on established fundamental factors (size, etc.) and their proprietary scoring measure on the volatility of a company's economic profit. The lower the EVA-based volatility score, the lower the required return on invested capital (largely cost of equity capital). Other things the same, the higher the company specific risk score, the higher the CSAM assessed cost of (equity) capital.

In addition, there are well-known factor-based equity models that can be used in lieu of the single-factor CAPM. In this context, the analyst might consider the benefits of using a multi-factor approach to estimating the firm's expected return on common stock, and (therefore) the required return on invested capital. Prominent fundamental and macro-factor equity models used by major investment players are covered in a later chapter. Fundamental factor models (like BARRA) have been used to build forecasts of equity returns based on beta, size, earnings momentum, and book-to-price ratios — among other "common factors" that influence security return. Macro-factor models — such as Burmeister, Ibbotson, Roll, and Ross — have been used in practice to estimate the expected return on common stocks in the context of interest rate and economywide changes in corporate profits, among other macro-factors.

## Exhibit 7: Security Selection Analysis: Decomposition of Expected Return on (Equity) Capital

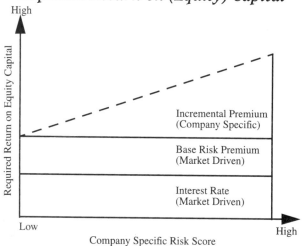

Source: James A. Abate, "Select Economic Value Portfolios," *U.S. Equity Product Overview* (Credit Suisse Asset Management, January 1998).

---

[25] See Abate, "Select Economic Value Portfolios."

# CASH FLOW RETURN ON INVESTMENT

Although EVA is perhaps the most popular *value-based* metric, it is not the only one used in practice by corporate managers and investors. Another prominent measure that is also consistent with the principles of wealth maximization is cash flow return on investment (CFROI). This metric is used by two consulting advisory firms — Holt Value Associates, LP (dealing primarily with investment management firms) and Boston Consulting Group (on the corporate side). Although differences exist, Holt's CFROI measure is similar in concept to the well-known internal rate of return (IRR) method used in capital budgeting analysis.

In principle, CFROI can be viewed as the after-tax internal rate of return on the firm's existing assets. CFROI is that rate which sets the present value of the after-tax cash flows generated by the firm's existing assets equal to their investment cost. As a result, the firm's net present value is positive if CFROI exceeds the "hurdle rate" or cost of capital, while the firm's NPV is negative when the Holt estimated CFROI metric falls short of the required return on the firm's existing capital.

Since Holt's CFROI metric is based on both current *and* distant cash flows while Stern Stewart & Co.'s EVA measure appears — on the surface — to be a snapshot of the firm's current economic profit, it is tempting to argue that the former firm's measure is more closely aligned with promoting shareholder value added over the long term. Such a comparative interpretation is incorrect however when one realizes that economic profit (EVA) is the *annualized* equivalent of the firm's net present value (see below). Also, if for some reason the firm's managers compare CFROI to a hurdle rate that is inconsistent with the required return on the firm's capital, COC, then a wealth-destroying *agency* problem exists between the firm's managers and owners.

## Wealth Equivalency of CFROI and EVA

Although Stern Stewart and Holt/BCG like to promote their respective metrics as the "best" among today's value-based measures, it is important to emphasize that EVA and CFROI are theoretically equivalent ways of looking at the firm's net present value (or shareholder value add). This wealth equivalency between the two value-based methodologies is based on the following considerations: on the Stern Stewart side of the wealth creator ledger, the firm's NPV can always be viewed as the present value of its anticipated economic profit stream. In this context, EVA is the *yearly* equivalent of the firm's net present value.

Additionally, on the Holt/BCG side of the wealth creator ledger, the firm's NPV is positive when CFROI or the internal rate of return exceeds the corporate-wide hurdle rate. But EVA, and therefore NPV, is positive *if and only if* the firm's residual or surplus return on capital (IRR *minus* COC) is greater than zero. To see how this works, we'll show in a simple manner that the firm's net present value is in fact equal to the present value of its anticipated future economic profit (EVA). We'll then show that, in principle, the firm's cash flow return on investment (CFROI) is the internal rate of return (IRR) that drives the *sign* of the firm's EVA when measured relative to its cost of capital.

## The NPV-EVA Link

Consider a simple "two period" model where the firm's total capital investment, TC, generates a one-time after-tax cash flow, CF(1), in the future period. From a capital budgeting perspective, the firm's net present value (NPV) is equal to the discounted value of the anticipated future cash flow less the initial capital investment:

$$NPV = \frac{CF(1)}{1 + COC} - TC$$

In turn, the firm's after-tax cash flow can be expressed as the initial total capital times (one plus) the after-tax return on capital, ROC. Substituting and rearranging the basic NPV formula yields:

$$NPV = \frac{TC \times (1 + ROC)}{1 + COC} - \frac{TC \times (1 + COC)}{1 + COC}$$

$$= \frac{TC \times (ROC - COC)}{1 + COC}$$

$$= \frac{EVA(1)}{1 + COC}$$

Since the numerator in the above valuation expression is the firm's anticipated future EVA, this shows that the firm's net present value is in fact the present value of the anticipated future economic profit. For example, with an initial capital investment of $100, an expected cash flow in the forthcoming year of $125, and a cost of capital of 10%, the firm's anticipated future economic profit (EVA) is $15, and its net present value is $13.64, as shown by:

$$NPV = \frac{\$15}{1.1} = \$13.64$$

In this basic setting, the firm's total market value (capitalization) is $113.64 ($100 + $13.64).

## The NPV-CFROI Link

In principle, the firm's CFROI is that rate which sets the net present value of the firm's anticipated future cash flows (less initial investment) equal to zero. In our simple two period illustration, the firm's CFROI is that rate (or IRR) which sets the discounted value of the expected future cash flow less investment cost, TC, equal to zero:

$$0 = \frac{CF(1)}{(1 + CFROI)} - TC$$

This development shows that the firm's expected cash flow, CF(1), can be expressed in terms of the initial capital investment, TC, and its CFROI measure according to:

$$CF(1) = TC \times (1 + CFROI)$$

Upon substituting this cash flow expression into the original NPV formula, one sees the formal relationship between the firm's net present value and its CFROI when measured relative to the cost of capital:

$$NPV = \frac{TC \times (1 + CFROI)}{(1 + COC)} - TC$$

$$= \frac{TC \times (CFROI - COC)}{1 + COC} = \frac{EVA(1)}{1 + COC}$$

As expected, in this expression the firm's net present value is positive *if and only if* its CFROI (or expected IRR) is greater than the cost of capital, COC. Otherwise, wealth is destroyed when CFROI falls short of the weighted average cost of debt *and* equity capital, COC. But these anticipated capital return versus capital cost conditions are the same wealth creating (or destroying) conditions that drive the assessed residual return on capital, RROC, and the sign and level (when linked to the initial capital investment) of the firm's economic profit, EVA.

Based on the simple example, the firm's expected cash flow return on investment, CFROI, is 25% (25/100). With a cost of capital of 10% (10/100), the firm's assessed RROC is 15%. Since CFROI exceeds the cost of capital, the firm's assessed economic profit is positive, EVA of $15, and its net present value is also positive at $13.64.

$$NPV = \frac{TC \times (CFROI - COC)}{1 + COC}$$

$$= \left( \frac{\$100 \times (0.25 - 0.10)}{1.1} = \$13.64 \right)$$

Hence, the firm is a wealth "creator" due to its *jointly* attractive CFROI (measured relative to COC) *and* therefore EVA condition. At 1.14 ($113.64/$100), the firm's value to economic capital ratio is greater than unity because of its positive net present value opportunity.

## CFROI: Real World Considerations

Pamela Peterson and David Peterson point out that the proprietary CFROI measure is very informative yet more complex than a typical IRR calculation.[26] The estimation difficulty arises because the inputs to the model are stated in *real* as opposed to nominal dollars.

---

[26] See Peterson and Peterson, *Company Performance and Measures of Value Added.*

### Exhibit 8: Nominal CFROI Inputs for Hershey Foods Corporation for 1993

| | | |
|---|---|---|
| Gross Cash Investment | = | $2,925.863 million |
| Gross Cash Flow (payment) | = | $427.156 million |
| Nondepreciating Asset (future value) | = | $522.968 million |
| Asset Life | = | 18 years |
| IRR | = | 13.31% |

Source: Pamela P. Peterson and David R. Peterson, *Company Performance and Measures of Value Added* (Charlottesville, VA: The Research Foundation of the Institute of Chartered Financial Analysts, 1996).

Using the 1993 Annual Report for Hershey Foods Corporation, they provide an insightful discussion on how to calculate CFROI (as well as EVA) along with the important issues that arise when interpreting the results. After intensive examination of Hershey's financial statements, Peterson and Peterson discover the gross cash flow and investment items that are pertinent to the CFROI calculation. Their *nominal* findings from information gleaned from the Hershey Corporation financial reports at year-end 1993 are shown in Exhibit 8.

Based on the information provided in Hershey's 1993 Annual Report, they find that the internal rate of return on the firm's *existing* assets is 13.31%. Although many calculations were involved to arrive at this point, the estimated IRR percentage is *not* the firm's actual CFROI. As noted by Peterson and Peterson, there are two practical differences between the standard IRR and CFROI calculations. First, the inputs to the CFROI model are stated in current monetary equivalents: past investments are "grossed up" to the current period by a historical inflation factor while gross cash flows are inflation-adjusted back to the present time period.

In light of the current dollar adjustments supplied by Holt Value Associates (to Peterson and Peterson), the CFROI measure for Hershey Foods Corporation drops from 13.31% to 10.25%. This percentage estimation difference is important. If the firm's "hurdle rate" were somewhere between the two figures, the unsuspecting (or less informed) analyst with a CFROI estimate of 13.31% might incorrectly gauge the firm as a "wealth creator" with positive NPV. Second, in the Holt/BCG approach, the firm's CFROI is actually stated in *real* terms as opposed to nominal terms. Hence, the real CFROI measure is impacted by the inflation assumption used by the analyst in the future cash flow and gross investment estimation processes (aside from the many nominal accounting adjustments that were already mentioned in calculating a firm's economic profit).

Peterson and Peterson also point out that CFROI measurement concerns arise because the estimated *real* return on the firm's existing assets is *not* compared to an inflation-adjusted cost of capital measure using the standard COC formulation. If correct, then the Holt/BCG approach to shareholder value added may give rise to an agency conflict between managers and owners, unless of course their estimated "hurdle rate" — perhaps in light of the many empirical challenges to CAPM — is somehow a more descriptive measure of the *equilibrium* required rate of return on the firm's economic capital. Given the proprietary nature of the Holt/BCG cost of capital benchmark, one is left wondering how the market would generally know this in setting the equilibrium real rate in the first instance.

# THE EMPIRICAL EVIDENCE

There is a growing body of empirical research that shows that value-based metrics like EVA have a statistically significant impact on stock prices. For instance, at the economywide level, Goldman Sachs U.S. Research Group finds that about 27% of the movement in the S&P Industrials share price is explained by variations in EVA over the 1978 to 1997 (estimate) years.[27] Exhibit 9 shows that this percentage of price variation explained ($R^2$) for the market rises to 35% for the more recent decade covering 1986 to 1997E. This finding is also consistent with Grant's EVA findings, although he shows that the percentage of cross sectional NPV explained in the capital market by the economic profit measure is higher when the dependent and independent regression variables were adjusted by total capital.[28]

Although the percentage of variation in the economywide NPV over time (Goldman Sachs) and in the cross section of large U.S. firms (Grant) might seem low — because some 65% of fluctuations in the economywide NPV remain unexplained in the single-factor regressions — it is important to note that the findings mask some powerful economic profit happenings for wealth creators and destroyers. In this context, Exhibit 10 reports the NPV-to-Capital ratios versus the EVA-to-Capital ratios for selected deciles (100 firms) in the Performance 1000 Universe at year-end 1994 — as reported in the Grant study.

---

## Exhibit 9: Goldman Sachs U.S. Research Group
### Regression Analysis

A simple linear regression that correlates *changes* in EVA® to changes in share price for the S&P Industrials from 1978-1997E reflects an $R^2$ of about 27%. The regression line indicates statistical significance and can be expressed as*

S&P Industrials' Share Price =   1.00   + 0.08EVA®;$R^2$ = 27.1%
                                (13.79)    (2.58)

The $R^2$ is about 35% over the 1986-1997E period. The regression line can be expressed as

S&P Industrials' Share Price =   1.07   + 0.11EVA®;$R^2$ = 35.4%
                                (9.92)     (2.34)

* *t*-values reported in parentheses.
   Source: Reported on page 3 of Steven G. Einhorn, Gabrielle Napolitano, and Abby Joseph Cohen of Goldman Sachs, "EVA® and Valuation of the S&P," *U.S. Research* (January 8, 1998). Copyright 1998 by Goldman Sachs.

---

[27] See Steven G. Einhorn, Gabrielle Napolitano, and Abby Joseph Cohen, "EVA® and Valuation of the S&P," *U.S. Research* (Goldman Sachs, January 8, 1998).
[28] See Grant, *Foundations of Economic Value Added.*

*Exhibit 10: Regression Statistics for Selected Deciles in Performance 1,000 Universe at Year-End 1994*

NPV/Capital = Alpha + Beta × EVA/Capital

| Decile Number | Intercept | EVA Beta* | Adjusted $R^2$ |
|---|---|---|---|
| 1 | 0.96 | 18.57 | 67.37% |
| | (7.25) | (14.26) | |
| 5 | 1.14 | 11.72 | 39.74% |
| | (9.16) | (8.06) | |
| 6 | 0.90 | 2.99 | 10.57 |
| | (12.95) | (3.55) | |
| 10 | −0.12 | 0.46 | 7.47 |
| | (−9.46) | (3.00) | |

* *t*-values reported in parentheses.

Exhibit 10 shows that 67% of the variation in the NPV-to-Capital ratios for the top 100 U.S. wealth creators at year-end 1994 is explained by *contemporaneous* movements in the EVA-to-Capital ratios. The percentage of NPV variation explained in the cross section is about 40% and 11% for fifth and sixth decile firms, respectively, while only 7% of the NPV variation is explained for the last 100 firms. In each decile, the "EVA betas" are statistically significant as the "*t*-values" exceed the significance benchmark of 2. As Grant points out, the low $R^2$ value between the NPV/Capital and EVA/Capital ratios in the last decile of the Performance 1000 may be due to the "clattering of conflicting financial sounds" and the "abundance of managerial noise" at these wealth destroying firms.

In general, the empirical research suggests that firms and investors have an incentive to discover those firms that will experience positive momentum in their real economic profit over time. Grant's empirical research also demonstrates that during the 1990 to 1994 period about 60% to 80% of movement in the relative NPV ratio of firms is explained by cross-sectional variations in relative economic profit for the top 50 wealth creators listed in the Performance Universe. A representative "scatter" of the NPV-to-Capital versus the EVA-to-Capital ratios for 50 wealth-creating firms is shown in Exhibit 11.

## Value-Based Versus Traditional Financial Metrics

Before proceeding to demonstrate how EVA can be used in a security selection context, it is important to note that empirical research to date does *not* seem to verify — in a statistically-meaningful way — the proposition that value-based metrics *per se* have relative information content over traditional financial metrics. After extensive comparative analysis on the pricing role of value-based versus traditional metrics (operating earnings-to-assets and return on asset ratios, for examples), Peterson and Peterson conclude that "The commonly used value-added measures, economic profit and market value added (unadjusted), which have gained much attention in the financial press, are only slightly more correlated with stock returns than the traditional measures and thus may not be better gauges of performance than traditional measures." This absence of relative information content of value-based metrics over traditional financial measures is also consistent with the findings observed in the EVA-based study by Gary Biddle, Robert Bowen, and James Wallace.[29]

In fairness though, it should be noted that the return on capital (ROC) component of the firm's *residual* return on capital (a key value-based measure) is based on accounting data that are also used to calculate traditional financial metrics such as "earning power (operating earnings/assets)" and return on asset ratios. As we will see shortly, much of the variability in the *surplus* capital return can in fact be traced to inherent volatility in the firm's after-tax capital return. In this context, the lack of *relative* information content of value-based metrics over traditional measures in explaining stock price movements is not a particularly surprising finding. Moreover, *too* much emphasis on the relative measurement question misses a key benefit offered by the emerging measures of corporate financial success: Value-based metrics like EVA have evolved out of the classical theory of the firm, and are therefore (at the very least) consistent with the NPV principles of wealth maximization.

## Exhibit 11: NPV-to-Capital versus EVA-to-Capital Ratio: 50 Largest Wealth Creators in Performance Universe at Year End 1994

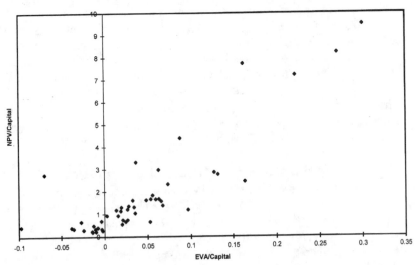

[29] For rigorous studies that focus on the *relative* information content of value-based metrics, see Peterson and Peterson cited previously as well as Gary C. Biddle, Robert M. Bowen, and James S. Wallace, "Evidence on the Relative and Incremental Information Content of EVA®, Residual Income, Earnings, and Operating Cash Flow," (Working paper, University of Washington, 1996).

## EVA Versus REVA

As a final layer of complexity, there is even a debate within the economic profit camp as to whether EVA should be estimated in the standard form employed by Stern Stewart *et al* or whether a refined version — called "Refined Economic Value Added" (REVA) — should be used in company-based research. As shown in this chapter, EVA is calculated by dividing UNOPAT by total economic capital employed within the firm. In this way, EVA measures the dollar "surplus" generated by the firm's (present and anticipated future) operating capital. Hence, in present value terms, it represents the value-added (or net present value) to the firm's physical (and human) capital.

As such, REVA — which in effect measures the firm's unlevered net operating profit after tax (UNOPAT) over the market value of the firm — is not as firmly rooted in the NPV theory of the firm. For an insightful discussion of the EVA *versus* REVA controversy, the interested reader is referred to articles published in the *Financial Analysts Journal* by Bacidore, Boquist, Milbourn, and Thakor (for REVA) and Ferguson and Leistikow (for conventional EVA).[30] Again though, we believe that the researcher needs to be careful about getting too tangled up in the details of (1) the value versus traditional metrics debate, and possibly (2) the EVA versus REVA debate when evaluating the NPV merits of a value-based approach to equity (and debt) securities analysis.

## A CLOSER LOOK AT REAL-WORLD WEALTH CREATORS (AND DESTROYERS)

The regression findings shown in Exhibits 9 and 10 are helpful in giving the analyst a measure of confidence in knowing that value-based metrics have a meaningful impact on corporate valuation. However, they don't really give the analyst a "bottom up" perspective on the economic profit happenings at the company level. To help fill this gap, we'll look at some real world wealth creators and, unfortunately, firms that have destroyed wealth.

In this context, Exhibits 12 and 13, show the after tax return on capital (ROC) versus the cost of capital (COC) for the top and bottom 10 firms listed in the Stern Stewart Performance Universe at year-end 1995. In this annual survey, 1,000 companies are ranked according to their *aggregate* net present value (MVA in Stern Stewart terminology). NPV (or MVA) is the difference between the firm's market value (including debt and equity capitalization) and the operating capital employed in the business.[31]

---

[30] The case for REVA is discussed by Jeffrey Bacidore, John Boquist, Todd Milbourn, and Anjan Thakor, "The Search for the Best Financial Performance Measure," *Financial Analysts Journal* (May/June 1997). The "back to basics" case for EVA is covered by Robert Ferguson and Dean Leistikow, "Search for the Best Financial Performance Measure: Basics are Better," *Financial Analysts Journal* (January/February 1998).

[31] It should also be emphasized that the firm's net present value (NPV) can be expressed as the present value of it's anticipated future EVA stream. In this context, EVA can be viewed as the *annualized* equivalent of the firm's NPV. For a rigorous discussion of the conceptual and empirical linkages between a firm's net present value and its discounted EVA stream, see Grant, *Foundations of Economic Value Added.*

## Exhibit 12: ROC versus COC: Top 10 Wealth Creators in Performance Universe for 1995

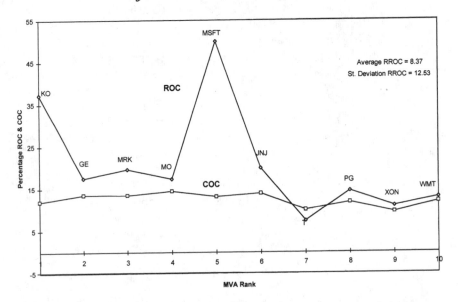

## Exhibit 13: ROC versus COC: Top 10 Wealth Destroyers in Performance Universe for 1995

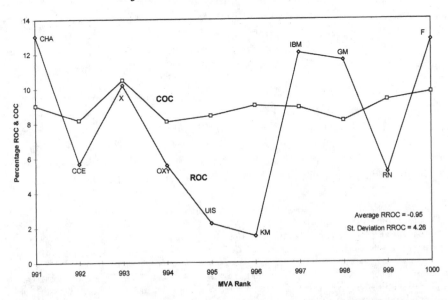

Consistent with financial theory, Exhibit 12 shows that 9 of the top 10 wealth creators at year-end 1995 had after-tax capital returns that exceeded their overall capital costs. On the high side, Microsoft and Coca-Cola's ROC figures were 49.98% and 37.25%, respectively. Meanwhile, the cost of capital figures for these powerful wealth creators were noticeably lower, at 13.11% and 11.96%. Both Merck and Johnson & Johnson posted some strong financial results too. The respective ROC figures, near 19.5%, for the two health care companies exceeded the weighted average capital costs by some 600 basis points.

On the lower-side of the *top* wealth creator list, AT&T's after tax return on capital, 7.33%, fell short of its weighted average cost of debt and equity capital, 9.89%. As a result, this telecommunications giant had a negative residual capital return, at −2.56%, for 1995. On average, the return on capital (ROC) for the first 10 firms listed in the Performance Universe at year-end 1995 was 20.69%. This capital return figure is noticeably higher than the average capital cost of 12.32%. As shown in Exhibit 12, the average residual return on capital (RROC) for powerful wealth creators at year-end 1995 was 8.37%, with a standard deviation of 12.53%. This cross-sectional volatility figure for the top 10 wealth creators is largely driven by the fluctuating ROC figures about the comparably stable cost of capital (COC) percentages.

## Top 10 Wealth Destroyers for 1995

Exhibit 13 gives a comparison of the after tax return on capital and the cost of capital for the 10 firms listed at the *bottom* of the Stern Stewart (MVA) rankings at year-end 1995. In this exhibit, it is interesting to see that 6 out of the 10 firms shown had ROC figures that — although consistently positive — fell short of the respective weighted average cost of capital. For examples, Kmart, Unisys, and RJR Nabisco Holdings, Corp. were at the bottom of the heap with negative residual capital returns at −7.51%, −6.2%, and −4.16%, respectively. Occidental Petroleum was also problematic for that year with an after tax return on capital of 5.58% in the presence of a weighted capital cost percentage of 8.11%.

On the positive side, it is interesting to see (Exhibit 13) that firms like Champion International Corp., International Business Machines, General Motors, and Ford Motor Company had capital returns that were somewhat higher than their after-tax capital costs. For instance, Champion's post-tax return on capital (ROC) was 13.04%, while its COC was 9.03%. For 1995, General Motors had a return on capital, 11.63%, that was some 350 basis points higher than its weighted debt and equity capital costs. Likewise, IBM's residual capital return (RROC) at year-end 1995 was 3.16%.

Despite the good news for these "value-oriented" companies, the 1995 average return on capital for the 10 wealth wasting firms was 7.99%, while the average COC figure was 8.94%. As shown in Exhibit 13, this results in a negative average residual return on capital, at −0.95%, with a residual return volatility of 4.26%. As with powerful wealth creators (Exhibit 12), the cross-sectional movement in the RROC figures for wealth destroyers is largely due to the movement in their after-tax capital returns — as the COC figures in Exhibit 13 are quite stable about the cross-sectional average of 8.94%.

Moreover, that 4 of the bottom 10 firms listed in the Performance Universe at year-end 1995 had positive RROC figures may be due, in part, to the strong growth in the U.S. economy — since 8 of the largest wealth wasters in the Stern Stewart survey for 1994 had negative residual returns. One should not rule out the possibility, however, that firms like Champion, et al were possibly "real value" opportunities within the value universe of securities at year-end 1995.

# COMPANY SELECTION USING EVA®

If the capital market is pricing efficient, then the firm's anticipated future EVA will be reflected in its current net present value (MVA in Stern Stewart terminology). This means that "growth stocks" will have high price relatives (price/earnings and price/book ratios) because they *should* have, while the so-called "value stocks" will have low price relatives because their poor EVA outlook leads to currently negative net present value. For value stocks, this adverse pricing circumstance happens because their anticipated return on capital falls short of the weighted average cost of debt *and* equity capital. Moreover, in such a rational world investors have little incentive to engage in active management activities as security prices "fully reflect" the EVA-generating opportunities of firms in the marketplace.[32]

Suppose, however, that pockets of pricing inefficiency are present in the capital market. In this context, the active investor has an incentive to seek out those companies having attractive EVA potential given their current valuation. To operationalize this concept, the active investor could choose those securities — among a conventional universe of value and growth stocks — that offer the dual characteristics of (1) maximum EVA potential for their current relative valuation, and (2) minimum relative valuation for their projected level of economic value added. By selecting securities in this way, pro-active investors maximize the likelihood of active reward (positive EVA alpha) while minimizing the active risk of paying too much for the mispriced (debt and equity) shares of companies in the capital market.

## Towards an EVA Growth Portfolio

Exhibit 14 shows a scatter plot of the profitability index ratio (after-tax return on capital/cost of capital) versus the value-to-capital ratio for the top 50 wealth-creating firms listed in the Performance 1,000 Universe at year-end 1995. With a value/capital ratio near 1.8, it's interesting to see in the exhibit that Columbia/HCA and Motorola had EVA characteristics at year-end 1995 that were much more attractive than the residual earnings prospects of companies like Chevron and Boeing. At 1.38 and 1.47, the profitability index ratio for the two wealth creators were noticeably higher than those figures observed for Boeing and Chevron, at 0.26 and 0.40, respectively.

---

[32] For an extensive discussion on how to select companies and industries in an economic profit context, see Grant, *Foundations of Economic Value Added*. Additional analysis of the EVA-based approach to security selection can be found in Martin M. Herzberg, "Employing EBO/EVA® Analysis in Stock Selection," *Journal of Investing* (Spring 1998), and Abate, "Select Economic Value Portfolios."

*Exhibit 14: Profitability Index Ratio versus Value/Cap Ratio for 50 Largest U.S. Wealth Creators at Year-End 1995*

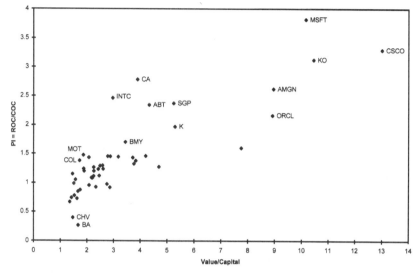

Likewise, with a value/capital ratio in the 3 to 4 range, Intel and Computer Associates had EVA characteristics that were considerably more attractive than the real earnings offered by Bristol Myers Squibb. For example, Intel's profitability index ratio at year-end 1995 was 2.46 while the same ratio for Bristol Myers Squibb was 1.7. At the high end of the relative valuation spectrum, one sees (Exhibit 14) that Amgen had a profitability index ratio of 2.61, that exceeded the 2.15 figure for Oracle. Also, at 3.81, Microsoft's exceptionally high profitability index ratio outdistanced the favorable capital return/capital cost ratio for Coca Cola at 3.11.

Taken together, these wealth-creating firms at year-end 1995 trace out a set of active growth opportunities, whereby the selected firms had maximum EVA prospects for given levels of the value/capital ratio. If the investor were to form a portfolio of say 10 growth-oriented stocks with attractive EVA/valuation prospects, this portfolio might have consisted of firms like Columbia/HCA and Motorola with relative valuations slightly below 2, along with Intel, Computer Associates, Abbot Labs, and Schering Plough with price/book ratios in the 3 to 5 range. Also, the high growth component of this active portfolio would have consisted of powerful EVA producers like Amgen, Coca Cola, Microsoft Corporation, and Cisco Systems with relative corporate valuations in the 9 to 13 range.

Indeed, at year-end 1995, these wealth creating firms had profitability index ratios ranging from 2.61 for Amgen on up to 3.28 for Cisco Systems and 3.81 for Microsoft Corporation. Moreover, this EVA-based portfolio defines the *fundamental* tenets of a modern-day growth portfolio since each company had attractive residual return prospects for their given valuation in the marketplace.

### Exhibit 15: Profitability Index Ratio versus Value/Cap Ratio for 50 Largest Wealth Destroyers at Year-End 1995

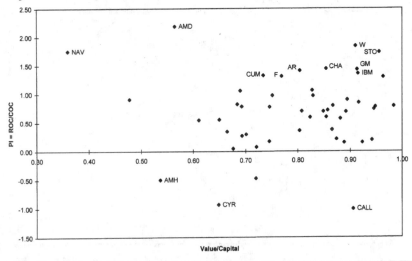

## Towards an EVA Value Portfolio

The EVA-based approach to security analysis can also be applied to identify the active opportunity set of "value" stocks. In this context, Exhibit 15 presents a scatter plot of the profitability index ratio (return on capital/cost of capital) versus the value/capital ratio for the *bottom* 50 firms listed in the Performance 1,000 Universe at year-end 1995. By conventional standards, these firms would normally be considered as "value-oriented" companies because their price/book ratios — measured by the corporate value-to-aggregate book capital ratio — were not only relatively low, but they were also consistently below unity.

In economic terms, one can say that the 50 largest wealth destroyers in the Performance Universe at year-end 1995 had *negative* net present value because their market values fell short of the total capital employed in the respective businesses. Not surprisingly, most of these wealth destroying firms had contemporaneously negative EVA as revealed by the fact that their profitability index ratios were largely less than one. Viewed in efficient market terms, these so called "value-oriented" companies had low price/book ratios because they *should* have. That is, the bottom firms in the Performance Universe had market-assessed negative net present value because their after-tax return on capital (PI ratio below one) fell short of the weighted average cost of debt and equity capital.

From a *real* value perspective, it's interesting to see in Exhibit 15 that 10 firms had negative NPV in the presence of their currently positive EVA. Firms like Navistar International and Advanced Micro Devices had attractive profitability index ratios, at 1.75 and 2.19, in the presence of their negative market-assessed NPVs. Also, the exhibit shows that firms like Cummins Engine and Ford

Motor Co., on over to Westvaco, Stone Container, General Motors, and International Business Machines had positive EVA prospects at year-end 1995 — revealed by profitability index ratios that exceeded unity — in the presence of their corporate valuations that fell substantially below the operating capital employed in these well-known U.S. companies.

If pricing inefficiencies existed in the capital market then the 10 firms shown in Exhibit 15 — with jointly positive EVA in the presence of their currently negative NPV — could have been used to define a set of *real* value opportunities at year-end 1995. In this context, Navistar International and Advanced Micro Devices were exceptionally attractive "value opportunities" at that time. Indeed, with a value/capital ratio of only 0.36, Navistar's after-tax return on capital was some 75% higher than its cost of capital (PI ratio equal 1.75). Likewise, Advanced Micro Device's profitability index ratio was 2.19 in the presence of its market value that was some 44% below total book capital (value/capital ratio equal 0.56). In effect these two firms were real value opportunities at year-end 1995 because they offered the dual characteristic of maximum EVA prospects while minimizing the active risk of paying too much for possibly mispriced equity shares in the marketplace.

Exhibit 15 also shows that Cummins Engine was the better value opportunity at that time in comparison with companies like Ford, to General Motors and International Business Machines. Cummins looked like the better "buy" opportunity because it offered similar EVA prospects — with a profitability index ratio at 1.32 — in the presence of a value/capital ratio of 0.73 that was considerably lower than the price/book ratios observed on General Motors and IBM, both at 0.91. From a corporate valuation perspective, Exhibit 15 shows that the selection of this engine manufacturer seems to minimize the active risk of paying too much for the potentially mispriced shares of firms having profitability index ratios in the 1.3 to 1.4 range.

Moreover, if the active investor was looking for diversification within the overall universe of value stocks, then the set of 10 firms having positive EVA in the presence of their contemporaneously negative NPV could be used to define the set of "real value" opportunities within the bottom 50 firms listed in the Performance Universe. Although many of the remaining 40 firms had positive after tax capital returns at year-end 1995, they would have been excluded from this suggested active value set because their positive capital returns were not sufficiently high enough to cover their overall capital costs. Indeed, firms like Amdahl, Cray Research, and Nextell (CALL) were wealth wasters because their capital returns at that time were actually negative.

## Top 10 Company Picks at Year-End 1995

Exhibit 16 shows a "top 10" scatter of firms that were culled from the top and bottom samples of 50 firms listed in the Performance Universe at year-end 1995. Common to each of these security selections is the recognition that they have *maximum* EVA potential for any *given* level of the value/capital ratio. For firms having a relative valuation below unity, it was apparent in Exhibit 15 that Navistar International and Advanced Micro Devices were attractive opportunities within the set of so-called "value stocks" having negative market-assessed NPV. With a price/book ratio in the 3 to 5 range, Exhibit 14 revealed that four firms had exceptional profitability index ratios at year-end 1995. These active opportunities included Intel, Computer Associates, Abbot Labs, and Schering Plough.

Of course at the high end of the valuation spectrum, one would be remiss to leave out of the "top 10" portfolio selections at year-end 1995 the high EVA producers like Coca Cola, Microsoft, and Cisco Systems. Among the 100 firms shown in Exhibits 14 and 15, these powerful wealth creators had the highest profitability index ratios at that time. For 1995, the after-tax capital return over the capital cost figures for Coke and Microsoft were 3.11 and 3.81, respectively.

From a diversification perspective, Amgen was added to the "top 10" portfolio holdings shown in Exhibit 16 to help fill the relative valuation gap in the 6 to 9 range. Although this biotechnology firm offered attractive residual earnings potential (profitability index ratio at 2.61) for a price/book ratio near 9, this security selection does *not* minimize the active risk of paying too much for the EVA prospects of wealth creating firms. From a *strict* security selection perspective, Exhibit 16 shows that Amgen is dominated by Intel, Abbot Labs, and Shering Plough since these latter wealth creators had noticeably lower price/book ratios for firms having similarly positioned profitability index ratios, near 2.5.

## Exhibit 16: Top 10 Company Picks for 1995: Culled from Top 50 and Bottom 50 Samples in Performance 1,000 Universe

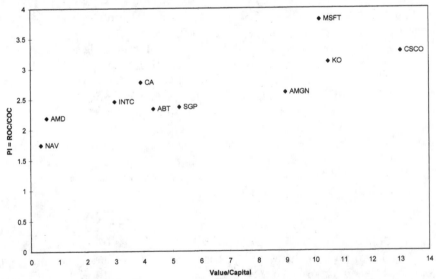

## Caveats

A word of caution to the active investor: it is important to note that if the capital market were in fact pricing efficient, then the anticipated EVA prospects of the 10 firms shown in Exhibit 16 would have already been "fully reflected" in their market values at that time. In this context, the fact that Navistar International and Advanced Micro Devices had contemporaneously negative NPV (value/cap ratio below one) with positive EVA (profitability index ratio greater than one) could be explained by investor pessimism about the *future* EVA prospects of firms that were *correctly* perceived by the market to be wealth destroyers.

Likewise, Microsoft's and Cisco's relative valuation would be high because the abnormal earnings growth has already been factored into their current market prices. From an efficient market perspective, their high price/book ratios would be correctly explained by continued investor optimism about the future EVA prospects of these powerful wealth creating firms. With pricing efficiency, the revealed *alpha* values for the top 10 company value and growth-oriented security selections at year-end 1995 would be statistically indistinguishable from zero. Alas, even with the emergence of value-based metrics like EVA, we are right back to the timeless question about the investment merits of active versus passive investing.

## SUMMARY

EVA and related value-based metrics are making significant inroads on how companies and even industries are being evaluated in a securities analysis context. The classical NPV model of corporation finance is the cornerstone of this new company-based approach to financial analysis. Aided by financial tools such as EVA and CFROI, wealth creating firms are identified by their fundamental ability to invest in real assets (both physical and human) having after-tax capital returns that exceed the required return on capital. Wealth destroyers on the other hand have negative residual capital returns because their post-tax capital returns fall short of the overall cost of capital. For wealth wasters, this adverse residual return on capital situation happens even though the firm's after-tax capital returns are sufficiently high enough to cover the cost of debt financing.

The economic approach to measuring corporate profit is different from the accounting approach in many important ways. Unlike traditional measures, such as EBITD, EBIT, and even net income, EVA — and similarly designed value-based metrics — attempts to estimate the firm's *economic income* by accounting for both the cost of debt *and* equity financing. The benefit of assessing corporate profits in this "top down" company way is that managers are required to assess the feasibility of their capital investment decisions as if they were in fact shareholders. Projects having (discounted) positive economic profit should get funded because they enhance the firm's net present value, while negative-average

EVA investments in real capital should be rejected as they ultimately destroy shareholder wealth.

This approach to measuring the firm's real corporate profitability can be used to actively select investment securities. Companies experiencing positive economic profit announcements should see noticeable increases in their stock price, as shareholders give a welcome response to the firm's positive growth opportunities. On the other hand, troubled firms with negative EVA outlooks — or firms with CFROI *less* than COC situations — are possibly sell or short-sell candidates as their adverse residual capital returns will eventually result in falling share price. As with other fundamental approaches to security analysis and equity portfolio management, the abnormal gains (if any) received from a value-based metrics strategy are limited by the degree of pricing efficiency in the capital market.

# APPENDIX

## VALUATION CONSIDERATIONS: "OK-BEVERAGE COMPANY"

In this chapter, we used the income and balance sheets for a hypothetical "OK-Beverage Company" to calculate economic profit (EVA) in a basic financial setting. However, nothing was said at that point about the market value of OK-B as an ongoing corporation. Without getting into extensive valuation considerations, some simple pricing insights are obtained by assuming that investors pay an NPV (net present value) multiple of, say, 10-times the estimated EVA of "OK-B-like" companies. In the ensuing pricing development, it is also helpful to note that the firm's overall market value, $V_F$, can be expressed as the sum of (1) the total operating capital employed in the business and (2) the market value added (MVA=NPV) from the firm's existing assets and future growth opportunities. That is,

$$V_F = TC + NPV$$

With an EVA multiplier of *10-times* OK-B's revised aggregate EVA of $84 (−$3,876 + $3,960), the firm's market value added is $840. Upon adding this NPV figure to its total operating capital (*with* the $20,000 growth opportunity), one obtains:

$$V_F = TC + NPV$$
$$= 158,000 + \$840 = \$158,840$$

Summarizing these basic valuation findings: with positive real growth, OK-B has moved from a wealth waster to a wealth neutral firm. The firm's zero-expected *total* EVA is generated by a return on capital, ROC, that now equals the weighted average cost of capital — even though ROC is higher than the firm's pre- and post-tax cost of corporate debt financing. Because of OK-B's wealth-neutral position, the firm's value-to-capital (or price-book ratio) is near unity. Incidentally, at this point, the firm's profitability index ratio (ROC/COC) is also close to one.

## Estimating OK-B's Stock Price

OK-B's stock price can always be viewed as its equity capitalization divided by total shares outstanding. Although simple enough in concept, the stock price calculation is complicated by the fact that the firm will have to issue more shares in order to finance the positive growth opportunity. Let's begin the share valuation process by recognizing that the $20,000 investment cost will be financed according to OK-B's target capital structure proportions, assumed at 30% debt and 70% equity, respectively.

$$\Delta TC = \Delta D + \Delta E$$
$$= w_d \times \Delta TC + (1 - w_d) \times \Delta TC$$
$$= 0.3 \times \$20,000 + 0.7 \times \$20,000 = \$20,000$$

In this financing expression, $\Delta TC$ is the change in the firm's operating capital due to the proposed investment opportunity, and $w_d$ (at 30%) is OK-B's presumed *target* debt weight in the firm's capital structure. As shown, the amount of new debt $(\Delta D)$ is $6,000 and the equity capital $(\Delta E)$ requirement is $14,000.

The amount of new equity $(\Delta E)$ raised by the firm to finance real growth can be viewed as the number of new OK-B shares issued, $n^*$, times the estimated price per share. As mentioned before, the *intrinsic* worth of the stock can be estimated by dividing the firm's aggregate equity capitalization (with the growth opportunity taken into account) by total shares outstanding — including the original 6,250 plus new shares issued. With these considerations, the equity financing formula becomes:

$$\Delta E = n^* \times \text{Stock Price}$$
$$= n^* \times \left[ \frac{V_F - D}{6{,}250 + n^*} \right]$$

Substituting the known values for $\Delta E$, $V_F$, and $D$ into the above expression yields:

$$\$14{,}000 = n^* \times \left[ \frac{\$158{,}840 - \$47{,}400}{6{,}250 + n^*} \right]$$

Upon solving the equity financing formula for $n^*$, one obtains 898 *new* shares of common stock (rounded). With 7,148 total shares outstanding, OK-B's stock price — with the *positive* NPV opportunity — is $15.59.

$$\text{Stock Price} = \frac{\text{Equity Cap}}{\text{Total Shares}}$$
$$= \frac{\$111{,}440}{6{,}250 + n^*} = \frac{\$111{,}440}{7{,}148} = \$15.59$$

Not surprisingly, OK-B's estimated stock price is close to the new book value of its outstanding common stock. At $15.47, this figure is obtained by dividing the firm's *revised* book capital, $110,600 ($96,600 + $14,000), by the 7,148 common shares outstanding. In economic terms, OK-B's stock price is close to book-value per share because the firm's overall net present value — due to zero-total expected EVA — is now near zero. In the absence of any further changes in OK-B's growth opportunities (whereby ROC exceeds COC), the firm's price/book ratio should rise in the marketplace from 0.72 (shown later) to 1; and remain at that relative valuation figure until any further economic changes.

It should also be noted though that corporate actions that give OK-B's shareholders the "illusion of value creation" — such as arbitrarily splitting the firm's stock, or possibly swapping the outstanding shares for more debt to give a falsely-higher EPS signal — will still lead to a stock price that returns to the *intrinsic* value associated with the firm's wealth-neutrality position. That is, in a well-functioning capital market, only real growth opportunities — whereby firms have positive *residual* capital returns — will cause the market value of the firm and its outstanding (debt and) equity shares to rise in the marketplace.

# DISCOVERING THE REAL VALUE IN "VALUE STOCKS"

Let's look again at OK-B to find the "real value" in this beverage company. In the status quo, or no-growth position, it was discovered that the firm's existing assets generated negative EVA. Assuming that investors pay an EVA multiple of 10 for "OK-B-like" companies — in the *range* where EVA is either positive or negative — that places the firm's initial market value at $99,240, as shown below.

$$V_F = TC + NPV$$
$$= \$138,000 + 10 \times (-\$3,876) = \$99,240$$

In this negative EVA situation, OK-B's value-to-capital ratio (or price/book ratio) is less than unity:[33]

$$\frac{V_F}{TC} = 1 + \frac{NPV}{TC}$$

$$= 1 + \frac{-\$38,760}{\$138,000} = 0.72$$

This finding is interesting since conventional wisdom holds that "value stocks" have *low* price relatives, along with high dividend yields. In OK-B's case though, its corporate valuation (as well as its stock price) seems low when measured relative to earnings and book value because the firm's valuation *should* be (low). Although popular wisdom might view the outstanding equity as a "value stock" investment, the underlying firm itself is hardly an active value opportunity in its *status quo* position with negative NPV.

## OK-B's Real Value Opportunities

However, when OK-B's real growth opportunity is factored into the research analysis, the stock can be viewed as a value stock with *positive* earnings (EVA) momentum. If investors are generally slow in either discovering or reacting to these economic changes, then the firm's shares could be an active *buy* opportunity for some period of time. Along this security selection theme, Exhibit A shows the research benefit of making a distinction between a value stock *per se* — like OK-B in its status quo position — and an active value opportunity, whereby, investors have not fully discounted the firm's wealth-producing EVA potential.

---

[33] The corporate value-to-capital ratio for OK-Beverage Company is consistent with the relative valuation approach discussed by Fairfield. See Patricia Fairfield, "P/E, P/B, and the Present Value of Future Dividends," *Financial Analysts Journal* (July/August 1994).

## Exhibit A: OK-B's Real Value Opportunities

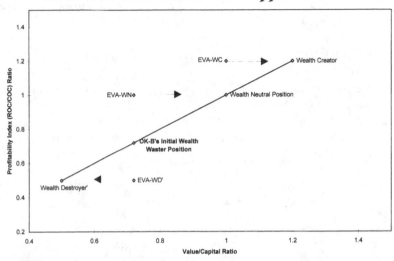

Previous calculations have shown that OK-B is a wealth waster if it simply remains as is. In this static situation, the firm's after-tax return on existing operating capital (ROC) is *not* sufficiently high enough to cover the overall capital costs of 10.2%. Consequently, the firm's negative-average EVA produces a value-to-capital ratio that is justifiably *less* than unity. By conventional standards, OK-B might be considered a value stock primarily because of the low, 0.72, price-to-book value ratio. In sharp contrast, the modern insight reveals — due to the *adverse* EVA projections on the firm's existing assets — that OK-B has a seemingly low relative valuation because it *should* have.

With the positive EVA-growth opportunity ($3,960), the firm's overall profitability index ratio (measured by the ROC/COC ratio) should rise to unity. If the capital market were highly efficient — in the sense of *fully* reflecting the pricing importance of classical NPV analysis — then the firm's price/book ratio would instantly rise to unity. Based on the previous assumptions (primarily, an EVA-multiplier of 10), OK-B's existing market value would rise from $99,240 to $158,840, and its stock price would soar from $9.25 [($99,240 − $41,400)]/6,250), to around $15.59.

On the other hand, if the capital market were slow to react to OK-B's real growth announcement, then its outstanding stock (and possibly bonds) would be an active value opportunity for informed investors. The firm's delayed price response could be caused by various pricing inefficiencies, including the possibility that investors were unfamiliar with the practical aspects of EVA-linked NPV analysis, or that given OK-B's track record, they were unwilling to believe that the firm would ever experience any meaningful future growth.[34]

---

[34] It is, of course, an interesting question as to whether the *real-world* relationship between the profitability index ratio(ROC/COC) and the revealed value/capital ratio is linear or nonlinear.

With pricing delays in mind, Exhibit A provides two reasons why OK-B may be considered an active value opportunity. The beverage company is a potential buy opportunity because its estimated profitability index ratio — with the positive growth opportunity — is higher than the required PI ratio for a wealth destroying firm having a value-to-capital ratio of 0.72. Alternatively, for the projected profitability index ratio (shown as EVA-WN) at unity, Exhibit A indicates that the stock should be attractive to informed investors because the actual or *status-quo* price-to-book value ratio falls short of the required value/cap ratio for wealth neutral firms. In the absence of a timely price response, OK-B would therefore be undervalued in the marketplace.

Exhibit A also reveals dynamic pricing implications that are consistent with the principles of shareholder wealth maximization. Suppose, for instance, that after becoming a wealth neutral firm — with average profitability index ratio and value/cap ratios at unity — OK-B announces a second growth opportunity such that the PI ratio rises from 1 to 1.2 (see EVA-WC point in the exhibit). Again, in the absence of an instantaneous price response, the firm's equity (and possibly risky debt) securities would be a buy opportunity for active investors. This happens because OK-B's estimated profitability index ratio, 1.2, would now be consistent with the PI ratio for a wealth creating firm. Therefore, its value/cap ratio should rise in the marketplace by some 20% to reflect the firm's movement from a wealth neutral (with the first positive NPV project) to a wealth enhancing firm (with the second real growth opportunity).

In contrast, if OK-B were to announce a negative NPV project at, say, the firm's *initial* wealth destroyer position in Exhibit A, then the firm's price-book ratio would fall in the capital market in response to the adverse EVA happening (see EVA-WD in the exhibit). With a delayed pricing response, the firm's outstanding securities (both equity and debt) would be viewed as a sell or short-selling opportunity for active investors.

On balance, the value-based insights show that security prices can rise *and* fall in response to fundamental changes in the firm's real investment opportunities — whereby its future capital returns exceed the weighted average cost of debt and equity capital.

# QUESTIONS

1. a. What are value-based metrics such as EVA® and CFROI®?
   b. Why were they created and how do they differ from traditional financial metrics such as earnings per share and return on equity?

2. What are the differences and similarities between the value-based metrics and traditional approaches to equity securities analysis (We covered the traditional fundamental approach to equity securities analysis in Chapter 6.)

3. In 1974, Joel Stern published a now classic article titled "Earnings Per Share Don't Count" (*Financial Analysts Journal*, July-August 1974).

   a. What do you think is meant by the title of his article from a value-based metrics perspective?
   b. If Stern is correct about the pricing irrelevancy of EPS (and ROE) in the evaluation of equity securities, then why does "Wall Street" still embrace the importance of earnings announcements, consensus earnings estimates, and estimates of earnings momentum?

4. Economic profit differs from accounting profit in several important ways. Discuss how the following accounting "expense" items should be treated from a value (or shareholder)-based metrics perspective:

   a. Research and development expenditures
   b. Marketing expenditures
   c. Corporate training expenditures
   d. Goodwill arising from acquisitions
   e. Restructuring charges
   f. Depreciation

5. In a major study using common stock returns during the 1941-1990 period, Eugene Fama and Kenneth French (*Journal of Finance*, June 1992) conclude that the traditionally celebrated CAPM relationship between average returns and beta risk is "weak," and "perhaps nonexistent."

   What are the implications of the Fama-French study for the calculation of a value-based metric such as EVA. Be sure to discuss (i) which component of EVA — namely, UNOPAT or the cost of capital, COC — is impacted by the apparent limitation of CAPM as an equilibrium expected return model, and (ii) whether or not CAPM limitations severely limit the usefulness of value-based metrics more generally.

6. What are the value-based implications of the following quotation from Professor Merton Miller (from his Nobel Memorial Prize Lecture, December 7, 1990) concerning the impact of corporate debt policy on the market value of firms and its outstanding equity shares.

> "The M&M (Miller and Modigliani) propositions are the finance equivalents of conservation laws. What gets conserved in this case is the risk of the earning stream generated by the firm's operating assets. Leveraging or deleveraging the firm's capital structure serves mainly to partition that risk among all of the firm's security holders."

Be sure to discuss the impact (or lack thereof) of corporate leverage on the firm's economic value added — including its unlevered net operating profit after tax, UNOPAT, and the weighted average cost of capital — in answering this question.

7. a. The value-based metrics approach to equity securities analysis provides a way to discover the "real" value within the universe of so-called value stocks. Use the following relative value formula to discuss why a stock having a low price-to-book ratio (a fundamental factor used to identify a value stock) may in fact be a "value trap" using the value-based metrics approach to equity securities analysis.

   Value/Capital = 1 + NPV/Capital

   where NPV is the net present value.

   b. Look again at Exhibit 11. Notice that some of the largest U.S. wealth creators in the Stern Stewart Performance Universe have jointly positive NPV-to-Capital ratio in the presence of their currently negative EVA-to-Capital ratio. What is the efficient capital market interpretation of this NPV-EVA finding? If, on the other hand, the capital market were inefficient, would these firms having jointly positive NPV-to-Capital and negative EVA-to-Capital ratios be potential buy or sell candidates?

   c. Take another look at Exhibit 13. Why was IBM a potential "real" value (or buy) opportunity among the universe of "wealth destroyers" at year-end 1995? What is your pricing interpretation as to why IBM had a poor MVA (or NPV) rank in the presence of a positive residual return on capital for that year?

8. The following cross-sectional regression results were estimated by the authors between the MVA-to-Capital (independent or $y$ variable) and the EVA-to-Capital (the dependent or $x$-variable) ratios for the 50 largest U.S. wealth creators in the 1998 Stern Stewart Performance 1000 Universe:

*Regression test #1:* Simple linear model

MVA/Capital = 1.78 + 26.53 × (EVA/Capital) $R^2$ = 92.69%

*Regression test #2:* Non-linear model

MVA/Capital = 1.30 + 36.57 × (EVA/Capital) − 6.01 × (EVA/Capital)$^2$

$R^2$ = 93.73%

a. What is the economic significance of the estimated linear model for large U.S. wealth creators?
b. What is the economic meaning of the empirical results for these firms using the non-linear MVA-EVA model?
c. Based on the statistical findings for wealth creators at year-end 1998, is a linear economic value added model sufficient to describe the relationship between EVA and MVA, or is a non-linear model required in determining the fundamental relationship?
d. If the capital base for a wealth creator were "100" (for 100% of any initial capital base) and its EVA were "3," then what would the simple linear model predict that the firm's MVA (or NPV) be? In turn, what would the firm's MVA using the non-linear estimated EVA model be?
e. Based on the information provided in part (d), calculate the market value of the firm using the linear and non-linear EVA models, respectively. Do these corporate valuation findings differ in any material way?

# Chapter 8

# Discounted Cash Flow Equity Valuation Models

Equity valuation is the ultimate goal of the analysis of securities. To this end, equity analysts use traditional and/or modern financial metrics as data input to an equity *valuation model*. If the resulting "intrinsic value" is greater than the current market price, then the stock seems presently undervalued — since the assessed future cash flow potential of the firm is greater than that expected by consensus investors. If the intrinsic value falls short of the current market price, then the stock may be overvalued due to the firm's relatively low cash flow potential. The stock is priced "just right" when the intrinsic value estimate from an equity valuation model lies within a non-profitable (or no-arbitrage) trading range that is consistent with the firm's current stock price.[1]

Before delving into the mechanics of equity valuation models, it is important for analysts to realize that regardless of the model chosen, the market value of the firm and its outstanding shares are independent of the specific valuation procedure employed. In this sense, corporate value is ultimately determined by the firm's discounted future stream of cash flow — whether measured directly or indirectly by investors and corporate managers in terms of future dividends, free cash flow, economic profit, or yearly sales franchise, economic measures that are explained in this chapter. Moreover, this pricing equivalency between competing equity valuation models is based on the recognition that in an efficient capital market, equilibrium security prices are set such that equivalent-risk securities provide investors with the same one-period expected return.[2]

Although other pricing models exist, the focus in this chapter is on theory and application of *present value* approaches to equity valuation. In this context, we cover the following discounted cash flow models: (1) dividend discount model, (2) free cash flow model, (3) economic profit model, and (4) sales franchise model. Factor models are another widely used (and quantitative) approach to equity securities valuation. We cover factor model approaches to equity valuation in Chapter 9.

---

[1] The *non*-arbitrage trading band that is placed around the intrinsic value of a stock is based on two considerations: (1) transaction costs arising from research and trading costs, and (2) recognition that the estimated stock price is itself a stochastic random variable. For an insightful discussion of the role of confidence limits in the equity valuation process, see William J. Hurley and Lewis D. Johnson, "Confidence Intervals for Stochastic Dividend Discount Models," unpublished paper.

[2] For a rigorous discussion of "equal rate of return principle," and the equity valuation models that can be derived from this financial concept, see Chapter 2 in Eugene F. Fama and Merton H. Miller, *The Theory of Finance* (Holt, Rinehart, and Winston: 1972).

# DIVIDEND DISCOUNT MODELS[3]

We begin the equity valuation journey by looking at various forms of the classic "dividend discount" model. The basis for the *dividend discount model* is simply the application of present value analysis, which asserts that the fair price of an asset is the present value of the expected cash flows.[4] In the case of common stock, the cash flows can be expressed in terms of expected dividend payouts. The basic model is:

$$P = \frac{D_1}{(1+r_1)} + \frac{D_2}{(1+r_2)^2} + \dots \tag{1}$$

where

$\quad P \;$ = the fair value or theoretical value of the stock
$\quad D_t$ = the expected dividend for period $t$
$\quad r_t \;$ = the appropriate discount or capitalization rate for period $t$

We call equation (1) the *general dividend discount model*. This model has an infinite number of parameters, so various assumptions must be made to make the valuation calculation tractable.

## The Finite Life General Model

One common approach is to estimate dividends for a finite time period (say $T$ periods), and then assume some terminal value, $P_T$, intended to capture the future value of all subsequent dividends. The general model then becomes:

$$P = \frac{D_1}{(1+r_1)} + \frac{D_2}{(1+r_2)^2} + \dots + \frac{D_T}{(1+r_T)^T} + \frac{P_T}{(1+r_T)^T} \tag{2}$$

where

$\quad P_T$ = the expected sale price (or terminal price) at the horizon (period $T$)
$\quad T \;\;$ = the number of periods in the horizon
$\quad r_t \;\;$ = the appropriate discount or capitalization rate for period $t$

Equation (2) is called the *finite-life general model*. The benefit of this model is that the dividend stream to be estimated is finite and within a reasonable forecast horizon (say, a business cycle). However, the model begs the question of how one estimates the terminal value, and still requires estimation of period-specific discount rates.

The first level of abstraction is to assume that the discount rate will be the same for all future periods. This is a fairly innocuous assumption, analogous

---

[3] This section draws from pages 108 to 115 in William J. Hurley and Frank J. Fabozzi, "Dividend Discount Models," Chapter 7 in Frank J. Fabozzi (ed.), *Selected Topics in Equity Portfolio Management* (New Hope, PA; Frank J. Fabozzi Associates, 1998).
[4] John B. Williams, *The Theory of Investment Value* (Cambridge, MA: Harvard University Press, 1938).

to those associated with the term structure of interest rates. That is, we know that the year-by-year rate on a 10-year bond is not the same in each period (except for the case of a flat term structure), yet we use the 10-year yield, as a geometrically weighted average of the yearly rates, to describe the yield on that bond. In the same way, we can think of the constant discount rate, $r$, as being a (very) long-term weighted average of individual period discount rates. Any bias induced by this assumption is liable to be minimal in comparison with the estimation errors inherent in predicting individual period discount rates far into the future. Hence we posit the constant discount rate version of the finite-life model:

$$P = \frac{D_1}{(1+r)} + \frac{D_2}{(1+r)^2} + \ldots + \frac{D_T}{(1+r)^T} + \frac{P_T}{(1+r)^T} \tag{3}$$

For example, suppose that the following data are determined by an analyst for stock XYZ:

$$D_1 = \$2.00 \quad D_2 = \$2.20 \quad D_3 = \$2.30 \quad D_4 = \$2.55 \quad D_5 = \$2.65$$
$$P_5 = \$26 \quad T = 5 \quad r = 0.10$$

Given the assumption of a constant discount rate, the fair price of stock XYZ based on the constant discount rate version of the finite-life model given by equation (3) is:

$$P = \frac{\$2.00}{(1.10)} + \frac{\$2.20}{(1.10)^2} + \frac{\$2.30}{(1.10)^3} + \frac{\$2.55}{(1.10)^4} + \frac{\$2.65}{(1.10)^5} + \frac{\$26.00}{(1.10)^5} = \$24.90$$

The constant discount rate version of the finite-life model requires three forecasts as inputs to calculate the fair value of a stock:

1. the expected terminal price ($P_T$)
2. the dividends up to period $T$ ($D_1$ to $D_T$)
3. the discount rate ($r$)

Thus the relevant question is, How accurately can these inputs be forecasted?

The terminal price is the most difficult of the three forecasts. According to theory, $P_T$ is the present value of all future dividends after $T$; that is, $D_{T+1}$, $D_{T+2}$, ... , $D_{\text{infinity}}$. Also, the discount rate ($r$) must be estimated. In practice, forecasts are made of either dividends ($D_T$) or earnings ($E_T$) first, and then the price $P_T$ is estimated by assigning an "appropriate" requirement for yield, price-earnings ratio, or capitalization rate. Note that the present value of the expected terminal price $P_T/(1+r)^T$ in equation (3) becomes very small if $T$ is very large. In practice, the value for $r$ is typically generated from the capital asset pricing model (CAPM). Recall that CAPM provides the expected return for a company based on its systematic risk (beta). Of course, this one-factor model is not the only approach to measuring the required return on common stock.

Given the fair price derived from a dividend discount model, the assessment of the stock proceeds along the following lines. If the market price is below the intrinsic value derived from the model, then the stock is potentially *underval-*

*ued* or *cheap*. The opposite holds for a stock whose market price is greater than the model-derived price. In this case, the stock is said to be *overvalued* or *expensive*. A stock trading equal to or close to its fair price is said to be *fairly valued*.

The DDM tells us the relative value but does not tell us when the price of the stock should be expected to move to its fair price. That is, the model says that based on the inputs generated by the analyst, the stock may be cheap, expensive, or fair. However, it does not tell the analyst that if it is mispriced how long it will take before the market recognizes the mispricing and corrects it. As a result, a manager may hold a stock perceived to be cheap for an extended period of time and may underperform a benchmark during that period.

Practitioners rarely use the DDM as given by equation (3). Instead, the specialized DDMs described below are used.

## Constant Dividend Growth Models

If it assumed there is a constant growth in dividends over the life of the stock, then the finite-life dividend discount model assuming a constant discount rate can be modified further.

### *Geometric Dividend Growth Model*

Dividend growth can be assumed to be geometric or additive. If future dividends are assumed to grow at an assumed rate ($g$) and a single discount rate is used, then the dividend discount model given by equation (3) becomes

$$P = \frac{D_1}{(1+r)} + \frac{D_1(1+g)^1}{(1+r)^2} + \frac{D_1(1+g)^2}{(1+r)^3} + \dots + \frac{D_1(1+g)^{T-1}}{(1+r)^T} + \frac{P_T}{(1+r)^T} \quad (4)$$

and it can be shown that as $T$ approaches infinity, equation (4) reduces to:

$$P = \frac{D_1}{r-g} \quad (5)$$

Equation (5) is called the *constant dividend growth model*. It also referred to as the *Gordon model*, named after Myron Gordon who was one of its earliest advocates.[5] An equivalent formulation for the constant growth model is

$$P = \frac{D_0(1+g)}{r-g} \quad (6)$$

where $D_0$ is the current dividend and therefore $D_1$ is equal to $D_0(1+g)$.

Let's apply the model as given by equation (6) to estimate the price of three utilities, Bell Atlantic, Bell South, and Cincinnati Bell, as of 1994. The discount rate for each telephone utility was estimated using the capital asset pricing model assuming (1) a market risk premium of 5% and (2) a risk-free rate of 6%.

---

[5] Myron J. Gordon, *The Investment, Financing and Valuation of the Corporation* (Homewood, IL: Richard D. Irwin, 1952).

The beta estimate for each telephone utility was obtained from Value Line (0.90 for Bell Atlantic, 0.80 for Bell South, and 0.95 for Cincinnati Bell). The discount rate, $r$, for each telephone utility based on the CAPM was then:

Bell Atlantic    $r = 0.06 + 0.90\ (0.05) = 0.105$ or $10.5\%$
Bell South    $r = 0.06 + 0.80\ (0.05) = 0.100$ or $10.0\%$
Cincinnati Bell   $r = 0.06 + 0.95\ (0.05) = 0.1075$ or $10.75\%$

The dividend growth rate can be estimated by using the compounded rate of growth of historical dividends. The dividend history for the three telephone utilities ending in 1994 is shown in Exhibit 1. The data needed for the calculations are summarized below:

| | Starting in | Dividend | 1994 dividend | No. of years |
|---|---|---|---|---|
| Bell Atlantic | 1984 | $1.60 | $2.80 | 10 |
| Bell South | 1984 | $1.72 | $2.88 | 10 |
| Cincinnati Bell | 1977 | $0.22 | $0.84 | 17 |

The compound growth rate, $g$, is found using the following formula:

$$\left(\frac{1994\ \text{dividend}}{\text{Starting dividend}}\right)^{1/\text{no. of years}} - 1$$

## Exhibit 1: Annual Dividend and Dividend Changes for Bell Atlantic, Bell South, and Cincinnati Bell

| Year | Bell Atlantic Dividend | Bell Atlantic % Change* | Bell South Dividend | Bell South % Change* | Cincinnati Bell Dividend | Cincinnati Bell % Change* |
|---|---|---|---|---|---|---|
| 1977 | | | | | 0.22 | |
| 1978 | | | | | 0.27 | 22.73 |
| 1979 | | | | | 0.30 | 11.11 |
| 1980 | | | | | 0.32 | 6.67 |
| 1981 | | | | | 0.33 | 3.13 |
| 1982 | | | | | 0.34 | 3.03 |
| 1983 | | | | | 0.35 | 2.94 |
| 1984 | 1.60 | | 1.72 | | 0.37 | 5.71 |
| 1985 | 1.70 | 6.25 | 1.88 | 9.30 | 0.42 | 13.51 |
| 1986 | 1.80 | 5.88 | 2.04 | 8.51 | 0.44 | 4.76 |
| 1987 | 1.92 | 6.67 | 2.20 | 7.84 | 0.48 | 9.09 |
| 1988 | 2.04 | 6.25 | 2.36 | 7.27 | 0.56 | 16.67 |
| 1989 | 2.20 | 7.84 | 2.52 | 6.78 | 0.68 | 21.43 |
| 1990 | 2.36 | 7.27 | 2.68 | 6.35 | 0.76 | 11.76 |
| 1991 | 2.52 | 6.78 | 2.76 | 2.99 | 0.80 | 5.26 |
| 1992 | 2.60 | 3.17 | 2.76 | 0 | 0.80 | 0 |
| 1993 | 2.68 | 3.08 | 2.76 | 0 | 0.80 | 0 |
| 1994 | 2.80 | 4.48 | 2.88 | 4.35 | 0.84 | 5.00 |

* The percent change is found as follows:

$$\frac{\text{Dividend in year } t}{\text{Dividend in year } t-1} - 1$$

Substituting the values from the table into the formula we get:

$$g \text{ for Bell Atlantic} = \left(\frac{\$2.80}{\$1.60}\right)^{1/10} - 1 = 0.0576$$

$$g \text{ for Bell South} = \left(\frac{\$2.88}{\$1.72}\right)^{1/10} - 1 = 0.0529$$

$$g \text{ for Cinc. Bell} = \left(\frac{\$0.84}{\$0.22}\right)^{1/17} - 1 = 0.0820$$

The value of $D_0$, the estimate for $g$, and the discount rate $r$ for each electric utility are summarized below:

|                  | $D_0$  | $g$    | $r$    |
|------------------|--------|--------|--------|
| Bell Atlantic    | $2.80 | 0.0576 | 0.1050 |
| Bell South       | $2.88 | 0.0529 | 0.1000 |
| Cincinnati Bell  | $0.84 | 0.0820 | 0.1075 |

Substituting these values into equation (6) we obtain:

$$\text{Bell Atlantic estimated price} = \frac{\$2.80 \ (1.0576)}{0.105 - 0.0576} = \$62.47$$

$$\text{Bell South estimated price} = \frac{\$2.88 \ (1.0529)}{0.10 - 0.0529} = \$64.38$$

$$\text{Cinc. Bell estimated price} = \frac{\$0.84 \ (1.0820)}{0.1075 - 0.0820} = \$35.64$$

A comparison of the estimated price and the actual price is given below:

|                  | Estimated price | Actual price |
|------------------|-----------------|--------------|
| Bell Atlantic    | $62.47          | $61          |
| Bell South       | $64.38          | $60          |
| Cincinnati Bell  | $35.64          | $22          |

Notice that the simple constant dividend growth model gives a decent estimate of price for Bell Atlantic and Bell South, but is considerably off the mark for Cincinnati Bell. The reason can be seen in Exhibit 1 which shows the annual percentage change in dividends for the three utilities. The dividend growth pattern for none of the three utilities appears to suggest a constant growth rate. However, the Bell Atlantic and Bell South appear to be more in conformity with a constant growth than Cincinnati Bell.

## Additive Dividend Growth Model

It is also possible that dividend growth follows an additive process. For instance, suppose the current dividend is $D_0$ and the dividend in one period's time is $D_0 + d$ where $d$ is the dollar change in dividends. The dividend in two period's time is $D_0$

+ 2d, the dividend in three period's time is $D_0 + 3d$, and so on, *ad infinitum*. The present value of this dividend stream is[6]

$$P = \frac{D_0 + d}{r} + \frac{d}{r^2} \tag{7}$$

Equation (7) is termed the *additive dividend growth model.*

## Multi-Phase Dividend Growth Models

Most multiperiod dividend growth models try to model the life cycle concept. In the simplest case, a model may recognize a finite period of accelerated growth followed by a more stable growth phase. An extension to this approach is to allow for a period of transition between the high and stable growth phases. These approaches are often called the *two-phase* and *three-phase dividend discount models*, respectively.

### *Two-Phase Model*

The two-phase geometric growth model recognizes that high growth rates can only be sustained for a finite period (say until the end of period $T$), and then the firm will face more stable growth prospects from period $T + 1$ to infinity. Hence we suppose that dividends grow at a geometric rate $g_1$ over the first $T$ periods and, thereafter, at a geometric rate $g_2$. Under this assumption, the present value of future dividends can be shown to be:[7]

$$P = \frac{D_1}{r - g_1}\left[1 - \left(\frac{1 + g_1}{1 + r}\right)^T\right] + \frac{1}{(1 + r)^T}\left(\frac{D_T(1 + g_2)}{r - g_2}\right) \tag{8}$$

where $D_T = D_1(1 + g_1)^{T-1}$

The first term in equation (8) gives the value of the dividends paid during the high growth phase, while the second term gives the value of the dividends paid from period $T+1$ to infinity.

### *Three-Phase Model*

A simple variation of the two-phase model incorporates a transition phase in recognition of the fact that changes in growth rates are gradual and not abrupt. This is the three-phase growth model. Hence, suppose that dividends grow at a high geometric rate $g_1$ over the first $T$ periods, at a geometric rate $g_2$ over the next $M$ periods, and, thereafter, at a long-run steady state geometric rate $g_3$. Under this assumption, the present value of future dividends is[8]

---

[6] William J. Hurley and Lewis D. Johnson, "Generalized Markov Dividend Discount Models," *Journal of Portfolio Management* (Fall 1998).

[7] This model and its derivation are from Eric Sorensen and David Williamson, "Some Evidence on the Value of Dividend Discount Models," *Financial Analysts Journal* (November-December 1985),pp. 60-69.

[8] This model, also from Sorensen and Williamson ("Some Evidence on the Value of Dividend Discount Models"), is most closely associated with Nicholas Moldovsky. (See, Nicholas Moldovsky, Catherine May, and Sherman Chattiner, "Common Stock Valuation — Principles, Tables, and Applications," *Financial Analysts Journal* (March-April 1965).)

$$P = \frac{D_1}{r - g_1}\left[1 - \left(\frac{1 + g_1}{1 + r}\right)^T\right] + \frac{1}{(1 + r)^M}\left(\frac{D_T(1 + r)^T}{r - g_2}\right)\left(1 - \frac{(1 + g_2)^M}{1 + r}\right)$$

$$+ \frac{1}{(1 + r)^{T+M}}\left(\frac{D_{T+M}(1 + r)^T}{r - g_3}\right) \tag{9}$$

where

$$D_T = D_0 (1 + g_1)^T$$
$$D_{T+M} = D_0 (1 + g_1)^T (1 + g_2)^M$$

The three-phase model is reasonably intuitive if one recognizes that the first term in equation (9) grosses up the original dividend at the high growth rate, the second term (the transition period) increases the dividend at a decreasing rate, and the third term is again the constant growth model discounted back to the present.

Different companies are assumed to be at different phases in the three-phase model. An emerging growth company would have a longer growth phase than a more mature company. Some companies are considered to have higher initial growth rates and hence longer growth and transition phases. Other companies may be considered to have lower current growth rates and hence shorter growth and transition phases.

In the typical investment organization, analysts supply the projected earnings, dividends, growth rates for earnings, and dividend and payout ratios using fundamental security analysis. The growth rate at maturity for the entire economy is applied to all companies. As a generalization, approximately 25% of the expected return from a company (projected by the DDM) comes from the growth phase, 25% from the transition phase, and 50% from the maturity phase. However, a company with high growth and low dividend payouts shifts the relative contribution toward the maturity phase, while a company with low growth and a high payout shifts the relative contribution toward the growth and transition phases.

A three-phase model is used in practice by Salomon Brothers Inc. This organization is a broker/dealer that provides research to clients. The three-phase model that it developed is called the E-MODEL (E for earnings).[9]

## FREE CASH FLOW MODEL

In recent years there has been an increased focus by investors and corporate managers on equity valuation procedures that begin by looking at the firm's aggregate corporate value and then its stock price. One of the more popular corporate valuation procedures used by equity analysts is the traditional *free cash flow model*. In

---

[9] For a discussion of this model, see Eric H. Sorensen and Steven B. Kreichman, "Valuation Factors: Introducing the E-MODEL," Salomon Brothers Inc., May 12, 1987.

the most general form of this valuation model, the firm's market value, $V$, is expressed as the present value of its anticipated free cash flow according to:

$$V = \sum \frac{FCF_t}{(1 + r)^t} \tag{10}$$

where $FCF_t$ is the estimated free cash flow at time period $t$, and $r$ is the firm's expected return or weighted-average cost of capital. Unless otherwise noted, $t$ runs from 1 to infinity.

In turn, the firm's anticipated free cash flow can be expressed in one of two ways. One approach looks at the firm's free cash flow in terms of its *gross* operating profit after tax, GOPAT, less *gross* capital investment (including working capital additions) during time period $t$:[10]

$$\begin{aligned} FCF_t &= GOPAT_t - Gross\ Investment_t \\ &= [EBIT_t(1-t_u) + D] - [Net\ Inv._t + D] \\ &= [NOPAT_t + D] - [Net\ Inv._t + D] \end{aligned} \tag{11}$$

The first term in the second cash flow expression of equation (11) shows that *GOPAT* is equal to the (unlevered) firm's tax-adjusted *EBIT* plus depreciation, while gross investment is the sum of its net investment plus depreciation. Investment expenditures are included in free cash flow model because the firm cannot expect to grow its future earnings — beyond that generated on its maintained existing assets — without making future investments in real operating capital (including tangible and intangible assets, as well as human capital).

Equivalently, upon subtracting depreciation, $D$ (presumed equal to an appropriate charge for economic obsolescence), from both right hand side terms of the gross cash flow formulation, we express the firm's free cash flow in terms of its familiar *net* operating profit after tax, *NOPAT*, and *net* capital investment (namely, gross investment — including working capital additions — minus a yearly depreciation charge) according to equation (12):

$$\begin{aligned} FCF_t &= EBIT_t(1 - t_u) - Net\ Investment_t \\ &= NOPAT_t - Net\ Inv._t \end{aligned} \tag{12}$$

As Fama and Miller point out, the gross operating profit, GOPAT, and net operating profit, NOPAT, approaches to free cash flow estimation differ only in form rather than substance.[11]

---

[10] In the free cash flow expression that follows, it should also be noted that GOPAT can be expressed as:

$$GOPAT = EBITD(1-t_u) + t_u D$$

where *EBITD* is the firm's operating profit before interest, taxes, and depreciation, and $t_u D$ is the yearly tax subsidy received by the *unlevered* firm from the deductibility of depreciation in computing corporate taxes — at the unlevered corporate tax rate, $t_u$.

[11] See Chapter 2 in Fama and Miller, *The Theory of Finance* — with the understanding that our cash flow labels are different.

## Two-Stage Free Cash Flow Model

To operationalize the free cash flow model, we'll express the firm's market value in terms of (1) the intrinsic value of its ability to generate free cash flow during a finite growth period, $T$, plus (2) the present value of mature or competitive growth in the firm's remaining cash flow for years $T+1$ to infinity. This two-phase interpretation of the FCF model can be expressed as:[12]

$$V = \frac{\sum\limits_{t}^{T} FCF_t}{(1+r)^t} + \frac{1}{(1+r)^T} \frac{NOPAT_T}{r} \tag{13}$$

where, the first term on the right hand side of equation (13) is the assessed value of the firm's estimated free cash flow during its finite growth years when "discounted" back to the current period at the firm's weighted average cost of capital, $r$.

As shown, the firm's "residual value" at $T$ is based on the simplifying assumption that capital investment (beyond maintenance of existing assets) ends at that time. That is, during the post-horizon years, gross annual investment is equal to depreciation while net capital investment equals zero. The *NOPAT/r* term is therefore the "residual value" of the firm at time period $T$. Discounting this residual value figure back to the current time period gives the present value contribution of the firm's anticipated free cash flows from years $T+1$ to infinity.

## *Free Cash Flow Estimation: Horizon Years*

When using the free cash flow model, the equity analyst needs to know how to calculate the firm's cash flow over the estimated horizon years (and thereafter). To assist in this development, we'll employ a sales forecasting model with simple assumptions about the firm's (1) anticipated revenue growth, $g$, (2) pre-tax *net* (of depreciation) operating margin, $p$, (3) unlevered tax rate, $t_u$, (4) *net* capital investment (gross investment less depreciation) as function $f$ of increased sales, and (5) working capital additions as function $w$ of increased revenue.[13] We'll also show how the firms' free cash flow can be expressed in two equivalent ways: the NOPAT and GOPAT approaches.

Based on the sales forecasting parameters, the firm's estimated free cash flow, $FCF(t)$, during the horizon years (period 1 to $T$) can be expressed in NOPAT form as equation (14):

---

[12] We could of course describe the firm's market value in the context of a two-phase geometric FCF model like that used in equation (8). However, in the application that follows, we estimate the year-to-year free cash flow during the horizon years ($T$).

[13] For consistency with the traditional approach to free cash flow estimation, we employ the sales forecasting technique described by Rappaport. (See, Alfred Rappaport, "Strategic Analysis for More Profitable Acquisitions," *Harvard Business Review* (July/August 1979).)

$$FCF_t = S_{t-1}(1 + g)p(1 - t_u) - (w + f)(S_t - S_{t-1})$$
$$= EBIT_t(1 - t_u) - (w + f)(S_t - S_{t-1})$$
$$= NOPAT_t - Net\ Investment_t \tag{14}$$

where the first term on the right hand side of the sales forecasting equation is the firm's (accounting) net operating profit after tax (NOPAT) and the second term reflects the horizon year's *net* capital investment and working capital additions as a proportion of increased (or decreased) dollar revenue.[14]

Based on this traditional sales forecasting technique, Exhibit 2 shows 10 years of free cash flow figures based on (1) a revenue base of 100, (2) annualized revenue growth of 15%, (3) pre-tax net operating margin of 20%, (4) net capital investment at 20% of increased sales, and (5) working capital additions at 10% of anticipated sales change. A corporate tax rate of 35% (for equivalent unlevered firm) is also used in the cash flow illustration. Also, the free cash flow representation in Exhibit 2 is important because it causes the equity analyst to realize that future investment — beyond that required to maintain existing assets — is required to generate a future stream of revenue and earnings. In this context, the *net* capital investment figures — defined by $f(S_t - S_{t-1})$ — for years 1 through 10 represent gross capital investment less a "depreciation" charge associated with maintaining the productive capacity of the firm's existing assets.

Exhibit 3 shows that the firm's free cash flow can also be expressed in the context of its GOPAT less gross capital additions (including working capital). To estimate the firm's free cash flow this way, recall that GOPAT can be expressed as:

$$GOPAT_t = EBIT_t(1 - t_u) + D$$
$$= NOPAT_t + D \tag{15}$$

## Exhibit 2: Estimating Free Cash Flow: NOPAT Approach

| Period | 1 | 2 | 3 | 4 | 5 | 6 | 7 | 8 | 9 | 10 |
|---|---|---|---|---|---|---|---|---|---|---|
| Sales | 115.00 | 132.25 | 152.09 | 174.90 | 201.14 | 231.31 | 266.00 | 305.90 | 351.79 | 404.56 |
| Op. Exp. | 92.00 | 105.80 | 121.67 | 139.92 | 160.91 | 185.04 | 212.80 | 244.72 | 281.43 | 323.64 |
| EBIT | 23.00 | 26.45 | 30.42 | 34.98 | 40.23 | 46.26 | 53.20 | 61.18 | 70.36 | 80.91 |
| Taxes | 8.05 | 9.26 | 10.65 | 12.24 | 14.08 | 16.19 | 18.62 | 21.41 | 24.63 | 28.32 |
| NOPAT | 14.95 | 17.19 | 19.77 | 22.74 | 26.15 | 30.07 | 34.58 | 39.77 | 45.73 | 52.59 |
| NCapInv. | 3.00 | 3.45 | 3.97 | 4.56 | 5.25 | 6.03 | 6.94 | 7.98 | 9.18 | 10.55 |
| Work Cap | 1.50 | 1.73 | 1.98 | 2.28 | 2.62 | 3.02 | 3.47 | 3.99 | 4.59 | 5.28 |
| Net Inv. | 4.50 | 5.18 | 5.95 | 6.84 | 7.87 | 9.05 | 10.41 | 11.97 | 13.77 | 15.83 |
| FCF | 10.45 | 12.02 | 13.82 | 15.89 | 18.28 | 21.02 | 24.17 | 27.80 | 31.97 | 36.76 |

[14] Consistent with the free cash flow approach employed by Rappaport, $f$ is net of depreciation cost to maintain existing assets. See Rappaport, "Strategic Analysis for More Profitable Acquisitions."

## Exhibit 3: Estimating Free Cash Flow: GOPAT Approach

| Period | 1 | 2 | 3 | 4 | 5 | 6 | 7 | 8 | 9 | 10 |
|---|---|---|---|---|---|---|---|---|---|---|
| Sales | 115.00 | 132.25 | 152.09 | 174.90 | 201.14 | 231.31 | 266.00 | 305.90 | 351.79 | 404.56 |
| Op. Exp. | 92.00 | 105.80 | 121.67 | 139.92 | 160.91 | 185.04 | 212.80 | 244.72 | 281.43 | 323.64 |
| EBIT | 23.00 | 26.45 | 30.42 | 34.98 | 40.23 | 46.26 | 53.20 | 61.18 | 70.36 | 80.91 |
| Taxes | 8.05 | 9.26 | 10.65 | 12.24 | 14.08 | 16.19 | 18.62 | 21.41 | 24.63 | 28.32 |
| NOPAT | 14.95 | 17.19 | 19.77 | 22.74 | 26.15 | 30.07 | 34.58 | 39.77 | 45.73 | 52.59 |
| Deprec. | 0.90 | 1.04 | 1.19 | 1.37 | 1.57 | 1.81 | 2.08 | 2.39 | 2.75 | 3.17 |
| GOPAT | 15.85 | 18.23 | 20.96 | 24.11 | 27.72 | 31.88 | 36.66 | 42.16 | 48.49 | 55.76 |
| G.CapInv. | 3.90 | 4.49 | 5.16 | 5.93 | 6.82 | 7.84 | 9.02 | 10.37 | 11.93 | 13.72 |
| Work Cap | 1.50 | 1.73 | 1.98 | 2.28 | 2.62 | 3.02 | 3.47 | 3.99 | 4.59 | 5.28 |
| Gross Inv | 5.40 | 6.21 | 7.14 | 8.21 | 9.44 | 10.86 | 12.49 | 14.36 | 16.52 | 19.00 |
| FCF | 10.45 | 12.02 | 13.82 | 15.89 | 18.28 | 21.02 | 24.17 | 27.80 | 31.97 | 36.76 |
| NCapInv. | 3.00 | 3.45 | 3.97 | 4.56 | 5.25 | 6.03 | 6.94 | 7.98 | 9.18 | 10.55 |

Upon *adding* back depreciation in equation (15) to the firm's accounting-based NOPAT, we can express the firm's yearly free cash flow figures in terms of its gross operating profit after taxes and *gross* capital investment at $t$. This GOPAT way of estimating the firm's free cash flow during the horizon years is shown in Exhibit 3. Since the firm's annual depreciation charge $(D)$ is added back to NOPAT, it must also be added back to the firm's *net* capital investment for each year.

## Free Cash Flow Estimation: Residual Period

In the two-stage free cash flow model — as well as other multi-stage versions — some assumption needs to be made about cash flow generation after the finite horizon period $(T)$. One simplifying assumption employed by equity analysts assumes that the firm's existing assets in place at $T$ generate a NOPAT perpetuity thereafter. In this context, the firm's *gross* capital investment in the post horizon years is assumed to equal depreciation, while working capital additions are assumed to equal zero. That is, gross capital additions in years $T+1$ to infinity are just enough to maintain (measured by depreciation) the productive capacity of the firm's existing assets in place at termination of the finite horizon period. This, of course, implies that the firm's net capital investment in the post horizon years is zero.

With a zero growth assumption, we can represent the firm's free cash flow for the post horizon or residual years (years $T+1$ to infinity) as equation (16):

$$FCF_t = NOPAT_T - Net\ Investment_t$$
$$= NOPAT_T - (D - D)$$
$$= NOPAT_T \tag{16}$$

## Present Value of Free Cash Flows

Exhibit 4 shows how to "roll up" the firm's free cash flow estimates — for years 1 to infinity — into the estimated market value of the firm and its outstanding shares.

In this context, the top portion of Exhibit 4 shows the "intrinsic value," at $116.98 million, of the estimated yearly free cash flow sequence during the horizon period — namely, years 1 through 10. As shown, this figure results from first calculating the present value of each free cash flow estimate at an assumed cost of capital of 10%, and then cumulating or summing-up the yearly present value results. In turn, the lower portion of Exhibit 4 shows how to calculate the firm's "residual value" — which is equal to the present value of the firm's expected corporate value at year 10.

With zero growth at termination of the horizon period, the firm's expected value at $T$ (for 10 years) can be expressed as equation (17):

$$V_T = \frac{NOPAT_T}{r} = \frac{\$52.59}{0.1} = \$525.90 \tag{17}$$

Discounting $525.90 back 10 years at 10% yields the firm's residual value in the current period, at $202.76. Upon adding the two present value figures ($116.98 + $202.76), we obtain the firm's overall intrinsic value, $V$, at $319.74.

If we assume that long-term debt is, say, $12 million, and the firm has 5 million common shares outstanding, then the intrinsic worth of its stock is currently $61.55. This per share figure is calculated by dividing the firm's estimated equity capitalization, $E$, by its outstanding shares according to equation (18):

$$\text{Stock Price} = \frac{\text{Corporate Value} - \text{LT Debt}}{n} = \frac{E}{n}$$

$$= \frac{(\$319.74 - \$12)}{5} = \$61.55 \tag{18}$$

## Exhibit 4: Free Cash Flow Valuation

| Year | NOPAT | Net Invest | FCF | Pres. Val. 10% | Cum. PV 0.00 |
|------|-------|-----------|------|-------|-------|
| 1 | 14.95 | 4.5 | 10.45 | 9.50 | 9.50 |
| 2 | 17.19 | 5.18 | 12.01 | 9.93 | 19.43 |
| 3 | 19.77 | 5.95 | 13.82 | 10.38 | 29.81 |
| 4 | 22.74 | 6.84 | 15.9 | 10.86 | 40.67 |
| 5 | 26.15 | 7.87 | 18.28 | 11.35 | 52.02 |
| 6 | 30.07 | 9.05 | 21.02 | 11.87 | 63.88 |
| 7 | 34.58 | 10.41 | 24.17 | 12.40 | 76.29 |
| 8 | 39.77 | 11.97 | 27.8 | 12.97 | 89.26 |
| 9 | 45.73 | 13.77 | 31.96 | 13.55 | 102.81 |
| 10 | 52.59 | 15.83 | 36.76 | 14.17 | 116.98 |
| 11 Plus | 52.59 | | | | |

| | | |
|---|---|---|
| Residual Value | 525.9 | 202.76 |
| Corporate Value | | 319.74 |
| LT Debt | | 12.00 |
| Equity | | 307.74 |
| Share OS | | 5.00 |
| Price | | 61.55 |

## Exhibit 5: Cost of Capital Sensitivity Analysis
### Free Cash Flow Model

| Rate % | Basis Pt. Change | Horiz. Val. | Resid. Val. | Corp. Val. | % Change Corp. Val. |
|---|---|---|---|---|---|
| 8 | -200 | 130.46 | 304.49 | 434.95 | 36.03 |
| 8.5 | -150 | 126.89 | 273.65 | 400.54 | 25.27 |
| 9 | -100 | 123.46 | 246.83 | 370.29 | 15.81 |
| 9.5 | -50 | 120.16 | 223.38 | 343.54 | 7.44 |
| 10 | 0 | 116.98 | 202.76 | 319.74 | 0 |
| 10.5 | 50 | 113.92 | 184.54 | 298.46 | -6.66 |
| 11 | 100 | 110.97 | 168.38 | 279.35 | -12.63 |
| 11.5 | 150 | 108.13 | 153.98 | 262.11 | -18.03 |
| 12 | 200 | 105.39 | 141.11 | 246.50 | -22.91 |

The two-stage free cash model could of course be expanded to more than two stages. The only difference is that more than one abnormal free cash flow growth rate would be used in the corporate valuation process, up to the termination of the overall finite growth years, $T$. Either zero or long-term constant growth in free cash flow is generally assumed thereafter (years $T+1$ to infinity).

## Cost of Capital Change: FCF Model

When the firm's free cash flow estimates were discounted at 10% — a standard rate used in many present value illustrations — we found that the firm's corporate value was $319.74. Exhibits 5 and 6 (table and graph, respectively) show what happens to the firm's market value when the cost of capital rises and falls in increments of 50 basis points from a base rate of 10%. The corporate pricing relationships shown in these exhibits are consistent with the principles of financial theory in a number of interesting respects. First, Exhibit 5 shows that an *inverse* relationship exists between corporate value and the weighted average cost of capital. As the discount rate rises in the marketplace — due perhaps to a rise in either the risk-free rate of interest or the business risk premium required by investors in the unlevered firm — the market value of the firm goes down. Conversely, when the firm's cost of capital goes down — due this time to either a fall in the risk-free rate or a decline in the required business risk premium — corporate value goes up.

Second, it's also interesting to see that the relationship between corporate value and the cost of capital is *convex*. For example, when the cost of capital rises by 100 basis points — from 10% to 11% — the market value of firm falls by 12.63%. In contrast, when the corporate discount rate falls by 100 basis points — from 10% to 9% — the market value of firm rises by 15.81%. Likewise, an asymmetric pricing response arises when the cost of capital rises or falls by 200 basis points. These corporate valuation findings are consistent with well-known pricing relationships in the bond market. In effect, the "convexity" in the corporate value-cost of capital relationship reveals that firm values are more sensitive to cost of capital (or interest rate) declines than to equivalent basis point increases in the weighted average cost of capital.

## Exhibit 6: Corporate Valuation and the Cost of Capital: Free Cash Flow Model

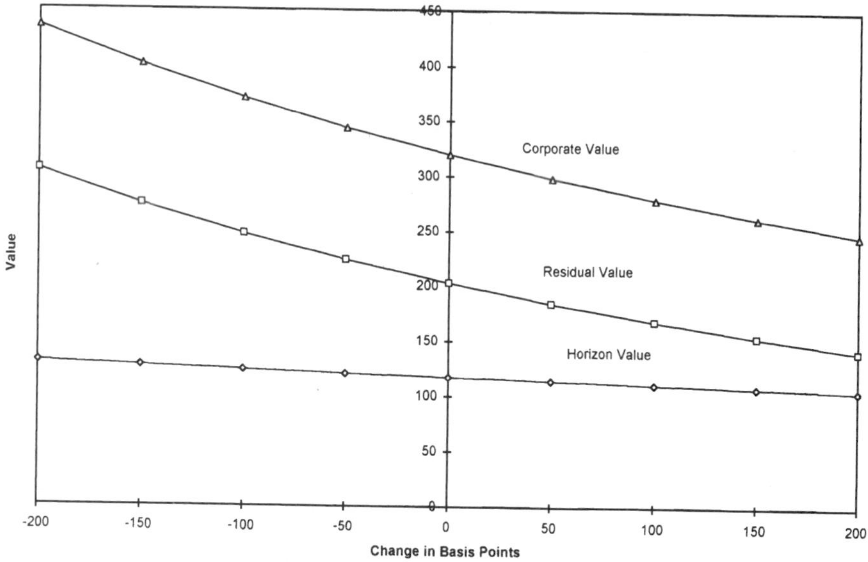

Additionally, Exhibit 6 shows that the residual value function is more sensitive to cost of capital changes than the horizon value function. This is also consistent with known present value relationships in the sense that long *duration* assets are more sensitive to interest rate changes than short duration assets. In our illustration, the residual value function is a present value reflection of distant cash flows generated in the post horizon years, $T+1$ to infinity. Consequently, the firm's residual value is like a long duration asset that is highly sensitive to cost of capital changes. In contrast, the firm's horizon value can be viewed as a relatively short duration asset, and thereby less sensitive to cost of capital change. For instance, when the firm's cost of capital declines by 100 basis points, the firm's residual value rises by 21.74% ($246.83/$202.76), while its horizon value increases by a much smaller percentage, at 5.54% ($123.46/$116.98).

## ECONOMIC PROFIT MODEL

The *economic profit approach* to equity valuation also looks at the firm's aggregate value, $V$. As described in Chapter 7 where we cover value-based metrics, the firm's corporate value (debt plus equity capitalization) is expressed as the sum of its total economic capital ($TC$) *plus* the net present value ($NPV$) generated by the firm's existing and anticipated future assets. That is,

$$V = Debt\ Value + Equity\ Value = TC + NPV \tag{19}$$

In contrast with the dividend discount model and free cash flow approaches described earlier in this chapter, the economic profit model provides a *direct* assessment of whether the firm's managers are investing in wealth-creating (namely, positive NPV) or wealth-destroying (negative NPV) investment projects.[15]

## NPV and Economic Profit

In principle, the firm's net present value is equal to the present value of anticipated economic profit, or economic value added, that is generated by both its existing and expected future assets. In this context, we can express the firm's NPV in terms of its discounted stream of anticipated economic value added according to:[16]

$$
\text{NPV} = \sum \frac{\text{EVA}_t}{(1+r)^t} \tag{20}
$$

where $\text{EVA}_t$ in equation (20) is the firm's expected economic value added at period $t$, and $r$ is the firm's weighted average cost of capital (assumed constant for all future years). As with the dividend discount and free cash flow approaches covered before, we can operationalize the economic profit model by looking at two distinct stages of growth; in this instance, EVA growth during the anticipated horizon years, $T$, followed by competitive or mature economic profit growth for years $T+1$ to infinity.

With two stages of economic profit growth, the firm's aggregate net present value can be expressed as equation (21):[17]

$$
\text{NPV} = \sum_{}^{T} \frac{\text{EVA}_t}{(1+r)^t} + \frac{1}{(1+r)^T} \frac{\text{EVA}_{T+1}}{r - g_{LT}} \tag{21}
$$

where EVA and $r$ were defined before, and $g_{LT}$, is the firm's long-term economic profit growth rate. This value is assumed to be equal to zero in the two-stage economic profit illustration that follows.

## Estimating Economic Profit

At this point, it is helpful to note that the firm's economic value added for any given year is equal to its *unlevered* net operating profit after tax less the dollar

---

[15] This does *not* mean that the economic profit model gives a valuation answer that is different from the dividend discount and free cash flow models. Indeed, these equity valuation procedures are all derived from the "equal rate of return principle" cited earlier.

[16] For a theoretical and empirical foundation on the economic profit approach to equity valuation, see Grant, *Foundations of Economic Value Added.*

[17] Applications of the two-stage EVA growth model are covered by: (1) Al Jackson, Michael J. Mauboussin, and Charles R. Wolf, "EVA Primer," *Equity-Research Americas* (CS First Boston: February 20, 1996), (2) Steven G. Einhorn, Gabrielle Napolitano, and Abby Joseph Cohen, "EVA: A Primer," *U.S. Research* (Goldman Sachs, September 10, 1997), and (3) Grant, *Foundations of Economic Value Added.*

capital charge on the firm's economic capital at the start of period $t$ (equivalently, the end of period $t-1$), \$COC. For consistency with estimation procedures used by Stern Stewart and Goldman Sachs, we express the firm's economic profit in terms of its accounting-based NOPAT and total capital.[18] In their economic profit models, NOPAT is net of the firm's accounting depreciation, while TC is a reflection of the firm's *net* physical capital (gross plant and equipment *less* accumulated depreciation) and short-term operating capital (current assets less *non*-interest bearing short-term liabilities). We show this as equation (22):

$$EVA_t = NOPAT_t - rTC_{t-1}$$
$$= EBIT_t(1 - t_u) - rTC_{t-1} \qquad (22)$$

Given the net operating profit after tax and net investment information shown in Exhibit 2, we now show that the economic profit and free cash flow approaches yield the same aggregate value of the firm and, thereby, are equivalent estimates of its stock price. The difference between the two approaches to equity valuation is largely one of interpretation — where (1) the free cash flow model looks at the firm's after-tax profitability *net* of required yearly investment to sustain a growing earnings stream, and (2) the economic profit model (in its most meaningful form) provides a *direct* present value assessment of whether the firm is a wealth creator or wealth waster. The firm's wealth creator status is in turn determined by the sign of its net present value generated by existing and anticipated future assets not currently in place.

Exhibit 7 provides the yearly EVA estimates for illustration of the economic profit approach to equities security valuation. As shown, the economic profit estimate for any given year is obtained by subtracting the total dollar capital charge from the firm's net operating profit estimate for that year. With an initial capital base of \$40 million, and a cost of capital of 10%, the firm's capital charge for year 1 is \$4 million. Subtracting this figure from the corresponding NOPAT estimate, \$14.95 million, we obtain the firm's anticipated economic profit for year 1, at \$10.95. The economic profit estimates shown in Exhibit 7 for the rest of the horizon period — namely, years 2 through 10 — are obtained in a similar manner.

Also, with zero-expected growth in the firm's economic profit *beyond* the horizon period, the firm's estimated economic profit for years 11 to infinity is forecasted at \$39.45 million. This EVA perpetuity is calculated by subtracting the firm's dollar cost of capital (cost of capital *times* economic capital in place at end of year 10), at \$13.14 million, from its estimated net operating profit after tax perpetuity (NOPAT in this case), at \$52.59 million. We use NOPAT in the *post* horizon years under the assumption that the firm's depreciation tax subsidy is used to maintain the productivity of existing assets in place at year $T$.

---

[18] The "NOPAT" approach to estimating the firm's economic profit is described in (1) G. Bennett Stewart III, *The Quest for Value* (Harper Collins, New York: 1991), and (2) Einhorn, Napolitano, and Cohen, "EVA: A Primer."

## Exhibit 7: Estimation of Economic Profit
### Cost of Capital = 10%

| Year | Yearly Net Inv. | Total Net Capital | NOPAT | Capital Charge | Economic Profit |
|------|------|------|------|------|------|
| 0 | | 40 | | | |
| 1 | 4.5 | 44.5 | 14.95 | 4.00 | 10.95 |
| 2 | 5.18 | 49.68 | 17.19 | 4.45 | 12.74 |
| 3 | 5.95 | 55.63 | 19.77 | 4.97 | 14.80 |
| 4 | 6.84 | 62.47 | 22.74 | 5.56 | 17.18 |
| 5 | 7.87 | 70.34 | 26.15 | 6.25 | 19.90 |
| 6 | 9.05 | 79.39 | 30.07 | 7.03 | 23.04 |
| 7 | 10.41 | 89.8 | 34.58 | 7.94 | 26.64 |
| 8 | 11.97 | 101.77 | 39.77 | 8.98 | 30.79 |
| 9 | 13.77 | 115.54 | 45.73 | 10.18 | 35.55 |
| 10 | 15.83 | 131.37 | 52.59 | 11.55 | 41.04 |
| 11 Plus | | | 52.59 | 13.14 | 39.45 |

## Exhibit 8: Valuation of Economic Profit

| Year | EVA | Pres.Val. | Cum. PV 0 |
|------|------|------|------|
| 1 | 10.95 | 9.95 | 9.95 |
| 2 | 12.74 | 10.53 | 20.48 |
| 3 | 14.80 | 11.12 | 31.60 |
| 4 | 17.18 | 11.73 | 43.34 |
| 5 | 19.90 | 12.36 | 55.69 |
| 6 | 23.04 | 13.00 | 68.70 |
| 7 | 26.64 | 13.67 | 82.37 |
| 8 | 30.79 | 14.36 | 96.73 |
| 9 | 35.55 | 15.08 | 111.81 |
| 10 | 41.04 | 15.82 | 127.63 |
| Residual Value | 394.53 | | 152.11 |
| NPV | | | 279.74 |
| Capital | | | 40.00 |
| Corp.Val | | | 319.74 |
| LT Debt | | | 12.00 |
| Equity | | | 307.74 |
| Share OS | | | 5.00 |
| Price | | | 61.55 |

## Present Value of Economic Profit

Exhibit 8 illustrates the pricing results of our application of the two-stage economic profit approach to corporate valuation. The top portion of the exhibit shows how to calculate the *net* present value of the firm's estimated economic profit during the horizon years, 1 though 10, when discounted at 10%. As shown, the cumulative present value of that anticipated EVA stream is $127.63 million. In turn, the residual value at *T* (equivalently, the net present value at *T*) of the firm's estimated

EVA stream in the post-horizon years is $394.53. This residual value estimate is calculated by discounting the EVA perpetuity (assuming *zero*-growth for convenience) by the firm's weighted average cost of capital according to equation (23):[19]

$$\text{NPV}_T = \frac{\text{EVA}_{T+1}}{r} = \frac{\$39.453}{0.1} = \$394.53 \tag{23}$$

Discounting the residual value figure (at *T*) back to the current period yields the intrinsic value of the firm's anticipated EVA stream in the post-horizon years, at $152.11 (rounded). Upon summing the NPV of the firm's EVA stream during *both* horizon and post-horizon periods — $127.63 and $152.11 respectively — we obtain the firm's estimated *total* net present value in the current period of $279.74. This expected NPV figure represents the aggregate value added to the firm's initial capital of $40 million due to positive economic profit that is generated by the firm's existing assets and anticipated future assets *not* currently in place. In our valuation illustration, the firm is a "wealth creator" because the positive stream of economic profit is the underlying source of its positive net present value.

At $319.74, the firm's estimated market value is equal to the sum of its initial economic capital, $40, plus the overall value added by the firm's manager's as given by equation (19):[20]

$$V = TC + NPV = \$40 + \$279.74 = \$319.74$$

Upon subtracting the firm's (assumed) long-term debt, $12 million, from its intrinsic corporate value, we obtain the firm's equity capitalization of $307.74 million. Dividing this latter figure by the assumed number of common shares outstanding yields the intrinsic worth of the firm's stock, at $61.55. That is,

$$\text{Stock Price} = \frac{\text{Equity Capitalization}}{n} = \frac{\$307.75}{5} = \$61.55$$

As expected, the underlying value of the firm and its outstanding shares are the same as the figures obtained previously using the free cash flow approach to corporate valuation. In principle, the same valuation result could be derived using the dividend discount model covered at the outset of this chapter — as the respective security valuation procedure — dividend discount, free cash flow, and economic profit approaches — are derived from the same risk-adjusted equal rate of return principle.[21]

---

[19] With mature growth, it should be apparent that the firm's EVA capitalization rate (in the valuation expression that follows) becomes $1/(r-g_{LT})$: where $g_{LT}$ is the firm's long-term EVA growth rate covering the post-horizon years.

[20] This valuation statement must be qualified by the fact that corporate value is also influenced by sector and macroeconomic forces (such as interest rate changes) that are independent of managerial decision making.

[21] See Fama and Miller, *The Theory of Finance*, Chapter 2.

### Exhibit 9: Cost of Capital Sensitivity Analysis
#### Economic Profit Model

| Rate % | Basis Pt. Change | NPV | Tot. Cap. | Corp. Val. | % Change Corp. Val. |
|---|---|---|---|---|---|
| 8 | -200 | 394.95 | 40.00 | 434.95 | 36.03 |
| 8.5 | -150 | 360.54 | 40.00 | 400.54 | 25.27 |
| 9 | -100 | 330.29 | 40.00 | 370.29 | 15.81 |
| 9.5 | -50 | 303.54 | 40.00 | 343.54 | 7.44 |
| 10 | 0 | 279.74 | 40.00 | 319.74 | 0.00 |
| 10.5 | 50 | 258.46 | 40.00 | 298.46 | -6.66 |
| 11 | 100 | 239.35 | 40.00 | 279.35 | -12.63 |
| 11.5 | 150 | 222.11 | 40.00 | 262.11 | -18.03 |
| 12 | 200 | 206.50 | 40.00 | 246.50 | -22.91 |

### Exhibit 10: Corporate Valuation and the Cost of Capital: Economic Profit Model

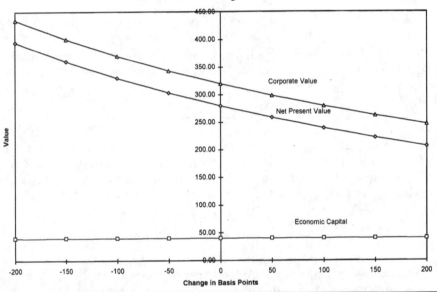

## Cost of Capital Change: Economic Profit Model

When discounting the firm's anticipated economic profit by 10% (our *initial* economic profit illustration), the firm's market value was estimated to be $319.74. Exhibits 9 and 10 (table and graph, respectively) show the pricing impact of cost of capital variation on both the firm's net present value and corporate value in the economic profit model. This time, the corporate value-cost of capital relationship manifests itself in the inverse relationship between the firm's net present value and its underlying weighted average cost of capital. This happens because corporate value in the economic profit approach is equal to the sum of the firm's initial economic capital (a fixed amount) and the aggregate NPV generated by the firm's existing and anticipated future assets.

Although the *absolute* price changes in NPV and corporate value are the same in response to fluctuations in the cost of capital, the percentage responses — or duration estimates — are of dissimilar magnitude. For example, Exhibit 9 shows that if the cost of capital declines by 100 basis points — from 10% to 9% — then corporate value rises from $319.74 to $370.29. This represents an absolute price change of $50.55 and a percentage change of 15.81%. In response to the 100 basis point decrease in the cost of capital, the firm's underlying NPV rises from $279.74 to $330.29. This too represents a price change of $50.55, yet a percentage change of 18.07%. The difference in price elasticity is explained by the fact that the firm's NPV makes up 87.5% of its corporate valuation while the initial capital accounts for the remaining capitalization weight ($40/319.74 \times 100 = 12.5\%$).

Also, since the firm's net present value is derived from the present value of its anticipated economic profit stream (again, from existing and expected future assets), the sensitivity of the firm's market value is fundamentally related to the sensitivity of its economic profit stream to underlying changes in the corporate-wide hurdle rate. Moreover, the source of the cost of capital variations shown in Exhibits 9 and 10 may be due to unforeseen changes in the risk-free rate of interest (which in many instances are linked to unanticipated changes in the inflation rate) and investors' (debt and equity holders in total) perception of the required premium for bearing the firm's underlying business risk.

## Macro-Application of Economic Profit Model

The economic profit approach has recently been applied to value both companies and the general market. Exhibit 11 shows how one prominent supplier of economic profit information, Goldman Sachs, uses economic profit analysis to estimate the intrinsic or "fair" value of the S&P Industrials share price.[22] In their macro-valuation analysis for January 5, 1998, they use the following assumptions about EVA-related parameters during the horizon or "forecast period" covering year-end 1997 to year 2002: (1) adjusted capital employed by S&P Industrial firms grows by the long-term capital growth rate of 6.7% per year, (2) an average U.S. return on capital of 12.7%, also equal to their ROC estimate for 1997, and (3) U.S. cost of capital estimate of 8%.

During the long-term phase of the valuation analysis, Goldman Sachs assumes that adjusted capital for the S&P Industrials will grow at 5.5% — the long-term, trend line nominal growth in U.S. gross domestic product — in the presence of a residual capital return (in perpetuity) equal to that estimated for 1998. These economic profit assumptions beyond year 2002 result in a 5.5% long-term growth rate in the *dollar* level of economywide EVA. As with the "forecast"

---

[22] For a complete discussion of this macro-EVA application, see Steven G. Einhorn, Gabrielle Napolitano, and Abby Joseph Cohen, "EVA® and Valuation of the S&P," U.S. Research (Goldman Sachs, January 8, 1998).

period (years 1998 through 2001), a weighted average cost of capital estimate of 8% is employed to value the S&P Industrials economic profit for the long term.

As of January 5, 1998, Goldman analysis indicates that the intrinsic "share" price of the S&P Industrials was $1315.02. This figure results from adding the aggregate net present value for the S&P Industrials of $975.45 ($885.85 plus $89.60) to the 1997 economic capital estimate of $547.57, and then subtracting "net debt" of $208.00 from the estimated S&P Industrials' "corporate value" of $1523.02. In light of the abnormal growth rate in U.S. equity prices during the past 5- and 10-year time periods, it is particularly noteworthy that economic profit analysis provides a rationale for arguing that the U.S. stock market was at a level consistent with macroeconomic fundamentals pertaining to (1) U.S. long-term capital growth rate, (2) after-tax average return on U.S. productive capital, and (3) the U.S. required rate of return.[23]

Indeed, the macroeconomic profit analysis shown in Exhibit 11 suggests that the U.S. stock market may have been *undervalued* during January 1998. At $1,130.55, the actual level of the S&P Industrials share price on January 5 fell short of its estimated intrinsic worth by some 14%. This sizable undervaluation though is due in large part to the presumption by Goldman Sachs that their 1998 residual capital return (ROC − COC) estimate of 4.45% will remain constant forever — a permanent "EVA-spread" assumption that seems especially optimistic, since *all* 20 of their residual capital return estimates for the 1978 to 1997 period are below 4.45%. Moreover, Goldman Sachs employs an equity risk premium of only 3% for the S&P Industrials, which is some 200 to 300 basis points below the 5% to 6% convention that is often used in both traditional and modern applications of the capital asset pricing model.

## SALES FRANCHISE MODEL

Due to competitive aspects of the global economy, Martin Leibowitz believes that firms can rapidly shift their production activities to the most efficient, least-cost producing nations. If correct, this competitiveness condition suggests that the firm's (positive) net present value is largely derived from a yearly "sales franchise" that results from brand differentiation, patents, copyrights, and country-specific trade and/or regulatory barriers to free entry. From a valuation perspective, this implies that the equity analyst should pay particular attention to the firm's "top-line" *revenue* growth as opposed to its "bottom-line" earnings per share.

In its most general form, the Leibowitz *sales franchise model* can be expressed as:[24]

---

[23] This view that the level of the U.S. stock market in recent years is consistent with that implied by economic profit fundamentals such as the "surplus return" on U.S. capital is emphasized in Grant, *Foundations of Economic Value Added.*

[24] For a complete discussion of the sales franchise approach to equity valuation, see Martin L. Leibowitz, "Franchise Margins and the Sales-Driven Franchise Value," *Financial Analysts Journal* (November-December 1997), pp. 43-53.

## Exhibit 11: S&P Industrials EVA® Valuation — Terminal Value Model

(Assuming a prospective average WACC of 8%, constant ROC-COC spread, and nominal growth in adjusted capital employed and EVA® of 5.5% in perpetuity)

| Year | (1) Capital Employed (a) | (2) NOPAT (b) | (3) (%) Return on Capital Employed (r*) | (4) (%) WACC (c) | (5) Spread (r-WACC) | (6) EVA (d) ($ per share) | (7) PV of Estimated EVA (e) ($ per share) | (8) Cumulative PV of Estimated EVA (e) ($ per share) |
|---|---|---|---|---|---|---|---|---|
| 1977 | 136.45 | 13.55 | NA | 8.8 | NA | NA | | |
| 1978 | 151.34 | 17.03 | 12.48 | 9.4 | 3.04 | 4.14 | | |
| 1979 | 169.71 | 21.06 | 13.92 | 10.4 | 3.52 | 5.33 | | |
| 1980 | 189.92 | 22.49 | 13.25 | 12.5 | 0.80 | 1.37 | | |
| 1981 | 208.56 | 23.89 | 12.58 | 14.2 | -1.63 | -3.10 | | |
| 1982 | 221.83 | 20.04 | 9.61 | 13.7 | -4.07 | -8.50 | | |
| 1983 | 223.96 | 20.30 | 9.15 | 12.3 | -3.10 | -6.89 | | |
| 1984 | 238.14 | 22.75 | 10.16 | 13.2 | -3.01 | -6.74 | | |
| 1985 | 257.52 | 24.70 | 10.37 | 11.6 | -1.24 | -2.96 | | |
| 1986 | 265.83 | 24.26 | 9.42 | 9.4 | 0.02 | 0.04 | | |
| 1987 | 286.08 | 29.85 | 11.23 | 10.0 | 1.28 | 3.42 | | |
| 1988 | 367.88 | 39.37 | 13.76 | 10.0 | 3.72 | 10.63 | | |
| 1989 | 408.00 | 42.48 | 11.55 | 9.8 | 1.75 | 6.43 | | |
| 1990 | 445.72 | 41.51 | 10.17 | 9.6 | 0.62 | 2.54 | | |
| 1991 | 443.38 | 31.61 | 7.09 | 9.2 | -2.14 | -9.52 | | |
| 1992 | 447.42 | 33.31 | 7.51 | 8.7 | -1.14 | -5.04 | | |
| 1993 | 461.83 | 37.63 | 8.41 | 7.7 | 0.71 | 3.16 | | |
| 1994 | 457.38 | 45.06 | 9.76 | 8.8 | 0.94 | 4.36 | | |
| 1995 | 475.82 | 54.07 | 11.82 | 8.5 | 3.31 | 15.16 | | |
| 1996 | 500.30 | 58.92 | 12.38 | 8.5 | 3.90 | 18.54 | | |
| 1997E | 547.57 | 63.70 | 12.73 | 8.5 | 4.23 | 21.16 | | |
| FORECAST PERIOD | | | | | | | | |
| 1998E | 584.32 | 68.16 | 12.45 | 8.0 | 4.45 | 24.36 | 22.55 | 22.55 |
| 1999E | 623.54 | 72.93 | 12.48 | 8.0 | 4.48 | 26.19 | 22.45 | 45.00 |
| 2000E | 665.39 | 78.04 | 12.52 | 8.0 | 4.52 | 28.15 | 22.35 | 67.35 |
| 2001E | 710.06 | 83.50 | 12.55 | 8.0 | 4.55 | 30.27 | 22.25 | 89.60 |
| 2002E | 757.72 | 89.34 | 12.58 | 8.0 | 4.58 | 32.54 | 22.15 | 111.74 |

Equity ("Fair") Value of S&P Industrials =

| | |
|---|---|
| + PV of EVA Terminal Value (f) | 885.85 |
| + Cumulative PV of Estimated EVA from 1998-2001 (see Column 8): | 89.60 |
| + Beginning Capital Employed (See Column 1): | 547.57 |
| = Corporate Value: | 1,523.02* |
| Less Net Debt: | 208.00 |
| = Equity Value: | 1,315.02 |
| 1/5/98 S&P Industrials Closing Price (Per Share): | 1,130.55 |
| CURRENT UNDERVALUATION | 14% |

(a) Estimates for 1998 through 2002 are based on the 20-year CAGR of 6.7%.
(b) Estimates for 1998 through 2002 are based on a normalized CAGR of 7.0%.
(c) Estimates for 1998 through 2002 reflect a projected WACC of 8%.
(d) Defined as (spread) × (beginning capital employed).
(e) Based on a projected WACC of 8%.
(f) Reflects a WACC of 8%, constant ROC-COC spread, and growth in adjusted capital (and $-EVA) of 5.5% beyond the year 2002. PV of EVA terminal value = PV of estimated EVA in 2002/(WACC - long-term growth in EVA) [i.e., $22.15/(0.08-0.055)].
*Correction to original.

Source: Table 1 on page 2 of Steven G. Einhorn, Gabrielle Napolitano, and Abby Joseph Cohen of Goldman Sachs, "EVA and Valuation of the S&P," *U.S. Research* (January 8,1998).
Copyright 1998 by Goldman Sachs.

$$V = TC + NPV(YSF)$$

$$= TC + \sum \frac{YSF_t}{(1+r)^t} \tag{24}$$

where $V$ is the intrinsic value of the firm, and NPV(YSF) is the *net* creation of wealth that is created by the firm's yearly sales franchise, YSF. For convenience, we'll look at the corporate valuation implications of Leibowitz's sales franchise model using our previous data.

## Illustration of Sales Franchise Model

Since we assumed initially that the firm's operating expenses and future net investment and working capital additions were a function of the annual sales forecast (or change therein), we can easily show how to derive the market value of the firm and its outstanding shares in terms of the Leibowitz sales franchise model. In this context, Exhibit 12 shows the firm's yearly sales franchise in terms of (1) forecasted sales, (2) the net profit margin, $p$, and (3) the *net* investment and working capital percentages, $f$ and $w$, respectively. A quick look at the yearly sales franchise column reveals that these dollar figures are the same economic profit values that were shown in Exhibit 7.

### Exhibit 12: Sales Franchise Model

| Year | Forecast Sales | Pretax Operating Margin | EBIT | Unlevered Tax Rate | NOPAT | Cap. Chg. Fraction Sales | Dollar Capital Charge | Yearly Sales Franchise |
|------|------|------|------|------|------|------|------|------|
| 1 | 115 | 0.2 | 23.00 | 0.35 | 14.95 | 0.0348 | 4.00 | 10.95 |
| 2 | 132.25 | 0.2 | 26.45 | 0.35 | 17.19 | 0.0336 | 4.45 | 12.74 |
| 3 | 152.09 | 0.2 | 30.42 | 0.35 | 19.77 | 0.0327 | 4.97 | 14.80 |
| 4 | 174.90 | 0.2 | 34.98 | 0.35 | 22.74 | 0.0318 | 5.56 | 17.17 |
| 5 | 201.14 | 0.2 | 40.23 | 0.35 | 26.15 | 0.0311 | 6.25 | 19.90 |
| 6 | 231.31 | 0.2 | 46.26 | 0.35 | 30.07 | 0.0304 | 7.03 | 23.04 |
| 7 | 266.00 | 0.2 | 53.20 | 0.35 | 34.58 | 0.0298 | 7.94 | 26.64 |
| 8 | 305.90 | 0.2 | 61.18 | 0.35 | 39.77 | 0.0294 | 8.98 | 30.79 |
| 9 | 351.79 | 0.2 | 70.36 | 0.35 | 45.73 | 0.0289 | 10.18 | 35.56 |
| 10 | 404.56 | 0.2 | 80.91 | 0.35 | 52.59 | 0.0286 | 11.55 | 41.04 |
| 11 Plus | 404.56 | 0.2 | 80.91 | 0.35 | 52.59 | 0.0325 | 13.14 | 39.45 |
|  |  |  |  |  |  | NPV(YSF) |  | $279.74 |
|  |  |  |  |  |  | Capital |  | $40.00 |
|  |  |  |  |  |  | Corp Val. |  | $319.74 |
|  |  |  |  |  |  | LT Debt |  | 12 |
|  |  |  |  |  |  | Equity |  | $307.74 |
|  |  |  |  |  |  | Share OS |  | 5 |
|  |  |  |  |  |  | Price |  | 61.55 |

Moreover, since the firm's estimated yearly sales franchise is the same as its economic profit stream (during both horizon and post-horizon years), the intrinsic worth of its annual sales franchise — generated by existing and expected future revenue-earning franchises — is $279.74. This pricing figure is of course the same as the firm's aggregate net present value. It is now a simple matter to show that the firm's estimated corporate value is $319.74:

$$V = TC + NPV(YSF)$$
$$= \$40 + \$279.74 = \$319.74$$

Not surprisingly, the firm's estimated stock price is $61.55. Should the market price of the company's outstanding shares fall short of this pricing estimate, then the stock is potentially undervalued, while the firm's stock price seems overvalued if market price is significantly higher than that implied by the intrinsic worth of its anticipated yearly sales franchise.

## SUMMARY

Equity valuation models can be used to calculate the intrinsic worth of the firm's securities. In this chapter, we examined the pricing significance of four prominent equity valuation models: (1) dividend discount model, (2) free cash flow model, (3) economic profit model, and (4) sales franchise model. Among the findings, it was noted that regardless of the particular model chosen, the firm's market value and share price are fundamentally related to the cash flow potential of its existing and anticipated future assets (not currently in place). This wealth equivalence among equity valuation models is based on the equal rate of return principle, whereby equivalent-risk securities must — in a well-functioning capital market — provide investors with the *same* one-period expected rate of return.

We also noted that there exists an *inverse* relationship between changes in corporate value — whether measured by present value of anticipated free cash flow or the firm's expected economic profit stream — and the firm's weighted average cost of capital. The sensitivity of corporate value to cost of capital change displays standard "fixed income" characteristics in the sense that firm value rises by a greater percentage when cost of capital goes down as compared with the (absolute value of) percentage decline in corporate value when interest rates go up. Since cost of capital changes in most instances are influenced by macroeconomic factors — such as fluctuations in risk-free interest rate and the business risk premium — that are outside of the control of management, the firm's corporate valuation and share price can change *independently* of firm-specific actions taken by management.

From a comparative perspective, the key benefit of the Leibowitz sales franchise model is that it makes a *specific* statement about a major source of the firm's economic profit — namely, revenue growth derived from patents, copyrights, and country-specific trade barriers. On the other hand, the model may be more restrictive than economic profit and free cash flow approaches to equity valuation since fluctuations in corporate value can be explained by other economic factors such as heightened interest rate uncertainty. Also, an undue focus on revenue growth may cause equity analysts and corporate managers alike to *mistakenly* conclude that revenue maximization and wealth maximization are equivalent.

Now that the equity analyst has a solid background in the theory and application of equity valuation techniques, we turn our attention to fundamental- and macroeconomic factor approaches to equity portfolio management.

# QUESTIONS

1. What is the underlying principle of the dividend discount model?

2. When does the dividend discount model tell the analyst that the stock will achieve its fair model?

3. Explain the difficulties of applying the dividend discount model.

4. Suppose that the following data are determined by a security analyst for the NotReal.Com Corporation:

$$D_1 = \$4.00 \quad D_2 = \$4.20 \quad D_3 = \$4.30 \quad D_4 = \$4.50 \ D_5 = \$4.70$$
$$P_5 = \$48 \quad T = 5$$
$$r_1 = r_2 = r_3 = r_4 = r_5 = 0.12$$

a. Using the dividend discount model, what is the fair price of NotReal.Com's stock price?

b. Suppose NotReal.Com Corporation's stock is selling for $39.68, is the stock undervalued or overvalued given your answer to part a?

c. If the required return is 9% instead of 12%, what is the fair price of Not-Real.Com Corporation's stock?

d. Suppose that NotReal.Com Corporation's stock price is selling for $39.68. What is the expected return?

e. If the required return is 13% is NotReal.Com Corporation's stock undervalued or overvalued?

5. Suppose an investor applies the constant-growth version of the dividend discount model to estimate the price of the TelTex Corporation. The current dividend per share is $3.

a. Assuming the current dividend will grow at a constant rate of 10% per year and the discount rate is 12%, what is the estimated value of a share of Tel-Tex Corporation?

b. Suppose the market price of a share of TelTex Corporation is $12. What spread between the discount rate and the growth rate is consistent with the current dividend, the observed market price, and the constant-growth version of the dividend discount model?

6. What are the assumptions underlying the three-phase dividend discount model?

7. This equity valuation question is based on the stock valuation exercise using the dividend growth model for Bell Atlantic, Bell South, and Cincinnati Bell.

a. Use the actual stock prices given in the chapter for the three telephone companies to solve for the expected rate of return, given knowledge of their current dividend and anticipated dividend growth rates.

b. Show where Bell Atlantic, Bell South, and Cincinnati Bell plot on the "Securities Market Line." Recall that the SML shows the relationship between the discount rate using CAPM (vertical axis) and the level of systematic risk, beta, for the stock (horizontal axis).

c. "Alpha" — a measure of abnormal return — can be viewed as the difference between the expected stock return (see part a) and the CAPM return. Show where the alpha values for the three stocks plot in the SML graph, and explain whether the shares of these telephone companies were overvalued or undervalued at that time based on the model.

8. Use the free cash flow forecasting model to develop a set of 5-year forecasts for ABC Growth Company.

> *ABC Growth Company:*
> Revenue base = $50 million
> Estimated sales growth $(g) = 30\%$
> Pre-tax operating margin $(p) = 25\%$
> Income tax rate for unlevered firm $(t) = 35\%$
> Annual capital investment (per dollar of sales increase) $(f) = 20\%$
> Working capital additions (per dollar of sales increase) $(w) = 10\%$

Your financial "spreadsheet" should show the year-to-year details of how you arrived at the free cash flow estimates, including (1) revenue, (2) EBIT, (3) NOPAT, (4) annual capital investment, (5) working capital additions, and (6) the annual free cash flow estimates.

9. a. What is the "horizon value" of the free cash flow estimates for ABC Growth Company (see the previous question). Assume a discount rate — or weighted average cost of capital — of 8% in answering this question.

b. What is the "residual value" of ABC Growth Company at the end of year 5? Assume, for convenience, that revenue growth ceases at the end of year 5, annual capital spending is equal to economic depreciation, and that no further working capital additions are needed beyond year 5.

c. What are the intrinsic value estimates of ABC Growth Company and its shares of common stock? Assume that long-term debt is equal to 10% of the estimated worth of the growth company, and that ABC has 10 million shares of common stock outstanding.

d. If the common stock of ABC Growth Company is selling for $20, is the stock potentially overvalued or undervalued? Also, if ABC shares are in fact mispriced, does your discounted cash flow (DCF) analysis say anything about when the shares would rise or fall in the marketplace? Explain your reasoning.

e. In principle, by what percent would a 100 basis point decrease in the cost of capital for ABC Growth Company cause its stock price to rise? Show the calculation.

f. In principle, by what percent would a 100 basis point rise in the cost of capital cause the firm's market value to fall? Show the calculation.

g. Illustrate your corporate valuation findings in parts e and f graphically, and explain why there is an asymmetric corporate pricing response to variations in the discount rate (or weighted average cost of capital).

10. INTEL Corporation: Free Cash Flow Analysis

*Background:* Recall the Value Line report for Intel Corporation (dated April 23, 1999) that we used to review the traditional measures of corporate financial success in Chapter 6 on page 151. Let's now use the 1999 report to estimate the intrinsic worth of Intel Corporation and its stock using the free cash flow (question 10) and economic profit (see question 11) approaches to equity valuation.

The following additional information is provided to help construct the free cash flow estimates using the Value Line report:

- Assume that the mid-point of the column titled "02-04" shown at the top of the Value Line table represents the year "03" (for year-end 2003).
- EBIT for any year can be estimated by multiplying "Sales" times "Operating (Profit) Margin."
- Use the "Income Tax Rate" listed on the Value Line report to calculate NOPAT for any given year. Note that the capital structure box indicates that Intel is for all practical purposes an "unlevered" firm.
- Gross (annual) capital investment can be estimated by multiplying "Capital Spending per share" times "Common Shares Outstanding." Note that implied annual capital spending for the years 2001 and 2002 can be estimated from the growth in gross annual capital spending for the years 2000 to 2003.
- Economic depreciation is measured by "Depreciation" shown in the Value Line table. Note that implied depreciation estimates for the years 2001 and 2002 can be estimated from known depreciation figures for the years 2000 and 2003.
- Working capital additions can be estimated by the change in "Working Capital" for any two years. (As with gross annual capital spending and depreciation, implied changes in working capital can be calculated from otherwise known working capital changes at years 2000 and 2003).

a. Develop a set of free cash flow estimates for Intel Corporation for the four years 2000 to 2003.

b. What is the "horizon value" of Intel's free cash flow estimates at year-end 1999? Assume a cost of capital (discount rate) of 8% in answering this question.

c. What is Intel's estimated "residual value" at year-end 2003? For convenience, use the zero-growth assumption to estimate the firm's free cash flow estimates beyond year 2003.

d. What is the intrinsic value (or enterprise value) of Intel Corporation at year-end 1999? What is the intrinsic worth of Intel stock at year-end 1999? (Note: Use Intel's estimated "Long-Term Debt" figure for 1999 and "Common Shares Outstanding" at that time in estimating Intel's stock price for 1999.)

e. Based on the price shown on the Value Line report, is Intel stock overvalued or undervalued for 1999? Why?

11. INTEL Corporation: Economic Profit Analysis

Use the Value Line report for Intel Corporation to review some of the key features of the economic profit approach to equity valuation:

a. Develop a set of economic value added (EVA) estimates for Intel Corporation for the years 2000 to 2003. Use beginning of year total capital estimates ("Long-Term Debt" plus "Shareholders' Equity") from the Value Line report to estimate capital charges for the years 2000 to 2003. Note that implied total capital figures for the years 2001 and 2002 will need to be calculated.

b. What is the "horizon value" at year-end 1999 of Intel's economic profit (EVA) estimates for the four years spanning 2000 to 2003? Assume an 8% cost of capital (as before).

c. What is the net present value of Intel Corporation at year-end 1999? (Note: We can estimate the NPV of this semi-conductor firm by (simply) subtracting its total capital from the estimated 1999 "enterprise value" of Intel obtained in question 10. In principle, the two equity valuation approaches—free cash flow and economic profit models—are equivalent.)

d. What forward-looking EVA multiple, or "EVA capitalization rate," at year-end 2003 would make the economic profit and free cash flow approaches yield the same intrinsic share price for Intel Corporation at year-end 1999?

# Chapter 9

# Factor-Based Portfolio Models

An important analytical tool used by equity managers for portfolio construction and risk control is a factor model. This quantitative approach to portfolio management is referred to as a *factor-based approach*. In this chapter, we'll see what a factor model is and how it can be used by both active and passive managers.

As we will see, a factor model tries to explain stock returns. Because of this, a factor model can be used to evaluate the performance of a portfolio manager in addition to its role in portfolio construction and risk control. We learned in Chapters 2 and 3 that the single index market model is a convenient tool for assessing the systematic and unsystematic return elements of an equity portfolio. However, this model does not reveal any information about the underlying factors that may lead to abnormally high (or low) average returns. In Chapter 14, we'll see how an equity factor model can be used to assess a manager's performance.

## SNAPSHOT VIEW OF FACTOR MODELS

Before examining the types of factor models used by practitioners, let's first look at the basic characteristics of a factor model — sometimes referred to as a *multi-factor model*. Russell Fogler provides a helpful introduction to factor models.[1] In an insightful article, he notes that the return on any stock or portfolio can always be decomposed into both market and *non*-market effects based on: (1) overall market direction as determined by the beta effect, (2) "common factors" that impact groups of stock such as size, price/book ratio, price/earnings ratio, and dividend yield, (3) industry or sector effects, and (4) company specific return effects that uniquely impact the performance of a particular stock.

To illustrate this statistical concept, Fogler describes a multi-factor equity model having three "common factors" according to:

$$R_i = b_0 + b_1(\text{Beta}) + b_2(\text{Size}) + b_3(E/P) + b_4(D/P)$$
$$+ b_5(\text{Industrial}) + b_6(\text{Non-Industrial}) + e_i$$

where the set of "$b$-coefficients" (or slope measures) represent the stock (or portfolio) return sensitivities to the set of factors described in the equation. These factors include Beta for systematic market factor, and size, earnings yield (E/P), and dividend yield for systematic *non*-market or "common factors" that influence the

---

[1] H. Russell Fogler, "Common Stock Management in the 1990s," *Journal of Portfolio Management* (Winter 1990), pp. 26-35.

stock or portfolio return over time. Also, the Industrial and Non-Industrial terms are "dummy variables" having a value of either one or zero.

If a company operates in the financial services sector of the economy, then the Non-Industrial exposure would be *one* while the Industrial measure would, by definition, be zero. As with all regression models, the error term, $e_i$, is assumed to be a normally distributed random variable. Fogler adds that this company specific term is the heart of *real* security analysis, as its *non*-random components (if any) can only be known to few active investors. Otherwise, the information content of the $e_i$ term would lead to another systematic *non*-market factor.

# TYPES OF FACTOR MODELS

There are three types of factor models being used today to manage equity portfolios: statistical factor models, macroeconomic factor models, and fundamental factor models.[2] We describe these three factor models below.

## Statistical Factor Models

In a *statistical factor model,* historical and cross-sectional data on stock returns are tossed into a statistical model. The statistical model used is *principal components analysis* which is a special case of a statistical technique called *factor analysis.* The goal of the statistical model is to best explain the observed stock returns with "factors" that are linear return combinations and uncorrelated with each other.

For example, suppose that monthly returns for 1,500 companies for ten years are computed. The goal of principal components analysis is to produce "factors" that best explain the observed stock returns. Let's suppose that there are six "factors" that do this. These "factors" are statistical artifacts. The objective in a statistical factor model then becomes to determine the economic meaning of each of these statistically derived factors.

Because of the problem of interpretation, it is difficult to use the factors from a statistical factor model for valuation and risk control. Instead, practitioners prefer the two other models described below, which allow them to prespecify meaningful factors, and thus produce a more intuitive model.

## Macroeconomic Factor Models

In a *macroeconomic factor model*, the inputs to the model are historical stock returns and observable macroeconomic variables. That is, the raw descriptors are macroeconomic variables. The goal is to determine which macroeconomic variables are pervasive in explaining historical stock returns. Those variables that are

---

[2] Gregory Connor, "The Three Types of Factor Models: A Comparison of Their Explanatory Power," *Financial Analysts Journal* (May-June 1995), pp. 42-57.

pervasive in explaining the returns are then the factors and included in the model. The responsiveness of a stock to these factors is estimated using historical time series data.

We will discuss three proprietary macroeconomic factor models here: (1) the Burmeister, Ibbotson, Roll, and Ross (BIRR) model,[3] (2) the Salomon Brothers' Risk Attribute Model,[4] and (3) the Northfield Macroeconomic Equity Risk Model.[5]

In the BIRR model, there are five macroeconomic factors that reflect unanticipated changes in the following macroeconomic variables:

- investor confidence (confidence risk)
- interest rates (time horizon risk)
- inflation (inflation risk)
- real business activity (business cycle risk)
- a market index (market timing risk)

Exhibit 1 explains each of these macroeconomic factor risks

In the U.S. version of the Salomon Brothers RAM model, the following six macroeconomic factors have been found to best describe the financial environment and are therefore the factors used:

- change in expected long-run economic growth
- short-run business cycle risk
- long-term bond yield changes
- short-term Treasury bill changes
- inflation shock
- dollar changes versus trading partner currencies

In addition, there is another factor called "residual market beta" which is included to capture macroeconomic factors after controlling for the other six macroeconomic factors. Exhibit 2 provides a brief description of each macroeconomic factor.

Like BIRR and Salomon, Northfield Information Services has developed a proprietary macroeconomic equity risk model. The Northfield model looks at the pricing impact of *unanticipated* changes in seven macroeconomic factors to assess security and portfolio return performance. Their macro equity risk factors include:

---

[3] Edwin Burmeister, Roger Ibbotson, Richard Roll, and Stephen A. Ross, "Using Macroeconomic Factors to Control Portfolio Risk," unpublished paper. The information used in this chapter regarding the BIRR model is obtained from various pages of the BIRR website (*www.birr.com*).

[4] This model is described in Eric H. Sorensen, Joseph J. Mezrich, and Chee Thum, *The Salomon Brothers U.S. Risk Attribute Model, Salomon Brothers*, Quantitative Strategy, October 1989, and Joseph J. Mezrich, Mark O'Donnell, and Vele Samak, *U.S. RAM Model: Model Update*, Salomon Brothers, Equity Portfolio Analysis, April 8, 1997.

[5] Northfield factor models are covered in two separate product reports for 1998: (1) Northfield Macroeconomic Equity Risk Model, and (2) Northfield Fundamental Equity Risk Model. We cover their fundamental equity risk model later in this chapter.

## Exhibit 1: Macroeconomic Factor Risks in the BIRR Factor Model

### Confidence Risk

Confidence Risk exposure reflects a stock's sensitivity to unexpected changes in investor confidence. Investors always demand a higher return for making relatively riskier investments. When their confidence is high, they are willing to accept a smaller reward than when their confidence is low. Most assets have a positive exposure to Confidence Risk. An unexpected increase in investor confidence will put more investors in the market for these stocks, increasing their price and producing a positive return for those who already held them. Similarly, a drop in investor confidence leads to a drop in the value of these investments. Some stocks have a negative exposure to the Confidence Risk factor, however, suggesting that investors tend to treat them as "safe haven" when their confidence is shaken.

### Time Horizon Risk

Time Horizon Risk exposure reflects a stock's sensitivity to unexpected changes in investors' willingness to invest for the long term. An increase in time horizon tends to benefit growth stocks, while a decrease tends to benefit income stocks. Exposures can be positive or negative, but growth stocks as a rule have a higher (more positive) exposure than income stocks.

### Inflation Risk

Inflation Risk exposure reflects a stock's sensitivity to unexpected changes in the inflation rate. Unexpected increases in the inflation rate put a downward pressure on stock prices, so most stocks have a negative exposure to Inflation Risk. Consumer demand for luxuries declines when real income is eroded by inflation. Thus, retailer, eating places, hotels, resorts, and other "luxuries" are harmed by inflation, and their stocks therefore tend to be more sensitive to inflation surprises and, as a result, have a more negative exposure to Inflation Risk. Conversely, providers of necessary goods and services (agricultural products, tire and rubber goods, etc.) are relatively less harmed by inflation surprises, and their stocks have a smaller (less negative) exposure. A few stocks attract investors in times of inflation surprise and have a positive Inflation Risk exposure.

### Market Timing Risk

Market Timing Risk exposure reflects a stock's sensitivity to moves in the stock market as a whole that cannot be attributed to the other factors. Sensitivity to this factor provides information similar to that of the CAPM Beta about how a stock tends to respond to changes in the broad market. It differs in that the Market Timing factor reflects only those surprises that are not explained by the other four factors.

### Business Cycle Risk

Business Cycle Risk exposure reflects a stock's sensitivity to unexpected changes in the growth rate of business activity. Stocks of companies such as retail stores that do well in times of economic growth have a higher exposure to Business Cycle Risk than those that are less affected by the business cycle, such as utilities or government contractors. Stocks can have a negative exposure to this factor if investors tend to shift their funds toward those stocks when news about the growth rate for the economy is not good.

Source: Reproduced from pages of the BIRR website (*www.birr.com*).

## Exhibit 2: Macroeconomic Factors in the Salomon Brothers U.S. Risk Attribute Model

*Economic Growth*[a]

Monthly change in industrial production as measured concurrently with stock returns.

*Business Cycle*[b]

The change in the spread between the yield on 20-year investment-grade corporate bonds and 20-year Treasury bonds is used as a proxy for the shorter-term cyclical behavior of the economy. Changes in the spread capture the risk of default resulting from the interaction of earnings cyclicality and existing debt structure.

*Long-Term Interest Rates*[b]

The change in interest rates is measured by the change in the 10-year Treasury yield. Changes in this yield alters the relative attractiveness of financial assets and therefore induces a change in the portfolio mix.

*Short-Term Interest Rates*[b]

The change in short-term interest rates is measured by changes in the 1-month Treasury bill rate.

*Inflation Shock*[a]

Inflation is measured by the Consumer Price Index. The inflation shock component is found by subtracting expected inflation from realized inflation. Expected inflation is measured using a proprietary econometric model.

*U.S. Dollar*[b]

The impact of currency fluctuations on the market is measured by changes in the basket of currencies. Specifically, a 15-country, trade-weighted basket of currencies is used.

[a] Adapted from Joseph J. Mezrich, Mark O'Donnell, and Vele Samak, *U.S. RAM Model: Model Update*, Salomon Brothers, Equity Portfolio Analysis, April 8, 1997, p. 1.
[b] Adapted from the discussion on page 4 of Eric H. Sorensen, Joseph J. Mezrich, and Chee Thum, *The Salomon Brothers U.S. Risk Attribute Model*, Salomon Brothers, Quantitative Strategy, October 1989.

- unanticipated change in inflation rate
- changes in industrial production
- oil price changes
- change in housing starts
- exchange rate variation
- change in credit risk premiums
- change in slope of treasury yield curve

A summary description of each macroeconomic factor used by Northfield Information Services along with the percentage change descriptors for the seven macro-factors is shown in Exhibit 3.

### Parameter Estimation in a Macro Factor Model

We'll now use the Salomon Brothers and Northfield models to explain the statistical procedures that are often seen in a macroeconomic factor model.[6] First, we'll discuss the parameter estimation and standardization procedure used in Salomon Brothers' Risk Attribute Model.

---

[6] We also describe and illustrate the standardization procedure used in a fundamental equity risk model in a later section.

## Exhibit 3: Northfield Macroeconomic Factor Model Economic Variable Definitions

*Unexpected Inflation (UI)*
Monthly unexpected inflation is calculated as the negative of the change in the *real* rate of interest. The inflation rate for a month is estimated as 12 times the percentage change in the Consumer Price Index from the prior month. The short-term interest rate for a month is defined as the three-month Treasury bill bond-equivalent yield as of the beginning of the month. The real rate of interest is simply the interest rate *minus* the inflation rate.
UI calculation for month $t$:

$$\text{Inflation}_t = [(CPI_t/CPI_{t-1})-1] \times 100 \times 12$$
$$\text{Real Rate}_t = \text{TBill Yield}_{t-1} - \text{Inflation}_t$$
$$UI_t = (RR_t - RR_{t-1}) \times (-1)$$

*Industrial Production (IP)*
The Industrial Production Index is the one published by the Federal Reserve Board. This index is periodically re-indexed to a new base, and Northfield takes care to use figures that are comparable in construction of the IP index.
IP calculation for month $t$:

$$\% \text{ Change } IP_t = [(IP_t/IP_{t-1}) - 1] \times 100$$

*Oil Prices (OP)*
The Oil Price is defined as the settlement price of the futures contract for crude oil on the New York Mercantile Exchange that is closest to expiration. The units are dollars per barrel.
OP calculation for month $t$:

$$\% \text{ Change } OP_t = [(OP_t/OP_{t-1}) - 1] \times 100$$

*Housing Starts (HS)*
The Housing Starts value is the announced rate of new housing starts, expressed in thousands of units.
HS calculation for month $t$:

$$\% \text{ Change } HS_t = [(HS_t/HS_{t-1}) - 1] \times 100$$

*Exchange Value of the U.S. Dollar*
The Exchange Value is based on the same cash index upon which the New York Futures Exchange U.S. Dollar futures contract is based.
EV calculation for month $t$:

$$\% \text{ Change } EV_t = [(EV_t/EV_{t-1}) - 1] \times 100$$

*Credit Risk Premium (CRP)*
The Credit Risk Premium is defined as the yield on Barrons "Best Grade" Corporate Bond Index, less the yield on the Barrons "Intermediate-Grade" Corporate Bond Index. The constituents of these indices correspond roughly to AAA and BAA.
CRP calculation for month $t$:

$$CRP_t = \text{BAA Yield}_t - \text{AAA Yield}_t$$
$$\text{Change in Credit Risk Premium} = CRP_t - CRP_{t-1}$$

## Exhibit 3 (Continued)

*Slope of Term Structure (STS)*

The slope of the term structure is defined as the yield-to-maturity of the 20-year U.S. Treasury bond minus the bond-equivalent yield of the one-year Treasury bill. If more than one issue of the 20-year bond is trading, the issue that is nearest par is utilized. If no issue is trading with a 20-year maturity, a hypothetical 20-year maturity yield is interpolated using a second-order curve fit to the yield curve. Since yields are being used, the change in slope of the yield curve is a simple subtraction:

$$STS_t = \text{20-year } YTM_t - \text{1-year } YTM_t$$
$$\text{Change Slope of Yield Curve} = STS_t - STS_{t-1}$$

*Special Symbols*

Northfield also uses *special* symbols to represent the average characteristics of the stocks in a particular industry. There are 55 industry classifications. All special symbols are assumed to represent one "share" outstanding at a "price" of $1000.

Source: Adapted from *Macroeconomic Equity Risk Model*, Northfield Information Services, 1998 product report, pp. 11-13.

For each stock in the universe used by Salomon Brothers (about 3,500) a multiple regression is estimated. The dependent variable is the stock's monthly return. The independent variables are the six macroeconomic factors, the residual market factor, and other market factors. The size and statistical significance of the regression coefficients of each of the macroeconomic factors is examined. Then for all stocks in the universe the regression coefficient for each of the macroeconomic factors is standardized. The purpose of standardizing the estimated regression coefficients is that it makes a comparison of the relative sensitivity of a stock to each macroeconomic factor easier.

The standardization methodology is as follows. For a given macroeconomic factor, the average value and standard deviation of the estimated regression coefficient from all the stocks in the universe are computed. The standardized regression coefficient for a stock with respect to a given macroeconomic factor is then found by calculating the difference between the estimated regression coefficient and the average value and then dividing this value by the standard deviation. The standardized regression coefficient is restricted to a value between −5 and +5.

A stock's standardized regression coefficient for a given macroeconomic factor is then the measure of the sensitivity of that stock to that risk factor. The standardized regression coefficient is therefore the factor sensitivity. If a stock has a factor sensitivity for a specific macroeconomic factor of zero, this means that it has average response to that macroeconomic factor. The more the factor sensitivity deviates from zero, the more responsive the stock is to that risk factor. For example, consider the economic growth factor. A positive value for this macroeconomic factor means that if all other factors are unchanged, a company is likely to outperform market returns if the economy improves. A negative value for the economic growth factor means that if all other factors are unchanged, a company is likely to underperform market returns if the economy improves.

Moreover, the sensitivity for the factors are estimated so that they are statistically independent. This means that there will be no double counting the influence of a factor.

Northfield Information Services employs multiple regression techniques on nearly 8,000 stocks when estimating the parameters in their macroeconomic factor model. In the Northfield Macroeconomic Equity Risk Model, the monthly return sensitivities — or "factor loadings" — on the macroeconomic factors are estimated in two distinct stages. First, monthly stock returns are regressed against four of the seven factors covered in their economywide risk model. These are familiar macroeconomic risk factors that are also seen in macro-equity risk models like BIRR — including, *unexpected* changes in inflation, industrial production, credit or default risk premiums, and the slope of the Treasury yield curve. According to Northfield Information Services, the goal of the first stage regression is to preserve the results of original macroeconomic research in this area, and to avoid a statistical problem caused by multicollinearity among the macroeconomic factors.

In the second stage, Northfield regresses monthly security return "residuals" on *unexpected* changes in the three remaining factors — including unanticipated changes in oil prices, housing starts, and changes in the U.S. dollar exchange rate. According to Northfield officials, this two-stage regression procedure helps to reduce estimation bias in the regression coefficients (due to multicollinearity in the macro factors) since the two most highly correlated variables — namely, oil prices and inflation — appear in separate regression equations.

## Fundamental Factor Models

Fundamental factor models use company and industry attributes and market data as raw descriptors. Examples are price/earnings ratios, book/price ratios, estimated economic growth, and trading activity. The inputs into a fundamental factor model are stock returns and the raw descriptors about a company. Those fundamental variables about a company that are pervasive in explaining stock returns are then the raw descriptors retained in the model. Using cross-sectional analysis the sensitivity of a stock's return to a raw descriptor is estimated.

As determined by Jacobs and Levy,[7] many of these descriptors are highly correlated. Adding highly correlated factors to a model neither enhances returns nor lowers risk. Factors that by themselves seem to be important may be unimportant when combined with other factors; factors that by themselves seem not to be important may be important when combined with other factors. A manager must be able to untangle these relationships.

Two of the most well-known and commercially available fundamental factor models are the BARRA and the Wilshire models. The BARRA E2 model

---

[7] Bruce I. Jacobs and Kenneth N. Levy, "Disentangling Equity Return Regularities: New Insights and Investment Opportunities," *Financial Analyst Journal* (May-June 1988), pp. 18-43.

begins with raw descriptors.[8] It then combines raw descriptors to obtain risk indexes to capture related company attributes. For example, raw descriptors such as debt-to-asset ratio, debt-to-equity ratio, and fixed-rate coverage are measures that capture a company's financial leverage. These measures would be combined to obtain a risk index for financial leverage.

The BARRA E2 fundamental factor model has 13 risk indexes and 55 industry groups. For 12 of the risk indexes and the 55 industry groups, the model is estimated for BARRA's HICAP universe (1,000 of the largest-capitalization companies plus selected slightly smaller companies to fill underrepresented industry groups) using statistical techniques. The universe has varied from 1,170 to 1,300 companies.

Exhibit 4 reproduces the information about the 13 risk indexes as published by BARRA. Also shown in the exhibit are the raw descriptors used to construct each risk index. For example, the earnings-to-price ratio is a combination of the following raw descriptors: current earnings-to-price ratio, earnings-to-price ratio for the past five years, and IBES earnings-to-price ratio projection. Before each raw descriptor in Exhibit 4 is a plus or minus sign. The sign indicates how the raw descriptor influences a risk index. The 55 industry classifications are shown in Exhibit 5.

## Exhibit 4: BARRA E2 Model Risk Index Definitions*

1. Variability In Markets (VIM)

This risk index is a predictor of the volatility of a stock based on its behavior and the behavior of its options in the capital markets. Unlike beta, which measures only the response of a stock to the market, Variability in Markets measures a stock's overall volatility, including its response to the market. A high beta stock will necessarily have a high Variability in Markets exposure. However, a high exposure will not necessarily imply a high beta; the stock may be responding to factors other than changes in the market.

This index uses measures such as the cumulative trading range and daily stock price standard deviation to identify stocks with highly variable prices. BARRA uses different formulas for three categories of stocks.

a. Optioned stocks — all stocks having listed options.

b. Listed stocks — all stocks in the HICAP universe that are listed on an exchange but do not have listed options.

c. Thin stocks — all stocks that are traded over the counter or are outside the HICAP universe, except those with listed options.

Optioned stocks are distinct for several reasons. First, the option price provides an implicit forecast of the total standard deviation of the stock itself. Second, optioned stocks tend to be those with greatest investor interest and with the most effective trading volume. Stock trading volume descriptors understate the effective volume because they omit option volume.

---

[8] The BARRA E2 model is BARRA's second generation U.S. equity model. In 1997, BARRA released its third generation U.S. equity model (BARRA E3). The discussion in this chapter and the information provided in Exhibits 4 and 5 are based on the BARRA E2 model. The E3 model closely resembles the E2 model in structure, but with improved industry and risk index definitions.

# Exhibit 4 (Continued)

Thin stocks, about ten percent of the basic sample, are broken out because they tend to trade differently from other stocks. Over-the-counter stocks and other thinly traded securities show price behavior inconsistent with efficient and timely prices. Thin stocks are less synchronized with market movements, and exhibit frequent periods in which no meaningful price changes occur as well as occasional outlying price changes that are promptly reversed. These influences cause some indicators of stock price variability to be biased.

In calculating this index, BARRA standardizes the formulas for the three stock categories relative to one another to provide one index for the total population.

A. Optioned Stock Descriptors
  + Cumulative Range, 12 months
  + Beta * Sigma
  + Option Standard Deviation
  + Daily Standard Deviation
B. Listed Stock Descriptors
  + Beta * Sigma
  + Cumulative Range, 12 months
  + Daily Standard Deviation
  + Trading Volume to Variance
  − Log of Common Stock Price
  + Serial Dependence
  − Annual Share Turnover
C. Thin Stock Descriptors
  + Beta * Sigma
  + Cumulative Range, 12 months
  + Annual Share Turnover
  − Log of Common Stock Price
  − Serial Dependence

2. Success (SCS)
The Success index identifies recently successful stocks using price behavior in the market (measured by historical alpha and relative strength) and, to a lesser degree, earnings growth information. The relative strength of a stock is significant in explaining its volatility.

  + Relative Strength
  + Historical Alpha
  + Recent Earnings Change
  + IBES Earnings Growth
  − Dividend Cuts, 5 years
  + Growth in Earnings per Share

3. Size (SIZ)
The Size index values total assets and market capitalization to differentiate large stocks from small stocks. This index has been a major determinant of performance over the years as well as an important source of risk.

  + Log of Capitalization
  + Log of Total Assets
  + Indicator of Earnings History

## *Exhibit 4 (Continued)*

4. Trading Activity (TRA)

Trading activity measures the relative activity of a firm's shares in the market, or the "institutional popularity" of a company. The most important descriptors are the share turnover variables. In addition, this index includes the ratio of trading volume to price variability, the logarithm of price, and the number of analysts following the stock, as reported in the IBES database. The stocks with more rapid share turnover, lower price, and signs of greater trading activity are generally the higher risk stocks.

+ Annual Share Turnover
+ Quarterly Share Turnover
+ Share Turnover, 5 years
+ Log of Common Stock Price
+ IBES Number of Analysts
+ Trading Volume to Variance

5. Growth (GRO)

The Growth index is primarily a predictor of a company's future growth but also reflects its historical growth. BARRA estimates earnings growth for the next five years using regression techniques on a comprehensive collection of descriptors, all of which are distinct elements of the growth concept. The Growth index includes descriptors of payout, asset growth and historical growth in earnings, the level of earnings to price, and variability in capital structure.

− Payout, 5 years
− Earnings to Price Ratio, 5 years
+ Earnings Growth
+ Capital Structure Change
− Normalized Earnings to Price Ratio
+ Recent Earnings Change
− Dividend Yield, 5 years
+ IBES Earnings Change
− Yield Forecast
+ Indicator of Zero Yield
− Earnings to Price Ratio
− IBES Earnings to Price Ratio
+ Growth in Total Assets

6. Earnings to Price Ratio (EPR)

The Earnings to Price Ratio measures the relationship between company earnings and market valuation. To compute the Earnings to Price Ratio, BARRA combines measures of past, current, and estimated future earnings.

+ Current Earnings to Price Ratio
+ Earnings to Price Ratio, 5 years
+ IBES Earnings to Price Ratio Projection

7. Book to Price Ratio (BPR)

This index is simply the book value of common equity divided by the market capitalization of a firm.

8. Earnings Variability (EVR)

The Earnings Variability index measures a company's historical earnings variability and cash flow fluctuations. In addition to variance in earnings over five years, it includes the relative variability of earnings forecasts taken from the IBES database, and the industry concentration of a firm's activities.

# Exhibit 4 (Continued)

---

+ Variance in Earnings
+ IBES Standard Deviation to Price Ratio
+ Earnings Covariability
+ Concentration
+ Variance of Cash Flow
+ Extraordinary Items

9. Financial Leverage (FLV)

The Financial Leverage index captures the financial structure of a firm as well as its sensitivity to interest rates using the debt to assets ratio, the leverage at book value, and the probability of fixed charges not being covered. Bond market sensitivity is included only for financial companies.

- Bond Market Sensitivity
+ Debt to Assets Ratio
+ Leverage at Book (Debt to Equity)
+ Uncovered Fixed Charges

10. Foreign Income (FOR)

This index reflects the fraction of operating income earned outside the United States. It is a measure of sensitivity to currency exchange rate changes.

11. Labor Intensity (LBI)

This index estimates the importance of labor, relative to capital, in the operations of a firm. It is based on ratios of labor expense to assets, fixed plant and equipment to equity, and depreciated plant value to total plant cost. A higher exposure to Labor Intensity indicates a larger ratio of labor expense to capital costs and can be a gauge of sensitivity to cost-push inflation.

+ Labor Share
- Inflation-adjusted Plant to Equity Ratio
- Net Plant to Gross Plant

12. Yield (YLD)

The Yield index is simply a relative measure of the company's annual dividend yield.

1 3. LOCAP

The LOCAP characteristic indicates those companies that are not in the HICAP universe. It permits the factors in the model to be applied across a broader universe of assets than that used to estimate the model. The LOCAP factor is, in part, an extension of the Size index, allowing the returns of approximately 4500 smaller companies to deviate from an exact linear relationship with the Size index.

---

*In 1997, BARRA released its E3 model which closely resembles the E2 model but with improved risk index definitions.

Source: *United States Equity Model Handbook* (Berkeley, CA: BARRA, 1996), pp. 19-23.

## Exhibit 5: BARRA E2 Model Industry Classifications*

| The industry classifications in the U.S. Model are: | | |
|---|---|---|
| 1. Aluminum | 20. Containers | 39. Railroads, Transit |
| 2. Iron & Steel | 21. Producer Goods | 40. Air Transport |
| 3. Precious Metals | 22. Pollution Control | 41. Transport by Water |
| 4. Misc. Mining, Metals | 23. Electronics | 42. Retail (Food) |
| 5. Coal & Uranium | 24. Aerospace | 43. Retail (All Other) |
| 6. International Oil | 25. Business Machines | 44. Telephone, Telegraph |
| 7. Dom. Petroleum Reserves | 26. Soaps, Housewares | 45. Electric Utilities |
| 8. For. Petroleum Reserves | 27. Cosmetics | 46. Gas Utilities |
| 9. Oil Refining, Distribution | 28. Apparel, Textiles | 47. Banks |
| 10. Oil Service | 29. Photographic, Optical | 48. Thrift Institutions |
| 11. Forest Products | 30. Consumer Durables | 49. Miscellaneous Finance |
| 12. Paper | 31. Motor Vehicles | 50. Life Insurance |
| 13. Agriculture, Food | 32. Leisure, Luxury | 51. Other Insurance |
| 14. Beverages | 33. Health Care (Non-drug) | 52. Real Property |
| 15. Liquor | 34. Drugs, Medicine | 53. Mortgage Financing |
| 16. Tobacco | 35. Publishing | 54. Services |
| 17. Construction | 36. Media | 55. Miscellaneous |
| 18. Chemicals | 37. Hotels, Restaurants | |
| 19. Tires & Rubber | 38. Trucking, Freight | |

* In 1997, BARRA released its E3 model which has improved industry classifications.
Source: *United States Equity Model Handbook* (Berkeley, CA: BARRA, 1996), pp. 32.

As with the macroeconomic factor model, the raw descriptors are standardized or normalized. The risk indices are in turn standardized. The sensitivity of each company to each risk index is standardized.

The Wilshire Atlas model uses six fundamental factors, one market factor sensitivity, and 39 industry factors to explain stock returns. The six fundamental factors and the market factor sensitivity are listed in Exhibit 6, along with their definitions.

The BARRA and Wilshire models are commercially available. Now we'll look at two proprietary fundamental equity risk models including (1) the model used by Goldman Sachs Asset Management (GSAM) in managing client equity portfolios and (2) the Northfield Fundamental Equity Risk Model.

In the GSAM fundamental model, there are nine descriptions used in the process of portfolio construction and risk control. As described in Exhibit 7, these fundamental equity risk factors include:

- book-to-price ratio
- forecast retained earnings-to-price ratio
- EBITD-to-enterprise value ratio
- analysts earnings revisions
- stock price momentum
- sustainable growth rate

## Exhibit 6: Fundamental Factors and Market Sensitive Factor Definitions for Wilshire Atlas Factor Model

| 1.Earnings/price ratio | Sum of the most recent four quarters' earnings per share divided by the closing price. |
|---|---|
| 2. Book value/price ratio | Book value per share divided by stock price. |
| 3. Market capitalization | The natural logarithm of the product of a security's price multiplied by the number of shares outstanding. |
| 4. Net earnings revision | Analysts momentum measure: Net earnings revision, based on I/B/E/S data, measures analysts' optimism of earnings. Net earnings revision is the percentage of analysts who are feeling more optimistic about earnings in the next period. The higher the net earnings revision number, the more optimistic analysts are about an increase in that company's earnings. |
| 5. Reversal | Price momentum measure: Reversal captures the mean reversion tendencies of stocks. It is a measure of the difference between a security's actual return in the last period and the expected return with respect to its beta. If a stock has a positive reversal this means that it had a higher than expected return in the last period given its beta. Thus, this security is expected to have a lower than expected return in the next period so that the returns for this security will conform to the norm expectations over the long run. |
| 6. Earnings torpedo | Earnings momentum measure: Earnings torpedo, based on I/B/E/S data, is a measure of the estimated growth in earnings for a security relative to historical earnings. Earnings torpedo is based on the ratio of next years estimated earnings per share versus its historical earnings per share. The securities in the universe are then ranked by the estimate and given an earnings torpedo score. A security with a high earnings torpedo score is considered to be vulnerable to a large drop in price if earnings do not meet the higher earnings estimates forecasted by analysts in the next period. |
| 7. Historical beta | Classic measure of security volatility. Measured for each security by regressing the past 60 months worth of excess returns against the S&P500. A minimum of 38 months are required for the data to be valid. |

Source: Adapted from *U.S. Equity Risk Model* (Santa Monica, CA: Wilshire Associates, July 1997 draft).

- systematic or relative risk (beta)
- residual risk
- earnings disappointment risk

These factors fall into three distinct categories: (1) value measures, (2) growth and momentum measures, and (3) equity risk measures. Specifically, the first three factors are traditional value factors, while the last three measures are equity risk factors. Analysts revisions and sustainable growth rate are momentum and growth measures.

Northfield Information Services has developed a fundamental equity risk model that is similar in structure to the BARRA E2 model. Yet, construction of the "common factors" in Northfield model is not as complex as that revealed in BARRA's Fundamental Risk Measurement Service (FRMS). However, this effort toward factor simplicity may be a "mixed blessing" in the sense that BARRA uses numerous accounting and market-based measures in construction of their fundamental equity risk indexes. The 11 "endogeneous" or common factors used in Northfield's Fundamental Equity Risk Model are shown in Exhibit 8. Consistent with BARRA E2, the Northfield fundamental risk model has 55 industry designators.

Like others, Northfield Information Services goes through a rigorous statistical procedure to estimate the monthly alphas on individual securities and portfolios. In this context, Northfield employs a three-step regression procedure to obtain the monthly alphas on individual securities and portfolio.

First, the individual security betas are estimated from a time series regression between the stock's historical monthly return and the market return. Next, for the particular month in review, the "market model" betas are regressed on *standardized* values of the fundamental factors used in their equity risk model — such as equity size, book/price ratio, price momentum, earnings growth, and other pervasive endogenous factors. The "fitted betas" from this cross-sectional regression are then used by Northfield to calculate the estimated monthly alpha for each security according to:

$$\alpha_j = (R_j - R_f) - (R_m - R_f)\beta_j$$

## Exhibit 7: Factor Definitions for the Goldman Sachs Asset Management Factor Model

| Factor | Definition |
| --- | --- |
| Book/Price | Common equity per share divided by price |
| Retained EPS/Price | Year-ahead consensus EPS forecast less indicated annual dividend divided by price. One-year forecast EPS is a weighted average of the forecasts for the current and next fiscal years. |
| EBITD/Enterprise Value | Earnings before interest, taxes and depreciation divided by total capital. Total capital is equity at market plus long-term debt at book. |
| Estimate Revisions | The number of estimates raised in the past three months, less the number lowered, divided by the total number of estimates. |
| Price Momentum | Total return over the last 12 months, less the return for the latest month (to adjust for short-term reversals). |
| Sustainable Growth | The consensus long-term growth forecast. |
| Beta | The regression coefficient from a 60-month regression of the stock's excess returns (above the T-bill rate) against the market's excess returns. |
| Residual Risk | The "unexplained" variation from the above regression; the standard error of the regression. |
| Disappointment Risk | The risk that actual earnings will not meet projections. Stocks with high expected one-year earnings growth have high disappointment potential; stocks with low expectations have less disappointment risk. |

Source: Table 4 in *Select Equity Investment Strategy*, Goldman Sachs Asset Management, February 1997, p. 4.

## Exhibit 8: Northfield Fundamental Equity Risk Model: Endogeneous Factor Definitions

*Earnings/Price*
The ratio of earnings per share to the most recent month-end market price. EPS is defined as trailing twelve month earnings as reported on the most recent quarterly report.

*Book/Price*
The ratio of book value per share as reported on the most recent quarterly report to the most recent month-end market price.

*Dividend Yield*
The trailing twelve month cash dividends paid per share divided by the most recent month-end market price.

*Trading Activity*
The ratio of the average weekly trading volume during the past month divided by shares outstanding as reported in the most recent quarterly report.

*12-month Relative Strength*
The ratio of the percentage price change for the security to the percentage gain for the S&P 500 index for the last 12-month period.

*Logarithm of Market Capitalization*
The logarithm (base 10) of total market value of common shares outstanding using the most recent month and market price and the shares outstanding as reported on the most recent quarterly report.

*Earnings Variability*
The numerical value "one" minus the R-squared statistic for a trend line of the most recent five years of fiscal year earnings per share.

*EPS Growth Rate*
The annual percentage growth rate of reported earnings per share over the past five fiscal years.

*Revenue/Price*
The ratio of trailing twelve-month revenues per share as reported on the most recent quarterly report to the most recent month-end market price.

*Debt/Equity*
The ratio of long term debt outstanding to corporate net worth (total book value) as reported on the most recent quarterly report.

*Price Volatility*
A price volatility index calculated as the (52 week high price minus 52 week low price) divided by the (52 week high price plus the 52 week low price).

The Northfield Fundamental Equity Risk Model also has 55 industry designations.

Source: *Fundamental Equity Risk Model*, Northfield Information Services, 1998 product report, pp. 6-7.

where $\alpha_j$ is the estimated abnormal return (alpha) on security $j$ for month in review, $(R_j - R_f)$ and $(R_m - R_f)$ are the security and index return premiums, respectively, and $\beta_j$ is the "fundamental beta" for the current time period. It is important to emphasize that both the estimated alpha and fundamental beta are monthly regression estimates that can (and do) vary over time.

Finally, the estimated alpha's on individual securities are regressed cross sectionally on the fundamental risk variables — again, the standardized (or "t scores") values for equity size, earnings/price ratio, price momentum, earnings growth, etc. Upon repeating this three step regression procedure — specifically, a time series regression to obtain the initial "raw" betas, followed by two cross-sectional regressions to obtain the fitted betas and alphas, respectively — the portfolio manager is able to see possible patterns or trends in the fundamental risk factors that impact portfolio alpha. In this way, the portfolio manager can determine whether the time-wise factor loadings on size and book/price ratio, for examples, are consistent over time — such that an active "tilt" either towards or away from these fundamental risk factors might generate systematic *non*-market reward.

## THE OUTPUT AND INPUTS OF A FACTOR MODEL

Now that we have identified the types of factor models, let's look at the output of the model and the inputs to the model after the estimation has taken place. The output of a factor model is found by first multiplying a factor sensitivity by the assumed value for the factor measure (assumed risk factor).[9] This gives the contribution to the model's output from a given risk factor exposure. Summing up over all risk factors gives the output. For a $K$-factor model this is expressed mathematically as follows:

$$\text{Output} = \text{Beta}_1 \times (\text{Factor}_1 \text{ measure}) + \text{Beta}_2 \times (\text{Factor}_2 \text{ measure}) + ...$$
$$+ \text{Beta}_K \times (\text{Factor}_K \text{ measure})$$

Let's look first at the Beta's. These are the factor sensitivities and are estimated statistically. As explained earlier, they are commonly standardized or normalized.

The output varies by model. For example, in the BIRR macroeconomic factor model, the output is the *expected excess return* given the estimated factor sensitivities and the assumed values for the factor measures. The expected excess return is the expected return above the risk-free rate. In contrast, in the Salomon Brothers RAM factor model, the output is a score that is used to rank the outcome given the estimated factor sensitivities and assumed values for the factor measures.

The factor measures vary by model. In the BIRR macroeconomic factor model, for example, a factor measure is the estimated market price of the risk factor expressed in percent per year. For the Salomon Brothers RAM factor model, a factor measure is the normalized value for the factor.

Let's use the two macroeconomic models described earlier to show how the output is obtained. First, the BIRR model. The estimated risk exposure profile

---

[9] For an example of quantitative estimation of returns to the size factor using economic variables, see Bruce I. Jacobs and Kenneth N. Levy, "Forecasting the Size Effect," *Financial Analysts Journal* (May-June 1989), pp.61-78.

for Reebok International Limited and the assumed values for the risk factors (expressed in percent per year) are shown below:

| Risk factor | Estimated factor sensitivity | Estimated market price of risk (%) |
|---|---|---|
| Confidence risk | 0.73 | 2.59 |
| Time horizon risk | 0.77 | −0.66 |
| Inflation risk | −0.48 | −4.32 |
| Business cycle risk | 4.59 | 1.49 |
| Market timing risk | 1.50 | 3.61 |

The expected excess return is then found as follows:

Expected excess return for Reebok = 0.73 (2.59) + 0.77 (−0.66) + (−0.48) (−4.32) + 4.59 (1.49) + 1.50 (3.61) = 15.71%

To obtain the expected return, the risk-free rate must be added. For example, if the risk-free rate is 5%, then the expected return is 20.71% (15.71% plus 5%).

In the Salomon Brothers RAM model, the set of forecasts for the factor measures are called *scenario factors*. Based on scenario factors, the sensitivity of a stock to each factor can be calculated. Adding up the sensitivity of a stock to each factor gives a stock's *scenario score*. Recall that in this factor model there are six macroeconomic factors (described in Exhibit 2) and the residual beta. Each factor is expressed in normalized or standardized form. For Pepsico (in October 1989) the factor betas and a factor scenario for a weakening economy are given below:[10]

| Risk factor | Estimated factor sensitivity | Factor scenario (Weakening economy) |
|---|---|---|
| Economic growth | −1.8 | −1.0 |
| Business cycle | −0.9 | −0.5 |
| Long rate | 0.0 | 0.5 |
| Short rate | 0.1 | 0.3 |
| Inflation rate | −0.3 | 0.1 |
| U.S. dollar | 0.1 | 0.3 |
| Residual beta | −1.1 | −0.5 |

The scenario score for Pepsico is then:

Pepsico scenario score = −1.8 (−1.0) + (−0.9) (−0.5) + 0 (0.5) + 0.1 (0.3) + (−0.3) (0.1) + 0.1 (0.3) + (−1.1) (−0.5) = 1.7

This scenario score is then compared to the scenario score of other stocks in the universe of purchase or short-sale candidates of a portfolio manager.

---

[10] Sorensen, Mezrich, and Thum, "The Salomon Brothers U.S. Stock Risk Attribute Model," p. 6.

*Exhibit 9: Factor Value Positions in Unit Normal Distribution*

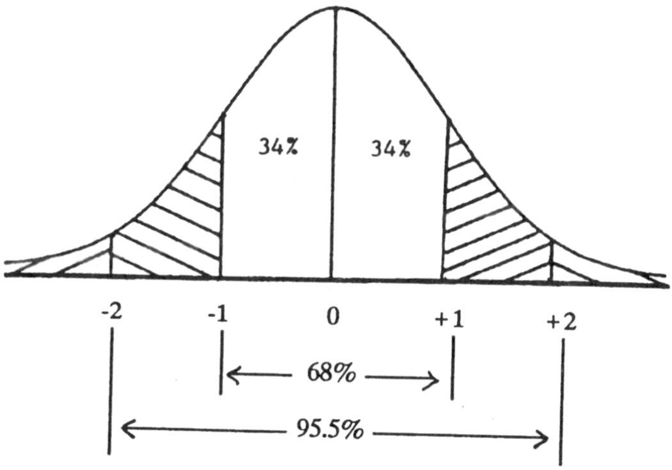

## Graphical Illustration of a Fundamental Factor Model

We can also gain some key insight about the meaning of a factor model by looking at the factor measures and return sensitivities in a graphical context. To illustrate this, Exhibits 9 through 11 provide a visual representation of a fundamental factor model — like those employed by BARRA, Wilshire, and Northfield Information Services.

Exhibit 9 shows that the factor values themselves — such as equity size, earnings/price ratio, and dividend yield — are each standardized according to their relative position in the "unit normal distribution." As shown in Exhibit 9, this means that if the stock of a particular company has, say, size characteristics (often measured by equity capitalization) that are similar to that of representative company in the benchmark portfolio (S&P 500, for example), then the equity size factor for this company would, by definition, be zero. If the observed size measure were negative, then the stock of the company in review would be smaller in size than the representative company in the benchmark index.

Conversely, a large company such as General Electric or Microsoft Corporation would be *atypical* of firms in the benchmark because of a standardized size measure greater than zero. From a size perspective, these firms are among the "top 5" companies in terms of equity capitalization in the S&P 500. Therefore, their standardized size measure would be considerably higher than that of the typical firm in the U.S. large cap benchmark. Exhibit 9 also shows that about 68% of the possible size outcomes in the unit normal distribution lie within −1 and +1 standard deviation from zero, while some 95% of the possible equity size outcomes would fall within two standard deviation units (±2, in numerical terms) from the standardized mean of zero. The 68% and 95% "confidence intervals" also apply to the standardized values of all other fundamental risk factors.

## Exhibit 10: Abnormal Return from the Size Factor in Month t

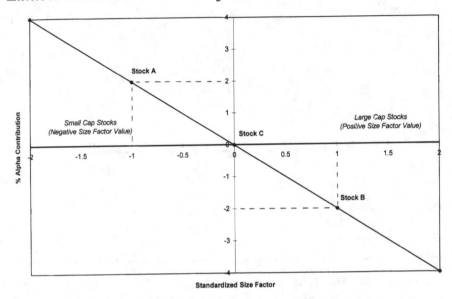

## Exhibit 11: Abnormal Return Percent from the Book Yield Factor in Month t

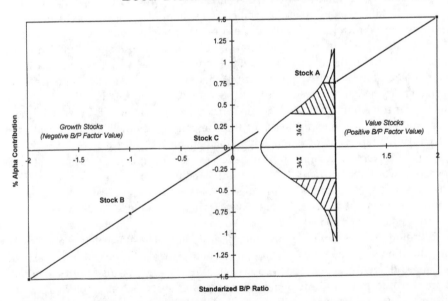

# A Closer Look at Potential Return Contribution

In a fundamental factor model — like macro-factor portfolio risk models — the contribution that a "common factor" such as size or earnings and book/price ratios makes to security or portfolio return is determined by *multiplying* the factor sensitivity (or loading) by the standardized value of the factor in the unit normal distribution. As a real world illustration, it is well known that size and value-oriented factors have abnormal return potential when measured relative to the single-factor CAPM.[11] Along this line, H. Russell Fogler finds that size alone during the 1980s generated 3.07% per year of excess portfolio return, while the earnings and book yield factors each had annualized alpha contributions of about 0.95%.[12] Assuming that past performance is somewhat descriptive of the future — at least for the purpose of our illustration — let's see how the active investor might use annualized factor return estimates in assessing future portfolio performance.

Exhibit 10 shows the potential return contribution due to the size factor for three representative common stocks. If the estimated size sensitivity (or factor loading) were, say, −2 (for 200 basis points of *annualized* monthly performance), then the common stock of  "small cap" company A, with a negative size factor of −1 would make a 2% (unweighted) active return contribution to an investor's portfolio. In a symmetric manner, if the standardized size measure for "large cap" company B were unity, then this "common factor" would offer a −2% (or −200 basis points) return contribution to the active portfolio. In a related manner, the stock of company C would have *no* excess (alpha) return potential since its size measure, at zero, is the same as that of the average firm — viewed cross sectionally — in the benchmark index (S&P 500, for example).

Exhibit 11 shows the ex ante alpha potential for the three stocks due to the book/price factor. If the estimated book yield sensitivity were 0.75% (for 75 basis points), then the stock of high (book) yield company A, having a standardized B/P factor of 1.0, would make a positive 75 basis point return contribution to the active investor's abnormal portfolio performance. Likewise, if the standardized book/price factor for stock B were −1, then this common factor would offer a negative 75 basis points (again, unweighted) of annualized monthly return to the active investor's portfolio. As with size, this book yield  performance is beyond that of the risk-adjusted market return. The book yield factor for Stock C would of course make *no* meaningful contribution to assessed portfolio alpha since its book/price ratio is typical of that of other firms in the benchmark.

---

[11] Fama and French emphasize the empirical relevance of *two* fundamental risk factors — including equity size and book/price ratio — in explaining cross section of security returns over the long term. See Eugene F. Fama and Kenneth R. French, "The Cross Section of Expected Stock Returns," *Journal of Finance* (June 1992).

[12] Among others, Fogler finds that equity size as well as earnings and book yield are relevant "common factors" in describing security and portfolio return performance. See "Common Stock Management in the 1990s."

Based on the fundamental factor model shown in Exhibit 11, we can alternatively say that high price-to-book ratio stocks — namely, growth stocks — have negative assessed "alpha" due to the assumed *positive* return sensitivity (or factor loading) on the book/price factor, at 0.75%, while the common stock of companies having low price/book ratio — such as value stocks — offer active reward opportunities from this "common factor." This happens because growth stocks have a standardized book yield factor that is negative, while so-called value stocks have a B/P factor value (in the unit normal distribution) that is largely greater than zero.[13]

## PORTFOLIO CONSTRUCTION WITH FACTOR MODELS

Now let's see how factor models are used in portfolio construction. Specifically, based on expectations about the future outcomes of the factors, an active equity manager can construct a portfolio to add value relative to some benchmark should those outcomes be realized.

### Portfolio Expected Excess Returns and Risk Exposure Profiles

In factor models in which the output is an expected excess return for a stock, the expected excess return for a portfolio can be easily computed. This is the weighted average of the expected excess return for each stock in the portfolio. The weights are the percentage of a stock value in the portfolio relative to the market value of the portfolio. Similarly, a portfolio's sensitivity to a given factor risk is a weighted average of the factor sensitivity of the stocks in the portfolio. The set of factor sensitivities is then the portfolio's risk exposure profile. Consequently, the expected excess return and the risk exposure profile can be obtained from the stocks comprising the portfolio.

Since a stock market index is nothing more than a portfolio that includes the universe of stocks making up the index, an expected excess return and risk exposure profile can be determined for an index. This allows a manager to compare the expected excess return and the risk profile of a stock and/or a portfolio to that of a stock market index whose performance the portfolio manager is measured against. For example, in the BIRR model, the risk exposure profile for the S&P 500 is shown below, as well as that of Reebok for comparative purposes:

---

[13] From an efficient market perspective, the revealed *average* of estimated factor sensitivities over time must be zero. If this overall pricing efficiency requirement were not met, then it would be possible for many investors to earn high risk-adjusted returns for extended periods of time, simply by "tilting" their equity allocation toward (away from) those common factors that offered abnormally positive (or negative) expected return.

The average equilibrium pricing condition can be seen in Exhibit 11 where the estimated return sensitivity on the book/yield factor is presumed drawn from a normal distribution with mean (or long-term) factor loading of zero.

| | Estimated factor sensitivity for | |
|---|---|---|
| Risk factor | S&P 500 | Reebok |
| Confidence risk | 0.27 | 0.73 |
| Time horizon risk | 0.56 | 0.77 |
| Inflation risk | −0.37 | −0.48 |
| Business cycle risk | 1.71 | 4.59 |
| Market timing risk | 1.00 | 1.50 |

By comparing the risk exposure profile of Reebok to the S&P 500, a portfolio manager can see the relative risk exposure. Using the same assumed values for the risk factors as used earlier for Reebok, the expected excess return for the S&P 500 is 8.09% compared to 15.71% for Reebok.

In factor models such as the Salomon Brothers RAM model where the output is a *scenario score*, the risk exposure profile of a portfolio and market index is calculated in the same manner as when the model's output is the expected excess return. However, in scenario score models the portfolio's and market index's output is a ranking.

The power of a factor model regardless of the type of output is that given the risk factors and the factor sensitivities, a portfolio's risk exposure profile can be quantified and controlled. The examples below show how this can be done with a fundamental factor model. This allows managers to avoid making unintended bets.

## Assessing the Exposure of a Portfolio

A fundamental factor model can be used to assess whether the current portfolio is consistent with a manager's strengths. In this application of factor models and the one that follows, we will use the BARRA factor model.[14] Exhibit 12 is a list of the holdings of manager X as of July 31, 1990.[15] There are 15 stocks held with a total market value of $111.9 million.

Exhibit 13 assesses the risk exposure of manager X's portfolio relative to the risk exposure of the S&P 500. The boxes in the second column of the exhibit indicate the significant differences in the exposure of manager X's portfolio relative to the S&P 500. There are two risk indices boxed — success and foreign income — and two industry groupings boxed — business machines and miscellaneous finance. Exhibit 4 describes the risk indices. The −0.45 exposure to the success risk index reveals that manager X's portfolio exhibits low relative strength as measured by stock price and earnings momentum — a style characteristic. Consequently, the success risk index indicates an exposure to style. Thus, we can see that manager X is making a style bet. The 0.62 exposure to the foreign income risk index tells manager X that the companies in the portfolio tend to earn a significant portion of their operating income abroad. Consequently, manager X is making an international bet. In terms of industry exposure, manager X is extremely more aggressive in his or her holdings of business machine stocks and miscellaneous finance stocks.

---

[14] The illustrations are adapted from Chapter VI of *United States Equity Model Handbook* (Berkeley, CA: BARRA, 1996).
[15] This was an actual portfolio of a BARRA client.

## Exhibit 12: Portfolio Holdings for Manager X

```
BARRA Microcomputer Products:    Interactive PORCH                           Page    1
Portfolio: SAMPLE                Market: SAP500                    Pricing Date: 07-31-90

    IDENT    NAME                         SHARES    PRICE    %WGT    BETA    %YLD    IND

    1 FDX    FEDERAL EXPRESS CORP          80700    41.625    3.00    1.15    0.00   AIR
    2 NEM    NEWMONT MNG CORP              67500    49.500    2.98    0.76    1.21   GOLD
    3 I      FIRST INTST BANCORP         167700    33.000    4.94    1.32    9.09   BANKS
    4 HWP    HEWLETT PACKARD CO          126900    43.125    4.89    1.15    0.97   BUS MN
    5 IBM    INTERNATIONAL BUS MACH      141400   111.500   14.08    1.01    4.34   BUS MN

    6 F      FORD MTR CO DEL             273100    41.500   10.12    0.98    7.17   MOT VH
    7 HCSG   HEALTHCARE SVCS GRP IN       93000    24.250    2.01    1.29    0.28   SERVCS
    8 TXN    TEXAS INSTRS INC             81500    32.000    2.33    1.41    2.25   ELCTRN
    9 S      SEARS ROEBUCK & CO          342900    33.625   10.30    1.09    5.94   RET OT
   10 AXP    AMERICAN EXPRESS CO         291900    29.125    7.59    1.20    3.15   FINANC

   11 JNJ    JOHNSON & JOHNSON           205800    70.625   12.98    1.02    1.92   HEALTH
   12 EK     EASTMAN KODAK CO            324800    38.125   11.06    1.10    5.24   PHOTOG
   13 WMX    WASTE MGMT INC              185900    41.375    6.87    1.24    0.86   POLL C
   14 PCI    PARAMOUNT COMMUNICATIO      118900    39.500    4.20    1.14    1.77   PUBLSH
   15 TAN    TANDY CORP                   79800    36.750    2.62    1.26    1.63   RET OT
```

Source: The information in this exhibit is adapted from Figure VI-1 of *United States Equity Model Handbook* (Berkeley, CA: BARRA, 1996), p. 40.

Notice in this example how the manager is able to identify where the bets are made. Manager X has made a style bet, an international bet, and a bet on two industries. If the manager did not intend to make these bets, the portfolio can be rebalanced to eliminate any unintended bets.

## Tilting a Portfolio

Now let's look at how an active manager can construct a portfolio to make intentional bets. Suppose that manager Y seeks to construct a portfolio that generates superior returns relative to the S&P 500 by tilting it toward high-success stocks. At the same time, the manager does not want to increase tracking error risk significantly. An obvious approach may seem to be to identify all the stocks in the universe that have a higher than average success risk index. The problem with this approach is that it introduces unintentional bets with respect to the other risk indices.

Instead, an optimization method combined with a factor model can be used to construct the desired portfolio. The input to this process is the tilt exposure sought, the benchmark stock market index, and the number of stocks to be included in the portfolio. The BARRA optimization model also requires a specification of the excess return sought. In our illustration, the tilt exposure sought is high success stocks, the benchmark is the S&P 500, and the number of stocks to be included in the portfolio is 50. While we do not report the holdings of the optimal portfolio here, Exhibit 14 provides an analysis of that portfolio by comparing the risk exposure of the 50-stock optimal portfolio to that of the S&P 500.

## Exhibit 13: Analysis of Manager X Portfolio's Exposure Relative to the S&P 500

```
Comparison Summary Report                          Date: 07-31-90

Portfolio              SAMPLE
Comparison Port.       SAP500
Market                 SAP500

Number of Assets            15
Port. Value      111,940,087.50
Predicted Yield           3.78
Alpha                     0.00
Utility                  -0.36
Tracking Error            7.25
```

| FACTORS | SAMPLE | SAP500 | DIFF | MCTE |
|---|---|---|---|---|
| VARIABILITY IN MARKETS | 0.02 | -0.06 | 0.09 | 0.010 |
| SUCCESS | -0.45 | 0.01 | -0.47 | -0.021 |
| SIZE | 0.54 | 0.29 | 0.26 | 0.004 |
| TRADING ACTIVITY | 0.22 | 0.00 | 0.22 | -0.002 |
| GROWTH | -0.12 | -0.05 | -0.07 | 0.016 |
| EARNINGS/PRICE | 0.08 | 0.01 | 0.08 | 0.007 |
| BOOK/PRICE | 0.18 | -0.02 | 0.20 | 0.001 |
| EARNINGS VARIATION | 0.00 | -0.05 | 0.05 | 0.003 |
| FINANCIAL LEVERAGE | 0.28 | 0.03 | 0.25 | -0.001 |
| FOREIGN INCOME | 0.62 | 0.12 | 0.51 | -0.001 |
| LABOR INTENSITY | 0.30 | 0.01 | 0.29 | -0.003 |
| YIELD | 0.16 | 0.02 | 0.14 | 0.007 |
| LOCAP | 0.02 | 0.00 | 0.02 | -0.005 |
| ALUMINUM | 0.00 | 0.60 | -0.60 | 0.099 |
| IRON AND STEEL | 0.00 | 0.30 | -0.30 | 0.081 |
| PRECIOUS METALS | 1.25 | 0.42 | 0.83 | 0.071 |
| MISC. MINING, METALS | 0.54 | 0.61 | -0.07 | 0.073 |
| COAL AND URANIUM | 0.00 | 0.40 | -0.40 | 0.013 |
| INTERNATIONAL OIL | 0.00 | 4.49 | -4.49 | -0.033 |
| DOM PETROLEUM RESERVES | 0.51 | 3.46 | -2.96 | -0.047 |
| FOR PETROLEUM RESERVES | 0.69 | 2.25 | -1.56 | -0.037 |
| OIL REFINING, DISTRIBUTN | 0.00 | 1.29 | -1.29 | -0.011 |
| OIL SERVICE | 0.00 | 1.02 | -1.02 | -0.017 |
| FOREST PRODUCTS | 0.00 | 0.30 | -0.30 | 0.120 |
| PAPER | 0.00 | 2.06 | -2.06 | 0.082 |
| AGRICULTURE, FOOD | 0.00 | 4.99 | -4.99 | 0.047 |
| BEVERAGES | 0.00 | 1.41 | -1.41 | 0.066 |
| LIQUOR | 0.00 | 1.05 | -1.05 | 0.050 |
| TOBACCO | 0.00 | 1.38 | -1.38 | 0.067 |
| CONSTRUCTION | 0.00 | 0.88 | -0.88 | 0.098 |
| CHEMICALS | 1.99 | 3.44 | -1.45 | 0.083 |
| TIRE & RUBBER | 0.00 | 0.10 | -0.10 | 0.101 |
| CONTAINERS | 0.00 | 0.17 | -0.17 | 0.069 |
| PRODUCERS GOODS | 0.02 | 4.49 | -4.47 | 0.086 |
| POLLUTION CONTROL | 6.87 | 1.13 | 5.75 | 0.124 |
| ELECTRONICS | 2.21 | 2.39 | -0.18 | 0.126 |
| AEROSPACE | 0.00 | 2.47 | -2.47 | 0.089 |
| BUSINESS MACHINES | 19.07 | 4.80 | 14.26 | 0.130 |
| SOAPS, HOUSEWARE | 0.00 | 1.99 | -1.99 | 0.084 |
| COSMETICS | 4.54 | 0.94 | 3.60 | 0.096 |
| APPAREL, TEXTILES | 0.00 | 0.77 | -0.77 | 0.080 |
| PHOTOGRAPHIC, OPTICAL | 6.75 | 0.55 | 6.20 | 0.114 |
| CONSUMER DURABLES | 0.00 | 0.99 | -0.99 | 0.104 |
| MOTOR VEHICLES | 8.91 | 2.42 | 6.49 | 0.114 |
| LEISURE, LUXURY | 0.00 | 0.18 | -0.18 | 0.096 |
| HEALTH CARE (NON-DRUG) | 5.06 | 1.85 | 3.21 | 0.070 |
| DRUGS, MEDICINE | 5.70 | 6.81 | -1.12 | 0.066 |
| PUBLISHING | 2.10 | 1.48 | 0.62 | 0.090 |
| MEDIA | 2.10 | 1.67 | 0.43 | 0.079 |
| HOTELS, RESTAURANTS | 0.00 | 1.75 | -1.75 | 0.094 |
| TRUCKING, FREIGHT | 0.00 | 0.13 | -0.13 | 0.098 |
| RAILROADS, TRANSIT | 0.00 | 0.92 | -0.92 | 0.046 |
| AIR TRANSPORT | 3.00 | 0.59 | 2.41 | 0.139 |
| TRANSPORT BY WATER | 0.00 | 0.03 | -0.03 | 0.039 |
| RETAIL (FOOD) | 0.00 | 0.85 | -0.85 | 0.062 |
| RETAIL (ALL OTHER) | 6.12 | 5.19 | 0.93 | 0.098 |
| TELEPHONE, TELEGRAPH | 0.00 | 8.26 | -8.26 | 0.036 |
| ELECTRIC UTILITIES | 0.00 | 4.37 | -4.37 | 0.024 |
| GAS UTILITIES | 0.00 | 1.17 | -1.17 | 0.019 |
| BANKS | 6.49 | 2.93 | 3.56 | 0.063 |
| THRIFT INSTITUTIONS | 0.00 | 0.28 | -0.28 | 0.073 |
| MISC. FINANCE | 10.87 | 2.20 | 8.67 | 0.094 |
| LIFE INSURANCE | 0.00 | 0.92 | -0.92 | 0.061 |
| OTHER INSURANCE | 2.37 | 2.24 | 0.13 | 0.059 |
| REAL PROPERTY | 0.82 | 0.19 | 0.63 | 0.107 |
| MORTGAGE FINANCING | 0.00 | 0.00 | -0.00 | 0.068 |
| SERVICES | 2.01 | 1.89 | 0.12 | 0.070 |
| MISCELLANEOUS | 0.00 | 0.56 | -0.56 | 0.053 |

Source: The information in this exhibit is adapted from Figure VI-3 of *United States Equity Model Handbook* (Berkeley, CA: BARRA, 1996), p. 42.

## Exhibit 14: Analysis of a 50-Stock Portfolio Constructed to be Tilted Toward High Success Stocks

```
Comparison Summary Report                          Date: 07-31-90

Portfolio            SUCCESS
Comparison Port.     SAP500
Market               SAP500

Number of Assets           50
Port. Value        99,999,723.50
Predicted Yield          3.04
Alpha                    0.31
Utility                  0.18
Tracking Error          [4.19]
```

| FACTORS | US50 | SAP500 | DIFF |
|---|---|---|---|
| VARIABILITY IN MARKETS | 0.10 | -0.06 | 0.16 |
| SUCCESS | 0.77 | 0.01 | 0.76 |
| SIZE | 0.24 | 0.29 | -0.05 |
| TRADING ACTIVITY | -0.06 | 0.00 | -0.07 |
| GROWTH | 0.10 | -0.05 | 0.15 |
| EARNINGS/PRICE | -0.00 | 0.01 | -0.01 |
| BOOK/PRICE | -0.16 | -0.02 | -0.14 |
| EARNINGS VARIATION | 0.00 | -0.05 | 0.05 |
| FINANCIAL LEVERAGE | -0.16 | 0.03 | -0.19 |
| FOREIGN INCOME | -0.10 | 0.12 | -0.21 |
| LABOR INTENSITY | -0.04 | 0.01 | -0.05 |
| YIELD | -0.11 | 0.02 | -0.13 |
| LOCAP | 0.00 | 0.00 | -0.00 |
| ALUMINUM | 1.98 | 0.60 | 1.38 |
| IRON AND STEEL | 0.00 | 0.30 | -0.30 |
| PRECIOUS METALS | 0.50 | 0.42 | 0.07 |
| MISC. MINING, METALS | 0.47 | 0.61 | -0.14 |
| COAL AND URANIUM | 0.42 | 0.40 | 0.02 |
| INTERNATIONAL OIL | 4.36 | 4.49 | -0.13 |
| DOM PETROLEUM RESERVES | 2.45 | 3.46 | -1.01 |
| FOR PETROLEUM RESERVES | 3.19 | 2.25 | 0.94 |
| OIL REFINING, DISTRIBUTN | 1.44 | 1.29 | 0.15 |
| OIL SERVICE | 1.79 | 1.02 | 0.77 |
| FOREST PRODUCTS | 0.03 | 0.30 | -0.27 |
| PAPER | 1.07 | 2.06 | -0.99 |
| AGRICULTURE, FOOD | 5.29 | 4.99 | 0.30 |
| BEVERAGES | 0.00 | 1.41 | -1.41 |
| LIQUOR | 0.37 | 1.05 | -0.68 |
| TOBACCO | 3.13 | 1.38 | 1.75 |
| CONSTRUCTION | 2.27 | 0.88 | 1.39 |
| CHEMICALS | 3.39 | 3.44 | -0.05 |
| TIRE & RUBBER | 0.00 | 0.10 | -0.10 |
| CONTAINERS | 0.00 | 0.17 | -0.17 |
| PRODUCERS GOODS | 4.36 | 4.49 | -0.14 |
| POLLUTION CONTROL | 2.38 | 1.13 | 1.25 |
| ELECTRONICS | 4.24 | 2.39 | 1.84 |
| AEROSPACE | 3.11 | 2.47 | 0.64 |
| BUSINESS MACHINES | 1.39 | 4.80 | -3.42 |
| SOAPS, HOUSEWARE | 4.79 | 1.99 | 2.80 |
| COSMETICS | 0.29 | 0.94 | -0.66 |
| APPAREL, TEXTILES | 0.98 | 0.77 | 0.21 |
| PHOTOGRAPHIC, OPTICAL | 0.00 | 0.55 | -0.55 |
| CONSUMER DURABLES | 0.73 | 0.99 | -0.27 |
| MOTOR VEHICLES | 4.35 | 2.42 | 1.94 |
| LEISURE, LUXURY | 0.00 | 0.18 | -0.18 |
| HEALTH CARE (NON-DRUG) | 2.10 | 1.85 | 0.25 |
| DRUGS, MEDICINE | 4.60 | 6.81 | -2.21 |
| PUBLISHING | 0.00 | 1.48 | -1.48 |
| MEDIA | 0.16 | 1.67 | -1.51 |
| HOTELS, RESTAURANTS | 0.59 | 1.75 | -1.16 |
| TRUCKING, FREIGHT | 0.00 | 0.13 | -0.13 |
| RAILROADS, TRANSIT | 0.00 | 0.92 | -0.92 |
| AIR TRANSPORT | 0.00 | 0.59 | -0.59 |
| TRANSPORT BY WATER | 0.00 | 0.03 | -0.03 |
| RETAIL (FOOD) | 4.78 | 0.85 | 3.93 |
| RETAIL (ALL OTHER) | 9.80 | 5.19 | 4.62 |
| TELEPHONE, TELEGRAPH | 0.00 | 8.26 | -8.26 |
| ELECTRIC UTILITIES | 12.31 | 4.37 | 7.95 |
| GAS UTILITIES | 1.03 | 1.17 | -0.14 |
| BANKS | 0.00 | 2.93 | -2.93 |
| THRIFT INSTITUTIONS | 0.00 | 0.28 | -0.28 |
| MISC. FINANCE | 2.10 | 2.20 | -0.10 |
| LIFE INSURANCE | 1.67 | 0.92 | 0.75 |
| OTHER INSURANCE | 1.55 | 2.24 | -0.69 |
| REAL PROPERTY | 0.23 | 0.19 | 0.04 |
| MORTGAGE FINANCING | 0.00 | 0.00 | -0.00 |
| SERVICES | 0.19 | 1.89 | -1.70 |
| MISCELLANEOUS | 0.15 | 0.56 | -0.42 |

Source: The information in this exhibit is adapted from Figure VI-7 of
*United States Equity Model Handbook* (Berkeley, CA: BARRA, 1996), p. 47.

### Exhibit 15: Summary of Perfect Foresight Tests Two Strategies Using Factor Models: 12-Month Rolling Value Added (%) from January 1987 to July 1995

| Country | Long Stock Strategy | | | Market Neutral Strategy | | |
|---|---|---|---|---|---|---|
| | High | Low | Average | High | Low | Average |
| United States | 82% | 39% | 55% | 195% | 75% | 138% |
| United Kingdom | 131 | 52 | 82 | 326 | 50 | 155 |
| Japan | 106 | 56 | 74 | 236 | 66 | 121 |
| Canada | 91 | 63 | 77 | — | — | — |

Source: Table 15 from David J. Leinweber, Robert D. Arnott, and Christopher G. Luck, "The Many Sides of Equity Style," Chapter 11 in T. Daniel Coggin, Frank J. Fabozzi, and Robert D. Arnott (eds.), *The Handbook of Equity Style Management* (New Hope, PA: Frank J. Fabozzi Associates, 1997).

## Fundamental Factor Models and Equity Style Management

In Chapter 5, we covered equity style management. Notice that the factors used in fundamental factor models such as the BARRA factor model (Exhibit 4), Wilshire factor model (Exhibit 6), and the GSAM factor model (Exhibit 7) are the same characteristics used in style management. Since the factors can be used to add value and control risk, this suggests that factor models can be used in style management for the same purposes.

## RETURN PERFORMANCE POTENTIAL OF FACTOR MODELS

It is interesting to see how well a portfolio constructed using a factor model would have performed with perfect foresight. For example, suppose we are examining monthly returns. We look at the actual factor return for the month and use that as our expectation at the beginning of the month. Given the forecasts an optimization model can be used to design the optimal portfolio.

Leinweber, Arnott, and Luck performed this experiment for several countries using the BARRA factor model for those countries — United States, United Kingdom, Japan, and Canada — for the period January 1987 to July 1995.[16] Transaction costs for rebalancing a portfolio each month were incorporated. A 12-month rolling value added return was calculated. A value added return is the return above a broad-based stock index for the country.

Two strategies were followed. One was simply a long position in the stocks. The second was a market neutral long-short strategy.[17] Exhibit 15 reports

---

[16] David J. Leinweber, Robert D. Arnott, and Christopher G. Luck, "The Many Sides of Equity Style," Chapter 11 in T. Daniel Coggin, Frank J. Fabozzi, and Robert D. Arnott (eds.), *The Handbook of Equity Style Management* (New Hope, PA: Frank J. Fabozzi, 1997).

[17] See Bruce I. Jacobs and Kenneth N. Levy, "The Long and Short on Long-Short," *Journal of Investing* (Spring 1997), pp. 73-86.

the results of the perfect foresight tests. With perfect foresight, the BARRA factor model would have added significant value for each country stock portfolio. For example, in the United States even in the worst 12-month rolling period the factor-based model added 39% for the long stock strategy and 75% for the market neutral long-short strategy.

Eric Sorensen, Joseph Mezrich, and Chee Thum performed two backtests of the Salomon Brothers RAM (a macroeconomic factor model) to assess the model. The tests were basically event studies.[18] In the first backtest, these researchers looked at daily returns following an unexpected announcement regarding an inflation measure. Specifically, on July 14, 1989 the Producer Price Index that was announced was sharply less than anticipated. As a result, the yield on Treasury bills with one month to maturity fell on that day from 8.6% to 8.4%. An optimized portfolio that had a high sensitivity to inflation was constructed. The inflation sensitive tilted portfolio outperformed the S&P 500 by 46 basis points from the day prior to the event (July 13, 1989) through the day after the event (July 15, 1989). This result supports the position that the factor model was an important tool for constructing a portfolio based on expectations.

The second backtest was based on a longer period of time. The event in this case was the movement of the U.S. dollar during the spring of 1989. Specifically, there was an unexpected strengthening (i.e., appreciation) of the U.S. dollar relative to the German mark from May 12 to June 2, 1989. An optimized portfolio was constructed that was tilted towards stocks that benefited from a stronger U.S. dollar. The RAM-based portfolio tilted with this bias outperformed the S&P 500 by 62 basis points.

## SUMMARY

There are three types of factor models: statistical factor models, macroeconomic factor models, and fundamental factor models. Statistical factor models use a statistical technique called principal components analysis to identify which raw descriptors best explain stock returns. The resulting factors are statistical artifacts and are therefore difficult to interpret. Consequently, a statistical factor model is rarely used in practice. The more common factor models are the macroeconomic factor model and the fundamental factor model.

In a factor model, the sensitivity of a stock to a factor is estimated. The risk exposure profile of a stock is identified by a set of factor sensitivities. The risk exposure profile of a portfolio is the weighted average of the risk exposure profile of the stocks in the portfolio. Similarly, the risk exposure profile of a market index can be obtained.

The output of a factor model can be either the expected excess return or a scenario score. The expected excess return of a stock is found by multiplying each

---

[18] Sorensen, Mezrich, and Thum, *The Salomon Brothers U.S. Risk Attribute Model.*

factor sensitivity by the assumed value for the risk factor and summing over all risk factors. The expected return is the expected excess return plus the risk-free rate. The expected excess return for a portfolio and a market index is just the weighted average of the expected excess return of the stocks comprising the portfolio or the market index.

The power of a factor model is that given the risk factors and the factor sensitivities, a portfolio's risk exposure profile can be quantified and controlled. Applications of factor models include the ability to assess whether or not the current portfolio is consistent with a manager's strengths and to construct a portfolio with a specific tilt without making unintentional bets. Since many factors in a fundamental model are the same characteristics used in style management, factor models can be used in controlling risk in a style management strategy.

# QUESTIONS

1. a. What is a macroeconomic factor model?

   b. What are the similarities and differences among the major players and vendors that use or offer these models — including the macroeconomic factor models of BIRR, Salomon, and Northfield Information Services?

2. a. What is a fundamental factor model?

   b. What are the similarities and differences among the models used or offered by major players and vendors — including, the fundamental factor models of BARRA, Wilshire, and Goldman Sachs Asset Management?

   c. Is there any empirical evidence that supports the fundamental factors that we often see in these quantitative approaches to equity portfolio management? (Hint: recall the empirical results that we presented in Chapter 5 on equity management styles).

3. a. How are the factors standardized in a fundamental or macroeconomic factor model?

   b. How does an investor determine the contribution that a fundamental or macro-factor — such as book/price ratio or business cycle risk factor — makes to the expected return on a portfolio?

4. What is your view of the following statement by H. Russell Fogler that appeared in the Winter 1990 issue of the *Journal of Portfolio Management* regarding the relative performance merit of multiple factor portfolio models?

   > Once we appreciate the simplicity and power of multiple factor models (such as BARRA), single index measurement will join the archives of performance measurement history, where it belongs.

   Specifically, what single index model(s) does Fogler call into question, and do you agree with his assessment about the relative merit of multiple factor versus single factor equity portfolio models? If so, why — if not, why not?

5. Consider the following multi-factor regression model:

   $$R = b_0 + b_1(\text{Beta}) + b_2(\text{Size}) + b_3(\text{P/BV}) + b_4(\text{Yield}) + b_5(\text{Industrial}) + b_6(\text{Non-Industrial}) + e$$

   where

   | | |
   |---|---|
   | $R$ | = return on a stock |
   | Beta | = estimated value from the single-index market model |
   | P/BV | = price to book value ratio |

Yield          = ratio of the dividend to stock price
Industrial     = 1 if the company is an industrial firm and 0 otherwise
Non-Industrial = 1 if the company is a non-industrial firm and 0 otherwise

a. What is the systematic risk factor in this multiple factor model?
b. What are the "common factors" (systematic non-market) factors in the model?
c. What single index model emerges if the coefficients (the "$b$" terms) on the common factors are equal to zero?
d. If the factor sensitivity on size ($b_2$) were equal to −0.01, would portfolio performance be enhanced by an active tilt toward large cap or small cap stocks? Explain your answer in the context of a standardized size factor at, say, −1 and 1, respectively.
e. If the factor sensitivity (regression coefficient) on price/book value ratio (P/BV) and dividend yield were −0.03 and 0.02, respectively, would the investor's portfolio benefit from an active tilt toward value or growth stocks? Again, use standardized factor values of −1 and 1, respectively, in your explanation of portfolio performance.
f. If the Industrial factor value were zero, and the Non-Industrial factor were (therefore) one, which industries or sectors of the economy would benefit from the common factors that are assumed to benefit portfolio performance in the multi-factor regression analysis?

6. James Abate of Credit Suisse Asset Management employs a dual strategy to finding the best stocks in the marketplace. His "top-down" approach looks at how dominant macroeconomic factors (interest rates, commodity prices) impact the stocks of companies in the financial and energy sectors, while his "bottom up" analysis focuses on fundamental economic profit trends for companies operating in the health care and technology sectors of the economy.

   Discuss how a synthesized multiple factor model having both macroeconomic and fundamental factors might be developed and employed to identify active opportunities across the spectrum of equity securities. What would the multi-factor model look like, and what are the factors that you would include in a factor model having both fundamental and macroeconomic tenets?

7. Suppose that Unidentified Portfolio X has the following factor exposure to the primary fundamental factors listed below:

| Factor | Standardized Factor Exposure |
|---|---|
| Size | 2.0 |
| E/P Ratio | −1.0 |
| B/P Ratio | −2.0 |
| Yield | −0.8 |
| Foreign Income | 1.8 |

a. Does Unidentified Portfolio X mostly consist of large cap stocks or small to medium cap stocks?

b. Is Unidentified Portfolio X tilted toward value or growth stocks? Use the factor exposures for E/P, B/P, and Dividend Yield in explaining your answer.

c. Do the companies represented in Unidentified Portfolio X largely generate their earnings from domestic U.S. sources or international sources?

d. What is the meaning of the factor exposures to the standardized E/P and B/P factors? Are they conveying a consistent message about the equity management style of Unidentified Portfolio X?

7. The following quotations is from Bruce Jacobs and Kenneth Levy ("Investment Analysis: Profiting from a Complex Equity Market," Chapter 2 in Frank J. Fabozzi (ed.) *Active Equity Portfolio Management*, Frank J. Fabozzi Associates):

> Simultaneous analysis of all relevant variables via multivariate regression takes into account and adjusts for such (fundamental) relationships. The result is the return to each variable separately, controlling for all related variables. A multi-variate analysis for low P/E, for example, will provide a measure of the excess return to a portfolio that is market-like in all respects except for having a lower-than-average P/E ratio. Disentangled returns are "pure" returns.

a. What are Jacobs and Levy referring to when they argue that "Disentangled returns are 'pure' returns?"

b. How can a factor model be employed to "disentangle" the real effects as opposed to spurious factor influences that impact portfolio performance and portfolio risk control?

8. a. How can a factor model be used to assist in the development and maintenance of a market index fund? Be sure to focus on the role of multiple factor models in portfolio risk control.

b. How can a multiple factor model be used to assist in a strategy that involves active style tilting?

c. How can a multi-factor model be employed to assist a portfolio manager who uses an "enhanced indexing" approach to equity management? (We defined this limited active risk strategy in Chapter 4.)

# Chapter 10

# Profiles in Equity Management

We now have looked at the equity management process from several different — yet related — angles including (1) value versus growth styles of equity management, (2) traditional and value-based approaches to equity management, (3) cash flow valuation approaches to the analysis of equity securities, and (4) quantitatively based factor model approaches to equity portfolio management. In this chapter, we profile the active management strategies of several portfolio managers who have developed innovative approaches to equity management. Based on both personal interviews and published research/product reports, we cover the active strategies of the following investment management firms:[1]

- Jacobs Levy Equity Management
- State Street Global Advisors
- Boston Partners Asset Management
- Credit Suisse Asset Management
- Columbia Management Company

The appendix to this chapter provides information about these investment management firms.

## JACOBS LEVY EQUITY MANAGEMENT

The active investment approach employed by Bruce Jacobs and Kenneth Levy of Jacobs Levy Equity Management evolves out of their deeply rooted philosophical view of the equity market.[2] In their view, the equity market is "complex" in the sense that it is neither deterministic — like the dynamics of a pendulum — nor completely random — like the Brownian motion of gas molecules. Jacobs and Levy argue that in reality the equity market operates somewhere between these extremes, such that the stock market should be evaluated from an integrated prism that is designed to "disentangle" real investment opportunities from those that are illusory or spurious.

---

[1] It is important to mention that the active strategies that we profile in this chapter do not necessarily constitute the entire active policy of the money management firms shown in the text. Our goal is to provide readers with a diversity of portfolio managers that employ innovative approaches to equity securities analysis and portfolio management.

[2] For a further discussion of Jacobs and Levy's view of the "complex" stock market, see Bruce I. Jacobs and Kenneth N. Levy, "Investment Analysis: Profiting from a Complex Equity Market," *Active Equity Portfolio Management*, Frank J. Fabozzi (ed.) (New Hope, PA: Frank J. Fabozzi Associates, 1998), pp. 21-35.

## Exhibit 1: Return Effects Form a Tangled Web

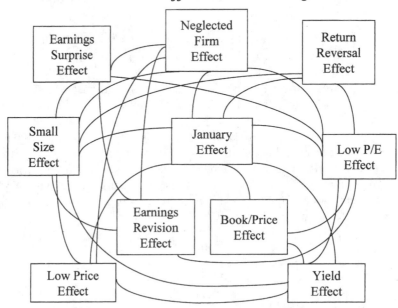

Source: Exhibit 1 in Bruce I. Jacobs and Kenneth N. Levy, "Investment Analysis: Profiting from a Complex Equity Market," Chapter 2 in Frank J. Fabozzi (ed.), *Active Equity Portfolio Management* (New Hope, PA: Frank J. Fabozzi Associates, 1998), p. 26.

## Disentangling Equity Returns

Central to the Jacobs Levy model is the recognition that the equity market is permeated by a complex web of interrelated — although not entirely predictable — return effects that impact all securities in the marketplace. In this context, Exhibit 1 shows a series of return regularities that have been "discovered" by academic researchers since the efficient markets hypothesis was first proposed by Eugene Fama and others during the early 1970s. The major benefit of the "complex market" approach used by Jacobs and Levy is that it employs an integrated quantitative approach to help identify the pure return effects and relationships from the web of investment opportunities shown in Exhibit 1.

## A Unified Approach

Jacobs and Levy emphasize the importance of disentangling security returns within a unified approach. To see the importance of this idea, consider the typical value, growth, and small capitalization representation of the equity market. By viewing the world of equity management in a compartmentalized fashion, the active manager may miss the information content that, say, macroeconomic factors such as economic growth and inflation have for all securities. By estimating the regression coefficient in a model that looks at the relationship between the return to value stocks and inflation, for example, one should recognize that the robustness of such a locally estimated statistical model is limited by the fact that inflation impacts all securities along a continuum — whether value or growth stocks.

According to Jacobs and Levy, what is needed is a globally estimated model where the regression return sensitivities are estimated from a complex model that exploits the information content of economic factors for all securities. By analogy, they point out that if a researcher were trying to predict employment trends in the Northeast region of the United States, then employment growth happenings in the Southeastern part of the country would be useful information in building a clear picture of employment patterns in the former region. More to the point, they correctly ponder what the active manager should do if the locally estimated model reveals that, say, Ford Motor Company's stock looks attractive relative to General Motors while the regression coefficients on fundamental and macroeconomic factors from a globally estimated statistical model indicate the contrary.

## Pure Effects

The Jacobs Levy complex market approach to equity management also emphasizes that economic and fundamental factors impact securities within a particular equity classification in a way that can only be seen by *disentangling* the various return effects. Recall from Chapter 5 that prominent value and growth indexes are constructed using the price-to-book ratio as the primary fundamental factor for deciding which stocks fall into growth and value categories, respectively. Indeed, as we discussed in Chapter 5, the price/book screen is the only fundamental factor that is used in construction of the S&P/BARRA Large Cap Growth and Value indexes.

Exhibit 2 shows the benefit of looking at the pure effect of stocks with relatively high price-to-book ratios — holding other fundamental factors at their respective market averages — versus a value index that sorts simply by naive price-to-book ratio, unadjusted for the effects of other factors. As Jacobs and Levy point out, the disentangled P/B return series is noticeably higher than the naive P/B portfolio — emphasizing the return improvement that can be attained with finer definitions of "value" — and is also less variable about the overall trend. In effect, the pure return series has more "signal" and less "noise" than the conventional value series.

Additionally, Exhibits 3 and 4 show the benefit of disentangling the following three size dimensions: small cap, analyst neglect, and low stock price. Exhibit 3 shows the "naive" cumulative returns to the various size measures. Each of these return series is constructed from a univariate regression between security returns and the specific size measure without accounting for possible correlation effects among fundamental and industry factors that impact all securities. In contrast, Exhibit 4 is based on a multivariate regression that estimates pure returns to the size factor with full accounting for the correlative return impact of fundamental forces.

## Exhibit 2: Naive and Pure Returns to High Book-to-Price Ratio

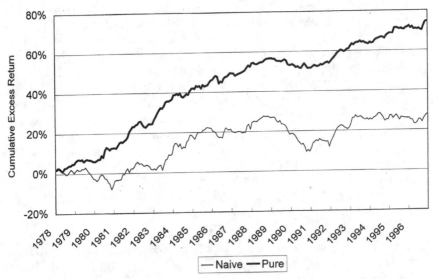

Source: Exhibit 2 in Bruce I. Jacobs and Kenneth N. Levy, "Investment Analysis: Profiting from a Complex Equity Market," Chapter 2 in Frank J. Fabozzi (ed.), *Active Equity Portfolio Management* (New Hope, PA: Frank J. Fabozzi Associates, 1998), p. 27.

## Exhibit 3: Naive Returns Can Hide Opportunities: Three Size-Related Variables

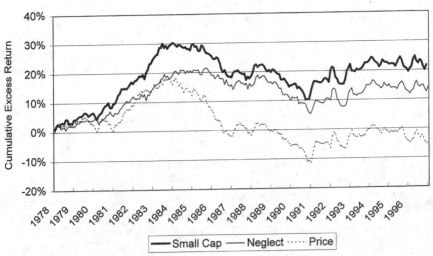

Source: Exhibit 3 in Bruce I. Jacobs and Kenneth N. Levy, "Investment Analysis: Profiting from a Complex Equity Market," Chapter 2 in Frank J. Fabozzi (ed.), *Active Equity Portfolio Management* (New Hope, PA: Frank J. Fabozzi Associates, 1998), p. 28.

## Exhibit 4: Pure Returns Can Reveal Opportunities: Three Size-Related Variables

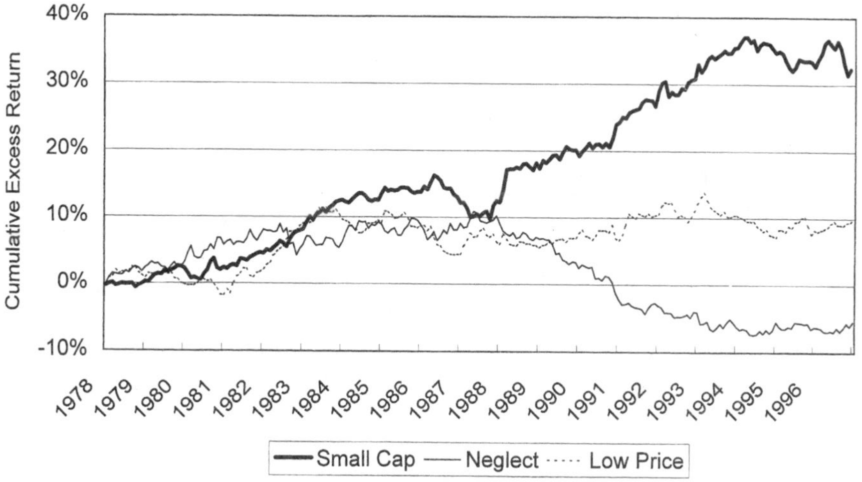

Source: Exhibit 5 in Bruce I. Jacobs and Kenneth N. Levy, "Investment Analysis: Profiting from a Complex Equity Market," Chapter 2 in Frank J. Fabozzi (ed.), *Active Equity Portfolio Management* (New Hope, PA: Frank J. Fabozzi Associates, 1998), p. 29.

The naive returns shown in Exhibit 3 are quite misleading. For example, the unadjusted cumulative return series for small cap and analyst neglect are highly correlated. This leaves the equity manager with the impression that these fundamental dimensions are close proxies. In sharp contrast, the disentangled return series shown in Exhibit 4 reveals that the real return-enhancing factor was actually small cap, while the analyst neglect factor had a negative impact on cumulative returns. Since the pure returns are "additive," this finding suggests that a portfolio consisting of small (equity) cap stocks having a negative tilt on the analyst neglect factor (above-average following by analysts) would have generated beneficial abnormal returns during the reporting period.

Exhibit 4 also shows that low price stocks had a largely neutral impact on portfolio performance during the sample years while the naive return series shown in Exhibit 3 suggests — incorrectly — that the cumulative return to low price stocks was negative. Hence, the Jacobs Levy quantitative approach to the analysis of equity securities shows that even simple fundamental factors such as equity size and price-to-book ratio (recall Exhibit 2) need — in a complex market environment — to be examined in a framework that accounts for the possible impacts of other related influences on equity return.

## What's Behind Pure Return Effects?

Jacobs and Levy believe that returns to pure effects are driven by a combination of economic fundamentals, such as interest rates, industrial production, inflation, and investor behavior, including overreaction and herding. The effects of these variables can differ across different types of stock and over different market environments. Changes in interest rate spreads, for example, are more important for financial stocks. Earnings surprises and earnings estimate revisions are more important for growth stocks. Stocks with high dividend-discount-model values tend to perform better in bull markets than bear markets, whereas high-yield stocks experience the reverse.

Jacobs and Levy also monitor signals by informed agents, including stock splits, corporate buybacks, and insider trading activity. Furthermore, they take into account nonlinearities in relationships between stock returns and relevant variables. The effects of positive earnings surprises, for example, tend to be arbitraged away quickly, whereas negative earnings surprises are more long-lasting (perhaps because sales of stock are limited to investors who already own the stock and a relatively small number of short sellers). Relationships may also change over time; ongoing research on new inefficiencies, new sources of data, and new statistical techniques ensures model robustness.

Jacobs and Levy use all the dimensions found relevant by the valuation model to construct optimized portfolios to meet various client needs.[3] Use of multiple dimensions maximizes potential profit opportunities and enhances risk control. The aim in construction of all Jacobs Levy portfolios is to take no more risk than is warranted by the expected incremental return.

Although their research, valuation, and optimization processes are heavily reliant on sophisticated computer modeling, Jacobs and Levy emphasize the importance of the human element. One criterion they use in considering variables to model, for example, is that the predicted effect-return relationships respond in intuitively satisfying ways to macroeconomic events and to detected modes of investor behavior. Furthermore, while trading at Jacobs Levy takes advantage of lower-cost electronic venues, hands-on analysis of ongoing corporate news ensures that circumstances are conducive to desired trades.

## Long-Short Investing

The empirical findings revealed in Exhibit 4 indicate that investment rewards were available to active investors who were long on stocks having jointly below average equity capitalization and above average following by equity analysts — namely, small cap stocks with negative analyst neglect. Jacobs and Levy also employ a market-neutral strategy whereby active portfolio rewards can be obtained by going long on stocks having positive expected returns (based on, say, the pure price/book or small cap effects) while shorting those securities with a fundamental factor (like analyst neglect) having negative anticipated return effects.[4]

---

[3] Strategies offered by Jacobs Levy Equity Management include large cap core, designed to deliver active returns above large cap indices such as the S&P 500; small cap core; large and small cap growth and value; insight-weighted; and long-short.

Specifically, Jacobs and Levy argue that by simultaneously going long on stocks with high expected returns and short on similar-risk (equity beta) stocks with low expected returns, the active manager anticipates gains on the combined portfolio of longs and shorts — as long position stock prices rise and short position stock prices fall in view of the manager's correctly assessed positive and negative return expectations. If the risk and market positions of the longs and shorts are of similar magnitude, then the overall portfolio will be "immunized" against unanticipated price movements in the stock market as a whole. In this sense, the active investor anticipates earning a true return from security selection that is not constrained by index-related weighting considerations that typically impede a long-only portfolio.

### *Jacobs Levy's Long-Short Example[5]*

Exhibit 5 reproduces the basics of the long-short strategy as explained by Jacobs and Levy. In this context, consider an institutional investor who deposits $10 million in a prime broker's custodial account for long-short investing. With a 50% initial margin requirement, the investor has sufficient equity capital to support a long-short portfolio consisting of $10 million longs and $10 million shorts. Upon purchasing $9 million in designated stocks with high expected returns — leaving a $1 million liquidity buffer — the prime broker then arranges with a securities lender — for example, a bank having established custody operations — to borrow $9 million of designated (as determined by the investor's security selection decisions) securities for short-sale. Upon selling the securities, the prime broker then deposits the proceeds from the short-sale into a collateral account held by the securities lender.

The investor will receive short-term interest on (1) the short sale proceeds held as collateral at the securities lender and (2) the liquidity buffer account, at $1 million, that is held at the equity manager's prime brokerage firm. In effect, the investor earns the short-term interest rate on the entire $10 million in up-front equity capital.[6] Exhibit 5 (upper and lower portions) shows the financial detail of what happens to the institutional investor's "market neutral" portfolio when the stock market rises by 30% or falls by 15% in the presence of a long-short return spread of 6% (long return exceeds the return on short side of the active portfolio by 600 basis points).

The upper portion of Exhibit 5 shows that when the stock market goes up by 30%, the long side of the portfolio rises presumably by 33%. Accordingly, the $9 million invested long rises to $11.97 million (1.3 × $9 million) for a capital gain of $2.97 million. On the short side, the relatively lower expected return securities rise by 27%, from $9 million to $11.43 million, which results in a loss on the investor's short positions of $2.43 million.

---

[4] For an insightful discussion of the Jacobs Levy market neutral approach to equity management, see Bruce I. Jacobs and Kenneth N. Levy, "The Long and Short on Long-Short," *The Journal of Investing* (Spring 1997) pp. 73-86.

[5] This example is from Jacobs and Levy, "The Long and Short on Long-Short."

[6] For convenience, Jacobs and Levy omit the securities lender fee of about 25 to 30 basis points of annualized return (among other minor charges) in their illustration of long-short investing.

## Exhibit 5: Market-Neutral Long-Short Hypothetical Performance: Bull and Bear Markets

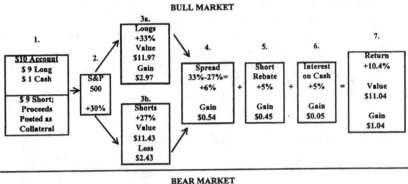

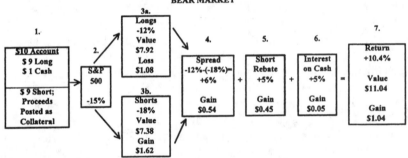

Source: Exhibit 2 from Bruce I. Jacobs and Kenneth N. Levy, "The Long and Short on Long-Short," *The Journal of Investing* (Spring 1997), p. 75.
This copyrighted material is reprinted with permission from Institutional Investor, Inc. *The Journal of Investing*, 488 Madison Avenue, New York, NY 10022.

Also, upon summing (1) the $0.54 million gain from long-short securities transactions ($2.97 million less $2.43 million), (2) the 5% short rebate, at $0.45 million, earned on the $9 million of collateral posted at the securities lender, and (3) the 5% interest, at $0.05 million, earned on the liquidity buffer held at the prime broker, the investor receives a dollar gain of $1.04 million on the long-short strategy. This results in an overall return of 10.4% on the investor's initial $10 million ($1.04/$10). As we will shortly see (no pun intended), the 10.4% return on the investor's long-short portfolio is largely due to the $0.54 million net gain (or 6% of $9 million) earned jointly from both the long and short securities transactions.

The lower portion of Exhibit 5 shows what happens to the long-short portfolio when the market declines by 15%. In this example, securities held long decline by 12% while the stock prices of securities that were shorted decline by 18% — maintaining the long-short spread of 6%. The longs are now worth $7.92 million while the shorted securities are worth $7.38 million. This results in a loss of $1.08 million on the long side of the transaction and a $1.62 gain on the short side.

On balance, the long-short spread of $0.54 million (again, 6% of $9 million) combined with the $0.50 million ($0.45 plus $0.05) earned on deposited funds (held at the securities lender and prime broker, respectively) result in an overall gain of $1.04 million, or 10.4%, on the investor's initial capital. As revealed in Exhibit 5, the investor's long-short, or market neutral, portfolio is expected to earn the same return regardless of the future direction — namely, bull or bear market — of the stock market. According to Jacobs and Levy, the long-short investor can expect to capture the information content of his or her underlying analysis of equity securities having high expected rates of return (the longs) and low expected returns (the shorts), respectively.

## STATE STREET GLOBAL ADVISORS

The history of active equity management at State Street Global Advisors (SSgA) is jointly a history of innovation in the field of portfolio management and a history of money management startups that emerged from knowledge either acquired or developed at State Street Asset Management.[7] Pioneered by Peter Stonberg (among others), the U.S. Active Equity Group at State Street Global Advisors follows a disciplined fundamental approach to active equity management. Termed "Matrix Equity," the large cap core investment product of SSgA incorporates a value (for *valuation*) and growth perspective in the analyses and selection of equity securities. Exhibit 6 provides a historical perspective on the evolution of active strategies and technology employed by the equity management group at SSgA.[8]

Underlying the active strategy at SSgA has been an evolving emphasis on two equity factors — current valuation and growth. During the early 1980s, State Street recognized the pricing significance of combining traditional fundamental analysis with earnings estimate revisions as a way of identifying mispriced securities in the marketplace. The basic idea is simple and compelling: Stocks with attractive company fundamentals and positive earnings momentum are viewed as buy opportunities while the stocks of companies having poor fundamentals and negative earnings momentum are considered sell or short-sell opportunities. In more complex terms, Exhibit 6 shows that the core value/growth strategy has evolved with numerous quantitative enhancements including multi-factor valuation analysis, estimate revision enhancement features, industry and sector risk controls, and transaction cost modeling.

---

[7] While SSgA's Core Matrix strategy is explained in the text, it is interesting to note that several quantitative-oriented money management firms evolved out of the earlier-named State Street Asset Management Group. These portfolio management firms include Franklin Portfolio Associates (John Nagorniak), Boston International Advisors (Lyle Davis and David Umstead), and Numeric Investors (John Bogle and Langdon Wheeler).

[8] The exhibits presented in this section were obtained from an SSgA product report — "U.S. Active Equity Overview," State Street Global Advisors, 1998. We are grateful to Peter Stonberg and Jane Cupp for supplying this internal information.

## Exhibit 6: Evolution of the Investment Strategy at State Street Global Advisors

| Year | Enhancement | Year | Enhancement |
|------|-------------|------|-------------|
| 1984 | Estimate revision and value | 1995 | Estimate revision momentum |
| 1987 | Sector controls | | Projected E/P value |
| | Multi-factor value | | Added negative stock offsets |
| 1988 | Single formula value model | 1996 | Industry skill adjustments |
| 1990 | Linear optimizer | | Incorporated BARRA E3 industry classifications |
| | Capitalization, beta and yield controls | 1997 | Enhanced capitalization controls |
| 1991 | Relative value | 1998 | Industry clustering |
| 1992 | Industry controls | | Earnings stability |
| 1993 | Transaction cost modeling | | Lead analyst identification |
| | Detailed estimate revision | | |
| | Enhanced value model | | |

Source: SSgA presentation, *U.S. Active Equity Overview.*

## Exhibit 7: State Street Global Advisors' Investment Process

Source: SSgA presentation, *U.S. Active Equity Overview.*

## Matrix Equity

A flowchart of the systematic process used by State Street Global Advisors is shown in Exhibit 7. SSgA's investable universe for its large cap core matrix strategy is the Russell 1000 universe. For each stock, SSgA engages in a quantitative assessment of the pricing significance of traditional fundamental factors. This includes the linkage between earnings-to-price ratio and revenue growth (among others), combined with a detailed assessment of the earnings growth characteristics of a company's stock as reflected in analysts' estimate revisions.

## Exhibit 8: State Street Global Advisors'
## Investment Process to Identify Undervalued Securities with
## Superior Growth Potential

*Stock Evaluation*
*Value:*
   Traditional fundamental analysis
*Growth:*
   Capturing expectations through earnings estimate revisions

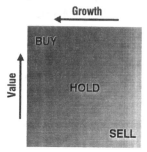

Source: SSgA presentation, *U.S. Active Equity Overview.*

Before including a stock in the portfolio, the research team at SSgA also engages in a qualitative review of each security. This added layer of scrutiny is performed to see if recent corporate actions might adversely impact what was previously viewed as an attractive buy opportunity based on quantitative assessment of the company's valuation/growth characteristics. In this disciplined context, Exhibit 7 shows that the large cap core matrix strategy at SSgA consists of:

   • an investable universe of large cap stocks
   • a quantitative assessment of primary valuation and growth factors
   • a qualitative review of security selection candidates
   • portfolio construction and risk control

Exhibit 8 shows the matrix synthesis used by SSgA to identify potentially undervalued securities with superior growth potential. On the vertical axis one sees fundamental security valuation as determined by the research team at SSgA. Undervalued stocks point in a northward direction, while potentially overvalued securities — based on a quantitative assessment of fundamental value considerations — point southward. On the horizontal axis one sees the growth scaling as determined by an extensive review of earnings estimate revisions. Stocks of companies having surprise positive earnings announcements — relative to consensus estimates — are deemed attractive and therefore point westward in the matrix, while those companies having unanticipated negative earnings announcements are deemed unattractive and point eastward along the estimate revision dimension.

Integrating the value and growth results, Exhibit 8 reveals that the best security selection opportunities lie in the northwest portion of the equity matrix.

Companies that plot in this region look attractively priced based on an assessment of their revenue growth and cash flow plowback (among other value factors), while at the same time experiencing positive earnings momentum that was unanticipated by consensus investors. Conversely, the stocks of firms located in the southeast portion of the equity matrix are sell or short-sell candidates. Firms showing up in this section of the large cap equity matrix have jointly poor assessed relative value (vertical axis) in the presence of recent corporate earnings announcements that are unfavorable.

Exhibit 8 also reveals that companies that fall in the middle of the equity matrix give conflicting buy and sell signals. That is, stocks located in the northeastern part of the equity matrix have attractive company fundamentals combined with negative earnings estimate revisions. In a similar manner, securities that fall in the southwest portion of the equity matrix have unattractive investment fundamentals along with positive earnings surprise. In both instances, there is no consistency in the quantitative factors that would lead to a buy or sell decision.

## A Closer Look at Valuation and Growth

SSgA looks at two primary elements to determine a company's current value: expected future earnings and current capital (or asset) structure. Evaluation of a company's future earnings potential is made by assessing the relationship between a relative earnings-to-price ratio and the firm's projected sales growth and changes in operating margins. The goal here is to avoid overpaying for a company's anticipated future growth opportunities. Along the asset structure dimension (the second current value consideration), SSgA examines the fundamental relationship between the firm's price-to-book ratio and its underlying ability to generate both favorable return on equity (ROE) and excess cash flow. In SSgA's framework, earnings estimates and stock prices are updated daily to enhance the responsiveness of the active equity model.

From a growth perspective, SSgA has used earnings estimate revisions in its security selection and portfolio construction process since inception of Matrix Equity during the early 1980s. Their research on this growth factor reveals three issues that drive a comprehensive earnings estimate revision analysis:

- change in earnings estimate relative to price
- consensus opinion among equity analysts
- momentum in analyst earnings revision relative to consensus view

Exhibit 9 illustrates the importance of looking at "lead" analyst earnings estimate detail relative to consensus opinion. In this illustration, the analyst's initial earnings forecast lies below the median earnings forecast. According to State Street, there are three potential estimate revision paths that the analyst can take over time: (1) the analyst becomes even more pessimistic about the future earnings prospects of the firm, (2) the analyst moves toward the consensus opinion, and (3) the analyst changes course from pessimistic to optimistic about the firm's future earnings prospects.

## *Exhibit 9: Earnings Estimate Revisions versus Consensus Opinion*

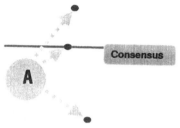

Source: SSgA presentation, *U.S. Active Equity Overview.*

If the analyst becomes more pessimistic about a firm's future earnings potential, then SSgA views this to be important since the analyst is willing to move further away from the consensus opinion. A movement in the analyst's estimate revision toward the median forecast would not convey any material information that was not already anticipated by equity analysts. On the other hand, a crossing in the analyst's estimate revision from below to above the median forecast would be viewed by SSgA as very significant—as the estimate revision itself is likely to represent new information about the firm's improving economic prospects. Exhibit 10 illustrates SSgA's sell decisions on Western Digital stock in the presence of persistent downward earnings estimate revisions by equity analysts at prominent Wall Street (i.e., sell side) firms.

Most importantly, a synthesis of the primary value and growth factors results in the set of buy and sell opportunities that form the basis of the large cap core equity strategy. As mentioned before, a final qualitative review is employed by the SSgA research team before implementation of any buys and sells. A representative display of companies that emerged from a matrix equity synthesis of current valuation and growth factors is shown in Exhibit 11. Stocks that lie in the northwest region of the matrix form the basis for long-only portfolios, while a long-short strategy is obtained with a combination of stocks that fall in the northwest and southeast portions of the equity matrix, respectively.[9]

## Matrix Equity Risk Controls

Active portfolio construction at SSgA is designed to stay within a tolerable range of fundamental and sector characteristics of the market benchmark. In this context, Exhibit 12 shows the investment fundamentals for Matrix Equity compared with the S&P 500 Index as of June 30, 1998. A snapshot of the two diversified portfolios reveals the same beta (at 1) and dividend yield (at 1.4%), along with a similarity in price/earnings and price/book ratios. Moreover, both of these U.S. equity portfolios are weighted toward giant or maxi-capitalization stocks.

[9] SSgA's Matrix Equity strategy is also employed in numerous "long-only" products including Large Cap Growth, Large Cap Value, MidCap, Special Small Cap, Small Cap, and U.S. Aggressive Growth portfolios. Their active Long-Short U.S. Equity portfolio employs matrix equity tenets and is headed (at the time of this writing) by David Hanna.

*Exhibit 10: Western Digital Corporation*

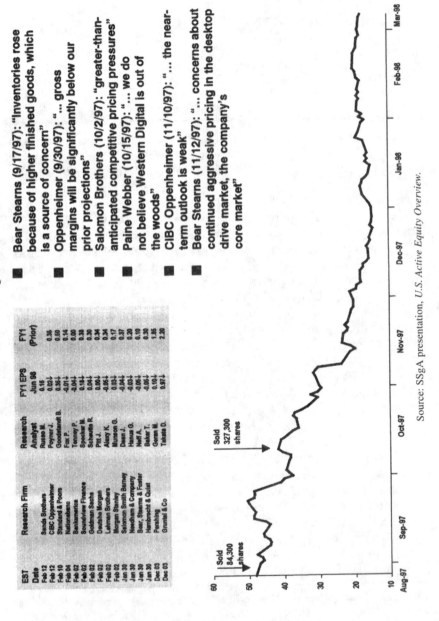

Source: SSgA presentation, *U.S. Active Equity Overview.*

*Exhibit 11: State Street Global Advisors' Portfolio Graphics*
*Large Cap Core Matrix Equity Strategy*

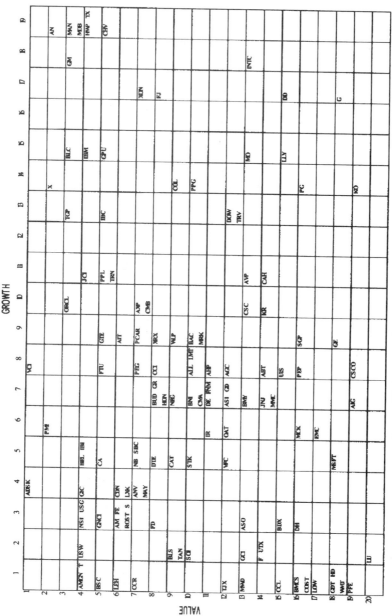

Source: SSgA presentation, *U.S. Active Equity Overview.*

## Exhibit 12: Portfolio Characteristics
### Large Cap Core Matrix Equity Strategy as of June 30, 1998
#### Fund Characteristics

|  | Portfolio | S&P 500 Index |
|---|---|---|
| Forward P/E | 19.3 | 21.8 |
| Yield (%) | 1.4 | 1.4 |
| P/B | 4.7 | 4.5 |
| Beta | 1.00 | 1.00 |
| Projected 5 Year Growth (%) | 13.7 | 14.1 |
| Average Cap ($) | 63.9 B | 70.9 B |
| Turnover (%) | 100 | — |
| # of holdings | 131 | 500 |

### Top Ten Holdings

| Name | Portfolio Weight (%) | Index Weight (%) |
|---|---|---|
| Microsoft Corporation | 3.57 | 3.01 |
| General Electric Company | 2.81 | 3.34 |
| Lucent Technologies Inc. | 2.35 | 1.23 |
| Chase Manhattan Corp. | 2.07 | 0.73 |
| Pfizer Inc. | 2.06 | 1.60 |
| Nationsbank Corp. | 2.05 | 0.83 |
| Exxon Corporation | 1.96 | 1.97 |
| Coca-Cola Company | 1.86 | 2.38 |
| Morgan Stanley Dean Witter | 1.81 | 0.62 |
| Bristol-Myers Squibb | 1.78 | 1.29 |

Source: SSgA presentation, *U.S. Active Equity Overview.*

SSgA's Matrix Equity should not be confused with indexing. To the extent that differences exist between the portfolio and market index, they are exploited with the goal of earning a positive abnormal return (alpha) on the overall active portfolio. From this perspective, it's interesting to see that the average equity capitalization for Matrix Equity diverges from that of the S&P 500 by some $7 billion ($63.9 – $70.9). Although this capitalization difference might not seem large — since both numbers are indicative of maxi-cap stocks — one should keep in mind that a $7 billion size difference cuts across the entire small cap to large cap spectrum used by *Morningstar* when classifying mutual funds by equity size. Also noteworthy in Exhibit 12 is the 100% turnover rate for Matrix Equity along with a portfolio having 131 stocks versus 500 stocks for the S&P benchmark.

As a final layer of portfolio analysis, Exhibit 13 shows the Matrix Equity sector weights as of June 30, 1998. From a risk control perspective, it is interesting to see that within a tolerable range the active sector weights for Matrix Equity are similar to those of the S&P 500 benchmark. However, the active overweighting on capital goods, consumer cyclical, and technology stocks combined with the underweighting on basic material, energy, and consumer staple stocks is presumably significant enough to generate abnormal returns (namely, positive alpha) on the matrix equity portfolio — where, as explained before, each sector is evaluated along both value and growth-oriented (earnings estimate revisions) dimensions.

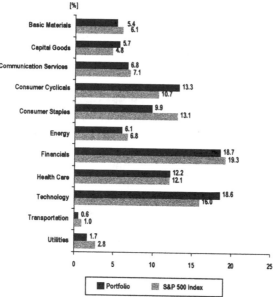

### Exhibit 13: Portfolio Characteristics
*Large Cap Core Matrix Equity Strategy as of June 30, 1998 — Sector Weights*

Source: SSgA presentation, *U.S. Active Equity Overview.*

## BOSTON PARTNERS ASSET MANAGEMENT

Wayne Archambo, Principal and Equity Portfolio Manager, directs the small cap and mid cap value products at Boston Partners Asset Management. His active management philosophy has evolved over the years, and can be summed up in two qualified words: namely, value works! Over time, he believes that statistically inexpensive stocks (as measured by the price/earnings or price/book ratio) having a positive catalyst for earnings change, outperform statistically expensive stocks. In this context, he emphasizes the *dual* importance of relative valuation and business momentum, as a so-called "cheap" stock can get cheaper, and an inexpensive stock can stay inexpensive for long periods of time.

Moreover, fledging companies with a low stock price fall into what Archambo calls the "value trap." To avoid that pitfall, he buys statistically inexpensive stocks of companies having (1) attractive return and growth characteristics, and (2) a visible business catalyst — such as favorable inventory and receivable turnover ratios — to identify the fundamental value of a security.

### Equity Valuation at Boston Partners

In determining what a company is worth, the equity analysts at Boston Partners closely monitor its free cash flow. Given distortions created by today's accounting standards — and some companies' willingness to aggressively apply these standards — accounting earnings are deemed (in Boston Partners' view) to be almost meaningless. To derive free cash flow, equity analysts look at the operating cash flow that a company generates minus the annual capital expenditure required to maintain the firm's productive assets. Exhibit 14 shows a basic illustration of the free cash flow estimation procedure used by Boston Partners Asset Management. The exhibit reveals that a company's economic earnings can differ significantly from its reported accounting profit (net income).

When evaluating a company's stock, Boston Partners also determines the growth rate of the firm's free cash flow and the sustainability of that growth rate. In determining projected growth rates, and consistency thereof, the equity analysts carefully examine a company's historical return on capital and the projected marginal return on invested capital. High return companies generate capital that can be deployed back into the business. If this capital is allocated to projects with above average corporate returns, then growth can be sustained. If, however, the capital is deployed into real investment projects with marginal returns that are lower than average corporate returns, then growth — in Boston Partners' view — will decelerate.

Additionally, the return on capital that a company generates is a function of the industry within which it operates and the skill of management. Therefore, to uncover promising investment ideas, Boston Partners deems it important to understand both industry dynamics and management quality. In this context, portfolio manager Archambo periodically interviews the management of companies in the small cap and mid cap portfolios. Recognizing that company visits are both time intensive and costly, he emphasizes that it is vital for active money managers to understand how management plans to allocate capital and what returns they can realistically expect on capital investment projects.

## Exhibit 14: Boston Partners (BP): Free Cash Flow Estimation
### ABC Cable Company (in $ Millions)

| | | |
|---|---|---|
| Net Income | | $500 |
| + Depreciation Expense | 200 | |
| − Maintenance Capital Expenditure | 500 | |
| + Amortization of Goodwill | 25* | |
| = Free Cash Flow | | $225 |
| (Economic Earnings) | | |

*Depreciation and Maintenance Capital Assumptions:*
Gross Plant = $5000
GAAP Useful Life (assumption) = 25 years
Boston Partners Estimate Useful Life = 10 years**

Depreciation Expense = $200 = Gross Plant/GAAP Useful Life
Maintenance Capital  = $500 = Gross Plant/BP Estimated Useful Life

* Goodwill amortization resulting from recent corporate acquisition.
** Difference between assumed GAAP useful plant life and Boston Partners estimates due to technological innovation in the cable industry.

Once Boston Partners has a firm grasp of a company's economic earnings (measured by free cash flow) and its growth prospects, it then determine an appropriate multiple of estimated earnings. In general, Boston Partners prefers to buy the stocks of companies having attractive returns combined with stock price that trades at a significant discount to both its peer group and the market as a whole. However, Archambo warns managers that inexpensive stocks can stay inexpensive for long periods of time. Therefore, when Boston Partners has identified an undervalued stock — based on traditional equity fundamentals — it also looks for a visible business catalyst to find the value of that security.

## Identifying Fundamental Catalysts

According to Boston Partners, there are several potential catalysts the equity analyst can look for. Examples include rising earnings estimates, a change in senior management, the disposition of under-performing assets, insider buying trends, and attractive corporate acquisitions, to name a few. In this realm of equity analysis, Boston Partners pays close attention to a company's balance sheet. The reason for this special balance sheet focus is that sell side equity analysts get paid mostly to predict the income statement (namely, EPS), not a company's balance sheet. In certain industries though — particularly retail and technology — balance sheet improvement or deterioration can portend positive or negative earnings trends. For example, a build-up in accounts receivables or inventories may be a precursor to a slowdown in a firm's growth rate of sales.

Along this line, Archambo stresses that companies struggling to meet "top line" revenue projections often stuff their distribution channels. This can create a substantial increase in days receivable outstanding. If the goods are not sold out of the channel, distributors will cancel new orders, thereby negatively impacting future earnings. Inventories present another area of concern for equity analysts. When inventories increase relative to realistic production levels, part of the additional cost is placed on the balance sheet rather than being reported in income. The resulting artificial boost to earnings will reverse when inventories decline again. In addition, high inventories can become obsolete and require a write down in the future. Therefore, an increase in days of production in inventory should be a warning sign that earnings are artificially inflated and likely to be disappointing in the future.

Archambo also notes that determining the importance of a catalyst is not pure science; there is a certain art in understanding the relevance and investment impact of certain catalysts. He further emphasizes that a change in senior management can be a positive or negative catalyst depending on whether the new management has (1) a clearly articulated and realistic plan for change, and (2) adequate incentives to carry out the plan successfully.

Archambo points to the case of Federal Mogul as a company that fits into his active approach to equity fundamental analysis. Specifically, when Richard Snell was named CEO of Federal Mogul during the Fall of 1996, he laid out a credible plan to improve the returns of the company. Initially, he decided to dispose of non-core, low-return assets such as Federal Mogul's international retail business. Snell then implemented initiatives designed to improve inventory turnover and decrease days receivables outstanding — two powerful business catalysts according to Boston Partners. Finally, Snell embarked on a meaningful cost cutting program. All of these actions resulted in improved company returns, better cash flow, and an improved outlook for corporate growth. Also, Federal Mogul's top management had incentives — in the form of stock options — to maximize the performance of the company and therefore improve the value of the stock.

Another key part of Archambo's active strategy for Boston Partners' small cap and mid cap portfolios can be summed up like this: "know what you don't know." By this, he means that active portfolio managers should not spend excessive amounts of time analyzing factors that are inherently not knowable. Instead, Archambo suggests that the equity analyst should assess the risks associated with truly unknown factors and then make a reasonable attempt at adjusting the price target to factor in these uncertainties. One example of an unknowable, he argues, is trying to predict the outcome of corporate litigation. Another example is trying to predict quarterly earnings two years out for a volatile (commodity) technology company.

This does not mean that Boston Partners — in the context of their small and mid cap value portfolios — will not buy the stocks of highly unpredictable companies. However, in such cases, the portfolio manager should feel adequately compensated for bearing the excess risk associated with the unknown variables. As an anecdotal comment, Archambo feels that some equity analysts — particularly those with high intelligence quotients — spend far too much time trying to quantify multiple unknown factors, while in the process missing the active stock selection opportunities that may be revealed with a simple, yet disciplined, equity strategy — such as a value strategy with a fundamental catalyst.

## Illustration of Boston Partner's Active Strategy

Exhibit 15 provides a visual display of how Boston Partners uses fundamental equity analysis to identify opportunities in the small cap and mid cap universes. Above the midpoint on the vertical axis are companies with high rate of return on capital, and below this point are low return-generating firms. Also, to the right of the midpoint on the horizontal axis are expensive companies — as measured by the price-to-book ratio — while to the left of this point in the exhibit are inexpensive companies.

In turn, the active management role of each quadrant shown in Exhibit 15 can be summarized as follows:

- Quadrant I – *Opportunistic Value*. Companies in this quadrant generate high returns and yet trade at discount stock valuations. In principle, consistently high returns should generate superior growth, and be rewarded with a premium stock valuation. In analyzing companies in Quadrant I, it is necessary to understand the importance of the marginal return on capital (that is, change in operating income divided by change in operating assets). If the marginal return is below the average return, it is likely that the company is moving from Quadrant I to Quadrant IV. Boston Partners tries to avoid companies whose valuations seem "cheap," but whose capital return characteristics are deteriorating. Boston Partners also recognizes a regression tendency to the mean. Competitive advantages facilitating abnormally high returns can dissipate over time. Therefore, Boston Partners looks for companies having attractive stock valuations, and whose competitive advantages are likely to be sustainable over the investment horizon.

- Quadrant II – *High Expectations*. Companies in Quadrant II have superior return characteristics, but their stock is richly valued in the capital market. To capture active value here, Boston Partners generally sells stock as they move from Quadrant I into Quadrant II. Quadrant II is the traditional domain of growth companies, as measured by high revenue and earnings growth expectations. For stocks to stay in Quadrant II, the underlying company return and growth rates must be sustained at abnormally high levels.

- Quadrant III – *Fallen Growth*. Stocks in Quadrant III are richly valued, but they have low returns. Generally stocks in this quadrant are growth favorites whose businesses have taken a turn for the worse. Also, corporate valuations stay high for a while as active managers hold out hope for a return to the "glory days." Ultimately, however, prices compress and the stocks move into Quadrant IV. Boston Partners tries to avoid such "fallen angel" stocks.

## Exhibit 15: Boston Partners Equity Strategy

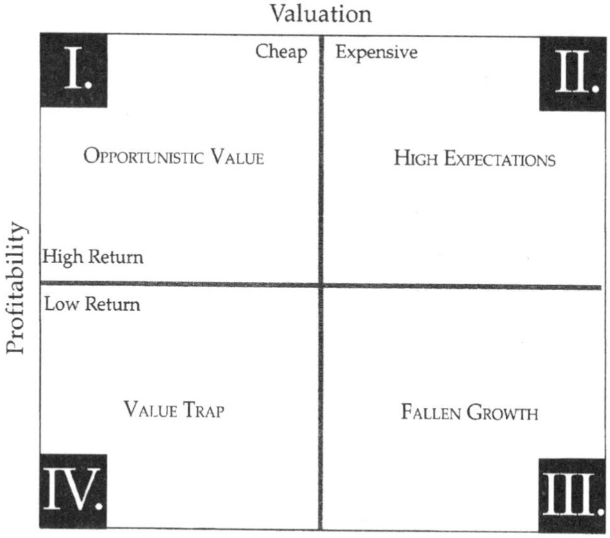

Valuation

Source: Boston Partners Asset Management, L.P.

• Quadrant IV – *Value Trap*. Stocks in this quadrant are inexpensive — yet they deserve to be because of low company returns. According to portfolio manager Archambo, there is a high opportunity cost associated with lugging around broken, cheap stocks waiting for an improvement. Boston Partners does not wait for such improvement (since it could take two or three years) and therefore only buy stocks in Quadrant IV that show evidence of real corporate improvement. The equity analyst must pay close attention to the emerging fundamental catalyst (if any) to find outstanding stock opportunities in this quadrant. If a tangible catalyst is in place that will improve corporate earnings prospects, stocks can move from Quadrant IV to Quadrant I. Successful stock picking therefore requires close examination of the marginal return on capital and the developing fundamental catalyst.

On balance, Boston Partners Asset Management focuses on investigating and understanding fundamental factors that have a decisive impact on equity security selection and portfolio performance. Simply put, this money management firm attempts to buy inexpensive stocks — with attractive growth and return characteristics — that have a visible profit catalyst in place to ensure both short- to medium-term stock price performance.

## CREDIT SUISSE ASSET MANAGEMENT

Credit Suisse Asset Management (CSAM) has found the economic profit framework (see Chapter 7) particularly effective in its ability to describe both changes in corporate valuation and in their active attempt at capturing abnormal returns on securities of firms operating in different sectors of the economy.[10] The concept of economic profits utilized by CSAM (like the commercial EVA® measure of corporate success) is defined as the after-tax operating cash flow return earned by a firm in *excess* of what its owners of equity and debt expect to earn on their invested capital. The firm's required rate of return (or weighted average cost of capital) is based on an assessment of market risk factors as well as company-specific risk considerations.

### Bottom-Up Approach

In Credit Suisse Asset Management's "bottom-up" approach to security selection, the estimated economic profit is examined in terms of a firm's relationship with market or investor expectations of future returns. From this perspective, CSAM's economic profit approach to equity management is an excellent way of gauging how effective the company's decision-making has been in allocating resources

---

[10] A complete discussion of CSAM's economic profit approach to security analysis can be found in James A. Abate, "Select Economic Value Portfolios," *U.S. Equity Product Overview* (Credit Suisse Asset Management, January 1998). The economic profit model discussed here is also consistent with the EVA-based company analysis approach discussed in Chapter 7.

which will lead to shareholder wealth creation and changes in market value. The follow-on bridge is to identify not only good companies (corporate perspective), but the proper entry points so that those good companies are also good stock selection candidates (investment perspective).

The three key pricing elements used by Credit Suisse Asset Management to assess the value of a firm's anticipated economic profits include: (1) capital growth rate, (2) after-tax operating return on invested capital, and (3) the required return on invested capital (weighted average cost of capital). CSAM's desire is to isolate the market expectations for a company that are implied by its current market value.

Growth is crucial in Credit Suisse Asset Management's bottom-up pricing assessment. This is where CSAM analysts attempt to capture a reasonable and sustainable growth rate for a company in terms of revenues and profits. This is also where linking the balance sheet to the income statement is deemed important since the growth rate for revenues and profits is a function of investment, whether it is in new plant and equipment or intangible assets. CSAM analysts also recognize that the after-tax operating return on invested capital is crucial when compared to the required return on invested capital. While this return spread is often referred to as the "residual return on capital" or the "surplus return on capital," Credit Suisse Asset Management refers to the difference between the firm's after-tax operating return and the required (or expected) rate of return as the "excess return on invested capital."

In the CSAM approach, the economic profit, capital growth, and valuation linkage is transparent: Those companies that generate positive excess returns on invested capital should continue to invest and grow their businesses, while firms having negative residual returns should not. In essence, the assessed spread between a company's operating return on capital and the required return on capital measures how much "economically profitable" reinvestment a firm can generate. Deprivation of growth in a high return on capital business is viewed as a signalling event that future revenue and economic growth rates may slow. From a corporate valuation perspective, any company that is deemed attractive from an economically profitable and judicious capital growth standpoint should trade at a premium when measured relative to replacement cost of assets. In this context, CSAM recognizes that a company that generates an excess return on invested capital should trade at a premium to replacement value based upon market expectations of continued economically profitable reinvestment.

Economic profit analysis can be used to assess which companies are likely to generate positive abnormal returns. In the Credit Suisse Asset Management model, this profit/valuation assessment involves the calculation and/or research assessment of:

1. the excess return on invested capital (positive or negative)
2. the growth rate of capital
3. the ratio of market value to asset replacement cost
4. the relationship between market implied growth rates and CSAM's estimates through the use of an earnings discount model

## Excess Return on Invested Capital

The first step in CSAM valuation analysis is to calculate the spread between the firm's operating return on capital and the required return on capital. The estimation of the excess return on invested capital is explained below.

### Estimating the After-Tax Operating Return on Capital

An essential component of economic profit analysis involves arriving at a measure of pre-interest, after-tax operating earnings generated by a firm, relative to the amount of capital which was required to generate such operating return. This well-known profitability ratio is simply the firm's after-tax operating return on capital.

To arrive at after-tax operating earnings, Credit Suisse Asset Management deducts from revenues the cost of goods sold, selling and administrative expenses, marketing and promotional outlays, cash taxes on operating profits, and an amount to reflect required economic capital expenditures rather than "accounting" depreciation. This after-tax earnings calculation is used to approximate the firm's real operating cash flow.

In the CSAM model, the amount of invested capital is determined without regard to capital structure and from a replacement cost basis. In this calculation, the estimated current replacement cost of assets is used rather than an accounting figure in an effort to eliminate accounting distortions that have little bearing to economic reality. (Examples include restructuring charges, accumulated depreciation, and reserves.)

### Estimating the Required Return on Capital

Credit Suisse Asset Management uses a market-capitalization weighted average of the required return on equity and debt. Calculating some of the components in the required return on capital formula is a straightforward task. For example, the required return on debt can be determined mostly by the firm's credit rating. However, they also recognize that a significant, many times conflicting, amount of academic research has been focused on estimating the required return on equity.

To handle empirical regularities arising from systematic *non*-market phenomenon, CSAM has constructed a proprietary scoring model akin to more fundamentally oriented measures like credit ratings. This required return approach accounts for the shortcomings of an exclusively market based, backward looking measure of risk such as beta (in the CSAM view) to estimate company specific required rates of return on equity capital. The focus is on assessing stability in future economic profit by not only using firm size, but also growth and variability of earnings, financial leverage, and other measures to adequately capture the impact of risk on required return. In effect, the higher the embedded fundamental risk for a company, the higher the required return or cost of capital.

Along this line, Credit Suisse Asset Management does a sizable amount of proprietary analytical research on determining the market driven base risk premium, as well as the slope of the incremental premium, i.e., the difference between the least risky and most risky companies in the investable universe.

Other things the same (market and *non*-market factors such as size), firms having demonstrated stability in their economic profit are assigned a low company-specific risk "score" in comparison with those firms with volatile economic profits. An illustration of CSAM's "company specific" approach to estimating the required return on (equity) capital is shown in Exhibit 16.

### Growth Rate of Capital

According to Credit Suisse Asset Management, firms create economic profits by either investing in high return projects or by rationalizing underperforming assets in place. Invested capital management, otherwise referred to as capital budgeting analysis, is closely linked with changes in the level of economic profit — for it is corporate investments and/or divestitures that drive operating returns. Sources of funds (after-tax earnings, additional debt and equity financing, asset sales) when related to the ability to exceed the required rate of return on invested capital should be consistent with the use of funds (internal growth spending, corporate acquisitions, debt reduction, stock buybacks, and dividends).

The focus on value-creating firms by Credit Suisse Asset Management is therefore twofold: (1) those companies that CSAM analysts expect to experience an increase in market value when undertaking new projects, and (2) firms that CSAM expects to increase in market value when reducing operations by divestiture or abandonment of projects in place. Exhibit 17 presents a display of excess returns measured relative to the capital growth rate for a sample group of companies. Note that the intercept on the horizontal axis is above zero. This is to reflect a nominal growth hurdle rate to identify real growth within a peer set.

## Exhibit 16: Required Return versus Company Specific Risk Score

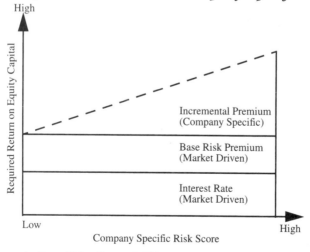

Source: James A. Abate, "Select Economic Value Portfolios," *U.S. Equity Product Overview* (Credit Suisse Asset Management, January 1998).

## Exhibit 17: Excess Returns Relative to Capital Growth Rate Used by CSAM

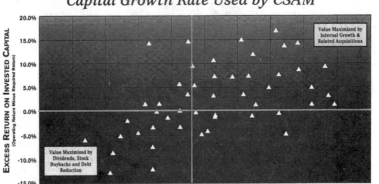

Source: James A. Abate, "Select Economic Value Portfolios," *U.S. Equity Product Overview* (Credit Suisse Asset Management, January 1998).

### Market Value-to-Asset Replacement Cost

Credit Suisse Asset Management also looks at the market value-to-asset replacement cost ratio when assessing the investment merits of equity securities. As stated previously, it is not only important to identify good companies but also those that are good stock investments at today's price. Market value is defined as the current freely tradable value of equity, debt, preferred stock, and minority interests. The value of cash and marketable securities is subtracted from market value and invested capital if it is viewed as *abnormal* relative to working capital requirements and linked to a specific timetable for distribution to shareholders.

A market value-to-asset replacement cost ratio in excess of one implies that existing and anticipated future capital investments have economic value added. Therefore, companies with ratios that exceed unity must achieve economic profit improvement at least at the growth rate which is implied within the current market value or a detrimental revaluation in the market value/asset replacement cost ratio will occur. Also, those firms with excess returns on invested capital that consistently surprise positively will receive a favorable revaluation (higher ratio). A representative display of the excess return on invested capital versus the market value-to-asset replacement cost ratio is shown in Exhibit 18.

### Analyzing Market Implied Growth Rates

In attempting to accurately value a company and thereby conclude whether or not a bottom-up market inefficiency exists, market implied growth rates are compared to both past and forward-looking estimates for operating performance. For specific securities, CSAM calculates market *implied* expectations of future economically profitable growth by using an earnings (after-tax operating cash flow) discount model, thought of sometimes as the discounted cash flow method. In this way, CSAM examines the firm's market value as it relates earnings growth to its excess return on invested capital.

Credit Suisse Asset Management employs a constant growth or earnings discount model. In this present value framework, the market value of the firm can be expressed as:

$$V = \text{Earnings}/(r - g)$$

where $V$ is the firm's market capitalization (including debt and equity), $r$ is the required return on capital, and $g$ is the long-term sustainable earnings growth rate. Next, with knowledge of the firm's market value, after-tax operating earnings, and required return on capital, it is possible to estimate the market *implied* long-term growth rate, $g$, according to:

$$g = r - \text{Earnings}/V$$

That is, Credit Suisse Asset Management backs into the market's *implied* expected growth rate for a company with knowledge of its after-tax operating earnings, market valuation of invested capital, and the required return on capital. The market's *implied* growth rate, $g$, for a company is then compared to a growth estimate — based upon CSAM's assessment of trends in capital growth as it relates to revenue and economic profit generation. If there is a *positive* spread between the CSAM assessed growth rate and market-implied earnings growth, then there is a potential buy opportunity. In contrast, if CSAM-assessed earnings growth falls short of market implied earnings growth rate then a potential sell opportunity exists. In this latter instance, upside surprise to the implied growth rate is not transparent. Therefore, economic profit growth appears to be expensively priced. In addition, a target price is calculated based upon Credit Suisse Asset Management's growth expectations to determine the degree of opportunity, if any.

## Exhibit 18: Risk-Adjusted Cash on Cash Valuation Used by CSAM

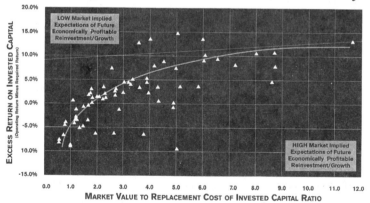

Source: James A. Abate, "Select Economic Value Portfolios," *U.S. Equity Product Overview* (Credit Suisse Asset Management, January 1998).

This is where Credit Suisse Asset Management in its actively managed U.S. equity portfolios attempts to add value for clients from a *bottom up* perspective. Through use of proprietary models, CSAM attempts to find those companies that are generating returns in excess of required return on invested capital. This tells CSAM's analysts (1) which companies are gaining the most from their capital spending, and (2) those firms that are capable of using their cost of capital as a competitive advantage. Credit Suisse Asset Management's detailed valuation analysis permits it to get a truer understanding of which, why, and to what extent, companies are selling for more than their asset replacement cost. In this way, CSAM hopes to find the good, fast-growing companies with low disappointment risk and potential restructuring opportunities. That goal is especially important in an economic cycle where capital spending, mergers and acquisitions, and asset rationalizations are an integral part of corporate planning.

We have attempted to illustrate the significant *value drivers* in the Credit Suisse Asset Management economic profit model. In actuality, an in-depth analysis of the relevant variables and their sub-components (e.g., operating return equals operating profit margin times asset utilization) is conducted through a variety of techniques. As part of the analysis, CSAM uses (1) company-specific historical trend analysis, (2) multi-period benchmarking to peer firms, (3) compilation of qualitative information, including company visits and management meetings, and (4) determination of competitive advantage persistency in its bottom-up approach to equity securities analysis.

## CSAM's "Top-Down" Approach

One of the distinguishing characteristics of Credit Suisse Asset Management's U.S. portfolio management effort is its research focus on sector-specific economic profit influences. In its so-called *non-nucleus* or *peripheral sectors*, the principal driver of sector and individual stock selection process are macroeconomic profit trends that tend to affect most stocks in the sector in a somewhat equal manner. In other words, CSAM's analyst will model the entire industry, first to assess opportunities before attempting to identify the best stocks. By nature, peripheral sectors tend to be commodity price and interest rate sensitive industries, generally those where no individual company's competitive advantage is dominant.

For instance, in sectors like oil (part of energy) and chemicals (part of basic materials), Credit Suisse Asset Management finds that stocks are highly correlated with trailing periods capital spending and commodity prices. Thus, analysis of macro trends such as global capacity changes, GDP growth, utilization rates, and currency values adds more value to the portfolio decision than a purely bottom-up approach to security selection. In other words, the macro trend overwhelmingly influences the level of industry or sector-based economic profits (measured *net* of capital costs) and does so in a homogeneous way across the sector. The fundamental premise of economic profit generation is still intact — proper allocation of capital being essential to shareholders — but poor decisions by one or more companies can have great "headwind" effect on even the best companies within an industry, oil and mining being good examples.

## Exhibit 19: Growth of $100 Invested in Two Companies in Financial Services (Banking) Sector

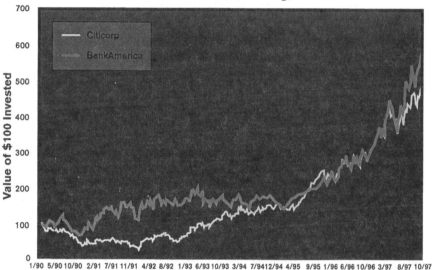

Source: James A. Abate, "Select Economic Value Portfolios," *U.S. Equity Product Overview* (Credit Suisse Asset Management, January 1998).

Thus, the portfolio peripherals consist of a group of sectors where macro *themes* drive stock price to a great degree. For these industries, a *top-down* macro-economic profit approach is first used in stock selection. Since these companies share many of the common influencing factors of operating and investment performance — such as commodity price or interest rate effects — stock price comovement is usually tight in the peripheral sectors. CSAM's peripheral sectors include financial services, energy, utilities, basic materials and precious metals, transportation, and real estate trusts. To illustrate the peripheral comovement theme, Exhibits 19 and 20 show how $100 invested in two companies in the banking and utilities sectors, respectively, *jointly* moved in value over time.

In general, Credit Suisse Asset Management's approach to sector analysis has three key elements. First, CSAM feels that it is crucial to understand what point sectors are at in the economic or competitive development cycle. Second, it is important to identify how the respective sectors stand to benefit or be hurt from current economic profit trends in the economy. Third, CSAM deems it important to engage in a detailed analysis and modeling of particular macro variables for each of the peripheral sectors.

### Sector Deviation from Benchmark

From Credit Suisse Asset Management's view, sector emphasis or de-emphasis should *not* be made by a conventional value or growth style of investing. In fact, the style should be a derivative of the sector calls and the abundance of a sector's stockpicking opportunities — *not* the other way around. For example, if an investment manager is labeled as a traditional growth manager, then according to the S&P/BARRA Growth Index, that manager is taking on significant benchmark risk unless he or she is consistent with a 20% or so current weight in health care stocks.

At the opposite end of the spectrum, the weight of health care in the S&P/BARRA Value Index stands at approximately 3%. In other words, the manager is almost forced to make an investment in a sector based solely on the style or investment label that is attributed to him which are driven by valuation measures such as price-to-book ratio, but not related to an appropriate fundamental measure such as excess return on operating capital. These sector deviations from benchmark issues can arise in many other industries as well.

Rather than focus on value or growth stocks *per se*, the primary task in determining sector emphasis results from an assessment of volatility and return comovement of stocks within various industry groups. In this way, CSAM determines whether or not a "bottom-up" economic profit framework for individual stock selection works best in comparison with a "top-down" approach that allows the portfolio manager to emphasize a factor's homogeneous influence on stock prices within the sector. The result is what Credit Suisse Asset Management calls a "true value" equity portfolio.

## Exhibit 20: Growth of $100 Invested in Two Companies in the Utilities Sector

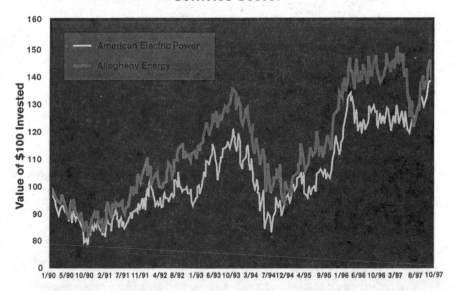

Source: James A. Abate, "Select Economic Value Portfolios," *U.S. Equity Product Overview* (Credit Suisse Asset Management, January 1998).

### Exhibit 21: Columbia Management Company's Top-Down Investment Decision Process

**INVESTMENT TEAM**

**INVESTMENT ENVIRONMENT**

**ECONOMIC INDICATORS**
GDP, Productivity, Employment, Inflation, Earnings

**FINANCIAL FACTORS**
Money Supply, Federal Reserve Policy, Interest Rates

**GOVERNMENT POLICIES**
Taxation, Budget, Regulation, Legislation

**VALUATION**
Current/Historical, Absolute/Relative

**INVESTMENT THEMES**
Developed from analysis of the
Investment environment

**FAVORED SECTORS**
Industries and representative companies
impacted by identified themes

**FAVORED STOCKS**
Subject to fundamental
technical analysis

Source: Exhibit 3 in Lawrence S. Viehl, "Top Down/Thematic Equity Management," Chapter 3 in
T. Daniel Coggin and Frank J. Fabozzi (eds.), *Applied Equity Valuation* (New Hope, PA:
Frank J. Fabozzi Associates, 1998), p. 42.

## COLUMBIA MANAGEMENT COMPANY

As explained in this book, fundamental equity analysis often begins with a bottom-up look at the investment merit (or lack thereof) of a company's outstanding securities. In an interesting twist on equity fundamental analysis, Columbia Management Company (CMC) employs a top-down approach to equity management where macro themes are combined with traditional macroeconomic factors as the central focus in the portfolio research and construction process.[11] By taking a broad view of the macro investment environment to include economic, financial, and governmental policy happenings, CMC's top-down/thematic approach can be viewed as a macro fundamental approach to equity management.

### Columbia's Macro Thematic Model

Exhibit 21 shows the top-down investment decision process employed by Columbia Management Company. As shown, CMC's macro research and portfolio strategy consists of four key elements including:

---

[11] For a rigorous discussion of Columbia's top down/thematic approach to equity management, see Lawrence S. Viehl, "Top Down/Thematic Equity Management," Chapter 3 in T. Daniel Coggin and Frank J. Fabozzi (eds.), *Applied Equity Valuation* (New Hope, PA: Frank J. Fabozzi Associates, 1998).

- The Investment Environment
- The Set of Investment Themes
- Theme Sensitive Sectors and Industries
- Portfolio Construction with Theme Sensitive Stocks

CMC begins the investment process with a broad look at the macroeconomic and political environment (see Exhibit 21). In this step, CMC expands the scope of traditional top-down equity analysis to include (1) macroeconomic factors including gross domestic product, productivity of capital, inflation, and economywide earnings' outlook, (2) financial factors such as money supply, Federal Reserve policy, and global interest rate developments, and (3) governmental policies dealing with taxation, budget, regulation, and legislative developments and changes. This first step in CMC's top-down decision process also includes a look at standard market valuation measures such as price/earnings ratio in both absolute and relative terms.

In the second step of its active decision process, CMC seeks to identify pervasive investment themes that cut across multiple industries and sectors of the economy. In this context, CMC takes a closer look at the macro investment environment to assess the information content of the broad investment themes. In step three, CMC identifies and monitors those industries and sectors having either wealth increasing or wealth decreasing thematic exposure. The final step in CMC's top-down model involves a detailed screening of securities within the predetermined industries and sectors that are most likely to appreciate (or depreciate) in value due to wealth impact of the underlying pervasive theme.

As an illustration of a wealth destroying theme, Lawrence Viehl of CMC points to heightened uncertainty in health care stocks in the aftermath of the 1992 Presidential Election. At that time, a Presidential task force was assigned to examine both the delivery and cost of providing health care services in the United States — with a primary emphasis on cost containment in a reshaped health care market. Given the cost containment and possible regulatory focus of the task force, investors began dumping health care securities, fearing — whether justified or not — that the underlying companies would not be able to grow earnings at heretofore historic rates. In turn, health care stocks fell from 12% of the S&P 500 Index in 1991 down to 9% and 8% by the end of 1992 and 1993, respectively.

Conversely, when it became clear that major health care reform in the United States was losing political ground, health care securities began to rise as evidenced by the turnaround in health care stocks rising from 8% of the S&P 500 Index in 1993 up to 11% by the end of 1997. By recognizing that a powerful investment theme — compared with the traditional top down way of looking just at economywide forces such as productivity and inflation — was underway during the early 1990s, the top down/thematic approach would have alerted investors when these fundamental macro changes were occurring and with what intensity. From an active management perspective, investors should (therefore) buy the stocks of companies that are anticipated to have favorable macro themes, while selling or short-selling the stocks of firms having negative thematic exposure that lead directly or indirectly to lower stock price.

## Pervasive Macro Themes

According to CMC, the macro themes should ideally cut across several industries or sectors of the economy. In this context, Viehl points to three general themes that have (or will continue to have) a pervasive effect on security prices:

- Restructuring of "Corporate America"
- Agricultural shifts due to fundamental change in crop prices
- "Demographic aging" of the population

With corporate restructuring, the firm's managers presumably become more focused on creating shareholder value. If this shareholder wealth theme is pervasive — as it must be with globally competitive capital markets — then its financial impact will cut across multiple industries and sectors of the (world) economy. The security selection goal here is to determine beforehand those firms that are wealth maximizers in the first instance and those companies that systematically destroy shareholder value. In this fundamental sense, the value-based metrics covered in Chapter 7 could prove to be of considerable value to the thematic-oriented equity manager.

### Viehl's Thematic "Aging" Illustration

Viehl provides an insightful illustration of the top-down thematic approach to investing. He argues that demographic aging of the population has (or will have) a correlative thematic effect on several industries and sectors of the economy. In this context, U.S. Census projections for the 1995 to 2005 period suggest that the greatest growth in population will occur in the 45-54 and 55-64 age groups. Accordingly, this population aging theme is likely to impact company growth rates and therefore stock prices in numerous industries including health care, travel and entertainment, and financial services, for examples. If correct, then the top down/thematic strategy is to discover — and invest in the stock of — those industries and sectors that will likely benefit from demographic change as younger individuals move into the 45-54 age category and the representative 45-54 aged person grows older.

Exhibit 22 highlights the benefit of constructing a long-only portfolio of stocks based on the "Aging of America" theme. Among the findings, it is interesting to see that the theme-generated equity portfolio outperformed the S&P 500 Index in 1997 and was ahead of the market as of the first quarter of 1998. Indeed, at 49.8% in 1997, the theme-oriented portfolio performance was considerably higher than the percentage price change observed on the S&P 500 benchmark, at 31%. Second, with the exception of HMOs, the theme-based performance across sectors — including "asset gatherers" (financial services), drug manufacturers, and leisure time/travel sectors — was uniformly positive and quite attractive with returns in excess of 40% for 1997.

### Exhibit 22: Columbia Management Company's Portfolio Theme: Aging of America

| | % S&P 500 | % Price Change (Market Weighted) | |
|---|---|---|---|
| | | 1997 | First Quarter 1998 |
| Asset Gatherers/Financial Services | 2.1 | 61.0 | 17.6 |
| Merrill Lynch | 0.3 | 79.0 | 13.8 |
| Morgan, J.P. | 0.3 | 15.6 | 19.0 |
| Price, T.R. | 0.0 | 44.5 | 11.9 |
| Jefferson-Pilot | 0.1 | 37.5 | 14.2 |
| Lincoln National | 0.1 | 48.8 | 9.1 |
| Morgan Stanley/Dean Witter | 0.5 | 78.5 | 23.3 |
| Travelers | 0.8 | 78.1 | 11.4 |
| Drug Manufacturers | 7.5 | 55.9 | 15.0 |
| American Home Products | 0.7 | 30.5 | 24.7 |
| Warner-Lambert | 0.5 | 65.6 | 37.1 |
| Lilly, Eli | 0.9 | 90.8 | −14.4 |
| Pharmacia Upjohn | 0.3 | −7.6 | 19.5 |
| Bristol Meyers | 1.3 | 73.6 | 10.2 |
| Pfizer | 1.3 | 79.7 | 33.7 |
| Glaxo Holding ADS | 0.0 | 50.8 | 13.1 |
| Schering-Plough | 0.7 | 91.9 | 31.6 |
| Merck | 1.8 | 33.1 | 20.9 |
| Drug Retail | 0.5 | 55.2 | 13.6 |
| Walgreen | 0.2 | 55.9 | 12.4 |
| Rite Aid | 0.1 | 47.8 | 16.6 |
| CVS | 0.2 | 54.8 | 17.9 |
| Hospital Supply | 1.3 | 30.2 | 12.4 |
| Abbot Laboratories | 0.7 | 29.1 | 15.0 |
| Bard C.R. | 0.0 | 11.8 | 17.4 |
| Baxter International | 0.2 | 23.0 | 9.3 |
| Becton Dickenson | 0.1 | 15.3 | 36.1 |
| Medtronic | 0.3 | 54.4 | −1.2 |
| U.S. Surgical | 0.0 | −25.6 | 12.6 |
| Assisted Living | 0.0 | 136.2 | 4.2 |
| ARV Assisted Living | 0.00 | 37.6 | −12.5 |
| Assisted Living Concept | 0.0 | 159.0 | 7.6 |
| Carematrix | 0.0 | 119.0 | 7.0 |
| Emeritus | 0.0 | −5.6 | 2.0 |
| Regent Assisted Living | 0.0 | 21.1 | 34.8 |
| Alternative Living | 0.0 | 105.7 | 12.1 |
| Death Care Services | 0.1 | 27.6 | 13.6 |
| Service Corp Intl | 0.1 | 31.3 | 15.5 |
| Hillenbrand Ind | 0.0 | 41.2 | 20.3 |
| Loewen Group | 0.0 | −34.2 | −1.9 |

## Exhibit 22 (Continued)

| | % S&P 500 | % Price Change (Market Weighted) | |
|---|---|---|---|
| | | 1997 | First Quarter 1998 |
| HMOs | 0.4 | −13.9 | 22.9 |
| Aetna | 0.2 | −11.8 | 18.2 |
| Humana | 0.1 | 9.2 | 19.6 |
| United Healthcare | 0.2 | 10.4 | 30.3 |
| Oxford Health Plans | 0.0 | −73.5 | −4.0 |
| Pacificare Health A | 0.0 | −38.2 | 47.3 |
| Nursing Homes | 0.2 | 41.6 | 2.7 |
| Beverly Enterprises | 0.0 | 44.6 | 2.4 |
| Manor Care | 0.0 | 29.6 | 5.7 |
| Health South | 0.1 | 43.7 | 1.1 |
| Leisure Time/Travel | 1.8 | 41.5 | 8.5 |
| American Express | 0.5 | 58.0 | 2.9 |
| Circus Circus | 0.0 | −40.4 | 3.0 |
| Disney | 0.9 | 41.9 | 7.8 |
| AMR | 0.2 | 45.8 | 11.4 |
| Mirage Resorts | 0.1 | 5.2 | 6.9 |
| Hilton Hotels | 0.1 | 13.3 | 7.1 |
| Marriott Intl | 0.1 | 25.3 | −46.3 |
| Carnival Cruise | 0.0 | 67.8 | 26.0 |
| Total S&P Weighting | 13.9 | | |
| Theme Performance* | | 49.8% | 15.4% |
| S&P Performance* | | 31.0% | 13.5% |

*Returns are based on price performance and do not include reinvested dividends.

Source: Data from BaseLine. Exhibit 4 in Lawrence S. Viehl, "Top Down/Thematic Equity Management," Chapter 3 in T. Daniel Coggin and Frank J. Fabozzi (eds.), *Applied Equity Valuation* (New Hope, PA: Frank J. Fabozzi Associates, 1998), p. 42.

On the other hand, the active manager needs to be aware that the dynamic aspects of sectors, industries, and companies are such that powerful *non*-thematic forces of an economic nature can cause portfolio performance to depart significantly from that implied by the macro theme. For example, consider the −73.5% and −38.2% price declines in the stock of Oxford Health Plans and Pacificare Health A (HMOs) and the −40.4% drop in the stock price of Circus Circus (Leisure Time/Travel). As Viehl correctly points out, this is where bottom-up fundamental analysis — as the final stage in CMC's portfolio construction process — is essential to see if there are any mitigating factors that might cause the selected securities to depart significantly in valuation terms from that implied by the top-down macro theme.

Thus, on balance, the active investor should purchase the stocks of companies that are likely to benefit from a specific macro theme, while selling or shorting the stock of companies having negative thematic price sensitivity. In practice, this could entail shorting stocks in multiple industries or sectors with negative thematic exposure. Indeed, as with previous equity management profiles covered in this chapter, one could construct both long-only and long-short portfolios. In a thematic context, the long-only and long-short portfolios would emerge from a top-down investment decision process that is focused on pervasive macroeconomic and political/legislative themes that systematically cut across the entire economy.

## SUMMARY

One of the most exciting aspects of today's world of equity management is the close association between investment theory and practice. To demonstrate this real-world connection, we profiled the equity management strategies of several money managers and their firms including (1) the Jacobs Levy view of the complex equity market, (2) State Street Global Advisors' Matrix Equity approach to security analysis, (3) Boston Partners' fundamental mid-cap and small-cap value approach, (4) Credit Suisse Asset Management's economic profit — or value-based metric — model of the U.S. equity market, and (5) Columbia Management Company's top-down/thematic approach to equity portfolio management.

Jacobs Levy set the active management stage by arguing that the stock market is neither 100% efficient in the sense that security prices reflect "full information," nor is it completely deterministic with unlimited profit opportunities. They argue that in the real world, the stock market is "complex" and it therefore needs to be examined with an integrated prism (or system), leading to a multidimensional and dynamic approach to equity investing. Along this line, Wayne Archambo at Boston Partners and Peter Stonberg of State Street Global Advisors recognize the dynamic nature of the equity market as their in-house valuation of stocks on the buy (or sell) side need to be confirmed with independent information — such as favorable (unfavorable) earnings estimate revisions in SSgA's case, and positive (negative) business catalyst in the case of Boston Partners Asset Management.

Moreover, James Abate's economic profit approach to equity management at Credit Suisse Asset Management reveals that value-based metrics of shareholder value can be employed in both a systematic bottom-up and top-down approach to equity securities analysis. Consistent with CSAM's top-down approach, Lawrence Viehl's thematic model at Columbia Management Company can be used to buy (or sell) those securities that are likely to benefit (or be hurt) from the broad economic and political/legislative themes that can have a common influencing effect on security prices. According to Viehl, pervasive investment themes in recent times include corporate restructuring/downsizing and the ongoing "Aging of America."

# APPENDIX
# HIGHLIGHTS OF INVESTMENT MANAGEMENT FIRMS
# PROFILED IN THIS CHAPTER

### Jacobs Levy Equity Management
*Portfolio Managers:*
  Bruce I. Jacobs, MS, MSIA, MA, Ph.D.
  Kenneth N. Levy, MBA, MA, Ph.D. Candidate
*Investment Strategy:* Equity valuation for a complex market
*Implementation of Active Strategy:* Portfolios designed to benefit from numerous identified profit opportunities simultaneously; include several long-only strategies and long-short.

### State Street Global Advisors
*Portfolio Manager:*
  Peter Stonberg, MBA, CFA
*Investment Strategy:* Matrix analysis of equity securities
*Implementation of Active Strategy:* Portfolio construction based on synthesis of fundamental valuation and earnings estimate revision

### Boston Partners Asset Management
*Portfolio Manager:*
  Wayne J. Archambo, MBA, CFA
*Investment Strategy:* Value style with business momentum
*Implementation of Active Strategy:* Quantitative screening with overlay of fundamental business catalyst

### Credit Suisse Asset Management
*Portfolio Manager:*
  James A. Abate, MBA, CPA, CFA
*Investment Strategy:* Fundamental analysis using value-based metrics
*Implementation of Active Strategy:* Synthesis of bottom-up and top-down economic profit analysis

### Columbia Management Company
*Portfolio Manager:*
  Lawrence S. Viehl, MBA, CFA
*Investment Strategy:* Thematic macro approach to equity security selection
*Implementation of Active Strategy:* Portfolio design based on fundamental top down with macroeconomic and political themes

# Chapter 11

# Equity Trading

A view shared by some managers is that the key to successful portfolio management is the selection of good stocks or the selection of a good style. As one well regarded money manager was quoted as saying: "Success in investment management comes from picking good stocks. The rest is just plumbing."[1] Today, there is greater recognition that the transaction costs associated with equity trading will have a significant impact on the relative performance of an equity portfolio versus its benchmark. What is the difference between equity portfolio management and equity trading? Two widely recognized experts on equity trading costs, Wayne Wagner and Mark Edwards, whose firm, Plexus Group, provide information for institutional investors regarding trading costs, explain the difference between "trading" and "portfolio management" as follows:

> The portfolio manager's process is analytic and hypothetical; trading is in-the-trenches reality....

> Trading is fundamentally different from portfolio management in that selecting stocks does not require the cooperation of anyone else. The trader, however, needs somebody to trade with, and thus we move from deductive exercise to a negotiation process. In a negotiation one gives something to get something. In securities trading, one can trade for either liquidity or for information. Thus a trader is constantly concerned that value is received for value given.[2]

In this chapter we look at equity trading and tie in the motivation and costs of equity trading to our discussion in earlier chapters of active versus passive management and equity styles.

## TRADING MECHANICS

In the United States, secondary trading of common stock occurs in a number of market trading systems: major national stock exchanges, regional stock exchanges, and the over-the-counter (OTC) market. In addition to these trading locations,

---

[1] Cited in Wayne H. Wagner and Mark Edwards, "Implementing Investment Strategies: The Art and Science of Investing," Chapter 11 in Frank J. Fabozzi *Active Equity Portfolio Management* (New Hope, PA: Frank J. Fabozzi Associates, 1998).

[2] Wagner and Edwards, "Implementing Investment Strategies."

independently operated electronic trading systems are available for trading common stock. The mechanics for trading stocks are explained below.

# Brokers and Dealers

Market trading systems rely on brokers and dealers. A *broker* is an entity that acts as the agent of an investor who wishes to execute orders; no position is taken by the broker in the stock that is the subject of the trade. In contrast, a *dealer* is an entity that stands ready and willing to buy a stock for its own account (i.e., add to its inventory of the stock) or sell from its own account (i.e., reduce its inventory of the stock). At a given time, dealers advertise their willingness to buy a stock at a price (its *bid price*) that is less than what they are willing to sell the same stock for (its *ask price* or *offer price*).[3] On an exchange, a dealer is referred to as a *specialist*.

## *Function of Dealers*

Because of the imbalance of buy and sell orders that may reach the market at a given time, the price of a stock may change abruptly from one transaction to the next, in the absence of any intervention. For example, suppose that the market price for Yahoo stock is $90 as determined by several recent trades, but a flow of buy orders without an accompanying supply of sell orders arrives in the market. This temporary imbalance could be sufficient to push the price of Yahoo stock to, say, $92. The cost of having to pay a price higher than $90 can be viewed as the price of "immediacy." By immediacy it is meant that buyers and sellers want to trade immediately rather than waiting for the arrival of sufficient orders on the other side of the trade so that the price is closer to the price of the last known transaction.

In the absence of any intervention, this temporary imbalance would have a destabilizing effect on a stock's price. A flurry of unbalanced buy orders, for instance, could drive a stock's price up. Rising prices could then trigger an avalanche of subsequent buying, based on the perception of rising value in the stock. Of course, the market would soon correct unsubstantiated prices, resulting in a steep decline.

Dealers help stabilize the market by acting as a buffer between the buy and sell sides of the market. Dealers can be properly viewed as the suppliers of immediacy (i.e., the ability to trade promptly) to the market.[4] The bid-ask spread can, in turn, be viewed as the price charged by dealers for supplying immediacy together with short-run price stability (i.e., continuity or smoothness) in the presence of

---

[3] It is not always necessary for two transactors to use the services of a broker or a dealer to execute a transaction. Today, computerized systems have been developed that allow institutional investors to cross trades (i.e., match buyers and sellers). The two major systems that handle large institution-to-institution trades are INSTINET and POSIT. The latter, which stands for Portfolio System for Institutional Investors, is a trading system developed by BARRA and Jefferies & Co. POSIT is more than a simple order-matching system; it matches the purchase and sale of portfolios in such a way so as to optimize the liquidity of the system.

[4] George Stigler, "Public Regulation of Securities Markets," *Journal of Business* (April 1964), pp. 117-134; and Harold Demsetz, "The Cost of Transacting," *Quarterly Journal of Economics* (October 1968), pp. 35-36.

short-term order imbalances. There are two other roles that dealers play: providing better price information to market participants and, in certain market structures, providing the services of an auctioneer in bringing order and fairness to a market.

The price stabilization role follows from what may happen to the price of a particular transaction in the absence of any intervention during a temporary imbalance of orders. By taking the opposite side of a trade when there are no other orders, the dealer prevents the price from materially diverging from the price at which a recent trade was consummated.

Not only are investors concerned with immediacy, but they also want to trade at prices that are reasonable, given prevailing conditions in the market. While dealers do not know with certainty the true price of a stock, they do have a privileged position in some market structures, with respect not just to market orders but also to limit orders (described later). The latter is particularly true in market structures where one or more dealers are entitled to keep the book of limit orders. Their privileged position allows them to be in a better position to affect the quality of price information that they signal to market participants through their bids and offers.

Finally, the dealer acts as an auctioneer in some market structures, thereby providing order and fairness in the operations of the market. For example, as discussed later the dealer for an exchange-traded stock performs this function both by organizing trading to make sure that the exchange rules for the priority of trading are followed and by keeping a limit book.

### Risks Faced by Dealers

A dealer's bid-ask spread is affected by its cost of doing business and by the risks it bears. One of the most important costs involves order processing costs. The costs of equipment necessary to do business and the administrative and operations staff are examples. Dealers also have to be compensated for bearing risk. A dealer's position may involve carrying inventory of a stock (a long position) or selling a stock that is not in inventory (a short position). Three types of risks are associated with maintaining a long or short position in a given stock. First, there is the uncertainty about the future price of the stock. A dealer that has a net long position in a stock is concerned that the price will decline in the future; a dealer that is in a net short position is concerned that the price will rise.

The second type of risk has to do with the expected time it will take the dealer to unwind a position and its uncertainty. And this, in turn, depends primarily on the prevailing rate at which buy and sell orders reach the dealer (i.e., the frequency of transactions).[5] The greater the frequency of transactions, the less time a dealer will expect that it has to maintain a position. For example, if a dealer has an inventory of a particular stock that is infrequently traded, then the dealer expects that it will have to hold that stock in inventory for a longer time period than if the stock is frequently traded. As a result, the dealer's risk that the stock's price will decline when it is held in inventory is greater for a stock that is infrequently traded.

---

[5] This is referred to as the *thickness* of the market.

Finally, while a dealer may have access to better information about order flows (that is, buy and sell orders) than the general public, there are some trades where the dealer takes the risk of trading with someone who has better information.[6] This results in the better-informed trader obtaining a better price at the expense of the dealer. Consequently, in establishing the bid-ask spread for a trade, a dealer will assess whether the counterparty to the trade might have better information. Some trades that we will discuss later can be viewed as "informationless trades." This means that the dealer knows or believes that a trade is being requested to accomplish an investment objective that is not motivated by the potential future price movement of the stock.

## Types of Orders

In this section we describe the various types of orders that an investor can place with a broker. An investor must provide certain information to the broker. The parameters that the investor must provide are the specific stock, the number of shares, and the type of order.

Stocks prices are quoted in 16ths of a point. This quotation system came into effect in 1997. Prior to that time, price quotes were in 8ths of a point Each point is $1. Thus, prices for stocks are in 6.25 cent or $0.0625 increments. A stock price of 22 1/16 is then $22.0625. A stock price of 61 13/16 is $61 plus 13 times $0.0625, or $61.8125.

### Market Orders

When an investor wants to buy or sell a share of stock, the price and conditions under which the order is to be executed must be communicated to a broker. The simplest type of order is the *market order*, an order executed at the best price available in the market. The best price is assured by requiring that when more than one buy order or sell order reaches the market at the same time, the order with the best price is given priority. Thus, buyers offering a higher price are given priority over those offering a lower price; sellers asking a lower price are given priority over those asking a higher price.

In the case of common stock traded on an organized exchange, another priority rule is needed to handle the receipt of more than one order at the same price. Most often, the priority in executing such orders is based on the time of arrival of the order — the first orders in are the first orders executed — although there may be a rule that gives higher priority to certain types of market participants over others who are seeking to transact at the same price. For example, an exchange may classify orders as either "public orders" or orders of those member firms dealing for their own account (both nonspecialists and specialists). Exchange rules require that public orders be given priority over orders of member firms of an exchange who are dealing for their own account.

---

[6] Walter Bagehot, "The Only Game in Town," *Financial Analysts Journal* (March-April 1971), pp. 12-14, 22.

## Limit Orders

The danger of a market order is that an adverse move may take place between the time the investor places the order and the time the order is executed. For example, suppose Mr. Hieber wants to buy the stock of Anheuser Busch at $50, but not at $53. If he places a market order when the stock is trading at $50, Mr. Hieber faces the risk that the price will rise before his order is carried out, and he will have to pay an unacceptable price. Similarly, suppose Ms. Morrison owns Ameritech and wants to sell the stock at its current price of $45, but not at $43. If Ms. Morrison places a market order to sell Ameritech at the same time the company announces a major event that may adversely impact future earnings, the stock would be sold at the best available price, but the price might be unacceptable.

To avoid the danger of adverse unexpected price changes, an investor can place a limit order that designates a price threshold for the execution of the trade. The limit order is a conditional order: It is executed only if the limit price or a better price can be obtained. A buy limit order indicates that the stock may be purchased only at the designated price or lower. A sell limit order indicates that the stock may be sold at the designated price or higher. For example, Mr. Hieber, who wants to purchase Anheuser Busch but will not want to pay more than $50, can place a buy limit order at $50. Ms. Morrison, who wants to sell Ameritech but does not want to sell it at a price less than $45, will place a sell limit order for $45.

The danger of a limit order is that there is no guarantee that it will be executed at all. The designated price may simply not be obtainable. A limit order that is not executable at the time it reaches the market is recorded in a limit order book that is maintained by the specialist. The orders recorded in this book are treated equally with other orders in terms of the priority described earlier.

## Stop Orders

Another type of conditional order is the *stop order*, which specifies that the order is not to be executed until the market moves to a designated price, at which time it becomes a market order. A stop order to buy specifies that the order is not to be executed until the market rises to a designated price (i.e., trades at or above, or is bid at or above, the designated price). A stop order to sell specifies that the order is not to be executed until the market price falls below a designated price (i.e., trades at or below, or is offered at or below, the designated price). Once the designated price in the stop order is reached, the order becomes a market order.

A stop order is useful when an investor cannot watch the market constantly. Profits can be preserved or losses minimized on a stock position by allowing market movements to trigger a trade. In a sell stop order the designated price is less than the current market price of the stock. In contrast, in a sell limit order, the designated price is greater than the current market price of the stock. In a buy stop order the designated price is greater than the current market price of the stock. However, in a buy limit order the designated price is less than the current market price of the stock.

For example, suppose Mr. Hieber is uncertain about buying the Anheuser Busch stock at its current price of $50 but wants to be sure that if the price moves up he does not pay more than $53. If he places a stop order to buy at $53, the order becomes a market order when the price reaches $53. In the case of the sale of Ameritech by Ms. Morrison, suppose she wants to assure that she will not sell at less than $40 a share. She can place a stop order to sell at $40.

Two dangers are associated with stop orders. Stock prices sometimes exhibit abrupt price changes, so the direction of a change in a stock's price may be quite temporary, resulting in the premature trading of a stock. Also, once the designated price is reached, the stop order becomes a market order and is subject to the uncertainty of the execution price noted earlier for market orders.

### Stop-Limit Orders

A *stop-limit order*, a hybrid of a stop order and a limit order, is a stop order that designates a price limit. In contrast to the stop order, which becomes a market order if the stop is reached, the stop-limit order becomes a limit order if the stop is reached. The order can be used to cushion the market impact of a stop order. The investor may limit the possible execution price after the activation of the stop. As with a limit order, the limit price may never be reached after the order is activated, which therefore defeats one purpose of the stop order — to protect a profit or limit a loss.

### Market-If-Touched Orders

An investor may also enter a *market-if-touched order*. This order becomes a market order if a designated price is reached. However, a market-if- touched order to buy becomes a market order if the market falls to a given price, while a stop order to buy becomes a market order if the market rises to a given price. Similarly, a market-if-touched order to sell becomes a market order if the market rises to a specified price, while the stop order to sell becomes a market order if the market falls to a given price. We can think of the stop order as an order designed to get out of an existing position at an acceptable price (without specifying the exact price), and the market-if-touched order as an order designed to get into a position at an acceptable price (also without specifying the exact price).

### Time-Specific Order

Orders may be placed to buy or sell at the open or close of trading for the day. An *opening order* indicates a trade to be executed only in the opening range for the day, and a closing order indicates a trade is to be executed only within the closing range for the day.

An investor may enter orders that contain order cancellation provisions. A fill-or-kill order must be executed as soon as it reaches the trading floor, or it is immediately canceled. Orders may designate the time period for which the order is effective — a day, week, or month, or perhaps by a given time within the day. An open order, or good-till-canceled order, is good until the order is specifically canceled.

## Size-Related Orders

For common stock, orders are also classified by their size. A round lot is typically 100 shares of a stock. An odd lot is defined as less than a round lot. For example, an order of 75 shares of Microsoft Corporation (MSFT) is an odd-lot order. An order of 350 shares of MSFT includes an odd-lot portion of 50 shares. A block trade is defined on the NYSE as an order of 10,000 shares of a given stock or a total market value of $200,000 or more.

# Exchange-Imposed Restrictions on Short-Selling

A portfolio strategy may involve the short-selling of stocks. For example, in Chapter 10, we discussed a long-short strategy that required short-selling. Portfolio strategies involving futures and cash market trading also require short-selling. An investor must recognize exchange rules for short selling.

Exchange-imposed restrictions specify when a short sale may be executed; they are intended to prevent investors from destabilizing the price of a stock when the market price is falling. These restrictions are the so-called *tick-test rules*. A short sale can be made only when either (1) the sale price of the particular stock is higher than the last trade price (referred to as an up-tick trade) or (2) in cases where there is no change in the last trade price of the particular stock, the previous trade price is higher than the trade price that preceded it (referred to as a zero up-tick). For example, if Ms. Stokes wanted to "short" Wilson Pharmaceuticals at a price of $20 and if the two previous trade prices were $20⅛ and then $20, she could not do so at that time because of the up-tick trade rule. If, however, the previous trade prices were $19⅞, $19⅞, and then $20, she could short the stock at $20 because of the up-tick trade rule. Suppose that the sequence of the last three trades is $19⅞, $20, and $20. Ms. Stokes could short the stock at $20 because of the zero up-tick rule.

# Margin Requirements

An investor can use margin to create leverage in a portfolio. The funds borrowed to buy the additional stock are provided by the broker, and the broker gets the money from a bank. The interest rate that banks charge brokers for these transactions is known as the *call money rate* (also called the *broker loan rate*). The broker charges the investor the call money rate plus a service charge.

The broker is not free to lend as much as it wishes to the investor to buy securities. The Securities and Exchange Act of 1934 prohibits brokers from lending more than a specified percentage of the market value of the securities. The initial margin requirement is the proportion of the total market value of the securities that the investor must pay for in cash. The 1934 act gives the Board of Governors of the Federal Reserve the responsibility to set initial margin requirements, which it does under Regulations T and U. The initial margin requirement varies for stocks and bonds and is currently 50%, though it has been below 40%. The Fed also establishes a maintenance margin requirement. This is the minimum amount of equity needed in the investor's margin account as compared with the total market value. If the investor's margin account falls below the minimum maintenance margin, the investor is required to put up additional cash. The investor receives a margin call from the broker specifying the additional cash to be put into the investor's margin account. If the investor fails to put up the additional cash, the securities are sold.

Investors who take positions in the futures market are also required to satisfy initial and maintenance margin requirements.[7] Margin requirements for the purchase of securities are different in concept from those in futures markets. In a margin transaction involving securities, the initial margin requirement is equivalent to a down payment; the balance is borrowed funds for which interest is paid (the call rate plus a service charge). In the futures market, the initial margin requirement is effectively "good-faith" money, indicating that the investor will satisfy the obligation of the futures contract. No money is borrowed by the investor.

## Special Trading Arrangements for Institutional Investors

The institutionalization of the stock market has resulted in the evolution of special arrangements for the execution of certain types of orders commonly sought by institutional investors: (1) block trades, meaning orders requiring the execution of a trade for a large number of shares of a given stock and (2) program trades, meaning orders requiring the execution of trades in a large number of different stocks at as near the same time as possible. An example of a block trade would be a mutual fund that seeks to buy 15,000 shares of IBM stock. An example of a program trade is a pension fund that seeks to buy shares of 200 "names" (by names we mean companies) at the end of a trading day.

The arrangement that has evolved to accommodate these two types of institutional trades is a network of trading desks for the major brokerage firms and institutional investors that communicate with each other by means of electronic display systems and telephones. This network is referred to as the *upstairs market*. Participants in the upstairs market play a key role, not only in providing liquidity to the market so that such institutional trades can be executed, but also through taking part in activities that help to integrate the fragmented stock market.

### Block Trades

*Block trades* are defined as trades of 10,000 shares or more of a given stock, or trades of shares with a market value of $200,000 or more. Because executing large numbers of block orders places strains on the trading systems of exchanges, procedures have been developed to handle them. An institutional customer contacts a salesperson at a brokerage firm, indicating that it wishes to place a block order. The salesperson then gives the order to the brokerage firm's block execution department. (Notice that the salesperson does not submit the order to be executed to the exchange where the stock might be traded or, in the case of an

---

[7] We cover derivative instruments such as futures and options in Chapters 12 and 13.

unlisted stock, try to execute the order on the NASDAQ system.) The sales traders in the block execution department then contact other institutions in the hope of finding one or more institutions that would be willing to take the other side of the order. That is, they use the upstairs market in their search to fill the block trade order. If this can be accomplished, the execution of the order is complete.

If, on the other hand, the sales traders cannot find enough institutions to take the entire block (e.g., if the block trade order is for 40,000 shares of IBM, but only 25,000 can be exchanged, or "crossed," with other institutions), then the balance of the block trade order is given to the firm's market maker. The market maker must then make a decision about how to handle the balance of the block trade order. There are two choices: (1) The brokerage firm can take a position in the stock, in which case it is committing its own capital, or (2) the unfilled order can be executed by using the services of competing market makers.

### Program Trades

*Program trades* involve the buying and/or selling of a large number of names simultaneously. Such trades are also called basket trades, because effectively a "basket" of stocks is being traded. An institutional investor may want to use a program trade for a variety of reasons, for example, deploying new cash into the stock market, implementing a decision to move funds between the bond market and the stock market, rebalancing the composition of a stock portfolio because of a change in investment strategy, or liquidating a stock portfolio built by a money manager whose services a plan sponsor has terminated.

There are several commission arrangements available to an institution for a program trade. Each has numerous variants. One consideration in selecting an arrangement (besides commission costs) is the risk of failing to realize the best execution price. Another is the risk that the brokerage firms to be solicited about executing the trade will use their knowledge of the trade to benefit from the anticipated price movement that might result (i.e., they will "frontrun" the transaction).

A *program trade* accomplished on an agency basis involves the selection of a brokerage firm solely on the basis of commission bids (cents per share) submitted by various brokerage firms. The brokerage firm selected uses its best efforts as an agent of the institutional client to obtain the best price. The disadvantage of an agency basis arrangement for a program trade is that, while commissions may be the lowest, the execution price may not be the best because of market impact costs (discussed later this chapter) and the potential frontrunning by the brokerage firms that were solicited to submit a commission bid.

In an *agency incentive arrangement*, a benchmark portfolio value is established for the portfolio that is the subject of the program trade. The price for each name in the program trade is determined as either the price at the end of the previous day or the average price of the previous day. If the brokerage firm can execute the trade on the next trading day such that a better-than-benchmark portfolio value results (i.e., a higher value in the case of a program trade involving selling, or a lower value in the case of a program trade involving buying), then the brokerage firm receives a specified commission plus some predetermined additional compensation.

What if the brokerage firm does not achieve the benchmark portfolio value? Here is where the variants come into play. One arrangement may call for the brokerage firm to receive only an agreed-upon commission. Other arrangements may involve sharing the risk of not realizing the benchmark portfolio value with the brokerage firm. That is, if the brokerage firm falls short of the benchmark portfolio value, it must absorb a portion of the shortfall. In these risk-sharing arrangements, the brokerage firm is risking its own capital. The greater the risk-sharing the brokerage firm must accept, the higher the commission it will charge.

One problem that remains is the possibility of frontrunning. If brokerage firms know that an institution will execute a program trade with the prices that were determined the previous day, they may take advantage of this knowledge. To minimize the possibility of frontrunning, other types of program trade arrangements have been used. They call for a brokerage firm to receive only enough information about key portfolio parameters to allow several brokerage firms to bid on the entire portfolio, without knowing specific names or quantities. The winning bidder is then selected and given the details of the portfolio. This increases the risk to the brokerage firm of successfully executing the program trade, but the brokerage firm can use derivative products to protect itself if the characteristics of the portfolio in the program trade are similar to those of the general market.

Brokerage firms can execute the trade in the upstairs market or send orders electronically to exchange floors or the NASDAQ system through automated order routing systems such as the NYSE SuperDOT System.

## BASIC COST OF EQUITY TRADING

Wayne Wagner and Mark Edwards provide an insightful framework for evaluating the basic cost of equity trading. They begin by recognizing that a critical distinction exists between invest*ment* management and the equity trad*ing* process.[8] In this context, Wagner and Edwards identify five questions for institutional investors when assessing the success of their security selection decisions:

1. What was the security selection idea worth?
2. What was the commission cost?
3. What was the cost of delay on the trade desk?
4. What was the market impact of the trade?
5. How much of the trade was left unexecuted?

The answer to the first question is of course a reflection of the manager's ability to pick "winning" stocks — namely, securities that rise in value following

---

[8] Wagner and Edwards, "Implementing Investment Strategies: The Art and Science of Investing."

the manager's active buy decision, or stocks that fall in value after the manager initiates a sell or short sell decision. This is a key component of what equity managers do in the context of investment management.

The answer to the remaining questions (2 through 5), reflects trading cost considerations that can impact in a material way the revealed "alpha" on the equity manager's portfolio. Wagner and Edwards separate these costs into the cost of trader timing, market or price impact cost, and the opportunity cost of unexecuted or failed trades. The latter trading cost arises when the trader is unable to locate shares to complete the trade or the stock price has moved out of a range that is acceptable to the equity manager.

## Equity Trading Cost: A Simple Example

Consider the following example to highlight the key cost components of an equity trade. Following completion of an institutional trade, suppose that the ticker tape for XYZ stock reveals that:[9]

*6,000 shares of XYZ stock were purchased at $82.00*

Although 6,000 XYZ shares were bought, Exhibit 1 indicates what may have happened behind the scenes — beginning with the initial security selection decision by the manager (the investment idea), to the release of the buy order by the equity trader, to the subsequent trade execution by the broker (the essential elements of trading implementation)

We can assess the cost of trading XYZ stock as follows. The commission charge is the easiest to identify — namely, $0.045 per share, or $270 on the purchase of 6,000 shares of XYZ stock.

Since the trade desk did not release the order to buy XYZ stock until it was selling for $81, the assessed *trader timing* cost is $1 per share. Also, the *price impact* is $1 per XYZ share traded, as the stock was selling for $81 when the order was received by the broker — just prior to execution of the 6,000 XYZ shares at $82.

---

## Exhibit 1: XYZ Trade Decomposition

Equity manager wants to buy 10,000 shares of XYZ at current price of 80.
Trade desk releases 8,000 shares to broker when price is 81.
Broker purchases 6,000 shares of XYZ stock at $82 plus $0.045 (per share) commission.
XYZ stock jumps to 85, and remainder of order is canceled.
15 days later the price of XYZ stock is 88.

---

[9] This trading cost illustration is similar to the example provided by Wagner and Edwards in "Implementing Investment Strategies."

The *opportunity cost* — resulting from unexecuted shares — of the equity trade is somewhat more problematic. Assuming that the movement of XYZ stock price from $80 to $88 can be largely attributed to information used by the equity manager in his/her security selection decision, it appears that the value of the investment idea to purchase XYZ stock was 10% ($88/$80 minus 1) over a 15-day trading interval. Since 40% of the initial buy order on XYZ stock was "left on the table," it seems that the opportunity cost of *not* purchasing 4,000 shares of XYZ stock is 4% (10% × 40%).

The basic trading cost illustration in Exhibit 1 suggests that without efficient monitoring of the equity trading process, it is possible that the value of the manager's investment ideas (gross alpha) can be impacted negatively by sizable trading costs in addition to commission charges — including trader timing, price or market impact, and opportunity cost considerations. Moreover, trading cost issues are especially important in a world where active equity managers are hard pressed to outperform a simple buy and hold approach such as that employed in a market index fund.

# TRANSACTION COSTS: A CLOSER LOOK[10]

Money managers are evaluated against various benchmarks, and that evaluation must take related costs into account. In an investment era where 50 basis points can make a difference in performance, the careful analysis and management of transaction costs can yield significant benefits. In order to effectively manage transaction costs, money managers need to understand the different components of these costs and the various ways they can be measured.

## Components of Transaction Costs

Investment costs include research costs and transaction costs. Research costs include the cost of analysts, computers, and programmers to develop valuation models and the costs to purchase data and maintain data bases. Transaction costs consist of commissions, fees, execution costs, and opportunity costs, which can be grouped as either fixed or variable components.

The fixed components of transaction costs are easily measurable and are represented by commissions charged by brokers, taxes, and fees. The fixed components are relatively small. *Commissions* are the monies paid to brokers to execute trades.[11] Commissions on securities trades are fully negotiable. Included in the category of fees are custodial fees and transfer fees. *Custodial fees* are the fees charged by an institution that holds securities in safekeeping for an investor. A *transfer fee* is a fee paid by the investor to transfer ownership of a stock.

---

[10] The discussion in this section draws from Bruce M. Collins and Frank J. Fabozzi, "A Methodology for Measuring Transactions Costs," *Financial Analysts Journal* (March-April 1991), pp. 27-36.
[11] For a more detailed discussion of commissions, see Alan D. Biller, "A Plan Sponsor's Guide to Commissions," Chapter 10 in Frank J. Fabozzi (ed.), *Pension Fund Investment Management: Second Edition* (New Hope, PA: Frank J. Fabozzi Associates, 1997).

While commissions and fees are easily measurable, variable transaction costs — execution costs and opportunity costs — are not.

## Execution Costs

*Execution costs* represent the difference between the execution price of a stock and the price that would have existed in the absence of a trade. Since these two conditions cannot exist simultaneously, true transaction costs are inherently not observable. Nevertheless, there are ways to measure costs that provide useful information for the money manager. No single measure tells the whole story, and it is necessary to provide a set of measurement benchmarks that capture the entire transaction process. Further complicating the measurement problem is the need to separate the impact of other investors and the structure of the market mechanism.

Execution costs can be further divided into *market* or *price impact* and *market timing* considerations. *Market impact costs* are the result of the bid-ask spread and a dealer's required price concession. The price concession arises because of the risk the dealer takes that the investor's trade is possibly motivated by information that the investor has but the dealer does not. (Such trades are referred to as *information-motivated trades*.) *Market timing costs* are those that arise from price movement of the stock during the time of the transaction which is attributed to other activity in the stock.

*Execution costs* arise out of the demand for immediate execution through both the demand for liquidity and the trading activity on the trade date. Execution costs may vary according to the investment style and the trading demands of the investor.

There is a distinction between information-motivated trades and informationless trades.[12] *Information-motivated trades* occur when an investor believes he or she possesses pertinent information not currently reflected in the stock's price. This style of trading tends to increase market impact because it emphasizes the speed of execution. It can involve the sale of one stock in favor of another. *Informationless trades* are the result of either a reallocation of wealth or an implementation of an investment strategy that only utilizes existing information.

An example of informationless trades is a pension fund's decision to invest cash in the stock market. Two other examples of informationless trades include portfolio rebalances and the investment of new money. Thus, in the case of informationless trades, the demand for liquidity alone should not lead the market maker to demand significant price concessions associated with new information. If the market maker believes a desired trade is driven by information, however, he or she will increase the bid-ask spread to provide some protection.

The problem with measuring execution costs is that the true measure, which is the difference between the price of the stock in the absence of a money manager's trade and the execution price, is not observable. Furthermore, the exe-

---

[12] See L.J. Cuneo and W. H. Wagner, "Reducing the Cost of Stock Trading," *Financial Analyst Journal* (November-December 1975), 835-843, for a further exposition of the distinction between these two classes of trades, and the implications for reducing costs.

cution prices are dependent on supply and demand conditions at the margin. Thus, the execution price may be influenced by competitive traders who demand immediate execution or by other investors with similar motives for trading. This means that the execution price realized by an investor is the consequence of the structure of the market mechanism, the demand for liquidity by the marginal investor, and the competitive forces of investors with similar motivations for trading.

### Opportunity Cost

The cost of not transacting represents an *opportunity cost*.[13] Opportunity costs may arise when a desired trade fails to be executed. This component of costs represents the difference in performance between a money manager's desired investment and his or her actual investment after adjusting for execution costs and commissions. Opportunity costs have been characterized as the hidden cost of trading, and it has been suggested that the shortfall in the performance of many actively managed portfolios is the consequence of failing to execute all desired trades.[14]

The measurement of opportunity costs is subject to the same problems as the measurement of execution costs. The true measure of opportunity cost is derived from knowing what the performance of a stock would have been if all desired trades were executed across an investment horizon at the desired time. Since these are the desired trades that a money manager could not execute, they are inherently not observable. Nevertheless, by monitoring the performance of the desired investment as if all trades were executed, a money manager can estimate opportunity costs.

## Trade-Offs

The components of transaction costs are summarized below:

Transaction costs = fixed costs + variable costs
Fixed costs = commissions + fees + taxes
Variable costs = execution costs + opportunity costs
Execution costs = market impact costs + market timing costs
Opportunity costs = desired returns − actual returns − execution costs
− fixed costs

The broadest definition of investment costs is the performance difference between expected and actual outcomes. The performance expectations of a strategy can be represented by an investment benchmark which reflects the desired investment. Investment costs are revealed when there is a significant performance difference between the benchmark and the actual investment over a measurement

[13] See Andre F. Perold, "The Implementation Shortfall: Paper versus Reality," *Journal of Portfolio Management* (April 1988), pp. 4-9, for an excellent presentation of opportunity costs, within the context of costs defined as the implementation shortfall of an investment strategy.

[14] See L. J. Treynor, "What Does It Take to Win the Trading Game?" *Financial Analyst Journal* (January–February 1981), pp. 55–60, and Perold, op. cit., for a discussion of the consequences of high opportunity costs.

period. The performance differential is then attributable to the cost of trading the strategy, which we refer to as execution costs, or the inability to implement the desired strategy as represented by the benchmark, which we refer to as opportunity cost. The performance shortfall, therefore, is a combination of commissions, execution costs, and opportunity costs.

All three sources of costs have to be considered in any cost management program. The reduction of one cost may be at the expense of another. For example, the dramatic decline in commission rates has altered the risk/reward characteristics for the upstairs market makers which we described earlier in this chapter. The consequence may be an increase in bid-ask spreads and execution costs, or in opportunity costs because of increased search costs associated with finding the other side of the trade. A reduction in execution costs can be achieved by reducing market impact. One way to reduce execution costs is to delay trading until the price is right; however, this process may lead to missed investment opportunities.

The trade-off between execution costs and opportunity costs is illustrated in Exhibit 2. The vertical axis represents unit costs, where the units could be cents per share, basis points, or dollars. The horizontal axis represents time periods, which could be minutes, hours, days, etc. The downward-sloping line represents execution costs. As the line indicates, execution costs are positively related to the immediacy of execution. That means that execution costs go down as immediacy decreases — that is, as time increases. The upward-sloping line represents opportunity costs. Opportunity costs are positively related to the delay in execution. The parabola represents total costs and suggests that total costs can be minimized by appropriately trading off execution costs and opportunity costs.

## Exhibit 2: Cost Trade-Offs: Execution versus Opportunity Costs

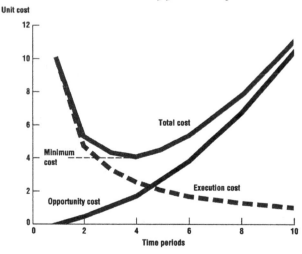

## Exhibit 3: Management Style versus Costs

| Management Style | Trading Motivation | Liquidity Demands | Execution Cost | Opportunity Cost |
|---|---|---|---|---|
| Value | Value | Low | Low | Low |
| Growth | Value | Low | Low | Low |
| Earnings surprise | Information | High | High | High |
| Index fund | | | | |
|    Large cap* | Passive | Variable | Variable | High |
|    Small cap | Passive | High | High | High |

* The costs associated with some investment strategies that utilize futures can be low despite high opportunity costs.

Exhibit 3 is a sample of approaches to investment management and related cost structures. Value managers and growth managers have longer investment horizons, lower demand for immediate execution, and a flatter opportunity cost curve than managers that employ an earnings surprise model. Consequently, value or growth-oriented managers need not pay a high immediacy cost. As a general rule, if the slope of a money manager's opportunity cost curve is less than the slope of his or her execution cost curve, it is better to wait to find a natural transactor on the other side of the trade. Investment strategies that meet this description can be used to offset the cost of liquidity.

## Measuring Transaction Costs

The measurement of transaction costs is critical for money managers in formulating investment strategies and for clients in assessing the performance of money managers. There are three dimensions to measuring transaction costs: commissions for a particular stock or trading style, determination of a benchmark for execution costs and opportunity costs, and separation of the influence of the trade from other factors.

Commission rates, taxes, and fees are readily observable and fixed for a *given* transaction. The measurement of other components of transaction costs, particularly the market impact component, has no unique solution.

Specifically, market impact arises when a trade induces a temporary price movement. This is the result of either immediate liquidity demands or the actions of a market maker who perceives that an investor's trade contains useful information. There are alternative approaches to measuring execution costs that capture useful information about the transaction process. In general, the cost of transacting is the difference between the execution price and a fair market benchmark. That is,

Costs = execution price − fair market price

The fair price of the stock is the price that would have prevailed had a money manager's trade not taken place. However, since that price is not observable, the fair price must be estimated or inferred. There are several working definitions of a fair price benchmark among practitioners. The choice of a benchmark may involve choosing either a price that represents the fair value of a stock in the absence of the money manager from the market or a price that represents the consequence of the money manager's presence in the market. We present three different approaches to measuring market impact, which we refer to as *pretrade measures*, *posttrade measures*, and *across-day* or *average measures*.

*Pretrade benchmarks* are prices occurring before or at the decision to trade, while *posttrade benchmarks* are prices occurring after the decision to trade. Average (across-day) measures use the average or representative price of a large number of trades. Essentially, all three approaches are attempts to measure the fair value of a stock at a point in time. Transaction costs emerge when the execution price deviates from the fair price. To the extent that any price represents an unbiased estimate of a fair price, the concept is valid. It does, however, assume that markets are efficient.

### Pretrade Benchmarks

Pretrade measures use a price that existed prior to the trade as a benchmark.[15] This price may be the previous night's close or the price at which the stock last traded. The premise behind pretrade benchmarks is that the only way of knowing the impact of a money manager's trade on the price of the stock is by comparing it with conditions prior to his or her arrival in the marketplace. One way to accomplish this is by comparing the execution price with the price at which the stock last traded. Alternatively, when a time lag to last sale exists, the midpoint of the bid-ask can be used. In either case, the argument follows that market conditions before the time of execution represent the reference point for evaluating any price movement induced by a money manager's entrance into the marketplace. A positive difference between the execution price and the benchmark is regarded as a cost.

Critics of pretrade benchmarks argue that using prior prices as a benchmark violates a fundamental requirement for a good measure of execution costs: the requirement that the benchmark be independent of the trading decision. In other words, the trader should not be able to game the trade. Gaming in this context refers to structuring a trade in such a way that it satisfies or accommodates a particular cost measure. That is, gaming is rigging the apparent costs by the person accountable for these costs so that the manager can show low costs by rigging the measurement criteria — and the client is none the wiser. A simple example of gaming is to execute easy trades and not difficult trades.

---

[15] See Andre Perold, "The Implementation Shortfall: Paper versus Reality," and Gary Beebower, "Evaluating Transaction Costs," Chapter 11 in Wayne H. Wagner (ed.), *The Complete Guide to Securities Transactions* (New York: John Wiley & Sons, 1989), for a discussion of pre-trade measures.

***Posttrade Benchmarks*** A second approach to measuring market impact costs is using posttrade benchmarks.[16] The premise underlying the use of a posttrade benchmark is that it avoids the problem of gaming because it is independent of the trading decision. One requirement, however, is a benchmark that lies outside the influence of the trade. Thus, the measurement interval is another parameter to consider. As is the case with pretrade benchmarks, there are several choices for posttrade benchmarks. These include the next trade immediately after a trade, the closing price on the trade date, or any price subsequent to the time of execution. A price reversal is indicative of positive execution costs. A price reversal is also indicative of liquidity-driven trades versus information-motivated trades where the price does not reverse.

### Average Measures

Another approach to establishing a fair price benchmark is to establish a representative price for the trade date. Two such measures are the average of the high and low and the trade-weighted average price.[17] The weakness of both measures as benchmarks for measuring execution costs is that they are subject to gaming. For example, the trade-weighted average price is gamed by spreading a trade out across the trading day — periodically transacting. A major proportion of the desired trade might be transacted around the opening, closing, and large-block trades. The trader participates but does not originate a trade. The trading style is reactive and not proactive. Thus, the use of this benchmark is essentially a promise by the trader to be mediocre and may not produce the best results. These averages are better indicators of the market timing portion of costs rather than execution costs. However, proponents argue that average cost benchmarks are better measures than market impact benchmarks because the former are more representative of an equilibrium price.[18]

### Other Factors

Other factors have been used to adjust costs. The movement of prices can be induced by general market movements.[19] For example, suppose several money managers would like to increase their exposure to the stock market. Suppose fur-

---

[16] For a discussion of posttrade measures of market impact, see Beebower, *op. cit.*, and G. Beebower and W. Priest, "The Tricks of the Trade," *Journal of Portfolio Management* (Winter 1980), pp. 36–42.

[17] See S. Berkowitz and D.E. Logue, "Study of the Investment Performance of ERISA Plans," U.S. Dept. of Labor, July 1986, and Berkowitz, Logue, and E.A. Noser, "The Total Cost of Transactions on the N.Y.S.E.," *Journal of Finance* (March 1988), pp.97-112, for a discussion of these measures.

[18] Peter Bernstein, consulting editor of the *Journal of Portfolio Management*, argues that the only reliable benchmarks are "representative price" benchmarks, which are essentially some form of average price, because they are more likely to represent an equilibrium price. Alternative benchmarks might incorporate market impact from competitive trades other than the one being evaluated.

[19] See Kathleen A. Condon, "Measuring Equity Transactions Costs," *Financial Analyst Journal* (September 1981), pp. 57–60, for a specification of this type of adjustment. See Stephen Bodurtha and T. Quinn, "Does Patient Trading Really Pay?" *Financial Analyst Journal* (April–May 1990), pp. 35–42, for an example of how to implement an adjustment for market changes.

ther that they all enter orders to buy certain stocks at the same time. As a result of these orders, the price may move between the time the order is entered and the time it is executed. Consequently, the cost of execution should be adjusted for changes in the market or other factors assumed to affect prices. The premise underlying this approach is to specify an unbiased estimate of a fair price in the money manager's absence from the market. The measure captures the residual effects of a money manager's trade on the movement in price by adjusting the benchmark. A positive residual is indicative of a cost. The expression below is an example of a cost estimator using this approach.

Cost = execution price − benchmark − market factor adjustment

Exhibit 4 summarizes the different approaches to measuring execution costs along with advantages and disadvantages.

## TRADING COSTS: SOME EMPIRICAL EVIDENCE

Wagner and Edwards provide some definitive findings on the range of equity trading costs according to: (1) price impact, (2) trader timing, and (3) opportunity cost resulting from failed trades. Based on nearly 700,000 trades by over 50 different management firms during the second half of 1996, their research points to an "iceberg" of equity trading costs — consisting of both observable and non-observable trading cost elements. Exhibit 5 reproduces the typical range of trading costs in basis points faced by institutional investors.

### Exhibit 4: Measurement Techniques

| Method | Benchmarks | Advantages | Disadvantages |
|---|---|---|---|
| Pretrade | Last sale<br>Previous close | Captures current market:<br>½ bid-ask spread | May affect trading decision |
| Posttrade | Next sale<br>Trade date close<br>N-day close | Avoids gaming | Neglects pretrade information<br>that is based on market effects |
| Intraday | Avg. high/low<br>Weighted average | Measures daily market timing | Subject to gaming |
| Factor-adjusted | Market<br>Industry | Captures residual effects | Difficult to measure |

## Exhibit 5: The "Iceberg" of Trading Costs
### (in basis points)

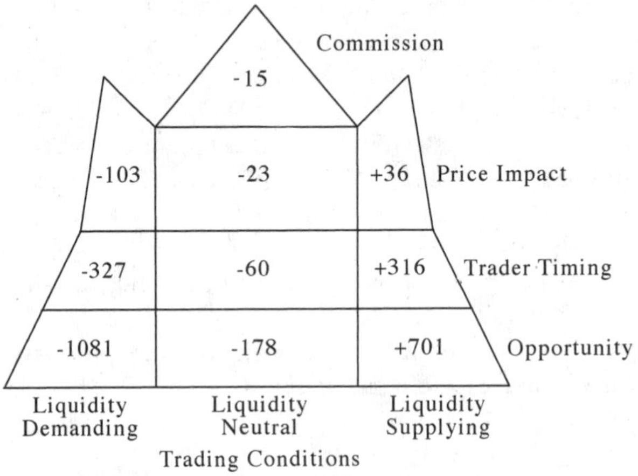

|  | Commission -15 |  |
|---|---|---|
| -103 | -23 | +36  Price Impact |
| -327 | -60 | +316  Trader Timing |
| -1081 | -178 | +701  Opportunity |
| Liquidity Demanding | Liquidity Neutral | Liquidity Supplying |

Trading Conditions

Source: Exhibit 2 in Wayne H. Wagner and Mark Edwards, "Implementing Investment Strategies: The Art and Science of Investing," Chapter 11 in Frank J. Fabozzi (ed.), *Active Equity Portfolio Management* (New Hope, PA: Frank J. Fabozzi Associates, 1998), p. 186.

Exhibit 5 shows that commission charges average about 15 basis points. Price impact — which is a reflection of dealer spread plus the price movement required to attract additional liquidity — can vary quite dramatically, depending on whether the trade is liquidity demanding, at −103 basis points, or liquidity supplying, at +36 basis points (for a trading cost reduction). A liquidity demanding trade occurs, for example, when an information trader requires immediate execution before prices move quickly to their new intrinsic value, while a liquidity supplying trade can be associated with a "value" manager who takes a contrarian position on a stock when market prices are falling — as the company fundamentals still look attractive in the eyes of the value-based manager. Based on the empirical findings of Wagner and Edwards, it's also interesting to see that a trading cost asymmetry exists between the cost of liquidity demanding and liquidity supplying trades.

Trader timing comprises another large component of the "iceberg" of equity trading costs. As shown in Exhibit 5, these costs can range from −327 basis points for a liquidity demanding trade, to +316 basis points when the trading desk is handling a liquidity supplying trade. At 60 basis points for a liquidity neutral trade, trader timing cost is 2.6 times (60/23) the normal trading cost associated with price impact.

As Wagner and Edwards point out, the final cost of trading is opportunity cost — that portion of the "iceberg" of equity trading costs that is never seen, but possibly the most damaging to investment performance. As revealed in Exhibit 5, the opportunity cost of unexecuted trades ranges from a whopping −1,081 basis points (10.81% drain on investment performance when compared to costless trading) to +701 basis points for a liquidity supplying trade. With liquidity neutral trades, the opportunity cost from failed trades is −178 basis points. This average opportunity cost is quite meaningful when one recognizes that such an inefficiency might cause an active equity manager — with otherwise positive alpha — to have revealed performance that is either the same as — or possibly short of — the return to passive indexing.

## Summary Definitions and Per Share Trading Cost

Wagner and Edwards also provide a set of definitions, computations, and experienced trading costs on a *per share* basis. Their trading cost definitions and (additional) research findings are shown in Exhibit 6. The trading cost definitions are also consistent with our earlier discussion.

Exhibit 6 indicates that the experienced trading cost for institutional managers generally includes (1) commission costs of 4.5 cents per share, (2) price impact of 8 cents per share, (3) trader timing cost of 23 cents per share, and (4) opportunity cost estimated at 71 cents over a 15-day trading horizon. According to Wagner and Edwards, the weighted average experienced cost — representing the difference between fully costed and costless returns — is 38 cents per share.

## EQUITY TRADING AND PORTFOLIO MANAGEMENT

By now it should be clear that equity trading should not be viewed as an adjunct to equity portfolio management. Indeed, the management of equity trading costs is an integral part of any successful investment management program. In this context, BARRA points out that superior investment performance is based on careful consideration of four key elements:[20]

## Exhibit 6: Definitions, Computations, and Experienced Cost

| Cost | Definition | Measurement | Experienced Costs |
|---|---|---|---|
| Commission | Explicit fee charged by a broker for services. | Provided for listed trades. | −4.5¢ |
| Impact | Cost of immediate execution. | The difference between the average execution price and the price at the time the order is revealed to the broker. | −8¢ |
| Timing | Cost of seeking liquidity. | Price change between the time the order goes to the trade desk and when it is released to the broker. | −23¢ |
| Opportunity | Cost of failing to find liquidity. | 15 day return for unexecuted shares. | −71¢ |
| Total | Difference between costless and fully costed returns | Weighted sum of the above | −38¢ |

Source: Exhibit 6 in Wayne H. Wagner and Mark Edwards, "Implementing Investment Strategies: The Art and Science of Investing," Chapter 11 in Frank J. Fabozzi (ed.), *Active Equity Portfolio Management* (New Hope, PA: Frank J. Fabozzi Associates, 1998), p. 188.

[20] The trading cost factor model described in this section is based on BARRA's Market Impact Model™. A basic description of the model is covered in a three-part newsletter series. See Nicolo Torre, "The Market Impact Model™," Equity Trading: Research , *BARRA Newsletters 165-167* (BARRA, 1998).

- forming realistic return expectations
- controlling portfolio risk
- efficient control of trading costs
- monitoring total investment performance

## Integrated Portfolio Management

Unfortunately, most discussions of equity portfolio management focus on the relationship between expected return and portfolio risk — with little if any emphasis on whether the selected securities in the "optimal" or target portfolio can be acquired in a cost efficient manner. To illustrate the seriousness of the problem that can arise with sub-optimal portfolio decisions, Exhibit 7 highlights what BARRA refers to as the "typical" versus "ideal" approach to (equity) portfolio management.

In the typical approach (top portion of Exhibit 7), portfolio managers engage in fundamental and/or quantitative research to identify the best securities in the marketplace — albeit with a measure of investment prudence (risk control) in mind. Upon completion, the portfolio manager reveals the list of securities that form the basis of the target portfolio to the senior trader. At this point, the senior trader informs the portfolio manager of certain untradable positions — which causes the portfolio manager to adjust the list of securities either by hand or some other *ad hoc* procedure. This, in turn, causes the investor's portfolio to be sub-optimal from an integrated portfolio management viewpoint.

Exhibit 7 also shows that as the trader begins to fill the portfolio with the now sub-optimal set of securities, an additional portfolio imbalance may occur as market impact causes the prices of some securities to "run away" during trade implementation. It should be clear that any *ad hoc* adjustments by the trader at this point will in turn build a systematic imbalance in the investor's portfolio — such that the portfolio manager's actual portfolio will depart permanently from that which would be efficient from a return-risk *and* trading cost perspective.

According to BARRA, the ideal approach to equity portfolio management (lower portion of Exhibit 7) requires a systematic integration of portfolio management and trading processes. In this context, the returns forecast, risk estimates, and trading cost program are jointly combined in determining the optimal investment portfolio. In this way, the portfolio manager knows up front if (complete) portfolio implementation is either not feasible or is too expensive when accounting for trading costs.

Accordingly, the portfolio manager can incorporate the appropriate trading cost information into the portfolio construction and risk control process — *before* the trading program begins. The portfolio manager is then able to build a portfolio of securities whereby actual security positions are consistent with those deemed to be optimal from an integrated portfolio context.

## BARRA's Market Impact Model

In previous sections we discussed the components of equity trading costs — including order processing (commissions, taxes, etc.) and market or price impact costs. We learned that market or price impact is an important component of equity trading costs.

Several vendors and broker/dealers have developed models based on systematic factors that determine the magnitude of market impact. BARRA, for example, developed a multifactor model based on factors that exhibit linear and non-linear characteristics. In BARRA's "Market Impact Model™," the *forecast* cost of a trade is expressed in terms of both trade- and asset-based factors.[21] The relevant factors include:

*Trade-based factors*:

- trade size, measured in terms of value
- the price of market liquidity (market tone)
- efficiency of investor's trading process (skill)

*Asset-based factors*:

- responsiveness of order flow to liquidity-provider price signals (elasticity)
- variability of the asset's price (volatility)
- frequency of asset trade (intensity)
- distribution of trade size (shape)

---

## Exhibit 7: Portfolio Management: Typical versus Ideal

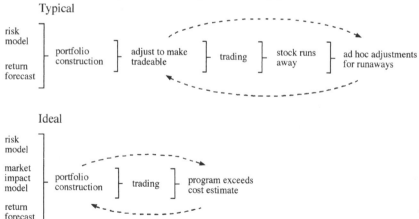

Source: Figure 4 in Nicolo Torre, "The Market Impact Model™ — First in a Series: The Market Impact Problem," Equity Trading: Research , *BARRA Newsletters 165* (BARRA, 1998), pp. 7-8.

---

[21] For a model developed by Salomon Smith Barney, see Eric H. Sorensen, Laurence J. Price, Keith Miller, Daniel E. Cox, and Samuel A. Birnhaum, "The Salomon Smith Barney Global Equity Impact Cost Model," Equity Research: Global Quantitative Research (Salomon Smith Barney, December 1998).

In a nutshell, BARRA's forecast cost of a trade is directly related to order size. The elasticity of order flow with respect to liquidity-provider price signals is dependent on the prevalence of "price takers" in the market — with more investors willing to trade at the current price for large cap stocks, for example, in comparison with small capitalization stocks where a greater uncertainty exists about true equilibrium price.

The result is that small cap stocks — with relatively fewer price takers — have higher forecast trading costs in comparison with the stocks of large capitalization companies. Not surprisingly, variability in the underlying price change for an asset also leads to higher trading costs. This is yet another factor which helps explain why the forecast trading cost of small cap companies is generally higher than the transaction cost for large cap firms. In addition, the intensity and shape of the distribution of trade size and order flow can have a material impact on equity transaction costs.

Exhibit 8 shows a market impact analysis for Boston Acoustics stock using BARRA's Market Impact Model. In this exhibit, the solid line represents the long-term average cost (measured in dollars) of transacting in Boston Acoustics stock — based on typical market conditions — while the thin line points to the "current" forecast cost of trading the stock due to short-term fluctuations in liquidity. Negative size values on the horizontal axis refer to a sell decision on Boston Acoustics stock, while positive trade size represent an increasing demand for the company stock. As shown, trade size (horizontal axis) is measured in thousands of dollars.

## Exhibit 8: Market Impact for Boston Acoustics Inc. (6/12/98)

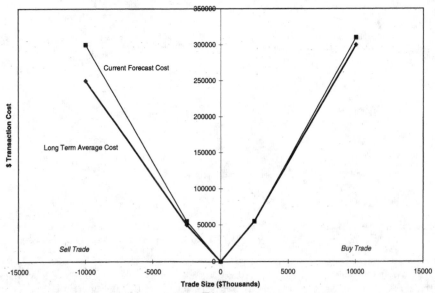

Source: "Market Impact Model™: Product Overview," BARRA, p. 1.

On the buy side, it appears that current trade conditions for Boston Acoustics stock were typical of that which generally prevail in the marketplace — since the (illustrated) current forecast cost of transacting at different sizes is largely consistent with the long-term average cost. This contrasts with current trading conditions when selling Boston Acoustics stock where there exists an ever-widening spread in the relationship between current market impact and historical trade cost — as the trading size on the horizontal axis gets more negative.

In numerical terms, Exhibit 8 reveals that the current market impact for a $10 million sell trade on Boston Acoustics stock was about $300,000 — or 3% of the trade value — while the benchmark average transaction cost was about $250,000 — representing a meaningful trading spread of 50 basis points on the sell side. Also, at $300,000, the historical cost of a $10 million buy on Boston Acoustics stock was similar to the *current* forecast cost of a comparably-sized sell decision on the firm's stock — while the current forecast cost of a comparable buy trade was slightly higher.

## SUMMARY

While previous chapters have focused on equity portfolio management, in this chapter we have looked at equity trading — the mechanics of trading stocks and the different components of transaction costs and their measurement.

Dealers provide four functions in markets: (1) opportunity for investors to trade immediately rather than waiting for the arrival of sufficient orders on the other side of the trade (i.e., immediacy), (2) maintenance of short-run price stability (i.e., continuity), (3) better price information to market participants, and (4) in certain market structures, the services of an auctioneer in bringing order and fairness to a market.

Stocks trades in 16ths of a point. When an investor directs a broker to buy or sell a stock, there are parameters that must be specified in addition to the number of shares. The different types of orders are markets orders, limit orders, stop orders, stop-limits orders, market-if-touched orders, time-specific orders, and size-related orders. There are exchanges imposed restriction on short selling (i.e., tick-test rules) and margin requirements for purchasing on margin.

To accommodate the trading needs of institutional investors, who tend to place orders of larger sizes and with a large number of names, special arrangements have evolved. Block trades are trades of 10,000 shares or more of a given stock or trades with a market value of $200,000 or more. Program trades, or basket trades, involve the buying and/or selling of a large number of names simultaneously. The institutional arrangement that has evolved to accommodate these needs is the upstairs market, which is a network of trading desks of the major brokerage firms and institutional investors that communicate with each other by means of electronic display systems and telephones.

In recent years, greater emphasis has been placed on the measurement and analysis of transaction costs. There are four general components to transactions costs: commissions, fees, execution costs, and opportunity costs. Execution costs represent the difference between the execution price of a stock and the price that would have existed in the absence of the trade, and arise out of the demand for immediate execution through both the demand for liquidity and the trading activity on the trade date. Opportunity costs arise when a desired trade fails to be executed. While commissions are fixed and measurable over a measurement period, there is no unique method to measure execution costs or opportunity costs.

# QUESTIONS

1. a. What is meant by a market order and why would one be placed when a trader wants immediate trading?
   b. What is meant by a limit order?
   c. What are the risks associated with a limit order?
   d. Suppose that a trader purchased the stock of company XYZ for $60 and that she sets a maximum loss that she will accept on this stock of $6. What type of order can she place?

2. a. What is meant by "shorting a stock"?
   b. What are the restrictions on shorting a stock?

3. What is the difference between a broker and dealer?

4. a. What is a program trade?
   b. What are the various types of commission arrangements for executing a program trade and the advantages and disadvantages of each?

5. a. Why would an investor purchase on margin?
   b. What is the call money rate?

6. The following two statements are taken from Greta E. Marshall's article "Execution Costs: The Plan Sponsor's View," which appears in *Trading Strategies and Execution Costs*, published by The Institute of Chartered Financial Analysts in 1988:

   a. "There are three components of trading costs. First there are direct costs which may be measured—commissions. Second, there are indirect—or market impact—costs. Finally, there are the undefined costs of not trading." What are market impact costs, and what do you think the "undefined costs of not trading" represent?
   b. "Market impact, unlike broker commissions, is difficult to identify and measure." Why is market impact cost difficult to measure?

7. a. What is meant by an information-motivated trade?
   b. Give an example of an information-motivated trade.
   c. What is meant by an informationless trade?
   d. Give an example of an informationless trade.

8. a. What are the difficulties of measuring execution costs.
   b. What are the various approaches to measuring market impact cost?
   c. What are the difficulties of measuring opportunity costs?
   d. What is the trade-off among the various types of transaction costs?

9. Consider the *simple* trade decomposition for LMN stock:

- Equity manager wants to buy 5,000 shares of LMN stock at $45.00
- Trade desk releases 3,000 shares to broker when price is $45.50
- Broker purchases 2,500 shares of LMN stock at $45.75, at $0.035 per share commission.
- LMN stock jumps to $48.00, prompting the rest of the order to be canceled
- 10 days later the price of LMN stock is $52.50

a. What would the ticker tape for LMN stock probably read?
b. What is the assessed trader timing cost per LMN share?
c. What is the assessed price impact cost per LMN share?
d. What is the percentage opportunity cost of an incomplete LMN trade?

10. Wagner and Edwards point to the following quote by a well-regarded money manager as one of the key reasons why active money managers have failed to keep up with index funds in the 1990s:

   "Success in investment management comes from picking good stocks. The rest is just plumbing."

   [Cited in Wayne H. Wagner and Mark Edwards, "Implementing Investment Strategies: The Art and Science of Investing," *Active Equity Portfolio Management* (New Hope, PA: Frank J. Fabozzi Associates, 1998)].

   Explain why Wagner and Edwards strongly disagree with this comment, and discuss how their empirical research could be used to enlighten today's active (and passive) equity portfolio managers.

11. Fill in the following table of investment management approaches and related cost structures. Use Exhibit 3 (Management Style versus Costs) as a guide to assessing trade motivation (value, information, passive), and liquidity demands, execution cost, and opportunity cost (high, low, or variable). For example, an "earnings surprise" strategy in Exhibit 3 would be classified as information motivated with high liquidity demands, execution costs, and opportunity costs, respectively.

| Management Style | Trade Motivation | Liquidity Demands | Execution Cost | Opportunity Cost |
|---|---|---|---|---|
| Yield: | | | | |
| Micro cap: | | | | |
| Consistent Growth: | | | | |
| Index fund: | | | | |
| Developed International: | | | | |
| Emerging Markets: | | | | |

12. a. What do Wagner and Edwards mean by the "iceberg of equity trading costs"?
   b. What is the estimated overall cost (in basis points) of a "liquidity demanding" trade?

c. What is the estimated overall cost of a "liquidity neutral" trade?

d. What is the estimated overall cost of a "liquidity supplying" trade?

e. Why does a liquidity demanding trade appear to be more expensive than a liquidity supplying trade?

13. a. What is the BARRA Market Impact Model (MIM)?

b. What are the primary factors used to quantify the dollar cost of market impact in BARRA's MIM?

c. What is the approximate historical trading cost of a $2.5 million buy trade on Boston Acoustics stock? (See Exhibit 8 in the chapter.)

d. What is the approximate current forecast trading cost of a $2.5 million buy trade on Boston Acoustics stock?

e. What is the trading cost spread (in basis points) between a $2.5 million buy (or sell) trade on Boston Acoustics stock?

# Chapter 12

# Derivative Instruments and Their Characteristics*

Derivative instruments, or simply derivatives, are contracts that essentially derive their value from the behavior of cash market instruments such as stocks, stock indexes, bonds, currencies, and commodities that underlie the contract. When the underlying for a derivative is a stock or stock index, the contract is called an *equity derivative*. The purpose of this chapter is to explain these instruments, their investment characteristics, and to provide an overview as to how they are priced. In the next chapter we look at how equity derivatives can be used in the management of equity portfolios.

## THE ROLE OF DERIVATIVES

Equity derivatives have several properties that provide economic benefits that make them excellent candidates for use in equity portfolio management. These properties are derived from the following four roles that derivatives serve in portfolio management: (1) to modify the risk characteristics of a portfolio (*risk management*); (2) to enhance the expected return of a portfolio (*returns management*); (3) to reduce transaction costs associated with managing a portfolio (*cost management*); and, (4) to achieve efficiency in the presence of legal, tax, or regulatory obstacles (*regulatory management*).

We can further reduce the role of derivatives to the single purpose of risk management and incorporate the other three roles into this one. Thus, one can argue that equity derivatives are used primarily to manage risk or to buy and sell risk at a favorable price. Risk management is a dynamic process that allows portfolio managers to identify, measure, and assess the current risk attributes of a portfolio and to measure the potential benefits from taking the risk. Moreover, risk management involves understanding and managing the factors that can have an adverse impact on the targeted rate of return. The objective is to attain a desired return for a given level of corresponding risk on an after-cost basis. This is consistent with the Markowitz efficient frontier and modern portfolio theory discussed in Chapter 2. The role of equity derivatives in this process is to shift the

---

* This chapter is adapted from various chapters in Bruce M. Collins and Frank J. Fabozzi, *Derivatives and Equity Portfolio Management* (New Hope, PA: Frank J. Fabozzi Associates, 1999).

frontier in favor of the investor by implementing a strategy at a lower cost, lower risk, and higher return or to gain access to an investment that was not available due to some regulatory or other restriction. We can, therefore, regard the management of equity portfolios as a sophisticated exercise in risk management.

Institutional equity investors have the means to accomplish investment objectives with a host of products and product structures. Pension funds, for example, can structure a product to meet their asset allocation targets, to access foreign markets, or to explicitly manage risk. Products that may meet their needs include listed stock index futures, equity swaps, or equity linked debt. The choice of an instrument depends on the specific investor needs and circumstances. In each case, the benefits from structuring a derivatives solution to an investment problem either involves cost reduction, risk management, or the management of certain legal or regulatory restrictions.

Equity derivatives give investors more degrees of freedom. In the past, the implementation and management of an investment strategy for pension funds, for example, was a function of management style and was carried out in the cash market. Pension funds managed risk by diversifying among management styles. Prior to the advent of the over-the-counter (OTC) derivatives market in the late 1980s, the first risk management tools available to investors were limited to the listed futures and options markets. Although providing a valuable addition to an investor's risk management tool kit, listed derivatives were limited in application due to their standardized features, limited size, and liquidity constraints. The OTC derivatives market gives investors access to longer-term products that better match their investment horizon and provides flexible structures to meet their exact risk/reward requirements. The number of unique equity derivative structures is essentially unlimited.

## EQUITY DERIVATIVES MARKET

The three general categories of derivatives are (1) futures and forwards, (2) options, and (3) swaps. The basic derivative securities are futures/forward contracts and options. Swaps and other derivative structures with more complicated payoffs are regarded as hybrid securities, which can be shown to be nothing more than portfolios of forwards, options, and cash instruments in varying combinations.

Equity derivatives can also be divided into two categories according to whether they are listed or OTC. The listed market consists of options, warrants, and futures contracts. The principal listed options market consists of exchange-traded options with standardized strike prices, expirations, and payout terms traded on individual stocks, equity indexes, and futures contracts on equity indexes. A FLexible EXchange (FLEX) Option was introduced by the CBOE in 1993 that provides the customization feature of the OTC market, but with the guarantee of the exchange. The listed futures market consists of exchange-traded equity index futures with standardized settlement dates and settlement terms.

OTC equity derivatives are not traded on an exchange and have an advantage over listed derivatives because they provide complete flexibility and can be tailored to fit an investment strategy. The OTC equity derivatives market can be divided into three components: OTC options and warrants, equity-linked debt investments, and equity swaps. OTC equity options are customized option contracts that can be applied to any equity index, basket of stocks or an individual stock. OTC options are privately negotiated agreements between an investor and an issuing dealer. The structure of the option is completely flexible in terms of strike price, expiration, and payout features.

A fundamental difference between listed and OTC derivatives, however, is that listed options and futures contracts are guaranteed by the exchange, while in the OTC market the derivative is the obligation of a non-exchange entity that is the counterparty. Thus, the investor is subject to credit risk or counterparty risk.

## LISTED EQUITY OPTIONS

Equity derivative products are either exchange-traded listed derivatives or over-the-counter derivatives. In this section we will look at listed equity options.

An *option* is a contract in which the option seller grants the option buyer the right to enter into a transaction with the seller to either buy or sell an underlying asset at a specified price on or before a specified date. The specified price is called the *strike price* or *exercise price* and the specified date is called the *expiration date*. The option seller grants this right in exchange for a certain amount of money called the *option premium* or *option price*.

The option seller is also known as the option writer, while the option buyer is the option holder. The asset that is the subject of the option is called the *underlying*. The underlying can be an individual stock, a stock index, or another derivative instrument such as a futures contract. The option writer can grant the option holder one of two rights. If the right is to purchase the underlying, the option is a *call option*. If the right is to sell the underlying, the option is a *put option*.

An option can also be categorized according to when it may be exercised by the buyer. This is referred to as the *exercise style*. A *European option* can only be exercised at the expiration date of the contract. An *American option* can be exercised any time on or before the expiration date.

The terms of exchange are represented by the contract unit, which is typically 100 shares for an individual stock and a multiple times an index value for a stock index. The terms of exchange are standard for most contracts. The contract terms for a FLEX option can be customized along four dimensions: underlying, strike price, expiration date, and settlement style. These options are discussed further below.

The option holder enters into the contract with an opening transaction. Subsequently, the option holder then has the choice to exercise or to sell the option. The sale of an existing option by the holder is a closing sale.

# Listed versus OTC Equity Options

There are three advantages of listed options relative to OTC options. First, the strike price and expiration dates of the contract are standardized. Second, the direct link between buyer and seller is severed after the order is executed because of the fungible nature of listed options. The Options Clearing Corporation (OCC) serves as the intermediary between buyer and seller. Finally, transaction costs are lower for listed options than their OTC counterparts.

There are many situations in which an institutional investor needs a customized option. Such situations will be identified when we discuss the applications of OTC options in the next chapter. The higher cost of OTC options reflects this customization. However, some OTC exotic option structures may prove to cost less than the closest standardized option because a more specific payout is being bought.

A significant distinction between a listed option and an OTC option is the presence of credit risk or counterparty risk. Only the option buyer is exposed to counterparty risk. Options traded on exchanges and OTC options traded over a network of market makers have different ways of dealing with the problem of credit risk. Organized exchanges reduce counterparty risk by requiring margin, marking to the market daily, imposing size and price limits, and providing an intermediary that takes both sides of a trade. The clearing process provides three levels of protection: (1) the customer's margin, (2) the member firm's guarantee, and (3) the clearinghouse. The OTC market has incorporated a variety of terms into the contractual agreement between counterparties to address the issue of credit risk and these are described when we discuss OTC derivatives.

For listed options, there are no margin requirements for the buyer of an option once the option price has been paid in full. Because the option price is the maximum amount that the option buyer can lose, no matter how adverse the price movement of the underlying, margin is not necessary. The option writer has agreed to transfer the risk inherent in a position in the underlying from the option buyer to itself. The writer, on the other, has certain margin requirements.

# Basic Features of Listed Options

The basic features of listed options are summarized in Exhibit 1. The exhibit is grouped into four categories with each option category presented in terms of its basic features. These include the type of option, underlying, strike price, settlement information, expiration cycle, exercise style, and some trading rules.

*Stock options* refer to listed options on individual stocks or American Depository Receipts (ADRs). The underlying is 100 shares of the designated stock. All listed stock options in the United States may be exercised any time before the expiration date; that is, they are American style options.

*Index options* are options where the underlying is a stock index rather than an individual stock. An index call option gives the option buyer the right to buy the underlying stock index, while a put option gives the option buyer the right to sell the underlying stock index. Unlike stock options where a stock can be delivered if the option is exercised by the option holder, it would be extremely complicated to settle an index option by delivering all the stocks that constitute the index. Instead, index options are cash settlement contracts. This means that if the option is exercised by the option holder, the option writer pays cash to the option buyer. There is no delivery of any stocks.

The most liquid index options are those on the S&P 100 index (OEX) and the S&P 500 index. Both trade on the CBOE. Index options can be listed as American or European. The S&P 500 index option contract is European, while the OEX is American. Both index option contracts have specific standardized features and contract terms. Moreover, both have short expiration cycles. There are almost 100 stock index option contracts listed across 26 separate exchanges and 20 countries. Among the latest arrivals are options traded on the Dow Jones STOXX 50 and the Dow Jones EURO 50 stock indexes. The indexes are comprised of 50 industrial, commercial, and financial European blue chip companies.

## Exhibit 1: Basic Features of Listed Equity Options
### Stock Options

| Option Type | Call or Put |
|---|---|
| Option Category | Equity |
| Underlying Security | Individual stock or ADR |
| Contract Value | Equity: 100 shares of common stock or ADRs |
| Strike Price | 2½ points when the strike price is between $5 and $25, 10 points when the strike price is over $200. Strikes are adjusted for splits, recapitalizations, etc. |
| Settlement and Delivery | 100 shares of stock |
| Exercise Style | American |
| Expiration Cycle | Two near-term months plus two additional months from the January, February or March quarterly cycles. |
| Transaction Costs | $1-$3 commissions and ⅛ market impact |
| Position and Size Limits | Large capitalization stocks have an option position limit of 25,000 contracts (with adjustments for splits, recapitalizations, etc.) on the same side of the market; smaller capitalization stocks have an option position limit of 20,000, 10,500, 7,500 or 4,500 contracts (with adjustments for splits, recapitalizations, etc.) on the same side of the market. |

### Index Options

| Option Type | Call or Put |
|---|---|
| Option Category | Indexes |
| Underlying Security | Stock index |
| Contract Value | Multiplier × index price |
| Strike Price | Five points. 10-point intervals in the far-term month. |
| Settlement and Delivery | Cash |
| Exercise Style | American |
| Expiration Cycle | Four near-term months. |
| Transaction Costs | $1-$3 commissions and ⅛ market impact |
| Position and Size Limits | 150,000 contracts on the same side of the market with no more than 100,000 of such contracts in the near-term series. |

## Exhibit 1 (Continued)
### LEAP Options

| Option Type | Call or Put |
|---|---|
| Option Category | LEAP |
| Underlying Security | Individual stock or stock index |
| Contract Value | Equity: 100 shares of common stock or ADRs |
| | Index: full or partial value of stock index |
| Strike Price | Equity: same as equity option |
| | Index: Based on full or partial value of index. ⅕ value translates into ⅕ strike price |
| Settlement and Delivery | Equity: 100 shares of stock or ADR |
| | Index: Cash |
| Exercise Style | American or European |
| Expiration Cycle | May be up to 39 months from the date of initial listing, January expiration only. |
| Transaction Costs | $1-$3 commissions and ⅛ market impact |
| Position and Size Limits | Same as equity options and index options |

### FLEX Options

| Option Type | Call, Put, or Cap |
|---|---|
| Option Category | Equity: E-FLEX option |
| | Index: FLEX option |
| Underlying Security | Individual stock or index |
| Contract Value | Equity: 100 shares of common stock or ADRs |
| | Index: multiplier × index value |
| Strike Price | Equity: Calls, same as standard calls |
| | Puts, any dollar value or percentage |
| | Index: Any index value, percentage, or deviation from index value |
| Settlement and Delivery | Equity: 100 shares of stock |
| | Index: Cash |
| Exercise Style | Equity: American or European |
| | Index: American, European, or Cap |
| Expiration Cycle | Equity: 1 day to 3 years |
| | Index: Up to 5 years |
| Transaction Costs | $1-$3 commissions and ⅛ market impact |
| Position and Size Limits | Equity: minimum of 250 contracts to create FLEX |
| | Index: $10 million minimum to create FLEX |
| | No size or position limits |

Source: Exhibit 3 in Chapter 2 of Bruce M. Collins and Frank J. Fabozzi, *Derivatives and Equity Portfolio Management* (New Hope, PA: Frank J. Fabozzi Associates, 1999).

The following mechanics should be noted for index options. The dollar value of the stock index underlying an index option is equal to the current cash index value multiplied by the contract's multiple. That is,

Dollar value of the underlying index = Cash index value × Contract multiple

For example, if the cash index value for the S&P 100 is 530, then the dollar value of the S&P 100 contract is 530 × $100 = $53,000.

For a stock option, the price at which the buyer of the option can buy or sell the stock is the strike price. For an index option, the strike index is the index value at which the buyer of the option can buy or sell the underlying stock index. The strike index is converted into a dollar value by multiplying the strike index by the multiple for the contract. For example, if the strike index is 510, the dollar value is $51,000 (510 × $100). If an investor purchases a call option on the S&P 100 with a strike index of 510, and exercises the option when the index value is 530, then the investor has the right to purchase the index for $51,000 when the market value of the index is $53,000. The buyer of the call option would then receive $2,000 from the option writer.

The other two categories listed in Exhibit 1, LEAPS and FLEX options, essentially modify an existing feature of either a stock option, an index option, or both. For example, stock option and index option contracts have short expiration cycles. Long-Term Equity Anticipation Securities (LEAPS) are designed to offer options with longer maturities. These contracts are available on individual stocks and some indexes. Stock option LEAPS are comparable to standard stock options except the maturities can range up to 39 months from the origination date. Index options LEAPS differ in size compared with standard index options having a multiplier of 10 rather than 100.

FLEX options allow users to specify the terms of the option contract for either a stock option or an index option. The value of FLEX options is the ability to customize the terms of the contract along four dimensions: underlying, strike price, expiration date, and settlement style. Moreover, the exchange provides a secondary market to offset or alter positions and an independent daily marking of prices. The development of the FLEX option is a response to the growing OTC market. The exchanges seek to make the FLEX option attractive by providing price discovery through a competitive auction market, an active secondary market, daily price valuations, and the virtual elimination of counterparty risk. The FLEX option represents a link between listed options and OTC products.

## Risk and Return Characteristics of Options

Now let's illustrate the risk and return characteristics of the four basic option positions — buying a call option (long a call option), selling a call option (short a call option), buying a put option (long a put option), and selling a put option (short a put option). We will use stock options in our example. The illustrations assume that each option position is held to the expiration date. Also, to simplify the illustrations, we assume that the underlying for each option is for 1 share of stock rather than 100 shares and we ignore transaction costs.

### Buying Call Options

Assume that there is a call option on stock XYZ that expires in one month and has a strike price of $100. The option price is $3. Suppose that the current or spot price of stock XYZ is $100. (The *spot price* is the cash market price.) The profit and loss will depend on the price of stock XYZ at the expiration date. The buyer of a call option benefits if the price rises above the strike price. If the price of stock XYZ is equal to $103, the buyer of a call option breaks even. The maximum loss is the option price, and there is substantial upside potential if the stock price rises above $103. Exhibit 2 shows using a graph the profit/loss profile for the buyer of this call option at the expiration date.

It is worthwhile to compare the profit and loss profile of the call option buyer with that of an investor taking a long position in one share of stock XYZ. The payoff from the position depends on stock XYZ's price at the expiration date. An investor who takes a long position in stock XYZ realizes a profit of $1 for every $1 increase in stock XYZ's price. As stock XYZ's price falls, however, the investor loses, dollar for dollar. If the price drops by more than $3, the long position in stock XYZ results in a loss of more than $3. The long call position, in contrast, limits the loss to only the option price of $3 but retains the upside potential, which will be $3 less than for the long position in stock XYZ. Which alternative is better, buying the call option or buying the stock? The answer depends on what the investor is attempting to achieve.

### Exhibit 2: Profit/Loss Profile at Expiration for a Short Call Position and a Long Call Position

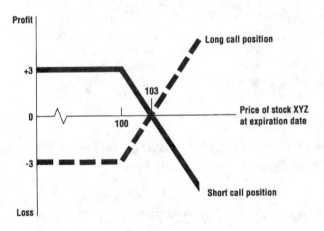

## Exhibit 3: Profit/Loss Profile at Expiration for a Short Put Position and a Long Put Position

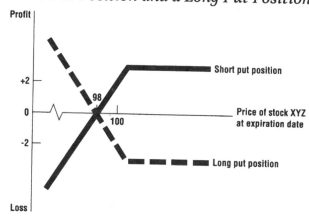

## Writing Call Options

To illustrate the option seller's, or writer's, position, we use the same call option we used to illustrate buying a call option. The profit/loss profile at expiration of the short call position (that is, the position of the call option writer) is the mirror image of the profit and loss profile of the long call position (the position of the call option buyer). That is, the profit of the short call position for any given price for stock XYZ at the expiration date is the same as the loss of the long call position. Consequently, the maximum profit the short call position can produce is the option price. The maximum loss is not limited because it is the highest price reached by stock XYZ on or before the expiration date, less the option price; this price can be indefinitely high. Exhibit 2 shows using a graph the profit/loss profile for the seller of this call option at the expiration date.

## Buying Put Options

To illustrate a long put option position, we assume a hypothetical put option on one share of stock XYZ with one month to maturity and a strike price of $100. Assume that the put option is selling for $2 and the spot price of stock XYZ is $100. The profit or loss for this position at the expiration date depends on the market price of stock XYZ. The buyer of a put option benefits if the price falls. Exhibit 3 shows using a graph the profit/loss profile for the buyer of this put option at the expiration date.

As with all long option positions, the loss is limited to the option price. The profit potential, however, is substantial: the theoretical maximum profit is generated if stock XYZ's price falls to zero. Contrast this profit potential with that of the buyer of a call option. The theoretical maximum profit for a call buyer cannot be determined beforehand because it depends on the highest price that can be reached by stock XYZ before or at the option expiration date.

To see how an option alters the risk/return profile for an investor, we again compare it with a position in stock XYZ. The long put position is compared with a short position in stock XYZ because such a position would also benefit if the price of the stock falls. While the investor taking a short stock position faces all the downside risk as well as the upside potential, an investor taking the long put position faces limited downside risk (equal to the option price) while still maintaining upside potential reduced by an amount equal to the option price.

### Writing Put Options

The profit and loss profile for a short put option is the mirror image of the long put option. The maximum profit to be realized from this position is the option price. The theoretical maximum loss can be substantial should the price of the underlying fall; if the price were to fall all the way to zero, the loss would be as large as the strike price less the option price the seller received. Exhibit 3 shows using a graph the profit/loss profile for the seller of this put option at the expiration date.

## The Value of an Option

Now we will look at the basic factors that affect the value of an option and discuss a well-known option pricing model.

### Basic Components of the Option Price

The price of an option is a reflection of the option's *intrinsic value* and any additional amount above its intrinsic value. The premium over intrinsic value is often referred to as the *time value*.

*Intrinsic Value* The intrinsic value of an option is its economic value if it is exercised immediately. If no positive economic value would result from exercising the option immediately, then the intrinsic value is zero. For a call option, the intrinsic value is positive if the spot price (i.e., cash market price) of the underlying is greater than the strike price. The intrinsic value is then the difference between the two prices. If the strike price of a call option is greater than or equal to the spot price of the underlying, the intrinsic value is zero. For example, if the strike price for a call option is $100 and the spot price of the underlying is $105, the intrinsic value is $5. That is, an option buyer exercising the option and simultaneously selling the underlying would realize $105 from the sale of the underlying, which would be covered by acquiring the underlying from the option writer for $100, thereby netting a $5 gain.

When an option has intrinsic value, it is said to be *in the money* (ITM). When the strike price of a call option exceeds the spot price of the underlying, the call option is said to be *out of the money* (OTM); it has no intrinsic value. An option for which the strike price is equal to the spot price of the underlying is said to be at the money. Both at-the-money and out-of-the-money options have an intrinsic value of zero because they are not profitable to exercise. Our call option with a strike price of $100 would be (1) in the money when the spot price of the underlying is greater than $100, (2) out of the money when the spot price of the underlying is less than $100, and (3) at the money when the spot price of the underlying is equal to $100.

For a put option, the intrinsic value is equal to the amount by which the spot price of the underlying is below the strike price. For example, if the strike price of a put option is $100 and the spot price of the underlying is $92, the intrinsic value is $8. The buyer of the put option who exercises the put option and simultaneously sells the underlying will net $8 by exercising since the underlying will be sold to the writer for $100 and purchased in the market for $92. The intrinsic value is zero if the strike price is less than or equal to the underlying's spot price.

For our put option with a strike price of $100, the option would be (1) in the money when the spot price of the underlying is less than $100, (2) out of the money when the spot price of the underlying exceeds $100, and (3) at the money when the spot price of the underlying is equal to $100

**Time Value** The *time value of an option* is the amount by which the option price exceeds its intrinsic value. The option buyer hopes that, at some time prior to expiration, changes in the market price of the underlying will increase the value of the rights conveyed by the option. For this prospect, the option buyer is willing to pay a premium above the intrinsic value. For example, if the price of a call option with a strike price of $100 is $9 when the spot price of the underlying is $105, the time value of this option is $4 ($9 minus its intrinsic value of $5). Had the current price of the underlying been $90 instead of $105, then the time value of this option would be the entire $9 because the option has no intrinsic value. Other factors being equal, the time value of an option will increase with the amount of time remaining to expiration, since the opportunity for a favorable change in the price of the underlying is greater.

There are two ways in which an option buyer may realize the value of a position taken in an option: the first is to exercise the option, and the second is to sell the option. In the first example above, since the exercise of an option will realize a gain of only $5 and will cause the immediate loss of any time value ($4 in our first example), it is preferable to sell the call. In general, if an option buyer wishes to realize the value of a position, selling will be more economically beneficial than exercising. However, there are circumstances under which it is preferable to exercise prior to the expiration date, depending on whether the total proceeds at the expiration date would be greater by holding the option or by exercising it and reinvesting any cash proceeds received until the expiration date.

### Factors That Influence the Option Price
The following six factors influence the option price:

## Exhibit 4: Summary of Factors that Effect the Price of an American Option

| | Effect of an Increase of Factor on | |
|---|---|---|
| Factor | Call Price | Put Price |
| Spot price of underlying | increase | decrease |
| Strike price | decrease | increase |
| Time to expiration of option | increase | increase |
| Expected price volatility | increase | increase |
| Short-term rate | increase | decrease |
| Anticipated cash dividends | decrease | increase |

1. spot price of the underlying
2. strike price
3. time to expiration of the option
4. expected price volatility of the underlying over the life of the option
5. short-term risk-free rate over the life of the option
6. anticipated cash dividends on the underlying stock or index over the life of
   the option

The impact of each of these factors depends on whether (1) the option is a call or a put and (2) the option is an American option or a European option. A summary of the effects of each factor on American put and call option prices is presented in Exhibit 4.

Notice how the expected price volatility of the underlying over the life of the option affects the price of both a put and a call option. All other factors being equal, the greater the expected volatility (as measured by the standard deviation or variance) of the price of the underlying, the more an investor would be willing to pay for the option, and the more an option writer would demand for it. This is because the greater the volatility, the greater the probability that the price of the underlying will move in favor of the option buyer at some time before expiration.

### Option Pricing Models

Several models have been developed to determine the theoretical value of an option. The most popular one was developed by Fischer Black and Myron Scholes in 1973 for valuing European call options.[1] Several modifications to their model have followed since then. We discuss this model here to give the reader a feel for the impact of the factors on the price of an option.

By imposing certain assumptions and using arbitrage arguments, the Black-Scholes option pricing model provides the fair (or theoretical) price of a European call option on a non-dividend-paying stock. Basically, the idea behind the arbitrage argument in deriving this and other option pricing models is that if

---

[1] Fischer Black and Myron Scholes, "The Pricing of Corporate Liabilities," *Journal of Political Economy* (May-June 1973), pp. 637-659.

the payoff from owning a call option can be replicated by (1) purchasing the stock underlying the call option and (2) borrowing funds, then the price of the option will be (at most) the cost of creating the replicating strategy.

The formula for the Black-Scholes model is

$$C = SN(d_1) - Xe^{-rt} N(d_2)$$

where

$$d_1 = \frac{\ln(S/K) + (r + 0.5s^2)t}{s\sqrt{t}}$$

$$d_2 = d_1 - s\sqrt{t}$$

$\ln$ = natural logarithm
$C$ = call option price
$S$ = price of the underlying
$K$ = strike price
$r$ = short-term risk-free rate
$e$ = 2.718 (natural antilog of 1)
$t$ = time remaining to the expiration date (measured as a fraction of a year)
$s$ = standard deviation of the change in stock price
$N(.)$ = the cumulative probability density[2]

Notice that five of the factors that we said earlier in this chapter influence the price of an option are included in the formula. However, the sixth factor, anticipated cash dividends, is not included because the model is for a non-dividend-paying stock. In the Black-Scholes model, the direction of the influence of each of these factors is the same as stated earlier. Four of the factors — strike price, price of underlying, time to expiration, and risk-free rate — are easily observed. The standard deviation of the price of the underlying must be estimated.

The option price derived from the Black-Scholes model is "fair" in the sense that if any other price existed, it would be possible to earn riskless arbitrage profits by taking an offsetting position in the underlying. That is, if the price of the call option in the market is higher than that derived from the Black-Scholes model, an investor could sell the call option and buy a certain quantity of the underlying. If the reverse is true, that is, the market price of the call option is less than the "fair" price derived from the model, the investor could buy the call option and sell short a certain amount of the underlying. This process of hedging by taking a position in the underlying allows the investor to lock in the riskless arbitrage profit. The number of shares necessary to hedge the position changes as the factors that affect the option price change, so the hedged position must be changed constantly.

---

[2] The value for $N(.)$ is obtained from a normal distribution function that is tabulated in most statistics textbooks or from spreadsheets that have this built-in function.

To illustrate the Black-Scholes model, assume the following values:

| | |
|---|---|
| Strike price | = $45 |
| Time remaining to expiration | = 183 days |
| Spot stock price | = $47 |
| Expected price volatility | = standard deviation = 25% |
| Risk-free rate | = 10% |

In terms of the values in the formula:

$$S = 47$$
$$K = 45$$
$$t = 0.5 \text{ (183 days/365, rounded)}$$
$$s = 0.25$$
$$r = 0.10$$

Substituting these values into the equations above, we get

$$d_1 = \frac{\ln(47/45) + [0.10 + 0.5(0.25)^2]0.5}{0.25\sqrt{0.5}} = 0.6172$$

$$d_2 = 0.6172 - 0.25\sqrt{0.5} = 0.4404$$

From a normal distribution table:

$$N(0.6172) = 0.7315 \text{ and } N(0.4404) = 0.6702$$

Then:

$$C = 47 (0.7315) - 45 (e^{-(0.10)(0.5)}) (0.6702) = \$5.69$$

Exhibit 5 shows the option value as calculated from the Black-Scholes model for different assumptions concerning (1) the standard deviation, (2) the risk-free rate, and (3) the time remaining to expiration. Notice that the option price varies directly with all three factors. That is, (1) the lower (higher) the volatility, the lower (higher) the option price; (2) the lower (higher) the risk-free rate, the lower (higher) the option price; and, (3) the shorter (longer) the time remaining to expiration, the lower (higher) the option price. All of this agrees with what is shown in Exhibit 4 about the effect of a change in one of the factors on the price of a call option.

How do we determine the value of put options? There is relationship that shows the relationship among the spot price of the underlying, the call option price, and the put option price. This is called the *put-call parity relationship*. If we can calculate the fair value of a call option, the fair value of a put with the same strike price and expiration on the same stock can be calculated from the put-call parity relationship.

# Exhibit 5: Comparison of Black-Scholes Call Option Price Varying One Factor at a Time

*Base Case*
Call option:
Strike price = $45
Time remaining to expiration = 183 days
Current stock price = $47
Expected price volatility = standard deviation = 25%
Risk-free rate = 10%

### Holding All Factors Constant Except Expected Price Volatility

| Expected Price Volatility | Call Option Price |
|---|---|
| 15% | 4.69 |
| 20 | 5.16 |
| 25 (base case) | 5.69 |
| 30 | 6.25 |
| 35 | 6.83 |
| 40 | 7.42 |

### Holding All Factors Constant Except the Risk-Free Rate

| Risk-Free Interest Rate | Call Option Price |
|---|---|
| 7% | 5.27 |
| 8 | 5.41 |
| 9 | 5.55 |
| 10 (base case) | 5.69 |
| 11 | 5.83 |
| 12 | 5.98 |
| 13 | 6.13 |

### Holding All Factors Constant Except Time Remaining to Expiration

| Time Remaining to Expiration | Call Option Price |
|---|---|
| 30 days | 2.82 |
| 60 | 3.52 |
| 91 | 4.14 |
| 183 (base case) | 5.69 |
| 273 | 7.00 |

## Sensitivity of the Option Price to a Change in Factors

In employing options in investment strategies, a manager would like to know how sensitive the price of an option is to a change in any one of the factors that affect its price. Let's discuss the sensitivity of a call option's price to changes in the price of the underlying, the time to expiration, and expected price volatility.

### The Call Option Price and the Price of the Underlying
A manager employing options for risk management wants to know how the option position will change as the price of the underlying changes. Exhibit 6 shows the theoretical price of a call option based on the price of the underlying. The horizontal axis is the price of the underlying at any point in time. The vertical axis is the theoretical

call option price. The shape of the curve representing the theoretical price of a call option, given the price of the underlying, would be the same regardless of the actual option pricing model used. In particular, the relationship between the price of the underlying and the theoretical call option price is convex.

The line from the origin to the strike price on the horizontal axis in Exhibit 6 is the intrinsic value of the call option when the price of the underlying is less than the strike price, since the intrinsic value is zero. The 45-degree line extending from the horizontal axis is the intrinsic value of the call option once the price of the underlying exceeds the strike price. The reason is that the intrinsic value of the call option will increase by the same dollar amount as the increase in the price of the underlying. For example, if the strike price is $100 and the price of the underlying increases from $100 to $101, the intrinsic value will increase by $1. If the price of the underlying increases from $101 to $110, the intrinsic value of the option will increase from $1 to $10. Thus, the slope of the line representing the intrinsic value after the strike price is reached is 1. Since the theoretical call option price is shown by the convex curve, the difference between the theoretical call option price and the intrinsic value at any given price for the underlying is the time value of the option.

Exhibit 7 shows the theoretical call option price, but with a tangent line drawn at the price p*. The tangent line in the exhibit can be used to estimate what the new option price will be (and therefore what the change in the option price will be) if the price of the underlying changes. Because of the convexity of the relationship between the option price and the price of the underlying, the tangent line closely approximates the new option price for a small change in the price of the underlying. For large changes, however, the tangent line does not provide as good an approximation of the new option price.

## Exhibit 6: Theoretical Call Price and Price of Underlying

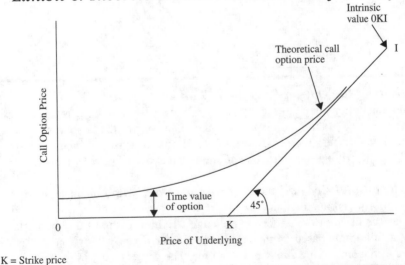

K = Strike price

## Exhibit 7: Estimating the Theoretical Option Price

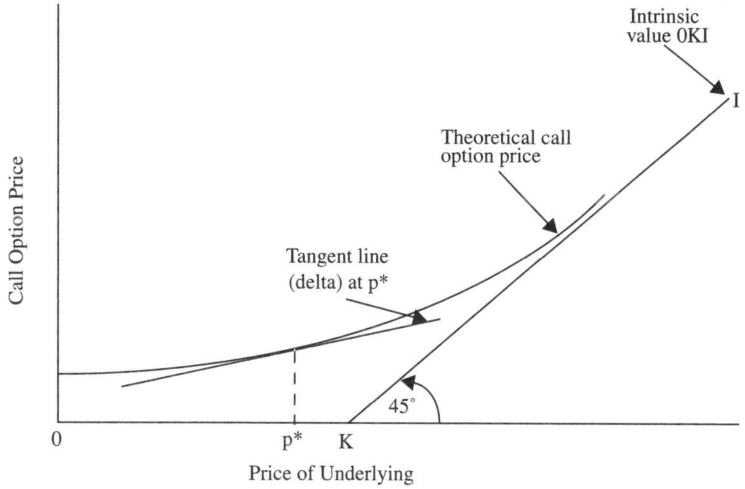

K = Strike price

---

The slope of the tangent line shows how the theoretical call option price will change for small changes in the price of the underlying. The slope of the tangent line is popularly referred to as the *delta* of the option. Specifically,

$$\text{Delta} = \frac{\text{Change in price of call option}}{\text{Change in price of underlying}}$$

For example, a delta of 0.4 means that a $1 change in the price of the underlying will change the price of the call option by approximately $0.40.

Exhibit 8 shows the curve of the theoretical call option price with three tangent lines drawn. The steeper the slope of the tangent line, the greater the delta. When an option is deep out of the money (that is, the price of the underlying is substantially below the strike price), the tangent line is nearly flat (see line 1 in Exhibit 8). This means that delta is close to zero. To understand why, consider a call option with a strike price of $100 and two months to expiration. If the price of the underlying is $20, the option price would not increase by much, if anything, should the price of the underlying increase by $1, from $20 to $21.

For a call option that is deep in the money, the delta will be close to 1. That is, the call option price will increase almost dollar for dollar with an increase in the price of the underlying. In Exhibit 8, the slope of the tangent line approaches the slope of the intrinsic value line after the strike price. As we stated earlier, the slope of that line is 1.

Thus, the delta for a call option varies from zero (for call options deep out of the money) to 1 (for call options deep in the money). The delta for a call option at the money is approximately 0.5.

## Exhibit 8: Theoretical Option Price with Three Tangents

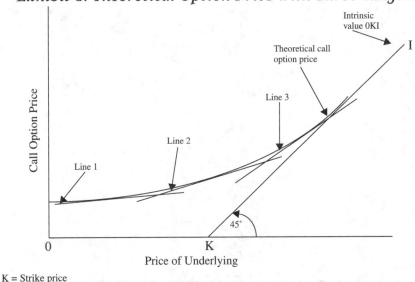

K = Strike price

The curvature of the convex relationship can also be approximated. This is the rate of change of delta as the price of the underlying changes. The measure is commonly referred to as *gamma* and is defined as follows:

$$\text{Gamma} = \frac{\text{Change in delta}}{\text{Change in price of underlying}}$$

**The Call Option Price and Time to Expiration** All other factors constant, the longer the time to expiration, the greater the option price. Since each day the option moves closer to the expiration date, the time to expiration decreases. The *theta* of an option measures the change in the option price as the time to expiration decreases, or equivalently, it is a measure of time decay. Theta is measured as follows:

$$\text{Theta} = \frac{\text{Change in price of option}}{\text{Decrease in time to expiration}}$$

Assuming that the price of the underlying does not change (which means that the intrinsic value of the option does not change), theta measures how quickly the time value of the option changes as the option moves toward expiration. Buyers of options prefer a low theta so that the option price does not decline quickly as it moves toward the expiration date. An option writer benefits from an option that has a high theta.

**The Call Option Price and Expected Price Volatility** All other factors constant, a change in the expected price volatility will change the option price. The vega (also called kappa) of an option measures the dollar price change in the price of the option for a 1% change in the expected price volatility. That is,

$$\text{Vega} = \frac{\text{Change in option price}}{1\% \text{ change in expected price volatility}}$$

# FUTURES CONTRACTS

A *futures contract* is an agreement between two parties, a buyer and a seller, where the parties agree to transact with respect to the underlying at a predetermined price at a specified date. Both parties are obligated to perform over the life of the contract, and neither party charges a fee. Once the two parties have consummated the trade, the exchange where the futures contract is traded becomes the counterparty to the trade, thereby severing the relationship between the initial parties.

Each futures contract is accompanied by an exact description of the terms of the contract, including a description of the underlying, the contract size, settlement cycles, trading specifications, and position limits. The fact is that in the case of futures contracts, delivery is not the objective of either party because the contracts are used primarily to manage risk or costs.

The nature of the futures contract specifies a buyer and a seller who agree to buy or sell a standard quantity of the underlying at a designated future date. However, when we speak of buyers and sellers, we are simply adopting the language of the futures market, which refers to parties of the contract in terms of the future obligation they are committing themselves to. The buyer of a futures contract agrees to take delivery of the underlying and is said to be *long futures*. Long futures positions benefit when the price of the underlying rises. Since futures can be considered a substitute for a subsequent transaction in the cash market, a long futures position is comparable to holding the underlying without the financial cost of purchasing the underlying or the income that comes from holding the underlying. The seller, on the other hand, is said to be *short futures* and benefits when the price of the underlying declines.

The designated price at which the parties agree to transact is called the *futures price*. The designated date at which the parties must transact is the *settlement date* or *delivery date*. Unlike options, no money changes hands between buyer and seller at the contract's inception. However, the futures broker and the futures exchange require initial margin as a "good faith" deposit. In addition, a minimum amount of funds referred to as *maintenance margin* is required to be maintained in the corresponding futures account. The initial margin and the maintenance margin can be held in the form of short-term credit instruments.

Futures are marked-to-the-market on a daily basis. This means that daily gains or losses in the investor's position are accounted for immediately and reflected in his or her account. The daily cash flow from a futures position is called *variation margin* and essentially means that the futures contract is settled daily. Thus, the buyer of the futures contract pays when the price of the underlying falls and the seller pays when the price of the underlying rises. Variation margin differs from other forms of margin because outflows must be met with cash.

Futures contracts have a settlement cycle and there may be several contracts trading simultaneously. The contract with the closest settlement is call the *nearby futures contract* and is usually the most liquid. The next futures contract is the one that settles just after the near contract. The contract with the furthest away settlement is called the *most distant futures contract.*

## Differences between Options and Futures

The fundamental difference between futures and options is that buyer of an option (the long position) has the right but not the obligation to enter into a transaction. The option writer is obligated to transact if the buyer so desires. In contrast, both parties are obligated to perform in the case of a futures contract. In addition, to establish a position, the party who is long futures does not pay the party who is short futures. In contrast, the party long an option must make a payment to the party who is short the option in order to establish the position. The price paid is the option price.

The payout structure also differs between a futures contract and an options contract. The price of an option contract represents the cost of eliminating or modifying the risk/reward relationship of the underlying. In contrast, the payout for a futures contract is a dollar-for-dollar gain or loss for the buyer and seller. When the futures price rises, the buyer gains at the expense of the seller, while the buyer suffers a dollar-for-dollar loss when the futures price drops.

Thus, futures payout is symmetrical, while the payout for options is skewed. The maximum loss for the option buyer is the option price. The loss to the futures buyer is the full value of the contract. The option buyer has limited downside losses but retains the benefits of an increase in the value in the position of the underlying. The maximum profit that can be realized by the option writer is the option price, which is offset by significant downside exposure. The losses or gains to the buyer and seller of a futures contract are completely symmetrical. Consequently, futures can be used as a hedge against symmetric risk, while options can be used to hedge asymmetric risk.

## Features of Futures

The key elements of a futures contract include the futures price, the amount or quantity of the underlying, and the settlement or delivery date. The underlying asset of a stock index futures contract is the portfolio of stocks represented by the index.

The value of the underlying portfolio is the value of the index in a specified currency times a number called a *multiplier.* For example, if the current value of the S&P 500 index is 1100, then the seller of a December S&P 500 futures contract is theoretically obligated to deliver in December a portfolio of the 500 stocks that comprise the index. The multiplier for this contract is 500. The portfolio would have to exactly replicate the index with the weights of the stocks equal to their index weights. The current value of one futures contract is $275,000 (= $1100 \times 250$).

## Exhibit 9: Selected Equity Futures Contracts Traded in the United States

| Index Futures Contract | Index Description | Exchange | Contract Size |
|---|---|---|---|
| Standard & Poor's 500 | 500 stocks, Cap weighed | CME | Index × $250 |
| Standard & Poor's Midcap | 400 stocks, Cap weighted | CME | Index × $500 |
| Russell 2000 Index | 2000 stocks, Cap weighted | CME | Index × $500 |
| Nikkei 225 Index | 225 stocks, Price weighted | CME | Index × $5 |
| Major Market Index | 20 stocks, Price weighted | CME | Index × $500 |
| S&P 500/BARRA Growth Index | 100+ stocks, Cap weighted | CME | Index × $250 |
| Standard & Poor's BARRA Value | 300+ stocks, Cap weighted | CME | Index × $250 |
| NASDAQ 100 Index | 100 stocks, Cap weighted | CME | Index × $100 |
| IPC Stock Index | 35 stocks, Cap weighted | CME | Futures × $25 |
| NYSE Composite Index | 2600+ stocks, Cap weighted | NYFE | Index × $500 |

However, because of the problems associated with delivering a portfolio of 500 stocks that exactly replicate the underlying index, stock index futures substitute cash delivery for physical delivery. At final settlement, the futures price equals the spot price and the value of a futures contract is the actual market value of the underlying replicating portfolio that represents the stock index. The contract is marked-to-market based on the settlement price, which is the spot price, and the contract settles.

Exhibit 9 provides a list of selected stock index futures traded in the United States.

## Pricing Stock Index Futures

Futures contracts are priced based on the spot price and cost of carry considerations. For equity contracts these include the cost of financing a position in the underlying asset, the dividend yield on the underlying stocks, and the time to settlement of the futures contract. The theoretical futures price is derived from the spot price adjusted for the cost of carry. This can be confirmed using risk-free arbitrage arguments.

The logic of the pricing model is that the purchase of a futures contract can be looked at as a temporary substitute for a transaction in the cash market at a later date. Moreover, futures contracts are not assets to be purchased and no money changes hands when the agreement is made. Futures contracts are agreements between two parties that establish the terms of a later transaction. It is these facts that lead us to a pricing relationship between futures contracts and the underlying. The seller of a futures contract is ultimately responsible for delivering the underlying and will demand compensation for incurring the cost of holding it. Thus, the futures price will reflect the cost of financing the underlying. However, the buyer of the futures contract does not hold the underlying and therefore does not receive the dividend. The futures price must be adjusted downward to take this into consideration. The adjustment of the yield for the cost of financing is what is called the *net cost of carry*. The futures price is then based on the net cost of carry, which is the cost of financing adjusted for the yield on the underlying. That is,

Futures price = Spot price + Cost of financing − Dividend yield

The borrowing or financing rate is an interest rate on a money market instrument and the yield in the case of stock index futures is the dividend yield on a portfolio of stocks that represent the stock index. The theoretical futures price derived from this process is a model of the fair value of the futures contract. It is the price that defines a no-arbitrage condition. The no-arbitrage condition is the futures price at which sellers are prepared to sell and buyers are prepared to buy, but no risk-free profit is possible.

The theoretical futures price expressed mathematically depends on the treatment of dividends. For individual equities with quarterly dividend payout, the theoretical futures price can be expressed as the spot price adjusted for the present value of expected dividends over the life of the contract and the cost of financing. The expression is given below as:

$$F(t,T) = [S(t) - D] \times [1 + R(t,T)]$$

where

$F(t,T)$ = futures price at time $t$ for a contract that settles in the future at time $T$

$S(t)$ = current spot price

$D$ = present value of dividends expected to be received over the life of the contract

$R(t,T)$ = borrowing rate for a loan with the same time to maturity as the futures settlement date

For example, if the current price of the S&P 500 stock index is 1175, the borrowing rate is 6%, the time to settlement is 60 days, and the index is expected to yield 2.071%. An annualized dividend yield of 2.071% corresponds to 4 index points when the S&P 500 stock index is 1175:

$$1175 \times [0.02071 \times (60/365)] = 4 \text{ index points}$$

The theoretical futures price can be calculated as follows:

$$D = 4/(1 + 0.06)^{60/365} = 3.96$$

$$R = (1 + 0.06)^{60/365} - 1 = 0.009624 \text{ or } 0.9624\%$$

$$F(t,60) = [1175 - 3.96] \times 1.009624 = 1182.31$$

If the actual futures price is above or below 1182.31, then risk-free arbitrage is possible. For actual futures prices greater than fair value, the futures contract is overvalued. Arbitrageurs will sell the futures contract, borrow enough funds to purchase the underlying stock index, and hold the position until fair value is restored or until the settlement date of the futures contract.

If, for example, we assume the actual futures price is 1188, then the following positions would lead to risk-free arbitrage:

- sell the overvalued futures at 1188
- borrow an amount equivalent to 1175
- purchase a stock portfolio that replicates the index for the equivalent of 1175

The position can be unwound at the settlement date in 60 days at no risk to the arbitrageur. At the settlement date, the futures settlement price equals the spot price. Assume the spot price is unchanged at 1175. Then,

- collect 4 in dividends
- settle the short futures position by delivering the index to the buyer for 1175
- repay 1186.31 ($1175 \times 1.009624$) to satisfy the loan (remember the interest rate for the 60 days is 0.9624%)

The net gain is [1188 + 4] − 1186.31 = 5.69. That is, the arbitrageur "earned" 5.69 index points or 48 basis points (5.69/1175) without risk or without making any investment. This activity would continue until the price of the futures converged on fair value.

It does not matter what the settlement price for the index is at the settlement date. This can be clearly shown by treating the futures position and stock position separately. The futures position delivers the difference between the original futures price and the settlement price or 1188 − 1175, which equals 13 index points. The long stock position earned only the dividends and no capital gain. The cost of financing the position in the stock is 11.31 and the net return to the combined short futures and long stock position is 13(futures) + 4(stock) less the 11.31 cost of financing, which is a net return of 5.69. Now consider what happens if the spot price is at any other level at the settlement date. Exhibit 10 shows the cash flows associated with the arbitrage. We can see from the results that regardless of the movement of the spot price, the arbitrage profit is preserved.

For actual futures prices less than fair value, the futures contract is undervalued. Arbitrageurs will buy the futures contract, short or sell the underlying, lend the proceeds, and hold the position until fair value is restored or until settlement date of the futures contract. If, for example, we assume the actual futures price is 1180, then the following positions would lead to risk-free arbitrage:

- buy the undervalued futures at 1180
- sell or short the stock index at 1175 and collect the proceeds
- lend the proceeds from the stock transaction at 6%

### Exhibit 10: Arbitrage Cash Flows
### Overvalued Futures*

| Futures Stock Index Settlement Price | Futures Cash Flows | Stock Cash Flows | Costs | Profit |
|---|---|---|---|---|
| 1200 | 1188 – 1200 = –12 | 25 + 4 = 29 | 11.31 | 5.69 |
| 1190 | 1188 – 1190 = –2 | 15 + 4 = 19 | 11.31 | 5.69 |
| 1188 | 1188 – 1188 = 0 | 13 + 4 = 17 | 11.31 | 5.69 |
| 1180 | 1188 – 1180 = 8 | 5 + 4 = 9 | 11.31 | 5.69 |
| 1175 | 1188 – 1175 = 13 | 0 + 4 = 4 | 11.31 | 5.69 |
| 1160 | 1188 – 1160 = 28 | –15 + 4 = –11 | 11.31 | 5.69 |

\* Short futures at 1188

### Undervalued Futures**

| Futures Stock Index Settlement Price | Futures Cash Flows | Stock Cash Flows | Interest Income | Profit |
|---|---|---|---|---|
| 1200 | 1200 – 1180 = 20 | –25 – 4 = –29 | 11.31 | 2.31 |
| 1190 | 1190 – 1180 = 10 | –15 – 4 = –19 | 11.31 | 2.31 |
| 1188 | 1188 – 1180 = 8 | –13 – 4 = –17 | 11.31 | 2.31 |
| 1180 | 1180 – 1180 = 0 | –5 – 4 = –9 | 11.31 | 2.31 |
| 1175 | 1175 – 1180 = –5 | 0 – 4 = –4 | 11.31 | 2.31 |
| 1160 | 1160 – 1180 = –20 | 15 – 4 = 11 | 11.31 | 2.31 |

\*\* Buy futures at 1180

Once again the position can be unwound at the settlement date at no risk to the arbitrageur. At that time the futures settlement price equals the spot price. Regardless of the settlement price of the index, the arbitrage is preserved in this case as well. Exhibit 10 presents a sample of settlement price outcomes. The following process applies to the arbitrage regardless of the direction of the stock market:

- settle the short stock position by taking futures delivery of the stock index
- pay the 4 index points in dividends due the index
- receive the proceeds from the loan (remember the term interest rate is 0.9624%)

In this example, the arbitrageur "earned" 20 basis points (2.31/1175) or 2.31 index points without risk or without making any investment. This activity would continue until the price of the futures converged on fair value.

The theoretical futures price can also be expressed mathematically based on a security with a known dividend yield. For equities that pay out a constant dividend over the life of a futures contract, this rendition of the model is appropriate. This may apply to stock index futures contracts where the underlying is an equity index of a large number of stocks. Rather than calculating every dividend, the cumulative dividend pay out or the weighted-average dividend produces a constant and known dividend yield. The cost of carry valuation model is modified to reflect the behavior of dividends. This is expressed in the following equation:

$$F(t,T) = S(t) \times [1 + R(t,T) - Y(t,T)]$$

where $Y(t,T)$ is the dividend yield on the underlying over the life of the futures contract and $F(t,T)$, $S(t)$, and $R(t,T)$ are as defined earlier.

For example, if the current price of a stock is 1175, the borrowing rate is 6%, the time to settlement is 60 days, and the annualized dividend yield is 1.38%, the theoretical futures price can be calculated as follows:

$$Y = (1 + 0.0138)^{60/365} - 1 = 0.002256 \text{ or } 0.2256\%$$

$$R = (1 + 0.06)^{60/365} - 1 = 0.009624 \text{ or } 0.9624\%$$

$$F(t,60) = 1175 \times [1 + (0.009624 - 0.002256] = 1183.66$$

In practice, it is important to remember to use the borrowing rate and dividend yield for the term of the contract and not the annual rates. The arbitrage conditions outlined above still hold in this case. The model is specified differently, but the same outcome is possible. When the actual futures price deviates from the theoretical price suggested by the futures pricing model, arbitrage would be possible and likely. The existence of risk-free arbitrage profits will attract arbitrageurs.

In practice, there are several factors that may violate the assumptions of the futures valuation model. Because of these factors, arbitrage must be carried out with some degree of uncertainty and the fair value futures price is not a single price, but actually a range of prices where the upper and lower prices act as boundaries around an arbitrage-free zone. Furthermore, the violation of various assumptions can produce mispricing and risk that reduce arbitrage opportunities.

The futures price ought to gravitate toward fair value when there is a viable and active arbitrage mechanism. Arbitrage activity will only take place beyond the upper and lower limits established by transaction and other costs, uncertain cash flows, and divergent borrowing and lending rates among participants. The variability of the spread between the spot price and futures price, known as the *basis*, is a consequence of mispricing due to changes in the variables that influence the fair value.

The practical aspects of pricing produce a range of prices. This means that the basis can move around without offering a profit motive for arbitrageurs. The perspective of arbitrageurs in the equity futures markets is based on dollar profit but can be viewed in terms of an interest rate. The borrowing or financing rate found in the cost of carry valuation formula assumes borrowing and lending rates are the same. In practice, however, borrowing rates are almost always higher than lending rates. Thus, the model will yield different values depending on the respective borrowing and lending rates facing the user. Every futures price corresponds to an interest rate. We can manipulate the formula and solve for the rate implied by the futures price, which is called the *implied futures rate*. For each market participant there is a theoretical fair value range defined by its respective borrowing and lending rates and transaction costs.

# OTC EQUITY DERIVATIVES

An OTC equity derivative can be delivered on a stand-alone basis or as part of a structured product. Structured products involve packaging standard or exotic options, equity swaps, or equity-linked debt into a single product in any combination to meet the risk/return objectives of the investor and may represent an alternative to the cash market even when cash instruments are available.

The three basic components of OTC equity derivatives are OTC options, equity swaps, and equity-linked debt. These components offer an array of product structures that can assist investors in developing and implementing investment strategies that respond to a changing financial world. The rapidly changing investment climate has fundamentally changed investor attitudes toward the use of derivative products. It is no longer a question of what can an investor gain from the use of OTC derivatives, but how much is sacrificed by avoiding this marketplace. OTC derivatives can assist the investor with cost minimization, diversification, hedging, asset allocation, and risk management

Before we provide a product overview, let's look at counterparty risk. For exchange listed derivative products counterparty or credit risk is minimal because of the clearing house associated with the exchange. However, for OTC products there is counterparty risk. For parties taking a position where performance of both parties is required, both parties are exposed to counterparty risk. The OTC market has incorporated a variety of terms into the contractual agreement between counterparties to address the issue of credit risk. These include netting arrangements, position limits, the use of collateral, recouponing, credit triggers, and the establishment of Derivatives Product Companies (DPCs).

*Netting arrangements* between counterparties are used in master agreements specifying that in the event of default, the bottom line is the net payment owed across all contractual agreements between the two counterparties. *Position limits* may be imposed on a particular counterparty according to the cumulative nature of their positions and creditworthiness. As the OTC market has grown, the creditworthiness of customers has become more diverse. Consequently, dealers are requiring some counterparties to furnish collateral in the form of a liquid short-term credit instrument. *Recouponing* involves periodically changing the coupon such that the marked-to-market value of the position is zero. For long-term OTC agreements, a *credit trigger provision* allows the dealer to have the position cash settled if the counterparty's credit rating falls below investment grade. Finally, dealers are establishing DPCs as separate business entities to maintain high credit ratings that are crucial in competitively pricing OTC products.

## OTC Options

OTC options can be classified as first generation and second generation options. The latter are called *exotic options*. We describe each type of OTC option below.

### First Generation of OTC Options

The basic type of first generation OTC options either extends the standardized structure of an existing listed option or created an option on stocks, stock baskets, or stock indexes without listed options or futures. Thus, OTC options were first used to modify one or more of the features of listed options: the strike price, maturity, size, exercise type (American or European), and delivery mechanism. The terms were tailored to the specific needs of the investor. For example, the strike price can be any level, the maturity date at any time, the contract of any size, the exercise type American or European, the underlying can be a stock, a stock portfolio, or an equity index or a foreign equity index, and the settlement can be physical, in cash or a combination.

An example of how OTC options can differ from listed options is exemplified by an Asian option. Listed options are either European or American in structure relating to the timing of exercise. Asian options are options with a pay-out that is dependent on the average price of the spot price over the life of the option. Due to the averaging process involved, the volatility of the spot price is reduced. Thus, Asian options are cheaper than similar European or American options.

The first generation of OTC options offered flexible solutions to investment situations that listed options did not. For example, hedging strategies using the OTC market allow the investor to achieve customized total risk protection for a specific time horizon. The first generation of OTC options allow investors to fine tune their traditional equity investment strategies through customizing strike prices, and maturities, and choosing any underlying equity security or portfolio of securities. Investors could now improve the management of risk through customized hedging strategies or enhance returns through customized buy writes. In addition, investors could invest in foreign stocks without the need to own them, profit from an industry downturn without the need to short stocks.

### Exotics: Second Generation OTC Options

The second generation of OTC equity options includes a set of products that have more complex payoff characteristics than standard American or European call and put options. These second-generation options are sometimes referred to as "exotic" options and are essentially options with specific rules that govern the payoff.[3] Exotic option structures can be created on a stand-alone basis or as part of a broader financing package such as an attachment to a bond issue.

Some OTC option structures are path dependent, which means that the value of the option to some extent depends on the price pattern of the underlying asset over the life of the option. In fact, the survival of some options, such as barrier options, depends on this price pattern. Other examples of path dependent options include Asian options, lookback options, and reset options. Another group

---

[3] For a description of exotic options, see Chapter 10 in Bruce M. Collins and Frank J. Fabozzi, *Derivatives and Equity Portfolio Management* (New Hope, PA: Frank J. Fabozzi Associates, 1999).

of OTC option structures has properties similar to step functions. They have fixed singular payoffs when a particular condition is met. Examples of this include digital or binary options and contingent options. A third group of options is classified as multivariate because the payoff is related to more than one underlying asset. Examples of this group include a general category of rainbow options such as spread options and basket options.

Competitive market makers are now prepared to offer investors a broad range of derivative products that satisfy the specific requirements of investors. The fastest growing portion of this market pertaining to equities involves products with option-like characteristics on major stock indexes or stock portfolios.

Exhibit 11 provides a partial listing of exotic options together with a brief description, an accompanying equity investment strategy application, and a comment on pricing. The list of option structures is hardly exhaustive and is intended only to provide an introduction to some of the more common structures.

## Exhibit 11: Description of Some Basic Exotic Options

| Option Structure | Description | Use | Pricing Comment |
|---|---|---|---|
| Knockout call | One of a class of barrier options Option is canceled if the spot price violates barrier target price | Overwriting | Less expensive than standard call option |
| Knockout put | One of a class of barrier options Option is canceled if the spot price goes above barrier target | Hedging | Less expensive than standard put option |
| Compound Option | Option on an option, Call on a put Gives owner the option to buy the put | Hedging Speculating | Less expensive than standard call option |
| Spread Option | Payout depends on the difference in performance between two assets | Asset Allocation | Large risk premium due to correlation |
| Lookback Option | Option that gives the right to holder to buy or sell underlying at best price attained over the life of the option | Equity Exposure to volatile sectors | More expensive than standard options Market timing |
| Quanto Option | Quantity-adjusted option. Pay-out depends on underlying price and size in proportional to price. | Access to Foreign Markets with currency hedge. | Pricing depends on correlation of exchange Rate and spot price. |
| Chooser Option | Holder must choose to set the option as a call or put at some specific time | Similar to straddle | Less expensive than straddle |
| Asian Option | Pay-out depends on average price of the underlying over a specified time period | Allows participation on average return | Less expensive than standard options Liability management |
| Basket Option | Similar to index options, Option written on basket of stocks | Hedging custom equity portfolios | Less expensive than portfolio of options |
| Binary Option | Cash or nothing | Market timing Asset or nothing | Less expensive than standard option |

Source: Exhibit 3 in Chapter 10 of Bruce M. Collins and Frank J. Fabozzi, *Derivatives and Equity Portfolio Management* (New Hope, PA: Frank J. Fabozzi Associates, 1999).

## *Exhibit 12: Equity Swaps*

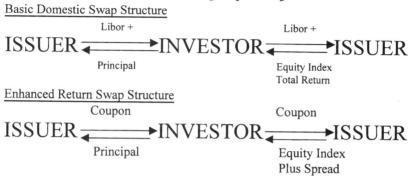

Basic Domestic Swap Structure

ISSUER ⟷ INVESTOR ⟷ ISSUER

Libor +

Principal

Libor +

Equity Index
Total Return

Enhanced Return Swap Structure

ISSUER ⟷ INVESTOR ⟷ ISSUER

Coupon

Principal

Coupon

Equity Index
Plus Spread

Source: Exhibit 9 in Chapter 10 of Bruce M. Collins and Frank J. Fabozzi,
*Derivatives and Equity Portfolio Management* (New Hope, PA: Frank J. Fabozzi Associates, 1999).

## Equity Swaps

Equity swaps are agreements between two counterparties which provide for the periodic exchange of a schedule of cash flows over a specified time period where at least one of the two payments is linked to the performance of an equity index, a basket of stocks, or a single stock. In a standard or plain vanilla equity swap one counterparty agrees to pay the other the total return to an equity index in exchange for receiving either the total return of another asset or a fixed or floating interest rate. All payments are based on a fixed notional amount and payments are made over a fixed time period.

Equity swap structures are very flexible with maturities ranging from a few months to 10 years. The returns of virtually any asset can be swapped for another without incurring the costs associated with a transaction in the cash market. Payment schedules can be denominated in any currency irrespective of the equity asset and payments can be exchanged monthly, quarterly, annually, or at maturity. The equity asset can be any equity index or portfolio of stocks, and denominated in any currency, hedged or unhedged.

Variations of the plain vanilla equity swap include: international equity swaps where the equity return is linked to an international equity index; currency-hedged swaps where the swap is structured to eliminate currency risk; and call swaps where the equity payment is paid only if the equity index appreciates (depreciation will not result in a payment from the counterparty receiving the equity return to the other counterparty because of call protection).

A basic swap structure is illustrated in Exhibit 12. In this case, the investor owns a short-term credit instrument that yields LIBOR plus a spread. The investor then enters into a swap to exchange LIBOR plus the spread for the total return to an equity index. The counterparty pays the total return to the index in exchange for LIBOR plus a spread. Assuming the equity index is the Nikkei 225, a U.S. investor could swap dollar-denominated LIBOR plus a spread for cash flows from the total return to the Nikkei denominated in yen or U.S. dollars. The index could be any foreign or domestic equity index. A swap could also be structured to generate superior returns if the financing instrument in the swap yields a higher return than LIBOR.

Equity swaps have a wide variety of applications including asset allocation, accessing international markets, enhancing equity returns, hedging equity exposure, and synthetically shorting stocks.

An example of an equity swap is a 1-year agreement where the counterparty agrees to pay the investor the total return to the S&P 500 Index in exchange for dollar-denominated LIBOR on a quarterly basis. The investor would pay LIBOR plus a spread × 91/360 × notional amount. This type of equity swap is the economic equivalent of financing a long position in the S&P 500 Index at a spread to LIBOR. The advantages of using the swap are no transaction costs, no sales or dividend withholding tax, and no tracking error or basis risk versus the index.

The basic mechanics of equity swaps are the same regardless of the structure. However, the rules governing the exchange of payments may differ. For example, a U.S. investor wanting to diversify internationally can enter into a swap and, depending on the investment objective, exchange payments on a currency-hedged basis. If the investment objective is to reduce U.S. equity exposure and increase Japanese equity exposure, for example, a swap could be structured to exchange the total returns to the S&P 500 Index for the total returns to the Nikkei 225 Index. If, however, the investment objective is to gain access to the Japanese equity market, a swap can be structured to exchange LIBOR plus a spread for the total returns to the Nikkei 225 Index. This is an example of diversifying internationally and the cash flows can be denominated in either yen or dollars. The advantages of entering into an equity swap to obtain international diversification are that the investor exposure is devoid of tracking error, and the investor incurs no sales tax, custodial fees, withholding fees, or market impact associated with entering and exiting a market. This swap is the economic equivalent of being long the Nikkei 225 financed at a spread to LIBOR at a fixed exchange rate.

## Equity-Linked Debt Investments

*Equity-linked debt* (ELD) investments are typically privately placed debt instruments. They differ from conventional debt instruments because the principal, coupon payment, or both are linked to the performance of an established equity index, a portfolio of stocks, or an individual stock. Consistent with other OTC equity derivative securities, equity-linked products have extremely flexible structures. For example, the equity component of the product can assume the characteristics of a call or a put or some combination. The payout can be more complex mixing exotic-type option payout with a bond.

In addition to providing flexible structures, equity-linked products also offer the investor the potential for higher returns than conventional debt instruments of similar credit risk. Other characteristics include: more volatile cash flows, the principal guaranteed by issuers with investment grade credit, and the avoidance of certain regulatory restrictions that prevent investors from entering into futures contracts, options, or swap agreements. Equity-linked products are typically longer-term investments and therefore have limited liquidity.

Equity-linked debt investments are also referred to as equity-linked notes. Examples of these are Equity Participation Notes (EPNs), Stock Upside Notes (SUNs), Structured Upside Participating Equity Receipt (SUPER), and Synthetic High Income Equity Linked Security (SHIELDS). Equity-linked notes are issued by banks, corporations, and government sponsored enterprises, and have maturities ranging from 1 year to 10 years. The coupon can be fixed or floating, linked to an equity index, a portfolio of stocks, or a single stock and denominated in any currency. The equity-linked payment is typically equal to 100% of the equity appreciation, and redemption at maturity is the par value of the bond plus the equity appreciation.

The conventional ELD instrument is simply a portfolio consisting of a zero-coupon bond and an index call option. This structure can be extended to include a put or an exotic option. The cash flows associated with an ELD structure are as follows. At issuance, the investor purchases the note, which represents the initial cash flow. Periodic cash flows are derived exclusively from the performance of the linked equity index. For example, if the index appreciated 10% for the year and equity participation is 100%, then assuming that the notional amount is $1 million, the investor would receive $100,000 as a periodic cash flow. The final cash flow includes the return of principal and the final equity payment.

Often, however, cash flows are subject to a cap, which limits the upside participation. SUNs, for example, provide 100% of principal at maturity and pay an annual coupon based on 133% of the year-over-year appreciation in the S&P 500 index subject to a cap of 10%. Thus, the maximum appreciation is 13.3% per annum. If an investor believes the S&P 500 will appreciate by more, this is not the appropriate investment vehicle.

The use of an ELD is particularly attractive to domestic insurance companies subject to risk-based capital guidelines, which mandate higher capital requirements for investing in equity than for debt. ELDs are carried as debt, but have their performance linked to equity. Thus, insurance companies can maintain the capital requirements associated with debt instruments and still obtain equity market exposure. Pension funds also can benefit by using ELDs to gain access to foreign equity markets. Direct foreign equity investments subject pension funds to withholding taxes. The use of ELD structures, where the equity component is a foreign index, allows pension funds to avoid withholding taxes. The note has the same structure flexibility as conventional ELD instruments and can also include a currency hedge.

An example of such an equity-linked note is one that combines a zero-coupon bond and an at-the-money call option on the FTSE-100 Index. The redemption value of the note is the higher of par value or the product of par value times the ratio of the value of the FTSE-100 Index at maturity and its value when the note is purchased. This equity-linked note creates a debt instrument with payments based on the returns to the FTSE-100 Index, while eliminating all unwanted risks and costs associated with holding U.K. equities.

As in the case of OTC options, equity-linked debt structures are extremely flexible. The investor can decide upon the amount of equity participation, whether to include a coupon or not, whether to target levels of equity appreciation over the life of the product when the target is realized, or whether to create a synthetic convertible bond.

# QUESTIONS

1. What are the four roles of derivatives in portfolio management?

2. a. What is the difference between a put option and a call option?
   b. What is the difference between an American option and a European option?
   c. Why do stock index options involve cash settlement rather than delivery of the underlying stocks?

3. a. Suppose a call option on a stock has a strike price of $80 and a cost of $12, and suppose you buy the call. Identify the profit at the expiration date for each of these values of the underlying stock: $35, $80, $110, $200.
   b. Suppose you had sold the call option in part a. What would your profit be at the expiration date for each of those stock prices?

4. Suppose you bought an index call option for 5.50 that has a strike price of 200 and that at expiration you exercised it. Suppose, too, that, at the time you exercised the call option, the index has a value of 240.

   a. If the index option has a multiple of $100, how much money does the writer of this option pay you?
   b. What profit did you realize from buying this call option?

5. a. Suppose the current price of a stock is $46. A call option on that stock with a strike price of $50 is selling for $9. What is the intrinsic value and time premium of this call option?
   b. Suppose the current price of a stock is $84. A put option on that stock with a strike price of $95 is selling for $13. What is the intrinsic value and time premium of this put option.

6. a. What is the time premium of an out-of-the money option?
   b. What is the time premium of an option at the expiration date?

7. "The option price depends on the volatility of the underlying stock. Since capital market theory asserts that the appropriate measure of volatility is a stock's beta, then the option price should depend on the stock's beta." Explain why you agree or disagree with this statement.

8. a. Assuming the values below for a European call option, calculate the theoretical option price using the Black-Scholes model:

| | | |
|---|---|---|
| Strike price | = | $100 |
| Current stock price | = | $100 |
| Dividend | = | $0 |

| Risk-free rate | = | 8% |
|---|---|---|
| Expected price volatility | = | 20% |
| Time to expiration | = | 91 days |

b. What is the intrinsic value and time premium for this call option?

9. For the call option in the previous question, what would be the theoretical option price, intrinsic value, and time premium if:
   a. The current stock price is $55 instead of $100?
   b. The current stock price is $150 instead of $100?

10. a. Calculate the option value for a two-period European call option with the following terms:

| Current price of underlying asset | = | $100 |
|---|---|---|
| Strike price | = | $10 |
| One-period risk-free rate | = | 5% |

   The stock price can either go up or down by 10% at the end of one period.
   b. Recalculate the value for the option when the stock price can move either up or down by 50% at the end of one period. Compare your answer with the calculated value in part a. Why is the answer different from what you might have expected?

11. a. What does the delta of an option measure?
    b. Why would you expect that the delta of a deep out-of-the-money call option would be close to zero?
    c. Why is the delta of an option not constant over the life of the option?
    d. What is meant by the gamma of an option?
    e. What is the theta of an option measure?
    f. A seller of a call option would prefer an option with a low theta. Do you agree with this statement?

12. a. How do margin requirements in the futures market differ from margin requirements in the cash market?
    b. What is the difference between initial margin and maintenance margin?

13. Suppose that the S&P 500 index is trading at 1380 and that the expected cash dividend yield is 1.9% for the 90 days. Assume also that the investor can borrow at a rate of 5% per annum.
    a. What is the borrowing rate for 90 days given an annual borrowing rate of 5%?
    b. What is the dividend in index points for the next 90 days if the expected cash dividend yield for the next 90 days is 1.9%?
    c. What is the theoretical value of an S&P 500 futures contract that settles in 90 days?

d. Given your answer in part c, if the S&P 500 futures contract settling in 90 days is selling for 1400, the contract is overvalued. What position would you take to realize the arbitrage opportunity?

e. What is the arbitrage profit that can be realized if the futures contract is trading at 1400?

f. Show that if at the settlement date any of the prices for the S&P 500 cash index shown in the table below are realized, the arbitrage profit found in part e will be realized. (Note: at the settlement date the futures price is equal to the cash market price.) Use the table below to demonstrate this.

| Future price at settlement date | Futures cash flows | Stocks cash flows | Interest cost | Profit |
|---|---|---|---|---|
| 1420 | | | | |
| 1410 | | | | |
| 1400 | | | | |
| 1380 | | | | |
| 1350 | | | | |
| 1330 | | | | |

g. Given your answer in part c, if the S&P 500 futures contract settling in 90 days is selling for 1382 the contract is undervalued. What position would you take to realize the arbitrage opportunity?

h. What is the arbitrage profit that can be realized if the futures contract is trading at 1382?

i. Show that if at the settlement date any of the prices for the S&P 500 cash index shown in the table below are realized, that the arbitrage profit found in part e will be realized. (At the settlement date the futures price is equal to the cash market price.) Use the table below to demonstrate this.

| Future price at settlement date | Futures cash flows | Stocks cash flows | Interest income | Profit |
|---|---|---|---|---|
| 1420 | | | | |
| 1410 | | | | |
| 1400 | | | | |
| 1380 | | | | |
| 1350 | | | | |
| 1330 | | | | |

14. a. Why is there counterparty risk in over-the-counter derivatives?
    b. Is the seller of an OTC option exposed to counterparty risk?

15. a. What is an equity swap?
    b. What is an equity-linked debt instrument?

# Chapter 13

# Applications of Derivatives to Equity Portfolio Management*

In the previous chapter we described the basic characteristics of the different types of equity derivatives. We identified four primary roles for derivatives: (1) to modify the risk characteristics of an investment portfolio; (2) to enhance the expected return of a portfolio; (3) to reduce transaction costs associated with managing a portfolio; and, (4) to circumvent regulatory obstacles. In this chapter, we will discuss several basic applications of these instruments to equity portfolio management.

## PORTFOLIO APPLICATIONS OF LISTED OPTIONS

Investors can use the listed options market to address a range of investment problems. We'll discuss the use of OTC options later. Advantages of listed options relative to OTC options are that they provide accurate and consistent information about pricing and virtually eliminate credit risk. Moreover, because of these characteristics and the standardization of products, listed options often have low transaction costs and moderate to high liquidity. The issue of transaction costs and liquidity can play an important role in the decision to use derivatives as part of the investment process.

### Risk Management Strategies

Risk management in the context of equity portfolio management focuses on price risk. Consequently, the strategies discussed here in some way address the risk of a price decline or a loss due to adverse price movement. Options can be used to create asymmetric risk exposures across all or part of the core equity portfolio. This allows the investor to hedge downside risk at a fixed cost with a specific limit to losses should the market turn down.

The most common strategy for risk management is a *protective put buying strategy*. This strategy is used by investors who currently hold a long position in the underlying security or investors who desire upside exposure and downside protection. The motivation is either to hedge some or all of the total risk. Index put options hedge mostly market risk, while put options on an individual stock hedge the total risk associated with a specific stock. This allows portfolio managers to use protective put strategies for separating tactical and strategic strategies.

---

* This chapter is adapted from various chapters in Bruce M. Collins and Frank J. Fabozzi, *Derivatives and Equity Portfolio Management* (New Hope, PA: Frank J. Fabozzi Associates, 1999).

Consider, for example, a manager who is concerned about non-financial events increasing the level of risk in the marketplace. Furthermore, assume the manager is satisfied with the core portfolio holdings and the strategic mix. Put options could be employed as a tactical risk reduction strategy designed to preserve capital and still maintain strategic targets for portfolio returns.

Thus, any investor concerned about downside risk is a candidate for a protective put strategy. Nonetheless, protective put strategies may not be suitable for all investors. The value of protective put strategies, however, is that they provide the investor with the ability to invest in volatile stocks with a degree of desired insurance and unlimited profit potential over the life of the strategy.

The protective put involves the purchase of a put option combined with a long stock position. The put option is comparable to an insurance policy written against the long stock position. The option price is the cost of the insurance premium and the amount the option is out-of-the-money is the deductible. Just as in the case of insurance, the deductible is inversely related to the insurance premium. The deductible is reduced as the strike price increases, which makes the put option more in-the-money or less out-of-the-money. The higher strike price causes the put price to increase and makes the insurance policy more expensive.

## Cost Management Strategies

Options can be used to manage the cost of maintaining an equity portfolio in a number of ways. Among the strategies are the use of short put and short call positions to serve as a substitute for a limit order in the cash market. Cash-secured put strategies can be used to purchase stocks at the target price, while covered calls or overwrites can be used to sell stocks at the target price. The target price is the one consistent with the portfolio manager's valuation or technical models and the price intended to produce the desired rate of return.

In addition, synthetic strategies may allow the investor to implement a position at a lower cost than a direct investment in the cash market. For example, foreign investors subject to dividend withholding taxes may find a synthetic long stock position using options an attractive alternative to the cash investment. Moreover, there is always an alternative method of creating a position. Synthetic calls, for example, can be created by borrowing, investing in stock, and buying put options. Likewise, a synthetic protective put strategy can be established by buying call options and discount bonds.

### Cash-Secured Put

The motivation behind a *cash-secured put strategy* is to reduce market impact costs associated with the purchase of a stock. The strategy can be used by managers to transact in the cash market without bearing the total cost of the perceived risk to the seller. The demand for the stock may bid up the price of the security regardless of the motivation behind the trade. If, for example, the manager believes that the stock is attractive at or below a particular price, a cash-secured put can be established using a strike price consistent with the target price. If the purchase is not motivated by firm-specific information, but is strategic in nature, part of a passive rebalancing, or based on relative valuation models, then using an option mechanism to purchase the stock may make sense.

The strategy is similar to a limit order in the cash market with two notable differences. First, the option approach pays the buyer a premium, while no such premium exists for a limit order. Second, the limit order can be ended at any time, while the option is only extant over the life of the contract.

A cash market transaction may bid up the price of the stock because sellers believe the trade is motivated by new information. The use of short put options is a means to convey the intent of the buyer. The put seller indicates to the market a willingness to accept the downside risk of a further stock price decline. Consequently, this makes it clear to the market that the interested party does not expect an immediate increase in the stock price. This may reduce the immediacy cost of market impact.

Thus, the short put mechanism of purchasing stock may be appropriate for managers with strategic interest in the stock, but no compelling need for immediate execution. The short put premium provides some downside cushion, which further reduces the effective cost of the stock. If the stock rises over the life of the option and the put expires worthless, then an overvalued stock has become more overvalued. If, on the other hand, the manager wants to own the stock immediately, then a put option strategy is not appropriate.

### Naked Calls

Similarly, short calls can be used as a mechanism for selling current holdings at a price consistent with the rate of return objective of the manager. The intention is twofold: (1) to reduce market impact costs and (2) to receive a favorable price for selling the stock shares.

Consider a manager who currently holds a number of stocks based on a quantitative valuation model. The model has created a sell price for each holding based on the investment horizon under consideration. The alternative methods for selling a substantial holding are to work it upstairs through a broker/dealer or establish a short call position with a strike price consistent with investment objectives. The disadvantage of a sizable cash market transaction is that the buyer will interpret the sale as information motivated and adjust the price accordingly. This could result in a meaningful decline in price and lower the return contribution of the stock to the overall portfolio.

A naked call can be written with a strike price as a substitute for a limit order. The investor selling the stock is conveying a clearer message to the market regarding intent. The stock is being sold for reasons other than the possession of adverse information regarding the company's future. The seller's intent is clearer for more aggressive OTM strike prices because it requires a rise in price for exercise. The effect of the overwrite position on portfolio performance is positive for neutral to slightly rising markets and negative for declining markets. The trade will undoubtedly incur transaction costs of some kind in either market. However, the prudent use of options is a useful way to be more specific about the motivation behind the trade.

## Return Enhancement Strategies

The most popular return enhancement strategies employing listed options are *covered call strategies*. If the investor currently owns the stock and writes a call on that stock, the strategy has been referred to as an "overwrite." If the strategy is implemented all at once (simultaneously buying the stock and selling the call), it is referred to as a "buy write." The essence of the covered call is to trade price appreciation for income. The strategy is appropriate for slightly bullish investors who don't expect much out of the stock and want to produce additional income. These are investors who are willing either to limit upside appreciation for limited downside protection or to manage the costs of selling the underlying stock. The primary motive is to generate additional income from owning the stock.

Although the call premium provides some limited downside protection, this is not an insurance strategy because it has significant downside risk. Consequently, investors should proceed with caution when considering a covered call strategy.

A covered call is less risky than buying the stock because the call premium lowers the break-even recovery price. The strategy behaves like a long stock position when the stock price is below the strike price. On the other hand, the strategy is insensitive to stock prices above the strike price and is therefore capped on the upside. The maximum profit is given by the call premium and the OTM amount of the call option.

## Regulatory Issues

The regulation of derivatives markets and equity markets is quite extensive in the United States. The Securities and Exchange Commission (SEC) is the primary regulator of equity markets and option markets. One focus of the SEC is to protect the investor by making certain that brokers identify the suitability of the investor for trading in options. This has mostly been a problem for smaller investors and not for institutional investors. However, numerous institutional inventors are still subject to a variety of antiquated restrictions that prohibit such investment management choices as short selling. Options can be used to establish a synthetic short position held in lieu of a short position in the cash market. In addition, options can be useful to foreign investors subject to local tax consequences by avoiding a cash market transaction.

## PORTFOLIO APPLICATIONS OF STOCK INDEX FUTURES

Now let's look at how stock index futures can work with equity investment strategies. Our focus is on how stock index futures can be used to manage all types of equity strategies more efficiently. We begin by examining how futures can help change equity exposure in order to achieve the desired level of exposure at the lowest possible cost. The two strategies examined are hedging strategies (a special case of risk management) and asset allocation strategies.

Stock index futures contracts are often ideal instruments for managing equity exposure due to their liquidity, flexibility, and low transaction costs. An equity position of comparable dollar value can be managed in the stock index futures market at a fraction of the cost in the cash market. The futures market is also an alternative means of implementing an investment strategy to the cash market.

The choice of whether to use the cash market or the futures market to alter equity exposure depends on the objectives of the manager and the size of the equity exposure. Despite apparent cost advantages, there are limits to the amount of stock index futures available to large institutional investors such as pension funds due to regulatory, size, and liquidity constraints. Nonetheless, stock index futures can still be an effective and valuable tool for portfolio management.

The motivation behind the choice to change equity exposure is important in deciding between the cash market or the stock index futures market. If the decision is a strategic asset allocation decision then it can be viewed as long term. If, on the other hand, the decision is tactical, it is a short-term situation. Stock index futures allow managers to quickly adjust imbalances in their asset allocation positions effectively without the need to purchase individual stocks. This effectively allows portfolio managers to increase or decrease equity exposure without altering the status of their core portfolio or disturbing their long-term investment objectives.

The appropriate way to analyze the cash and futures alternatives is to compare the costs of the two transactions.

## Hedging Market Risk

A common use of stock index futures from the introduction of these instruments is to hedge market risk. Hedging involves the transfer of risk from one party to another. Stock index futures serve as a valuable hedging instrument for both domestic and global equity portfolio managers. The global proliferation of viable futures contracts has brought the capability from the traditional S&P 500 type funds to a broad range of hedging possibilities. The methodology is identical except that hedging foreign equity positions requires currency hedges as well.

Hedging strategies involve cross-hedging when the hedging instrument is not perfectly correlated with the investor's equity portfolio. A perfectly hedged position is one without risk. If the underlying index is the same as the portfolio being hedged, then the hedge is an arbitrage and will generate a certain profit. If the futures contract is fairly priced at the risk-free rate, then the hedge is comparable to a risk-free investment and it will produce the risk-free rate of return. If the portfolio being hedged has some tracking error versus the underlying index, then the rate of return is comparable to a money market instrument with small levels of tracking error.

For equity portfolios designed to track known indexes with corresponding futures contracts, tracking error is not a huge problem. Alternative equity portfolios may have significant tracking error versus any particular hedging instrument that will subject the hedge to significant risk.

Hedging is not limited to long positions. Stock index futures provide a means to manage risk for those holding long or short positions in the equity market. By taking the opposite side of their position, equity managers can insulate the performance of their equity position from market movements. The residual performance is directly related to the level of non-market risk in the portfolio. The most sophisticated hedging techniques do not completely eliminate risk because the gains or losses on the futures side do not precisely offset the gains or losses on the cash equity portfolio. Nonetheless, the hedged position is clearly a low risk strategy particularly when the equity portfolio is highly correlated with the index underlying the stock index futures contract.

Stock index futures contracts in which the underlying is a broad-market index give managers the ability to hedge systematic risk and take advantage of superior stock selection ability that will produce a positive return even in declining markets. Stock index futures can be used to isolate the non-market component of total risk. This feature benefits active managers who have the ability to pick high performance stocks, but who do not necessarily like the market. There is no need to stay out of equities. The manager can use stock index futures to remove the market component from the strategy. Over the investment horizon, the returns to the hedged portfolio will include an incremental return to the selected stocks versus the market and any dividends from the stocks.

Stock index futures can only insulate an equity portfolio from some portion of total risk. If the equity portfolio happens to be a broad market index fund, then S&P 500 index futures can pretty much take care of total risk because non-market risk was eliminated through diversification. However, when this is not the case and the equity portfolio is subject to significant non-market risk, then it exposes the hedging strategy to those same risks.

### Hedge Ratios

In order to hedge a position, the amount of the position to be taken in the stock index futures contract must be determined. That is, a risk equivalent position of the cash market portfolio is needed for the stock index futures position in order to hedge the portfolio. The *hedge ratio* indicates the amount of the futures position that must be taken to hedge the cash market portfolio. For example, using the S&P 500 futures contract, a hedge ratio of 1 means that if a manager wants to hedge a $10 million stock portfolio, a $10 S&P 500 futures position must be sold. If the hedge ratio is 0.9, this means that $9 million of S&P 500 futures contracts must be sold to hedge a $10 stock portfolio.

It is tempting to use the portfolio's beta as a hedge ratio because it is an indicator of the sensitivity of the portfolio returns to the stock index returns. It appears, then, to be an ideal sensitivity adjustment. However, applying beta relative to a stock index as a sensitivity adjustment to a stock index futures contract assumes that the index and the futures contract have the same volatility. If futures always sold at their fair value, this would be a reasonable assumption. However, mispricing is an extra element of volatility in a stock index futures contract. Since the stock index futures contract is more volatile than the underlying stock index, using a portfolio beta as a sensitivity measure would result in a portfolio being over-hedged.

The most accurate sensitivity adjustment would be the beta of a portfolio relative to the futures contract. It can be shown that the beta of a portfolio relative to a stock index futures contract is equivalent to the product of the portfolio relative to the underlying index and the beta of the index relative to the futures contract.[1] The beta in each case is estimated using regression analysis in which the data are historical returns for the portfolio to be hedged, the stock index, and the stock index futures contract. The regressions estimated are:

$$r_P = a_P + B_{PI}\, r_I + e_P$$

where

$r_P$ = the return on the portfolio to be hedged
$r_I$ = the return on the stock index
$B_{PI}$ = the beta of the portfolio relative to the stock index
$a_P$ = the intercept of the relationship
$e_P$ = the error term

and

$$r_I = a_I + B_{IF}\, r_F + e_I$$

where

$r_F$ = the return on the stock index futures contract
$B_{IF}$ = the beta of the stock index relative to the stock index futures contract
$a_I$ = the intercept of the relationship
$e_I$ = the error term

Given $B_{PI}$ and $B_{IF}$, the minimum risk hedge ratio can then be found by:

Hedge ratio = $h = B_{PI} \times B_{IF}$

The hedge ratio $h$ in the above expression is referred to as a *minimum risk hedge ratio* (also called an *optimal hedge ratio*) because the ratio minimizes the variance of returns to the hedged position.

There is a special case where the portfolio beta can be used as the hedge ratio. This is the case if the manager can hedge the portfolio until the settlement date. This is because the return to mispricing is no longer an unknown factor when the portfolio can be held to the futures settlement date.

---

[1] Edgar Peters, "Hedged Equity Portfolios: Components of Risk and Return," *Advances in Futures and Options Research*, Vol. 1B, 1987, pp. 75-92.

Given the hedge ratio, the manager must determine the number of stock index futures contracts to sell. The number needed can be calculated using the following three steps after $B_{PI}$ and $B_{IF}$ are estimated:

*Step 1.* Determine the "equivalent market index units" of the market by dividing the market value of the portfolio to be hedged by the current value of the futures contract:

$$\text{Equivalent market index units} = \frac{\text{Market value of the portfolio to be hedged}}{\text{Current value of the futures contract}}$$

*Step 2.* Multiply the equivalent market index units by the hedge ratio to obtain the "beta-adjusted equivalent market index units":

Beta-adjusted equivalent market index units
= Hedge ratio × Equivalent market index units

or,

$$B_{PI} \times B_{IF} \times \text{Equivalent market index units}$$

*Step 3.* Divide the beta-adjusted equivalent index units by the multiple specified by the stock index futures contract:

$$\text{Number of contracts} = \frac{\text{Beta-adjusted equivalent market index units}}{\text{Multiple of the contract}}$$

## Asset Allocation

All investment decisions ultimately are asset allocation decisions. The choice to invest new cash in a domestic index fund instead of a global portfolio or the choice to reduce bond exposure are clear examples. If the decision is a long-term one, then it is a strategic asset allocation decision. Strategic decisions are made with the careful analysis of a client's long-term needs. If, instead, the decision is short-term, it is a tactical asset allocation decision. Tactical asset allocation (TAA) is actually a short-term to intermediate-term timing strategy designed to benefit from identifiable misevaluation in an asset class and seeks to add value to the overall fund performance. TAA could also include a defensive strategy to avoid adverse market movements. The classic example is a shift from equities to bonds or equity to cash in anticipation of a market correction. Asset allocation is not limited to domestic financial assets, but reaches into foreign markets as well.

The mechanics of implementing asset allocation decisions depend upon the investor's choice of an instrument. Whether managers choose to diversify internationally or not, superior security selection may be blown over by the adverse winds of a bear market. There are several ways that managers can respond to tactical asset allocation models that signal a danger of a market reversal. Tactical asset allocation is comparable to dynamic hedging. The choice to reduce or increase exposure to an asset class effectively hedges one risk in favor of another or none. The instruments to hedge market risk are also available for asset allocation decisions.

Managers have a choice of vehicles and methods to implement an asset allocation strategy. The stock index futures solution is available across a number of countries and asset classes, enabling managers to manage the systematic risk of equity portfolios regardless of the country of origin. The derivatives solutions to the asset allocation decision allows managers to separate the security selection decision from the market timing or the asset allocation decision. Later in this chapter we discuss the OTC derivatives alternative to stock index futures.

The choice of whether to use cash or futures to accomplish an allocation-related strategy was discussed earlier. Once again the choice comes down to whether the decision is long term or short term.

## Creating an Index Fund

An index fund is a portfolio of securities designed to exactly replicate the returns and risk profile of an established index. Equity indexing is an investment strategy that involves investing funds in a stock portfolio designed to track the performance of an established equity index. Index funds were originally developed as a low-cost passive alternative to active management and as part of a strategic asset allocation plan. As such, plain vanilla index funds were created where the benchmark was the most widely accepted stock market proxy — the S&P 500 Index.

To this day, the most basic index fund is designed to track the S&P 500 stock index. Recently however, indexing has taken on many different forms and doesn't fit perfectly into the traditional description. The most obvious development has been the use of numerous new benchmarks to represent more narrowly defined stock indexes and foreign stock indexes. However, it wasn't until the last few years that a global proliferation of stock index futures developed to accompany the new equity benchmark investments.

Traditionally, the only approach to establishing an index fund was to purchase a replicating portfolio in the cash market designed to track the S&P 500. With the arrival of equity index derivatives in the early 1980s, synthetic index funds were created. The return distribution of the S&P 500 Index could be replicated using stock index futures and a money market instrument. The early experience of the S&P 500 Index fund and its synthetic counterpart in the stock index futures market can now be extended to a host of other indexes. Some candidates are indexes with a narrower equity focus and foreign indexes.

As an alternative to holding a cash index fund, a synthetic index fund can be created using stock index futures contracts. The investor purchases stock index futures as a substitute for the cash index and invests the proceeds in a money market instrument. The advantages and disadvantages of using a synthetic index fund versus a cash index fund are the same as those discussed earlier. Based on the assumption of no transaction costs and efficient markets, we know that a synthetic index fund should generate the same returns as a cash index fund. In our next example, however, we relax the assumptions and compare the practical differences between the two applications.

The choice of using the futures market versus the cash market can only be determined by evaluating the trade-offs between costs and risks. The outcome of the synthetic strategy can only match the cash strategy if the following conditions are met:

- the investment amount corresponds to an exact futures amount
- interest rates are constant over the investment horizon
- expected dividends are realized
- the futures price is fairly valued when the strategy is initiated
- all subsequent futures prices are fairly valued.

In practice, these conditions are not exactly met. However, with good estimates of expectations and making the appropriate adjustments to the futures position, under normal market conditions, the risks can be minimized.

The risks of holding a synthetic index fund, for example, must be weighed against the risks of the cash index fund. The two primary sources of risk for using futures are variation margin and price risk. A technique known as "tailing" can be used to minimize the impact of variation margin on returns.[2] Price risk refers to the risk of mispriced futures contracts when the fund is initiated and during times when the position must be rolled into the next settlement cycle. On the other hand, one prominent advantage of a synthetic index fund over a cash index fund is cost. A cash index fund costs 30-40 basis points to initiate, while a synthetic index fund costs 2.5 basis points. The cash index fund is also subject to the cost of periodic rebalancings and to cash drag resulting from a delay in investing new cash.

In practice, many index funds hold a replicating portfolio to represent the benchmark and use stock index futures to manage cost and minimize cash drag. The prudent use of futures can provide the means of achieving the investment objective of matching the returns to the benchmark.

### Enhanced Index Funds

An index fund is a passive approach to investing where the objective is to exactly or closely match the performance of an agreed upon benchmark. The most common index fund is a plain vanilla S&P 500 index fund. The index fund manager attempts to match the performance of the S&P 500 index on a total return basis.

---

[2] Tailing is a technique designed to minimize the impact of variation margin on returns. The tailing or adjustment factor is applied to the original position such that slightly fewer contracts are bought or sold. The futures position is adjusted by the following formula:.

Tailing factor = 1/Term interest rate

The appropriate interest rate is either the term interest rate until expiration of the futures contract, or the term interest rate until the hedge is lifted. Fund managers prefer not to use tailing because it may put a drag on the strategy when the position is moving favorably.

The purpose of an enhanced index fund is to do better than the benchmark index without incurring additional risk.

It is difficult to outperform a benchmark without incurring tracking error risk. Tracking error risk will usually emerge whenever the replicating portfolio is not an exact replica of the benchmark. However, the incremental returns more than compensate for the small increase in risk. Naturally, over time, the enhanced index fund is expected to perform better than the benchmark on a risk-adjusted basis.

There are two basic approaches to enhanced indexing. The first involves changing the composition of the replicating portfolio in order take advantage of valued-added situations. This may include stock selection, sector selection, or a different weighting scheme. The resulting portfolio is usually constructed to minimize tracking error. The replicating portfolio is "tilted" toward superior performance in some way that is expected to provide it with the economic fuel to perform better than the benchmark. The replicating portfolio is put on common ground with the benchmark by trying to match its risk characteristics and not its expected return.

Alternatively, the index fund manager can use a stock replacement program to take advantage of misevaluation in the futures market in order to enhance return. The performance of the index fund is "enhanced" through stock index arbitrage and a stock replacement program. The incremental return is the result of futures pricing inefficiencies rather than estimated misevaluation of equities. The index fund has an additional opportunity for incremental return by reversing the arbitrage at a favorable price as well. In fact, some index funds may enter into a stock replacement program aggressively in order to take advantage of opportunities on the other side of the cash/futures swap.

Consequently, plain vanilla indexing can be viewed as an application of futures in the form of cost management. Enhanced indexing by seeking to capitalize on the mispricing between futures and cash is an example of a return enhancing strategy.

## Foreign Market Access

As investment strategies have become international in scope, stock index futures have become an effective means of managing equity exposure and risk exposure in a global portfolio. Once a decision is made to develop and maintain a global investment strategy, the equity manager has to decide how to treat currency risk. The choice to invest internationally subjects the equity portfolio to currency risk and market risk in the country where the investment takes place. The manager is now faced with the task of making prudent investment choices and developing an opinion on currency rates. The risk to the portfolio is that the manager's investment decision was correct, but not realized due to an appreciation in the domestic currency.

The use of stock index futures for implementing a global equity investment strategy can reduce currency risk. The reason is that currency risk is confined to initial margin payments and variation margin. These payments are usually much smaller than the initial value of the equity portfolio. Thus, stock index futures are a viable and important alternative for foreign equity investment compared to investing in the foreign stocks themselves.

The use of stock index futures in a global context shares the same advantages of using stock index futures in a domestic equity investment context. These include high liquidity, rapid execution, low transaction costs, single purchase for broad market exposure, no tracking error, and no custodial costs. A few additional features particularly applicable to foreign investment are that cash settlement avoids the risk of delivery, using stock index futures for country allocation avoids the different settlement periods that may exist between two or more countries, and using futures may avoid withholding taxes. Moreover, in some countries the use of stock index futures allows foreign investors to avoid restrictions on capital movements.

### Foreign Stock Index Futures Strategies

There are a number of ways to make an investment in foreign equities. One strategy is to invest in stock index futures and a money market instrument denominated in the local currency. This is a true synthetic index fund that is fully exposed to currency risk and is referred to as the "unhedged strategy."

A second strategy also buys, or goes long, stock index futures, but only converts enough of the domestic currency to satisfy initial margin payments and subsequent variation margin. The amount of currency risk is substantially reduced, which is why we refer to the strategy as a "partial hedge strategy." The amount of currency risk does not apply to the entire exposure as is the case with an investment in a foreign equity portfolio. The risk of loss due to an appreciation in the dollar is limited to the actual dollars put up as margin and all subsequent gains.

For example, consider two alternative investments: purchasing one CAC-40 stock index futures contract valued at FF680,000 (3400 × FF200) or purchasing an equivalent amount of French stocks. Furthermore, assume the current exchange rate is FF5.6/$, the investment horizon is 60 days and the rate on a domestic money market instrument is 5%. For the futures strategy, FF10,000 are necessary to meet the initial margin requirement. This means that $1,786 (FF10,000/5.6) is needed to meet the margin in French francs, which compares to $121,429 (FF680,000/5.6) for the alternative investment in the stocks. Assume the investment returns 10% at the settlement date of the contract in local currency and the dollar appreciates to FF6/$. The dollar return to the futures strategy is broken up as follows:[3]

| | | |
|---|---|---|
| Futures return | (FF10,000 + FF68,000)/6 | = $13,000 |
| Money market instrument return | $119,643 × 1.008219 | = $120,626 |
| Total return | | = $133,626 or 10.05% |
| Cash market return | FF680,000 × 1.10 | = FF748,000 |
| Dollar return | FF748,000/6 | = $124,667 or 2.7% |

The return to the cash market alternative is lost due to adverse currency movements while the futures position is not because of the limited currency risk.

## Exhibit 1: Strategy Performance
## Foreign Index Fund Using Stock Index Futures

U.K. Market rises 5% to 6510

| Exchange Rate | Unhedged Strategy | Partial Hedged Strategy | Hedged Strategy |
|---|---|---|---|
| Dollar falls to $1.65 | 8.64% | 5.41% | 5.35% |
| Dollar unchanged | 5.35 | 5.27 | 5.35 |
| Dollar rises to $1.55 | 2.06 | 5.12 | 5.35 |

U.K. Market falls 5% to 5890

| Exchange Rate | Unhedged Strategy | Partial Hedged Strategy | Hedged Strategy |
|---|---|---|---|
| Dollar falls to $1.65 | −1.67% | −4.56% | −4.65% |
| Dollar unchanged | −4.65 | −4.73 | −4.65 |
| Dollar rises to $1.55 | −7.63 | −4.91 | −4.65 |

A third strategy extends the first strategy to include a currency hedge against the entire position and is referred to as the "hedged strategy." The entire domestic currency value is converted to a foreign money market instrument. Initial margin and variation margin are satisfied in the local currency and the currency hedge is adjusted when the position changes.

The unhedged strategy is fully exposed to currency risk in contrast to the fully hedged strategy. The partial hedged strategy has some currency risk because the daily cash flows are denominated in the foreign currency, while the money market instrument is in the domestic currency.

The currency impact on the alternative strategies is demonstrated in Exhibit 1, which considers a U.S. investor who wants to diversify into U.K. equities. At the time of the investment, the FT-SE 100 stock index is 6200, the stock index futures contract is trading at 6225, and the marginal lending rate is 5.5% in the United Kingdom and 5% in the United States. The investment horizon is 60 days when the futures contract settles and the spot currency rate is $1.60/pound and the 60-day forward rate is $1.6007.

The results reported in Exhibit 1 do not include transaction costs because all are similarly affected. Thus, we lose nothing when comparing the currency impact. We also assume that the variation margin impact is negligible from a financing and currency standpoint. What we do see is that the first strategy performs best when the dollar falls regardless of the performance of the U.K. market. The partial hedge strategy has less volatility than the unhedged strategy, but more than the hedged strategy. When the dollar is unchanged, the partial hedged strategy has lower returns because the domestic money market rate is lower.

---

[3] The 60-day domestic interest rate is 0.8219% (5% × 60/365). At $119,643, the domestic money market investment in the partial hedged strategy is equal to the initial position value, at $121,429 (680,000/5.6) less the dollar-based margin requirement on the position, at $1,786.

Dollar returns in the illustration are measured relative to the initial value of the cash (and futures) position of $121,429. Consequently, the dollar return to the futures strategy is 10.5% (133,626/121,429 − 1), while the cash market return is only 2.7%.

## Exhibit 2: The Use of OTC Derivatives for Equity Strategies

| Equity Strategy | Purpose | Product Candidate |
|---|---|---|
| Return-enhancement strategies | Outperform benchmark | Equity Swap |
| Hedging strategies | Risk Management | Exotics, Swaps, Debt* |
| Spread strategies | Risk Management | Equity Swaps, Exotics |
| Market access strategies | Reduce Costs | Swaps, Debt, Warrants, Exotics |
| Changing Equity Exposure | Reduce Costs | Swaps, Debt, Exotics |
| Index funds | Outperform benchmark | Swaps, Debt |
|     Standard | | |
|     Enhanced | | |
|     Style | | |
| Asset allocation | Risk management | Swaps |
| Active manager transition. | Cost management | Swaps, Exotics |

\* Debt refers to equity-linked debt products.

Source: Exhibit 2 in Chapter 11 of Bruce M. Collins and Frank J. Fabozzi, *Derivatives and Equity Portfolio Management* (New Hope, PA: Frank J. Fabozzi Associates, 1999).

The choice of how to establish a global asset allocation policy depends on the orientation of the investor. The decision regarding the best way to implement the strategy ought to include stock index futures because of their many advantages. The cost of implementing a strategy in the cash market would have higher costs and lower returns. In non-U.S. cash markets, transaction costs are higher and the savings substantial using the stock index futures alternative. The decision to use stock index futures to gain foreign market access is strongly motivated by convenience and cost. Equity futures contracts can be effective tools for managing exposure to equity asset classes throughout the world.

## APPLICATIONS OF OTC EQUITY DERIVATIVES

The array of OTC derivative-based equity portfolio management strategies cuts across the two primary categories of investment philosophy — active and passive management. We consider several strategies in this section, which are listed in Exhibit 2, together with the purpose of using an OTC derivatives and a product candidate.

Exhibit 3 summarizes various OTC equity derivative structures in terms of the role of derivatives for long-term investors and hedgers. A broad spectrum of equity investment activities emanating from the role of derivatives can benefit from these three basic categories of OTC equity derivative structures.

Exhibit 11 in the previous chapter provided some examples of how an institutional investor can use specific products and structures to implement an equity investment strategy and how they might benefit. The concern facing most investors is to perform better than an appropriate benchmark. Saving 50 basis points in costs or enhancing returns by that amount due to taking advantage of derivative markets can go a long way to facilitate equity investment performance.

## Exhibit 3: OTC Derivative Structures and Investment Management

| Derivative Structure | Investor | Role | Application |
|---|---|---|---|
| OTC Options and Exotics | Long-term<br>Index Funds<br>Style Funds<br>Active Managers<br>Strategic Asset Allocators | Risk Management | Customized protective puts<br>Collar structures<br>Portfolio insurance<br>Currency hedging<br>Asset exposure<br>Probability exposure |
| | | Return Management | Index arbitrage<br>Option writing<br>Volatility forecasting<br>Intra-asset allocation<br>Leverage strategies |
| | | Cost Management | Option writing<br>Market access<br>Valuation estimation<br>Structured products |
| | | Regulatory Management | Foreign market exposure<br>Tax deferral<br>Asset exposure |
| Equity-Linked Debt | Long-term<br>Index Funds<br>Style Funds<br>Active Managers<br>Strategic Asset Allocators | Risk Management | Customized structures<br>Collar structures<br>Portfolio insurance<br>Currency hedging<br>Asset exposure |
| | | Return Management | Spread premiums |
| | | Cost Management | Foreign market cost avoidance<br>Asset allocation |
| | | Regulatory Management | Asset exposure<br>Foreign market exposure<br>Capital requirement |
| Equity Swaps | Long-term<br>Index Funds<br>Style Funds<br>Active Managers<br>Strategic Asset Allocators | Risk Management | Diversification<br>Asset allocation<br>Minimize tracking error<br>Currency hedging |
| | | Return Management | Tracking portfolio<br>Spread premium |
| | | Cost Management | Foreign market cost avoidance<br>Asset allocation |
| | | Regulatory Management | Foreign market exposure<br>Tax deferral<br>Asset exposure |

Source: Exhibit 3 in Chapter 11 of Bruce M. Collins and Frank J. Fabozzi, *Derivatives and Equity Portfolio Management* (New Hope, PA: Frank J. Fabozzi Associates, 1999).

## Exhibit 4: Hedging With Derivatives

| Hedging Strategy | Hedging Instrument | |
|---|---|---|
| | Listed | OTC |
| Reduce Market Risk | Stock index futures | Option, swap, debt |
| Reduce Total Risk | Multiple SIFs contracts | Option, swap, debt |
| Change Risk Components | Stock index futures | Option, swap, debt |
| Reduce Currency Risk | Quanto futures | Option, swap, debt |
| Reduce Interest Rate Risk | Interest rate derivatives | Option, swap, debt |
| Reduce Inflation Risk | Interest rate derivatives | Option, swap, debt |
| | Commodity index derivatives | |

Source: Exhibit 4 in Chapter 11 of Bruce M. Collins and Frank J. Fabozzi, *Derivatives and Equity Portfolio Management* (New Hope, PA: Frank J. Fabozzi Associates, 1999).

# Risk Management Strategies

As we have noted, a common use of derivatives is to hedge financial risk. Stock index futures can only insulate an equity portfolio from some portion of total risk. If the equity portfolio happens to be a broad market index fund, then S&P 500 index futures can pretty much take care of total risk because non-market risk was eliminated through diversification. However, when this is not the case and the equity portfolio is subject to significant non-market risk, then it exposes the hedging strategy to those same risks.

Stock index futures contracts in which the underlying is a broad market index allow portfolio managers the ability to hedge systematic risk and take advantage of superior stock selection ability that will produce a positive return even in declining markets. Stock index futures can be used to isolate the non-market component of total risk. This feature benefits active managers who have the ability to pick high performance stocks, but who have little market timing skills. There is no need to stay out of equities during volatile markets. The manager can use stock index futures to hedge market risk.

Consequently, over the investment horizon, the returns to the hedged portfolio will include an incremental return to the selected stocks versus the market and any dividends from the stocks. However, the resulting strategy may go beyond the desired risk-return tradeoff. OTC derivative structures can be designed to address all these issues and achieve the exact hedged position desired. All costs can be known upfront with no additional risk to investors, with the exception of some credit risk and market failure risk that accompanies all financial transactions.

Despite the benefits of using stock index futures, listed index futures products do not provide a full range of hedging choices for equity investors. OTC equity derivatives go a long way to fill this gap. Investors can choose among equity swaps, equity-linked debt, and a structured option-like product to hedge with greater precision the specific risk they want to shed and to acquire the risk they want to bear. Exhibit 4 provides a list of derivative alternatives for hedging equity portfolios.

## Exhibit 5: Alternative Investment Vehicles
## Global Asset Allocation Strategy

| Investment Category | Vehicle | Advantages | Disadvantages |
|---|---|---|---|
| Cash Market | Stock Portfolio | Ownership | Costs and Management |
| Listed Derivatives | Stock Index Futures | Cost | Managing futures |
| | Stock Index Options | Listed | Size, Standardization |
| | FLEX Options | Flexibility, Listed | Size, Tracking Error |
| OTC Options | Baskets | No tracking error | Cost |
| | Spread | Any Market | Cost |
| | Barriers | Low Cost | Volatile Markets |
| | Compound | Low Cost | Multiple Transactions |
| Swaps | Equity Swap | Quick, Efficient | Negative Payments |
| | International Swap | | Credit Risk |

Source: Exhibit 5 in Chapter 11 of Bruce M. Collins and Frank J. Fabozzi, *Derivatives and Equity Portfolio Management* (New Hope, PA: Frank J. Fabozzi Associates, 1999).

With the advent of second-generation "exotic" options, investors can now implement a hedging strategy with the degree of precision they desire. Market risk can be hedged in any country using any derivative structure. Equity swaps can exchange the total return of a portfolio for another less risky asset class. The structure can be designed to hedge currency risk if necessary and desired.

A structured product using exotics can design a payout that is contingent on certain market activity. For example, a barrier put option can be used to obtain a specific degree of protection without paying extra for outcomes that are not relevant. Ladder options can lock in a market decline, while flexible strike options can ratchet up when the market moves opposite to expectations.

Once again, the bottom line is that structured OTC equity derivative products can overcome the risk inherent in cash or futures market hedging strategies. Investors have the means to hedge all or a specific part of total risk.

## Asset Allocation

The mechanics of implementing asset allocation decisions depend upon the investor's choice of an investment vehicle. Exhibit 5 presents a list of candidates for a global asset shift which changes foreign equity exposure in the overall asset allocation strategy using listed derivatives and OTC derivatives.

The problem is the same one presented in an earlier discussion of equity investment strategies. The choices unfold similarly. The option-based solution may suffer from high costs due to a highly volatile portfolio or due to significant liquidity risk. However, exotic option structures provide a means to fine-tune the strategy to reflect very precisely forecasted returns. Basket options, such as index options, are cheaper than a portfolio of options. They also provide a portfolio manager with a means of eliminating tracking error between the underlying for the hedging vehicle and the equity portfolio.

Listed options have the additional problem of size limits for standardized contracts. FLEX options resolve some but not all of those limitations. The stock index futures alternative comes with some administrative issues and risks. The equity swap solution incorporates the asset allocation decision into a single transaction, but necessitates a counterparty and has credit risk. The derivatives solution to the asset allocation decision allows fund managers or portfolio managers to separate the security selection decision from the market timing or the asset allocation decision. The choice of what mechanism to use to accomplish the investment objective depends on whether the decision is long term or short term and the relative costs.

## Return Management Strategies

Return management strategies focus on structuring an investment strategy to increase returns but not risk. Here we include passive index funds and enhanced index funds because they are investment strategies designed to meet the performance criterion of matching or exceeding a benchmark. We could just as easily think of index funds as a means to match the risk characteristics of a benchmark, which is one of the features of this strategy. However, once the risk profile is established, the focus of index funds is performance relative to a benchmark.

The modified index fund strategies might also be called return-enhancement strategies. The purpose behind return-enhancement strategies is to increase return without an accompanying increase in risk. This means that an "enhanced" index fund ought to do better than the benchmark index without incurring additional risk. However, it may not be an easy task to outperform a benchmark without incurring tracking error risk. This risk will usually emerge whenever the replicating portfolio does not exactly mimic the composition of the benchmark. Nonetheless, the incremental returns are expected to more than compensate for the small increase in risk and, over time, the enhanced index fund is expected to outperform the benchmark on a risk-adjusted basis.

The goal of indexing is to construct a portfolio to exactly match the performance of the benchmark. When this is accomplished, tracking error is zero. In addition to performance reasons, plan sponsors are attracted to index funds because they provide investment diversification and are a means to control costs. Many plan sponsors have combined active and passive management using index funds as a risk management tool. Index funds can also provide a means for market-timing. Thus we see that index funds can fall into return management, risk management, or cost management categories. Part of the reason is that the use of index funds makes performance attribution and cost control more manageable because of the use of an established index as a benchmark. For the plan sponsor, an index fund can represent an entire asset class within the framework of its strategic asset allocation strategy or as part of an intra-asset allocation strategy that mixes active and passive management.

Recently, indexing has taken on many different forms that have broad applications. If we generalize our definition of index funds as a portfolio of stocks designed to match or exceed the returns of a benchmark while maintaining the same risk exposure, then there are many extensions of the original index fund. The many applications of index funds provide a rich landscape for using derivatives to further reduce costs. In fact, the prudent use of equity derivatives can reduce transaction costs to near zero. We regard the reduction of costs as any increase in after-cost return without changing the fundamental composition of the portfolio. This means that the returns are derived from the same sources in the cash market. Thus, it is comparable to getting a better execution in the cash market. Superior execution leads to lower costs, which increases return. The following is a list of index fund applications.

*Extended Funds* An *extended funds strategy* involves constructing a portfolio linked to an index that "extends" beyond the traditional S&P 500 index and may include a significantly larger group of stocks. The purpose of this strategy is to gain U.S. equity diversification. The universe of over 5,000 stocks across many sectors is more representative of the U.S. equity market and the U.S. economy. In addition, it provides a means of reducing risk versus a more narrow view represented by the S&P 500 index. No real liquid listed derivatives are available to create a synthetic fund. OTC derivative structures such as equity swaps and equity-linked debt instruments can provide an alternative investment vehicle to an exclusive cash approach.

*Non-S&P 500 Index Funds* A non-S&P 500 index funds strategy involves constructing a portfolio linked to a broad-based non-S&P 500 stock index. The strategy underlying these funds is to expand U.S. equity market exposure. Investors who currently have an S&P 500 index fund can combine it with a separate index fund that captures a neglected portion of the market. The end result can effectively be an extended fund with the added advantage of making intra-asset allocation rebalancings when desired. Once we travel outside the plain vanilla index fund, using listed derivatives becomes more difficult. OTC equity derivatives are available for implementing and managing non-S&P 500 index funds.

*Foreign or International Index Funds* A foreign or international index funds strategy seeks to design a portfolio that is linked to a foreign or international stock index. Thus, investors who do not invest beyond the borders of the United States are ignoring about half of world equities. The strategy objective of foreign investments is to gain international diversification. Furthermore, as global financial markets continue to deregulate and integrate, emerging markets in other parts of the world will provide additional opportunities. There are, however, direct investment expenses associated with owning foreign securities that exceed similar domestic investments. These may include larger commissions and spreads, stamp taxes, dividend withholding taxes, custody fees, and research fees. Many of these costs can be better managed through the use of OTC index derivatives.

*Special-Purpose Index Funds* A portfolio can be constructed to be linked to the performance of a sub-index, such as a market sector, or a portfolio with the same risk profile as a benchmark but with a tilt toward a specific parameter such as yield or price-earnings ratio. This strategy is called a *special-purpose index funds strategy.* Tilted portfolios are designed to enhance the returns to an index fund without assuming additional risk. Sometimes referred to as "enhanced" index funds, this strategy may also involve the use of futures or options to provide incremental return. An enhanced index fund begins with a traditional index fund and then utilizes financing techniques and derivative strategies to enhance return.

Having decided on a passive investment strategy and an appropriate benchmark, the investor's next consideration is how to implement the strategy. A cash market solution needs to address the design and construction of a replicating or tracking portfolio. In the presence of transaction costs, the optimal portfolio may still underperform the benchmark. Thus, in order to overcome the risk of underperformance the investor may have to assume more tracking error risk. The final choice of a replicating portfolio must be made within a cost management framework. The trade-off can be represented by expected tracking error versus expected trading costs. Costs are related to portfolio size and liquidity. Part of the skill of portfolio construction is to find the optimal balance between costs and risk. The marginal trade-off between risk and cost is greater for small sized portfolios.

Earlier we discussed the benefits of using stock index futures to manage an index fund. Synthetic index funds can be created using stock index futures that exactly replicate the returns to the underlying index. Recently, OTC index derivatives have been developed for investors with restrictions on using derivatives. These include equity-linked debt instruments and equity swaps. Equity swaps are important because they are the economic equivalent of financing an equity investment with a fixed-income security, typically a LIBOR-based security.

There are some index funds that use futures almost exclusively. It is not practical for large pension funds to rely exclusively on synthetic index funds due to market constraints. Thus, some combination of the cash market and futures market is appropriate. Index funds can be developed as a more dynamic strategy, and can be used as a risk management tool and a platform for better performance. However, stock index futures have their own administrative considerations and are limited in application because they have a linear pay off.

In order to provide a richer body of choices for implementing and managing index funds over the long haul, the use of OTC derivative structures provides the missing link to more complete and effective global risk management solutions to the investment problem. Equity-linked debt structures or equity swaps can be used to create the exact desired equity exposure in a single transaction, which makes them convenient, cost effective, and economically sound.

## Return Enhancement Strategies

There are two basic approaches to enhanced indexing which apply to other investment strategies as well. The first approach involves changing the composition of the equity portfolio in order to position the portfolio to take advantage of stocks, stock sectors, some different weighting allotments, or other criteria that the manager believes will cause the portfolio to perform better than a passive benchmark. In the case of index funds, the equity portfolio is the replicating portfolio. Changing the portfolio involves modifying the content of the portfolio and yet maintaining the current level of risk. The resulting portfolio is typically designed to minimize tracking error. For return management strategies, the equity portfolio is designed to match the risk characteristics of a benchmark and not its expected return.

In the second approach, index fund managers can use a stock index futures arbitrage to increase or enhance returns. The strategy is formalized as a stock replacement program, which invests in the less expensive of the cash portfolio or futures. The incremental return is the result of futures pricing inefficiencies rather than estimated mispricing of equities.

OTC equity derivatives can be a useful tool to modify the composition of the portfolio at low cost. The use of derivatives would enter the picture as part of the implementation process. The investor would first establish the necessary rebalancing to achieve the desired exposure to a new set of stocks on either an individual basis, an industry sector basis, or with the intent to modify a portfolio parameter such as price-earnings ratio. In any case, the result in the cash market is a set of sell orders and a set of buy orders. The investor is shedding some risks in favor of others. The rebalanced portfolio represents the right equity exposure to add incremental return necessary to improve performance with no added risk.

## Cost Management and Regulatory Management Strategies

We can apply the cost and regulatory management strategies explained earlier using listed options to OTC derivatives as well. The OTC applications extend the benefits further by providing additional flexibility when structuring a strategy. There are also a number of strategies that fall under this category simply because implementing them using derivatives results in lower costs than the cash market alternative. Moreover, in the case of some strategies, implementation in the cash market may have prohibitive regulatory obstacles. An example of both are foreign market access strategies. Derivatives provide investors a means to invest in foreign equities while avoiding some of the costs, tax consequences, and regulatory obstacles simultaneously or separately. This holds true for U.S. investors in equities outside the United States or foreigners investing in U.S. companies.

Here we review some of the listed option strategies discussed earlier in this chapter, but now using OTC derivatives. We explained the use of short puts as a means of buying stocks using derivatives as a substitute for a limit order in the cash market. This strategy is equally applicable to OTC options, which provide the additional advantage of customization to achieve the specific price and time horizon that meet the investor's needs. Similarly, short calls are a means of selling stocks currently held and targeted for sale. The advantages of the OTC market apply here as well.

In addition to these basic applications, OTC structures can be developed as alternatives to cash market transactions that are tailored to reflect very specific investment opinions or forecasts. These may include any structure that is the economic equivalent of a long or short cash position, but does not require the direct purchase or sale of stock. Other applications which could reduce cost involve an array of exotic structures that are priced lower than standard options. Barrier options can be structured to knock-in under conditions that reflect the price targets of the stock. Spread options allow the manager to generate the performance differential between the current situation and the desired situation without actually buying or selling the stock. Basket options can accomplish the result of buying or selling a basket of stocks simultaneously. Equity swaps can achieve the economic equivalent by an exchange of cash flows. OTC derivatives are equally applicable to cost management or regulatory management.

# QUESTIONS

1. "There's no real difference between options and futures. Both are hedging tools, and both are derivative products. It's just that with options you have to pay an option premium, while futures require no upfront payment except for 'good faith' margin. I can't understand why anyone would use options." Do you agree with this statement?

2. Why is a protective put buying strategy a risk management strategy?

3. What is the motivation for a cash-secured strategy?

4. The following excerpt is from an article entitled "Scudder Writes Covered Calls on S&P 500" that appeared in the July 13, 1992 issue of *Derivatives Week*, p. 7:

> Scudder, Stevens & Clark writes covered calls on the S&P 500 Index to enhance the return of some of its equity portfolios, according to Harry Hitch, principal at Scudder. Hitch, who advises Scudder's equity portfolio managers on derivatives use, said that the S&P 500 has been in a trading range since the beginning of the year, making it a good candidate for covered call writing. Half of the index is made up of growth stocks, a group that Scudder sees as overbought, whereas the other half is probably increasing in price. The combination of one half appreciating with the other half depreciating creates the range, rather than a decided one-way movement.
>
> The goal is to write calls at the top of the trading range, take the premium and wait for the options to expire worthless. ... Typically, Scudder takes 1,000 contract positions, worth around $42 million.

Explain the risks and rewards of the strategy discussed in this excerpt.

5. You are meeting with a pension plan sponsor who has asked you for advice on several investment policy guidelines that it has formulated for its managers. One of the guidelines involves the use of options for hedging and specifies the following:

> Protective put buying and covered call writing strategies are recognized by the investment community as means for hedging a stock position. The former will not be permitted by any of our fund managers because it involves a cost that may not be recouped if the put option is not exercised. We will permit covered call writing because there is no cost generated to protect the portfolio.

What advice would you give the plan sponsor concerning this investment policy guideline?

6. Suppose a portfolio manager wants to implement a protective put buying strategy for a stock she owns that has a current market price of $160. She is told that there are three 90-day put options available on that stock with strike prices of $156, $158, and $160.

   a. Which put option will give her the greatest price protection?
   b. Which put option will be the most expensive?
   c. Which put option should be selected?

7. What naked strategy or strategies would an investor pursue if she thought that a stock's price was going to rise?

8. The quote following is from the June 22, 1992 issue of *Derivatives Week*, p. 4:

> Aetna Investment Management, the London-based fund management arm of U.S. insurer Aetna Life & Casualty, expects to start using derivatives within weeks in more than £200 million of U.K. equity holdings, according to Tom Chellew, director. The firm has not used derivatives before in its total of £700 million under management in the U.K.
>
> Aetna is talking to trustees over the next two weeks and expects to get approval to start dealing thereafter, he said. Initially, it will only use derivatives in its more than £200 million of U.K. holdings in its £250 million of unit trusts under management.
>
> Chellew said initial strategies are likely to include writing covered calls and writing puts on stock Aetna doesn't mind buying. The firm will likely be interested in both U.K. index and individual stock options.
>
> Subsequently, Aetna expects to expand use into other holdings — specifically, equity and later possibly fixed income — and into pension and life insurance money under management, he said. Aetna will use derivatives to enhance yields and for risk reduction, and will trade futures for asset allocation.

   a. What does Mr. Chellew mean by writing puts on "stock Aetna doesn't mind buying"?
   b. How can options be used to "enhance yields and for risk reduction"?
   c. How can futures be used "to trade futures for asset allocation"?

9. The following is from an article entitled "Analytic Uses Options to Protect Tenneco Position," that appeared in the November 16, 1992 issue of *Derivatives Week*, p. 7:

> Analytic Investment Management in Irvine, Ca., last Monday sold 70 Nov. 40 puts and bought 70 Feb. 35 puts on Tenneco for its Ana-

lytic Optioned Equity Fund — a derivatives-driven mutual fund, according to Chuck Dobson, the fund's executive v.p. By selling and buying an equal number of exchange-traded puts, the firm maintained a fully-hedged position while using profits on its options to counterbalance paper losses on the 7,000 Tenneco shares it owns for a net gain of 1 7/8 per option, Dobson said.

Though Dobson could not give the price at which the stock was bought, he noted that since Tenneco was trading around $35 last Monday, the 7,000 shares were worth roughly $245,000, or about 0.27% of the total $91 million portfolio. Dobson explained that the firm takes a non-directional approach to picking stock, relying instead on the stock's volatility, option premium and dividends.

Dobson explained that the fund, which contains 130-140 mostly high capitalization stocks, is governed by four basic derivatives-linked strategies: 1) buy a stock and sell a call on the stock; 2) buy a stock and a put on the stock; 3) sell a put and place the exercise price in a cash reserve fund and 4) buy a call and place the exercise price in a money market fund.

a. Explain the option strategy cited in the first paragraph of this excerpt. Be sure to explain what Mr. Dobson meant by the "firm maintained a fully hedged position."

b. What does Mr. Dobson mean in the second approach when he says the "firm takes a non-directional approach to picking stock, relying instead on the stock's volatility."

c. Explain the first two strategies listed in the third paragraph.

10. a. What is a hedge ratio?
b. What is meant by "a minimum risk hedge ratio"?

11. a. Explain why it is not appropriate to use a portfolio's beta as a hedge ratio?
b. When is it reasonable to use a portfolio's beta as a hedge ratio?

12. Suppose that on July 1, 1986 the portfolio manager of a $10 million portfolio that is identical to the S&P 500 wanted to hedge against a possible market decline. More specifically, the manager wanted to hedge the portfolio until August 31, 1986. To hedge against an adverse market move during the period July 1, 1986 to August 31, 1986, the manager decided to enter into a hedge by selling the S&P 500 futures contracts that settled in September 1986. On July 1, 1986, the September 1986 futures contract was trading at 253.95.

Suppose further that the beta relative to the futures contract ($B_{IF}$) was estimated to be 0.745.

a. Given that the portfolio to be hedged is identical to the S&P 500, explain why the beta of the portfolio relative to the index $(B_{PI})$ is 1.
b. What is the hedge ratio for this portfolio?
c. Using the three steps explained in the chapter, show that approximately 59 S&P 500 futures contracts are needed to hedge the $10 million portfolio. Be sure to show your computation of the equivalent market index units and the beta-adjusted equivalent market index units. (Recall that the multiple for the S&P 500 contract is 500.)

13. Suppose that a money manager owned all the stocks in the Dow Jones Industrial Average on July 1, 1986. The market value of the portfolio held was $100 million. Also assume that the manager wanted to hedge the position against a decline in stock prices from July 1, 1986 to August 31, 1986, using the September 1986 S&P 500 futures contract.

When the hedge was placed on July 1, 1986, the September 1986 futures contract was trading at 253.95. The beta of the index relative to the futures contract $(B_{IF})$ was 0.745. The Dow Jones Index in a regression analysis was found to have a beta relative to the S&P 500 of 1.05 (with a coefficient of determination of 0.93).

a. What is the hedge ratio for this portfolio?
b. Using the three steps explained in the chapter, show that approximately 616 S&P 500 futures contracts are needed to hedge the $100 million portfolio. Be sure to show your computation of the equivalent market index units and the beta-adjusted equivalent market index units. (Recall that the multiple for the S&P 500 contract is 500.)

14. The following excerpt is from the September 7, 1992 issue of *Derivatives Week*, in an article entitled "Trafalgar Reproduces EAFE with Futures":

> Ontario-based Trafalgar Capital Management has been using equity index futures from five different countries to replicate the performance of the EAFE index, according to Vidis Vaicunas, v.p.-investment systems and trading at the firm. The EAFE index tracks the performance of 18 different equity markets in Europe, Australia and the Far East.

a. What is the advantage of using this approach rather than by buying individual shares in each country?
b. What are the risks associated with this approach?

15. a. How can a manager synthetically create an S&P 500 index fund using stock index futures?

b. What major factor should be considered in determining whether an index fund should be created using cash market stocks or stock index futures contracts?

c. What are the primary risks associated with using stock index futures to create a synthetic S&P 500 index fund?

16. a. Why can plain vanilla indexing be viewed as an application of futures in the form of cost management?

b. Why can enhanced indexing be viewed as an application of futures in the form of return enhancement?

17. Give an example of how OTC derivatives can be used in each of the following strategies:

a. risk management strategies.

b. asset allocation strategies.

c. return management strategies

d. return enhancement strategies

e. cost management strategies

# Chapter 14

# Performance Evaluation

Now that we seen how to manage an equity portfolio, let's turn to the important question of evaluating the performance of a manager. A client wants to know how well the manager it has retained has performed. The chief investment officer will want to know how well the managers responsible for the different portfolios under the firm's control have performed.

In this chapter we will see how to evaluate the investment performance of a manager. This process involves two steps: performance measurement and performance evaluation. *Performance measurement* involves the calculation of the return realized by a manager over some time interval which we call the *evaluation period*. As we will see, there are several important issues that must be addressed in developing a methodology for calculating a portfolio's return. Because different methodologies are available and these methodologies can lead to quite disparate results, it can be quite difficult to compare the performances of managers. Consequently, there is a great deal of confusion concerning the meaning of the data provided by managers to their clients and prospective clients that they are soliciting. This has lead to abuses by some managers in reporting performance results that are better than actual performance. To mitigate this problem the Committee for Performance Standards for the Association of Investment Management and Research has established standards for calculating performance results and how to present those results.

*Performance evaluation* is concerned with two issues. The first issue is determining whether the manager added value by outperforming the established benchmark. The second issue is determining how the money manager achieved the calculated return. For example, there are several strategies that an equity money manager can employ. Did the money manager achieve the return by market timing, by buying undervalued stocks, by buying low capitalization stocks, by overweighting specific industries, etc.? The decomposition of the performance results to explain the reasons why those results were achieved is called *performance attribution analysis*. Moreover, performance evaluation requires the determination of whether a manager achieved superior performance (i.e., added value) by skill or luck.

## PERFORMANCE MEASUREMENT

The starting point for evaluating the performance of a manager is measuring return. This might seem quite simple, but there are several practical issues that make the task complex.

393

# Alternative Return Measures

The *dollar return* realized on a portfolio for any evaluation period (i.e., a year, month, or week), is equal to the sum of

      1. the difference between the market value of the portfolio at the end of the evaluation period and the market value at the beginning of the evaluation period, and

      2. any distributions made from the portfolio.

It is important that any capital or income distributions from the portfolio to a client or beneficiary of the portfolio be included.

The *rate of return*, or simply return, expresses the dollar return in terms of the amount of the market value at the beginning of the evaluation period. Thus, the return can be viewed as the amount (expressed as a fraction of the initial portfolio value) that can be withdrawn at the end of the evaluation period while maintaining the initial market value of the portfolio intact.

In equation form, the *portfolio's return* can be expressed as follows:

$$R_p = \frac{MV_1 - MV_0 + D}{MV_0} \tag{1}$$

where

    $R_p$ = the return on the portfolio
    $MV_1$ = the portfolio market value at the end of the evaluation period
    $MV_0$ = the portfolio market value at the beginning of the evaluation period
    $D$ = the cash distributions from the portfolio to the client during the evaluation period

To illustrate the calculation of a return, assume the following information for an external manager for a pension plan sponsor: the portfolio's market value at the beginning and end of the evaluation period is $25 million and $28 million, respectively, and during the evaluation period $1 million is distributed to the plan sponsor from investment income. Thus:

$$MV_1 = \$28{,}000{,}000, \; MV_0 = \$25{,}000{,}000, \text{ and } D = \$1{,}000{,}000$$

then,

$$R_p = \frac{\$28{,}000{,}000 - \$25{,}000{,}000 + \$1{,}000{,}000}{\$25{,}000{,}000} = 0.16 = 16\%$$

There are three assumptions in measuring return as given by equation (1). First, it assumes that cash inflows into the portfolio from dividends and interest that occur during the evaluation period but are not distributed are reinvested in the portfolio. For example, suppose that during the evaluation period $2 million is received from dividends. This amount is reflected in the market value of the port-folio at the end of the period.

The second assumption is that if there are distributions from the portfolio, they occur at the end of the evaluation period, or are held in the form of cash until the end of the evaluation period. In our example, $1 million is distributed to the plan sponsor. But when did that distribution actually occur? To understand why the timing of the distribution is important, consider two extreme cases: (1) the distribution is made at the end of the evaluation period, as assumed by equation (1), and (2) the distribution is made at the beginning of the evaluation period. In the first case, the money manager had the use of the $1 million to invest for the entire evaluation period. By contrast, in the second case, the money manager loses the opportunity to invest the funds until the end of the evaluation period. Consequently, the timing of the distribution will affect the return, but this is not considered in equation (1).

The third assumption is that there is no cash paid into the portfolio by the client. For example, suppose that sometime during the evaluation period the plan sponsor gives an additional $1.5 million to the external manager to invest. Conse-quently, the market value of the portfolio at the end of the evaluation period, $28 million in our example, would reflect the contribution of $1.5 million. Equation (1) does not reflect that the ending market value of the portfolio is affected by the cash paid in by the sponsor. Moreover, the timing of this cash inflow will affect the calculated return.

Thus, while the return calculation for a portfolio using equation (1) can be determined for an evaluation period of any length of time such as one day, one month or five years, from a practical point of view, the assumptions discussed above limit its application. The longer the evaluation period, the more likely the assumptions will be violated. For example, it is highly likely that there may be more than one distribution to the client and more than one contribution from the client if the evaluation period is five years. Thus, a return calculation made over a long period of time, if longer than a few months, would not be very reliable because of the assumption underlying the calculations that all cash payments and inflows are made and received at the end of the period.

Not only does the violation of the assumptions make it difficult to com-pare the returns of two money managers over some evaluation period, but is also not useful for evaluating performance over different periods. For example, equa-tion (1) will not give reliable information to compare the performance of a 1-month evaluation period and a 3-year evaluation period. To make such a compari-son, the return must be expressed per unit of time, for example, per year.

The way to handle these practical issues is to calculate the return for a short unit of time such as a month or a quarter. We call the return so calculated the *subperiod return*. To get the return for the evaluation period, the subperiod returns are then averaged. So, for example, if the evaluation period is one year and 12 monthly returns are calculated, the monthly returns are the subperiod returns and they are averaged to get the 1-year return. If a 3-year return is sought and 12 quarterly returns can be calculated, quarterly returns are the subperiod returns and they are averaged to get the 3-year return. The 3-year return can then be converted into an annual return by the straightforward procedure described later.

There are three methodologies that have been used in practice to calculate the average of the subperiod returns: (1) the arithmetic average rate of return, (2) the time-weighted rate of return (also called the geometric rate of return), and (3) the dollar-weighted return.

### Arithmetic Average Rate of Return

The *arithmetic average rate of return* is an unweighted average of the subperiod returns. The general formula is:

$$R_A = \frac{R_{P1} + R_{P2} + \ldots + R_{PN}}{N} \tag{2}$$

$R_A$  = the arithmetic average rate of return
$R_{Pk}$ = the portfolio return for subperiod $k$ as measured by equation (1), $k = 1, \ldots, N$
$N$   = the number of subperiods in the evaluation period

For example, if the portfolio returns [as measured by equation (1)] were -10%, 20%, and 5% in months July, August, and September, respectively, the arithmetic average monthly return is 5%, as shown below:

$$N = 3, \ R_{P1} = -0.10, \ R_{P2} = 0.20, \text{ and } R_{P3} = 0.05$$

$$R_A = \frac{-0.10 + 0.20 + 0.05}{3} = 0.05 = 5\%$$

There is a major problem with using the arithmetic average rate of return. To see this problem, suppose the initial market value of a portfolio is $28 million and the market values at the end of the next two months are $56 million and $28 million, and assume that there are no distributions or cash inflows from the client for either month. Then using equation (1) the subperiod return for the first month ($R_{P1}$) is 100% and the subperiod return for the second month ($R_{P2}$) is −50%. The arithmetic average rate of return using equation (2) is then 25%. Not a bad return! But think about this number. The portfolio's initial market value was $28 million. Its market value at the end of two months is $28 million. The return over this 2-month evaluation period is zero. Yet, equation (2) says it is a whopping 25%.

Thus, it is improper to interpret the arithmetic average rate of return as a measure of the average return over an evaluation period. The proper interpretation is as follows: *it is the average value of the withdrawals (expressed as a fraction of the initial portfolio market value) that can be made at the end of each subperiod while keeping the initial portfolio market value intact.* In our first example above in which the average monthly return is 5%, the investor must add 10% of the initial portfolio market value at the end of the first month, can withdraw 20% of the initial portfolio market value at the end of the second month, and can withdraw 5% of the initial portfolio market value at the end of the third month. In our second example, the average monthly return of 25% means that 100% of the initial portfolio market value ($28 million) can be withdrawn at the end of the first month and 50% must be added at the end of the second month.

### Time-Weighted Rate of Return

The *time-weighted rate of return* measures the compounded rate of growth of the initial portfolio market value during the evaluation period, assuming that all cash distributions are reinvested in the portfolio. It is also commonly referred to as the *geometric mean return* since it is computed by taking the geometric average of the portfolio subperiod returns computed from equation (1). The general formula is:

$$R_T = [(1 + R_{P1})(1 + R_{P2}) \ldots\ldots (1 + R_{PN})]^{1/N} - 1 \qquad (3)$$

where $R_T$ is the time-weighted rate of return and $R_{Pk}$ and $N$ are as defined earlier.

For example, let us assume the portfolio returns were −10%, 20%, and 5% in July, August and September, as in the first example above, then the time-weighted rate of return as given by equation (3) is:

$$R_T = [(1 + (-0.10))(1 + 0.20)(1 + 0.05)]^{1/3} - 1$$
$$= [(0.90)(1.20)(1.05)]^{1/3} - 1 = 0.043$$

Since the time-weighted rate of return is 4.3% per month, one dollar invested in the portfolio at the beginning of July would have grown at a rate of 4.3% per month during the 3-month evaluation period.

The time-weighted rate of return in the second example is 0%, as expected, as shown below:

$$R_T = [(1 + 1.00)(1 + (-0.50))]^{1/2} - 1$$
$$= [(2.00)(0.50)]^{1/2} - 1 = 0\%$$

In general, the arithmetic and time-weighted average returns will give different values for the portfolio return over some evaluation period. This is because in computing the arithmetic average rate of return, the amount invested is assumed to be maintained (through additions or withdrawals) at its initial portfolio market value. The time-weighted return, in contrast, is the return on a portfolio that varies in size because of the assumption that all proceeds are reinvested.

In general, the arithmetic average rate of return will exceed the time-weighted average rate of return. The exception is in the special situation where all the subperiod returns are the same, in which case the averages are identical. The magnitude of the difference between the two averages is smaller the less the variation in the subperiod returns over the evaluation period. For example, suppose that the evaluation period is four months and that the four monthly returns are as follows:

$$R_{P1} = 0.04, \, R_{P2} = 0.06, \, R_{P3} = 0.02, \, \text{and} \, R_{P4} = -0.02$$

The average arithmetic rate of return is 2.5% and the time-weighted average rate of return is 2.46%. Not much of a difference. In our earlier example in which we calculated an average rate of return of 25% but a time-weighted average rate of return of 0%, the large discrepancy is due to the substantial variation in the two monthly returns.

## Dollar-Weighted Rate of Return

The *dollar-weighted rate of return* is computed by finding the interest rate that will make the present value of the cash flows from all the subperiods in the evaluation period plus the terminal market value of the portfolio equal to the initial market value of the portfolio. The cash flow for each subperiod reflects the difference between the cash inflows due to investment income (i.e., dividends and interest) and contribution made by the client to the portfolio, and the cash outflows reflecting distributions to the client. Notice that it is not necessary to know the market value of the portfolio for each subperiod to determine the dollar-weighted rate of return.

The dollar-weighted rate of return is simply an internal rate of return calculation and, hence it is also called the *internal rate of return*. The general formula for the dollar-weighted rate of return is:

$$V_0 = \frac{C_1}{(1 + R_D)} + \frac{C_2}{(1 + R_D)^2} + \ldots + \frac{C_N + V_N}{(1 + R_D)^n} \tag{4}$$

where

$\quad R_D \quad$ = the dollar-weighted rate of return
$\quad V_0 \quad$ = the initial market value of the portfolio
$\quad V_N \quad$ = the terminal market value of the portfolio
$\quad C_k \quad$ = the cash flow for the portfolio (cash inflows minus cash outflows) for subperiod $k$, $k = 1, 2,\ldots, N$

For example, consider a portfolio with a market value of $100 million at the beginning of July, capital withdrawals of $5 million at the end of months July, August, and September, no cash inflows from the client in any month, and a market value at the end of September of $110 million. Then

$V_0 = \$100,000,000, \, N = 3, \, C_1 = C_2 = C_3 = \$5,000,00,$ and
$V_3 = \$110,000,000$

$R_D$ is the interest rate that satisfies the following equation:

$$\$100,000,000 = \frac{\$5,000,000}{(1 + R_D)} + \frac{\$5,000,000}{(1 + R_D)^2} + \frac{\$5,000,000 + \$110,000,000}{(1 + R_D)^3}$$

It can be verified that the interest rate that satisfies the above expression is 8.08%. This, then, is the dollar-weighted rate of return.

The dollar-weighted rate of return and the time-weighted rate of return will produce the same result if no withdrawals or contributions occur over the evaluation period and all investment income are reinvested. The problem with the dollar-weighted rate of return is that it is affected by factors that are beyond the control of the manager. Specifically, any contributions made by the client or withdrawals that the client requires will affect the calculated return. This makes it difficult to compare the performance of managers.

To see this, suppose that a pension plan sponsor engaged two managers, A and B, with $10 million given to A to manage and $200 million to B. Suppose that (1) both managers invest in identical portfolios (that is, the two portfolio have the same securities and are held in the same proportion), (2) for the following two months the rate of return on the two portfolios is 20% for month 1 and 50% for month 2, and (3) the amount received in investment income is in cash. Also assume that the plan sponsor does not make an additional contribution to the portfolio of either manager. Under these assumptions, it is clear that the performance of both managers would be identical. Suppose, however, that the plan sponsor withdraws $4 million from A at the beginning of month 2. This means that A could not invest the entire amount at the end of month 1 and capture the 50% increase in the portfolio value. A's net cash flow would be as follows: (1) in month 1 the net cash flow is −$2 million since $2 million is realized in investment income and $4 million is withdrawn by the plan sponsor. The dollar-weighted rate of return is then calculated as follows:

$$\$10,000,000 = \frac{-\$2,000,000}{(1 + R_D)} + \frac{\$12,000,000}{(1 + R_D)^2} = 0\%$$

For B, the cash inflow for month 1 is $40 million ($200 million times 20%) and the portfolio value at the end of month 2 is $360 million ($240 million times 1.5). The dollar-weighted rate of return is:

$$\$200,000,000 = \frac{\$40,000,000}{(1 + R_D)} + \frac{\$360,000,000}{(1 + R_D)^2} = 44.54\%$$

These are quite different results for two managers we agreed had identical performance. The withdrawal by the plan sponsor and the size of the withdrawal relative to the portfolio value had a significant affect on the calculated return. Notice also that even if the plan sponsor had withdrawn $4 million from B at the beginning of month 2, this would not have had as significant an impact as it did for A. The problem would also have occurred if we assumed that the return in month 2 is −50% and that instead of A realizing a withdrawal of $4 million, the plan sponsor contributed $4 million.

Despite this limitation, the dollar-weighted rate of return does provide information. It indicates information about the growth of the fund which a client will find useful. This growth, however, may not be attributable solely to the performance of the manager because of contributions and withdrawals.

### Annualizing Returns

The evaluation period may be less than or greater than one year. Typically, return measures are reported as an average annual return. This requires the annualization of the subperiod returns. The subperiod returns are typically calculated for a period of less than one year for the reasons described earlier. The subperiod returns are then annualized using the following formula:

$$\text{Annual return} = (1 + \text{Average period return})^{\text{Number of periods in year}} - 1 \qquad (5)$$

So, for example, suppose the evaluation period is three years and a monthly period return is calculated. Suppose further that the average monthly return is 2%. Then the annual return would be:

$$\text{Annual return} = (1.02)^{12} - 1 = 26.8\%$$

Suppose instead that the period used to calculate returns is quarterly and the average quarterly return is 3%. Then the annual return is:

$$\text{Annual return} = (1.03)^{4} - 1 = 12.6\%$$

## AIMR Performance Presentation Standards

As explained above, there are subtle issues in calculating the return over the evaluation period. There are also industry concerns as to how managers should present results to clients and how they should disclose performance data and records to prospects from whom they are seeking to obtain funds to manage.[1]

The Committee for Performance Presentation Standards (CPPS) of the Association for Investment Management and Research (AIMR) was charged with developing standards for disclosure. The standards adopted by the AIMR (effective 1993) "are a set of guiding ethical principles intended to promote full disclosure and fair representation by investment managers in reporting their investment results."[2] A secondary objective of the standards is to ensure uniformity in the presentation of results so it is easier for clients to compare the performance of managers. It is important to emphasize that the AIMR standards deal with the presentation of the data and what must be disclosed, not with how the manager should be evaluated.

---

[1] See the concerns expressed in Claude N. Rosenberg Jr., panel discussion, as reported in *Performance Measurement: Setting Standards, Interpreting the Numbers* (Charlottesville, VA: The Institute for Chartered Financial Analysts, 1989), p. 15.

[2] *Performance Presentation Standards: 1993* (Charlottesville, VA: Association for Investment Management and Research, 1993).

## Exhibit 1: Mandatory Practices and Disclosures for AIMR Compliance

To be considered in compliance with the standards, the following practices and disclosures *must* be followed:[1]

- Calculate performance on a total return basis.
- Employ accrual accounting rather than cash accounting in calculating return (except for dividends and calculations of performance for periods prior to 1993).
- Calculate return using the time-weighted rate of return methodology, with valuation on at least a quarterly basis and geometric linking of period returns.[2]
- Include all actual fee-paying, discretionary portfolios in one composite or aggregate measure. This prevents a manager from showing to a client it is soliciting only the performance of selective accounts that have performed well. The number of portfolios and amount of assets in the composite, and the percentage of the firm's total assets the composite represents must be disclosed. The firm must also disclose the existence of any minimum size below which portfolios are excluded from a composite and the inclusion of any non-fee-paying portfolios in the composite.
- No linking of the results of simulated and model portfolios with actual portfolio performance is permitted. That is, only actual portfolio performance, not the performance that would have been realized if a certain strategy had been employed, can be reported.
- Deduct all trading costs in calculating the return.
- Disclose whether the performance results are calculated gross or net of management fees. If net results are reported, then the average weighted management fee must be disclosed.
- Disclose the tax rate assumption if the results are reported after taxes.
- Present at least a 10-year performance record. If the firm has been in existence for less than 10 years, then the performance since inception must be reported.
- Present annual returns for all years.
- Provide a complete list and description of all the firm's composites.

*Notes:*

[1] There are other required practices and disclosures dealing with the reporting of results of accounts that have been terminated, the treatment of new portfolios added to a composite, and special requirements for international portfolios.

[2] The process of geometric linking of returns is explained in the text.

---

In developing these standards, the CPPS recognized that in practice there is no single ideal set of performance presentation standards that are applicable to all users. There are provisions in the standards to prevent certain abusive practices. Rather than mandating other practices, the standards provide guidelines and recommendations for reporting. Thus, the standards can be broken down into (1) the requirements and mandatory disclosures for compliance and (2) practices recommended. Exhibit 1 lists the practices and disclosures that must be followed. To be considered in compliance with the standards. Some of the practices that the AIMR encourages are summarized in Exhibit 2.

## Exhibit 2: AIMR Recommended Guidelines and Disclosures

Some of the practices that the AIMR encourages are:

- Revalue a portfolio whenever cash flows in or out of the portfolio and market action combine to distort performance.
- Present performance gross of management fees in one-on-one presentation to clients. The results should be presented before taxes.
- Treat convertible and other hybrid securities consistently across and within composites.
- Disclose external risk measures such as standard deviation of composite returns across time.
- Disclose benchmarks that parallel the risk or investment style the client is expected to track.
- For leveraged portfolios, disclose the results on an unleveraged basis where possible.

### Calculating Returns Under the Standards

In our illustrations of the various ways to measure portfolio return, we used the same length of time for the subperiod (e.g., a month or a quarter). The subperiod returns were averaged with the preferred method being geometric averaging. The AIMR standards require that the return measure minimize the effect of contributions and withdrawals so that cash flow beyond the control of the manager is minimized. If the subperiod return is calculated daily, the impact of contributions and withdrawals will be minimized. The time-weighted return measure can then be calculated from the daily returns.

From a practical point of view, the problem is that calculating a daily return requires that the market value of the portfolio be determined at the end of each day. While this does not present a problem for a mutual fund that must calculate the net asset value of the portfolio each business day, it is a time-consuming administrative problem for other managers.

An alternative to the time-weighted rate of return has been suggested. This is the dollar-weighted rate of return, which as we noted earlier is less desirable in comparing the performance of managers because of the affect of withdrawals and contributions beyond the control of the manager. The advantage of this method from an operational perspective is that market values do not have to be calculated daily. The affect of withdrawals and contributions is minimized if they are small relative to the length of the subperiod. However, if the cash flow is over 10% at any time, the AIMR standards require that the portfolio be revalued on that date.[3]

Once the subperiod returns in an evaluation period are calculated, they are compounded. The AIMR standards specify that for evaluation periods of less than one year returns should *not* be annualized. Thus, if the evaluation period is seven months and the subperiod returns calculated are monthly, the 7-month return should be reported by calculating the compounded 7-month return instead.

---

[3] For a further discussion of the implementation of the AIMR Standards, see Deborah H. Miller, "How to Calculate the Numbers According to the Standards," in *Performance Reporting for Investment Managers: Applying the AIMR Performance Presentation Standards* (Charlottesville, VA: AIMR, 1991).

# EVALUATING PERFORMANCE

In the previous section, we concentrated on performance measurement and the AIMR performance reporting standards. But a performance measure does not answer two questions: (1) How did the manager perform after adjusting for the risk associated with the active strategy employed? and (2) How did the manager achieve the reported return?

The answer to these two questions is critical in assessing how well or how poorly the manager performed relative to some benchmark. In answering the first question, we must draw upon the various measures of risk (beta and standard deviation, for examples) that we described in Chapter 2. The answer to the second question tells us how the manager achieved a return. The reason this is important is that a manager may tell a client that he or she plans to pursue one of the active strategies described in this book. The client would then expect that any superior return accomplished is a result of such a strategy. But how can the client be certain? For instance, suppose a manager solicits funds from a client by claiming he can achieve superior common stock performance by selecting underpriced stocks. Suppose also that this manager does generate a superior return compared to the S&P 500 index. The client should not be satisfied with this performance until the return realized by the manager is decomposed into the various components that generated the return. A client may find that the superior performance is due to the manager's timing of the market (i.e., revising the beta in anticipation of market movements) rather than due to selecting underpriced stocks. In such an instance, the manager may have outperformed the S&P 500 (even after adjusting for risk), but not by following the strategy that the manager told the client that he intended to pursue.

Below we look at the state-of-the art technology for adjusting returns for risk so as to determine whether a superior return was realized and to decompose the actual return of a portfolio so as to determine the reasons why a return was realized. We refer to this analysis as performance evaluation.

We begin with a discussion of the various benchmarks that can be used to evaluate the performance of a manager.

## Benchmark Portfolios

To evaluate the performance of a manager, a client must specify a benchmark against which the manager will be measured. There are four types of benchmarks that have been used in practice: (1) market indexes, (2) generic investment style indexes, (3) Sharpe benchmarks, and (4) normal portfolios. We discussed the various types of market indexes in Chapter 5. The other types of benchmarks are discussed below.

### *Generic Investment Style Indexes*

Developed by various consulting firms, a generic investment style index measures the various investment styles described in Chapter 5. The problem with these indexes is that it is often difficult to classify a manager by a particular investment style.

To illustrate this problem, suppose a manager buys equal amounts of 80 stocks — the 40 highest dividend yield stocks in the Russell 1000 index and the 40 lowest price-earnings stocks in the Russell 2000 index.[4] The Russell 1000 index includes the largest capitalization stocks. So, the manager could be classified as following a large-capitalization style. Conversely, the stocks selected from within this index have a high dividend yield, a characteristic of stocks selected by a value manager. Thus, the manager can be classified as having this style. Finally, since half the portfolio is comprised of stocks in the Russell 2000 which includes the smallest capitalization stocks, this manager can be classified as following a small-capitalization style.

### Sharpe Benchmarks

Because of the difficulty of classifying a manager into any one of the generic investment styles, William Sharpe suggested that a benchmark can be constructed using multiple regression analysis from various specialized market indexes.[5] The rationale is that potential clients can buy a combination of tilted index funds to replicate a style of investing. A benchmark can be statistically created that adjusts for a manager's index-like tendencies. Such a benchmark is called a *Sharpe benchmark*.

The 10 mutually exclusive indexes suggested by Sharpe to provide asset class diversification are (1) the Russell Price-Driven Stock Index (an index of large value stocks), (2) the Russell Earnings-Growth Stock Index (an index of large growth stocks), (3) the Russell 2000 Small Stock Index, (4) the Salomon Brothers 90-Day Bill Index, (5) the Lehman Intermediate Government Bond Index, (6) the Lehman Long-Term Government Bond Index, (7) the Lehman Corporate Bond Index, (8) the Lehman Mortgage-Backed Securities Index, (9) the Salomon Brothers Non-U.S. Government Bond Index, and (10) the Financial Times Actuaries Euro-Pacific Index.

Later in this chapter we will see how to use the Sharpe benchmark to evaluate performance.

### Normal Portfolios

A *normal portfolio* is a customized benchmark that includes "a set of securities that contains all of the securities from which a manager normally chooses, weighted as the manager would weight them in a portfolio."[6] Thus, a normal portfolio is a specialized index. It is argued that normal portfolios are more appropriate benchmarks than market indexes because they control for investment management style thereby representing a passive portfolio against which a manager can be evaluated. In effect, the manager is being challenged to beat his or her average.

---

[4] This illustration is from H. Russell Fogler, "Normal Style Indexes — An Alternative to Manager Universes?" in *Performance Measurement: Setting the Standards, Interpreting the Numbers*, p. 97.

[5] William F. Sharpe, "Determining A Fund's Effective Asset Mix," *Investment Management Review* (September/October 1988), pp. 16-29.

[6] Jon Christopherson, "Normal Portfolios: Construction of Customized Benchmarks," in Chapter 6 in Frank J. Fabozzi (ed.), *Active Equity Portfolio Management* (New Hope, PA: Frank J. Fabozzi Associates, 1997), p.92.

## Exhibit 3: Example of Normal Portfolio Specification
### Section A: Screening Procedure
*Choose all stocks that meet the following criteria:*

1. Capitalization        ≥  $350,000,000 (i.e., large capitalization)
2. Yield                 ≤  5.00%
3. Book Price            ≤  0.5 Std. Deviation *(translates to Price/Book Ratio 1.00)*
4. Dividend Payout Ratio ≤  Market *(translates to less than or equal to the mean of the distribution)*
5. Historical Beta       ≥  0.85
6. Earnings Variability  ≥  (0.5) Std. Deviation *(translates to one-half standard deviation below* the mean of the distribution)

### Section B: Weight Scheme
*Equal Weight Within the Following Parameters*

|                            | % of Portfolio |
|----------------------------|----------------|
| $350 Million - $1 Billion  | 15%            |
| $1 Billion - $3 Billion    | 30%            |
| $3 Billion - $6 Billion    | 35%            |
| $6 Billion and up          | 15%            |
| IBM                        | 5%             |

### Section C: Rebalancing Scheme
Prior to 1989, the manager ran the screens semiannually and rebalanced position sizes monthly. After 1989, they do not rebalance monthly, rather they let the positions run for the full six months.

Source: Exhibit 1 in Jon Christopherson, "Normal Portfolios: Construction of Customized Benchmarks," in Chapter 6 in Frank J. Fabozzi (ed.), *Active Equity Portfolio Management* (New Hope, PA: Frank J. Fabozzi Associates, 1997), p.96

---

The construction of a normal portfolio for a particular manager is no simple task.[7] The principle is to construct a portfolio that, given the historical portfolios held by the manager, will reflect that manager's style in terms of assets and the weighting of those assets. The construction of a normal portfolio for a manager requires (1) defining the stocks to be included in the normal portfolio and (2) determining how these stocks should be weighted (i.e., equally weighted or capitalization weighted). The kind of information needed in order to create a normal portfolio is shown in Exhibit 3.

Defining the set of stocks to be included in the normal portfolio begins with discussions between the client and the manager to determine the manager's investment style. Based on these discussions, the universe of all publicly traded stocks is reduced to a subset that includes those stocks that the manager considers eligible given his investment style. For example, suppose that the manager's investment style is to invest in only stocks with a price/earnings ratio less than the average of all publicly traded stocks; all such stock would be included in the normal portfolio.

---

[7] See Mark Kritzman, "How to Build a Normal Portfolio in Three Easy Steps," *Journal of Portfolio Management* (Spring 1987), pp. 21-23.

Given these stocks, the next question is how they should be weighted in the normal portfolio. The choices are equal weighting, capitalization weighting, or a hybrid weighting scheme. In an equal weighting scheme, each stock is assigned the same portfolio percentage regardless of its market capitalization. In a capitalization weighted scheme, the total market capitalization of the stocks selected for the normal portfolio is computed. Then each stock is assigned a weight based on the market capitalization of the stock included in the normal portfolio and the total market capitalization. A hybrid weighting scheme may assign an equal weighting to stocks with a market capitalization that is less than some value and then a capitalization weight for all stocks above that value. Section B in Exhibit 3 shows a more complicated weighting scheme.

The weighting scheme selected can have a material impact on the performance benchmark. Most active managers do not structure their portfolios based on market capitalization. To see the effect of the weighting scheme, suppose that (1) the normal portfolio consists of the following six stocks, (2) these stocks are market capitalization weighted using the weights shown below, and (3) over the past year the return for each stock is as shown below:

| Stock | Capitalization weight | Return |
|-------|----------------------|--------|
| 1 | 35% | 18% |
| 2 | 25% | 12% |
| 3 | 20% | 10% |
| 4 | 10% | 8% |
| 5 | 5% | 8% |
| 6 | 5% | 6% |

The return for this normal portfolio for the one year is 12.8%.

Now suppose that Manager A whose benchmark is the 6-stock normal portfolio holds the same six stocks but in different proportions to the weights used in constructing the normal portfolio. Specifically, suppose that Manager A has a bias toward small capitalization stocks and the weights are as shown below (the return for the individual stocks is the same as above)

| Stock | Capitalization weight | Return |
|-------|----------------------|--------|
| 1 | 5% | 18% |
| 2 | 5% | 12% |
| 3 | 15% | 10% |
| 4 | 24% | 8% |
| 5 | 26% | 8% |
| 6 | 25% | 6% |

The return realized for Manager A's portfolio is 8.5%. The manager substantially underperformed the normal portfolio. The manager's alleged underperformance was due to the weighting scheme which was biased in favor of large capitalization stocks. For example, suppose Manager B who is evaluated against the 6-stock normal portfolio has a bias toward large capitalization stocks and holds the same six stocks in the proportions shown below:

| Stock | Capitalization weight | Return |
|-------|----------------------|--------|
| 1 | 40% | 18% |
| 2 | 30% | 12% |
| 3 | 15% | 10% |
| 4 | 4% | 8% |
| 5 | 6% | 8% |
| 6 | 5% | 6% |

The return for Manager B's portfolio is 13.4%, suggesting that this manager outperformed the normal portfolio.

Various methodologies can be used to determine the weights. These methodologies typically involve a statistical analysis of the historical holdings of a manager and the risk exposure contained in those holdings. For example, a consultant may suggest using a manager's month-end portfolios over the past five years as a guide in determining weights.[8] Plan sponsors work with pension consultants to develop normal portfolios for a manager. The consultants use commercially available systems that have been developed for performing the needed statistical analysis and the necessary optimization program to create a portfolio exhibiting similar factor positions to replicate the "normal" position of a manager.[9]

There are some who advocate the responsibility of developing normal portfolios should be left to the manager. However, many clients are reluctant to let their managers control the construction of normal portfolios because they believe that the managers will produce easily beaten, or "slow rabbit," benchmarks. Bailey and Tierney demonstrate that under reasonable conditions there is no-long term benefit for the manager to construct a "slow rabbit" benchmark and explain the disadvantage of a manager pursuing such a strategy.[10] In addition, they recommend that clients should let managers control the benchmarks. Clients, should, instead, focus their efforts on monitoring the quality of the benchmarks and the effectiveness of the managers' active management strategies.

## Single-Index Performance Evaluation Measures

In the 1960s, several single-index measures were used to evaluate the relative performance of managers. These measures of performance evaluation did not specify how or why a manager may have outperformed or underperformed a benchmark. The three measures, or indexes, are the *Treynor index,*[11] the *Sharpe index,*[12] and

---

[8] Edward P. Rennie and Thomas J. Cowhey, "The Successful Use of Benchmark Portfolios," in Darwin M. Bayston and H. Russell Fogler, (eds.), *Improving Portfolio Performance with Quantitative Models,* (Charlottesville: Institute of Chartered Financial Analysts, 1989), p. 34.

[9] The procedure for creating normals using the BARRA system is explained in the following two publications of the firm *The Normalbook* (September 1988) and Arjun Divecha and Richard Grinold, *Normal Portfolios: Issues for Sponsors, Managers, and Consultants* (February 1989).

[10] Jeffrey V. Bailey and David E. Tierney, "Gaming Manager Benchmarks," *Journal of Portfolio Management* (Summer 1993), pp. 37-41.

[11] Jack Treynor, "How to Rate Management of Investment Funds," *Harvard Business Review* (January-February 1965), pp. 63- 75.

[12] William F. Sharpe, "Mutual Fund Performance," *Journal of Business* (January 1966), pp. 119-138.

the *Jensen index*.[13] All three indexes assume that there is a linear relationship between the portfolio's return and the return on some broad-based market index.

In the early studies of investment managers, these measures were used to evaluate the performance of the managers of mutual funds. However, they are of very limited use in the evaluation of managers today because of the development of the performance attribution models discussed in the next section.

### Treynor Index

The *Treynor index* is a measure of the excess return per unit of risk. The excess return is defined as the difference between the portfolio's return and the risk-free rate of return over the same evaluation period. The risk measure in the Treynor index is the relative systematic risk as measured by the portfolio's beta which can be estimated statistically. Treynor argues that this is the appropriate risk measure since in a well-diversified portfolio the unsystematic risk is close to zero.

In equation form, the Treynor index is:

$$\frac{\text{Portfolio return} - \text{Risk-free rate}}{\text{Portfolio's beta}}$$

## Sharpe Index

As with the Treynor index, the *Sharpe index* is a measure of reward/risk ratio. The numerator is the same as in the Treynor index. The risk of the portfolio is measured by the standard deviation of the portfolio. The Sharpe index is thus:

$$\frac{\text{Portfolio return} - \text{Risk-free rate}}{\text{Standard deviation of portfolio}}$$

Thus the Sharpe index is a measure of the excess return relative to the total variability of the portfolio. The Sharpe and Treynor indexes will give identical rankings if the portfolios evaluated are well diversified. If they are poorly diversified, the rankings could be quite different.

### Jensen Index

The *Jensen index* uses the capital asset pricing model to determine whether the manager outperformed the market index. The empirical analogue of the CAPM is

$$R_p - R_F = \beta_p (R_M - R_F) + e$$

where

$$\begin{aligned}
R_p &= \text{the return on the portfolio} \\
R_F &= \text{the risk-free rate} \\
\beta_p &= \text{the beta of the portfolio}
\end{aligned}$$

---

[13] Michael C. Jensen, "The Performance of Mutual Funds in the Period 1945-1964," *Journal of Finance* (May 1968), pp. 389-416.

$$R_M \quad = \text{ return on the market}$$
$$e \quad = \text{ random error term}$$

In words:

Excess return = Beta × [Excess return on the market index]
+ Random error term

If the excess return produced by the manager does not exceed the excess return described by this formula, however, the manager has added nothing. After all, the historical beta of the portfolio represents an expectation of information-free performance; a random portfolio should perform this well. Jensen, then, added a factor to represent the portfolio's performance that diverges from its beta. This term, called *alpha,* is a measure of the manager's performance. Using time-series data for the return on the portfolio and the market index, the following equation can be estimated by regression analysis:

$$R_{pt} - R_{Ft} = \alpha_p + \beta_p \left[ (R_{Mt}) - R_{Ft} \right] + e_{pt}$$

The intercept term alpha, $\alpha_p$, in the above equation is the unique return realized by the manager. That is:

Excess return = Unique return + Beta × [Excess return on the market index]
+ Random error term

The Jensen measure is the alpha or unique return that is estimated from the above regression. If the alpha is not statistically different from zero, there is no unique return. A statistically significant alpha that is positive means that the manager out-performed the market index on a risk-adjusted basis; a negative value means that the manager underperformed the market index after risk consideration.

As with the Treynor index, the Jensen measure assumes that the portfolio is fully diversified so that the only risk remaining in the portfolio is systematic risk.

## Application of Traditional Performance Measures

Exhibit 4 reports some of the basic statistics that we covered in Chapter 3, as well as the single index performance measures that we explain in this chapter.[14] The respective performance measures include the average return, standard deviation, Jensen index (alpha), beta, $R^2$ (percentage of portfolio return variation explained), and the single index Sharpe measure. As mentioned before, the Jensen

---

[14] While we show in this section how to apply the traditional single index performance measures--such as the Jensen index, the Sharpe index, and the Treynor index — it should be emphasized that institutional managers largely use the multi-factor performance attribution approaches that we describe later. To the extent that single index performance measures are still in use today, they are used primarily in the evaluation of mutual funds — for example, see most any Morningstar mutual fund report.

index is a measure of risk adjusted portfolio performance, while the traditional Sharpe ratio looks at the average fund premium (average portfolio return less risk-free rate of interest) per unit of total portfolio risk (measured by rate of return standard deviation).[15]

Exhibit 4 shows portfolio statistics for two hypothetical funds — Market Fund X and Growth Fund Y. On the surface, it appears that the actively managed Growth Fund Y has outperformed the Market Fund X — since the average rate of return on the growth fund, 22%, exceeds the (assumed) return earned on the market index fund, 20%, by 200 basis points. In a total return sense, Growth Fund Y has in fact outperformed Market Fund X. However, on a portfolio risk scale, we see that the standard deviation of the return to the growth fund, at 15%, is higher than the risk level assumed on the Market Fund X, at 12%. In this context, Exhibit 4 reveals some "mixed" evidence as to whether Growth Fund Y outperformed the market index when one considers the additional risk.

A closer look at Exhibit 4 reveals that the Jensen index for the Market Fund X is zero. This alpha value should not be surprising given that the goal of an index fund is to track the performance of a market benchmark. Indeed, with a Jensen index at zero, and an $R^2$ at 100 (for 100%), that would speak loudly about just how well (as opposed to how poorly) the index fund manager was doing in achieving the stated risk management goal of the passive fund. In contrast, it is troubling — from a risk adjusted performance perspective — to see that the Jensen index for the Growth Fund Y is negative, at −200 basis points per year. With that alpha, and an "expense ratio" for actively managed funds that is often several times the standard fee associated with a passive fund, it is easy to see why investment moneys would move into the Market Fund X and away from an actively managed fund having risk-adjusted performance characteristics like Growth Fund Y.

---

### Exhibit 4: Traditional Performance Measures
### Passive versus Active Fund*

|  | Market Fund X | Growth Fund Y |
|---|---|---|
| Average Return % | 20 | 22 |
| Standard Deviation % | 12 | 15 |
| Alpha (Jensen index) % | 0.0 | −2 |
| Beta | 1.0 | 1.2 |
| $R^2$ % | 100 | 75 |
| Risk-free Rate | 5 | — |
| Sharpe index | 1.25 | 1.13 |

* Hypothetical funds and numerical example for illustration purposes only.

---

[15] In a later section to this chapter, we cover the conventional Sharpe benchmarks as a multiple index approach to performance attribution.

Exhibit 4 also reports the traditional Sharpe index for the two equity funds. At 1.13, the Sharpe index for the Growth Fund Y is lower than the corresponding risk-adjusted performance ratio for Market Fund X, at 1.25. In terms of capital market theory, discussed in Chapter 2, this means that the "slope" of the Capital Market Line — where the CML consists of a "two-asset" holding of U.S. Treasury bills (slightly levered) and the S&P 500 — is everywhere higher than the slope of a hypothetical line connecting the average return on Growth Fund Y with the risk-free rate of interest. In effect, the Sharpe index suggests that the risk-adjusted performance of the growth fund is lower than the corresponding average excess return (average portfolio return less risk-free rate) to portfolio risk ratio for the passively managed Market Fund X.

Although the Treynor index is not listed in Exhibit 4, we can easily calculate it according to:[16]

Treynor index = (Portfolio return – Risk-free return)/beta
= (Sharpe index × Portfolio standard deviation)/beta

Upon inserting the relevant portfolio statistics for Growth Fund Y and Market Fund X into the above formula, we obtain:

Treynor index (Growth Fund Y) = 1.13 × 15.00/1.20 = 14.13
Treynor index (Market Fund X) = 1.25 × 12.00/1.00 = 15.00

As with the single index Sharpe measure, the Treynor index reveals that Market Fund X has outperformed the Growth Fund Y on a risk-adjusted basis — where portfolio risk in the Treynor view is measured by the fund's "relative" risk in the market, or its beta.

Based on the overall performance findings revealed in Exhibit 4 it is evident that the investor should be more optimistic about the risk-adjusted performance results for Market Fund X when compared with the performance results for actively managed Growth Fund Y — even though the growth fund outperformed the market index fund on a total return basis. However, one of the serious limitations of the single index performance measures that we review here — including the Jensen index (alpha), Sharpe index, and the Treynor index — is that *none* of these measures tell the investor or portfolio manager anything about the underlying economic and/or financial factors that led to the revealed abnormal portfolio performance. Fortunately, the severe performance measurement limitation of single index models can be overcome with performance attribution models that are based on the fundamental and/or macroeconomic factor models that we described in Chapter 9.

---

[16] Morningstar, for example, does not report the Treynor index in its (single index) analysis of mutual fund performance. However, this firm does report well known "MPT (Modern Portfolio Theory) Statistics" such as the Jensen index (alpha), the Sharpe index, the standard deviation of portfolio return, and the portfolio beta.

# Equity Performance Attribution Models

In broad terms, the return performance of a common stock portfolio can be explained by four actions followed by a manager. The first is actively managing a portfolio so as to time movements in the market. For example, the manager can increase the beta of a portfolio when the market is expected to increase and decrease it when the market is expected to decline The second is actively managing a portfolio so as to capitalize on factors that are expected to perform better than other factors. For example, if a manager believes that low price-earnings stocks will outperform high price-earnings stock, the manager can tilt the portfolio in favor of low price-earnings stocks. The third is selecting the industries in which to invest. The fourth is actively managing the portfolio by buying stocks that are believed to be undervalued and selling (or shorting) stocks that are believed to be overvalued.

If it is possible to decompose the actual return of a portfolio into the reasons for the performance, we can answer questions such as: (1) What were the major sources of added value? (2) Was market timing statistically significant? (3) Was the manager in the right industries? (4) Was security selection statistically significant? The analysis must employ statistical analysis in order to determine whether the results are statistically significant or just a result of luck.

The methodology for answering these questions is called *performance attribution analysis.* The single-index performance evaluation measures discussed above do not help answer these questions. However, for stock portfolios, multi-factor models which we described in Chapter 9 can be used to answer the above questions.

The most popular model used by large plan sponsors and their consultants to evaluate the performance of equity managers is *BARRA's performance analysis (PERFAN) factor model.* We described the BARRA factor model in Chapter 9. The four sources of return (factors) of a common stock portfolio in terms of our discussion above are referred to in the BARRA model as "market timing," "risk indices," "industries," and "asset selection." Below we will illustrate this model with the analysis of a hypothetical portfolio as reported by Frank Jones and Ronald Kahn.[17] A discussion of the statistical analysis employed to derive the BARRA model for performance analysis is beyond the scope of this chapter.

Exhibit 5 reports the return on the portfolio and its decomposition based on BARRA's factor model. Notice that the return for the portfolio ("Total Managed Portfolio Return") was 20.6% while the return for the benchmark portfolio ("Benchmark Return") that this manager is evaluated against was 20.24%. Since the 20.24%, the Benchmark Return, can be accomplished without active management, the excess return of 36 basis points is referred to as the "Total Active Return." The key is to attribute the Total Active Return to the four factors in the BARRA model.

---

[17] Frank J. Jones and Ronald N. Kahn, "Stock Portfolio Attribution Analysis," Chapter 32 in Frank J. Fabozzi (ed.), *Handbook of Portfolio Management* (New Hope, PA: Frank J. Fabozzi Associates, 1998).

## Exhibit 5: Illustration of Decomposition of Total Return Using BARRA Stock Portfolio Factor Model

Returns

| Total Managed Portfolio | Benchmark |
|---|---|
| (+20.60%) | (+20.24%) |

Total Active
(+0.36%)

| Expected Active* | Total Exceptional Active |
|---|---|
| (−0.42%) | (+0.78%) |

| Market Timing | Risk Indices | Industries | Asset Selection |
|---|---|---|---|
| (−0.64%) | (+2.69%) | (+0.09%) | (−1.37%) |

* $(B_p-1) \times 6.0\% = -0.42\%$ where $B_p$, the portfolio beta equals 0.93, and where 6.0% is the expected excess market return (that is, in excess of the risk free rate).

Source: Exhibit 3 in Frank J. Jones and Ronald N. Kahn, "Stock Portfolio Attribution Analysis," Chapter 32 in Frank J. Fabozzi (ed.), *Handbook of Portfolio Management* (New Hope, PA: Frank J. Fabozzi Associates, 1998), p. 700.

---

Before doing this, the Total Active Return must be decomposed because a portion of the Total Active Return is due to the beta of the portfolio differing from that of the benchmark. The portion of the Total Active Return resulting from the deviation of the portfolio's beta and benchmark's beta is called the "Expected Active Return." The difference between the Total Active Return and the Expected Active Return is called the "Total Exceptional Active Return" and it is this return that will be further analyzed using the BARRA factors.

Let's first look at how the Expected Active Return is computed. We know from the capital asset pricing model the following:

$$E(R_p) = R_F + \beta_p [E(R_M) - R_F]$$

We are interested in the spread between the expected return for the portfolio, $E(R_p)$, and the expected return on the market, $E(R_M)$. This spread is the Expected Active Return. Solving for $E(R_p) - E(R_M)$ we have

$$E(R_p) - E(R_M) = (\beta_p - 1) [E(R_M) - R_F]$$

This equation tells us that the Expected Active Return is found by multiplying the portfolio's beta deviation from 1 by the market risk premium $[E(R_M) - R_F]$.

Thus, to determine the Expected Active Return it is necessary to not only compute the portfolio's beta, but to estimate what the market risk premium is. Studies have suggested that the market risk premium is 6% and this is the value used in the BARRA analysis. In our illustration, the portfolio's beta is 0.93. Therefore,

Expected Active Return = $(0.93 - 1) (0.06) = -0.0042 = -0.42\%$

Given the Expected Active Return, the Total Exception Active Return is found as follows:

Total Exceptional Active Return
= Total Active Return − Expected Active Return

Using the values from our illustration, we find:

Total Exceptional Active Return = 0.36% − (−0.42%) = 0.78%

Now the task is to find out how the manager generated the 78 basis points of Total Exceptional Active Return. The decomposition of the Total Exceptional Active Return is shown in Exhibit 5. A detailed breakdown in terms of the components of the four BARRA factors is provided in Exhibit 6. Exhibit 7 provides a summary of the analysis of the performance of this portfolio as described by Jones and Kahn.

## Performance Evaluation Using Sharpe Benchmarks

As explained earlier, Sharpe benchmarks are determined by regressing subperiod (e.g., monthly) returns on various market indexes. For example, a Sharpe benchmark was computed for an actual common stock portfolio. The evaluation period was for the period January 1981 through July 1988. After adjustments, the resulting Sharpe benchmark based on monthly observations was[18]

Sharpe benchmark = 0.43 × (FRC Price-Driven index)
+ 0.13 × (FRC Earnings-Growth index) + 0.44 × (FRC 2000 index)

where FRC is an index produced by Frank Russell Company.

Notice that the sum of the three coefficients is equal to one. The coefficient of determination for this regression was 97.6%. The intercept term for this regression is 0.365% which represents the average excess monthly return and is a statistic similar to Jensen's alpha explained earlier.

By subtracting the style benchmark's monthly return from the manager's monthly portfolio return, performance can be measured. This difference, which is referred to as "added-value residual," is what the manager added over the return from three "index funds" in the appropriate proportions. For example, suppose that in some month the return realized by this manager is 1.75%. In the same month, the return for the three indexes were as follows: 0.7% for the FRC Price-Driven index, 1.4% for the FRC Earnings-Growth index, and 2.2% for the FRC 2000 index. The added-value residual for this month would be calculated as follows. First, calculate the value of the Sharpe benchmark:

Sharpe benchmark = 0.43 × (0.7%) + 0.13 × (1.4%) + 0.44 × (2.2%)
= 1.45%

---

[18] See Fogler, "Normal Style Indexes — An Alternative to Manager Universes?" p. 102.

## Exhibit 6: Decomposition of Total Exceptional Active Return (0.7790%)

| Market Timing (-0.6370%) | | Risk Indices (+2.6936%) | | Industries (+0.0879%) | | Asset Selection (-1.3656%) | |
|---|---|---|---|---|---|---|---|
| | | *Size* | | *Sectors* | | | |
| - Average Active Equity Beta | -0.6030 | Size | -0.1032 | - Basic Mat'ls | -0.1496 | - Assets Held in portfolio | -0.435 |
| - Active Equity Beta Variation | -0.0340 | Size Non-Linearity | 0.0616 | - Energy | 0.1658 | . Over-weighted Assets | -0.435 |
| . Above Average Equity Beta | +0.0022 | Non-Est Universe | 0.0000 | . Cnsmr Non-cyclicals | 0.1859 | . Under-weighted Assets | +0.000 |
| . Below Average Equity Beta | -0.0362 | | -0.0416 | - Cnsmr Cyclicals | 0.0603 | | |
| - Equity Beta Policy | -0.6370 | *Growth/Value* | | - Cnsmr Services | 0.2311 | Benchmark Assets Not Held | -0.930 |
| | | Growth | 0.3940 | - Industrials | 0.0705 | | |
| | | Earnings Yield | 1.1492 | - Utility | -0.3071 | Total Asset Selection | -1.366 |
| | | Value | 0.6627 | - Transport | -0.0565 | | |
| | | Dividend Yield | -0.1477 | - Health Care | -0.2740 | | |
| | | | 2.0582 | - Technology | 0.0522 | | |
| | | *Risk* | | - Telecommunications | 0.0143 | | |
| | | Volatility | 0.1754 | - Commercial Services | -0.0349 | | |
| | | Momentum | -0.0575 | - Financial | 0.1299 | | |
| | | Trading Activity | 0.0141 | | | | |
| | | Earnings Variation | 0.2142 | Total Sector | 0.0879 | | |
| | | Leverage | 0.2634 | | | | |
| | | Currency Sensitivity | 0.0676 | (13 Sectors further subdivided into 52 Industries) | | | |
| | | | 0.6772 | | | | |
| | | *Total* | 2.6936 | | | | |

Source: Exhibit 4 in Frank J. Jones and Ronald N. Kahn, "Stock Portfolio Attribution Analysis," Chapter 32 in Frank J. Fabozzi (ed.), *Handbook of Portfolio Management* (New Hope, PA: Frank J. Fabozzi Associates, 1998), p. 701.

## Exhibit 7: Summary of Manager's Performance Based on Attribution Analysis

Given the results of the attribution analysis provided in Exhibits 4 and 5, evaluate the managed portfolio's performance over this period.

The answer is as follows. The managed portfolio returned +20.60% over this period, outperforming the benchmark's +20.24% return by +0.36% (the Total Active Return). This +0.36% overperformance was composed of an underperformance of 0.42% in the Expected Active Return based on (1) the portfolio's beta (0.93) and the average excess market return (6%) and (2) an overperformance of 0.78% in the Total Exceptional Active Return.

The Total Exceptional Active Return is composed of four components. The first component is Market Timing, in which there was an underperformance of 0.64%, almost all of which was due to the Average Active Equity Beta (0.60%). The remainder (0.04%) was due to an underperformance of 0.04% in below average equity beta — the above active equity beta outperformed by an insignificant 0.0022%.

The second component, the Risk Indices factor, was the largest positive contributor to Total Active Return with an outperformance of 2.69%. Of this, there was an overperformance of 2.06% due to the growth/value style factor. There was also an overperformance of 0.68% due to the Risk Index style factor and an underperformance of 0.04% due to the Size style factor. When decomposed into the 13 Risk Indices, the strongest and the weakest indices were as follows:

| Strong | | Weak | |
|---|---|---|---|
| Earnings Yield | 1.1492 | Yield | −0.1477 |
| Value | 0.6627 | Size | −0.1032 |
| Growth | 0.3940 | Momentum | −0.0575 |
| Leverage | 0.2634 | Non-Estimation Universe | 0.0000 |

Third, there was an overperformance of 0.09% due to the Industries factor. Among the 13 sectors, the three strongest and weakest sectors were as follows:

| Strong | | Weak | |
|---|---|---|---|
| Consumer Services | +0.2311% | Utility | −0.3071% |
| Consumer (non-cyclical) | +0.1859% | Health Care | −0.2740% |
| Energy | +0.1658% | Basic Materials | −0.1496% |

The 13 sectors are divided into 52 industries. While returns are attributed to the industries in the model, they are not included herein.

The fourth factor in the Total Exceptional Active Return is Asset Selection which provided an underperformance relative to the benchmark of 1.37%. This underperformance was caused by a 0.44% underperformance due to assets overweighted in the portfolio and an underperformance of 0.93% due to benchmark assets not held in the portfolio.

Overall, the rather small total active overperformance of +0.36% was the net effect of some much larger positive and negative performances as summarized in Exhibit 6 and as rank ordered below:

| | |
|---|---|
| Risk Indices: | +2.69% |
| Industries | +0.09% |
| Expected Active | −0.42% |
| Market Timing | −0.64% |
| Asset Selection | −1.37% |

The analysis suggests that this portfolio manager has been successful in "betting on" cheap earnings and book value (the Value and Earnings Yield Risk Indices) and unsuccessful in selecting individual stocks (Asset Selection) and market timing (Market Timing). This portfolio manager might be more successful if (1) more stocks were purchased to diversify and limit individual stock bets, (2) the portfolio beta was maintained to limit market timing, and (3) factors other than Value and Earnings Yield bets were controlled.

Source: Adapted from Frank J. Jones and Ronald N. Kahn, "Stock Portfolio Attribution Analysis," Chapter 32 in Frank J. Fabozzi (ed.), *Handbook of Portfolio Management* (New Hope, PA: Frank J. Fabozzi Associates, 1998), pp. 706-707.

The added-value residual is then

Added-value residual = Actual return − Sharpe benchmark return

Since the actual return for the month is 1.75%,

Added-value residual = 1.75% − 1.45% = 0.3%.

Notice that if this manager had been benchmarked against a single investment style index such as the FRC Price-Driven index, he would have outperformed the benchmark by a wide margin (1.05%). In contrast, if the FRC 2000 index is used as the benchmark, the manager would have underperformed by 0.45%.

# INFORMATION RATIO: A FITTING CONCLUSION

We conclude this chapter and book with a discussion of a performance measure concept known as the *information ratio* (IR). This performance ratio is a measure of the success of the investment process. As we learned in Chapter 1 (see Exhibit 2), the information ratio is related to the "depth" of equity manager insight and the "breadth" of equity manager insights — as reflected in either the number of investable ideas or the number of investment securities.

In more formal terms, the information ratio is a measure of risk-adjusted performance because it is a ratio of excess return (alpha) to residual risk (tracking error induced by a departure from benchmark holdings and weights). For example if a manager's excess return (relative to an agreed upon benchmark with a client) is 1.5%, with a residual risk (tracking error) of 3%, then the equity manager's information ratio is 0.5. A more highly skilled manager with a greater ability to select stocks would have an information ratio of 1 if the excess return is 3% (or 300 basis points relative to the benchmark) for the same (3%) tracking error.

Grinold and Kahn show that the information ratio is related to the depth of equity manager insight and the breadth of insights according to:[19]

$$IR = IC \times \sqrt{BR}$$

where $IR$ is the information ratio, $IC$ is the "information coefficient," and $BR$ is the breadth of equity manager insights. As mentioned above, $IR$ is a measure of the success of the investment process. In turn, the information coefficient, $IC$, is a quantitative measure of equity manager depth. It is measured by the correlation between the manager's forecasted excess return (relative to a benchmark) and the actual excess return.

---

[19] A rigorous examination of the information ratio in the context of equity manager depth and breadth of insights can be found in Richard C. Grinold and Ronald N. Kahn, *Active Portfolio Management* (Chicago, IL: Probus, 1995). An informative discussion of how depth of equity insight and breadth of opportunities combine to produce a constant IR can be found in Bruce I. Jacobs and Kenneth N. Levy, "Investment Management: An Architecture for the Equity Market," Chapter 1 in Frank J. Fabozzi (ed.), *Active Equity Portfolio Management* (New Hope, PA: Frank J. Fabozzi Associates, 1998).

## Exhibit 8: Iso-Information Ratio (IR) Curves

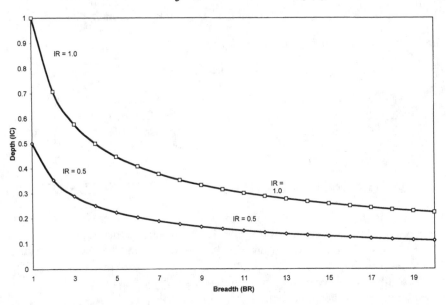

Exhibit 8 shows a pair of "iso-information ratio" curves, each having a constant measure of excess return-to-residual risk. The lower curve in the exhibit has an information ratio of 0.5, while the upper curve has an information ratio of 1.0. As we explained in Chapter 1, there are many combinations of depth (measured by the information coefficient) and breadth of investment insights (or securities) that can produce the same information ratio — as manifest in a constant excess return/residual risk ratio such as 0.5 or 1.0 shown in Exhibit 8.

With five securities (or insights), the lower curve in Exhibit 8 reveals that the manager would need to achieve a correlation of 0.2236 between forecasted excess returns and actual excess returns in order to produce an information ratio of 0.5. This same excess return/residual risk combination can be achieved with a portfolio of 15 securities (or insights) if the information coefficient declined to 0.1291. In contrast, the upper curve reveals that if the manager wants (or needs) to produce an information ratio of, say, 1 — whereby the excess return now equals the residual risk exposure — then this too can be achieved by several pair-wise combinations of depth and breadth.

Specifically, with five securities Exhibit 8 reveals that the equity manager would have to achieve a correlation of 0.4472 between forecasted excess returns and actual excess returns ($IC = 0.4472$) in order to produce a constant information ratio (excess reward/residual risk) of 1. This same information ratio can be achieved with 15 investable securities (or insights) as long as the depth of equity securities analysis ($IC$ ratio) is 0.2582.

This brings us to the end of our equity management journey. We hope that after reading this book that our readers will see a marked improvement in their own information ratios! — as revealed in a higher IR on managed institutional funds and/or their personal portfolios. The source of a possible rise in the information ratio for our readers may be due to (1) an expansion of investor depth of insight based on the innovative equity management strategies covered in this book—such as, the value-based metrics and factor-based approaches to equity securities analysis and portfolio management, and (2) an expansion of equity manager breadth due to opportunities that may arise from a greater understanding of the traditional and modern approaches to equity portfolio management explained in this book.

# QUESTIONS

1. What is the difference between performance measurement and performance evaluation?

2. Suppose that the monthly return for two money managers is as follows:

| Month | Manager A | Manager B |
|---|---|---|
| 1 | 9% | 25% |
| 2 | 13% | 13% |
| 3 | 22% | 22% |
| 4 | −18% | −24% |

    a. What is the arithmetic average monthly rate of return for the two managers?
    b. What is the time-weighted average monthly rate of return for the two managers?
    c. Why does the arithmetic average monthly rate of return diverge more from the time-weighted monthly rate of return for manager B than for manager A?

3. Stevens & Fortell is a money management firm. One of its clients gave the firm $50 million to manage. The market value for the portfolio for the four months after receiving the funds was as follows:

| End of month | Market value (in millions) |
|---|---|
| 1 | $25.0 |
| 2 | $75.0 |
| 3 | $37.5 |
| 4 | $50.0 |

    a. Calculate the rate of return for each month.
    b. Stevens & Fortell reported to the client that over the 4-month period the average monthly rate of return was 33.33%. How was that return obtained?
    c. Is the average monthly rate of return of 33.33% indicative of the performance of Stevens & Fortell? If not, what would be a more appropriate measure?

4. The X-tra Return Company is a money management firm that manages the funds of pension plan sponsors. For one of its clients it manages $50 million. The cash flow for this particular client's portfolio for the past three months was $5 million, −$2 million, and $1 million. The market value of the portfolio at the end of three months was $52 million.
    a. What is the dollar-weighted rate of return for this client's portfolio over the 3-month period?
    b. Suppose that the $2 million cash outflow in the second month was a result of withdrawals by the plan sponsor and that the cash flow after adjusting for this withdrawal is therefore zero. What would the dollar-weighted rate of return then be for this client's portfolio?

5. a. If the average monthly return for a portfolio is 0.92%, what is the annualized return?

   b. If the average quarterly return for a portfolio is 1.78%, what is the annualized return?

6. The Very Reliable Corporation is a money management firm that was started five years ago. The firm has 20 discretionary, fee paying accounts with an aggregate amount under management of $1.2 billion. In preparing a report for a client that it is prospecting for funds it has done the following:

   (i) presented the return for the past three years for five representative portfolios;

   (ii) Calculated the arithmetic average annual return over the past three years where the sub-period return was measured each year.

   (iii) disclosed what the return would have been for the past 10 years based on the actual performance for the past three years and simulated returns for the seven prior years using the same strategy it employed for the actual portfolio.

   (iv) calculated the return before transaction costs and management fees.

   Based on the above, explain whether or not Very Reliable Corporation is in compliance with the AIMR standards.

7. In *Performance Measurement: Setting the Standards, Interpreting the Numbers*, John Sherrerd, a member of the of the Performance Presentation Standards Committee of the AIMR, stated:

   It is important to keep in mind that the objective of these performance statistics is to measure the capabilities of the manager, not the cash flows. It is not an attempt to measure how many dollars the client has earned over a period of time. If the performance of the manager is being measured, those results should not be influenced by whether the client is taking money out and spending it, the way most endowments might, or leaving it in, as many corporations do.

   a. Why is the dollar-weighted rate of return affected by contributions and withdrawals by the client?

   b. What rate of return methodology does the AIMR standards require?

8. a. What is the performance evaluation role of a "normal portfolio"?

   b. What are the two principle requirements that are needed when constructing a normal portfolio?

c. Look again at Exhibit 3 Describe the quantitative (factor standardization and weighting) aspects of the screening procedure used to construct the normal portfolio shown in the illustration.

d. Explain how the screening criteria shown in Exhibit 3 could be modified to construct a normal portfolio for a large cap value manager. How would the screening fundamentals change for a large cap growth manager?

e. What are the conflicts (equity style drift, weighting schemes, for examples) that may arise between clients and managers when performance is benchmarked against a normal portfolio?

9. Use the following average return and risk estimates to calculate and interpret single index measures of investment performance for two mutual funds:

| Index/Portfolio | Average Return % | Standard Deviation % | Beta |
|---|---|---|---|
| Market index | 15 | 16 | 1.00 |
| Mutual fund A | 18 | 14 | 0.90 |
| Mutual fund B | 16 | 20 | 1.20 |
| Risk-free asset | 5 | — | — |

The two mutual funds are actively managed.

a. Calculate the Sharpe and Treynor indexes for the market index and mutual funds A and B.

b. Did mutual fund A or B outperform the market index on a total return basis?

c. Did mutual fund A or B outperform the market index on a "risk-adjusted" basis?

d. Is mutual fund A likely to be a "value" portfolio or a "growth" portfolio? How about mutual fund B?

e. Using single index measures as a basis for performance measurement, did the manager of mutual fund A or B generate a superior investment performance? Explain your reasoning.

f. What are the limitations of single index performance measures such as the traditional Sharpe index, the Treynor index, and the Jensen index?

10. The following statement was made by H. Russell Fogler in "Common Stock Management in the 1990s," *Journal of Portfolio Management* (Winter 1990), pp. 34:

> Once we appreciate the simplicity and power of multiple-factor models, single index measurement will join the archives of performance measurement history, where it belongs.

The Treynor index, Sharpe index, and Jensen index are examples of single index measurements. Indicate whether you agree with the statement made by Dr. Fogler.

11. a. What is a Sharpe benchmark used for?

   b. What is the quantitative procedure used to construct a Sharpe benchmark?

   c. Why is the Sharpe benchmark approach to measuring performance a potential improvement over generic value and growth style indexes?

12. a. Calculate the Sharpe benchmark for a portfolio using the model estimates shown below?

   *Estimated Model:* Sharpe Benchmark = 0.45 × FRC Price-Driven + 0.15 × FRC Earnings-Growth + 0.25 × FT Euro-Pacific + 0.15 × Lehman LT Government Bond

   | Index | Monthly Performance |
   |---|---|
   | FRC Price-Driven | 0.5% |
   | FRC Earnings-Growth | −2.0% |
   | FT Euro-Pacific | −5.5% |
   | Lehman LT Government Bond | 1.0% |

   b. What is the "added-value residual" for a hypothetical portfolio if the actual monthly return was 1%?

   c. What portfolio management implications can one draw from this finding?

13. a. Complete the exhibit provided below for a hypothetical portfolio showing the breakdown of total portfolio return using BARRA's *performance analysis (PERFAN) factor model.*

   | BARRA Decomposition of Portfolio Return % | | |
   |---|---|---|
   | | Total Managed Portfolio 17 | Benchmark 15 |
   | Total Active ? | | |
   | | Expected Active * ? | Total Exceptional Active ? |
   | | Market Timing 0.5 | Risk Indices 1.4 |
   | | Industries 0.2 | Asset Selection ? |

   * Portfolio beta of 1.4, and a market risk premium of 5%.

   b. Write a brief summary of the manager's performance based on the (partial) BARRA attribution analysis shown above. What additional information would you need to complete a detailed evaluation of the manager's active performance? (Hint: Recall the "Decomposition of Total Exceptional Active Return" shown in Exhibit 6 of this chapter.)

14. a. What is the information ratio (IR)?
   b. What is the value of the information ratio if the manager's excess return is −1.5%, with a tracking error (residual risk) of 3%? What are the client/manager implications of a negative information ratio?
   c. What is the relationship between the information ratio and the information coefficient (IC)?
   d. What is an "iso-information ratio" curve?

15. Calculate the required information coefficients that produce the constant information ratios in the table below. (Note that these are some of the IC values used to construct the "iso-information ratio" curves in Exhibit 8.)

Values to Produce Constant Information Ratio (IR)

IR = 0.5          IR = 1.0

| Breadth | Depth* | Breadth | Depth* |
|---------|--------|---------|--------|
| 1       |        | 1       |        |
| 5       | 0.2236 | 5       | 0.4472 |
| 10      |        | 10      |        |
| 15      | 0.1291 | 15      | 0.2582 |
| 20      |        | 20      |        |

\* Measured by information coefficient (IC)

# Index

70/30 solution, 74

## A

Abate, James A., 81, 156, 172, 284
Abnormal return, 66
Accounting-based measures, 153
Across-day measures, 317
Active portfolio strategy, 3
Active style management, 119
Additive dividend growth model, 205
Adjusted beta, 57
Agency incentive arrangement, 309
Alpha, 2, 31, 411
American Depository Receipts (ADRs), 334
American option, 333
Arbitrage Pricing Theory, 36, 66
Archambo, Wayne, 278
Arithmetic average rate of return, 44, 398
Arnott, Robert D., 113, 255
Asian option, 357
Ask price, 302
Asset allocation decisions, 383
Asset allocation, 374
Asset approach, 169
Asset pricing models, 11
Association for Investment Management and Research, 402
At-the-money option, 340
Automated order routing systems, 310
Average measures, 317, 318

## B

Bacidore, Jeffrey, 181
Bailey, Jeffrey V., 409
BARRA factor model, 256
BARRA model, 241
BARRA, 5, 9
BARRA's Market Impact Model, 321
BARRA's performance analysis (PERFAN) factor model, 414
Barrier put option, 383
Basic mechanics of equity swaps, 360
Basic swap structure, 359
Basic trading cost, 312
Basis, 355
Basket options, 383
Basket trades, 309
Bauman, W. Scott , 108, 119
Beebower, G., 318
Benchmark return, 414
Berkowitz, S., 318
Bernstein, Peter L., 89, 155, 318
Beta, 67
Beta-adjusted equivalent market index units, 374

Bid price, 302
Bid-ask spread, 304
Biddle, Gary, 180
Bienstock, Sergio, 102
Biller, Alan D., 312
Binary options, 358
Birnhaum, Samuel A., 323
Black, Fischer, 35, 342
Black-Scholes option pricing model, 342, 343
Block trades, 308
BLOOMBERG market model relationship, 59
Bloomberg, 57, 60, 133
Blume, Marshall E., 58
Bodurtha, Stephen, 318
Book value and asset growth, 125
Book value per share, 99
Boquist, John, 181
Boston Partners Asset Management, 9, 261, 278
Bottom up approach, 82
Bottom-up economic profit framework, 291
Bottom-up investing, 65
Bottom-up stock selection, 81
Bowen, Robert, 180
Breadth of manager insights, 6, 418, 419
Break-even recovery price, 370
Broker loan rate, 307
Brokers, 302
Brown, Keith, 89
Brown, Melissa, 104
Buffet, Warren, 83
Burmeister, Ibbotson, Roll, and Ross (BIRR) model, 82, 231
Business cycle risk, 231
Buy and hold strategy, 67
Buy limit order, 305
Buy write, 370

## C

Call money rate, 307
Call swaps, 359
Capital Asset Pricing Model, 25, 66, 140
Capital market line, 26, 70
Capital market theory, 11
Cash drag, 376
Cash Flow Return on Investment®, 9, 84, 153, 174
Cash flow yield, 101
Cash flow/price ratio, 101
Cash settlement contracts, 335
Cash-secured put strategy, 368
Chaos theory, 87
Chattiner, Sherman, 205
Christopherson, Jon A., 99, 204
Clearinghouse, 334
Clusters, 98

Coefficient of determination, 31, 52
Coefficient of variation, 46
Coggin, T. Daniel, 87
Cohen, Abby Joseph, 156, 214
Cohen, Kalman J., 21
College Retirement Equities Fund, 3
Collins, Bruce M., 312, 357
Columbia Management Company, 9, 261, 293
Commissions, 8, 312
Committee for Performance Standards for the Association for Investment Management and Research, 395, 402
Common factors, 83, 229, 249
Company-specific risk, 30
Condon, Kathleen A., 318
Confidence interval, 48
Confidence risk, 231
Connor, Gregory, 230
Consistent growth manager, 100
Constant dividend growth model, 202
Contingent options, 358
Contract's multiple, 337
Contrarian manager, 99
Controlling risk, 6
Corporate plowback ratio, 97, 136
Correlation, 20, 49
Cost of carry, 351
Cost of financing a position, 351
Counterparty risk, 334, 356
  credit triggers, 356
  netting arrangements, 356
  recouponing, 356
Covariance, 20
Covered call strategies, 370
Covered call, 370
Cowhey, Thomas J., 409
Cox, Daniel E., 323
Credit Suisse Asset Management, 9, 84, 172, 261, 284
  "bottom-up" approach, 284
Cross-hedging, 371
CS First Boston, 84, 165, 171
Cuneo, L.J., 313
Currency hedge, 379
Currency risk, 359
Current capital (or asset) structure, 272
Customer's margin, 334
Cyclical, 98

## D

Dealers, 302
DeBondt, Werner, 89
Degree of capital market efficiency, 65, 90
Degree of pricing inefficiencies, 80
Delta of an option, 347
Demsetz, Harold, 302

Derivative instruments, 2
  cost management strategies, 331, 367-368
  regulatory management strategies, 331, 337, 387
  return enhancement strategies, 370, 377, 384, 387
  return management strategies, 384
  risk management strategies, 331, 367, 382
Derivatives Product Companies, 356
Digital options, 358
Discounted cash flow models, 199
Discriminant analysis, 102
Divecha, Arjun, 409
Diversifiable risk, 30
Dividend discount model, 199, 200
Dividend growth, 125
Dividend yield, 97, 126
Dividend/price ratio, 101
Dodd, David, 83
Dollar-weighted rate of return, 400
Domestic-indexed strategy, 77
Dow Jones EURO 50 stock indexes, 335
Dupont formula, 128

E

Earnings and cash flow growth, 125
Earnings growth, 99
Earnings momentum growth manager, 100
Earnings variability, 101
Economic earnings, 279
Economic profit analysis, 285
Economic profit approach, 213
Economic profit model, 199, 288
Economic profit, 9, 83
Economic Value Added, 83, 153, 156
Edwards, Mark , 4, 8, 301
Effective debt tax subsidy rate, 171
Efficient portfolios, 3, 5, 12, 21
Ehrbar, Al, 153
Einhorn, Steven G.,156, 214
E-MODEL, 206
Energy, 98
Engineered approach to active portfolio management, 7
Enhanced index fund, 376, 377
  approaches to enhanced indexing, 377
Equilibrium market price of risk, 29
Equity derivative, 331
Equity management styles, 97, 98
Equity matrix, 272
Equity Participation Notes (EPNs), 361
Equity performance attribution models, 414
Equity risk measures 242
Equity swaps, 356, 359
Equity valuation model, 199
Equity-linked debt, 356, 360
Establishing investment policy, 1, 2

European option, 333
EVA®, 9
Evaluating performance, 405
Evaluation period, 395
Ex ante Markowitz efficient frontier, 34
Ex ante mean-variance efficient, 34
Ex ante return, 15
Ex post return, 14
Excess return, 66
Exchange-traded options, 332
Execution price, 314
Exercise price, 333
Exercise style, 333
Exotic option structures, 357, 383
Exotic options, 356
Expected active return, 415
Expected excess return, 245
Expected future earnings, 272
Expected portfolio return, 14
Expected price volatility, 342
Expected return, 14
Expected terminal price, 201
Expiration cycle, 334
Expiration date, 333
Extended funds, 385
Extended market index , 79
Extra-market covariance, 83

F

Fabozzi, Frank J., 160, 200, 312, 357
Factor analysis, 230
Factor model, 229
  scenario factors, 246
  scenario score, 246
Factor-based approach, 229
Fama, Eugene F., 28, 66, 69, 77, 99, 118, 157, 160, 199, 249
Farrell, James L. , Jr., 98
Fat tails, 44
Feasible portfolio, 22
Fees, 312
Ferguson, Robert , 181
Financial Times Actuaries Euro-Pacific Index, 406
Financing rate, 352
Finite-life general dividend discount model, 200
First Call, 133
FLEX options, 337
FLexible EXchange (FLEX) Option, 332
Focardi, Sergio , 87
Fogler, H. Russell, 229, 249, 406
Foreign equity index, 357
Foreign market access, 377
Foreign or International Index Funds, 385
Frank Russell Company, 102, 104
Free cash flow model, 199, 206
French, Kenneth R., 69, 77, 99, 118, 160, 249
FTSE-100 Index, 361
Fundamental factor model approach, 83

Fundamental factor models, 173, 236
Fundamental return on a firm's stock, 129
Fundamental stock return, 129
Forward contracts, 332
Futures contract, 349
  delivery date, 349
  difference between futures and options, 350
  futures market versus the cash market, 376
  maintenance margin requirements, 308, 349
  margin requirements, 307, 308
  marked-to-the-market on a daily basis, 349
  most distant futures contract, 350
  nearby futures contract, 350
  settlement date, 349
  variation margin, 349, 350
Futures pricing, 349
  arbitrage-free zone, 355
  cost of carry valuation model, 354
  no-arbitrage condition, 352

G

Gamma, 348
General dividend discount model, 200
Generic investment style indexes, 405
Geometric mean return, 399
Giant cap stocks, 78
Global asset allocation policy, 380
Global market efficiency, 68
Global risk management, 77
Global-indexed strategy, 77
Global-indexing, 68
Global-passive investing, 68
Goldman Sachs Asset Management model, 9, 241
Goldman Sachs, 84, 165, 169, 171
Gordon model, 202
Gordon, Myron J., 202
Graham, Benjamin, 83
Grant, James L., 84, 85, 107, 153, 160, 214
Grinold, Richard , 409, 417
Gross capital investment, 207
Gross operating profit after tax, 207
Growth and momentum measures, 242
Growth at a price managers, 100
Growth at a reasonable price managers, 100
Growth managers, 316
Growth rates, 125
Growth stock managers, 98
Growth stock strategy, 77
Growth, 98

H

Harlow, W. V., 89
Haugen, Robert A., 88, 119

Hedge against symmetric risk, 350
Hedge asymmetric risk, 350
Hedge ratio, 372
Hedged strategy, 379
Hedging foreign equity positions, 371
Hedging market risk, 371
    equivalent market index units, 374
Herding, 266
Herzberg, Martin M., 184
Hill, Joanne M., 120
Historical beta, 57
Holding period return, 14
Holt Value Associates, LP, 174
Homogeneous expectations assumption, 21
Howe, John, 89
Hurley, William J., 199, 200, 205
Hypothesis testing, 56

**I**

IBES, 133
Impact of contributions and withdrawals, 404
Implied futures rate, 355
Implied interest expense, 167
Implied long-term growth rate, 288
In the money, 340
Index fund, 375
    creating an index fund, 375
Index options, 334, 383
Inefficient portfolio, 70
Inflation risk, 231
Information coefficient, 6, 418
Information ratio, 417
Information trader, 320
Informationless trades, 304
Information-motivated trades, 313, 318
INSTINET, 302
Institutional Brokerage Estimates Survey, 102
Internal capital generation rate, 130
Internal rate of return, 51, 400
International equity swaps, 359
Intra-asset allocation strategy, 384
Intrinsic value, 83, 199
Investment costs, 314
Investment management process, 1

**J**

Jackson, Al, 156, 214
Jacobs Levy Equity Management, 9, 261
Jacobs, Bruce I., 6, 65, 68, 106, 119, 236, 245, 255, 267
Jefferies & Co., 302
Jensen index, 410
Jensen, Michael C., 10, 410
Johnson, Lewis D., 199, 205
Jonas, Caroline , 88
Jones, Robert C., 65, 91, 92
Jones, Thomas P., 157

**K**

Kahn, Ronald, 414, 417-
Kappa, 349
Kreichman, Steven B., 206
Kritzman, Mark, 407

**L**

Ladder options, 383
Lakonishok, Josef, 119
Large growth and small growth stocks, 104
Large growth, 98
Large value stocks, 104
Large value, 98
Large-cap indexing, 71
Lau, Sheila, 30
LEAPS, 337
LeBaron, Blake , 87
Lehman Corporate Bond Index, 406
Lehman Intermediate Government Bond Index, 406
Lehman Long-Term Government Bond Index, 406
Lehman Mortgage-Backed Securities Index, 406
Leibowitz, Martin L., 220
Leinweber, David J., 113, 255
Leistikow, Dean, 181
Levered firm, 145
Levered market index, 86
Levered portfolio, 27
Levy, Kenneth N., 6, 65, 68, 106, 119, 236, 245, 255, 267
Limit book, 303
Limit order, 305
Linear model, 67
Lintner, John, 28
Liquidity neutral trade, 320
Liquidity-driven trades, 318
Listed futures market, 332
Listed options market, 332
Listed options, 334
Local-indexing, 68
Loftus, John, 81
Logue, D.E., 318
Long call position, 338
Long futures, 349
Long put option position, 339
Long-short strategy, 267
Long-Term Equity Anticipation Securities (LEAPS), 337
Low price-to-earnings (P/E) ratio, 99
Low-P/E manager, 99
Luck, Christopher G., 113, 255
Lynch, Peter, 83

**M**

Macro themes, 291, 295
Macroeconomic factor model, 230, 256
Macroeconomic factors, 294
Madden, Bartley J., 153

Magellan Fund, 79
Marathe, Vinay, 83
Market indexes, 405
Market model, 30
Market order, 304, 305
Market risk parameter, 67
Market timing costs, 313
Market timing risk, 231
Market timing, 313
Market value-to-asset replacement cost ratio, 287
Market-if-touched order, 306
Market-neutral strategy, 266
Marking to the market daily, 334
Markowitz diversification, 19
Markowitz efficient frontier, 24
Markowitz efficient portfolios, 21, 22
Markowitz, Harry M., 15 69, 155
Markowitz-Sharpe framework, 69
Matrix Equity, 269, 277
Mauboussin, Michael J., 156, 214
May, Catherine, 205
Mean-variance efficient portfolio, 22
Measurement and evaluation of investment performance, 4
Measuring and evaluating performance, 1
Member firm's guarantee, 334
Merrill Lynch, 84
Mezrich, Joseph, 256
Micro-cap stocks, 78
Mid cap stocks, 78
Milbourn, Todd , 181
Miller, Deborah H., 404
Miller, Keith, 323
Miller, Merton H., 143, 155, 157, 171, 199
Miller, Robert E. 108, 119
Minimum risk hedge ratio, 373
Mobius Group, 99, 100
Modern portfolio theory, 2, 3, 9, 11, 25
Modigliani, Franco, 143, 154
Modigliani-Miller model, 145
Moldovsky, Nicholas, 205
Morgan Stanley-EAFE (Europe, Australia, and the Far East) index, 71
Morningstar, 60, 78, 277
Motives for trading, 314
Mott, Claudia, 104
MSCI-EASEA and KOKUSAI indexes, 91
Multi-factor model, 229

**N**

Naked calls, 369
Napolitano, Gabrielle, 214
Net capital investment, 207
Net cost of carry, 351
Net operating profit after tax, 207
Net present value, 214
Nonlinear dynamic models, 87
Nonlinear model, 67

Non-S&P 500 Index funds, 385
Normal portfolios, 405, 406
Northfield Fundamental Equity Risk
    Model, 241
Northfield Information Services
    Macroeconomic Factor model, 9
Northfield Macroeconomic Equity
    Risk Model, 231
NYSE SuperDOT System, 310

**O**

O'Byrne, Stephen F., 160
O'Neill & Company, 60
Odd-lot order, 307
Offer price, 302
Opening order, 306
Operationally-efficient, 65
Optimal hedge ratio, 373
Optimal portfolio, 12
Option premium, 333
Option price, 333
Option's intrinsic value, 340
Options Clearing Corporation, 334
Options, 332, 333
OTC derivatives market, 332
OTC equity derivative, 356
OTC exotic option structures, 334
OTC options, 334
    first generation OTC options, 357
    second generation OTC equity
        options, 357
Out-of-the-money options, 340
Overreaction hypothesis, 88, 89
Overreaction, 266
Over-the-counter (OTC) derivatives,
    332
Overwrite, 370

**P**

Partial hedge strategy, 378
Passive portfolio strategy, 3
Passive style management, 119
Passive-active investing, 9
Passive-active investor, 92
Performance attribution analysis,
    395
Performance evaluation, 395
Performance measurement, 395
Perold, Andre F., 314, 317
Peters, Edgar E., 87, 373
Peterson, David R., 126, 168, 176
Peterson, Pamela P., 126, 168, 176
Plain vanilla equity swap, 359
Plain vanilla indexing, 377
Pogue, Jerry A., 21
Portable alpha strategies, 92
Portfolio construction, 229
POSIT, 302
Premium over intrinsic value, 340
Price limits, 334
Price reversal, 318
Price risk, 376
Price stabilization, 303
Price, Laurence J., 323

Price/book value ratio, 125
Price/cash flow ratio, 125
Price/earnings ratio, 125
Price/revenue ratio, 125
Price-to-book value per share ratio,
    99
Pricing efficiency, 5, 65
Pricing model, 351
Priest, W., 318
Principal components analysis, 230
Profitability ratios, 125
Program trades, 308, 309
Protective put buying strategy, 367
Protective put strategy, 368
Prudential Securities Large Cap
    Growth, 105
PSI Small Cap Value, 110
Public orders, 304
Put option, 333
Put-call parity relationship, 344

**Q**

Quadratic programming, 21
Quinn, T., 318

**R**

Rappaport, Alfred , 208
Refined Economic Value Added,
    181
Regression analysis, 52
Regulations T and U, 307
Regulatory issues, 370
Relative valuation measures, 125
Rennie, Edward P., 409
Reported accounting profit, 279
Research costs, 312
Residual risk, 30
Return on assets or capital, 125
Return on equity, 125
Revenue growth, 125
Risk control, 229
Risk management context, 7
Risk of mispriced futures contracts,
    376
Risk premium, 29
Risk-averse investor, 12
Risk-free arbitrage arguments, 351
Riskless assets, 13
Risk-sharing arrangements, 310
Role of derivatives, 331
Roll, Richard , 9, 34, 77, 116
Rosenberg, Barr, 83
Rosenberg, Claude N., Jr. 402
Ross, Stephen, 9, 36
Round lot, 307
Russell 1000 index, 102
Russell 2000 index, 102
Russell 2000 small cap index
    futures contact, 92
Russell 2000 Small Stock Index,
    406
Russell 2000 Value Index, 79
Russell Earnings-Growth Stock
    Index, 406

Russell Price-Driven Stock Index,
    406

**S**

S&P 100 index, 335
S&P 500 Index Trust, 79
S&P/BARRA Growth, 105
S&P/BARRA indexes, 43
S&P/BARRA Large-Cap Value
    Index, 79
Sales franchise model, 199, 220
Sales franchise, 9
Salomon Brothers 90-Day Bill
    Index, 406
Salomon Brothers Non-U.S. Gov-
    ernment Bond Index, 406
Salomon Brothers' Risk Attribute
    Model, 231
Salomon Risk Attribute Model, 9
Sauter, Gus, 79
Scheinkman, José, 87
Schlarbaum,Gary G., 99
Scholes, Myron, 342
Security analysis, 82
Security market line, 32
Selecting an equity portfolio strat-
    egy, 1, 3
Sell limit order, 305
Semi-strong form market effi-
    ciency, 66
Semi-variance, 16
Setting investment objectives, 1
Settlement style, 333
Sharpe benchmarks, 405, 406
    performance evaluation using,
        416
Sharpe index, 409, 410
Sharpe ratio, 70
Sharpe, William F.,10, 21, 28, 29,
    155, 406, 409
Shleifer, Andrei, 119
Short call position, 339
Short futures, 349
Short put option, 340
Short sale, 307
Single factor model, 172
Single-index market model, 30
Single-index performance evalua-
    tion measures, 409
Sinquefield, Rex, 69
Slow rabbit benchmark, 409
Small capitalization stocks, 78
Small growth, 98
Small value stocks, 104
Small value, 98
Sorensen, Eric H., 102, 205, 206,
    256, 323
Sources of financing approach, 169
Specialist, 302
Special-purpose index funds strat-
    egy, 386
Spot price, 338, 351
Standard & Poor's 500, 4
State Street Corporation, 126

State Street Global Advisors, 9, 261, 269
Statistical factor model, 230
Stern Stewart & Co., 84, 165, 174
    bottom up approach, 167
    top down approach, 168
Stern, Joel, 156
Stewart, G. Bennett , III, 153, 156, 215
Stigler, George, 154, 302
Stock baskets, 357
Stock options, 334
Stock replacement program, 377
Stock selection, 3
Stock Upside Notes (SUNs), 361
Stonberg, Peter, 269
Stop order, 305, 306
Stop-limit order, 306
Strategic asset allocation decision, 371
Strike index, 337
Strike price, 333
Strong-form efficiency, 66
Structured OTC equity derivative products, 383
Structured product, 356
Structured Upside Participating Equity Receipt (SUPER), 361
Style classification system, 100
Style jitter, 101
Style of investing, 98
Style switching, 120
Style-passive investing, 68
Style-passive strategy, 77
Swaps, 332
Synthetic High Income Equity Linked Security (SHIELDS), 361
Synthetic index fund, 375
Systematic risk, 29

**T**

Tactical asset allocation, 374
Tactical style management, 119
Tailing, 376
Thakor, Anjan, 181
Thaler, Richard, 89
Theoretical futures price, 351, 352
Theory of choice, 12
Theta, 348
Thickness of the market, 303
Three-phase dividend discount models, 205
Thum, Chee, 256
Tick-test rules, 307
Tierney, David E., 409
Time horizon risk, 231
Time value of an option, 341
Time value, 340
Time-weighted average return, 51
Time-weighted rate of return, 399
Tobin's Q, 126
Top-down approach, 81, 291
Top-down investing, 65
Top-down macroeconomic profit approach, 291

Torre, Nicolo, 5, 321
Total active return, 414, 415
Total exception active return, 415
Total managed portfolio return, 414
Tracking error risk, 377
Tracking error, 371
Trade-off between execution costs and opportunity costs, 315
Trader timing costs, 8
Trader timing, 312, 320
Trading costs
    execution costs, 312, 313
    hidden cost, 314
    iceberg of equity trading costs, 320
    market impact, 313
    measuring execution costs, 319
    measuring transaction costs, 316
    opportunity cost, 8, 312, 313, 314
    posttrade benchmarks, 318
    posttrade measures, 317
    pretrade benchmarks, 317
    pretrade measures, 317
    price impact, 8, 313, 320
    price or market impact, 312
    transfer fee, 312
Trading mechanics, 301
Traditional fundamental analysis, 82
Traditional macroeconomic factors, 293
Traditional measures of performance, 10
    application of, 411
Traditional measures, 125
Traditional top-down equity analysis, 294
Transaction costs, 120
Treynor index, 409, 410
Treynor, Jack L.,10, 28,314, 409
True value equity portfolio, 291
Trzcinka, Charles, 87
T-statistic, 56
Tsu, Maria E., 120
Tully, Shawn, 165
Two-parameter model, 17
Two-phase dividend discount models, 205
Two-stage free cash flow model, 210

**U**

Underlying, 333
Undiversifiable risk or market risk, 29
Unhedged strategy, 378
Unique risk, 30
Unlevered firm, 145
Unlevered net operating profit after tax, 157
Unsystematic risk, 30
Upstairs market, 308
Up-tick trade rule, 307
Utility function, 12

**V**

Value drivers, 289
Value Line scoring system, 134
Value Line, 60, 133
Value managers, 316
Value measures, 242
Value stocks, 184
Value strategy, 77
Value trap, 278
Value/replacement cost ratio, 126
Value-based metrics, 9, 153
Vanguard Group, 79
Variance of returns, 46
Variance, 16
Vega, 349
Viehl, Lawrence S., 81, 293
Vishny, Robert, 119

**W**

Wagner, Wayne H., 4, 5, 8, 30, 301, 313, 317
Wallace, James, 180
Weak-form efficiency, 66
Wealth creators, 183, 184
West, Richard R., 65
Williams, C. Nola, 99
Williams, John B., 200
Williamson, David, 205
Wilshire 5000 index, 79
Wilshire Associates, 104
Wilshire Large Cap Growth, 105
Wilshire model, 241
Wilshire Small Cap Value, 110
Wilshire Top 2500, 104
Wilshire, 9
Wilshire's Institutional Services/ Equity Division, 104
Wolf, Charles R., 156, 214

**Y**

Yield manager, 100
Young, David, 154, 165

**Z**

Zacks, 133
Zero-beta CAPM model, 69
Zero-beta portfolio, 35

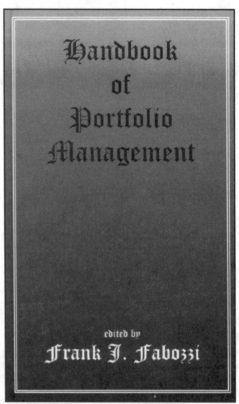

**HANDBOOK OF PORTFOLIO MANAGEMENT**
Frank J. Fabozzi, Editor
1998 Hardcover 748 Pages $89 ISBN 1-883249-41-4

Table of contents: 1. Overview of Portfolio Management; 2. Monetary Policy: How the Fed Set, Implements, and Measures Policy; 3. The Changing Framework and Methods of Investment Management; 4. Mean-Variance Optimization Models for Practitioners of Asset Allocation; 5. Foreign Exchange Hedging by Managers of International Fixed Income and Equity Portfolios; 6 Investment Management For Taxable Investors; 7. Investment Management: An Architecture for the Equity Market; 8. Investment Mangement: Profiting from a Complex Equity Market; 9. Dividend Discount Models; 10. Factor-Based Approach to Equity Portfolio Management; 11. Review of Financial Statements; 12. Introduction to Fundamental Analysis;13.Security Analysis Using EVA; 14. Overview of Equity Style Management; 15. Enhanced Equity Indexing; 16. The Asian Growth Paradigm as an Investment Tool; 17. Implementing Investment Strategies: The Art and Science of Investing; 18. Using Derivatives in Equity Portfolio Management; 19. Fixed Income Analytics: Valuation and Risk Management; 20. Quantitative Analysis of Fixed Income Portfolios Relative to Indices; 21. A Return Attribution Model for Fixed Income Securities; 22. Credit Analysis of Corporate Bonds; 23. Term Structure Factor Models; 24. Measuring and Managing Interest-Rate Risk; 25. Fixed Income Portfolio Investing: The Art of Decision Making; 6. Managing Indexed and Enhanced Indexed Bond Portfolios; 27. Global Corporate Bond Portfolio Management; 28. International Bond Portfolio Management; 29. Emerging Fixed Income and Local Currency: An Investment Management View; 30. Hedging Corporate Securities with Treasury and Derivative Instruments; 31. Index Total Return Swaps and Their Applications to Fixed Income Portfolio Management; 32. Stock Portfolio Attribution Analysis; 33. Fixed Income Return Attribution Analysis

**To order this book, please visit our web site at:**
**www.frankfabozzi.com**or call us at **(215) 598-8930**

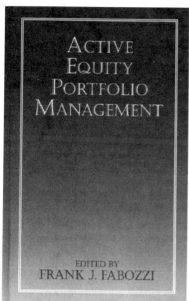